D1194577

Programming Game AI by Example

Mat Buckland

Wordware Publishing, Inc.

Library of Congress Cataloging-in-Publication Data

Buckland, Mat.
Programming game AI by example / by Mat Buckland.
p. cm.
Includes index.
ISBN 1-55622-078-2 (pbk.)
1. Computer games—Design. 2. Computer games—Programming. 3. Computer graphics. I. Title.
QA76.76.C672B85 2004
794.8'1526—dc22 2004015103

© 2005, Wordware Publishing, Inc.

An imprint of Jones and Bartlett Publishers

All Rights Reserved

1100 Summit Avenue, Suite 102
Plano, Texas 75074

No part of this book may be reproduced in any form or by any means without permission in writing from Wordware Publishing, Inc.

Printed in the United States of America

ISBN 10: 1-55622-078-2
ISBN 13: 978-1-55622-078-4

10 9 8 7 6 5 4 3 2 1
0409

Black & White, the Black & White logo, Lionhead, and the Lionhead logo are registered trademarks of Lionhead Studios Limited. Screenshots used with the permission of Lionhead Studios Limited. All rights reserved.
Impossible Creatures and Relic are trademarks and/or registered trademarks of Relic Entertainment, Inc.
NEVERWINTER NIGHTS © 2002 Infogrames Entertainment, S.A. All Rights Reserved. Manufactured and marketed by Infogrames, Inc., New York, NY. Portions © 2002 BioWare Corp. BioWare and the BioWare Logo are trademarks of BioWare Corp. All Rights Reserved. Neverwinter Nights is a trademark owned by Wizards of the Coast, Inc., a subsidiary of Hasbro, Inc. and is used by Infogrames Entertainment, S.A. under license. All Rights Reserved.
Unreal® Tournament 2003 ©2003 Epic Games, Inc. Unreal is a registered trademark of Epic Games, Inc. All rights reserved.
Other brand names and product names mentioned in this book are trademarks or service marks of their respective companies. Any omission or misuse (of any kind) of service marks or trademarks should not be regarded as intent to infringe on the property of others. The publisher recognizes and respects all marks used by companies, manufacturers, and developers as a means to distinguish their products.
This book is sold as is, without warranty of any kind, either express or implied, respecting the contents of this book and any disks or programs that may accompany it, including but not limited to implied warranties for the book's quality, performance, merchantability, or fitness for any particular purpose. Neither Wordware Publishing, Inc. nor its dealers or distributors shall be liable to the purchaser or any other person or entity with respect to any liability, loss, or damage caused or alleged to have been caused directly or indirectly by this book.

All inquiries for volume purchases of this book should be addressed to Wordware Publishing, Inc., at the above address. Telephone inquiries may be made by calling:

(972) 423-0090

Dedication

For Mum and Dad, who bought me my first computer, and therefore must share some responsibility for turning me into the geek that I am. ☺

"*Programming Game AI by Example* stands out from the pack by providing industrial-strength solutions to difficult problems, like steering and goal-oriented behavior. Mat guides the reader toward building a foundation robust enough for real games. This book is a must-have for anyone new to the field, and has tips for the seasoned professional as well. I wish I [had] read it eight years ago!"

Jeff Orkin
AI architect, Monolith Productions, No One Lives Forever 2 and F.E.A.R.

"…a nice combination of a lot of really useful information, put together in a way that doesn't make my brain leak."

Gareth Lewis
Project leader, Lionhead Studios, Black & White 2

"Each chapter of Mat's book gently introduces the reader to a fundamental game AI technology before expanding the new idea into a fully formed solution replete with extensive code and clearly worded examples. The tone of the book is uncomplicated and accessible to the reader, allowing a novice programmer the opportunity to get to grips with the basics of game AI programming by implementing their own systems direct from theory or expanding upon code examples offered to gain understanding in a sandbox environment. Once individual technologies are fully understood, the book goes on to combine these ideas into several complete game environments allowing the reader to understand the relationships between the interacting systems of an overarching game architecture."

Mike Ducker
AI programmer, Lionhead Studios, Fable

"Using easy-to-follow and well-described examples, this book shows you how to use most of the techniques professional AI programmers use. A great introduction for the beginner and an excellent reference for the more experienced!"

Eric Martel
AI programmer, Ubisoft, Far Cry (XBox)

"*Programming Game AI by Example* is an excellent book for the game programming neophyte, the intermediate programmer, and even the expert — it doesn't hurt to go over familiar ground, does it? The book concisely covers all of the important areas, including basic maths and physics through to graph theory and scripting with Lua, to arm any programmer with the tools needed to create some very sophisticated agent behaviours. Unusually for books of the type, *Programming Game AI by Example* is solid in its software engineering too, with the example code demonstrating game uses of familiar design patterns. I'd have no qualms about recommending *Programming Game AI by Example* to any programmer. It's an excellent read and an excellent springboard for ideas."

Chris Keegan
Technical director, Climax Studios (Solent)

Contents

Foreword

Draw the blinds. Turn off the TV set. Shut off your cell phone. Turn on a little background music. Pour yourself a cup of your favorite "programmer's drink," and find yourself a nice, cozy chair with your favorite laptop close at hand. You're about to go a-learnin'.

Welcome to *Programming Game AI by Example*.

I must confess I was surprised when Mat contacted me back in 2003 about this book. I wondered to myself, "He already covered all of the new techniques pretty well…what more is there to do?"

As we exchanged emails Mat expressed that he had a simple desire to follow up on his first book, *AI Techniques for Game Programming*, with something having a completely different focus. Whereas *Techniques* explored the more "exotic" biological technologies that a game AI programmer might be wondering about without bogging down in computer science minutiae, Mat wanted *Example* to focus more on what technologies are actually being used by most game AI programmers in their day-to-day work. New technologies and new approaches are always to be considered when it makes sense to do so of course, but developers must always have the basics at hand to build a firm foundation for any game AI engine. That's what this book is all about.

The Surge of Game AI's Importance

Game AI has undergone a quiet revolution in the past few years. No longer is it something that most developers consider only toward the end of a project when shipping deadlines loom and the publisher is pushing to have the game ship before the next holiday milestone. Now game AI is something that is *planned* for, something that developers are deliberately making as important a part of a game's development as the graphics or the sound effects. The market is rife with games of all kinds and developers are looking for every edge they can get to help their game get noticed. A game with truly *smart* opponents or non-player characters is one that gets noticed automatically, no matter what it looks like.

We've seen this in the enormous growth in books on the subject, in the surge in attendance at the Game Developers Conference AI roundtables, and in the explosion of game AI web sites across the Internet. Where a few years ago there were only a handful of books that covered AI techniques in terms that a programmer could understand, there are now dozens. Where a few years ago we weren't at all sure we could fill a single room at the GDC with people interested in talking about the techniques they used to build game AI engines, we now have to turn people away; we just can't fit everybody in the sessions. Where there were once only a small — very small — number of web pages dedicated to game AI on the Internet, there are now more than I can easily count; a quick Google search as I write this showed over a hundred dedicated in whole or in part to the topic. Amazing, absolutely amazing.

And every one of the developers who visits these pages, who comes to the roundtables, who buys the books is interested in the same things:

- What techniques do other developers use?
- What technologies have other developers found useful?
- What do different games do for AI? Are they all faking it, does everybody do the same thing, or is there room for improvement?
- What are the stumbling blocks that others have run into so I'm not surprised? More importantly, what are the solutions other people have developed so that *I* don't have to?
- How can I make my AIs smarter?
- Most importantly of all, how can I make my AIs more *fun*?

This book is for *those* people. The ones who seek hard, practical examples and hard, practical answers. There's more than pure theory here; this book is about real techniques with real, working examples.

About time, huh?

By Engineers, For Engineers

The most important thing to a good software engineer is to know about techniques that work and why. Theory is great, but demos and code are better; a developer can get right into the code and see *why* something works and how it might be adapted to his own problem. This is exactly the kind of thing that game AI developers have been pounding the walls for at every GDC AI roundtable. And this book delivers exactly this kind of information, and in spades.

From the initial chapters covering the sturdy finite state machine (FSM) to the chapters exploring the more exotic areas of fuzzy logic (FL), Mat has built a text that will serve as a ready reference and source of learning for a long time to come. Every major technique in use by developers is covered here, using the context of an innovative agent-based AI engine called Raven to show how a given approach works and why. Basic reactionary behaviors are the most obvious ones and Mat covers them in exhaustive detail, with code showing each evolutionary iteration and demos to help it all make sense.

Mat doesn't stop there as many books do, however. *Example* moves on to cover deeper approaches such as hierarchical goal-based agents, placing such technologies in the context of the Raven engine and building on previous examples to show how they can greatly improve a game's AI. These are techniques in use in only a handful of games on the market today, but they can make a game's AI truly stand out if done properly. This book will show you why they make a difference and how to use them. Mat even provides tips for better implementations than used in his examples and summarizes potential improvements to the techniques covered. To this end he offers up the occasional practical exercise to point the interested developer in ways to make a given technique better, helping readers to focus on how they might use the technology in their own games. After all, code is never *done*, it's just *done enough*.

All of this makes *Programming Game AI by Example* a book I think you're really going to find useful. If you're looking for hard code and real techniques, for a book that covers what game AI developers are really doing and how, then this is the book for you.

Have fun.

Steven Woodcock
ferretman@gameai.com

Acknowledgments

A *huge* thanks to Steve Woodcock (gameai.com) and Eric Martel (Ubisoft), who gave up much of their free time to help out with technical reviews of the text and code, and to Ron Wolfe (Sidney Fire Department), who volunteered to be my guinea pig. I owe you guys.

I'd also like to thank Craig Reynolds (Sony), Jeff Hannan (Codemasters), and William Combs (Boeing) for patiently answering my questions; and to the team at Wordware for all their expertise.

Thanks also to my old friend Mark Drury for checking over the math and physics chapter.

Finally, a big thank you and hug to my partner and best friend, Sharon, for the many hours she spent proofreading, and for all the times I must have stared vacantly at her moving lips whilst my mind was off visiting another planet. I don't know how she puts up with me.

Introduction

The objective of the book you hold in your hands is to provide a solid and practical foundation to game AI, giving you the confidence to approach new challenges with excitement and optimism. AI is an *enormous* topic, so don't expect to come away from this book an expert, but you will have learned the skills necessary to create entertaining and challenging AI for the majority of action game genres. Furthermore, you will have a sound understanding of the key areas of game AI, providing a solid base for any further learning you undertake. And let me tell you, the learning process is endless!

Being a good game AI programmer is not just about knowing how to implement a handful of techniques. Of course, individual techniques are important, but how they can be made to *work together* is more vital to the AI development process. To this end, this book spends a lot of time walking you through the design of agents capable of playing a team sports game (Simple Soccer) and a deathmatch type shoot-'em-up (Raven), demonstrating clearly how each technique is used and integrated with others. Furthermore, Simple Soccer and Raven provide a convenient test bed for further experimentation, and within the conclusions of many of the chapters are suggestions for future exploration.

Academic AI vs. Game AI

There is an important distinction to be made between the AI studied by academics and that used in computer games. Academic research is split into two camps: *strong* AI and *weak* AI. The field of strong AI concerns itself with trying to create systems that mimic human thought processes and the field of weak AI (more popular nowadays) with applying AI technologies to the solution of real-world problems. However, both of these fields tend to focus on solving a problem *optimally,* with less emphasis on hardware or time limitations. For example, some AI researchers are perfectly happy to leave a simulation running for hours, days, or even weeks on their 1000-processor Beowulf cluster so long as it has a happy ending they can write a paper about. This of course is an extreme case, but you get my point.

Game AI programmers, on the other hand, have to work with limited resources. The amount of processor cycles and memory available varies from platform to platform but more often than not the AI guy will be left, like Oliver holding out his bowl, begging for more. The upshot of this is that compromises often have to be made in order to get an acceptable level of performance. In addition, successful games — the ones making all the money — do one thing very well: They entertain the player (or they have a film license ☺). Ipso facto, the AI must be entertaining, and to achieve this must more often than not be *designed to be suboptimal.* After all, most players will quickly become frustrated and despondent with an AI that always gives them a whippin'. To be enjoyable, an AI must put up a good fight but lose more often than win. It must make the player feel clever, sly, cunning, and powerful. It must make the player jump from his seat shouting, "Take *that*, you little shit!"

The Illusion of Intelligence

But what is this mysterious thing we call artificial intelligence? With regard to game AI I am firmly of the opinion that if the player *believes* the agent he's playing against is intelligent, then it *is* intelligent. It's that simple. Our goal is to design agents that provide the *illusion of intelligence*, nothing more.

Because the illusion of intelligence is subjective, sometimes this takes very little effort at all. The designers of the AI for Halo, for instance, discovered their playtesters could be fooled into thinking the AI agents were more intelligent simply by increasing the number of hit points required to kill them. For one test session they allowed the agents to die really easily (low hit points); the result was that 36 percent of the testers thought the AI was too easy and 8 percent thought the AI were very intelligent. For the next test session the agents were made harder to kill (higher hit points). After just this small change 0 percent of the testers thought the AI was too easy and 43 percent thought the AI was very intelligent! This is an astonishing result and clearly shows the importance of playtesting throughout the game development cycle.

It has also been shown that a player's perception of the level of intelligence of a game agent can be considerably enhanced by providing the player with some visual and/or auditory clues as to what the agent is "thinking" about. For example, if the player enters a room and startles an agent, it should act startled. If your game is a "stealth-'em-up" like Thief and a game character hears something suspicious, then it should start to look around and maybe mumble a few words such as "What was that?" or "Is anyone there?" Even something simple like making sure that an agent tracks the movement of neighboring agents with its head can contribute significantly to a player's perception of the AI.

You must be careful though when designing your AI not to let the cloak of illusion slip, since once it does the player's belief in the game character will evaporate and the game becomes much less fun to play. This will happen if the AI is seen to act stupidly (running into walls, getting stuck in corners, not reacting to obvious stimuli) or is caught "cheating" (seeing through walls, requiring less gold to build units than the human player, hearing a pin drop at 500 meters), so you must take great pains to avoid either of these pitfalls.

A Word about the Code

Writing the accompanying source code for this book has necessitated a few compromises. For starters, the code must be formatted so each line fits in the width of the printed page. This seems like common sense, but I've seen many books where the formatting is hideous, with huge gaps and spaces everywhere, making the code difficult to follow as it meanders about the page. The bottom line is that, unlike your IDE, the printed page has a fixed width within which printed code must fit: Each line of code must have a maximum width of 82 characters. Restricting lines of code to this length can be challenging, particularly when using the STL and templates together with descriptive class and variable names. For this reason, I've had to keep several names shorter than I would have liked, but wherever this was necessary, I've taken the liberty of being generous with my commenting. You will also notice in some sections of the code a profusion of temporary variables. These are here to either make the code clearer to read or to split up long lines of code so they fit within the 82-character limit, or both.

The code and demo executables that accompany this book can be downloaded from www.wordware.com/files/ai. Then click on Buckland_AISource.zip and Buckland_AIExecutables.zip.

Appendix C provides instructions on how to set up your development environment in order to compile the projects.

Practice Makes Perfect

As with all skills, the more you practice using AI techniques and designing AI systems, the better you get. Those of you who have bought this book because you are already involved in the development of a game's AI can get started with what you learn immediately — you already have the perfect test bed to practice on. However, for those of you who are not currently involved in a project, I've included "practicals" at the end of most chapters for you to try your hand at. These encourage you to experiment with the knowledge you've learned, either by creating small stand-alone examples or by altering or building upon the Simple Soccer or Raven code projects.

Chapter 1

A Math and Physics Primer

There's no hiding from it — if you want to learn AI, it helps to know some mathematics and physics. Sure, you can use many AI techniques in a "cut and paste" fashion, but that's not doing yourself any favors; the moment you have to solve a problem slightly different from the one you've borrowed the code from you're going to run into difficulties. If you understand the theory behind the techniques, however, you will stand a much better chance of figuring out an alternative solution. Besides, it feels good to understand the tools you're working with. What better reason do you need to learn this stuff but that?

I'm going to write this chapter assuming you know hardly anything at all about math or physics. So forgive me if you already know most of it, but I figure this way I'll catch everyone, no matter what your experience is. Skim through the chapter until you come to something you don't know or you find a topic where you think your memory needs to be refreshed. At that point, start reading. If you are already comfortable with vector math and the physics of motion, I suggest you skip this chapter entirely and come back later if you find something you don't understand.

Mathematics

We'll start with mathematics because trying to learn physics without math is like trying to fly without wings.

Cartesian Coordinates

You are probably already familiar with the Cartesian coordinate system. If you've ever written a program that draws images to the screen then you will almost certainly have used the Cartesian coordinate system to describe the positions of the points, lines, and bitmaps that make up the image.

In two dimensions, the coordinate system is defined by two axes positioned at right angles to each other and marked off in unit lengths. The horizontal axis is called the *x*-axis and the vertical axis, the *y*-axis. The point where the axes cross is called the *origin*. See Figure 1.1.

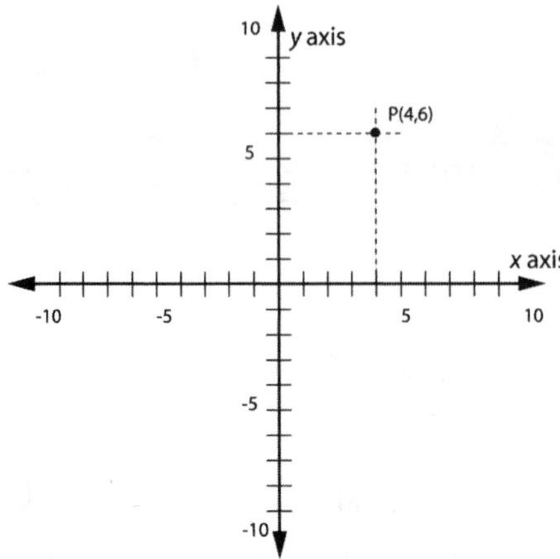

Figure 1.1. The Cartesian coordinate system

The arrowheads at each end of the axes in Figure 1.1 indicate they extend in each direction infinitely. If you imagine yourself holding an infinitely large sheet of paper with the x and y axes drawn on it, the paper represents the xy plane — the plane on which all points in the two-dimensional Cartesian coordinate system can be plotted. A point in 2D space is represented by a *coordinate pair* (x, y). The x and y values represent the distances along each of the respective axes. Nowadays, a series of points or lines plotted on the Cartesian coordinate system is usually referred to as a graph, which saves a lot of typing for sure. :o)

NOTE To represent three-dimensional space, another axis is needed — the z-axis. The z-axis extends from behind your screen to way behind your head, passing through the origin en route. See Figure 1.2.

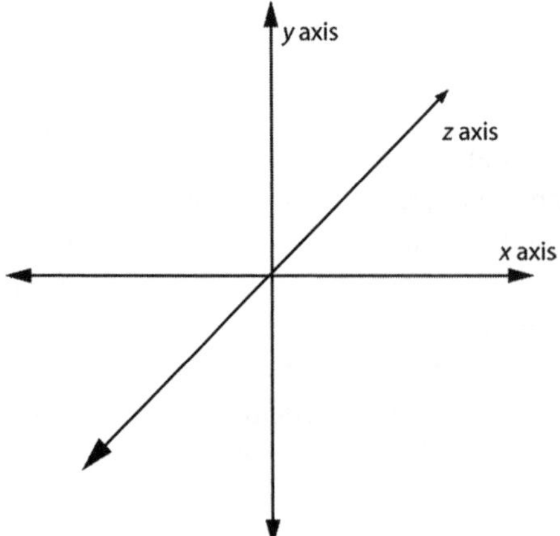

Figure 1.2. A three-axis (3D) coordinate system

Functions and Equations

The concept of functions is fundamental to mathematics. A *function* expresses the relationship between two (or more) terms called *variables*, and is typically written in the form of an *equation* (an algebraic expression set equal to another algebraic expression). Variables are named as such because, as the name implies, their values may vary. Variables are usually expressed with letters of the alphabet. The two most common variables you will see used in mathematical equations are x and y (although any letter or symbol is just as valid).

If each value of x can be associated with one value of y, then y is a function of x. y is said to be the *dependent* variable since its value depends on the value of x. Here are a couple of examples:

$$y = 2x \tag{1.1}$$

$$y = mx + c \tag{1.2}$$

In the second example, the m and the c represent *constants* (sometimes called coefficients) — values that never change no matter what the value of x is. They are effectively similar to the 2 in equation (1.1). Therefore, if $a = 2$, equation (1.1) can be written as follows:

$$y = ax \tag{1.3}$$

Given any value of x, the corresponding y value can be calculated by putting the x value into the function. Given $x = 5$ and $x = 7$ and the function $y = 2x$, the y values are:

$$\begin{aligned} y &= 2(5) = 10 \\ y &= 2(7) = 14 \end{aligned} \tag{1.4}$$

This type of function, where y is only dependent on one other variable, is called a *single-variable* function. Single-variable functions may be visualized by plotting them onto the xy Cartesian plane. To plot a function, all you have to do is move along the x-axis and for each x value use the function to calculate the y value. Of course, it's impossible to plot the graph for every value of x — that would take forever (literally) — so you must select a range of values.

The left-hand side of Figure 1.3 shows how function $y = 2x$ looks when plotted on the xy plane, using the range of x values between –5.0 and 5.0.

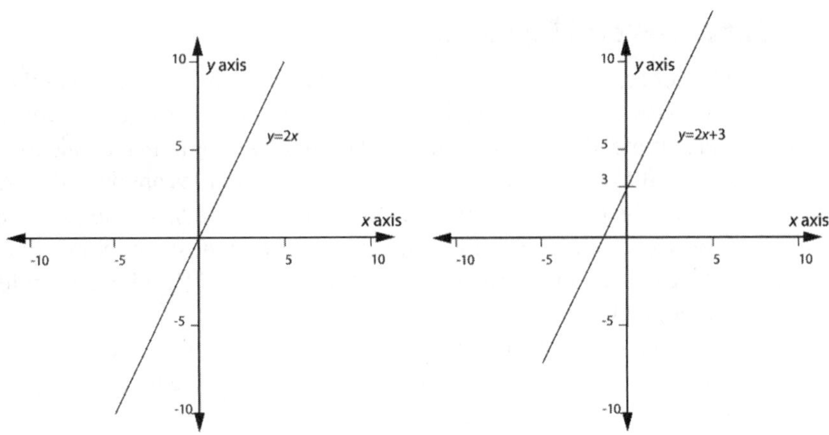

Figure 1.3. Functions plotted in Cartesian space

To plot the function $y = mx + c$ to a graph, you must first have some values for the constants m and c. Let's say $m = 2$ and $c = 3$, giving the function $y = 2x + 3$. The right-hand side of Figure 1.3 shows the resulting graph.

The graphs look very similar, don't they? That's because $y = mx + c$ is the function that defines all straight lines in 2D space. The constant m defines the line's gradient, or how steep the slope of the line is, and the constant c dictates where the line intersects the y-axis. The function $y = 2x$, shown on the left in the figure, is equivalent to the function $y = mx + c$, when $m = 2$ and $c = 0$. The plot on the right is almost identical but because its c value is 3, the point where it intersects the y-axis is shifted up by three units.

Sometimes you will see a function such as $y = mx + c$ written like this:

$$f(x) = mx + c \tag{1.5}$$

The notation $f(x)$ is stating that the dependent variable — in this example, the y — depends on the variable x in the expression given on the right-hand side, $mx + c$. Often, you will see symbols other than an f to represent the function, so don't become confused if you come across something like the following.

$$g(x) = x^2 + bx \tag{1.6}$$

The $g(x)$ represents exactly the same thing as if the equation was written as:

$$f(x) = x^2 + bx \tag{1.7}$$

Functions can depend on more than one variable. Take the calculation for the area of a rectangle for example. If its length is denoted by the letter l, and its width by w, then the area A is given by the equation:

$$A = lw \tag{1.8}$$

To plot a two-variable function like (1.8) on a graph, a third dimension, z, must be added, perpendicular to the other axes. Now it's possible to plot A to the z-axis, l to the x-axis, and w to the y-axis. See Figure 1.4.

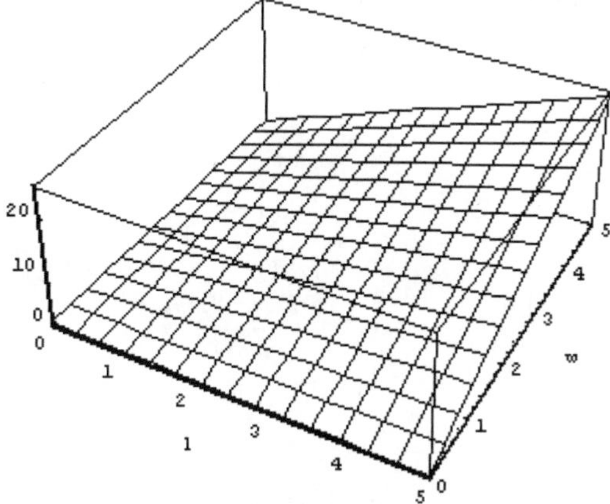

Figure 1.4. The function A = *lw* plotted in three dimensions

The volume of a cube is given by the three-variable function:

$$V = lwh \tag{1.9}$$

where the h represents the height of the cube. To plot this on a graph you need to add a fourth axis. Unfortunately, unless under the influence of psychotropic compounds, humans cannot see in more than three dimensions. However, we do have the ability to imagine them, so that's what you have to do if you want to plot functions with more than three variables on a graph. Mathematicians seem to find this easy to do, but many programmers, myself included, don't!

 **NOTE** The space an *n*-dimensional function occupies, where *n* is greater than 3, is often referred to as *hyperspace* by mathematicians.

Exponents and Powers

An exponential function is defined like this:

$$f(x) = a^x \tag{1.10}$$

The a is known as the *base* and the x as the *power*. If the equation is spoken, you would say that $f(x)$ equals a to the power x. This means that a is multiplied with itself x amount of times. So 7^2 is the same as writing 7x7, and 3^4 is the same as writing 3x3x3x3. A number to the power of 2 is known as the square of that number, and a number to the power of 3 is known as the cube. Therefore, the cube of 5 is:

$$5^3 = 5 \times 5 \times 5 = 125 \tag{1.11}$$

Figure 1.5 shows equation (1.10) plotted on a graph for $a = 2$. The curve clearly shows how the value of y increases rapidly with x. This type of curve is often referred to as *exponential growth*.

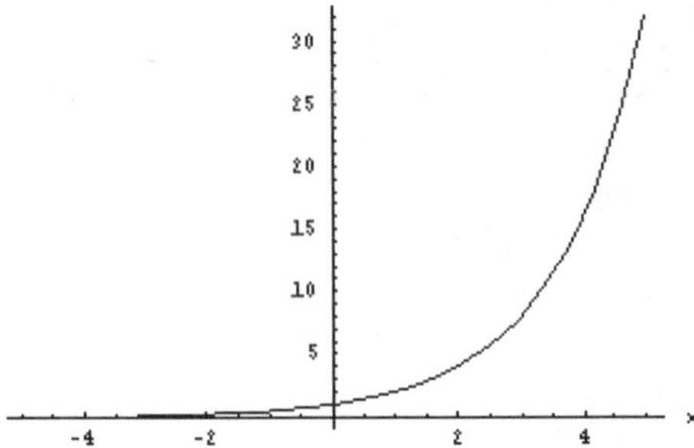

Figure 1.5. The function $f(x) = 2^x$ plotted on the xy plane

HISTORICAL NOTE For a reason lost to time, mathematicians decided they would use the latter part of the alphabet to represent variables and the rest of the alphabet to represent constants. This is why the axes in the Cartesian coordinate system are labeled x, y, and z.

Roots of Numbers (Radicals)

The *square root* of a number is a value that when multiplied by itself results in the original number. Square roots are written using the *radical* symbol $\sqrt{\ }$. Therefore, the square root of 4 is written as:

$$\sqrt{4} = 2 \tag{1.12}$$

We can square both sides of this equation to show the relationship between the power and the root:

$$4 = 2^2 \tag{1.13}$$

The square root of a number is also known as the *second root* of that number. We can also calculate the third, fourth, fifth, or any size root of a number. The third root of a number is known as its cube root and is written like this: $\sqrt[3]{\ }$. Notice how we need the 3 there to tell us that the root to be taken is the third. The cube root of a number gives a number that when multiplied to the power of three gives the original number. For instance:

$$\sqrt[3]{27} = 3 \tag{1.14}$$

Once again we can cube both sides of the equation to show the relationship between the power and the root:

$$27 = 3^3 \tag{1.15}$$

It's also possible to write the root of a number as a *fractional exponent*. For example, the square root of a number can be written as $x^{\frac{1}{2}}$, the third root as $x^{\frac{1}{3}}$, and so on.

Simplifying Equations

Often, to solve an equation you must first simplify it. One of the golden rules for achieving this is that you can add, subtract, divide, or multiply terms to either side. (There is one exception to this rule: The term must not be zero when multiplying or dividing.) As long as the same thing is done to *both* sides, then the sides will remain equal. This is best understood with the aid of a couple of examples.

Example 1

Consider the following equation:

$$3x + 7 = 22 - 2x \tag{1.16}$$

This equation can be simplified by subtracting 7 from both sides.

$$\begin{aligned} 3x + 7 - 7 &= 22 - 2x - 7 \\ 3x &= 15 - 2x \end{aligned} \tag{1.17}$$

It can be further simplified by adding $2x$ to both sides:

$$\begin{aligned} 3x + 2x &= 15 - 2x + 2x \\ 5x &= 15 \end{aligned} \tag{1.18}$$

We can also divide both sides by 5, giving us the answer for x:

$$\begin{aligned} \frac{5x}{5} &= \frac{15}{5} \\ x &= 3 \end{aligned} \tag{1.19}$$

Let's take a look at a slightly more complex example.

Example 2

Let's say we want to solve the following for *y*:

$$y = 2(3x - 5y) + \frac{x}{3} \tag{1.20}$$

First of all we can remove the parentheses by multiplying the term inside the parentheses $(3x - 5y)$, by the term outside (2), giving:

$$y = 6x - 10y + \frac{x}{3} \tag{1.21}$$

Next, it's a good idea to remove all fractional terms by multiplying all the terms on both sides with the denominators of the fractions (the denominators are the values beneath the line). In this example, multiplying all terms on both sides of equation (1.21) by 3 gives:

$$3y = 18x - 30y + x \tag{1.22}$$

At this point we have a *y* term on the left and *x and y* terms on the right. We need to transpose similar terms so they share the same side of the equation. In this example we can do this by adding $30y$ to both sides.

$$\begin{aligned} 3y + 30y &= 18x - 30y + x + 30y \\ 3y + 30y &= 18x + x \end{aligned} \tag{1.23}$$

Now that like terms are grouped together we can combine them. This gives:

$$33y = 19x \tag{1.24}$$

Finally, we should divide both sides by the coefficient in front of the unknown variable. In this example we are solving for *y* so we must divide both sides by 33, giving:

$$y = \frac{19}{33}x \tag{1.25}$$

Example 3

Here are a few more rules that come in handy when simplifying equations:

$$\frac{x}{y} = \frac{1}{y}(x) \tag{1.26}$$

$$\frac{a}{x} + \frac{b}{y} = \frac{ay + bx}{xy} \tag{1.27}$$

$$(x+y)^2 = x^2 + y^2 + 2xy \tag{1.28}$$

$$\left(\frac{x}{y}\right)^2 = \frac{x^2}{y^2} \tag{1.29}$$

$$\sqrt{\frac{x}{y}} = \frac{\sqrt{x}}{\sqrt{y}} \tag{1.30}$$

Let's take a look at some of the new rules in action. This time the equation to simplify is:

$$5x - 2y = \left(\frac{y-x}{\sqrt{x}}\right)^2 \tag{1.31}$$

Using rule (1.29) gives:

$$\begin{gathered} 5x - 2y = \frac{(y-x)^2}{\left(\sqrt{x}\right)^2} \\ 5x - 2y = \frac{(y-x)^2}{x} \end{gathered} \tag{1.32}$$

Multiplying both sides by x to dispose of the fractional part gives:

$$x(5x - 2y) = (y-x)^2 \tag{1.33}$$

Now to get rid of the parentheses on the left:

$$5x^2 - 2xy = (y-x)^2 \tag{1.34}$$

To remove the parentheses on the right we use the rule from (1.28):

$$5x^2 - 2xy = x^2 + y^2 - 2xy \tag{1.35}$$

Adding $2xy$ to both sides gives:

$$5x^2 = x^2 + y^2 \tag{1.36}$$

By subtracting x^2 from both sides and rearranging we get the simplified equation:

$$y^2 = 4x^2 \tag{1.37}$$

The final step is to take the square root of both sides:

$$y = 2x \tag{1.38}$$

Simplifying equations can get a lot harder than this of course, but these few rules are enough for you to understand any of the simplifications presented in this book.

Trigonometry

Trigonometry is based on the study of triangles. The word comes from the Greek words *trigon*, for triangle, and *metry*, for measure. It is an enormously useful field of mathematics and has many practical applications in computer science. In the game AI field, you will find it used for line-of-sight (LOS) calculations, collision detection, some aspects of pathfinding, etc. Lots of AI is really math-dependent when you boil it down; you will be wise to learn it well.

Rays and Line Segments

A *ray* is a line with one endpoint. It is of infinite length and is defined by a direction (usually expressed as a normalized vector; see the section on vectors later in this chapter) and an origin. Figure 1.6 shows a ray situated at the origin.

A *line segment* is a *piece* of a line and is defined by two endpoints. Figure 1.6 also shows a line segment defined by the two endpoints p1 and p2.

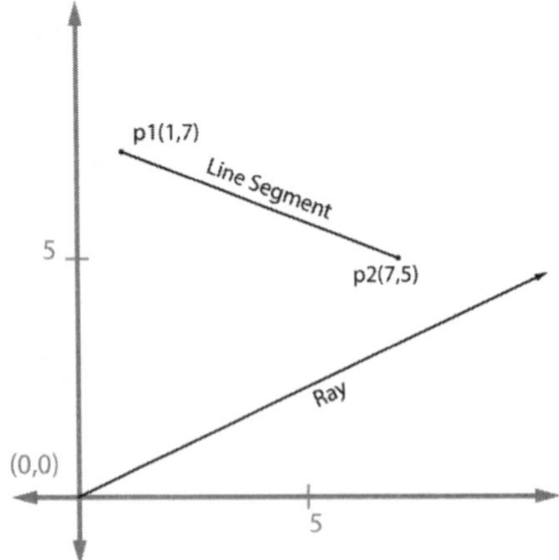

Figure 1.6. A line segment and a ray

Angles

An angle is defined as the measure of divergence of two rays that share the same origin. See Figure 1.7.

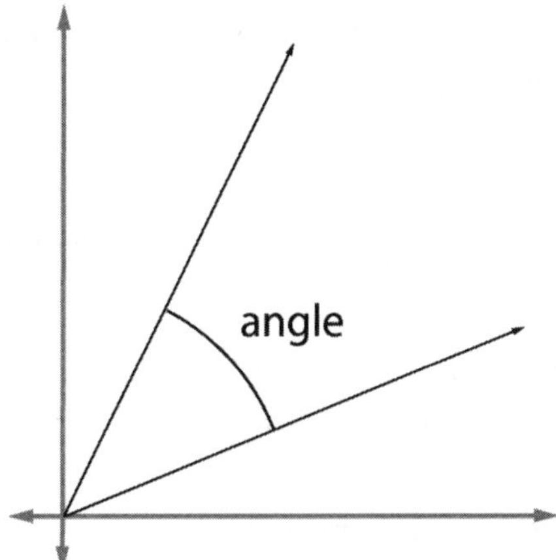

Figure 1.7. An angle

You may be used to thinking of angles in terms of degrees. Walls in most homes are typically at 90 degree angles, for example, and circles are 360 degrees around. Mathematicians prefer to measure the magnitude of an angle using *radians*. Radians are a unit of measurement based upon a circle of unit radius — a radius of 1 — centered at the origin. The radius of a circle is the distance from the center of the circle to its perimeter. Drawing the two rays from Figure 1.7 onto the same diagram as the unit circle, we get Figure 1.8. The length of the curved line segment between the two rays — shown in the diagram as a dotted line — is the angle measured in radians between them.

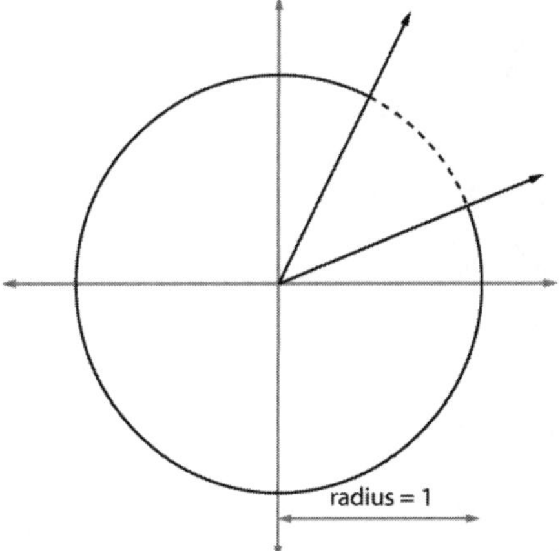

Figure 1.8. The length of the dotted line is the angle in radians between the two rays.

Now that you know what a radian is, let's calculate how many radians there are in a circle. You may remember the Greek symbol π (pi) from your school days. It's a well-known and frequently used mathematical constant, and has a value of 3.14159 (to five decimal places). You can use pi to calculate the circumference of a circle — the distance around the entire perimeter — using the equation:

$$perimeter = 2\pi r \quad (1.39)$$

Using this equation to determine the perimeter of a unit circle gives the number of radians in a circle. That's because the number of radians in a circle *is* the length of the perimeter of a circle with a radius of 1. So we just substitute 1 for r in equation (1.39) to get:

$$perimeter = 2\pi r = 2\pi(1) = 2\pi = num\ radians \quad (1.40)$$

Therefore, there are 2 π radians in every circle.

TIP Now that you know how many radians make up a circle, you can convert between radians and degrees if you ever have to. There are 360 degrees in a circle, so that means:

$360° = 2\pi$ rads

Dividing both sides by 360 we get:

$1° = 2\pi/360$ rads

Angles are usually denoted using the Greek letter *theta*, which looks like this: θ.

Triangles

A triangle consists of three line segments connected at their ends. A triangle's inner angles always add up to π radians (180 degrees). Figure 1.9 shows the different types of triangles you can encounter.

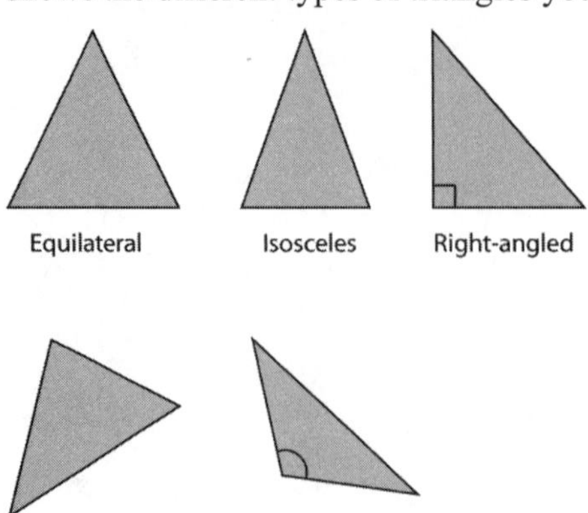

Figure 1.9. Different types of triangles

- An **equilateral** triangle has sides of equal length. Triangles with this property also have angles of equal sizes.
- An **isosceles** triangle has two sides and two angles of equal size.
- A **right-angled** triangle has one angle that is π/2 radians (90 degrees) — a *right angle*. The right angle is always represented by a box.
- An **acute** triangle's inner angles are all acute (less than π/2 radians).
- An **obtuse** triangle has one angle that is obtuse (greater than π/2 radians).

Pythagorean Theorem

The triangles you will be using most are of the right-angled variety. They have many interesting properties you can put to good use. Possibly the most famous property of right-angled triangles was discovered by Pythagoras, a Greek mathematician who lived from 569 to 475 BC. He was a very clever chap indeed, and is most famous for stating this:

> *The square of the hypotenuse of a right-angled triangle is equal to the sum of the squares of the other two sides.*

The hypotenuse of a triangle is its longest side, as shown in Figure 1.10.

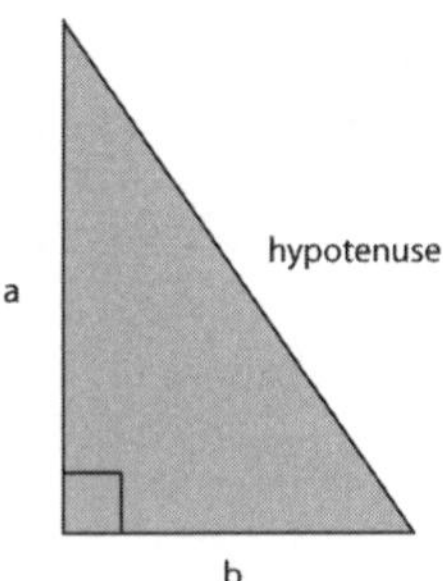

Figure 1.10

If the hypotenuse is denoted as h, the Pythagorean theorem can be written as:

$$h^2 = a^2 + b^2 \tag{1.41}$$

Taking the square root of both sides gives:

$$h = \sqrt{a^2 + b^2} \tag{1.42}$$

This means that if we know the length of any two sides of a right-angled triangle, we can easily find the third.

⌘ **TIP** When working on the AI for games you will frequently find yourself using the Pythagorean theorem to calculate if Agent A is closer to an object than Agent B. This would normally require two calls to the square root function, which, as we all know, is slow and should be avoided wherever possible. Fortunately, when comparing the lengths of the sides of two triangles, if side A is bigger than side B, then it will always be bigger, whether the lengths are squared or not. This means that we can avoid taking the square roots and just compare the squared values instead. This is known as working in *squared-distance space* and is something you will see frequently in the code shown in this book.

A Practical Example of the Pythagorean Theorem

Let's say you have an archer at position A (8, 4) and his target at position T (2, 1). The archer can only fire an arrow a maximum distance of 10 units. Consequently, to determine if he can hit the target, the distance between them must be calculated. This is easy to determine using the Pythagorean theorem. First, the lengths of the sides TP and AP shown in Figure 1.11 are calculated.

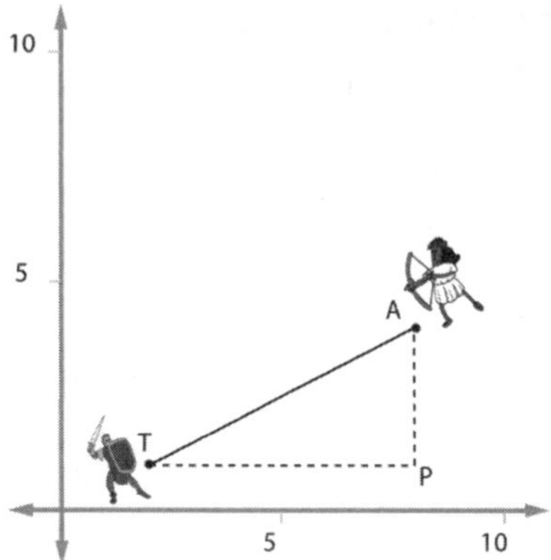

Figure 1.11

To find the distance AP, the y component of the archer's position is subtracted from the y component of the target's position:

$$AP = 4 - 1 = 3 \quad (1.43)$$

To find the distance TP, we do the same, but with the x components:

$$TP = 8 - 2 = 6 \quad (1.44)$$

Now that TP and AP are known, the distance from the archer to the target can be calculated using the Pythagorean theorem:

$$\begin{aligned} TA &= \sqrt{AP^2 + TP^2} \\ &= \sqrt{3^2 + 6^2} \\ &= \sqrt{9 + 36} \\ &= 6.71 \end{aligned} \tag{1.45}$$

Well within target range. Let that arrow fly!

The Mysteries of SohCahToa Unveiled

If you know the length of one of the sides of a right-angled triangle and one of the remaining two angles, you can determine everything else about the triangle using trigonometry. First, take a look at Figure 1.12. It shows the names of each side of a right-angled triangle.

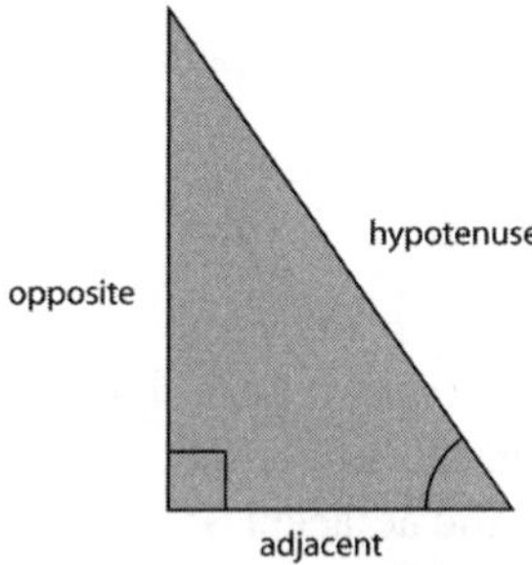

Figure 1.12. Names of the sides of a triangle

The side opposite the angle is called the *opposite* (surprise, surprise), and the side lying between the angle and the right angle is known as the *adjacent*. There are three trigonometric functions to help calculate the features of a right-angled triangle. You probably know them from school. They are sine, cosine, and tangent, and are often abbreviated to *sin*, *cos*, and *tan*. This is what they represent:

$$\sin(\theta) = \frac{opposite}{hypotenuse} \tag{1.46}$$

$$\cos(\theta) = \frac{adjacent}{hypotenuse} \tag{1.47}$$

$$\tan(\theta) = \frac{opposite}{adjacent} \tag{1.48}$$

It will pay you well to memorize these three relationships because you'll be using them frequently. My math teacher taught me to memorize them as a mnemonic: Soh-Cah-Toa, pronounced "sowcahtowa" (where "sow" and "tow" rhyme with "know"). Although it looks weird, it's easy to say, and very easy to remember.

The best way of seeing how the sine, cosine, and tangent functions can be utilized is by looking at some examples.

⌘ **TIP** When working out any of the following problems on a calculator, make sure it's set to work in radians, and not degrees!

Take a look at Figure 1.13.

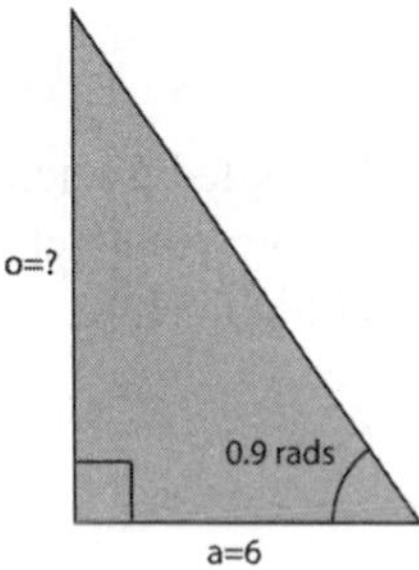

Figure 1.13

We want to calculate the length of the opposite given the length of the adjacent and the angle. From SohCahToa we can remember that the tangent of an angle is equal to the opposite divided by the adjacent. Rearranging the equation a little gives us:

$$o = aTan(\theta) \tag{1.49}$$

So all we have to do to get o is pick up a calculator (to determine the tangent) and plug in the numbers, like so:

$$\begin{aligned} o &= 6Tan(0.9) \\ &= 7.56 \end{aligned} \tag{1.50}$$

Easy peasy. Okay, let's try another, only this time you try to solve it first. Calculate the length of the side h shown in Figure 1.14

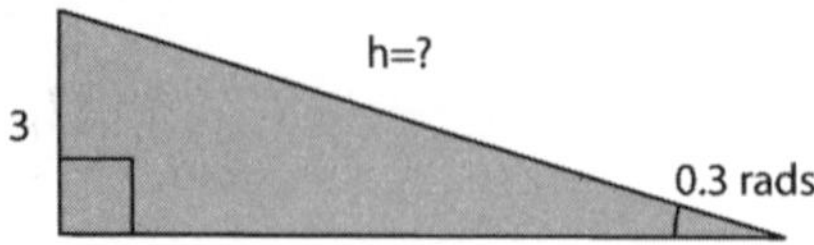

Figure 1.14

Did you manage it? In this example we know the angle and the opposite. Remembering SohCahToa, we see that it's the sine function that should be used because the sine of the angle is equal to the opposite divided by the hypotenuse. Rearranging the equation gives:

$$h = \frac{o}{\sin(\theta)} \tag{1.51}$$

And plugging in the numbers gives:

$$\begin{aligned} h &= \frac{3}{\sin(0.3)} \\ &= 10.15 \end{aligned} \tag{1.52}$$

So far so good. How about the problem shown in Figure 1.15? This time you have to find the angle given the lengths of the adjacent and hypotenuse.

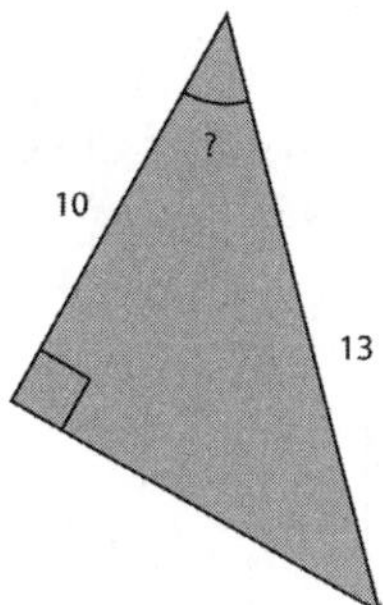

Figure 1.15

This time our friend is the cosine function, but plugging in the numbers creates a problem.

$$\cos(?) = \frac{10}{13} = 0.769 \tag{1.53}$$

We know that the *cosine* of the angle is 0.769, but what is the angle itself? How do we find that out? Well, the angle is determined using the *inverse cosine*. This is normally written as $\cos^{-1}$. So, all you do is use the inverse cosine button on a calculator (if you can't see $\cos^{-1}$ on your calculator, you may have to press the inverse button before the cosine button) to get the result:

$$? = \cos^{-1}(0.769) = 0.693\ \textit{radians} \tag{1.54}$$

At this point I'm going to end the lesson in trigonometry. Although it is a vast subject, the Pythagorean theorem and SohCahToa are all the trig theory you are going to need for the rest of this book.

Vectors

You'll be using vector math frequently when designing the AI for your games. Vectors are used everywhere from calculating which direction a game agent should shoot its gun to expressing the inputs and outputs of an artificial neural network. Vectors are your friend. You should get to know them well.

You have learned that a point on the Cartesian plane can be expressed as two numbers, just like this:

$$P = (x, y) \tag{1.55}$$

A 2D vector looks almost the same when written down:

$$\mathbf{v} = (x, y) \tag{1.56}$$

However, although similar, a vector represents two qualities: direction *and* magnitude. The right-hand side of Figure 1.16 shows the vector (9, 6) situated at the origin.

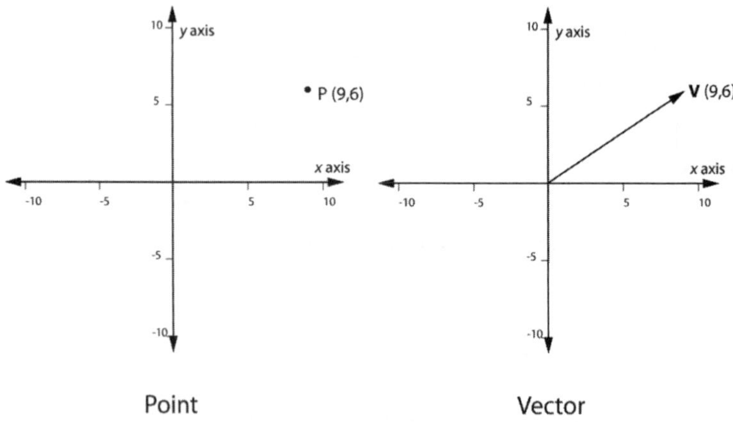

Figure 1.16. A point, P, and a vector, V

NOTE Vectors are typically denoted in bold typeface or as a letter with an arrow above it like so: $\vec{v}$. I'll be using the bold notation throughout this book.

The bearing of the arrow shows the direction of the vector and the length of the line represents the magnitude of the vector. Okay, so far so good. But what does this mean? What use is it? Well, for starters, a vector can represent the velocity of a vehicle. The magnitude of the vector represents the speed of the vehicle and the direction represents the heading of the vehicle. That's quite a lot of information from just two numbers (x, y).

Vectors aren't restricted to two dimensions either. They can be any size at all. You would use a 3D vector, (x, y, z) for example, to represent the velocity of a vehicle that moves in three dimensions, like a helicopter.

Let's take a look at some of the things you can do with vectors.

Adding and Subtracting Vectors

Imagine you are a contestant in a TV reality game. You are standing in a clearing in the jungle. Several other competitors stand beside you. You're all very nervous and excited because the winner gets to date Cameron Diaz… and the losers have to watch. Sweat is dripping from your forehead, your hands are clammy, and you cast nervous glances at the other competitors. The bronzed, anvil-chinned TV host steps forward and hands a gold-trimmed envelope to each competitor. He steps back and orders you all to rip open your envelopes. The first person to complete the instructions will be the winner. You frantically tear away at the paper. Inside is a note. It says:

> *I'm waiting for you in a secret location. Please hurry, it's very hot in here. You can reach the location by following the vectors (–5, 5), (0, –10), (13, 7), (–4, 3).*
>
> *Cameron*

With a smile on your face you watch the rest of the competitors sprint off in the direction of the first vector. You do a few calculations on the back of the envelope and then set off in a completely different direction at a leisurely stroll. By the time the other competitors reach Cameron's hideout, sweating like old cheese and gasping for breath, they can hear your playful giggles and the splash of cool shower water…

You beat the opposition because you knew how to add vectors together. Figure 1.17 shows the route all the other competitors took by following the vectors given in Cameron's note.

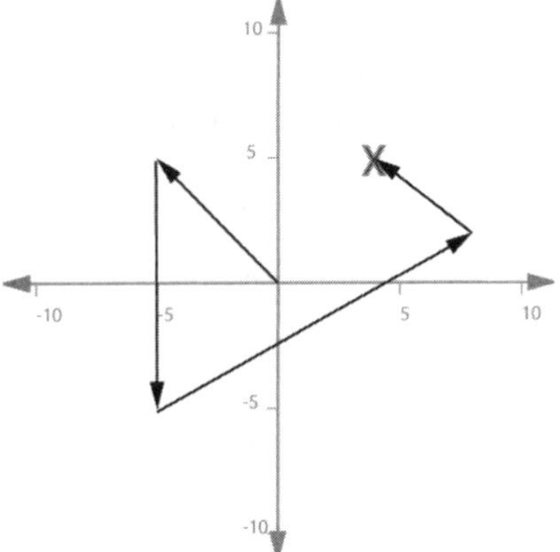

Figure 1.17. The route of the opposition

You knew, however, that if you added all the vectors together you would get a single vector as the result: one that takes you directly to the final destination. To add vectors together you simply add up all the x values to give the result's x component, and then do the same with the y values to get the y component. Adding the four vectors in Cameron's note together we get:

$$\begin{aligned} new\ x &= (-5) + (0) + (13) + (-4) = 4 \\ new\ y &= (5) + (-10) + (7) + (3) = 5 \end{aligned} \tag{1.57}$$

giving the vector (4, 5), exactly the same result as if we followed each vector individually. See Figure 1.18.

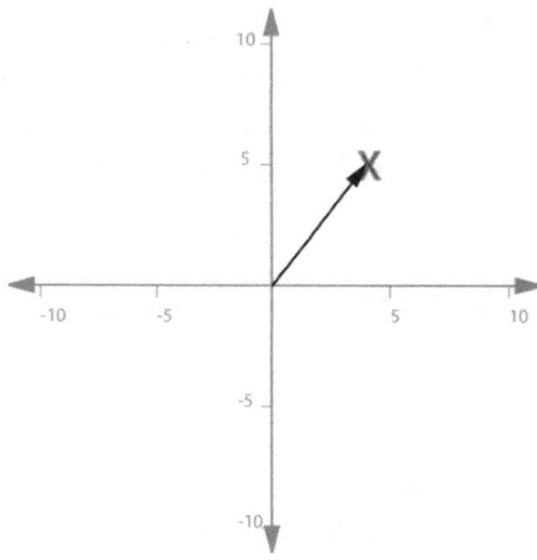

Figure 1.18. Your route

Multiplying Vectors

Multiplying vectors is a cinch. You just multiply each component by the value. For example, the vector **v** (4, 5) multiplied by 2 is (8, 10).

Calculating the Magnitude of a Vector

The *magnitude* of a vector is its length. In the previous example the magnitude of the vector **v** (4, 5) is the distance from the start point to Cameron's hideout.

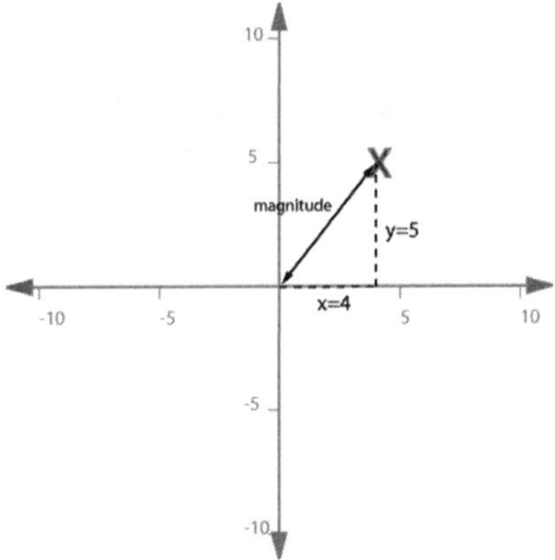

Figure 1.19. Finding the magnitude of a vector

This is easy to calculate using the Pythagorean theorem.

$$magnitude = \sqrt{4^2 + 5^2} = 6.403 \tag{1.58}$$

If you had a three-dimensional vector then you would use the similar equation:

$$magnitude = \sqrt{x^2 + y^2 + z^2} \tag{1.59}$$

Mathematicians place two vertical bars around a vector to denote its length.

$$magnitude = |\mathbf{v}| \tag{1.60}$$

Normalizing Vectors

When a vector is normalized, it retains its direction but its magnitude is recalculated so that it is of unit length (a length of 1). To do this you divide each component of the vector by the magnitude of the vector. Mathematicians write the formula like this:

$$\mathbf{N} = \frac{\mathbf{v}}{|\mathbf{v}|} \tag{1.61}$$

Therefore, to normalize the vector (4, 5) you would do this:

$$\begin{aligned} new\ x &= 4/6.403 = 0.62 \\ new\ y &= 5/6.403 = 0.78 \end{aligned} \tag{1.62}$$

This may seem a strange thing to do to a vector but in fact, normalized vectors are incredibly useful. You'll find out why shortly.

Resolving Vectors

It's possible to use trigonometry to resolve a vector into two separate vectors, one parallel to the *x*-axis and one to the *y*-axis. Take a look at the vector, **v**, representing the thrust of the jet-fighter shown in Figure 1.20.

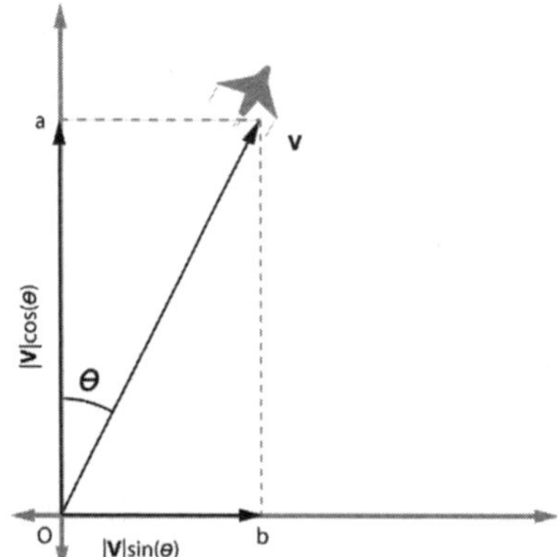

Figure 1.20

To resolve **v** into its *x*/*y* components we need to find Oa and Ob. This will give us the component of the aircraft's thrust that is acting along the *y*-axis, and the component along the *x*-axis, respectively. Another way of putting it is that Oa is the amount of thrust acting along the *x*-axis, and Ob is the amount along the *y*-axis.

First, let's calculate the amount of thrust along the *y*-axis: Oa. From trigonometry we know that:

$$\cos(\theta) = \frac{adjacent}{hypotenuse} = \frac{Oa}{|\mathbf{v}|} \tag{1.63}$$

Rearranged, this gives:

$$Oa = |\mathbf{v}| Cos(\theta) = y\ component \tag{1.64}$$

To calculate Ob this equation is used:

$$\sin(\theta) = \frac{opposite}{hypotenuse} = \frac{Ob}{|\mathbf{v}|} \tag{1.65}$$

Giving:

$$Ob = |\mathbf{v}| \sin(\theta) = x\ component \tag{1.66}$$

The Dot Product

The *dot product* gives the angle between two vectors — something you will need to calculate often when programming AI. Given the two 2D vectors **u** and **v**, the equation looks like this:

$$\mathbf{u} \bullet \mathbf{v} = \mathbf{u}_x \mathbf{v}_x + \mathbf{u}_y \mathbf{v}_y \tag{1.67}$$

The • symbol denotes the dot product. Equation (1.67) doesn't give us an angle though. I promised an angle, so you'll get one! Here's another way of calculating the dot product:

$$\mathbf{u} \bullet \mathbf{v} = |\mathbf{u}||\mathbf{v}|\cos(\theta) \tag{1.68}$$

Rearranging we get:

$$\cos(\theta) = \frac{\mathbf{u} \bullet \mathbf{v}}{|\mathbf{u}||\mathbf{v}|} \tag{1.69}$$

Remember, the vertical lines surrounding a vector indicate its magnitude. Now is the time when you discover one of the useful uses for normalizing vectors. If **v** and **u** are *both normalized*, then the equation simplifies enormously to:

$$\begin{aligned} \cos(\theta) &= \frac{\mathbf{u} \bullet \mathbf{v}}{1 \times 1} \\ &= \mathbf{u} \bullet \mathbf{v} \end{aligned} \tag{1.70}$$

Substituting in the equation from (1.67) for the right-hand side gives:

$$\cos(\theta) = \mathbf{u} \bullet \mathbf{v} = \mathbf{u}_x \mathbf{v}_x + \mathbf{u}_y \mathbf{v}_y \tag{1.71}$$

giving us an equation for the angle between the vectors.

One great use of the dot product is that it will quickly tell you if one entity is behind or in front of the facing plane of another. How so? Check out Figure 1.21.

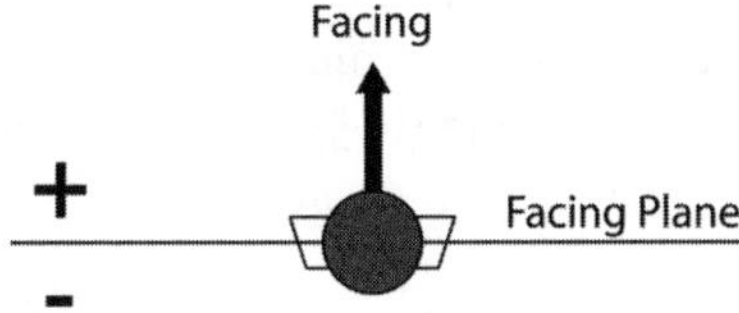

Figure 1.21

The figure shows a game agent facing directly north. The horizontal line is relative to the agent and describes the facing plane of the agent. Everything situated ahead of this line can be said to be in front of the agent.

Using the dot product it's easy to determine if an object is situated in front or behind the agent. The dot product of the agent's facing vector and the vector from the agent to the object will be positive if the object is forward of the facing plane of the agent and negative if it is behind.

A Practical Example of Vector Mathematics

Here's an example of some of the vector methods you've just learned about working together. Let's say you have a game agent, Eric the Troll, who stands at position *T* (the origin) and facing in the direction given by the normalized vector **H** (for heading). He can smell a helpless princess at position *P* and would very much like to throw his club at her, to tenderize her a little, before he rips her to pieces. To do this, he needs to know how many radians he must rotate to face her. Figure 1.22 shows the situation.

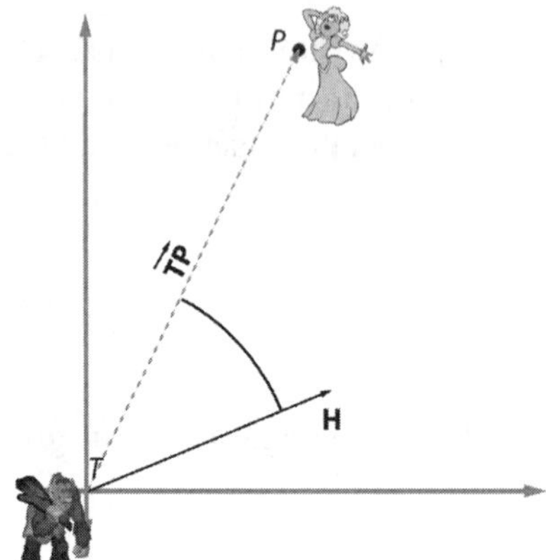

Figure 1.22

You've discovered that you can calculate the angle between two vectors using the dot product. However, in this problem you only have one vector to start with, **H**. Therefore we need to determine the vector $\overrightarrow{TP}$ — the vector that points directly at the princess. This is calculated by subtracting point *T* from point *P*. Because *T* is at the origin (0, 0), in this example $P-T = P$. However, the answer $P-T$ is a vector, so let's show this by typing it in bold and calling it **P**.

We know that the cosine of the angle the troll needs to turn to face the princess is equivalent to the dot product of **H** and **P**, provided both vectors are normalized. **H** is already normalized so we only need to normalize **P**. Remember, to normalize a vector its components are divided by its magnitude. Consequently, the normal of **P** ($\mathbf{N_P}$) is:

$$\mathbf{N}_\mathbf{p} = \frac{\mathbf{P}}{|\mathbf{P}|} \tag{1.72}$$

The dot product can now be used to determine the angle.

$$\cos(\theta) = \mathbf{N}_\mathbf{p} \bullet \mathbf{H} \tag{1.73}$$

So

$$\theta = \cos^{-1}\left(\mathbf{N}_\mathbf{p} \bullet \mathbf{H}\right) \tag{1.74}$$

To clarify the process, let's do the whole thing again but with some numbers. Let's say the troll is situated at the origin $T\,(0, 0)$ and has a heading of **H** (1, 0). The princess is standing at the point $P\,(4, 5)$. How many radians does the troll have to turn to face the princess?

We know that we can use equation (1.74) to calculate the angle but first we need to determine the vector, **TP**, between the troll and the princess and normalize it. To obtain **TP** we subtract T from P, resulting in the vector (4, 5). To normalize **TP** we divide it by its magnitude. This calculation was shown earlier in equation (1.62), resulting in $\mathbf{N}_{\mathrm{TP}}$ (0.62, 0.78).

Finally we plug the numbers into equation (1.74), substituting equation (1.71) for the dot product.

$$\theta = \cos^{-1}\left(\mathbf{N}_{TP} \bullet \mathbf{H}\right)$$
$$\theta = \cos^{-1}\left(\left(0.62 \times 1\right) + \left(0.78 \times 0\right)\right)$$
$$\theta = \cos^{-1}\left(0.62\right)$$
$$\theta = 0.902 \text{ radians}$$

The Vector2D Struct

All the examples given in this book make use of the `Vector2D` struct. It's very straightforward and implements all the vector operations we've discussed. I'll list the majority of its declaration here so you can familiarize yourself with it.

```
struct Vector2D
{
  double x;
  double y;

  Vector2D():x(0.0),y(0.0){}
  Vector2D(double a, double b):x(a),y(b){}

  //sets x and y to zero
  inline void Zero();

  //returns true if both x and y are zero
  inline bool      isZero()const;
```

```
  //returns the length of the vector
  inline double    Length()const;

  //returns the squared length of the vector (thereby avoiding the sqrt)
  inline double    LengthSq()const;

  inline void      Normalize();

  //returns the dot product of this and v2
  inline double    Dot(const Vector2D& v2)const;

  //returns positive if v2 is clockwise of this vector,
  //negative if counterclockwise (assuming the Y axis is pointing down,
  //X axis to right like a Window app)
  inline int       Sign(const Vector2D& v2)const;

  //returns the vector that is perpendicular to this one
  inline Vector2D  Perp()const;

  //adjusts x and y so that the length of the vector does not exceed max
  inline void      Truncate(double max);

  //returns the distance between this vector and the one passed as a parameter
  inline double    Distance(const Vector2D &v2)const;

  //squared version of above
  inline double    DistanceSq(const Vector2D &v2)const;

  //returns the vector that is the reverse of this vector
  inline Vector2D  GetReverse()const;

  //we need some operators
  const Vector2D& operator+=(const Vector2D &rhs);
  const Vector2D& operator-=(const Vector2D &rhs);
  const Vector2D& operator*=(const double& rhs);
  const Vector2D& operator/=(const double& rhs;
  bool operator==(const Vector2D& rhs)const;
  bool operator!=(const Vector2D& rhs)const;
};
```

Local Space and World Space

It's important you understand the difference between *local space* and *world space*. The world space representation is normally what you see rendered to your screen. Every object is defined by a position and orientation *relative to the origin of the world coordinate system* (see Figure 1.23). A soldier is using world space when he describes the position of a tank with a grid reference, for instance.

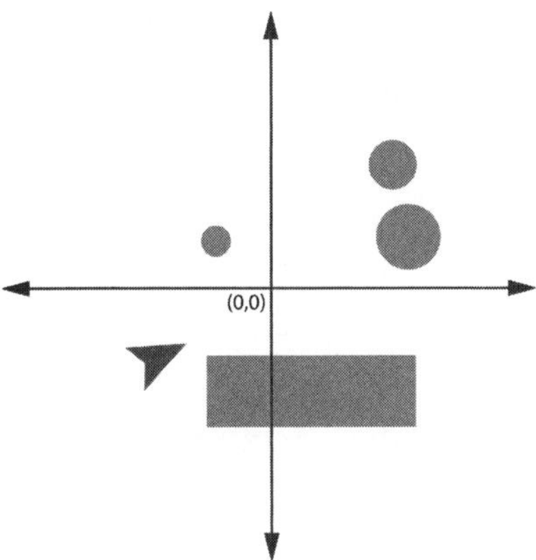

Figure 1.23. Some obstacles and a vehicle shown in world space

Local space, however, describes the position and orientation of objects relative to a specific entity's local coordinate system. In two dimensions, an entity's local coordinate system can be defined by a facing vector and a side vector (representing the local *x*- and *y*-axis, respectively), with the origin positioned at the center of the entity (for three dimensions an additional up vector is required). Figure 1.24 shows the axis describing the local coordinate system of the dart-shaped object.

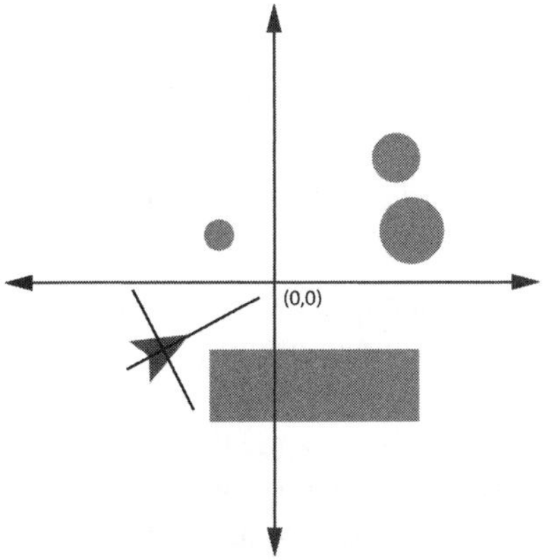

Figure 1.24. The vehicle's local coordinate system

Using this local coordinate system we can transform the world so that all the objects in it describe their position and orientation relative to it (see Figure 1.25). This is just like viewing the world through the eyes of the entity. Soldiers are using local space when they say stuff like "Target 50m away at 10 o'clock." They are describing the location of the target relative to their own position and facing direction.

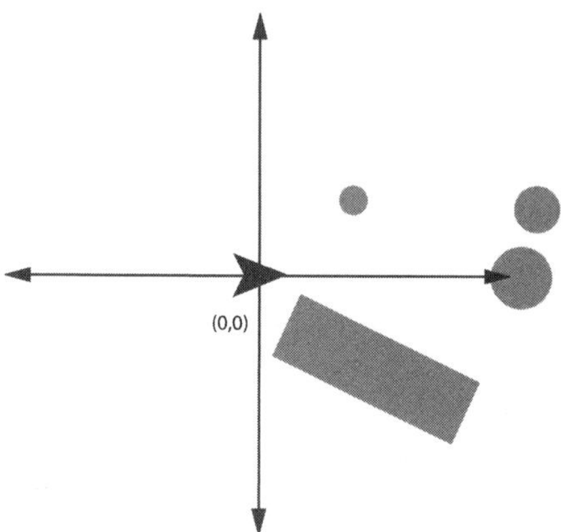

Figure 1.25. Objects transformed into the vehicle's local space

This ability to transform objects between local and world space can help simplify many calculations as you'll see later in the book. (Although you need to understand the concept, how it's actually done is beyond the scope of this book — check out the matrix transformations chapter of a computer graphics book.)

Physics

My dictionary defines the science of physics as:

> *The science of matter and energy and of the interactions between the two.*

As a game AI programmer you'll frequently be working with the laws of physics, and especially ones concerned with motion, which is what will be covered in this section. You'll often find yourself creating algorithms for predicting where an object or agent will be at some time in the future, for calculating what the best angle is to fire a weapon, or what heading and force an agent should kick a ball with to pass it to a receiver. This isn't AI per se of course, but it *is* all part of creating the illusion of intelligence and is normally part of the AI programmer's workload, so you need to know this stuff.

Let's take a look at some of the fundamental concepts used in physics.

Time

Time is a scalar quantity (completely specified by its magnitude and with no direction) measured in seconds, abbreviated to s. Until recently, a second was defined in terms of the rotational spin of the Earth, but as the

Earth's rotation is slowing down slightly every year, by the late sixties this became problematic for scientists who needed increasingly precise measurements for their experiments. Today, therefore, a second is measured as:

> *The duration of 9,192,631,770 periods of the radiation corresponding to the transition between the two hyperfine levels of the ground state of the cesium 133 atom.*

This definition provides today's scientists with the constant time interval they require for their precise experiments.

Time in computer games is measured in one of two ways: either in seconds (just as in the real world) or by using the time interval between updates as a kind of *virtual second*. The latter measurement can simplify many equations but you have to be careful because, unless the update rate is locked, the physics will differ between machines of varying speeds! Therefore, if you choose to use a virtual second, make sure your game's physics update frequency is locked to a reasonable rate — usually the rate of the slowest machine you're developing for.

NOTE Not all that long ago the majority of computer games used a fixed frame rate and every component — rendering, physics, AI, etc. — was updated at the same frequency. Many of today's sophisticated games, however, specify a unique rate for each component. For example, the physics might be updated 30 times a second, the AI 10 times a second, and the rendering code allowed to go as fast as the machine it runs on. Therefore, whenever I refer to an "update rate" in the text, if I don't specify a context, it will be in the context of the subject I'm talking about.

Distance

The standard unit of distance — a scalar quantity — is the meter, abbreviated to m.

Mass

Mass is a scalar quantity measured in kilograms, abbreviated to kg. Mass is the measure of an *amount* of something. This can be a confusing quality to measure since the mass of an object is calculated by weighing it, yet mass is not a unit of weight; it is a unit of *matter*. The weight of an object is a measurement of how much force gravity is exerting on that object. Because gravity varies from place to place (even here on Earth), this means the weight of an object can vary in different places, even though its mass never changes. So how can mass be measured accurately?

Scientists have overcome this problem by creating a platinum-iridium cylinder that everyone has agreed to call THE kilogram. This cylinder is kept in Paris and all measurements are made relative to it. In other words, you can go to France and have your own duplicate kilogram made, which weighs exactly the same as THE kilogram. Now you know that wherever you are located, no matter what the gravity, your duplicate will have exactly the same mass as THE kilogram back in France. Problem solved.

Position

You might think the position of an object is an easy property to measure, but *where exactly* do you measure its position from? For example, if you wanted to specify your body's position in space, from where would you take the measurement? Would it be from your feet, your stomach, or your head? This presents a problem because there would be a big discrepancy between the position of your head and that of your feet.

Physicists solve this problem by taking the location of the *center of mass* of the object as its position. The center of mass is the object's balance point. This would be the place where you could attach an imaginary piece of string to the object and it would balance in any position. Another good way of thinking about the center of mass is that it is the average location of all the mass in a body.

Velocity

Velocity is a vector quantity (a quantity that has magnitude *and* direction) that expresses *the rate of change of distance over time*. The standard unit of measurement of velocity is meters per second, abbreviated to m/s. This can be expressed mathematically as:

$$v = \frac{\Delta x}{\Delta t} \tag{1.75}$$

The Greek capital letter Δ, read as delta, is used in mathematics to denote a *change in quantity*. Therefore, Δt in equation (1.75) represents a change in time (a time interval) and Δx a change in distance (a displacement). Δ is calculated as the *after quantity minus the before quantity*. Therefore if an object's position at t = 0 is 2 (before) and at t = 1 is 5 (after), Δx is 5 – 2 = 3. This can also result in negative values. For instance if an object's position at t = 0 is 7 (before) and at t = 1 is 3 (after), Δx is 3 – 7 = –4.

NOTE Delta's little brother, the lowercase letter delta, written as δ, is used to represent very small changes. You often see δ used in calculus. Because δ looks similar to the letter *d*, to prevent confusion, mathematicians tend to avoid using *d* to represent distance or displacement in their equations. Instead, a less ambiguous symbol such as Δx is used.

Using equation (1.75), it's easy to calculate the average velocity of an object. Let's say you want to work out the average velocity of a ball as it rolls between two points. First calculate the displacement between the two points, then divide by the amount of time it takes the ball to cover that distance. For instance, if the distance between the points is 5 m and the time taken for the ball to travel between points is 2 s, then the velocity is:

$$v = \frac{5}{2} = 2.5 \text{ m/s} \tag{1.76}$$

It's also easy to calculate how far an object has traveled if we know its average speed and the length of time it has been traveling. Let's say you are driving your car at 35 mph and you'd like to know how far you've moved in the last half hour. Rearranging equation (1.75) gives:

$$\Delta x = v\Delta t \tag{1.77}$$

Popping in the numbers gives:

$$\text{distance traveled} = 35 \times \frac{1}{2} = 17.5 \text{ miles} \tag{1.78}$$

Relating this to computer games, if you have a vehicle at position **P** at time *t* traveling at constant velocity **V**, we can calculate its position at the next update step (at time *t* + *1*) by:

$$\mathbf{P}_{t+1} = \mathbf{P}_t + \mathbf{V}\Delta t \tag{1.79}$$

Where $\mathbf{V}\Delta t$ represents the displacement between update steps (from equation (1.77)).

Let's make this crystal clear by showing you a code example. Following is a listing for a `Vehicle` class that encapsulates the motion of a vehicle traveling with constant velocity.

```
class Vehicle
{
  //a vector representing its position in space
  vector m_vPosition;

  //a vector representing its velocity
  vector m_vVelocity;

public:

  //called each frame to update the position of the vehicle
  void Update(float TimeElapsedSinceLastUpdate)
  {
    m_vPosition += m_vVelocity * TimeElapsedSinceLastUpdate;
  }
};
```

Note that if your game uses a fixed update rate for the physics, as do many of the examples in this book, Δt will be constant and can be eliminated from the equation. This results in the simplified `Update` method as follows:

```
//update for a simulation using a constant update step
void Vehicle::Update()
{
  m_vPosition += m_vVelocity;
}
```

Remember though, that if you choose to eliminate Δt like this, the unit of time you will be using in any calculations is no longer the second but rather the time interval between update steps.

Acceleration

Acceleration is a vector quantity that expresses *the rate of change of velocity over time* and is measured in meters per second per second, written as m/s^2. Acceleration can be expressed mathematically as:

$$a = \frac{\Delta v}{\Delta t} \tag{1.80}$$

This equation is stating that acceleration is equivalent to the change in velocity of an object divided by the time interval during which the change in velocity occurred.

For example, if a car starts from rest and accelerates at 2 m/s^2, then every second, 2 m/s is added to its velocity. See Table 1.1.

Table 1.1

Time(s)	Velocity(m/s)
0	0
1	2
2	4
3	6
4	8
5	10

Plotting this data to a velocity versus time graph, we get Figure 1.26. If we examine a time interval, say the interval between $t = 1$ and $t = 4$, we can see that the gradient of the slope, given by $\frac{\Delta v}{\Delta t}$, is equivalent to the acceleration during that interval.

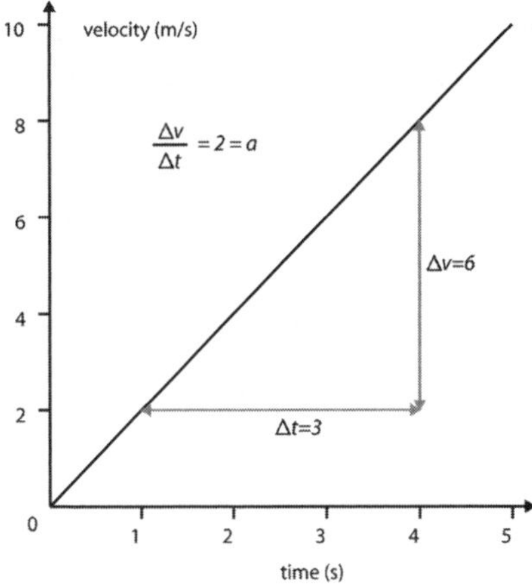

Figure 1.26. The velocity of the car plotted against time

You learned earlier how the equation $y = mx + c$ defines all straight lines in the 2D Cartesian plane, where m is the gradient and c the intersection on the y-axis. Because we can infer from Figure 1.26 that constant acceleration is always plotted as a straight line, we can relate that equation to the acceleration of the car. We know that the y-axis represents the velocity, v, and that the x-axis represents time, t. We also know that the gradient m relates to the acceleration. This gives the equation:

$$v = at + u \tag{1.81}$$

The constant u represents the velocity of the car at time $t = 0$, which can be shown as the intersection of the line on the y-axis. For instance, if the car in the example started off with a velocity of 3 m/s, then the graph would be identical but offset upward by 3 as shown in Figure 1.27.

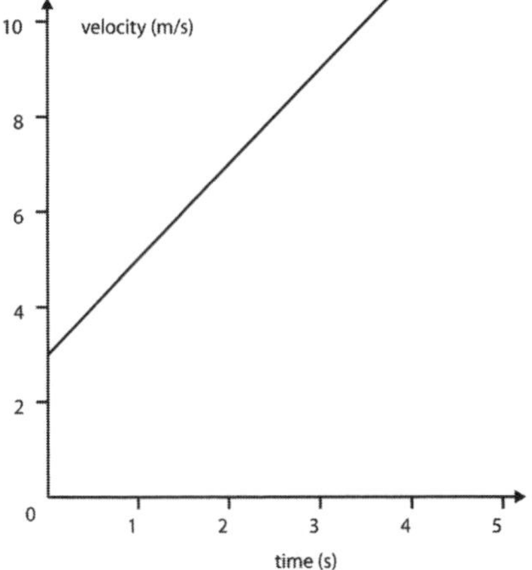

Figure 1.27. The same car but traveling with an initial velocity of 3 m/s at time $t = 0$

To test the equation let's determine what the velocity of a car starting with a velocity of 3 m/s and accelerating at 2 m/s^2 will be after 3 seconds. Plugging in the numbers to equation (1.81) gives:

$$\begin{aligned} v &= 2 \times 3 + 3 \\ v &= 9 \text{ m/s} \end{aligned} \tag{1.82}$$

This is exactly what we can infer from the graph. See Figure 1.28.

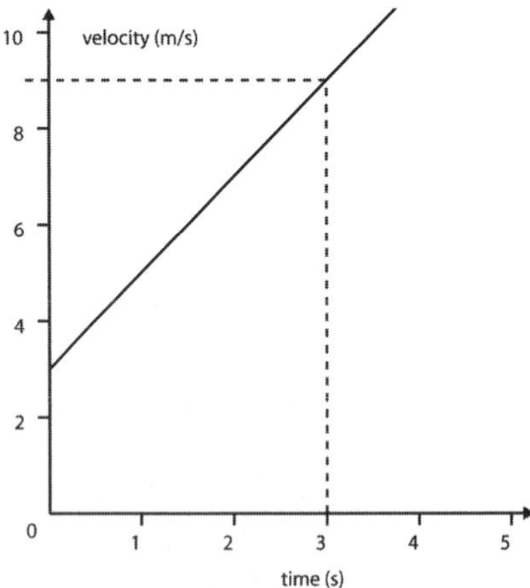

Figure 1.28

Another interesting thing about a velocity-time graph is that the area under the graph between two times is equivalent to the distance traveled by the object during that time. Let's look at a simple example first. Figure 1.29 shows the time versus velocity graph for a vehicle that spends 2 seconds at 4 m/s then stops.

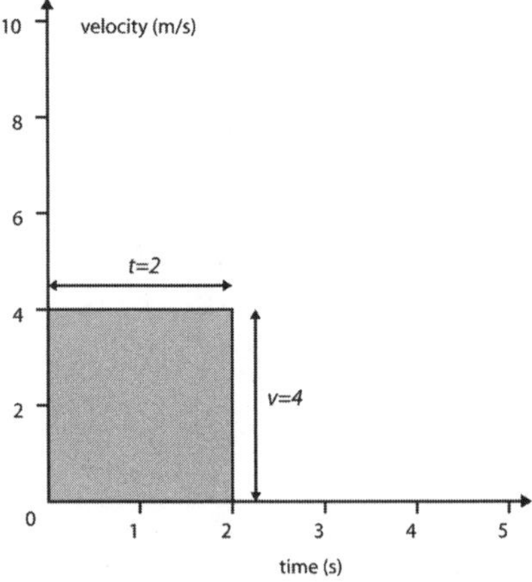

Figure 1.29

The area under the graph (the region shaded in gray) is given by height × width, which is equivalent to velocity × time, which as you can see gives the result of 8 meters. This is the same result from using the equation $\Delta x = v\Delta t$.

Figure 1.30 shows the example from earlier where a vehicle accelerates from rest with a constant acceleration of 2 m/s^2. Let's say we'd like to calculate the distance traveled between the times $t = 1$ and $t = 3$.

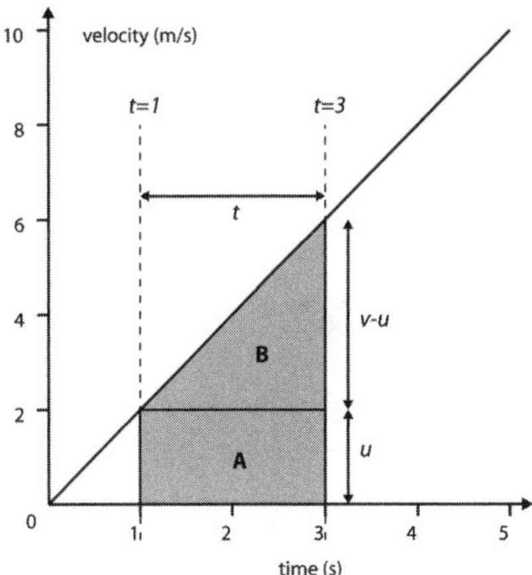

Figure 1.30

We know that the distance traveled between $t = 1$ and $t = 3$ is the area beneath the graph between those times. As is clearly shown in the figure, this is the sum of the areas of rectangle A and triangle B.

The area of A is given by the time displacement, t, multiplied by the starting velocity, u, written as:

$$Area(A) = \Delta t \times u \tag{1.83}$$

The area of B, a triangle, is half the area of the rectangle described by the sides of the triangle. The sides of the triangle are given by the time displacement, t, and the difference between the finish velocity and the start velocity, $v - u$. This can be written as:

$$Area(B) = \frac{1}{2}(v - u)\Delta t \tag{1.84}$$

Therefore, the total area under the graph between times $t = 1$ and $t = 3$, which is equivalent to the distance traveled, is the sum of these two terms, given as:

$$\Delta x = u\Delta t + \frac{1}{2}(v - u)\Delta t \tag{1.85}$$

We know that $v - u$ is equivalent to the change in velocity Δv, and that, from equation (1.80)

$$v - u = \Delta v = a\Delta t \tag{1.86}$$

This value for $v - u$ can be substituted into equation (1.85) to give us an equation that relates distance to time and acceleration.

$$\Delta x = u\Delta t + \frac{1}{2}a\Delta t^2 \tag{1.87}$$

Putting the numbers into this equation gives:

$$\begin{aligned} \Delta x &= 2 \times 2 + \frac{1}{2} \times 2 \times 2^2 \\ \Delta x &= 4 + 4 \\ \Delta x &= 8 \text{ m} \end{aligned} \tag{1.88}$$

We can do another useful thing with this equation: We can factor time out to give us an equation relating velocity to distance traveled. Here's how.

From equation (1.81) we know that:

$$\Delta t = \frac{v - u}{a} \tag{1.89}$$

We can substitute this value for Δt in equation (1.87) to give:

$$\Delta x = u\left(\frac{v - u}{a}\right) + \frac{1}{2}a\left(\frac{v - u}{a}\right)^2 \tag{1.90}$$

This nasty-looking equation can be simplified greatly. (If you are new to algebra I suggest trying to simplify it yourself. If you find yourself getting stuck, the full simplification is given at the end of the chapter.)

$$v^2 = u^2 + 2a\Delta x \tag{1.91}$$

This equation is extremely useful. For example, we can use it to determine how fast a ball dropped from the top of the Empire State Building will be traveling when it hits the ground (assuming no air resistance due to wind or velocity). The acceleration of a falling object is due to the force exerted upon it by the Earth's gravitational field and is equivalent to approximately 9.8 m/s^2. The starting velocity of the ball is 0 and the height of the Empire State Building is 381 m. Putting these values into the equation gives:

$$\begin{aligned} v^2 &= 0^2 + 2 \times 9.8 \times 381 \\ v &= \sqrt{7467.6} \\ v &= 86.41 \text{ m/s} \end{aligned} \tag{1.92}$$

The preceding equations hold true for all objects moving with a constant acceleration but of course it's also possible for objects to travel with varying acceleration. For example, an aircraft when taking off from a runway has a high acceleration at the beginning of its run (which you can feel as a force pushing you into the back of your seat), which decreases as the limits of its engine's power are reached. This type of acceleration would look something like that shown in Figure 1.31.

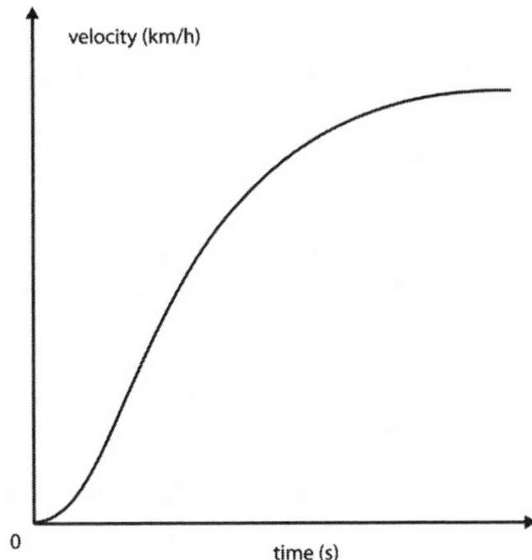

Figure 1.31. An aircraft accelerating up the runway

As another example, Figure 1.32 shows the velocity versus time graph for a car that accelerates to 30 km/h, brakes sharply to avoid a stray dog, and then accelerates back to 30 km/h.

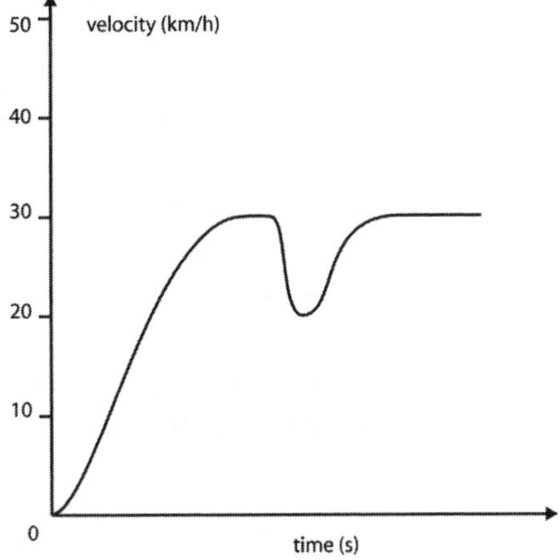

Figure 1.32

When you have varying accelerations like these it's only possible to determine the acceleration at a specific time. This is achieved by calculating the gradient of the tangent to the curve at that point.

Force

According to Isaac Newton:

> *An impressed force is an action exerted upon a body in order to change its state, either of rest, or of uniform motion in a right line.*

Therefore, force is that quality that can alter an object's speed or line of motion. Force has nothing to do with motion itself though. For example, a flying arrow does not need a constant force applied to it to keep it flying (as was thought by Aristotle). Force is only present where *changes in motion* occur, such as when the arrow is stopped by an object or when a drag racer accelerates along the strip. The unit of force is the Newton, abbreviated to N, and is defined as:

> *The force required to make a one-kilogram mass move from rest to a speed of one meter per second in one second.*

There are two different types of force: contact and non-contact forces. Contact forces occur between objects that are touching each other, such as the frictional force present between the snow and skis of a downhill skier. Non-contact forces are those that occur between objects not touching each other, such as the gravitational force of the Earth upon your body or the magnetic force of the Earth upon a compass needle.

It's important to note that many forces can act upon a single object simultaneously. If the sum of those forces equals zero, the object remains in motion with the same velocity in the same direction. In other words, if an object is stationary or moving in a straight line with a constant velocity, the sum of all the forces acting upon it must be zero. If, however, the sum of the forces is not equal to zero, the object will accelerate in the direction of the resultant force. This can be confusing, especially in relation to static objects. For instance, how can there be *any* forces acting upon an apple sitting on a table? After all, it's not moving! The answer is that there are two forces acting upon the apple: the force of gravity trying to pull the apple toward the Earth and an equal and opposite force from the table pushing it away from the Earth. This is why the apple remains motionless. Figure 1.33 shows examples of varying amounts of forces acting upon everyday objects.

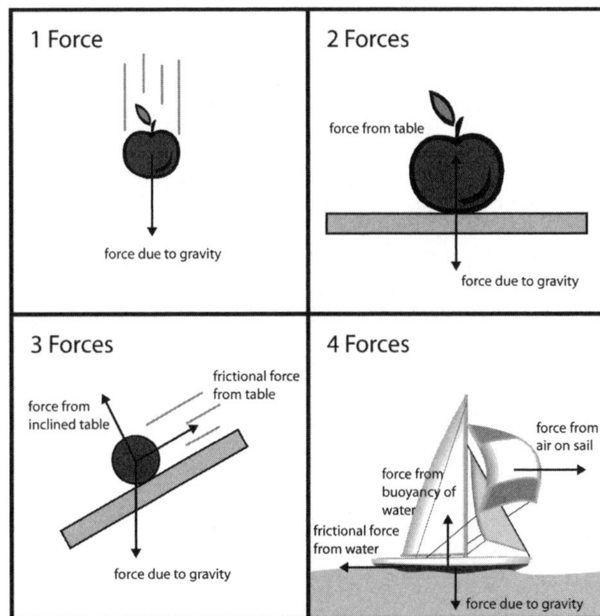

Figure 1.33. From left to right and top to bottom: a falling apple, an apple resting on a table, a ball rolling down an inclined table, and a yacht sailing on water

We know that if the sum of the forces acting upon an object is non-zero, an acceleration will be imparted in the direction of the force; but how much acceleration? The answer is that the amount of acceleration, *a*, is proportional to the object's mass, *m*, and to the total force applied, *F*. This relationship is given by the equation:

$$a = \frac{F}{m} \tag{1.93}$$

More commonly though, you will see this equation written as:

$$F = ma \tag{1.94}$$

Using this equation, if we know how fast an object is accelerating and its mass, we can calculate the total force acting upon it. For instance, if the boat in Figure 1.33 has a mass of 2000 kg, and it is accelerating at a rate of 1.5 m/s^2, the total force acting upon it is:

$$F_{total} = 2000 \times 1.5 = 3000 \text{ N}$$

Also using the equations for force, acceleration, velocity, and position, if we know how much force is acting on an object, we can determine the acceleration due to that force and update the object's position and velocity accordingly. For example, let's say you have a spaceship class with attributes for its mass, current velocity, and current position. Something like this:

```
class SpaceShip
{
private:

  vector m_Position;

  vector m_Velocity;

  float  m_fMass;

public:

  ...
};
```

Given the time interval since the last update and a force to be applied, we can create a method that updates the ship's position and velocity. Here's how:

```
void SpaceShip::Update(float TimeElapsedSinceLastUpdate, float ForceOnShip)
{
  float acceleration = ForceOnShip / m_fMass;
```

First of all, calculate the acceleration due to the force using equation (1.93).

```
  m_Velocity += acceleration * TimeElapsedSinceLastUpdate;
```

Next, update the velocity from the acceleration using equation (1.80).

```
  m_vPosition += m_Velocity * TimeElapsedSinceLastUpdate;
}
```

Finally, the position can be updated with the updated velocity using equation (1.77).

Summing Up

This chapter covers a lot of ground. If much of this stuff is new to you, you'll be feeling slightly confused and perhaps a little intimidated. Don't worry though. Soldier on and, as you read through the book, you'll see how each principle is applied to a practical problem. When you see the theory used in real-world contexts, you'll find it a lot easier to understand.

Simplification of Equation (1.90)

Let me show you how that pesky-looking equation is simplified. Here it is again in all its glory.

$$\Delta x = u\left(\frac{v-u}{a}\right) + \frac{1}{2}a\left(\frac{v-u}{a}\right)^2$$

First, let's work on the rightmost term. From the rule shown by equation (1.29) we can change the equation to read:

$$\Delta x = u\left(\frac{v-u}{a}\right) + \frac{1}{2}a\frac{(v-u)^2}{a^2}$$

We can now tidy up the a's a little:

$$\Delta x = u\left(\frac{v-u}{a}\right) + \frac{(v-u)^2}{2a}$$

Let's now dispose of the parentheses in the $(v-u)^2$ term using the rule given by equation (1.28).

$$\Delta x = u\left(\frac{v-u}{a}\right) + \frac{v^2+u^2-2vu}{2a}$$

Let's remove the other parentheses too.

$$\Delta x = \frac{uv-u^2}{a} + \frac{v^2+u^2-2vu}{2a}$$

Now to get rid of the fractional parts by multiplying every term by $2a$:

$$2a\Delta x = 2a\left(\frac{uv-u^2}{a}\right) + 2a\left(\frac{v^2+u^2-2vu}{2a}\right)$$

$$2a\Delta x = 2uv - 2u^2 + v^2 + u^2 - 2vu$$

Almost there now! We just need to group like terms together.

$$2a\Delta x = v^2 - u^2$$

And rearrange to give the final equation.

$$v^2 = u^2 + 2a\Delta x$$

Chapter 2

State-Driven Agent Design

Finite state machines, or FSMs as they are usually referred to, have for many years been the AI coder's instrument of choice to imbue a game agent with the illusion of intelligence. You will find FSMs of one kind or another in just about every game to hit the shelves since the early days of video games, and despite the increasing popularity of more esoteric agent architectures, they are going to be around for a long time to come. Here are just some of the reasons why:

They are quick and simple to code. There are many ways of programming a finite state machine and almost all of them are reasonably simple to implement. You'll see several alternatives described in this chapter together with the pros and cons of using them.

They are easy to debug. Because a game agent's behavior is broken down into easily manageable chunks, if an agent starts acting strangely, it can be debugged by adding tracer code to each state. In this way, the AI programmer can easily follow the sequence of events that precedes the buggy behavior and take action accordingly.

They have little computational overhead. Finite state machines use hardly any precious processor time because they essentially follow hard-coded rules. There is no real "thinking" involved beyond the if-*this*-then-*that* sort of thought process.

They are intuitive. It's human nature to think about things as being in one state or another and we often refer to ourselves as being in such and such a state. How many times have you "got yourself into a state" or found yourself in "the right state of mind"? Humans don't really work like finite state machines of course, but sometimes we find it useful to think of our behavior in this way. Similarly, it is fairly easy to break down a game agent's behavior into a number of states and to create the rules required for manipulating them. For the same reason, finite state machines also make it easy for you to discuss the design of your AI with non-programmers (with game producers and level designers for example), providing improved communication and exchange of ideas.

They are flexible. A game agent's finite state machine can easily be adjusted and tweaked by the programmer to provide the behavior required by the game designer. It's also a simple matter to expand the scope of an agent's behavior by adding new states and rules. In addition, as your AI skills grow you'll find that finite state machines provide a solid backbone with which you can combine other techniques such as fuzzy logic or neural networks.

What Exactly Is a Finite State Machine?

Historically, a finite state machine is a rigidly formalized device used by mathematicians to solve problems. The most famous finite state machine is probably Alan Turing's hypothetical device: the Turing machine, which he wrote about in his 1936 paper, "On Computable Numbers." This was a machine presaging modern-day programmable computers that could perform any logical operation by reading, writing, and erasing symbols on an infinitely long strip of tape. Fortunately, as AI programmers, we can forgo the formal mathematical definition of a finite state machine; a descriptive one will suffice:

> *A finite state machine is a device, or a model of a device, which has a finite number of states it can be in at any given time and can operate on input to either make transitions from one state to another or to cause an output or action to take place. A finite state machine can only be in one state at any moment in time.*

The idea behind a finite state machine, therefore, is to decompose an object's behavior into easily manageable "chunks" or states. The light switch on your wall, for example, is a very simple finite state machine. It has two states: on and off. Transitions between states are made by the input of your finger. By flicking the switch up it makes the transition from off to on, and by flicking the switch down it makes the transition from on to off. There is no output or action associated with the off state (unless you consider the bulb being off as an action), but when it is in the on state electricity is allowed to flow through the switch and light up your room via the filament in a lightbulb. See Figure 2.1.

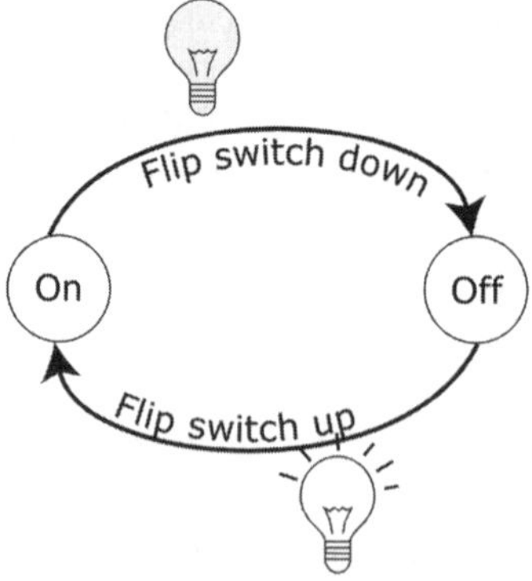

Figure 2.1. A light switch is a finite state machine. (Note that the switches are reversed in Europe and many other parts of the world.)

Of course, the behavior of a game agent is usually much more complex than a lightbulb (thank goodness!). Here are some examples of how finite state machines have been used in games.

- The ghosts' behavior in Pac-Man is implemented as a finite state machine. There is one Evade state, which is the same for all ghosts, and then each ghost has its own Chase state, the actions of which are implemented differently for each ghost. The input of the player eating one of the power pills is the condition for the transition from Chase to Evade. The input of a timer running down is the condition for the transition from Evade to Chase.
- Quake-style bots are implemented as finite state machines. They have states such as FindArmor, FindHealth, SeekCover, and RunAway. Even the weapons in Quake implement their own mini finite state machines. For example, a rocket may implement states such as Move, TouchObject, and Die.
- Players in sports simulations such as the soccer game FIFA2002 are implemented as state machines. They have states such as Strike, Dribble, ChaseBall, and MarkPlayer. In addition, the teams themselves are often implemented as FSMs and can have states such as KickOff, Defend, or WalkOutOnField.
- The NPCs (non-player characters) in RTSs (real-time strategy games) such as Warcraft make use of finite state machines. They have states such as MoveToPosition, Patrol, and FollowPath.

Implementing a Finite State Machine

There are a number of ways of implementing finite state machines. A naive approach is to use a series of if-then statements or the slightly tidier mechanism of a switch statement. Using a switch with an enumerated type to represent the states looks something like this:

```
enum StateType{RunAway, Patrol, Attack};

void Agent::UpdateState(StateType CurrentState)
{
  switch(CurrentState)
  {
  case state_RunAway:

     EvadeEnemy();

     if (Safe())
     {
       ChangeState(state_Patrol);
     }

     break;
```

```
  case state_Patrol:

    FollowPatrolPath();

    if (Threatened())
    {
      if (StrongerThanEnemy())
      {
        ChangeState(state_Attack);
      }
      else
      {
        ChangeState(state_RunAway);
      }
    }

    break;

  case state_Attack:

    if (WeakerThanEnemy())
    {
       ChangeState(state_RunAway);
    }

    else
    {
      BashEnemyOverHead();
    }

    break;

  }//end switch
}
```

Although at first glance this approach seems reasonable, when applied practically to anything more complicated than the simplest of game objects, the switch/if-then solution becomes a monster lurking in the shadows waiting to pounce. As more states and conditions are added, this sort of structure ends up looking like spaghetti very quickly, making the program flow difficult to understand and creating a debugging nightmare. In addition, it's inflexible and difficult to extend beyond the scope of its original design, should that be desirable… and as we all know, it most often is. Unless you are designing a state machine to implement very simple behavior (or you are a genius), you will almost certainly find yourself first tweaking the agent to cope with unplanned-for circumstances before honing the behavior to get the results you thought you were going to get when you first planned out the state machine!

Additionally, as an AI coder, you will often require that a state perform a specific action (or actions) when it's initially entered or when the state is exited. For example, when an agent enters the state RunAway you may want it to wave its arms in the air and scream "Arghhhhhhh!" When it finally escapes and changes state to Patrol, you may want it to emit a sigh, wipe its forehead, and say "Phew!" These are actions that only occur when the RunAway state is entered or exited and not during the usual update step. Consequently, this additional functionality must ideally be built into your state machine architecture. To do this within the framework of a switch or if-then architecture would be accompanied by lots of teeth grinding and waves of nausea, and produce very ugly code indeed.

State Transition Tables

A better mechanism for organizing states and affecting state transitions is a *state transition table*. This is just what it says it is: a table of conditions and the states those conditions lead to. Table 2.1 shows an example of the mapping for the states and conditions shown in the previous example.

Table 2.1. A simple state transition table

Current State	Condition	State Transition
Runaway	Safe	Patrol
Attack	WeakerThanEnemy	RunAway
Patrol	Threatened AND StrongerThanEnemy	Attack
Patrol	Threatened AND WeakerThanEnemy	RunAway

This table can be queried by an agent at regular intervals, enabling it to make any necessary state transitions based on the stimulus it receives from the game environment. Each state can be modeled as a separate object or function existing external to the agent, providing a clean and flexible architecture. One that is much less prone to spaghettification than the if-then/switch approach discussed in the previous section.

Someone once told me a vivid and silly visualization can help people to understand an abstract concept. Let's see if it works...

Imagine a robot kitten. It's shiny yet cute, and has wire for whiskers and a slot in its stomach where cartridges — analogous to its states — can be plugged in. Each of these cartridges is programmed with logic, enabling the kitten to perform a specific set of actions. Each set of actions encodes a different behavior; for example, "play with string," "eat fish," or "poo on carpet." Without a cartridge stuffed inside its belly the kitten is an inanimate metallic sculpture, only able to sit there and look cute... in a Metal Mickey kind of way.

The kitten is very dexterous and has the ability to autonomously exchange its cartridge for another if instructed to do so. By providing the rules that dictate when a cartridge should be switched, it's possible to string together sequences of cartridge insertions permitting the creation of all sorts of interesting and complicated behavior. These rules are programmed onto a tiny chip situated inside the kitten's head, which is analogous to the state transition table we discussed earlier. The chip communicates with the kitten's internal functions to retrieve the information necessary to process the rules (such as how hungry Kitty is or how playful it's feeling).

As a result, the state transition chip can be programmed with rules like:

IF Kitty_Hungry AND NOT Kitty_Playful
    SWITCH_CARTRIDGE eat_fish

All the rules in the table are tested each time step and instructions are sent to Kitty to switch cartridges accordingly.

This type of architecture is very flexible, making it easy to expand the kitten's repertoire by adding new cartridges. Each time a new cartridge is added, the owner is only required to take a screwdriver to the kitten's head in order to remove and reprogram the state transition rule chip. It is not necessary to interfere with any other internal circuitry.

Embedded Rules

An alternative approach is to *embed the rules for the state transitions within the states themselves*. Applying this concept to Robo-Kitty, the state transition chip can be dispensed with and the rules moved directly into the cartridges. For instance, the cartridge for "**play with string**" can monitor the kitty's level of hunger and instruct it to switch cartridges for the "**eat fish**" cartridge when it senses hunger rising. In turn the "**eat fish**" cartridge can monitor the kitten's bowel and instruct it to switch to the "**poo on carpet**" cartridge when it senses poo levels are running dangerously high.

Although each cartridge may be aware of the existence of any of the other cartridges, each is a self-contained unit and not reliant on any external logic to decide whether or not it should allow itself to be swapped for an alternative. As a consequence, it's a straightforward matter to add states or even to swap the whole set of cartridges for a completely new set (maybe ones that make little Kitty behave like a raptor). There's no need to take a screwdriver to the kitten's head, only to a few of the cartridges themselves.

Let's take a look at how this approach is implemented within the context of a video game. Just like Kitty's cartridges, states are encapsulated as objects and contain the logic required to facilitate state transitions. In addition, all state objects share a common interface: a pure virtual class named `State`. Here's a version that provides a simple interface:

```
class State
{
public:
```

```
  virtual void Execute (Troll* troll) = 0;
};
```

Now imagine a Troll class that has member variables for attributes such as health, anger, stamina, etc., and an interface allowing a client to query and adjust those values. A Troll can be given the functionality of a finite state machine by adding a pointer to an instance of a derived object of the State class, and a method permitting a client to change the instance the pointer is pointing to.

```
class Troll
{
  /* ATTRIBUTES OMITTED */

  State* m_pCurrentState;

public:

  /* INTERFACE TO ATTRIBUTES OMITTED */

  void Update()
  {
    m_pCurrentState->Execute(this);
  }

  void ChangeState(const State* pNewState)
  {
    delete m_pCurrentState;
    m_pCurrentState = pNewState;
  }
};
```

When the Update method of a Troll is called, it in turn calls the Execute method of the current state type with the this pointer. The current state may then use the Troll interface to query its owner, to adjust its owner's attributes, or to effect a state transition. In other words, how a Troll behaves when updated can be made completely dependent on the logic in its current state. This is best illustrated with an example, so let's create a couple of states to enable a troll to run away from enemies when it feels threatened and to sleep when it feels safe.

```
//----------------------------------State_RunAway
class State_RunAway : public State
{
public:

  void Execute(Troll* troll)
  {
    if (troll->isSafe())
    {
      troll->ChangeState(new State_Sleep());
    }
```

```
    else
    {
      troll->MoveAwayFromEnemy();
    }
  }
};

//-------------------------------State_Sleep
class State_Sleep : public State
{
public:

  void Execute(Troll* troll)
  {
    if (troll->isThreatened())
    {
      troll->ChangeState(new State_RunAway())
    }

    else
    {
      troll->Snore();
    }
  }
};
```

As you can see, when updated, a troll will behave differently depending on which of the states `m_pCurrentState` points to. Both states are encapsulated as objects and both provide the rules effecting state transition. All very neat and tidy.

This architecture is known as the *state design pattern* and provides an elegant way of implementing state-driven behavior. Although this is a departure from the mathematical formalization of an FSM, it is intuitive, simple to code, and easily extensible. It also makes it extremely easy to add enter and exit actions to each state; all you have to do is create `Enter` and `Exit` methods and adjust the agent's `ChangeState` method accordingly. You'll see the code that does exactly this very shortly.

The West World Project

As a practical example of how to create agents that utilize finite state machines, we are going to look at a game environment where agents inhabit an Old West-style gold mining town named West World. Initially there will only be one inhabitant — a gold miner named Miner Bob — but later in the chapter his wife will also make an appearance. You will have to imagine the tumbleweeds, creakin' mine props, and desert dust blowin' in your eyes because West World is implemented as a simple text-based console application. Any state changes or output from state actions will be sent as text to the console window. I'm using this plaintext-only approach as it demonstrates clearly the mechanism of a finite state machine without adding the code clutter of a more complex environment.

There are four locations in West World: a *gold mine*, a *bank* where Bob can deposit any nuggets he finds, a *saloon* in which he can quench his thirst, and *home-sweet-home* where he can sleep the fatigue of the day away. Exactly where he goes, and what he does when he gets there, is determined by Bob's current state. He will change states depending on variables like thirst, fatigue, and how much gold he has found hacking away down in the gold mine.

Before we delve into the source code, check out the following sample output from the WestWorld1 executable.

```
Miner Bob: Pickin' up a nugget
Miner Bob: Pickin' up a nugget
Miner Bob: Ah'm leavin' the gold mine with mah pockets full o' sweet gold
Miner Bob: Goin' to the bank. Yes siree
Miner Bob: Depositin' gold. Total savings now: 3
Miner Bob: Leavin' the bank
Miner Bob: Walkin' to the gold mine
Miner Bob: Pickin' up a nugget
Miner Bob: Ah'm leavin' the gold mine with mah pockets full o' sweet gold
Miner Bob: Boy, ah sure is thusty! Walkin' to the saloon
Miner Bob: That's mighty fine sippin liquor
Miner Bob: Leavin' the saloon, feelin' good
Miner Bob: Walkin' to the gold mine
Miner Bob: Pickin' up a nugget
Miner Bob: Pickin' up a nugget
Miner Bob: Ah'm leavin' the gold mine with mah pockets full o' sweet gold
Miner Bob: Goin' to the bank. Yes siree
Miner Bob: Depositin' gold. Total savings now: 4
Miner Bob: Leavin' the bank
Miner Bob: Walkin' to the gold mine
Miner Bob: Pickin' up a nugget
Miner Bob: Pickin' up a nugget
Miner Bob: Ah'm leavin' the gold mine with mah pockets full o' sweet gold
Miner Bob: Boy, ah sure is thusty! Walkin' to the saloon
Miner Bob: That's mighty fine sippin' liquor
Miner Bob: Leavin' the saloon, feelin' good
Miner Bob: Walkin' to the gold mine
Miner Bob: Pickin' up a nugget
Miner Bob: Ah'm leavin' the gold mine with mah pockets full o' sweet gold
Miner Bob: Goin' to the bank. Yes siree
Miner Bob: Depositin' gold. Total savings now: 5
Miner Bob: Woohoo! Rich enough for now. Back home to mah li'l lady
Miner Bob: Leavin' the bank
Miner Bob: Walkin' home
Miner Bob: ZZZZ...
Miner Bob: ZZZZ...
Miner Bob: ZZZZ...
Miner Bob: ZZZZ...
Miner Bob: What a God-darn fantastic nap! Time to find more gold
```

In the output from the program, each time you see Miner Bob change location he is changing state. All the other events are the actions that take place within the states. We'll examine each of Miner Bob's potential states in just a moment, but for now, let me explain a little about the code structure of the demo.

The BaseGameEntity Class

All inhabitants of West World are derived from the base class `BaseGameEntity`. This is a simple class with a private member for storing an ID number. It also specifies a pure virtual member function, `Update`, that must be implemented by all subclasses. `Update` is a function that gets called every update step and will be used by subclasses to update their state machine along with any other data that must be updated each time step.

The `BaseGameEntity` class declaration looks like this:

```
class BaseGameEntity
{
private:

  //every entity has a unique identifying number
  int          m_ID;

  //this is the next valid ID. Each time a BaseGameEntity is instantiated
  //this value is updated
  static int  m_iNextValidID;

  //this is called within the constructor to make sure the ID is set
  //correctly. It verifies that the value passed to the method is greater
  //or equal to the next valid ID, before setting the ID and incrementing
  //the next valid ID
  void SetID(int val);

public:

  BaseGameEntity(int id)
  {
    SetID(id);
  }

  virtual ~BaseGameEntity(){}

  //all entities must implement an update function
  virtual void  Update()=0;

  int          ID()const{return m_ID;}
};
```

For reasons that will become obvious later in the chapter, it's very important for each entity in your game to have a unique identifier. Therefore, on instantiation, the ID passed to the constructor is tested in the `SetID` method to make sure it's unique. If it is not, the program will exit with an assertion failure. In the example given in this chapter, the entities will use an enumerated value as their unique identifier. These can be found in the file EntityNames.h as `ent_Miner_Bob` and `ent_Elsa`.

The Miner Class

The `Miner` class is derived from the `BaseGameEntity` class and contains data members representing the various attributes a `Miner` possesses, such as its health, its level of fatigue, its position, and so forth. Like the troll example shown earlier in the chapter, a `Miner` owns a pointer to an instance of a `State` class in addition to a method for changing what `State` that pointer points to.

```
class Miner : public BaseGameEntity
{
private:

  //a pointer to an instance of a State
  State*                 m_pCurrentState;

  // the place where the miner is currently situated
  location_type          m_Location;

  //how many nuggets the miner has in his pockets
  int                    m_iGoldCarried;

  //how much money the miner has deposited in the bank
  int                    m_iMoneyInBank;

  //the higher the value, the thirstier the miner
  int                    m_iThirst;

  //the higher the value, the more tired the miner
  int                    m_iFatigue;

public:

  Miner(int ID);

  //this must be implemented
  void Update();

  //this method changes the current state to the new state
  void ChangeState(State* pNewState);

  /* bulk of interface omitted */
};
```

The `Miner::Update` method is straightforward; it simply increments the `m_iThirst` value before calling the `Execute` method of the current state. It looks like this:

```
void Miner::Update()
{
  m_iThirst += 1;

  if (m_pCurrentState)
  {
    m_pCurrentState->Execute(this);
  }
}
```

Now that you've seen how the `Miner` class operates, let's take a look at each of the states a miner can find itself in.

The Miner States

The gold miner will be able to enter one of four states. Here are the names of those states followed by a description of the actions and state transitions that occur within those states:

- **EnterMineAndDigForNugget**: If the miner is not located at the gold mine, he changes location. If already at the gold mine, he digs for nuggets of gold. When his pockets are full, Bob changes state to **VisitBankAndDepositGold**, and if while digging he finds himself thirsty, he will stop and change state to **QuenchThirst**.
- **VisitBankAndDepositGold**: In this state the miner will walk to the bank and deposit any nuggets he is carrying. If he then considers himself wealthy enough, he will change state to **GoHomeAnd-SleepTilRested**. Otherwise he will change state to **EnterMine-AndDigForNugget**.
- **GoHomeAndSleepTilRested**: In this state the miner will return to his shack and sleep until his fatigue level drops below an acceptable level. He will then change state to **EnterMineAndDigForNugget**.
- **QuenchThirst**: If at any time the miner feels thirsty (diggin' for gold is thusty work, don't ya know), he changes to this state and visits the saloon in order to buy a whiskey. When his thirst is quenched, he changes state to **EnterMineAndDigForNugget**.

Sometimes it's hard to follow the flow of the state logic from reading a text description like this, so it's often helpful to pick up pen and paper and draw a *state transition diagram* for your game agents. Figure 2.2 shows the state transition diagram for the gold miner. The bubbles represent the individual states and the lines between them the available transitions.

A diagram like this is better on the eyes and can make it much easier to spot any errors in the logic flow.

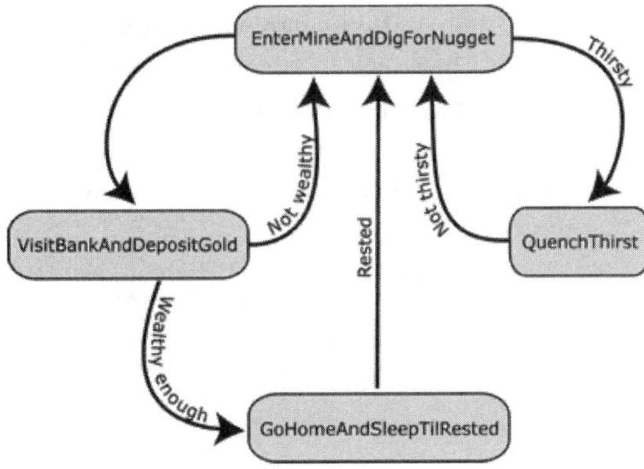

Figure 2.2. Miner Bob's state transition diagram

The State Design Pattern Revisited

You saw a brief description of this design pattern a few pages back, but it won't hurt to recap. Each of a game agent's states is implemented as a unique class and each agent holds a pointer to an instance of its current state. An agent also implements a `ChangeState` member function that can be called to facilitate the switching of states whenever a state transition is required. The logic for determining any state transitions is contained within each `State` class. All state classes are derived from an abstract base class, thereby defining a common interface. So far so good. You know this much already.

Earlier in the chapter it was mentioned that it's usually favorable for each state to have associated *enter* and *exit* actions. This permits the programmer to write logic that is only executed once at state entry or exit and increases the flexibility of an FSM a great deal. With these features in mind, let's take a look at an enhanced `State` base class.

```
class State
{
public:

  virtual ~State(){}

  //this will execute when the state is entered
  virtual void Enter(Miner*)=0;

  //this is called by the miner's update function each update step
  virtual void Execute(Miner*)=0;

  //this will execute when the state is exited
  virtual void Exit(Miner*)=0;
}
```

These additional methods are only called when a `Miner` changes state. When a state transition occurs, the `Miner::ChangeState` method first calls the `Exit` method of the current state, then it assigns the new state to the current state, and finishes by calling the `Enter` method of the new state (which is now the current state). I think code is clearer than words in this instance, so here's the listing for the `ChangeState` method:

```
void Miner::ChangeState(State* pNewState)
{
  //make sure both states are valid before attempting to
  //call their methods
  assert (m_pCurrentState && pNewState);

  //call the exit method of the existing state
  m_pCurrentState->Exit(this);

  //change state to the new state
  m_pCurrentState = pNewState;

  //call the entry method of the new state
  m_pCurrentState->Enter(this);
}
```

Notice how a `Miner` passes the `this` pointer to each state, enabling the state to use the `Miner` interface to access any relevant data.

⌘ **TIP** The state design pattern is also useful for structuring the main components of your game flow. For example, you could have a menu state, a save state, a paused state, an options state, a run state, etc.

Each of the four possible states a `Miner` may access are derived from the `State` class, giving us these concrete classes: `EnterMineAndDigForNugget`, `VisitBankAndDepositGold`, `GoHomeAndSleepTilRested`, and `QuenchThirst`. The `Miner::m_pCurrentState` pointer is able to point to any of these states. When the `Update` method of `Miner` is called, it in turn calls the `Execute` method of the currently active state with the `this` pointer as a parameter. These class relationships may be easier to understand if you examine the simplified UML class diagram shown in Figure 2.3.

Each concrete state is implemented as a singleton object. This is to ensure that there is only one instance of each state, which agents share (those of you unsure of what a singleton is, please read the sidebar on page 58). Using singletons makes the design more efficient because they remove the need to allocate and deallocate memory every time a state change is made. This is particularly important if you have many agents sharing a complex FSM and/or you are developing for a machine with limited resources.

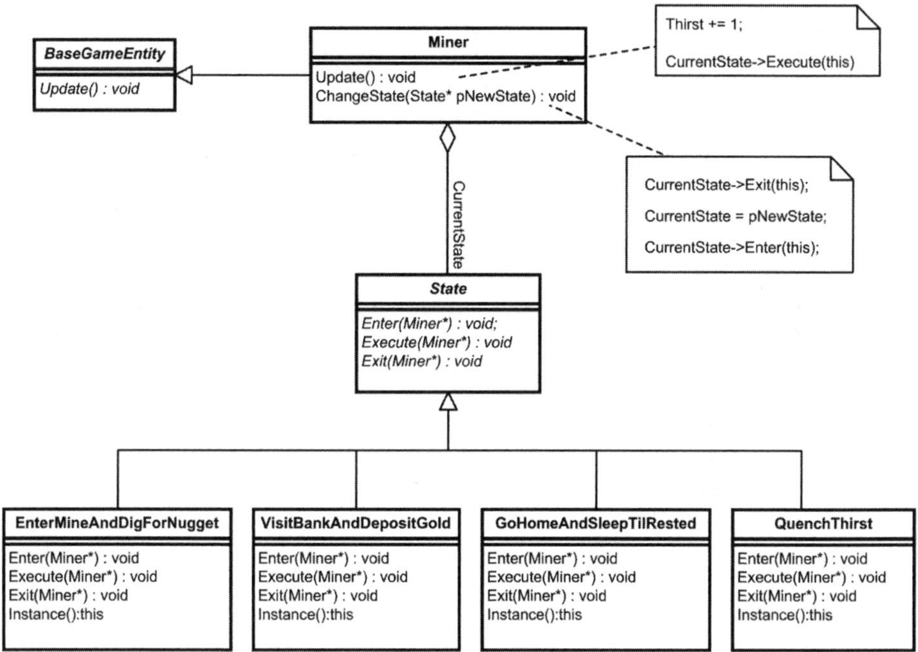

Figure 2.3. UML class diagram for Miner Bob's state machine implementation

NOTE I prefer to use singletons for the states for the reasons I've already given, but there is one drawback. Because they are shared between clients, singleton states are unable to make use of their own local, agent-specific data. For instance, if an agent uses a state that when entered should move it to an arbitrary position, the position cannot be stored in the state itself (because the position may be different for each agent that is using the state). Instead, it would have to be stored somewhere externally and be accessed by the state via the agent's interface. This is not really a problem if your states are accessing only one or two pieces of data, but if you find that the states you have designed are repeatedly accessing lots of external data, it's probably worth considering disposing of the singleton design and writing a few lines of code to manage the allocation and deallocation of state memory.

The Singleton Design Pattern

Often it's useful to guarantee that an object is only instantiated once and/or that it is globally accessible. For example, in game designs that have environments consisting of many different entity types — players, monsters, projectiles, plant pots, etc. — there is usually a "manager" object that handles the creation, deletion, and management of such objects. It is only necessary to have one instance of this object — a singleton — and it is convenient to make it globally accessible because many other objects will require access to it.

The singleton pattern ensures both these qualities. There are many ways of implementing a singleton (do a search at google.com and you'll see what I mean). I prefer to use a static method, Instance, that returns a pointer to a static instance of the class. Here's an example:

```
/* ------------------ MyClass.h -------------------- */
#ifndef MY_SINGLETON
#define MY_SINGLETON

class MyClass
{
private:

  // member data
  int m_iNum;

  //constructor is private
  MyClass(){}

  //copy ctor and assignment should be private
  MyClass(const MyClass &);
  MyClass& operator=(const MyClass &);

public:

  //strictly speaking, the destructor of a singleton should be private but some
  //compilers have problems with this so I've left them as public in all the
  //examples in this book
  ~MyClass();

  //methods
  int GetVal()const{return m_iNum;}
```

```
  static MyClass* Instance();
};

#endif

/* -------------------- MyClass.cpp ------------------- */

//this must reside in the cpp file; otherwise, an instance will be created
//for every file in which the header is included
MyClass* MyClass::Instance()
{
  static MyClass instance;

  return &instance;
}
```

Member variables and methods can now be accessed via the `Instance` method like so:

```
            int num = MyClass::Instance()->GetVal();
```

Because I'm lazy and don't like writing out all that syntax each time I want to access a singleton, I usually `#define` something like this:

```
            #define MyCls MyClass::Instance()
```

Using this new syntax I can simply write:

```
            int num = MyCls->GetVal();
```

Much easier, don't you think?

 **NOTE** If singletons are a new concept to you, and you decide to search the Internet for further information, you will discover they fuel many a good argument about the design of object-oriented software. Oh yes, programmers love to argue about this stuff, and nothing stokes a dispute better than the discussion of global variables *or objects that masquerade as globals*, such as singletons. My own stance on the matter is to use them wherever I think they provide a convenience and, in my opinion, do not compromise the design. I recommend you read the arguments for and against though, and come to your own conclusions. A good starting place is here:

http://c2.com/cgi/wiki?SingletonPattern

Okay, let's see how everything fits together by examining the complete code for one of the miner states.

The EnterMineAndDigForNugget State

> *In this state the miner should change location to be at the gold mine. Once at the gold mine he should dig for gold until his pockets are full, when he should change state to* ***VisitBankAndDepositNugget****. If the miner gets thirsty while digging he should change state to* ***QuenchThirst****.*

Because concrete states simply implement the interface defined in the virtual base class `State`, their declarations are very straightforward:

```
class EnterMineAndDigForNugget : public State
{
private:

  EnterMineAndDigForNugget(){}

  /* copy ctor and assignment op omitted */

public:

  //this is a singleton
  static EnterMineAndDigForNugget* Instance();

  virtual void Enter(Miner* pMiner);

  virtual void Execute(Miner* pMiner);

  virtual void Exit(Miner* pMiner);
};
```

As you can see, it's just a formality. Let's take a look at each of the methods in turn.

EnterMineAndDigForNugget::Enter

The code for the `Enter` method of `EnterMineAndDigForNugget` is as follows:

```
void EnterMineAndDigForNugget::Enter(Miner* pMiner)
{
  //if the miner is not already located at the gold mine, he must
  //change location to the gold mine
  if (pMiner->Location() != goldmine)
  {
    cout << "\n" << GetNameOfEntity(pMiner->ID()) << ": "
         << "Walkin' to the gold mine";

    pMiner->ChangeLocation(goldmine);
  }
}
```

This method is called when a miner first enters the **EnterMineAndDigForNugget** state. It ensures that the gold miner is located at the gold mine.

An agent stores its location as an enumerated type and the `ChangeLocation` method changes this value to switch locations.

EnterMineAndDigForNugget::Execute

The `Execute` method is a little more complicated and contains logic that can change a miner's state. (Don't forget that `Execute` is the method called each update step from `Miner::Update`.)

```
void EnterMineAndDigForNugget::Execute(Miner* pMiner)
{
  //the miner digs for gold until he is carrying in excess of MaxNuggets.
  //If he gets thirsty during his digging he stops work and
  //changes state to go to the saloon for a whiskey.
  pMiner->AddToGoldCarried(1);

  //diggin' is hard work
  pMiner->IncreaseFatigue();

  cout << "\n" << GetNameOfEntity(pMiner->ID()) << ": "
       << "Pickin' up a nugget";

  //if enough gold mined, go and put it in the bank
  if (pMiner->PocketsFull())
  {
    pMiner->ChangeState(VisitBankAndDepositGold::Instance());
  }

  //if thirsty go and get a whiskey
  if (pMiner->Thirsty())
  {
    pMiner->ChangeState(QuenchThirst::Instance());
  }
}
```

Note here how the `Miner::ChangeState` method is called using `QuenchThirst`'s or `VisitBankAndDepositGold`'s `Instance` member, which provides a pointer to the unique instance of that class.

EnterMineAndDigForNugget::Exit

The `Exit` method of `EnterMineAndDigForNugget` outputs a message telling us that the gold miner is leaving the mine.

```
void EnterMineAndDigForNugget::Exit(Miner* pMiner)
{
  cout << "\n" << GetNameOfEntity(pMiner->ID()) << ": "
       << "Ah'm leavin' the gold mine with mah pockets full o' sweet gold";
}
```

I hope an examination of the preceding three methods helps clear up any confusion you may have been experiencing and that you can now see how each state is able to modify the behavior of an agent or effect a transition into another state. You may find it useful at this stage to load up the WestWorld1 project into your IDE and scan the code. In particular, check out all the states in MinerOwnedStates.cpp and examine the `Miner` class to familiarize yourself with its member variables. Above all else, make sure you understand how the state design pattern works before you read any further. If you are a little unsure, please take the time to go over the previous few pages until you feel comfortable with the concept.

You have seen how the use of the state design pattern provides a very flexible mechanism for state-driven agents. It's extremely easy to add additional states as and when required. Indeed, should you so wish, you can switch an agent's entire state architecture for an alternative one. This can be useful if you have a very complicated design that would be better organized as a collection of several separate smaller state machines. For example, the state machine for a first-person shooter (FPS) like Unreal 2 tends to be large and complex. When designing the AI for a game of this sort you may find it preferable to think in terms of several smaller state machines representing functionality like "defend the flag" or "explore map," which can be switched in and out when appropriate. The state design pattern makes this easy to do.

Making the State Base Class Reusable

As the design stands, it's necessary to create a separate `State` base class for each character type to derive its states from. Instead, let's make it reusable by turning it into a class template.

```
template <class entity_type>
class State
{
public:

  virtual void Enter(entity_type*)=0;

  virtual void Execute(entity_type*)=0;

  virtual void Exit(entity_type*)=0;

  virtual ~State(){}
};
```

The declaration for a concrete state — using the **EnterMineAndDigForNugget** miner state as an example — now looks like this:

```
class EnterMineAndDigForNugget : public State<Miner>
{

public:

  /* OMITTED */
};
```

This, as you will see shortly, makes life easier in the long run.

Global States and State Blips

More often than not, when designing finite state machines you will end up with code that is duplicated in every state. For example, in the popular game The Sims by Maxis, a Sim may feel the urge of nature come upon it and have to visit the bathroom to relieve itself. This urge may occur in any state the Sim may be in and at any time. Given the current design, to bestow the gold miner with this type of behavior, duplicate conditional logic would have to be added to every one of his states, or alternatively, placed into the `Miner::Update` function. While the latter solution is acceptable, it's better to create a *global state* that is called every time the FSM is updated. That way, all the logic for the FSM is contained within the states and not in the agent class that owns the FSM.

To implement a global state, an additional member variable is required:

```
//notice how now that State is a class template we have to declare the entity type
State<Miner>* m_pGlobalState;
```

In addition to global behavior, occasionally it will be convenient for an agent to enter a state with the condition that when the state is exited, the agent returns to its previous state. I call this behavior a *state blip*. For example, just as in The Sims, you may insist that your agent can visit the bathroom at any time, yet make sure it always returns to its prior state. To give an FSM this type of functionality it must keep a record of the previous state so the state blip can revert to it. This is easy to do as all that is required is another member variable and some additional logic in the `Miner::ChangeState` method.

By now though, to implement these additions, the `Miner` class has acquired two extra member variables and one additional method. It has ended up looking something like this (extraneous detail omitted):

```
class Miner : public BaseGameEntity
{
private:

  State<Miner>*   m_pCurrentState;
  State<Miner>*   m_pPreviousState;
  State<Miner>*   m_pGlobalState;
  ...

public:

  void ChangeState(State<Miner>* pNewState);
  void RevertToPreviousState();
  ...
};
```

Hmm, looks like it's time to tidy up a little.

Creating a State Machine Class

The design can be made a lot cleaner by encapsulating all the state related data and methods into a state machine class. This way an agent can own an instance of a state machine and delegate the management of current states, global states, and previous states to it.

With this in mind take a look at the following `StateMachine` class template.

```
template <class entity_type>
class StateMachine
{
private:

  //a pointer to the agent that owns this instance
  entity_type*          m_pOwner;

  State<entity_type>*   m_pCurrentState;

  //a record of the last state the agent was in
  State<entity_type>*   m_pPreviousState;

  //this state logic is called every time the FSM is updated
  State<entity_type>*   m_pGlobalState;

public:

  StateMachine(entity_type* owner):m_pOwner(owner),
                                   m_pCurrentState(NULL),
                                   m_pPreviousState(NULL),
                                   m_pGlobalState(NULL)
  {}

  //use these methods to initialize the FSM
  void SetCurrentState(State<entity_type>* s){m_pCurrentState = s;}
  void SetGlobalState(State<entity_type>* s) {m_pGlobalState = s;}
  void SetPreviousState(State<entity_type>* s){m_pPreviousState = s;}

  //call this to update the FSM
  void  Update()const
  {
    //if a global state exists, call its execute method
    if (m_pGlobalState)   m_pGlobalState->Execute(m_pOwner);

    //same for the current state
    if (m_pCurrentState) m_pCurrentState->Execute(m_pOwner);
  }

  //change to a new state
  void  ChangeState(State<entity_type>* pNewState)
  {
    assert(pNewState &&
           "<StateMachine::ChangeState>: trying to change to a null state");
```

```
    //keep a record of the previous state
    m_pPreviousState = m_pCurrentState;

    //call the exit method of the existing state
    m_pCurrentState->Exit(m_pOwner);

    //change state to the new state
    m_pCurrentState = pNewState;

    //call the entry method of the new state
    m_pCurrentState->Enter(m_pOwner);
  }

  //change state back to the previous state
  void  RevertToPreviousState()
  {
    ChangeState(m_pPreviousState);
  }

  //accessors
  State<entity_type>*  CurrentState()  const{return m_pCurrentState;}
  State<entity_type>*  GlobalState()   const{return m_pGlobalState;}
  State<entity_type>*  PreviousState() const{return m_pPreviousState;}

  //returns true if the current state's type is equal to the type of the
  //class passed as a parameter.
  bool  isInState(const State<entity_type>& st)const;
};
```

Now all an agent has to do is to own an instance of a StateMachine and implement a method to update the state machine to get full FSM functionality.

The improved `Miner` class now looks like this:

```
class Miner : public BaseGameEntity
{
private:

  //an instance of the state machine class
  StateMachine<Miner>*  m_pStateMachine;

  /* EXTRANEOUS DETAIL OMITTED */

public:

  Miner(int id):m_Location(shack),
              m_iGoldCarried(0),
              m_iMoneyInBank(0),
              m_iThirst(0),
              m_iFatigue(0),
              BaseGameEntity(id)

  {
    //set up state machine
    m_pStateMachine = new StateMachine<Miner>(this);

    m_pStateMachine->SetCurrentState(GoHomeAndSleepTilRested::Instance());
    m_pStateMachine->SetGlobalState(MinerGlobalState::Instance());
  }

  ~Miner(){delete m_pStateMachine;}

  void Update()
  {
    ++m_iThirst;
    m_pStateMachine->Update();
  }

  StateMachine<Miner>* GetFSM()const{return m_pStateMachine;}

  /* EXTRANEOUS DETAIL OMITTED */
};
```

Notice how the current and global states must be set explicitly when a `StateMachine` is instantiated.

The class hierarchy is now like that shown in Figure 2.4.

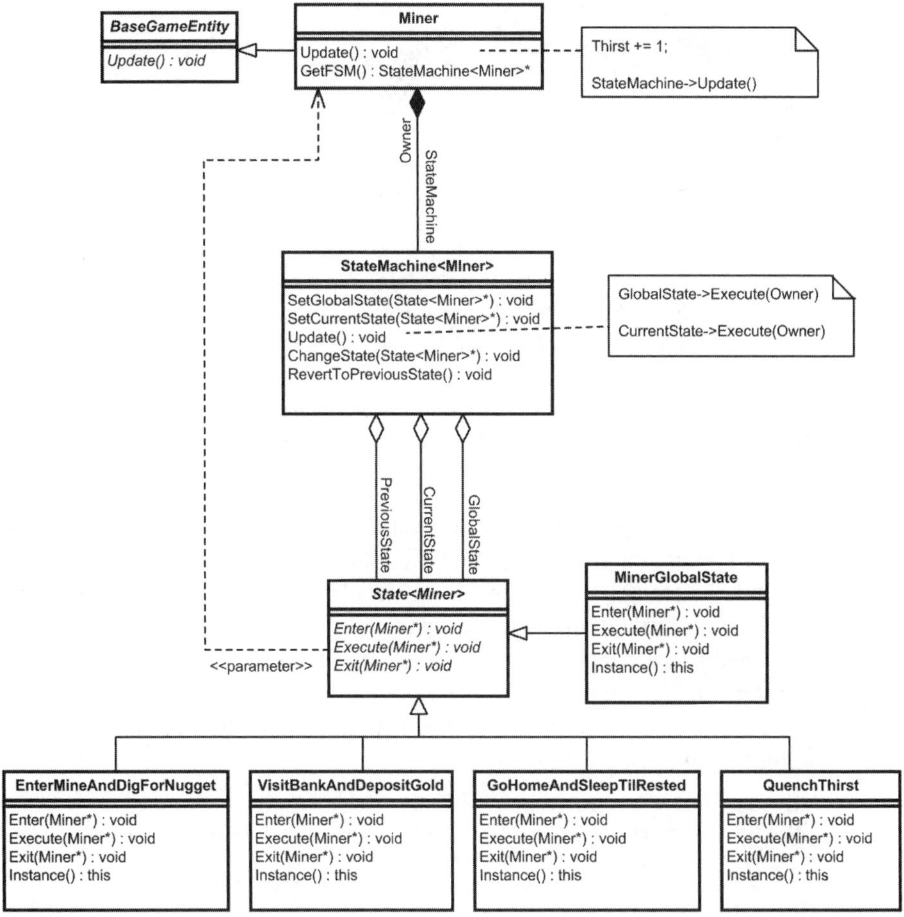

Figure 2.4. The updated design

Introducing Elsa

To demonstrate these improvements, I've created the second project for this chapter: WestWorldWithWoman. In this project, West World has gained another inhabitant, Elsa, the gold miner's wife. Elsa doesn't do much just yet; she's mainly preoccupied with cleaning the shack and emptying her bladder (she drinks way too much cawfee). The state transition diagram for Elsa is shown in Figure 2.5.

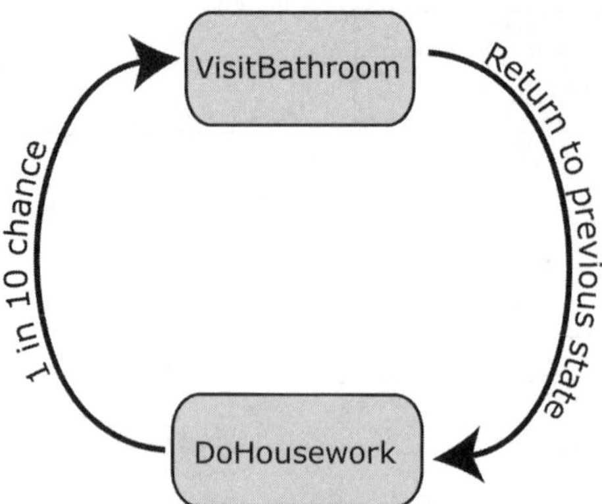

Figure 2.5. Elsa's state transition diagram. The global state is not shown in the figure because its logic is effectively implemented in any state and never changed.

When you boot up the project into your IDE, notice how the `VisitBathroom` state is implemented as a blip state (i.e., it always reverts back to the previous state). Also note that a global state has been defined, `WifesGlobalState`, which contains the logic required for Elsa's bathroom visits. This logic is contained in a global state because Elsa may feel the call of nature during any state and at any time.

Here is a sample of the output from WestWorldWithWoman. Elsa's actions are shown italicized.

```
Miner Bob: Pickin' up a nugget
Miner Bob: Ah'm leavin' the gold mine with mah pockets full o' sweet gold
Miner Bob: Goin' to the bank. Yes siree
Elsa: Walkin' to the can. Need to powda mah pretty li'l nose
Elsa: Ahhhhhh! Sweet relief!
Elsa: Leavin' the john
Miner Bob: Depositin' gold. Total savings now: 4
Miner Bob: Leavin' the bank
Miner Bob: Walkin' to the gold mine
Elsa: Walkin' to the can. Need to powda mah pretty li'l nose
Elsa: Ahhhhhh! Sweet relief!
Elsa: Leavin' the john
Miner Bob: Pickin' up a nugget
Elsa: Moppin' the floor
Miner Bob: Pickin' up a nugget
Miner Bob: Ah'm leavin' the gold mine with mah pockets full o' sweet gold
Miner Bob: Boy, ah sure is thusty! Walkin' to the saloon
Elsa: Moppin' the floor
Miner Bob: That's mighty fine sippin' liquor
Miner Bob: Leavin' the saloon, feelin' good
Miner Bob: Walkin' to the gold mine
Elsa: Makin' the bed
Miner Bob: Pickin' up a nugget
Miner Bob: Ah'm leavin' the gold mine with mah pockets full o' sweet gold
Miner Bob: Goin' to the bank. Yes siree
```

```
Elsa: Walkin' to the can. Need to powda mah pretty li'l nose
Elsa: Ahhhhhh! Sweet relief!
Elsa: Leavin' the john
Miner Bob: Depositin' gold. Total savings now: 5
Miner Bob: Woohoo! Rich enough for now. Back home to mah li'l lady
Miner Bob: Leavin' the bank
Miner Bob: Walkin' home
Elsa: Walkin' to the can. Need to powda mah pretty li'l nose
Elsa: Ahhhhhh! Sweet relief!
Elsa: Leavin' the john
Miner Bob: ZZZZ...
```

Adding Messaging Capabilities to Your FSM

Well-designed games tend to be event driven. That is to say, when an event occurs — a weapon is fired, a lever is pulled, an alarm tripped, etc. — the event is broadcast to the relevant objects in the game so that they may respond appropriately. These events are typically sent in the form of a packet of data that contains information about the event such as what sent it, what objects should respond to it, what the actual event is, a time stamp, and so forth.

The reason event-driven architectures are generally preferred is because they are efficient. Without event handling, objects have to continuously poll the game world to see if a particular action has occurred. With event handling, objects can simply get on with their business until an event message is broadcast to them. Then, if that message is pertinent, they can act upon it.

Intelligent game agents can use the same idea to communicate with each other. When endowed with the power to send, handle, and respond to events, it's easy to design behavior like the following:

- **A wizard throws a fireball at an orc**. The wizard sends a message to the orc informing it of its impending doom so it may respond accordingly, i.e., die horribly and in magnificent style.
- **A football player makes a pass to a teammate**. The passer can send a message to the receiver, letting it know where it should move to intercept the ball and at what time it should be at that position.
- **A grunt is injured**. It dispatches a message to each of its comrades requesting help. When one arrives with aid, another message is broadcast to let the others know they can resume their activities.
- **A character strikes a match to help light its way along a gloomy corridor**. A delayed message is dispatched to warn that the match will burn down to his fingers in thirty seconds. If he is still holding the match when he receives the message, he reacts by dropping the match and shouting out in pain.

Good, eh? The remainder of this chapter will demonstrate how agents can be given the ability to handle messages like this. But before we can figure out how to transmit them and handle them, the first thing to do is to define exactly what a message is.

The Telegram Structure

A message is simply an enumerated type. This could be just about anything. You could have agents sending messages like `Msg_ReturnToBase`, `Msg_MoveToPosition`, or `Msg_HelpNeeded`. Additional information also needs to be packaged along with the message. For example, we should record information about who sent it, who the recipient is, what the actual message is, a time stamp, and so forth. To do this, all the relevant information is kept together in a structure called `Telegram`. The code is shown below. Examine each member variable and get a feel for what sort of information the game agents will be passing around.

```
struct Telegram
{
  //the entity that sent this telegram
  int          Sender;

  //the entity that is to receive this telegram
  int          Receiver;

  //the message itself. These are all enumerated in the file
  //"MessageTypes.h"
  int          Msg;

  //messages can be dispatched immediately or delayed for a specified amount
  //of time. If a delay is necessary, this field is stamped with the time
  //the message should be dispatched.
  double       DispatchTime;

  //any additional information that may accompany the message
  void*        ExtraInfo;

  /* CONSTRUCTORS OMITTED */
};
```

The `Telegram` structure should be reusable, but because it's impossible to know in advance what sort of additional information future game designs will need to pass in a message, a void pointer `ExtraInfo` is provided. This can be used to pass any amount of additional information between characters. For example, if a platoon leader sends the message `Msg_MoveToPosition` to all his men, `ExtraInfo` can be used to store the coordinates of that position.

Miner Bob and Elsa Communicate

For the purposes of this chapter, I've kept the communication between Miner Bob and Elsa simple. They only have two messages they can use, and they are enumerated as:

```
enum message_type
{
  Msg_HiHoneyImHome,
  Msg_StewReady
};
```

The gold miner will send `Msg_HiHoneyImHome` to his wife to let her know he's back at the shack. `Msg_StewReady` is utilized by the wife to let herself know when to take dinner out of the oven and for her to communicate to Miner Bob that food is on the table.

The new state transition diagram for Elsa is shown in Figure 2.6.

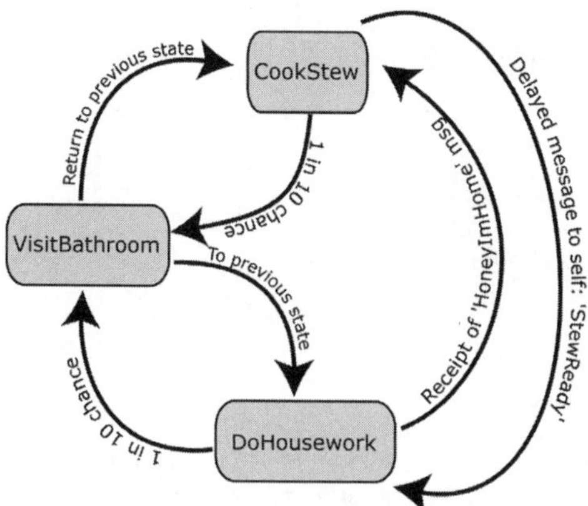

Figure 2.6. Elsa's new state transition diagram

Before I show you how telegram events are handled by an agent, let me demonstrate how they are created, managed, and dispatched.

Message Dispatch and Management

The creation, dispatch, and management of telegrams is handled by a class named `MessageDispatcher`. Whenever an agent needs to send a message, it calls `MessageDispatcher::DispatchMessage` with all the necessary information, such as the message type, the time the message is to be dispatched, the ID of the recipient, and so on. The `MessageDispatcher` uses this information to create a `Telegram`, which it either dispatches immediately or stores in a queue ready to be dispatched at the correct time.

Before it can dispatch a message, the MessageDispatcher must obtain a pointer to the entity specified by the sender. Therefore, there must be some sort of database of instantiated entities provided for the MessageDispatcher to refer to — a sort of telephone book where pointers to agents are cross-referenced by their ID. The database used for the demo is a singleton class called EntityManager. Its declaration looks like this:

```
class EntityManager
{
private:

  //to save the ol' fingers
  typedef std::map<int, BaseGameEntity*> EntityMap;

private:

  //to facilitate quick lookup the entities are stored in a std::map, in
  //which pointers to entities are cross-referenced by their identifying
  //number
  EntityMap           m_EntityMap;

  EntityManager(){}

  //copy ctor and assignment should be private
  EntityManager(const EntityManager&);
  EntityManager& operator=(const EntityManager&);

public:

  static EntityManager* Instance();

  //this method stores a pointer to the entity in the std::vector
  //m_Entities at the index position indicated by the entity's ID
  //(makes for faster access)
  void            RegisterEntity(BaseGameEntity* NewEntity);

  //returns a pointer to the entity with the ID given as a parameter
  BaseGameEntity* GetEntityFromID(int id)const;

  //this method removes the entity from the list
  void            RemoveEntity(BaseGameEntity* pEntity);
};

//provide easy access to the instance of the EntityManager
#define EntityMgr EntityManager::Instance()
```

When an entity is created it is registered with the entity manager like so:

```
  Miner* Bob = new Miner(ent_Miner_Bob); //enumerated ID
  EntityMgr->RegisterEntity(Bob);
```

A client can now request a pointer to a specific entity by passing its ID to the method EntityManager::GetEntityFromID in this way:

```
Entity* pBob = EntityMgr->GetEntityFromID(ent_Miner_Bob);
```

The client can then use this pointer to call the message handler for that particular entity. More on this in a moment, but first let's look at the way messages are created and routed between entities.

The MessageDispatcher Class

The class that manages the dispatch of messages is a singleton named MessageDispatcher. Take a look at the declaration of this class:

```
class MessageDispatcher
{
private:

  //a std::set is used as the container for the delayed messages
  //because of the benefit of automatic sorting and avoidance
  //of duplicates. Messages are sorted by their dispatch time.
  std::set<Telegram> PriorityQ;

  //this method is utilized by DispatchMessage or DispatchDelayedMessages.
  //This method calls the message handling member function of the receiving
  //entity, pReceiver, with the newly created telegram
  void Discharge(Entity* pReceiver, const Telegram& msg);

  MessageDispatcher(){}

public:

  //this class is a singleton
  static MessageDispatcher* Instance();

  //send a message to another agent.
  void DispatchMessage(double      delay,
                       int         sender,
                       int         receiver,
                       int         msg,
                       void*       ExtraInfo);

  //send out any delayed messages. This method is called each time through
  // the main game loop.
  void DispatchDelayedMessages();
};

//to make life easier...
#define Dispatch MessageDispatcher::Instance()
```

The MessageDispatcher class handles messages to be dispatched immediately and time stamped messages, which are messages to be delivered at a specified time in the future. Both these types of messages are created and managed by the same method: DispatchMessage. Let's go through the source. (In the companion file this method has some additional lines of code for outputting some informative text to the console. I've omitted them here for clarity.)

```
void MessageDispatcher::DispatchMessage(double      delay,
                                        int         sender,
                                        int         receiver,
                                        int         msg,
                                        void*       ExtraInfo)
{
```

This method is called when an entity sends a message to another entity. The message sender must provide as parameters the details required to create a `Telegram` structure. In addition to the sender's ID, the receiver's ID, and the message itself, this function must be given a time delay and a pointer to any additional info, if any. If the message is to be sent immediately, the method should be called with a zero or negative delay.

```
  //get a pointer to the receiver of the message
  Entity* pReceiver = EntityMgr->GetEntityFromID(receiver);

  //create the telegram
  Telegram telegram(delay, sender, receiver, msg, ExtraInfo);

  //if there is no delay, route the telegram immediately
  if (delay <= 0.0)
  {
    //send the telegram to the recipient
    Discharge(pReceiver, telegram);
  }
```

After a pointer to the recipient is obtained via the entity manager and a `Telegram` is created using the appropriate information, the message is ready to be dispatched. If the message is for immediate dispatch, the `Discharge` method is called straight away. The `Discharge` method passes the newly created `Telegram` to the message handling method of the receiving entity (more on this shortly). Most of the messages your agents will be sending will be created and immediately dispatched in this way. For example, if a troll hits a human over the head with a club, it could send an instant message to the human telling it that it had been hit. The human would then respond using the appropriate action, sound, and animation.

```
  //else calculate the time when the telegram should be dispatched
  else
  {
    double CurrentTime = Clock->GetCurrentTime();

    telegram.DispatchTime = CurrentTime + delay;

    //and put it in the queue
    PriorityQ.insert(telegram);
  }
}
```

If the message is to be dispatched at some time in the future, then these few lines of code calculate the time it should be delivered before inserting the new telegram into a priority queue — a data structure that keeps its elements sorted in order of precedence. I have utilized a `std::set` as the priority queue in this example because it automatically discards duplicate telegrams.

Telegrams are sorted with respect to their time stamp and to this effect, if you take a look at Telegram.h, you will find that the < and == operators have been overloaded. Also note how telegrams with time stamps less than a quarter of a second apart are to be considered identical. This prevents many similar telegrams bunching up in the queue and being delivered en masse, thereby flooding an agent with identical messages. Of course, this delay will vary according to your game. Games with lots of action producing a high frequency of messages will probably require a smaller gap.

The queued telegrams are examined each update step by the method `DispatchDelayedMessages`. This function checks the front of the priority queue to see if any telegrams have expired time stamps. If so, they are dispatched to their recipient and removed from the queue. The code for this method looks like this:

```
void MessageDispatcher::DispatchDelayedMessages()
{
  //first get current time
  double CurrentTime = Clock->GetCurrentTime();

  //now peek at the queue to see if any telegrams need dispatching.
  //remove all telegrams from the front of the queue that have gone
  //past their sell-by date
  while( (PriorityQ.begin()->DispatchTime < CurrentTime) &&
         (PriorityQ.begin()->DispatchTime > 0) )
  {
    //read the telegram from the front of the queue
    Telegram telegram = *PriorityQ.begin();

    //find the recipient
    Entity* pReceiver = EntityMgr->GetEntityFromID(telegram.Receiver);

    //send the telegram to the recipient
    Discharge(pReceiver, telegram);

    //and remove it from the queue
    PriorityQ.erase(PriorityQ.begin());
  }
}
```

A call to this method must be placed in the game's main update loop to facilitate the correct and timely dispatch of any delayed messages.

Message Handling

Once a system for creating and dispatching messages is in place, the handling of them is relatively easy. The `BaseGameEntity` class must be modified so any subclass can receive messages. This is achieved by declaring another pure virtual function, `HandleMessage`, which all derived classes must implement. The revised BaseGameEntity base class now looks like this:

```
class BaseGameEntity
{
private:

  int          m_ID;

  /* EXTRANEOUS DETAIL REMOVED FOR CLARITY*/

public:

  //all subclasses can communicate using messages.
  virtual bool  HandleMessage(const Telegram& msg)=0;

 /* EXTRANEOUS DETAIL REMOVED FOR CLARITY*/
};
```

In addition, the State base class must also be modified so that a BaseGameEntity's states can choose to accept and handle messages. The revised State class includes an additional OnMessage method as follows:

```
template <class entity_type>
class State
{
public:

  //this executes if the agent receives a message from the
  //message dispatcher
  virtual bool OnMessage(entity_type*, const Telegram&)=0;

  /* EXTRANEOUS DETAIL REMOVED FOR CLARITY*/
};
```

Finally, the StateMachine class is modified to contain a HandleMessage method. When a telegram is received by an entity, it is first routed to the entity's current state. If the current state does not have code in place to deal with the message, it's routed to the entity's global state's message handler. You probably noticed that OnMessage returns a bool. This is to indicate whether or not the message has been handled successfully and enables the code to route the message accordingly.

Here is the listing of the StateMachine::HandleMessage method:

```
bool  StateMachine::HandleMessage(const Telegram& msg)const
{
  //first see if the current state is valid and that it can handle
  //the message
  if (m_pCurrentState && m_pCurrentState->OnMessage(m_pOwner, msg))
  {
    return true;
  }

  //if not, and if a global state has been implemented, send
  //the message to the global state
```

```
    if (m_pGlobalState && m_pGlobalState->OnMessage(m_pOwner, msg))
    {
      return true;
    }

    return false;
  }
```

And here's how the `Miner` class routes messages sent to it:

```
bool Miner::HandleMessage(const Telegram& msg)
{
  return m_pStateMachine->HandleMessage(msg);
}
```

Figure 2.7 shows the new class architecture.

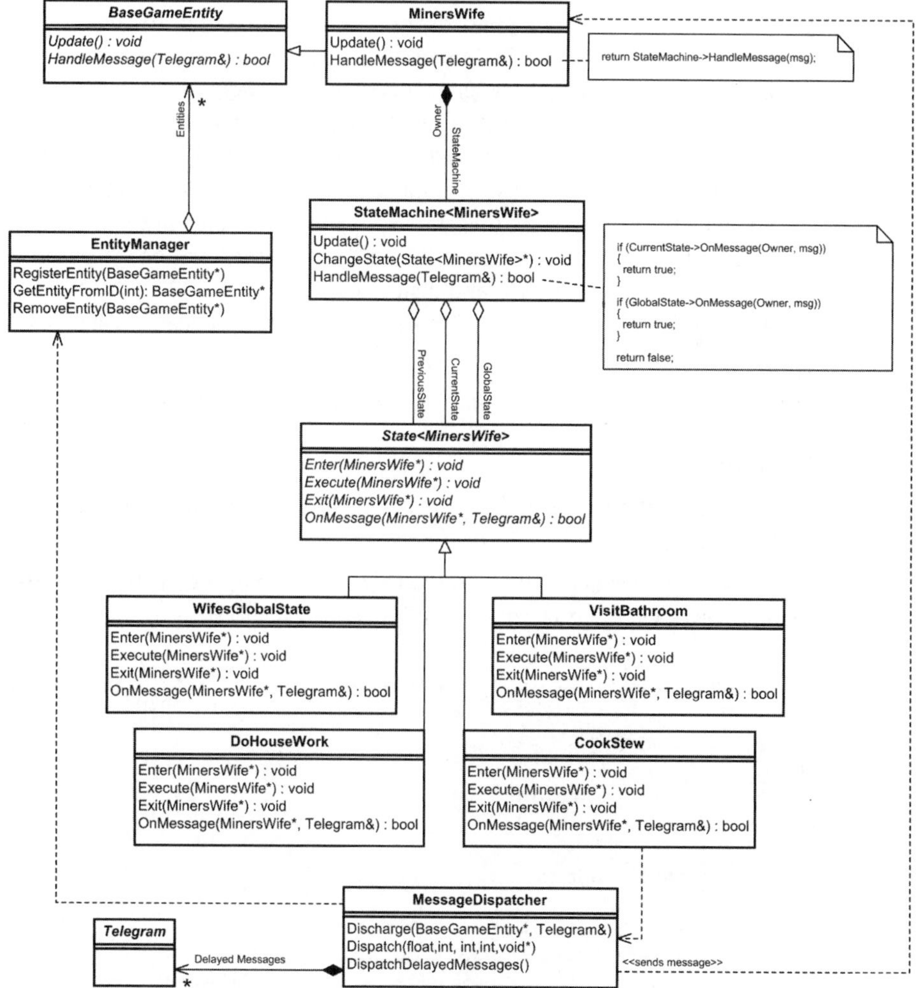

Figure 2.7. The updated design incorporating messaging

Elsa Cooks Dinner

At this point it's probably a good idea to take a look at a concrete example of how messaging works, so let's examine how it can be integrated into the West World project. In the final version of this demo, WestWorldWith-Messaging, there is a message sequence that proceeds like this:

1. Miner Bob enters the shack and sends a `Msg_HiHoneyImHome` message to Elsa to let her know he's arrived home.
2. Elsa receives the `Msg_HiHoneyImHome` message, stops what she's currently doing, and changes state to **CookStew**.
3. When Elsa enters the **CookStew** state, she puts the stew in the oven and sends a delayed `Msg_StewReady` message to herself to remind herself that the stew needs to be taken out of the oven at a specific time in the future. (Normally a good stew takes at least an hour to cook, but in cyberspace Elsa can rustle one up in just a fraction of a second!)
4. Elsa receives the `Msg_StewReady` message. She responds to this message by taking the stew out of the oven and dispatching a message to Miner Bob to inform him that dinner is on the table. Miner Bob will only respond to this message if he is in the **GoHomeAndSleepTilRested** state (because in this state he is always located at the shack). If he is anywhere else, such as at the gold mine or the saloon, this message would be dispatched and dismissed.
5. Miner Bob receives the `Msg_StewReady` message and changes state to **EatStew**.

Let me run through the code that executes each of these steps.

Step One

Miner Bob enters the shack and sends a `Msg_HiHoneyImHome` *message to Elsa to let her know he's arrived home.*

Additional code has been added to the `Enter` method of the **GoHomeAndSleepTilRested** state to facilitate sending a message to Elsa. Here is the listing:

```
void GoHomeAndSleepTilRested::Enter(Miner* pMiner)
{
  if (pMiner->Location() != shack)
  {
    cout << "\n" << GetNameOfEntity(pMiner->ID()) << ": "
         << "Walkin' home";

    pMiner->ChangeLocation(shack);

    //let the wife know I'm home
    Dispatch->DispatchMessage(SEND_MSG_IMMEDIATELY,  //time delay
                              pMiner->ID(),          //ID of sender
                              ent_Elsa,              //ID/name of recipient
```

```
                              Msg_HiHoneyImHome,      //the message
                              NO_ADDITIONAL_INFO);    //no extra info attached
  }
}
```

As you can see, when Miner Bob changes to this state the first thing he does is change location. He then dispatches `Msg_HiHoneyImHome` to Elsa by calling the `DispatchMessage` method of the `MessageDispatcher` singleton class. Because the message is to be dispatched immediately, the first parameter of `DispatchMessage` is set to zero. No additional information is attached to the telegram. (The constants `SEND_MSG_IMMEDIATELY` and `NO_ADDITIONAL_INFO` are defined with the value 0 in the file MessageDispatcher.h to aid legibility.)

⌘ **TIP** You don't have to restrict the messaging system to game characters such as orcs, archers, and wizards. Provided an object is derived from a class that enforces a unique identifier (like `BaseGameEntity`) it's possible to send messages to it. Objects such as treasure chests, traps, magical doors, or even trees are all items that may benefit from the ability to receive and process messages.

For example, you could derive an `OakTree` class from the `BaseGameEntity` class and implement a message handling function to react to messages such as HitWithAxe or StormyWeather. The oak tree can then react to these messages by toppling over or by rustling its leaves and creaking. The possibilities you can construct with this sort of messaging system are almost endless.

Step Two

Elsa receives the `Msg_HiHoneyImHome` *message, stops what she's currently doing, and changes state to* **CookStew**.

Because she never leaves the shack, Elsa should respond to `Msg_HiHoneyImHome` when in any state. The easiest way to implement this is to let her global state take care of this message. (Remember, the global state is executed each update along with the current state.)

```
bool WifesGlobalState::OnMessage(MinersWife* wife, const Telegram& msg)
{
  switch(msg.Msg)
  {
  case Msg_HiHoneyImHome:
   {
     cout << "\nMessage handled by " << GetNameOfEntity(wife->ID())
          << " at time: " << Clock->GetCurrentTime();

     cout << "\n" << GetNameOfEntity(wife->ID()) <<
          ": Hi honey. Let me make you some of mah fine country stew";

     wife->GetFSM()->ChangeState(CookStew::Instance());
   }

   return true;

  }//end switch
```

```
  return false;
}
```

Step Three

When Elsa enters the **CookStew** *state, she puts the stew in the oven and sends a delayed* `Msg_StewReady` *message to herself as a reminder to take the stew out before it burns and upsets Bob.*

This is a demonstration of how delayed messages can be used. In this example, Elsa puts the stew in the oven and then sends a delayed message to herself as a reminder to take the stew out. As we discussed earlier, this message will be stamped with the correct time for dispatch and stored in a priority queue. Each time through the game loop there is a call to `MessageDispatcher::DispatchDelayedMessages`. This method checks to see if any telegrams have exceeded their time stamp and dispatches them to their appropriate recipients where necessary.

```
void CookStew::Enter(MinersWife* wife)
{
  //if not already cooking put the stew in the oven
  if (!wife->Cooking())
  {
    cout << "\n" << GetNameOfEntity(wife->ID())
         << ": Puttin' the stew in the oven";

    //send a delayed message to myself so that I know when to take the stew
    //out of the oven
    Dispatch->DispatchMessage(1.5,                     //time delay
                              wife->ID(),              //sender ID
                              wife->ID(),              //receiver ID
                              Msg_StewReady,           //the message
                              NO_ADDITIONAL_INFO);     //no extra info attached

    wife->SetCooking(true);
  }
}
```

Step Four

Elsa receives the `Msg_StewReady` *message. She responds by taking the stew out of the oven and dispatching a message to Miner Bob to inform him that dinner is on the table. Miner Bob will only respond to this message if he is in the* **GoHomeAndSleepTilRested** *state (to ensure he is located at the shack).*

Because Miner Bob does not have bionic ears, he will only be able to hear Elsa calling him for dinner if he is at home. Therefore, Bob will only respond to this message if he is in the **GoHomeAndSleepTilRested** state.

```
bool CookStew::OnMessage(MinersWife* wife, const Telegram& msg)
{
```

```
  switch(msg.Msg)
  {
    case Msg_StewReady:
    {
      cout << "\nMessage received by " << GetNameOfEntity(wife->ID()) <<
           " at time: " << Clock->GetCurrentTime();
      cout << "\n" << GetNameOfEntity(wife->ID())
           << ": Stew ready! Let's eat";

      //let hubby know the stew is ready
      Dispatch->DispatchMessage(SEND_MSG_IMMEDIATELY,
                                wife->ID(),
                                ent_Miner_Bob,
                                Msg_StewReady,
                                NO_ADDITIONAL_INFO);

      wife->SetCooking(false);

      wife->GetFSM()->ChangeState(DoHouseWork::Instance());
    }

    return true;

  }//end switch

  return false;
}
```

Step Five

Miner Bob receives the `Msg_StewReady` *message and changes state to* **EatStew**.

When Miner Bob receives `Msg_StewReady` he stops whatever he's doing, changes state to **EatStew**, and settles down at the table ready to eat a mighty fine and fillin' bowl of stew.

```
bool GoHomeAndSleepTilRested::OnMessage(Miner* pMiner, const Telegram& msg)
{
   switch(msg.Msg)
   {
   case Msg_StewReady:

     cout << "\nMessage handled by " << GetNameOfEntity(pMiner->ID())
     << " at time: " << Clock->GetCurrentTime();

     cout << "\n" << GetNameOfEntity(pMiner->ID())
          << ": Okay hun, ahm a-comin'!";

     pMiner->GetFSM()->ChangeState(EatStew::Instance());

     return true;

   }//end switch
```

```
   return false; //send message to global message handler
}
```

Here is some example output from the WestWorldWithMessaging program. You can see clearly where the preceding message sequence occurs.

```
Miner Bob: Goin' to the bank. Yes siree
Elsa: Moppin' the floor
Miner Bob: Depositin' gold. Total savings now: 5
Miner Bob: Woohoo! Rich enough for now. Back home to mah li'l lady
Miner Bob: Leavin' the bank
Miner Bob: Walkin' home
Instant telegram dispatched at time: 4.20062 by Miner Bob for Elsa. Msg is
HiHoneyImHome
Message received by Elsa at time: 4.20062
Elsa: Hi honey. Let me make you some of mah fine country stew
Elsa: Puttin' the stew in the oven
Delayed telegram from Elsa recorded at time 4.20062 for Elsa. Msg is StewReady
Elsa: Fussin' over food
Miner Bob: ZZZZ...
Elsa: Fussin' over food
Miner Bob: ZZZZ...
Elsa: Fussin' over food
Miner Bob: ZZZZ...
Elsa: Fussin' over food
Queued telegram ready for dispatch: Sent to Elsa. Msg is StewReady
Message received by Elsa at time: 5.10162
Elsa: Stew ready! Let's eat
Instant telegram dispatched at time: 5.10162 by Elsa for Miner Bob. Msg is
StewReady
Message received by Miner Bob at time: 5.10162
Miner Bob: Okay hun, ahm a-comin'!
Miner Bob: Smells reaaal goood, Elsa!
Elsa: Puttin' the stew on the table
Elsa: Time to do some more housework!
Miner Bob: Tastes real good too!
Miner Bob: Thank ya li'l lady. Ah better get back to whatever ah wuz doin'
Elsa: Washin' the dishes
Miner Bob: ZZZZ...
Elsa: Makin' the bed
Miner Bob: All mah fatigue has drained away. Time to find more gold!
Miner Bob: Walkin' to the gold mine
```

Summing Up

This chapter has shown you the skills required to create very flexible and extensible finite state machines for your own games. As you have seen, the addition of messaging has enhanced the illusion of intelligence a great deal — the output from the WestWorldWithMessaging program is starting to look like the actions and interactions of two real people. What's more, this is only a very simple example. The complexity of the behavior you can create with finite state machines is only limited by your imagination. You don't have to restrict your game agents to just one finite state machine either. Sometimes it may be a good idea to use two FSMs working in parallel: one to control a character's movement and one to control the weapon selection, aiming, and firing, for example. It's even possible to have a state itself contain a state machine. This is known as a hierarchical state machine. For instance, your game agent may have the states **Explore**, **Combat**, and **Patrol**. In turn, the **Combat** state may own a state machine that manages the states required for combat such as **Dodge**, **ChaseEnemy**, and **Shoot**.

Practice Makes Perfect

Before you dash away and start coding your own finite state machines, you may find it good practice to expand the WestWorldWithMessaging project to include an additional character. For example, you could add a Bar Fly who insults Miner Bob in the saloon and they get into a fight. Before you write the code, grab a pencil and a sheet of paper and sketch out the state transition diagrams for each new character. Have fun!

Chapter 3

How to Create Autonomously Moving Game Agents

During the late '80s I remember watching a BBC Horizon documentary about state-of-the-art computer graphics and animation. There was lots of exciting stuff covered in that program, but the thing I remember most vividly was an amazing demonstration of the flocking behavior of birds. It was based on very simple rules, yet it looked so spontaneous and natural and was mesmerizing to watch. The programmer who designed the behavior is named Craig Reynolds. He called the flocking birds "boids," and the simple rules the flocking behavior emerged from he called "steering behaviors."

Since that time Reynolds has published a number of articles on various types of steering behaviors, all of them fascinating. Most, if not all, of his steering behaviors have direct relevance to games, which is why I'm going to spend a considerable amount of time describing them and showing you how to code and use them.

What Is an Autonomous Agent?

I've seen many definitions for what an autonomous agent is, but probably the best is this:

> *An autonomous agent is a system situated within and a part of an environment that senses that environment and acts on it, over time, in pursuit of its own agenda and so as to effect what it senses in the future.*

Throughout this chapter I will use the term "autonomous agent" in reference to agents that possess a degree of autonomous *movement*. If an autonomous agent stumbles upon an unexpected situation, like finding a wall in its way, it will have the ability to respond and adjust its motion accordingly. For example, you might design one autonomous agent to behave like a rabbit and one like a fox. If while munching happily on the fresh dewy grass, the rabbit happens to spot the fox, it will autonomously attempt to evade it. At the same time the fox will autonomously pursue the rabbit. Both these events occur without any further intervention from the programmer; once up and running, autonomous agents simply look after themselves.

This is not to say that an autonomous agent *should* be able to cope with absolutely any situation at all (although that might be one of your goals), but it is often very useful to be able to bestow an *amount* of autonomy. For example, a common problem when writing pathfinding code is how to deal with dynamic obstacles. Dynamic obstacles are those objects in your game world that move around or change position, like other agents, sliding doors, and so forth. Given a suitable environment, incorporating the correct steering behavior into a game character will preclude writing special pathfinding code to handle dynamic obstacles — an autonomous agent will have the ability to deal with them if and when it has to.

The movement of an autonomous agent can be broken down into three layers:

- **Action Selection**: This is the part of the agent's behavior responsible for choosing its goals and deciding what plan to follow. It is the part that says "go here" and "do A, B, and then C."
- **Steering**: This layer is responsible for calculating the desired trajectories required to satisfy the goals and plans set by the action selection layer. Steering behaviors are the implementation of this layer. They produce a steering force that describes where an agent should move and how fast it should travel to get there.
- **Locomotion**: The bottom layer, locomotion, represents the more mechanical aspects of an agent's movement. It is the *how* of traveling from A to B. For example, if you had implemented the mechanics of a camel, a tank, and a goldfish and then gave a command for them to travel north, they would all use different mechanical processes to create motion even though their intent (to move north) is identical. By separating this layer from the steering layer, it's possible to utilize, with little modification, the same steering behaviors for completely different types of locomotion.

Reynolds makes use of an excellent analogy to describe the roles of each of these layers in his paper "Steering Behaviors for Autonomous Characters."

> *"Consider, for example, some cowboys tending a herd of cattle out on the range. A cow wanders away from the herd. The trail boss tells a cowboy to fetch the stray. The cowboy says 'giddy-up' to his horse and guides it to the cow, possibly avoiding obstacles along the way. In this example, the trail boss represents action selection: noticing that the state of the world has changed (a cow left the herd) and setting a goal (retrieve the stray). The steering level is represented by the cowboy, who decomposes the goal into a series of simple sub-goals (approach the cow, avoid obstacles, retrieve the cow). A sub-goal corresponds to a steering behavior for the cowboy-and-horse team. Using various control*

signals (vocal commands, spurs, reins), the cowboy steers his horse toward the target. In general terms, these signals express concepts like: go faster, go slower, turn right, turn left, and so on. The horse implements the locomotion level. Taking the cowboy's control signals as input, the horse moves in the indicated direction. This motion is the result of a complex interaction of the horse's visual perception, its sense of balance, and its muscles applying torques to the joints of its skeleton. From an engineering point of view, legged locomotion is a very hard problem, but neither the cowboy nor the horse give it a second thought."

Not all is rosy and sweet in the world of autonomous agents though. The implementation of steering behaviors can beset the programmer with a truckload of new problems to deal with. Some behaviors may involve heavy manual tweaking, while others have to be carefully coded to avoid using large portions of CPU time. When combining behaviors, care usually must be taken to avoid the possibility that two or more of them may cancel each other out. There are means and ways around most of these problems though (well, all except for the tweaking — but that's fun anyway), and most often the benefits of steering behaviors far outweigh any disadvantages.

The Vehicle Model

Before I discuss each individual steering behavior I'm going to spend a little time explaining the code and class design for the vehicle model (the locomotion). `MovingEntity` is a base class from which all moving game agents are derived. It encapsulates the data that describes a basic vehicle with point mass. Let me run you through the class declaration:

```
class MovingEntity : public BaseGameEntity
{
protected:
```

The `MovingEntity` class is derived from the `BaseGameEntity` class, which defines an entity with an ID, a type, a position, a bounding radius, and a scale. All game entities from here onward in this book will be derived from `BaseGameEntity`. A `BaseGameEntity` also has an additional Boolean member variable, `m_bTag`, which will be utilized in a variety of ways, some of which will be described very shortly. I'm not going to list the class declaration here, but I recommend you take a quick look at the BaseGameEntity.h header sometime during your read through this chapter.

```
  SVector2D    m_vVelocity;

  //a normalized vector pointing in the direction the entity is heading.
  SVector2D    m_vHeading;

  //a vector perpendicular to the heading vector
  SVector2D    m_vSide;
```

The heading and side vectors define a local coordinate system for the moving entity. In the examples given in this chapter, a vehicle's heading will always be aligned with its velocity (for example, a train has a velocity aligned heading). These values will be used often by the steering behavior algorithms and are updated every frame.

```
  double        m_dMass;

  //the maximum speed at which this entity may travel.
  double        m_dMaxSpeed;

  //the maximum force this entity can produce to power itself
  //(think rockets and thrust)
  double        m_dMaxForce;

  //the maximum rate (radians per second) at which this vehicle can rotate
  double        m_dMaxTurnRate;

public:

  /* EXTRANEOUS DETAIL OMITTED */
};
```

Although this is enough data to represent a moving object, we still need a way of giving a moving entity access to the various types of steering behaviors. I have chosen to create a class, `Vehicle`, which inherits from `MovingEntity` and owns an instance of the steering behavior class, `SteeringBehaviors`. `SteeringBehaviors` encapsulates all the different steering behaviors I'll be discussing throughout this chapter. More on that in a moment though; first, let's take a look at the `Vehicle` class declaration.

```
class Vehicle : public MovingEntity
{
private:

  //a pointer to the world data enabling a vehicle to access any obstacle
  //path, wall, or agent data
  GameWorld*          m_pWorld;
```

The `GameWorld` class contains all the data and objects pertinent to the environment the agents are situated in, such as walls, obstacles, and so on. I won't list the declaration here to save space, but it might be a good idea to check out GameWorld.h in your IDE at some point to get a feel for it.

```
  //the steering behavior class
  SteeringBehaviors*  m_pSteering;
```

A vehicle has access to all available steering behaviors through its own instance of the steering behavior class.

```
public:

  //updates the vehicle's position and orientation
  void        Update(double time_elapsed);
```

```
  /* EXTRANEOUS DETAIL OMITTED */
};
```

You can see the class relationships clearly in the simplified UML diagram shown in Figure 3.1.

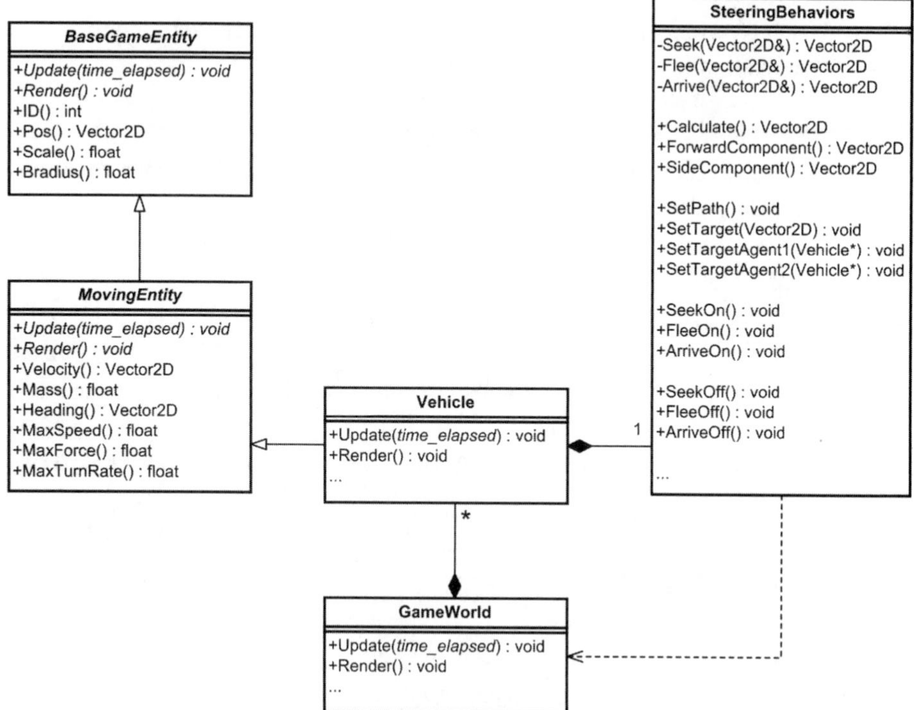

Figure 3.1. The `Vehicle` and `SteeringBehaviors` class relationships

Updating the Vehicle Physics

Before we move on to the steering behaviors themselves, I'd just like to walk you through the `Vehicle::Update` method. It's important that you understand every line of code in this function because it's the main workhorse of the `Vehicle` class. (If you do not know Newton's laws of force and motion, I would strongly recommend you read the relevant part of Chapter 1 before continuing.)

```
bool Vehicle::Update(double time_elapsed)
{
  //calculate the combined force from each steering behavior in the
  //vehicle's list
  SVector2D SteeringForce = m_pSteering->Calculate();
```

First the steering force for this simulation step is calculated. The `Calculate` method sums all a vehicle's active steering behaviors and returns the total steering force.

```
//Acceleration = Force/Mass
SVector2D acceleration = SteeringForce / m_dMass;
```

Using Newton's laws of physics, the steering force is converted into an acceleration (see equation 1.93, Chapter 1).

```
//update velocity
m_vVelocity += acceleration * time_elapsed;
```

Using the acceleration, the vehicle's velocity can be updated (see equation 1.81, Chapter 1).

```
//make sure vehicle does not exceed maximum velocity
m_vVelocity.Truncate(m_dMaxSpeed);

//update the position
m_vPos += m_vVelocity * time_elapsed;
```

The vehicle's position can now be updated using the new velocity (see equation 1.77, Chapter 1).

```
//update the heading if the vehicle has a velocity greater than a very small
//value
if (m_vVelocity.LengthSq() > 0.00000001)
{
  m_vHeading = Vec2DNormalize(m_vVelocity);

  m_vSide = m_vHeading.Perp();
}
```

As mentioned earlier, a `MovingEntity` has a local coordinate system that must be kept updated each simulation step. A vehicle's heading should always be aligned with its velocity so this is updated, making it equal to the normalized velocity vector. But — and this is important — *the heading is only calculated if the vehicle's velocity is above a very small threshold value*. This is because if the magnitude of the velocity is zero, the program will crash with a divide by zero error, and if the magnitude is non-zero but *very* small, the vehicle may (depending on the platform and operating system) start to move erratically a few seconds after it has stopped.

The side component of the local coordinate system is easily calculated by calling `SVector2D::Perp`.

```
  //treat the screen as a toroid
  WrapAround(m_vPos, m_pWorld->cxClient(), m_pWorld->cyClient());

}
```

Finally, the display area is considered to wrap around from top to bottom and from left to right (if you were to imagine it in 3D it would be toroidal — doughnut shaped). Therefore, a check is made to see if the updated position of the vehicle has exceeded the screen boundaries. If so, the position is wrapped around accordingly.

That's the boring stuff out of the way — let's move on and have some fun!

The Steering Behaviors

I'm now going to describe each steering behavior individually. Once I've covered all of them I'll explain the `SteeringBehaviors` class that encapsulates them and show you the different methods available for combining them. Toward the end of the chapter I'll demonstrate a few tips and tricks for getting the most out of steering behaviors.

Seek

The **seek** steering behavior returns a force that directs an agent toward a target position. It is very simple to program. The code looks like this (note that `m_pVehicle` points to the `Vehicle` that owns the `SteeringBehaviors` class):

```
Vector2D SteeringBehaviors::Seek(Vector2D TargetPos)
{
  Vector2D DesiredVelocity = Vec2DNormalize(TargetPos - m_pVehicle->Pos())
                            * m_pVehicle->MaxSpeed();

  return (DesiredVelocity - m_pVehicle->Velocity());
}
```

First the *desired velocity* is calculated. This is the velocity the agent would need to reach the target position in an ideal world. It represents the vector from the agent to the target, scaled to be the length of the maximum possible speed of the agent.

The steering force returned by this method is the force required, which when added to the agent's current velocity vector gives the desired velocity. To achieve this you simply subtract the agent's current velocity from the desired velocity. See Figure 3.2.

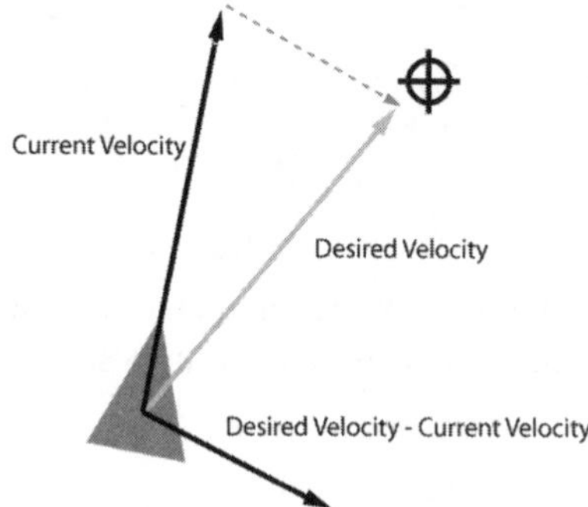

Figure 3.2. Calculating vectors for the seek behavior. The dotted vector shows how the addition of the steering force to the current velocity produces the desired result.

You can observe this behavior in action by running the Seek.exe executable. Click with the left mouse button to alter the position of the target. Notice how the agent will overshoot the target and then turn around to approach again. The amount of overshoot is determined by the ratio of MaxSpeed to MaxForce. You can change the magnitude of these values by pressing the Ins/Del and Home/End keys.

Seek comes in handy for all sorts of things. As you'll see, many of the other steering behaviors will make use of it.

Flee

Flee is the opposite of **seek**. Instead of producing a steering force to steer the agent toward a target position, **flee** creates a force that steers the agent away. Here's the code:

```
Vector2D SteeringBehaviors::Flee(Vector2D TargetPos)
{
  Vector2D DesiredVelocity = Vec2DNormalize(m_pVehicle->Pos() - TargetPos)
                            * m_pVehicle->MaxSpeed();

  return (DesiredVelocity - m_pVehicle->Velocity());
}
```

Note how the only difference is that the `DesiredVelocity` is calculated using a vector pointing in the opposite direction (`m_pVehicle->Pos() – TargetPos` instead of `TargetPos – m_pVehicle->Pos()`).

Flee can be easily adjusted to generate a fleeing force only when a vehicle comes within a certain range of the target. All it takes is a couple of extra lines of code.

```
Vector2D SteeringBehaviors::Flee(Vector2D TargetPos)
{
  //only flee if the target is within 'panic distance'. Work in distance
  //squared space.
  const double PanicDistanceSq = 100.0 * 100.0;
  if (Vec2DDistanceSq(m_pVehicle->Pos(), target) > PanicDistanceSq)
  {
    return Vector2D(0,0);
  }

  Vector2D DesiredVelocity = Vec2DNormalize(m_pVehicle->Pos() - TargetPos)
                            * m_pVehicle->MaxSpeed();

  return (DesiredVelocity - m_pVehicle->Velocity());
}
```

Notice how the distance to the target is calculated in distance squared space. As you saw in Chapter 1, this is to save calculating a square root.

Arrive

Seek is useful for getting an agent moving in the right direction, but often you'll want your agents to come to a gentle halt at the target position, and as you've seen, **seek** is not too great at stopping gracefully. **Arrive** is a behavior that steers the agent in such a way it *decelerates* onto the target position.

In addition to the target, this function takes a parameter of the enumerated type Deceleration, given by:

```
enum Deceleration{slow = 3, normal = 2, fast = 1};
```

Arrive uses this value to calculate how much time the agent desires to take to reach the target. From this value we can calculate at what speed the agent must travel to reach the target position in the desired amount of time. After that, the calculations proceed just like they did for **seek**.

```
Vector2D SteeringBehaviors::Arrive(Vector2D     TargetPos,
                                   Deceleration deceleration)
{
  Vector2D ToTarget = TargetPos - m_pVehicle->Pos();

  //calculate the distance to the target position
  double dist = ToTarget.Length();

  if (dist > 0)
  {
    //because Deceleration is enumerated as an int, this value is required
    //to provide fine tweaking of the deceleration.
    const double DecelerationTweaker = 0.3;

    //calculate the speed required to reach the target given the desired
    //deceleration
    double speed =  dist / ((double)deceleration * DecelerationTweaker);

    //make sure the velocity does not exceed the max
    speed = min(speed, m_pVehicle->MaxSpeed());

    //from here proceed just like Seek except we don't need to normalize
    //the ToTarget vector because we have already gone to the trouble
    //of calculating its length: dist.
    Vector2D DesiredVelocity = ToTarget * speed / dist;

    return (DesiredVelocity - m_pVehicle->Velocity());
  }

  return Vector2D(0,0);
}
```

Now that you know what it does, have a look at the demo executable. Notice how when the vehicle is far away from the target the **arrive** behavior acts just the same as **seek**, and how the deceleration only comes into effect when the vehicle gets close to the target.

Pursuit

Pursuit behavior is useful when an agent is required to intercept a moving target. It could keep **seeking** to the current position of the target of course, but this wouldn't really help to create the illusion of intelligence. Imagine you're a child again and playing tag in the schoolyard. When you want to tag someone, you don't just run straight at their current position (which is effectively **seeking** toward them); you predict where they are going to be in the future and run toward that offset, making adjustments as you narrow the gap. See Figure 3.3. This is the sort of behavior we want our agents to demonstrate.

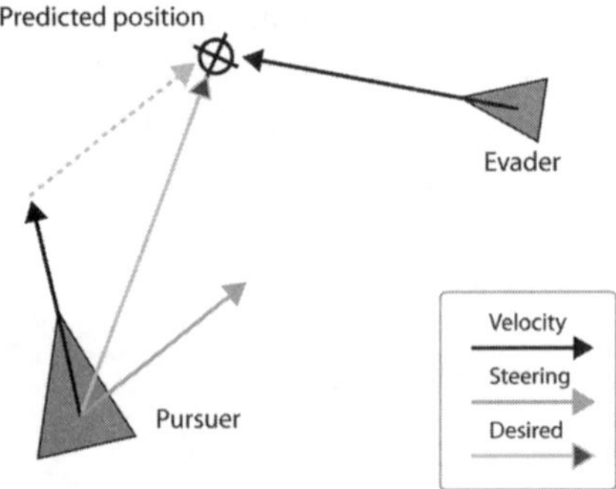

Figure 3.3. Calculating the vectors for the pursuit steering behavior. Once again, the dotted vector shows how the addition of the steering force to the current velocity produces the desired result.

The success of the pursuit function depends on how well the pursuer can predict the evader's trajectory. This can get very complicated, so a compromise must be made to obtain adequate performance without eating up too many clock cycles.

There is one situation the pursuer may face that enables an early out: If the evader is ahead and almost directly facing the agent, the agent should head directly for the evader's current position. This can be calculated quickly using dot products (see Chapter 1). In the example code, the evader's inverted heading must be within 20 degrees (approximately) of the agent's to be considered "facing."

One of the difficulties in creating a good predictor is deciding how far into the future the agent should predict. Clearly, the amount of look-ahead should be proportional to the separation between the pursuer and its evader, and inversely proportional to the pursuer's and evader's speeds. Once this time has been decided, an estimated future position can be calculated for the pursuer to **seek** to. Let's take a look at the code for this behavior:

```
Vector2D SteeringBehaviors::Pursuit(const Vehicle* evader)
{
  //if the evader is ahead and facing the agent then we can just seek
```

```
  //for the evader's current position.
  Vector2D ToEvader = evader->Pos() - m_pVehicle->Pos();

  double RelativeHeading = m_pVehicle->Heading().Dot(evader->Heading());

  if ((ToEvader.Dot(m_pVehicle->Heading()) > 0) &&
      (RelativeHeading < -0.95))  //acos(0.95)=18 degs
  {
    return Seek(evader->Pos());
  }

  //Not considered ahead so we predict where the evader will be.

  //the look-ahead time is proportional to the distance between the evader
  //and the pursuer; and is inversely proportional to the sum of the
  //agents' velocities
  double LookAheadTime = ToEvader.Length() /
                        (m_pVehicle->MaxSpeed() + evader->Speed());

  //now seek to the predicted future position of the evader
  return Seek(evader->Pos() + evader->Velocity() * LookAheadTime);
}
```

⌘ **TIP** Some locomotion models may also require that you factor in some time for turning the agent to face the offset. You can do this fairly simply by increasing the LookAheadTime by a value proportional to the dot product of the two headings and to the maximum turn rate of the vehicle. Something like:

```
LookAheadTime += TurnAroundTime(m_pVehicle, evader->Pos());
```

Where TurnAroundTime is the function:

```
double TurnaroundTime(const Vehicle* pAgent, Vector2D TargetPos)
{
  //determine the normalized vector to the target
  Vector2D toTarget = Vec2DNormalize(TargetPos - pAgent->Pos());

  double dot = pAgent->Heading().Dot(toTarget);

  //change this value to get the desired behavior. The higher the max turn
  //rate of the vehicle, the higher this value should be. If the vehicle is
  //heading in the opposite direction to its target position then a value
  //of 0.5 means that this function will return a time of 1 second for the
  //vehicle to turn around.
  const double coefficient = 0.5;

  //the dot product gives a value of 1 if the target is directly ahead and -1
  //if it is directly behind. Subtracting 1 and multiplying by the negative of
  //the coefficient gives a positive value proportional to the rotational
  //displacement of the vehicle and target.
  return (dot - 1.0) * -coefficient;
}
```

The **pursuit** demo shows a small vehicle being pursued by a larger one. The crosshair indicates the estimated future position of the evader. (The evader is utilizing a small amount of **wander** steering behavior to affect its motion. I'll be covering **wander** in just a moment.)

A pursuer's prey is set by passing the relevant method a pointer to the target in question. To set up a situation similar to the demo for this behavior you'd create two agents, one to pursue and the other to wander, just like this:

```
Vehicle* prey = new Vehicle(/* params omitted */);
prey->Steering()->WanderOn();

Vehicle* predator = new Vehicle(/* params omitted */);
predator->Steering()->PursuitOn(prey);
```

Got that? Okay, let's move on to **pursuit**'s opposite: **evade**.

Evade

Evade is almost the same as **pursuit** except that this time the evader **flees** from the estimated future position.

```
Vector2D SteeringBehaviors::Evade(const Vehicle* pursuer)
{
  /* Not necessary to include the check for facing direction this time */

  Vector2D ToPursuer = pursuer->Pos() - m_pVehicle->Pos();

  //the look-ahead time is proportional to the distance between the pursuer
  //and the evader; and is inversely proportional to the sum of the
  //agents' velocities
  double LookAheadTime = ToPursuer.Length() /
                         (m_pVehicle->MaxSpeed() + pursuer->Speed());

  //now flee away from predicted future position of the pursuer
  return Flee(pursuer->Pos() + pursuer->Velocity() * LookAheadTime);
}
```

Note that it is not necessary to include the check for facing direction this time.

Wander

You'll often find **wander** a useful ingredient when creating an agent's behavior. It's designed to produce a steering force that will give the impression of a random walk through the agent's environment.

A naive approach is to calculate a random steering force each time step, but this produces jittery behavior with no ability to achieve long persistent turns. (Actually, a rather nifty sort of random function, Perlin noise, can be used to produce smooth turning but this isn't very CPU friendly. It's still something for you to look into though if you get bored on a rainy day — Perlin noise has many applications.)

Reynolds' solution is to project a circle in front of the vehicle and steer toward a target that is constrained to move along the perimeter. Each time step, a small random displacement is added to this target, and over time it moves backward and forward along the circumference of the circle, creating a lovely jitter-free alternating motion. This method can be used to produce a whole range of random motion, from very smooth undulating turns to wild *Strictly Ballroom* type whirls and pirouettes depending on the size of the circle, its distance from the vehicle, and the amount of random displacement each frame. As they say, a picture is worth a thousand words, so it's probably a good idea for you to examine Figure 3.4 to get a better understanding.

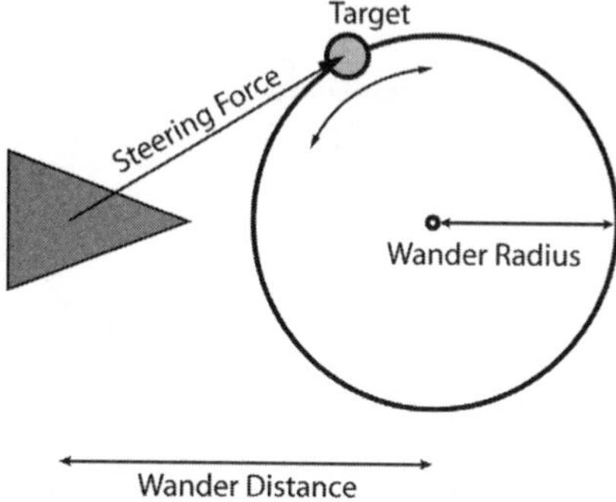

Figure 3.4

Let me take you through the code step by step. First there are three member variables wander makes use of:

```
double m_dWanderRadius;
```

This is the radius of the constraining circle.

```
double m_dWanderDistance;
```

This is the distance the wander circle is projected in front of the agent.

```
double m_dWanderJitter;
```

Finally, `m_dWanderJitter` is the maximum amount of random displacement that can be added to the target each second. Now for the method itself:

```
SVector2D SteeringBehaviors::Wander()
{
  //first, add a small random vector to the target's position (RandomClamped
  //returns a value between -1 and 1)
  m_vWanderTarget += SVector2D(RandomClamped() * m_dWanderJitter,
                               RandomClamped() * m_dWanderJitter);
```

`m_vWanderTarget` is a point constrained to the parameter of a circle of radius `m_dWanderRadius`, centered on the vehicle (`m_vWanderTarget`'s initial position is set in the constructor of `SteeringBehaviors`). Each time step, a small random displacement is added to the wander target's position. See Figure 3.5A.

```
  //reproject this new vector back onto a unit circle
  m_vWanderTarget.Normalize();
```

```
  //increase the length of the vector to the same as the radius
  //of the wander circle
  m_vWanderTarget *= m_dWanderRadius;
```

The next step is to reproject this new target back onto the wander circle. This is achieved by normalizing the vector and multiplying it by the radius of the wander circle. See Figure 3.5B.

```
  //move the target into a position WanderDist in front of the agent
  SVector2D targetLocal = m_vWanderTarget + SVector2D(m_dWanderDistance, 0);

  //project the target into world space
  SVector2D targetWorld = PointToWorldSpace(targetLocal,
                                            m_pVehicle->Heading(),
                                            m_pVehicle->Side(),
                                            m_pVehicle->Pos());


  //and steer toward it
  return targetWorld - m_pVehicle->Pos();
}
```

Finally, the new target is moved in front of the vehicle by an amount equal to `m_dWanderDistance` and projected into world space. The steering force is then calculated as the vector to this position. See Figure 3.5C.

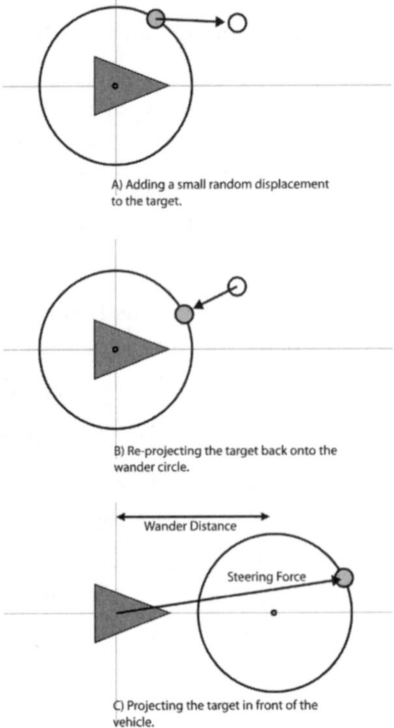

A) Adding a small random displacement to the target.
B) Re-projecting the target back onto the wander circle.
Wander Distance
Steering Force
C) Projecting the target in front of the vehicle.

Figure 3.5. Steps toward calculating the wander behavior

If you have a computer at hand I recommend you check out the demo for this behavior. The green circle is the constraining "wander circle" and the red dot the target. The demo allows you to adjust the size of the wander circle, the amount of jitter, and the wander distance so you can observe the effect they have on the behavior. Notice the relationship between the wander distance and the variation in angle of the steering force returned from the method. When the wander circle is far away from the vehicle, the method produces small variations in angle, thereby limiting the vehicle to small turns. As the circle is moved closer to the vehicle, the amount it can turn becomes less and less restricted.

⌘ **3D TIP** If you require your agents to wander in three dimensions (like a spaceship patrolling its territory), all you have to do is constrain the wander target to a *sphere instead of a circle*.

Obstacle Avoidance

Obstacle avoidance is a behavior that steers a vehicle to avoid obstacles lying in its path. An obstacle is any object that can be approximated by a circle (or sphere, if you are working in 3D). This is achieved by steering the vehicle so as to keep a rectangular area — a detection box, extending forward from the vehicle — free of collisions. The detection box's width is equal to the bounding radius of the vehicle, and its length is proportional to the vehicle's current speed — the faster it goes, the longer the detection box.

I think before I describe this process any further it would be a good idea to show you a diagram. Figure 3.6 shows a vehicle, some obstacles, and the detection box used in the calculations.

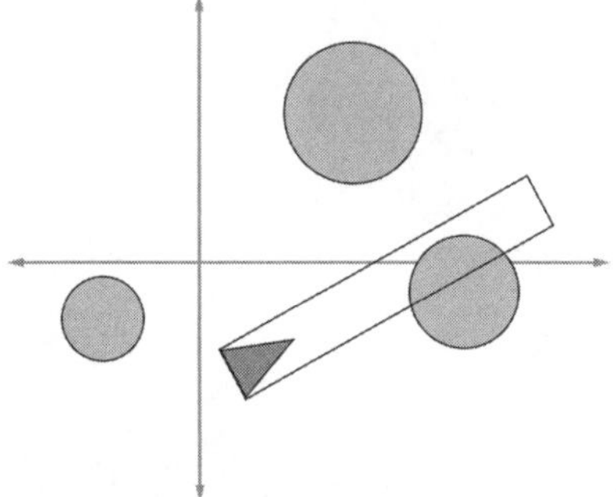

Figure 3.6. Setup for the obstacle avoidance steering behavior

Finding the Closest Intersection Point

The process of checking for intersections with obstacles is quite complicated, so let's take this step by step.

A) The vehicle should only consider those obstacles within range of its detection box. Initially, the **obstacle avoidance** algorithm iterates through all the obstacles in the game world and tags those that are within this range for further consideration.

B) The algorithm then transforms all the tagged obstacles into the vehicle's *local space* (for an explanation of local space, see Chapter 1). This makes life much easier as after transformation any objects with a negative local *x*-coordinate can be dismissed.

C) The algorithm now has to check to see if any obstacles overlap the detection box. Local coordinates are useful here as all you need to do is expand the bounding radius of an obstacle by half the width of the detection box (the vehicle's bounding radius) and then check to see if its local *y* value is smaller than this value. If it isn't, then it won't intersect the detection box and can subsequently be discarded from further consideration.

Figure 3.7 should help clear up these first three steps for you. The letters on the obstacles in the diagram correspond to the descriptions.

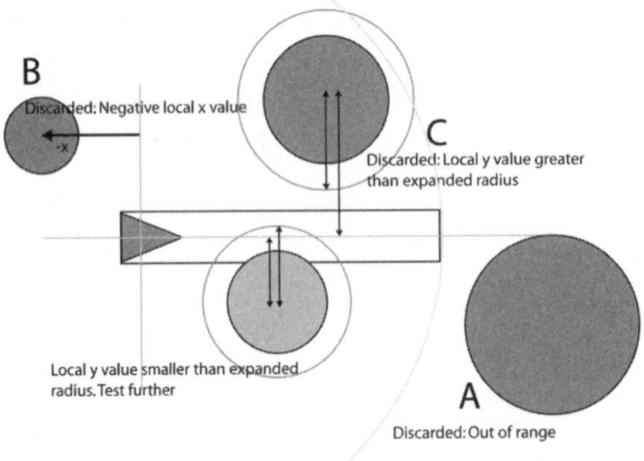

Figure 3.7. Steps A, B, and C

D) At this point there are only those obstacles remaining that intersect the detection box. It's now necessary to find the intersection point closest to the vehicle. Once more, local space comes to the rescue. Step C expanded an object's bounding radius. Using this, a simple line/circle intersection test can be used to find where the expanded circle intersects the *x*-axis. There will be two intersection points, as shown in Figure 3.8. (We don't have to worry about the case where there is one intersection tangent to the circle — the vehicle will appear to just glance off the obstacle.) Note that it is possible to have an obstacle in front of the vehicle, but it will have an intersection point to the rear of the vehicle. This is shown in the figure by obstacle A. The algorithm discards these cases and only considers intersection points laying on the positive *x*-axis.

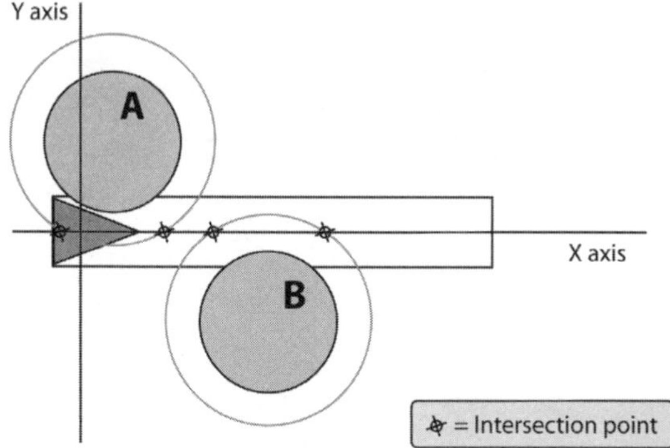

Figure 3.8. Intersection points

The algorithm tests all the remaining obstacles to find the one with the closest (positive) intersection point.

Before I show you how the steering force is calculated, let me list the part of the obstacle avoidance algorithm code that implements steps A to D.

```
Vector2D
SteeringBehaviors::ObstacleAvoidance(const std::vector<BaseGameEntity*>
     &obstacles)
{
  //the detection box length is proportional to the agent's velocity
  m_dDBoxLength = Prm.MinDetectionBoxLength +
                  (m_pVehicle->Speed()/m_pVehicle->MaxSpeed()) *
                  Prm.MinDetectionBoxLength;
```

All the parameters used by the project are read from an initialization file called Params.ini and stored in the singleton class `ParamLoader`. All the data in this class is public and is easily accessible through the #definition of `Prm` (`#define Prm (*ParamLoader::Instance())`). If further clarification is needed, see the ParamLoader.h file.

```
  //tag all obstacles within range of the box for processing
  m_pVehicle->World()->TagObstaclesWithinViewRange(m_pVehicle, m_dDBoxLength);

  //this will keep track of the closest intersecting obstacle (CIB)
  BaseGameEntity* ClosestIntersectingObstacle = NULL;
```

```
//this will be used to track the distance to the CIB
double DistToClosestIP = MaxDouble;

//this will record the transformed local coordinates of the CIB
Vector2D LocalPosOfClosestObstacle;

std::vector<BaseGameEntity*>::const_iterator curOb = obstacles.begin();

while(curOb != obstacles.end())
{
  //if the obstacle has been tagged within range proceed
  if ((*curOb)->IsTagged())
  {
    //calculate this obstacle's position in local space
    Vector2D LocalPos = PointToLocalSpace((*curOb)->Pos(),
                                           m_pVehicle->Heading(),
                                           m_pVehicle->Side(),
                                           m_pVehicle->Pos());

    //if the local position has a negative x value then it must lay
    //behind the agent. (in which case it can be ignored)
    if (LocalPos.x >= 0)
    {
      //if the distance from the x axis to the object's position is less
      //than its radius + half the width of the detection box then there
      //is a potential intersection.
      double ExpandedRadius = (*curOb)->BRadius() + m_pVehicle->BRadius();

      if (fabs(LocalPos.y) < ExpandedRadius)
      {
        //now to do a line/circle intersection test. The center of the
        //circle is represented by (cX, cY). The intersection points are
        //given by the formula x = cX +/-sqrt(r^2-cY^2) for y=0.
        //We only need to look at the smallest positive value of x because
        //that will be the closest point of intersection.
        double cX = LocalPos.x;
        double cY = LocalPos.y;

        //we only need to calculate the sqrt part of the above equation once
        double SqrtPart = sqrt(ExpandedRadius*ExpandedRadius - cY*cY);

        double ip = cX - SqrtPart;

        if (ip <= 0)
        {
          ip = cX + SqrtPart;
        }

        //test to see if this is the closest so far. If it is, keep a
        //record of the obstacle and its local coordinates
        if (ip < DistToClosestIP)
        {
          DistToClosestIP = ip;

          ClosestIntersectingObstacle = *curOb;
```

```
            LocalPosOfClosestObstacle = LocalPos;
          }
        }
      }
    }

    ++curOb;
  }
```

Calculating the Steering Force

Determining the steering force is easy. It's calculated in two parts: a *lateral force* and a *braking force*. See Figure 3.9.

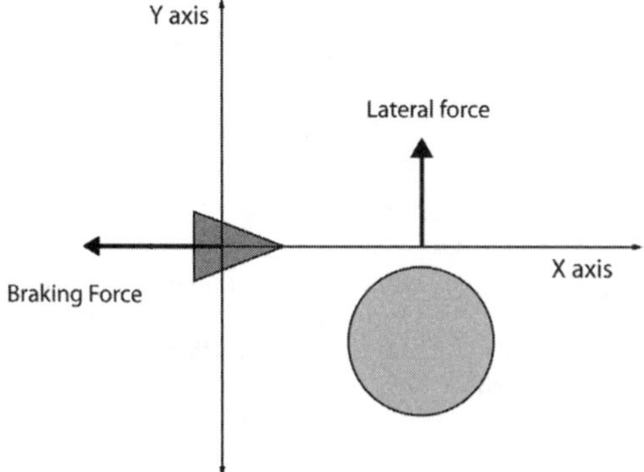

Figure 3.9. Calculating the steering force

There are a number of ways to calculate the lateral force but the one I prefer is to subtract the y value of the obstacle's local position from its radius. This results in a lateral steering force away from the obstacle that diminishes with the obstacle's distance from the *x*-axis. This force is scaled in proportion to the vehicle's distance from the obstacle (because the closer the vehicle is to an obstacle the quicker it should react).

The next component of the steering force is the braking force. This is a force acting backward, along the horizontal axis as shown in the figure, and is also scaled in proportion to the vehicle's distance from the obstacle.

The steering force is finally transformed into world space, resulting in the value returned from the method. The code is as follows

```
//if we have found an intersecting obstacle, calculate a steering
//force away from it
Vector2D SteeringForce;

if (ClosestIntersectingObstacle)
{
  //the closer the agent is to an object, the stronger the steering force
```

```
    //should be
    double multiplier = 1.0 + (m_dDBoxLength - LocalPosOfClosestObstacle.x) /
                        m_dDBoxLength;

    //calculate the lateral force
    SteeringForce.y = (ClosestIntersectingObstacle->BRadius()-
                       LocalPosOfClosestObstacle.y)  * multiplier;

    //apply a braking force proportional to the obstacle's distance from
    //the vehicle.
    const double BrakingWeight = 0.2;

    SteeringForce.x = (ClosestIntersectingObstacle->BRadius() -
                       LocalPosOfClosestObstacle.x) *
                       BrakingWeight;
  }

  //finally, convert the steering vector from local to world space
  return VectorToWorldSpace(SteeringForce,
                            m_pVehicle->Heading(),
                            m_pVehicle->Side());
}
```

⌘ **3D TIP** When implementing obstacle avoidance in three dimensions, use spheres to approximate the obstacles and a cylinder in place of the detection box. The math to check against a sphere is not that much different than that to check against a circle. Once the obstacles have been converted into local space, steps A and B are the same as you have already seen, and step C just involves checking against another axis.

Wall Avoidance

A wall is a line segment (in 3D, a polygon) with a normal pointing in the direction it is facing. **Wall avoidance** steers to avoid potential collisions with a wall. It does this by projecting three "feelers" out in front of the vehicle and testing to see if any of them intersect with any walls in the game world. See Figure 3.10. (The little "stub" halfway along the wall indicates the direction of the wall normal.) This is similar to how cats and rodents use their whiskers to navigate their environment in the dark.

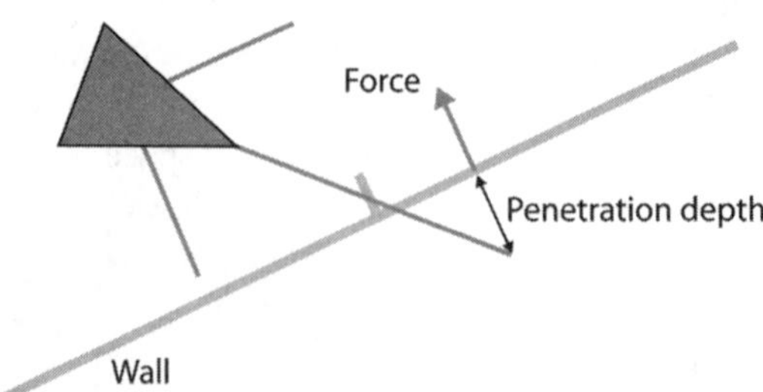

Figure 3.10. Wall avoidance

When the closest intersecting wall has been found (if there is one of course), a steering force is calculated. This is deduced by calculating how far the feeler tip has penetrated through the wall and then by creating a force of that magnitude in the direction of the wall normal.

```
Vector2D SteeringBehaviors::WallAvoidance(const std::vector<Wall2D>& walls)
{
  //the feelers are contained in a std::vector, m_Feelers
  CreateFeelers();

  double DistToThisIP    = 0.0;
  double DistToClosestIP = MaxDouble;

  //this will hold an index into the vector of walls
  int ClosestWall = -1;

  Vector2D SteeringForce,
           point,         //used for storing temporary info
           ClosestPoint;  //holds the closest intersection point

  //examine each feeler in turn
  for (int flr=0; flr<m_Feelers.size(); ++flr)
  {
    //run through each wall checking for any intersection points
    for (int w=0; w<walls.size(); ++w)
    {
      if (LineIntersection2D(m_pVehicle->Pos(),
                             m_Feelers[flr],
                             walls[w].From(),
                             walls[w].To(),
                             DistToThisIP,
                             point))
      {
        //is this the closest found so far? If so keep a record
        if (DistToThisIP < DistToClosestIP)
        {
          DistToClosestIP = DistToThisIP;

          ClosestWall = w;

          ClosestPoint = point;
        }
      }
    }//next wall


    //if an intersection point has been detected, calculate a force
    //that will direct the agent away
    if (ClosestWall >=0)
    {
      //calculate by what distance the projected position of the agent
      //will overshoot the wall
      Vector2D OverShoot = m_Feelers[flr] - ClosestPoint;

      //create a force in the direction of the wall normal, with a
```

```
      //magnitude of the overshoot
      SteeringForce = walls[ClosestWall].Normal() * OverShoot.Length();
    }

  }//next feeler

  return SteeringForce;
}
```

I have found the three feeler approach to give good results, but it's possible to achieve reasonable performance with just one feeler that continuously scans left and right in front of the vehicle. It all depends on how many processor cycles you have to play with and how accurate you require the behavior to be.

NOTE If you are the impatient sort and have already looked at the source code, you may have noticed that the final update function in the source is a little more complicated than the basic update function listed earlier. This is because many of the techniques I will be describing toward the end of this chapter involve adding to, or even changing, this function. All the steering behaviors listed over the next few pages, however, just use this basic skeleton.

Interpose

Interpose returns a steering force that moves a vehicle to the midpoint of the imaginary line connecting two other agents (or points in space, or of an agent and a point). A bodyguard taking a bullet for his employer or a soccer player intercepting a pass are examples of this type of behavior.

Like **pursuit**, the vehicle must estimate where the two agents are going to be located at a time *T* in the future. It can then steer toward that position. But how do we know what the best value of *T* is to use? The answer is, we don't, so we make a calculated guess instead.

The first step in calculating this force is to determine the midpoint of a line connecting the positions of the agents at the current time step. The distance from this point is computed and the value divided by the vehicle's maximum speed to give the time required to travel the distance. This is our *T* value. See Figure 3.11, top.

Using *T*, the agents' positions are extrapolated into the future. The midpoint of these predicted positions is determined and finally the vehicle uses the **arrive** behavior to steer toward that point. See Figure 3.11, bottom.

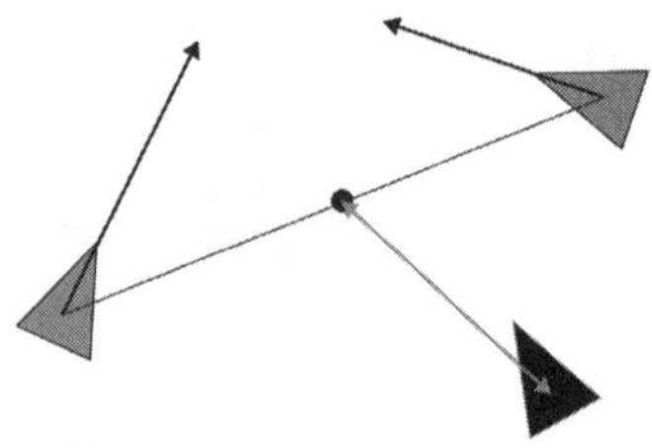

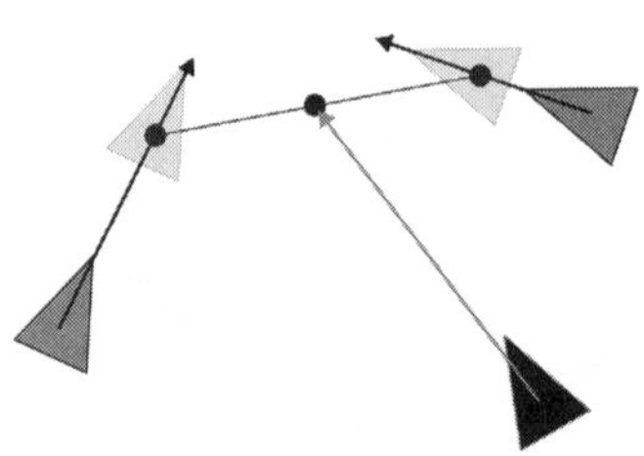

Figure 3.11. Predicting the interpose point

Here's the listing:

```
Vector2D SteeringBehaviors::Interpose(const Vehicle* AgentA,
                                      const Vehicle* AgentB)
{
  //first we need to figure out where the two agents are going to be at
  //time T in the future. This is approximated by determining the time
  //taken to reach the midway point at the current time at max speed.
  Vector2D MidPoint = (AgentA->Pos() + AgentB->Pos()) / 2.0;

  double TimeToReachMidPoint = Vec2DDistance(m_pVehicle->Pos(), MidPoint) /
                               m_pVehicle->MaxSpeed();

  //now we have T, we assume that agent A and agent B will continue on a
  //straight trajectory and extrapolate to get their future positions
  Vector2D APos = AgentA->Pos() + AgentA->Velocity() * TimeToReachMidPoint;
  Vector2D BPos = AgentB->Pos() + AgentB->Velocity() * TimeToReachMidPoint;

  //calculate the midpoint of these predicted positions
  MidPoint = (APos + BPos) / 2.0;

  //then steer to arrive at it
  return Arrive(MidPoint, fast);
}
```

Note that **arrive** is called with `fast` deceleration, allowing the vehicle to reach the target position as quickly as possible.

The demo for this behavior shows a red vehicle attempting to interpose itself between two blue wandering vehicles.

Hide

Hide attempts to position a vehicle so that an obstacle is always between itself and the agent — the hunter — it's trying to hide from. You can use this behavior not only for situations where you require an NPC to hide from the player — like find cover when fired at — but also in situations where you would like an NPC to sneak up on a player. For example, you can create an NPC capable of stalking a player through a gloomy forest, darting from tree to tree. Creepy!

The method I prefer to effect this behavior is as follows:

Step One. For each of the obstacles, a hiding spot is determined. See Figure 3.12.

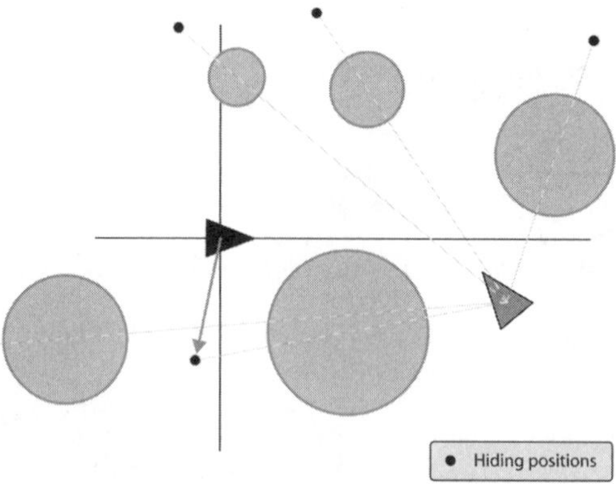

Figure 3.12. Potential hiding spots

These are calculated by the method GetHidingPosition, which looks like this:

```
SVector2D SteeringBehaviors::GetHidingPosition(const SVector2D& posOb,
                                               const double     radiusOb,
                                               const SVector2D& posTarget)
{
  //calculate how far away the agent is to be from the chosen obstacle's
  //bounding radius
  const double DistanceFromBoundary = 30.0;

  double DistAway = radiusOb + DistanceFromBoundary;

  //calculate the heading toward the object from the target
  SVector2D ToOb = Vec2DNormalize(posOb - posTarget);

  //scale it to size and add to the obstacle's position to get
  //the hiding spot.
  return (ToOb * DistAway) + posOb;
}
```

Given the position of a target and the position and radius of an obstacle, this method calculates a position DistanceFromBoundary away from the object's bounding radius and directly opposite the target. It does this by scaling the normalized "to obstacle" vector by the required distance away from the center of the obstacle and then adding the result to the obstacle's position. The black dots in Figure 3.12 show the hiding spots returned by this method for that example.

Step Two. The distance to each of these spots is determined. The vehicle then uses the **arrive** behavior to steer toward the closest. If no appropriate obstacles can be found, the vehicle **evades** the target.

Here's how it's done in code:

```
SVector2D SteeringBehaviors::Hide(const Vehicle*           target,
                                  vector<BaseGameEntity*>& obstacles)
{
  double     DistToClosest = MaxDouble
  SVector2D BestHidingSpot;

  std::vector<BaseGameEntity*>::iterator curOb = obstacles.begin();
  while(curOb != obstacles.end())
  {
    //calculate the position of the hiding spot for this obstacle
    SVector2D HidingSpot = GetHidingPosition((*curOb)->Pos(),
                                             (*curOb)->BRadius(),
                                             target->Pos());

    //work in distance-squared space to find the closest hiding
    //spot to the agent
    double dist = Vec2DDistanceSq(HidingSpot, m_pVehicle->Pos());

    if (dist < DistToClosest)
    {
      DistToClosest  = dist;

      BestHidingSpot = HidingSpot;
    }

    ++curOb;

  }//end while

  //if no suitable obstacles found then evade the target
  if (DistToClosest == MaxDouble)
  {
    return Evade(target);
  }

  //else use Arrive on the hiding spot
  return Arrive(BestHidingSpot, fast);
}
```

The demo executable shows two vehicles hiding from a slower, wandering vehicle.

There are a few modifications you can make to this algorithm:

1. You can allow the vehicle to hide only if the target is within its field of view. This tends to produce unsatisfactory performance though, because the vehicle starts to act like a child hiding from monsters beneath the bed sheets. I'm sure you remember the feeling — the "if you can't see it, then it can't see you" effect. It might work when you're a kid, but this sort of behavior just makes the vehicle look dumb. This can be countered slightly though by adding in a time effect so that the vehicle will hide if the target is visible *or* if it has

seen the target within the last *n* seconds. This gives it a sort of memory and produces reasonable-looking behavior.

2. The same as above, but this time the vehicle only tries to hide if the vehicle can see the target *and* the target can see the vehicle.
3. It might be desirable to produce a force that steers a vehicle so that it always favors hiding positions that are to the side or rear of the pursuer. This can be achieved easily using your friend the dot product to bias the distances returned from `GetHidingPosition`.
4. At the beginning of any of the methods a check can be made to test if the target is within a "threat distance" before proceeding with any further calculations. If the target is not a threat, then the method can return immediately with a zero vector.

Path Following

Path following creates a steering force that moves a vehicle along a series of waypoints forming a path. Sometimes paths have a start and end point, and other times they loop back around on themselves forming a never-ending, closed path. See Figure 3.13.

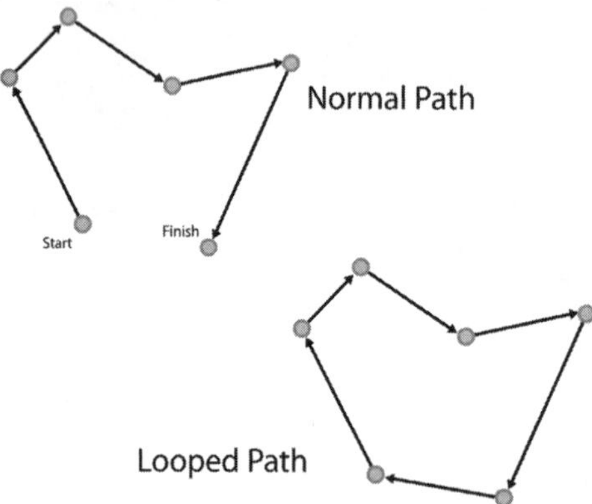

Figure 3.13. Different types of paths

You'll find countless uses for using paths in your game. You can use them to create agents that patrol important areas of a map, to enable units to traverse difficult terrain, or to help racing cars navigate around a racetrack. They are useful in most situations where an agent must visit a series of checkpoints.

The paths the vehicles described in this chapter follow are described by a `std::list` of `Vector2D`s. In addition, the vehicle also needs to know what the current waypoint is and whether it is a closed path or not to enable it to take the appropriate action when it reaches the final waypoint. If it is a closed path, it should head back to the first waypoint in the list and start all over again. If it's an open path, the vehicle should just decelerate to a stop (**arrive**) over the final waypoint.

`Path` is a class that looks after all these details. I'm not going to list it here but you may like to examine it in your IDE. You can find it in the file Path.h.

The simplest way of following a path is to set the current waypoint to the first in the list, steer toward that using **seek** until the vehicle comes within a target distance of it, then grab the next waypoint and **seek** to that, and so on, until the current waypoint is the last waypoint in the list. When this happens the vehicle should either **arrive** at the current waypoint, or, if the path is a closed loop, the current waypoint should be set to the first in the list again, and the vehicle just keeps on **seeking**. Here's the code for **path following**:

```
SVector2D SteeringBehaviors::FollowPath()
{
  //move to next target if close enough to current target (working in
  //distance squared space)
  if(Vec2DDistanceSq(m_pPath->CurrentWaypoint(), m_pVehicle->Pos()) <
                     m_WaypointSeekDistSq)
  {
    m_pPath->SetNextWaypoint();
  }

  if (!m_pPath->Finished())
  {
    return Seek(m_pPath->CurrentWaypoint());
  }

  else
  {
    return Arrive(m_pPath->CurrentWaypoint(), normal);
  }
}
```

You have to be very careful when implementing **path following**. The behavior is very sensitive to the max steering force/max speed ratio and also the variable `m_WaypointSeekDistSq`. The demo executable for this behavior allows you to alter these values to see what effect they have. As you will discover, it's easy to create behavior that is sloppy. How tight you need the **path following** to be depends entirely on your game environment. If you have a game with lots of gloomy tight corridors, then you're (probably) going to need stricter **path following** than a game set in the Sahara.

Offset Pursuit

Offset pursuit calculates the steering force required to keep a vehicle positioned at a specified offset from a target vehicle. This is particularly useful for creating formations. When you watch an air display, such as the British Red Arrows, many of the spectacular maneuvers require that the aircraft remain in the same relative positions to the lead aircraft. See Figure 3.14. This is the sort of behavior we want to emulate.

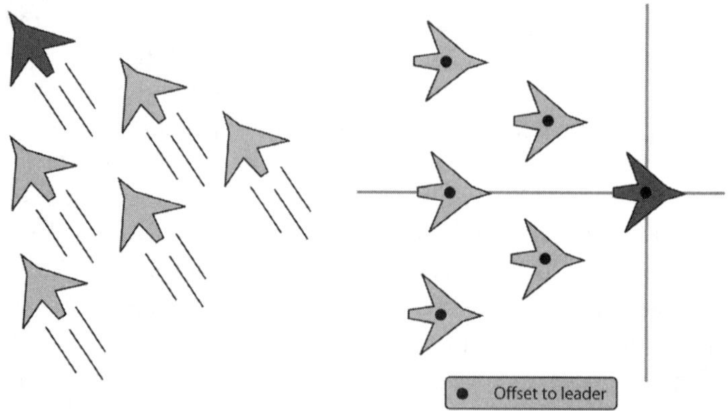

Figure 3.14. Offset pursuit. The leader is shown in dark gray.

The offset is always defined in "leader" space, so the first thing to do when calculating this steering force is to determine the offset's position in world space. After that the function proceeds similar to pursuit: A future position for the offset is predicted and the vehicle arrives at that position.

```
SVector2D SteeringBehaviors::OffsetPursuit(const Vehicle*  leader,
                                           const SVector2D offset)
{

  //calculate the offset's position in world space
  SVector2D WorldOffsetPos = PointToWorldSpace(offset,
                                               leader->Heading(),
                                               leader->Side(),
                                               leader->Pos());

  SVector2D ToOffset = WorldOffsetPos - m_pVehicle->Pos();

  //the look-ahead time is proportional to the distance between the leader
  //and the pursuer; and is inversely proportional to the sum of both
  //agents' velocities
  double LookAheadTime = ToOffset.Length() /
                         (m_pVehicle->MaxSpeed() + leader->Speed());

  //now arrive at the predicted future position of the offset
  return Arrive(WorldOffsetPos + leader->Velocity() * LookAheadTime, fast);
}
```

Arrive is used instead of **seek** as it gives far smoother motion and isn't so reliant on the max speed and max force settings of the vehicles. **Seek** can give some rather bizarre results at times — orderly formations can turn into what looks like a swarm of bees attacking the formation leader!

Offset pursuit is useful for all kinds of situations. Here are a few:

- Marking an opponent in a sports simulation
- Docking with a spaceship
- Shadowing an aircraft
- Implementing battle formations

The demo executable for **offset pursuit** shows three smaller vehicles attempting to remain at offsets to the larger lead vehicle. The lead vehicle is using **arrive** to follow the crosshair (click the left mouse button to position the crosshair).

Group Behaviors

Group behaviors are steering behaviors that take into consideration some or all of the other vehicles in the game world. The flocking behavior I described at the beginning of this chapter is a good example of a group behavior. In fact, flocking is a combination of three group behaviors — **cohesion**, **separation**, and **alignment** — all working together. We'll take a look at these specific behaviors in detail shortly, but first let me show you how a group is defined.

To determine the steering force for a group behavior, a vehicle will consider all other vehicles within a circular area of predefined size — known as the *neighborhood radius* — centered on the vehicle. Figure 3.15 should help clarify. The white vehicle is the steering agent and the gray circle shows the extent of its neighborhood. Consequently, all the vehicles shown in black are considered to be its neighbors and the vehicles shown in gray are not.

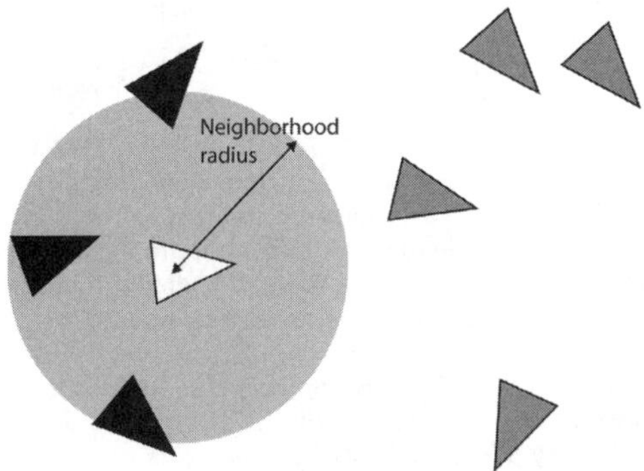

Figure 3.15. The neighborhood radius

Before a steering force can be calculated, a vehicle's neighbors must be determined and either stored in a container or tagged ready for processing. In the demo code for this chapter, the neighboring vehicles are tagged using the BaseGameEntity::Tag method. This is done by the TagNeighbors function template. Here's the code:

```
template <class T, class conT>
void TagNeighbors(const T* entity, conT& ContainerOfEntities, double radius)
{
  //iterate through all entities checking for range
  for (typename conT::iterator curEntity = ContainerOfEntities.begin();
       curEntity != ContainerOfEntities.end();
       ++curEntity)
  {
    //first clear any current tag
    (*curEntity)->UnTag();

    Vector2D to = (*curEntity)->Pos() - entity->Pos();

    //the bounding radius of the other is taken into account by adding it
    //to the range
    double range = radius + (*curEntity)->BRadius();

    //if entity within range, tag for further consideration. (working in
    //distance-squared space to avoid sqrts)
    if ( ((*curEntity) != entity) && (to.LengthSq() < range*range))
    {
      (*curEntity)->Tag();
    }

  }//next entity
}
```

Most of the group behaviors utilize a similar neighborhood radius, so we can save a little time by calling this method only once prior to a call to any of the group behaviors.

```
if (On(separation) || On(alignment) || On(cohesion))
{
  TagNeighbors(m_pVehicle, m_pVehicle->World()->Agents(), ViewDistance);
}
```

⌘ **TIP** You can pep up the realism slightly for group behaviors by adding a field-of-view constraint to your agent. For example you can restrict the vehicles included in the neighboring region by only tagging those that are within, say, 270 degrees of the heading of the steering agent. You can implement this easily by testing against the dot product of the steering agent's heading and the vector to the potential neighbor.

It's even possible to adjust an agent's FOV dynamically and make it into a feature of the AI. For example, in a war game a soldier's FOV may be detrimentally affected by its fatigue, thereby affecting its ability to perceive its environment. I don't think this idea has been used in a commercial game but it's certainly food for thought.

Now that you know how a group is defined let's take a look at some of the behaviors that operate on them.

Separation

Separation creates a force that steers a vehicle away from those in its neighborhood region. When applied to a number of vehicles, they will spread out, trying to maximize their distance from every other vehicle. See Figure 3.16, top.

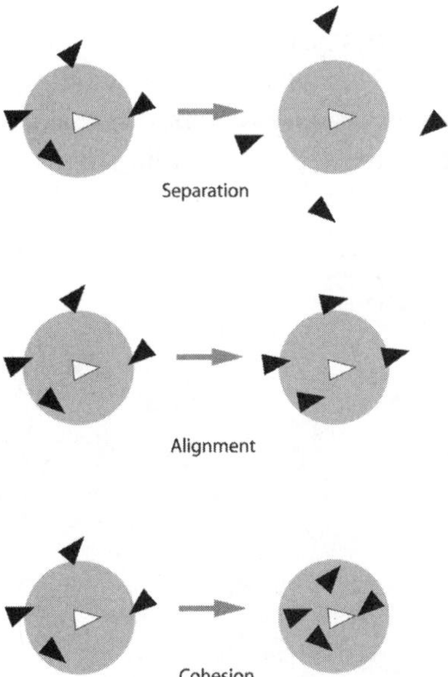

Figure 3.16. The separation, alignment, and cohesion group behaviors

This is an easy behavior to implement. Prior to calling **separation**, all the agents situated within a vehicle's neighborhood are tagged. **Separation** then iterates through the tagged vehicles, examining each one. The vector to each vehicle under consideration is normalized, divided by the distance to the neighbor, and added to the steering force.

```
Vector2D SteeringBehaviors::Separation(const std::vector<Vehicle*>& neighbors)
{
  Vector2D SteeringForce;

  for (int a=0; a<neighbors.size(); ++a)
  {
    //make sure this agent isn't included in the calculations and that
    //the agent being examined is close enough.
    if((neighbors[a] != m_pVehicle) && neighbors[a]->IsTagged())
    {
      Vector2D ToAgent = m_pVehicle->Pos() - neighbors[a]->Pos();

      //scale the force inversely proportional to the agent's distance
      //from its neighbor.
      SteeringForce += Vec2DNormalize(ToAgent)/ToAgent.Length();
```

```
    }
  }

  return SteeringForce;
}
```

Alignment

Alignment attempts to keep a vehicle's heading aligned with its neighbors. See Figure 3.16, middle. The force is calculated by first iterating through all the neighbors and averaging their heading vectors. This value is the desired heading, so we just subtract the vehicle's heading to get the steering force.

```
Vector2D SteeringBehaviors::Alignment(const std::vector<Vehicle*>& neighbors)
{
  //used to record the average heading of the neighbors
  Vector2D AverageHeading;

  //used to count the number of vehicles in the neighborhood
  int    NeighborCount = 0

  //iterate through all the tagged vehicles and sum their heading vectors
  for (int a=0; a<neighbors.size(); ++a)
  {
    //make sure *this* agent isn't included in the calculations and that
    //the agent being examined is close enough
    if((neighbors[a] != m_pVehicle) && neighbors[a]->IsTagged)
    {
      AverageHeading += neighbors[a]->Heading();

      ++NeighborCount;
    }
  }

  //if the neighborhood contained one or more vehicles, average their
  //heading vectors.
  if (NeighborCount > 0)
  {
    AverageHeading /= (double)NeighborCount;

    AverageHeading -= m_pVehicle->Heading();
  }

  return AverageHeading;
}
```

Cars moving along roads demonstrate **alignment** type behavior. They also demonstrate **separation** as they try to keep a minimum distance from each other.

Cohesion

Cohesion produces a steering force that moves a vehicle toward the center of mass of its neighbors. See Figure 3.16, bottom. A sheep running after its flock is demonstrating cohesive behavior. Use this force to keep a group of vehicles together.

This method proceeds similarly to the last, except this time we calculate the average of the position vectors of the neighbors. This gives us the center of mass of the neighbors — the place the vehicle wants to get to — so it **seeks** to that position.

```
Vector2D SteeringBehaviors::Cohesion(const std::vector<Vehicle*>& neighbors)
{
  //first find the center of mass of all the agents
  Vector2D CenterOfMass, SteeringForce;

  int NeighborCount = 0;

  //iterate through the neighbors and sum up all the position vectors
  for (int a=0; a<neighbors.size(); ++a)
  {
    //make sure *this* agent isn't included in the calculations and that
    //the agent being examined is a neighbor
    if((neighbors[a] != m_pVehicle) && neighbors[a]->IsTagged())
    {
      CenterOfMass += neighbors[a]->Pos();

      ++NeighborCount;
    }
  }

  if (NeighborCount > 0)
  {
    //the center of mass is the average of the sum of positions
    CenterOfMass /= (double)NeighborCount;

    //now seek toward that position
    SteeringForce = Seek(CenterOfMass);
  }

  return SteeringForce;
}
```

You might be a little disappointed that I haven't included demos for separation, cohesion, and alignment. Well, there's a reason for that: Like Itchy and Scratchy, they are not particularly interesting on their own; they are much better appreciated when they are *combined*, which takes us nicely into **flocking**.

Flocking

Flocking is the behavior I mentioned at the beginning of this chapter — the one I saw on the BBC documentary. It's a beautiful demonstration of what has become known as *emergent behavior*. Emergent behavior is behavior that looks complex and/or purposeful to the observer but is actually derived spontaneously from fairly simple rules. The lower-level entities following the rules have no idea of the bigger picture; they are only aware of themselves and maybe a few of their neighbors.

One good example of emergence is an experiment undertaken by Chris Melhuish and Owen Holland at the University of the West of England. Melhuish and Holland are interested in *stigmergy*, the field of science partly occupied with emergent behavior in social insects like ants, termites, and bees. They became interested in the way ants gather their dead, eggs, and other material into piles, and specifically the ant *Leptothorax*, because it lives among the cracks in rocks and operates, for all intents and purposes, in 2D… just like a wheeled robot. When observing *Leptothorax* in the laboratory, bustling about in their simulated crack — two sheets of glass — they noticed the ants had a tendency to push small granules of rock material together into clusters and wondered if they could design robots capable of doing the same.

After a little sweat and toil they managed to create robots operating on very simple rules, capable of gathering randomly scattered Frisbees into clusters. The robots had no knowledge of each other and didn't know what a cluster, or even a Frisbee, was. They couldn't even *see* the Frisbees. They could only push Frisbees using a U-shaped arm situated in front of them.

So how does the clustering behavior happen? Well, when the robots are switched on, they wander about until they bump into a Frisbee. A single Frisbee doesn't change a robot's behavior. However, when a Frisbee-pushing robot bumps into a second Frisbee, it immediately leaves the two Frisbees where they are, backs up a little, rotates by a random amount, and then wanders off again. Using just these simple rules and a little time, a few robots will push all the Frisbees into a few large clusters. Just like the ants.

Anyhow, let me abandon all this talk of Frisbees and get back to the flocking. Flocking, as originally described by Reynolds, is a combination of the three previously described group behaviors: **separation**, **alignment**, and **cohesion**. This works okay but, because of the limited view distance of a vehicle, it's possible for an agent to become isolated from its flock. If this happens, it will just sit still and do nothing. To prevent this from happening, I prefer to add in the **wander** behavior too. This way, all the agents keep moving all the time.

Tweaking the magnitudes of each of the contributing behaviors will give you different effects such as shoals of fish, loose swirling flocks of birds, or bustling close-knit herds of sheep. I've even managed to produce dense flocks of hundreds of tiny particles that are reminiscent of jellyfish. As this behavior is better seen than described, I recommend you open up the demo executable and play around for a while. Beware though — flocking is addictive! (Maybe that's why some animals like to do it so much...) You can adjust the influence of each behavior with the "A/Z," "S/X," and "D/C" keys. In addition you can view the neighbors of one of the agents by pressing the "G" key.

INTERESTING FACT Steering behaviors are often used to create special effects for films. The first film to use the flocking behavior was *Batman Returns*, where you can see flocks of bats and herds of penguins. The most recent films to use steering behaviors are *The Lord of the Rings* trilogy, directed by Peter Jackson. The movement of the orc armies in those films is created using steering behaviors via a piece of software called Massive.

Now that you've seen the benefits, let's take a look at exactly how steering behaviors can be combined.

Combining Steering Behaviors

Often you will be using a *combination* of steering behaviors to get the behavior you desire. Very rarely will you only use one behavior in isolation. For example, you might like to implement an FPS bot that will run from A to B (**path following**) while avoiding any other bots (**separation**) and walls (**wall avoidance**) that may try to impede its progress (see Chapter 7, "Raven: An Overview"). Or you might want the sheep you've implemented as a food resource in your RTS game to flock together (**flocking**) while simultaneously wandering around the environment (**wander**), avoiding trees (**obstacle avoidance**), and scattering (**evade**) whenever a human or dog comes near.

All the steering behaviors described in this chapter are methods of one class: `SteeringBehaviors`. A `Vehicle` owns an instance of this class and activates/deactivates the various behaviors by switching them on and off using accessor methods. For example, to set up one of the sheep for the situation described in the previous paragraph, you may do something like this (assuming a dog-like agent has already been created):

```
Vehicle* Sheep = new Vehicle();

Sheep->Steering()->SeparationOn();
Sheep->Steering()->AlignmentOn();
Sheep->Steering()->CohesionOn();
Sheep->Steering()->ObstacleAvoidanceOn();
Sheep->Steering()->WanderOn();
Sheep->Steering()->EvadeOn(Dog);
```

And from now on the sheep will look after itself! (You may have to shear it in the summer though.)

NOTE Because of the number of demos I've created for this chapter, the `SteeringBehaviors` class is enormous and contains much more code than would ever get used in a single project. Very rarely will you use more than a handful of behaviors for each game you design. Therefore, whenever I use steering behaviors in later chapters, I will use a cut-down version of the `SteeringBehaviors` class, custom made for the task at hand. I suggest you do the same. (Another approach is to define a separate class for each behavior and add them to a `std::container` as you need them.)

Inside the `Vehicle::Update` method you will see this line:

```
SVector2D SteeringForce = m_pSteering->Calculate();
```

This call determines the resultant force from all the active behaviors. This is not simply a sum of all the steering forces though. Don't forget that the vehicle is constrained by a maximum steering force, so this sum must be truncated in some way to make sure its magnitude never exceeds the limit. There are a number of ways you can do this. It's impossible to say if one method is better than another because it depends on what behaviors you need to work with and what CPU resources you have to spare. They all have their pros and cons. I strongly recommend you experiment for yourself.

Weighted Truncated Sum

The simplest approach is to multiply each steering behavior with a weight, sum them all together, and then truncate the result to the maximum allowable steering force. Like this:

```
SVector2D Calculate()
{
  SVector2D SteeringForce;

  SteeringForce += Wander()            * dWanderAmount;
  SteeringForce += ObstacleAvoidance() * dObstacleAvoidanceAmount;
  SteeringForce += Separation()        * dSeparationAmount;

  return SteeringForce.Truncate(MAX_STEERING_FORCE);
}
```

This can work fine, but the trade-off is that it comes with a few problems. The first problem is that because every active behavior is calculated every time step, this is a very costly method to process. Additionally, the behavior weights can be very difficult to tweak. (Did I say difficult? Sorry, I mean *very* difficult! ☺) The biggest problem, however, happens with conflicting forces — a common scenario is where a vehicle is backed up against a wall by several other vehicles. In this example, the separating forces from the neighboring vehicles can be greater than the repulsive force from the wall and the vehicle can end up being pushed through the wall boundary. This is almost certainly not going to be favorable. Sure you can make the weights for the wall avoidance huge, but then your vehicle may behave strangely next time it finds itself alone and next to a wall. Like I mentioned, tweaking the parameters for a weighted sum can be quite a juggling act!

Weighted Truncated Running Sum with Prioritization

What a mouthful! This is the method used to determine the steering forces for all the examples used in this book, chosen mainly because it gives a good compromise between speed and accuracy. This method involves calculating a *prioritized* weighted running total that is truncated after the addition of each force to make sure the magnitude of the steering force does not exceed the maximum available.

The steering behaviors are prioritized since some behaviors can be considered much more important than others. Let's say a vehicle is using the behaviors **separation**, **alignment**, **cohesion**, **wall avoidance**, and **obstacle avoidance**. The **wall avoidance** and **obstacle avoidance** behaviors should be given priority over the others as the vehicle should try not to intersect a wall or an obstacle — it's more important for a vehicle to avoid a wall than it is for it to align itself with another vehicle. If what it takes to avoid a wall is higgledy-piggledy alignment, then that's probably going to be okay and certainly preferable to colliding with a wall. It's also more important for vehicles to maintain some separation from each other than it is for them to align. But it's probably less important for vehicles to maintain separation than avoid walls. See where I'm going with this? Each behavior is prioritized and processed in order. The behaviors with the highest priority are processed first, the ones with the lowest, last.

In addition to the prioritization, this method iterates through every active behavior, summing up the forces (with weighting) as it goes. Immediately after the calculation of each new behavior, the resultant force, together with the running total, is dispatched to a method called `AccumulateForce`. This function first determines how much of the maximum available steering force is remaining, and then one of the following happens:

- If there is a surplus remaining, the new force is added to the running total.
- If there is no surplus remaining, the method returns `false`. When this happens, `Calculate` returns the current value of `m_vSteeringForce` immediately and without considering any further active behaviors.
- If there is still some steering force available, but the magnitude remaining is less than the magnitude of the new force, the new force is truncated to the remaining magnitude before it is added.

Here is a snippet of code from the `SteeringBehaviors::Calculate` method to help you better understand what I'm talking about.

```
SVector2D SteeringBehaviors::Calculate()
{
  //reset the force.
```

```
  m_vSteeringForce.Zero();

  SVector2D force;
  if (On(wall_avoidance))
  {
    force = WallAvoidance(m_pVehicle->World()->Walls()) *
            m_dMultWallAvoidance;

    if (!AccumulateForce(m_vSteeringForce, force)) return m_vSteeringForce;
  }

  if (On(obstacle_avoidance))
  {
    force = ObstacleAvoidance(m_pVehicle->World()->Obstacles()) *
            m_dMultObstacleAvoidance;

    if (!AccumulateForce(m_vSteeringForce, force)) return m_vSteeringForce;
  }

  if (On(separation))
  {
    force = Separation(m_pVehicle->World()->Agents()) *
            m_dMultSeparation;

    if (!AccumulateForce(m_vSteeringForce, force)) return m_vSteeringForce;
  }

  /* EXTRANEOUS STEERING FORCES OMITTED */
  return m_vSteeringForce;
}
```

This doesn't show all the steering forces, just a few so you can get the general idea. To see the list of all behaviors and the order of their prioritization, check out the `SteeringBehaviors::Calculate` method in your IDE. The `AccumulateForce` method may also be better explained in code. Take your time looking over this method and make sure you understand what it's doing.

```
bool SteeringBehaviors::AccumulateForce(Vector2D &RunningTot,
                                        Vector2D ForceToAdd)
{

  //calculate how much steering force the vehicle has used so far
  double MagnitudeSoFar = RunningTot.Length();

  //calculate how much steering force remains to be used by this vehicle
  double MagnitudeRemaining = m_pVehicle->MaxForce() - MagnitudeSoFar;

  //return false if there is no more force left to use
  if (MagnitudeRemaining <= 0.0) return false;

  //calculate the magnitude of the force we want to add
  double MagnitudeToAdd = ForceToAdd.Length();

  //if the magnitude of the sum of ForceToAdd and the running total
```

```
  //does not exceed the maximum force available to this vehicle, just
  //add together. Otherwise add as much of the ForceToAdd vector as
  //possible without going over the max.
  if (MagnitudeToAdd < MagnitudeRemaining)
  {
    RunningTot += ForceToAdd;
  }

  else
  {

    //add it to the steering force
    RunningTot += (Vec2DNormalize(ForceToAdd) * MagnitudeRemaining);
  }

  return true;
}
```

Prioritized Dithering

In his paper, Reynolds suggests a method of force combination he calls *prioritized dithering*. When used, this method checks to see if the first priority behavior is going to be evaluated this simulation step, dependent on a preset probability. If it is and the result is non-zero, the method returns the calculated force and no other active behaviors are considered. If the result is zero or if that behavior has been skipped over due to its probability of being evaluated, the next priority behavior is considered and so on, for all the active behaviors. This is a little snippet of code to help you understand the concept:

```
SVector2D SteeringBehaviors::CalculateDithered()
{
  //reset the steering force
  m_vSteeringForce.Zero();

  //the behavior probabilities
  const double prWallAvoidance     = 0.9;
  const double prObstacleAvoidance = 0.9;
  const double prSeparation        = 0.8;
  const double prAlignment         = 0.5;
  const double prCohesion          = 0.5;
  const double prWander            = 0.8;

  if (On(wall_avoidance) && RandFloat() > prWallAvoidance)
  {
    m_vSteeringForce = WallAvoidance(m_pVehicle->World()->Walls()) *
                       m_dWeightWallAvoidance / prWallAvoidance;

    if (!m_vSteeringForce.IsZero())
    {
      m_vSteeringForce.Truncate(m_pVehicle->MaxForce());

      return m_vSteeringForce;
```

```
  }
}

if (On(obstacle_avoidance) && RandFloat() > prObstacleAvoidance)
{
  m_vSteeringForce += ObstacleAvoidance(m_pVehicle->World()->Obstacles()) *
                      m_dWeightObstacleAvoidance / prObstacleAvoidance;

  if (!m_vSteeringForce.IsZero())
  {
    m_vSteeringForce.Truncate(m_pVehicle->MaxForce());

    return m_vSteeringForce;
  }
}

if (On(separation) && RandFloat() > prSeparation)
{
  m_vSteeringForce += Separation(m_pVehicle->World()->Agents()) *
                      m_dWeightSeparation / prSeparation;

  if (!m_vSteeringForce.IsZero())
  {
    m_vSteeringForce.Truncate(m_pVehicle->MaxForce());

    return m_vSteeringForce;
  }
}

/* ETC ETC */
```

This method requires far less CPU time than the others, but at the cost of accuracy. Additionally, you will have to tweak the probabilities a fair bit before you get the behavior just as you want it. Nevertheless, if you are low on resources and it's not imperative your agent's movements are precise, this method is certainly worth experimenting with. You can see the effect of each of the three summing methods I've described by running the demo Big Shoal/Big Shoal.exe. This demonstration shows a shoal of 300 small vehicles (think fish) being wary of a single larger wandering vehicle (think shark). You can switch between the various summing methods to observe how they affect the frame rate and accuracy of the behaviors. You can also add walls or obstacles to the environment to see how the agents handle those using the different summing methods.

Ensuring Zero Overlap

Often when combining behaviors, the vehicles will occasionally overlap one another. The **separation** steering force alone is not enough to prevent this from happening. Most of the time this is okay — a little overlap will go unnoticed by the player — but sometimes it's necessary to ensure that whatever happens, vehicles cannot pass through one another's bounding radii. This can be prevented with the use of a *non-penetration constraint.* This is a function that tests for overlap. If there is any, the vehicles are moved apart in a direction away from the point of contact (and without regard to their mass, velocity, or any other physical constraints). See Figure 3.17.

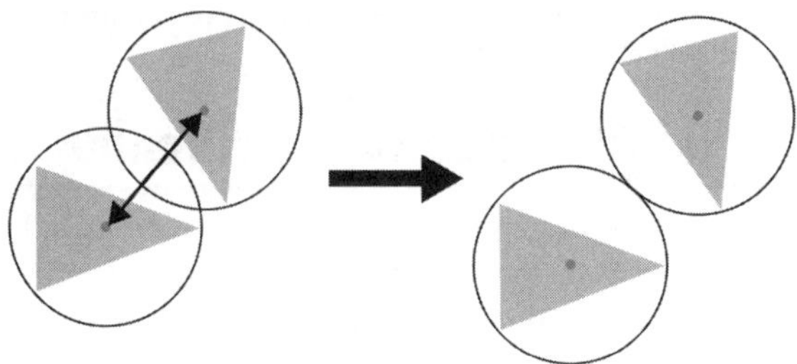

Figure 3.17. The non-penetration constraint in action

The constraint is implemented as a function template and can be used for any objects derived from a `BaseGameEntity`. You can find the code in the EntityFunctionTemplates.h header and it looks like this:

```
template <class T, class conT>
void EnforceNonPenetrationConstraint(const T&    entity,
                                     const conT& ContainerOfEntities)
{
  //iterate through all entities checking for any overlap of bounding radii
  for (typename conT::const_iterator curEntity =ContainerOfEntities.begin();
       curEntity != ContainerOfEntities.end();
       ++curEntity)
  {
    //make sure we don't check against the individual
    if (*curEntity == entity) continue;

    //calculate the distance between the positions of the entities
    Vector2D ToEntity = entity->Pos() - (*curEntity)->Pos();

    double DistFromEachOther = ToEntity.Length();

    //if this distance is smaller than the sum of their radii then this
    //entity must be moved away in the direction parallel to the
    //ToEntity vector
    double AmountOfOverLap = (*curEntity)->BRadius() + entity->BRadius() -
                             DistFromEachOther;
    if (AmountOfOverLap >= 0)
    {
      //move the entity a distance away equivalent to the amount of overlap.
      entity->SetPos(entity->Pos() + (ToEntity/DistFromEachOther) *
                     AmountOfOverLap);
    }
  }//next entity
}
```

You can watch the non-penetration constraint in action by running the craftily named Non Penetration Constraint.exe demo. Try altering the amount of separation to see what effect it has on the vehicles.

 **NOTE** For large numbers of densely packed vehicles such as you would see in big congested flocks, the non-penetration constraint will fail occasionally and there will be some overlap. Fortunately, this is not usually a problem as the overlap is difficult to see with the human eye.

Coping with Lots of Vehicles: Spatial Partitioning

When you have many interacting vehicles, it becomes increasingly inefficient to tag neighboring entities by comparing each one with every other one. In algorithm theory, something called *Big O* notation is used to express the relationship of time taken to the number of objects being processed. The all-pairs method we have been using to search for neighboring vehicles can be said to work in $O(n^2)$ time. This means that as the number of vehicles grows, the time taken to compare them increases in proportion to the square of their number. You can easily see how the time taken will escalate rapidly. If processing one object takes 10 seconds, then processing 10 objects will take 100 seconds. Not good, if you want a flock of several hundred birds!

Large speed improvements can be made by partitioning the world space. There are many different techniques to choose from. You've probably heard of many of them — BSP trees, quad-trees, oct-trees, etc. — and may even have used them, in which case you'll be familiar with their advantages. The method I use here is called *cell-space partitioning*, sometimes called bin-space partitioning (that's *not* short for binary space partitioning by the way; in this case "bin" really means bin). With this method, 2D space is divided up into a number of cells (or bins). Each cell contains a list of pointers to all the entities it contains. This is updated (in an entity's update method) every time an entity changes position. If an entity moves into a new cell, it is removed from its old cell's list and added to the current one.

This way, instead of having to test every vehicle against every other, we can just determine which cells lie within a vehicle's neighborhood and test against the vehicles contained in those cells. Here is how it's done step by step:

1. First of all, an entity's bounding radius is approximated with a box. See Figure 3.18.
2. The cells that intersect with this box are tested to see if they contain any entities.

3. All the entities contained within the cells from step 2 are examined to see if they are positioned within the neighborhood radius. If they are, they are added to the neighborhood list.

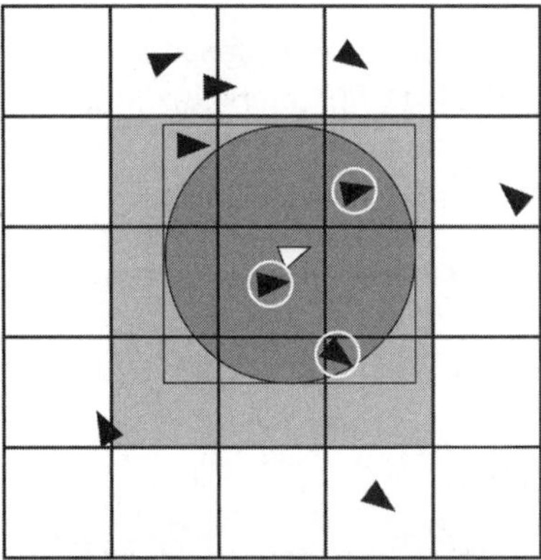

Figure 3.18. Cell-space partitioning. The circled vehicles are those within the white vehicle's neighborhood region.

3D NOTE If you are working in 3D, simply make the cells cubes and use a sphere as the neighborhood region.

If entities maintain a minimum separation distance from each other, then the number of entities each cell can contain is finite and cell space partitioning will operate in O(n) time. This means the time taken to process the algorithm is directly proportional to the number of objects it's operating on. If the number of objects is doubled, the time taken is only doubled and not squared as with O(n^2) algorithms. This implies the advantage you gain using space partitioning over the standard all-pairs technique is dependent on how many agents you have moving around. For small numbers, say less than fifty, there is no real advantage; but for large numbers, cell-space partitioning can be much faster. Even if the entities do not maintain a minimum separation distance and there is occasional overlap, on average the algorithm will perform much better than O(n^2).

I have implemented cell-space partitioning as a class template: `CellSpacePartition`. This class uses another class template, `Cell`, to define the cell structure.

```
template <class entity>
struct Cell
{
  //all the entities inhabiting this cell
  std::list<entity>    Members;

  //the cell's bounding box (it's inverted because the Windows' default
  //coordinate system has a y-axis that increases as it descends)
  InvertedAABBox2D     BBox;
```

```
  Cell(Vector2D topleft,
       Vector2D botright):BBox(InvertedAABBox2D(topleft, botright))
  {}
};
```

A Cell is a very simple structure. It contains an instance of a bounding box class, which defines its extents, and a list of pointers to all those entities that are situated within this bounding area.

The CellSpacePartition class definition is as follows:

```
template <class entity>
class CellSpacePartition
{
private:

  //the required number of cells in the space
  std::vector<Cell<entity> >      m_Cells;

  //this is used to store any valid neighbors when an agent searches
  //its neighboring space
  std::vector<entity>             m_Neighbors;

  //this iterator will be used by the methods next and begin to traverse
  //through the above vector of neighbors
  std::vector<entity>::iterator   m_curNeighbor;

  //the width and height of the world space the entities inhabit
  double  m_dSpaceWidth;
  double  m_dSpaceHeight;

  //the number of cells the space is going to be divided into
  int     m_iNumCellsX;
  int     m_iNumCellsY;

  double  m_dCellSizeX;
  double  m_dCellSizeY;


  //given a position in the game space, this method determines the
  //relevant cell's index
  inline int  PositionToIndex(const Vector2D& pos)const;

public:

  CellSpacePartition(double width,       //width of the environment
                     double height,      //height ...
                     int   cellsX,       //number of cells horizontally
                     int   cellsY,       //number of cells vertically
                     int   MaxEntitys);  //maximum number of entities to add

  //adds entities to the class by allocating them to the appropriate cell
  inline void AddEntity(const entity& ent);

  //update an entity's cell by calling this from your entity's Update method
```

```
  inline void UpdateEntity(const entity& ent, Vector2D OldPos);

  //this method calculates all a target's neighbors and stores them in
  //the neighbor vector. After you have called this method use the begin,
  //next, and end methods to iterate through the vector.
  inline void CalculateNeighbors(Vector2D TargetPos, double QueryRadius);

  //returns a reference to the entity at the front of the neighbor vector
  inline entity& begin();

  //this returns the next entity in the neighbor vector
  inline entity& next();

  //returns true if the end of the vector is found (a zero value marks the end)
  inline bool   end();

  //empties the cells of entities
  void        EmptyCells();
};
```

The class initializes m_Neighbors to have a maximum size equal to the total number of entities in the world. The iterator methods begin, next, and end and the CalculateNeighbors method manually keep track of valid elements inside this vector. This is to prevent the slowdown associated with the memory allocation and deallocation costs of repeatedly calling std::vector::clear() and std::vector::push_back() many times a second. Instead, previous values are simply overwritten and a zero value is used to mark the end of the vector.

Here is the listing for the CalculateNeighbors method. Notice how it follows the steps described earlier to determine a vehicle's neighbors.

```
template<class entity>
void CellSpacePartition<entity>::CalculateNeighbors(Vector2D TargetPos,
                                                    double   QueryRadius)
{
  //create an iterator and set it to the beginning of the neighbor list
  std::list<entity>::iterator curNbor = m_Neighbors.begin();

  //create the query box that is the bounding box of the target's query
  //area
  InvertedAABBox2D QueryBox(TargetPos - Vector2D(QueryRadius, QueryRadius),
                            TargetPos + Vector2D(QueryRadius, QueryRadius));

  //iterate through each cell and test to see if its bounding box overlaps
  //with the query box. If it does and it also contains entities then
  //make further proximity tests.
  std::vector<Cell<entity> >::iterator curCell;
  for (curCell=m_Cells.begin(); curCell!=m_Cells.end(); ++curCell)
  {
    //test to see if this cell contains members and if it overlaps the
    //query box
    if (curCell->pBBox->isOverlappedWith(QueryBox) &&
       !curCell->Members.empty())
    {
```

```
    //add any entities found within query radius to the neighbor list
    std::list<entity>::iterator it = curCell->Members.begin();
    for (it; it!=curCell->Members.end(); ++it)
    {
      if (Vec2DDistanceSq((*it)->Pos(), TargetPos) <
          QueryRadius*QueryRadius)
      {
        *curNbor++ = *it;
      }
    }
  }
}//next cell

  //mark the end of the list with a zero.
  *curNbor = 0;
}
```

You can find the full implementation of this class in Common/misc/CellSpacePartition.h. I have added cell space partitioning to the demo Big_Shoal.exe. It's now called Another_Big_Shoal.exe. You can toggle the partitioning on and off and see the difference it makes to the frame rate. There is also an option to view how the space is divided (default is 7 x 7 cells) and to see the query box and neighborhood radius of one of the agents.

⌘ **TIP** When applying the steering force to some vehicle types it can be useful to resolve the steering vector into forward and side components. For a car, for example, this would be analogous to creating the throttle and steering forces, respectively. To this end, you will find the methods `ForwardComponent` and `SideComponent` in the 2D `SteeringBehaviors` class used in this chapter's accompanying project file.

Smoothing

When playing with the demos, you may have noticed that sometimes a vehicle can twitch or jitter slightly when it finds itself in a situation with conflicting responses from different behaviors. For example, if you run one of the Big Shoal demos and switch the obstacles and walls on, you will see that sometimes when the "shark" agent approaches a wall or an obstacle, its nose shudders or trembles a little. This is because in one update step the **obstacle avoidance** behavior returns a steering force away from the obstacle but in the next update step there is no threat from the obstacle, so one of the agent's other active behaviors may return a steering force pulling its heading back toward the obstruction, and so on, creating unwanted oscillations in the vehicle's heading. Figure 3.19 shows how these oscillations can be started with just two conflicting behaviors: **obstacle avoidance** and **seek**.

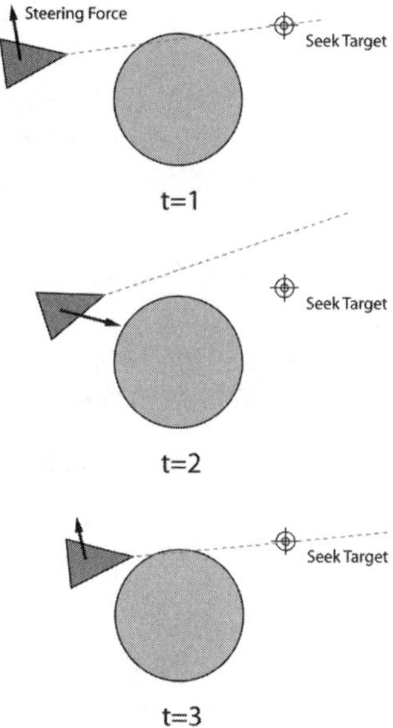

Figure 3.19. Conflicting behaviors can produce "judder."

This shakiness is usually not too noticeable. Occasionally though, there will be times when it will be preferable for the shaking not to occur. So how do you stop it? Well, as the vehicle's velocity is always aligned with its heading, stopping the shaking is not trivial. To negotiate the scenario given in Figure 3.19 successfully and smoothly, the vehicle needs to be able to foresee the conflict ahead of time and change behavior accordingly. Although this can be done, the solution can require a lot of calculation and additional baggage. A simple alternative suggested by Robin Green of Sony is to decouple the heading from the velocity vector and to average its value over several update steps. While this solution isn't perfect, it produces adequate results at low cost (relative to any other solution I know about). To facilitate this, another member variable is added to the `Vehicle` class: `m_vSmoothedHeading`. This vector records the average of a vehicle's heading vector and is updated each simulation step (in `Vehicle::Update`), using a call to an instance of a `Smoother` — a class that samples a value over a range and returns the average. This is what the call looks like:

```
if (SmoothingIsOn())
{
  m_vSmoothedHeading = m_pHeadingSmoother->Update(Heading());
}
```

This smoothed heading vector is used by the world transform function in the render call to transform a vehicle's vertices to the screen. The number of update steps the `Smoother` uses to calculate the average is set in params.ini and is assigned to the variable `NumSamplesForSmoothing`. When adjusting this value, you should try to keep it as low as possible to avoid unnecessary calculations and memory use. Using *very* high values produces weird behavior. Try using a value of 100 for `NumSamplesForSmoothing` and you'll see what I mean. It reminds me of a quote from *The Hitchhiker's Guide to the Galaxy*:

> *"You know," said Arthur with a slight cough, "if this is Southend, there's something very odd about it..."*
>
> *"You mean the way the sea stays steady and the buildings keep washing up and down?" said Ford. "Yes, I thought that was odd too."*

You can see the difference smoothing makes if you run the Another_Big_Shoal with Smoothing executable.

Practice Makes Perfect

In his paper "Steering Behaviors for Autonomous Characters," Reynolds describes a behavior called *leader following*. Leader following is a behavior that creates a steering force to keep multiple vehicles moving in single file behind a leader vehicle. If you've ever watched goslings follow their mother you'll know what I mean. To create this sort of behavior the followers must **arrive** at an offset position behind the vehicle in front while using **separation** to remain apart from one another. See Figure 3.20.

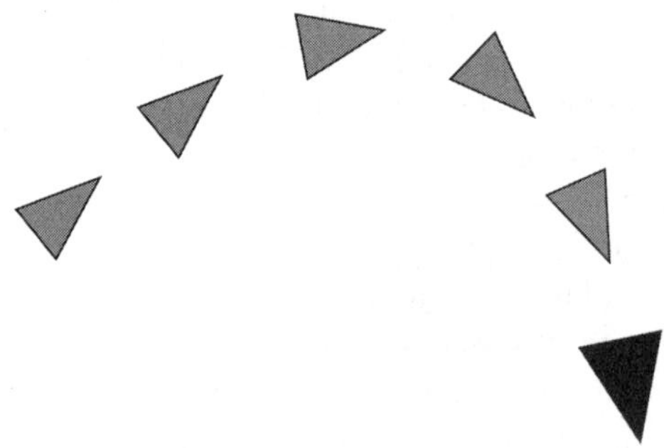

Figure 3.20. Leader following

Leader following can be improved further by creating a behavior that steers a vehicle laterally away from the direction of the leader if it finds itself in the leader's path.

Create a group of 20 vehicles that behave like a flock of sheep. Now add a *user-controlled vehicle* you can steer using the keyboard. Program your sheep so they believe the vehicle is a dog. Can you get the flock's behavior to look realistic?

Chapter 4

Sports Simulation — Simple Soccer

Designing team sport AI, and particularly AI to play soccer, is not easy. To create agents capable of playing a game anything like their professional human counterparts takes a serious amount of hard work. Many high-tech teams from notable universities around the world have been competing in a robotic soccer tournament, Robocup, since the early nineties. Although the ambitious goal of the tournament is to produce robots capable of winning the World Cup by the year 2050 (I'm not kidding), there is also a simulated soccer tournament running alongside the robotic one, where teams of simulated soccer players compete on virtual turf. Many of these teams use cutting-edge AI technology, much of it specially developed for soccer. If you were to attend a tournament, you would hear, between the cheers and the groans, teams discussing the merits of fuzzy-Q learning, the design of multi-agent coordination graphs, and situation-based strategic positioning.

Fortunately, as game programmers, we don't have to concern ourselves with all the detail of a properly simulated soccer environment. Our goal is not to win the World Cup but to produce agents capable of playing soccer well enough to provide an entertaining challenge to the game player. This chapter will walk you through the creation of game agents capable of playing a simplified version of soccer — Simple Soccer — using only the skills you've learned so far in this book.

My intention is not to demonstrate how every tactic and skill should be modeled, but to show you how to design and implement a team sports AI framework capable of supporting your own ideas. With this in mind, I've kept the game environment and the rules for Simple Soccer, well… very simple. I have also chosen to omit some obvious tactics. Partly because it will reduce the complexity of the AI and therefore make it easier for you to understand the flow of the state machine logic, but mainly because it will give you the opportunity of consolidating the skills you have learned in a proper, real-life, full-blown game AI project if you decide to tackle the exercises at the end of this chapter.

By the time you've finished this chapter you will have the ability to create AI agents capable of playing most team games. Ice hockey, rugby, cricket, American football, and even capture-the-flag — you name it, you'll be able to code an entertaining AI for it.

The Simple Soccer Environment and Rules

The rules of the game are uncomplicated. There are two teams: red and blue. Each team contains four *field players* and one *goalkeeper*. The objective of the game is to score as many *goals* as possible. A goal is scored by kicking the ball over the opposing team's goal line.

The sides of a Simple Soccer playing area (called a "pitch") are walled in (like ice hockey) so the ball cannot travel outside the playing area, but simply rebounds off the walls. This means that unlike normal soccer, there are no corners or throw-ins. Oh, and there's definitely no offside rule! Figure 4.1 shows the setup at the start of a typical game.

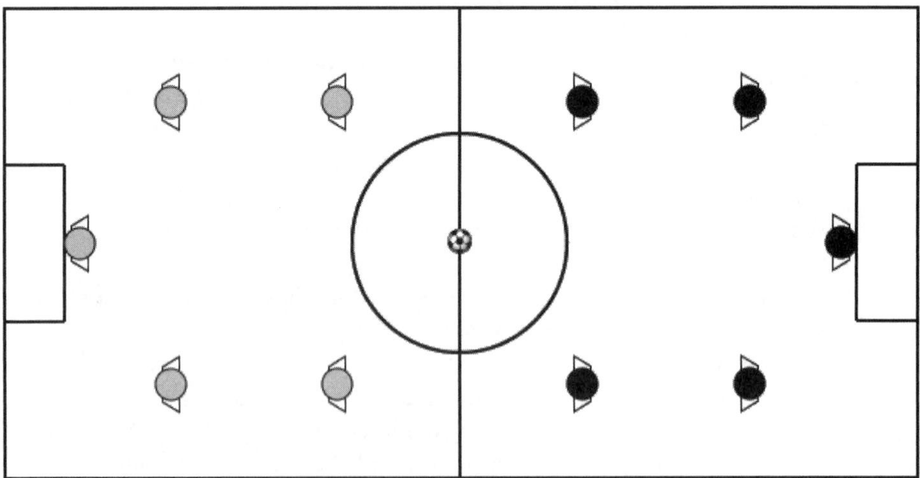

Figure 4.1. Kick-off positions (players are shown at increased scale for clarity)

The game environment consists of the following items:

- A soccer pitch
- Two goals
- One ball
- Two teams
- Eight field players
- Two goalkeepers

Each item type is encapsulated as an object. You can see how they are all related to each other by studying the simplified UML class diagram shown in Figure 4.2.

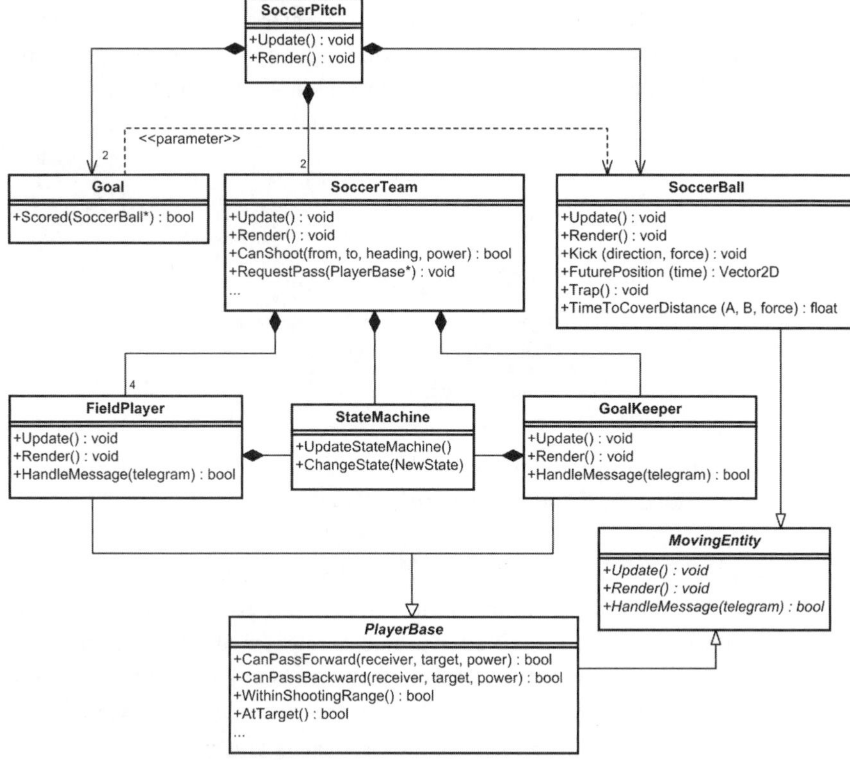

Figure 4.2. The Simple Soccer high-level object hierarchy

The player and goalkeeper objects are similar to the game agents you've already encountered in this book. I'll be describing them in detail very shortly, but first I'd like to show you how the soccer pitch, goals, and soccer ball are implemented. This should give you a feel for the environment the game agents occupy and then I can move on to the nitty-gritty of the AI itself.

The Soccer Pitch

The soccer pitch is a rectangular playing area enclosed by walls. At each of the short ends of the pitch, there is a goal centrally positioned. See Figure 4.1. The small circle at the center of the playing area is referred to as the *center-spot*. The ball is positioned on the center-spot prior to the start of the match. When a goal is scored both teams relinquish control of the ball and it's repositioned on the center-spot ready for another "kick-off." (For those soccer fans among my readers, please forgive my elaborate descriptions, but if I didn't go to this trouble I just *know* the moment this book is released I'll receive a dozen emails from the inhabitants of some hidden Himalayan valley wondering what on earth I'm talking about!)

The playing area is encapsulated by the class SoccerPitch. A single instance of this class is instantiated in main.cpp. The SoccerPitch object owns instances of SoccerTeam, SoccerBall, and Goal objects.

Here's the class declaration:

```
class SoccerPitch
{
public:

  SoccerBall*          m_pBall;

  SoccerTeam*          m_pRedTeam;
  SoccerTeam*          m_pBlueTeam;

  Goal*                m_pRedGoal;
  Goal*                m_pBlueGoal;
```

These first few members are self explanatory and I'll be describing the relevant classes in detail in a few pages.

```
  //container for the boundary walls
  std::vector<Wall2D> m_vecWalls;
```

The pitch boundaries in the Simple Soccer environment are represented by Wall2Ds. Walls are described by a line segment with two endpoints and a normal to the line segment representing the facing direction. You may remember them from the wall avoidance steering behavior description.

```
  //defines the dimensions of the playing area
  Region*               m_pPlayingArea;
```

A Region object is used to describe the dimensions of the soccer pitch. A Region stores the top left, right bottom, and center positions of the declared area, and also an identifying number (ID).

```
  std::vector<Region*> m_Regions;
```

Soccer players have to know where they are on the soccer pitch and although their *x*, *y* coordinates give a very specific position, it's also useful to split the pitch up into regions players can make use of to implement strategies. To facilitate this, the pitch is divided into eighteen areas as shown in Figure 4.3.

At the beginning of a game, each player is assigned a region to be its *home region.* This will be the region it returns to after a goal is scored or when it has finished making a play with the ball. A player's home region may vary during a game depending on the team strategy. For example, when attacking, it's advantageous for a team to occupy positions farther forward on the field (upfield) than when defending.

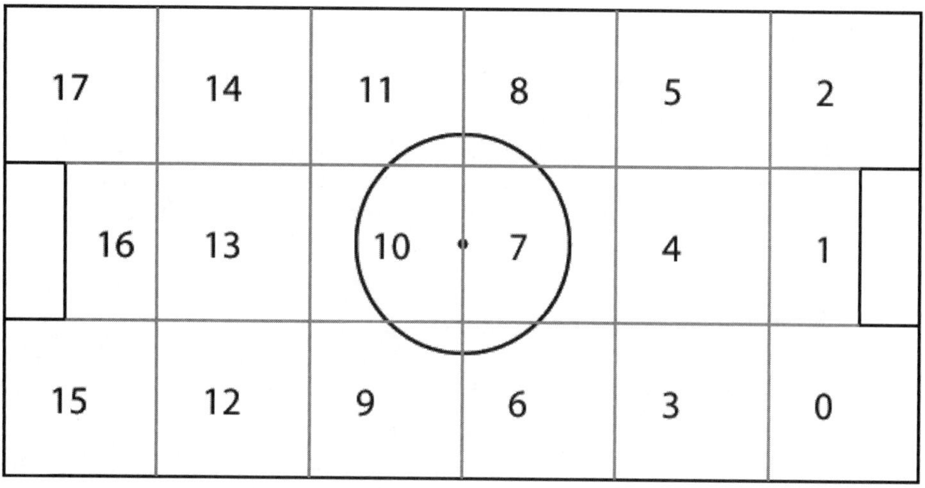

17	14	11	8	5	2
16	13	10	7	4	1
15	12	9	6	3	0

Figure 4.3. The pitch divided into regions

```
bool                    m_bGameOn;
```

Teams can query this value to see if the game is in play or not. (The game is not on if a goal has just been scored and all the players are returning to their kick-off positions.)

```
bool                    m_bGoalKeeperHasBall;
```

This value is set to true if either team's goalkeeper has the ball. Players can query this value to help them select an appropriate behavior. For example, if a goalkeeper has possession of the ball, a nearby opponent will not attempt to kick it.

```
  /* EXTRANEOUS DETAIL OMITTED */

public:

  SoccerPitch(int cxClient, int cyClient);

  ~SoccerPitch();

  void  Update();

  bool  Render();

  /* EXTRANEOUS DETAIL OMITTED */
};
```

The `SoccerPitch::Update` and `SoccerPitch::Render` functions are at the top of the update and render hierarchy. Each update step, these methods are called from within the main game loop and, in turn, the appropriate `Render` and `Update` methods of every other game entity is called.

The Goals

A goal on a real-life soccer pitch is defined by a left goal post and a right goal post. A goal is scored if any part of the ball crosses the goal line — the line connecting the goal posts. A rectangular area in front of each goal is drawn in the relevant team's color to make distinguishing each team's side easy. The goal line is the line that describes the rear of this box.

Here is the class declaration:

```
class Goal
{
private:

  Vector2D    m_vLeftPost;
  Vector2D    m_vRightPost;

  //a vector representing the facing direction of the goal
  Vector2D    m_vFacing;

  //the position of the center of the goal line
  Vector2D    m_vCenter;

  //each time Scored() detects a goal this is incremented
  int         m_iNumGoalsScored;

public:

  Goal(Vector2D left, Vector2D right):m_vLeftPost(left),
                                      m_vRightPost(right),
                                      m_vCenter((left+right)/2.0),
                                      m_iNumGoalsScored(0)
  {
    m_vFacing = Vec2DNormalize(right-left).Perp();
  }

  //Given the current ball position and the previous ball position,
  //this method returns true if the ball has crossed the goal line
  //and increments m_iNumGoalsScored
  inline bool Scored(const SoccerBall*const ball);

  /* ACCESSOR METHODS OMITTED */
};
```

Each time step, the `Scored` method of each team's goal is called from within `SoccerPitch::Update`. If a goal is detected, then the players and ball are reset to their start positions ready for kick-off.

The Soccer Ball

A soccer ball is a little more interesting. The data and methods to encapsulate a soccer ball are encoded in the `SoccerBall` class. A soccer ball moves, so its class inherits from the `MovingEntity` class we used in Chapter 3. In addition to the functionality provided by `MovingEntity`, `SoccerBall` also has data members for recording the ball's last updated position and methods for kicking the ball, testing for collisions, and calculating the future position of the ball.

When a real soccer ball is kicked it gently decelerates to rest because of the friction from the ground and the air resistance acting upon it. Simple Soccer balls don't live in the real world, but we can model a similar effect by applying a constant deceleration (a negative acceleration) to the ball's motion. The amount of deceleration is set in Params.ini as the value `Friction`.

Here is the complete declaration of the `SoccerBall` class followed by descriptions of a couple of its important methods.

```
class SoccerBall : public MovingEntity
{
private:

  //keeps a record of the ball's position at the last update
  Vector2D                   m_vOldPos;

  //a pointer to the player(or goalkeeper) who possesses the ball
  PlayerBase*                m_pOwner;

  //a local reference to the walls that make up the pitch boundary
  //(used in the collision detection)
  const std::vector<Wall2D>& m_PitchBoundary;

  //tests to see if the ball has collided with a wall and reflects
  //the ball's velocity accordingly
  void TestCollisionWithWalls(const std::vector<Wall2D>& walls);
```

The soccer ball only checks for collisions with the pitch boundary; it doesn't test for collisions against the players, as the ball must be able to move freely around and through their "feet."

```
public:

  SoccerBall(Vector2D                  pos,
             double                    BallSize,
             double                    mass,
             std::vector<Wall2D>& PitchBoundary):

      //set up the base class
      MovingEntity(pos,
                   BallSize,
                   Vector2D(0,0),
                   -1.0,                  //max speed - unused
                   Vector2D(0,1),
                   mass,
                   Vector2D(1.0,1.0),     //scale     - unused
                   0,                     //turn rate - unused
                   0),                    //max force - unused
    m_PitchBoundary(PitchBoundary),
    m_pOwner(NULL)
```

```
  {}

  //implement base class Update
  void      Update(double time_elapsed);

  //implement base class Render
  void      Render();

  //a soccer ball doesn't need to handle messages
  bool      HandleMessage(const Telegram& msg){return false;}

  //this method applies a directional force to the ball (kicks it!)
  void      Kick(Vector2D direction, double force);

  //given a kicking force and a distance to traverse defined by start
  //and finish points, this method calculates how long it will take the
  //ball to cover the distance.
  double    TimeToCoverDistance(Vector2D from,
                                Vector2D to,
                                double   force)const;

  //this method calculates where the ball will be at a given time
  Vector2D  FuturePosition(double time)const;

  //this is used by players and goalkeepers to "trap" a ball -- to stop
  //it dead. The trapping player is then assumed to be in possession of
  //the ball and m_pOwner is adjusted accordingly
  void      Trap(PlayerBase* owner){m_vVelocity.Zero(); m_pOwner = owner;}

  Vector2D  OldPos()const{return m_vOldPos;}

  //this places the ball at the desired location and sets its velocity to zero
  void      PlaceAtPosition(Vector2D NewPos);
};
```

Before I move on to describe the player and team classes, I'd just like to go over a couple of the `SoccerBall`'s public methods to make sure you understand the math they contain. These methods are frequently used by players to predict where the ball will be at some time in the future or to predict how long it will take the ball to reach a position. When you design the AI for a sports game/simulation you will be using your math and physics skills a lot. Oh yes! So if you don't know your theory, now's the time to head back to Chapter 1 and read up on it; otherwise you'll be more lost than a rapper in a rainforest.

3D Note: Although the demo has been coded in 2D, you would apply exactly the same techniques to a 3D game. There is a little more complexity because the ball will bounce and may travel above the players' heads, so you would have to add additional player skills for making chip shots and "heading" the ball, but these are mainly physics considerations. The AI is more or less the same; you would just have to add a few more states to the FSM and some additional logic to check for the height of the ball when calculating intercepts and the like.

SoccerBall::FuturePosition

Given a length of time as a parameter, FuturePosition calculates where the ball will be at that time in the future — assuming its trajectory continues uninterrupted. Don't forget that the ball experiences a frictional force with the ground, which must be taken into consideration. The frictional force is expressed as a constant acceleration acting opposite to the direction the ball is moving (deceleration, in other words). This constant is defined in params.ini as Friction.

To determine the position P_t of the ball at time t, we must calculate how far it travels using equation (1.87) from Chapter 1:

$$\Delta x = u\Delta t + \frac{1}{2}a\Delta t^2 \quad (4.1)$$

where Δx is the distance traveled, u is the velocity of the ball when kicked, and a is the deceleration due to friction.

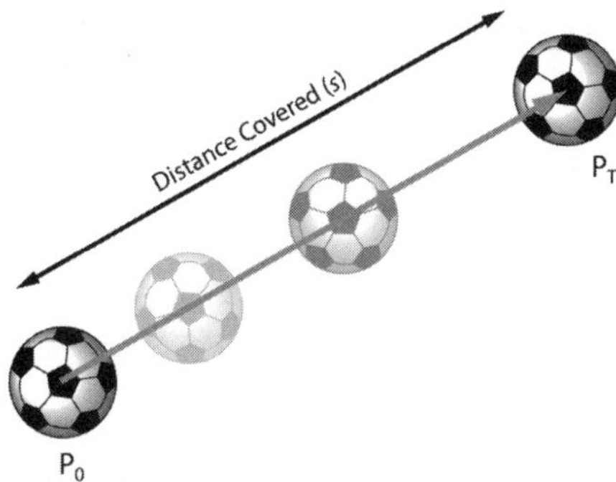

Figure 4.4. Calculating distance traveled

Once the distance traveled has been calculated, we know how much to add to the ball's position, but not in which direction. However, we *do* know the ball is traveling in the direction of its velocity vector. Therefore, if we normalize the ball's velocity vector and multiply it by the distance traveled, we end up with a vector that gives us the distance *and* direction. If this vector is added to the ball's position, the result is the predicted position. Here is the calculation in code:

```
Vector2D SoccerBall::FuturePosition(double time)const
{
  //using the equation x = ut + 1/2at^2, where x = distance, a = friction
  //u = start velocity

  //calculate the ut term, which is a vector
  Vector2D ut = m_vVelocity * time;

  //calculate the 1/2at^2 term, which is scalar
```

```
  double half_a_t_squared = 0.5 * Prm.Friction * time * time;

  //turn the scalar quantity into a vector by multiplying the value with
  //the normalized velocity vector (because that gives the direction)
  Vector2D ScalarToVector = half_a_t_squared * Vec2DNormalize(m_vVelocity);

  //the predicted position is the ball's position plus these two terms
  return Pos() + ut + ScalarToVector;
}
```

NOTE Many of the methods and functions shown throughout this book contain unnecessary temporary variables. They are there to aid your understanding, as their removal often obfuscates the underlying calculation(s) or makes the line of code too long to fit comfortably on the pages of this book.

SoccerBall::TimeToCoverDistance

Given two positions, A and B, and a kicking force, this method returns a `double` indicating how long it will take for the ball to travel between the two. Of course, given a large distance and a small kicking force, it may not be possible for the ball to cover the distance at all. In this event, the method returns a negative value.

This time the equation to use is this:

$$v = u + a\Delta t \tag{4.2}$$

Rearranging the variables gives the equation for time taken:

$$\Delta t = \frac{v - u}{a} \tag{4.3}$$

We know a = Friction, so we have to find v and u, where v = velocity at point B, and u will be the speed of the ball immediately after it has been kicked. In Simple Soccer, velocities are not accumulative. The ball is assumed to always have a zero velocity immediately prior to a kick. Although technically this is unrealistic — if the ball has just been passed to the kicking player, it will not have a zero velocity — in practice, this method results in easier calculations, while *still looking realistic to the observer.* With this in mind, u is equal to the instantaneous acceleration applied to the ball by the force of the kick. Therefore:

$$u = a = \frac{F}{m} \tag{4.4}$$

Now that u and a have been calculated, we only have to calculate v, and all three values can be popped into equation (4.3) to solve for Δt. To determine v (the velocity at point B), the following equation is used:

$$v^2 = u^2 + 2a\Delta x \tag{4.5}$$

Taking the square root of both sides gives:

$$v = \sqrt{u^2 + 2a\Delta x} \tag{4.6}$$

Don't forget Δx is the distance between A and B. If the term $u^2 + 2a\Delta x$ is negative, the velocity is not a real number (you can't calculate the square root of a negative number… well, you can, that's what complex numbers are for, but for the purposes of this book we'll pretend you can't). This means the ball cannot cover the distance from A to B. If the term is positive, then we have found v and it's a simple matter to put all the values into equation (4.3) to solve for Δt.

Below is the source code for you to examine.

```
double SoccerBall::TimeToCoverDistance(Vector2D A,
                                       Vector2D B,
                                       double   force)const
{
  //this will be the velocity of the ball in the next time step *if*
  //the player was to make the pass.
  double speed = force / m_dMass;

  //calculate the velocity at B using the equation
  //
  //  v^2 = u^2 + 2ax
  //

  //first calculate s (the distance between the two positions)
  double DistanceToCover =  Vec2DDistance(A, B);

  double term = speed*speed + 2.0*DistanceToCover*Prm.Friction;

  //if  (u^2 + 2ax) is negative it means the ball cannot reach point B.
  if (term <= 0) return -1.0;

  double v = sqrt(term);

  //it's possible for the ball to reach B and we know its speed when it
  //gets there, so now it's easy to calculate the time using the equation
  //
  //    t = v-u
  //        ---
  //         a
  //
  return (v-speed)/Prm.Friction;
}
```

Designing the AI

There are two types of soccer players on a Simple Soccer team: *field players* and *goalkeepers*. Both of these types derive from the same base class, `PlayerBase`. Both make use of a cut-down version of the `SteeringBehaviors` class you saw in the last chapter and both own finite state machines, with their own set of states. See Figure 4.5.

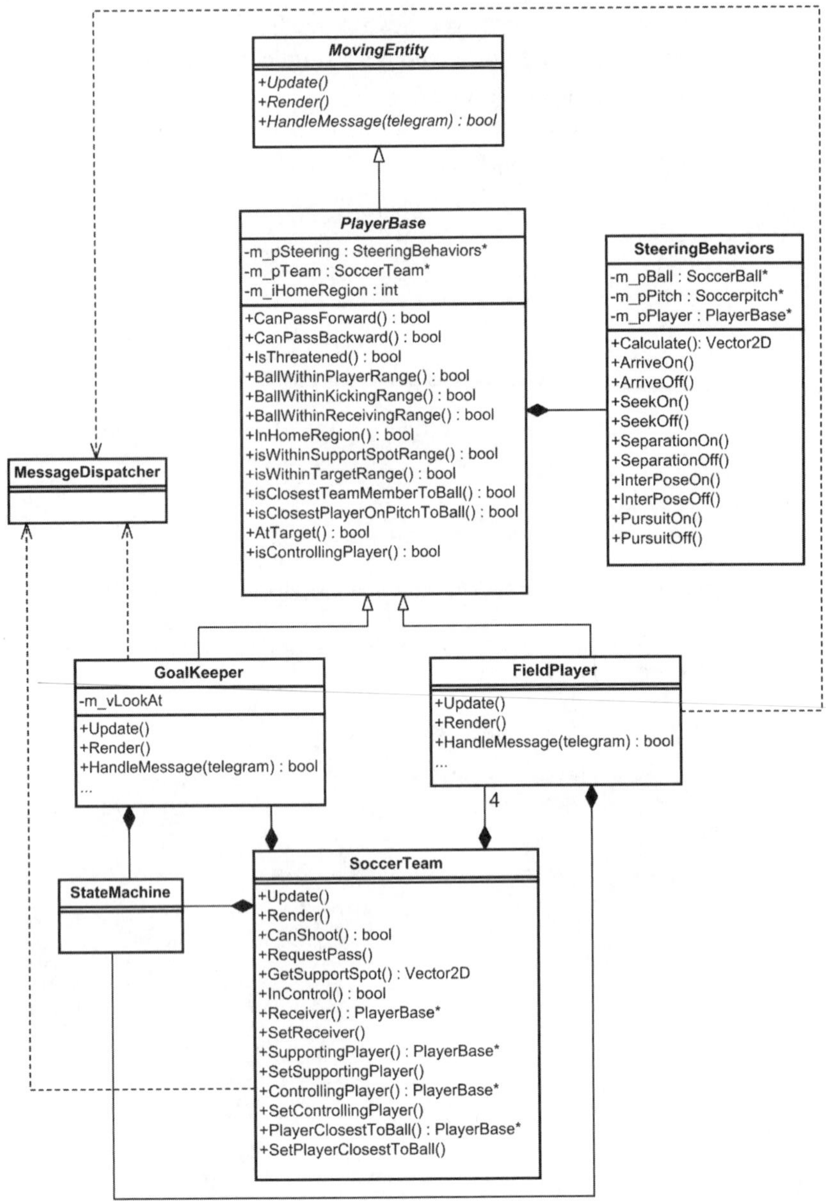

Figure 4.5. Class relationships at the agent level

Not all the methods of every class are shown, but it gives a good idea of the design. The majority of the methods that *are* listed for PlayerBase and SoccerTeam comprise the interface a player's state machine uses to route its AI logic. (I've omitted each method's parameters to permit me to fit the diagram on one page!)

Notice how a SoccerTeam also owns a StateMachine, giving a *team* the ability to change its behavior depending on the current state of play. Implementing AI at the team level in addition to the player level creates what is known as *tiered* AI. This type of AI is used in all sorts of computer games. You will often find tiered AI in real-time strategy (RTS) games where the enemy AI is commonly implemented in several layers at, say, the unit, troop, and commander levels.

Notice also how the players and their teams have the ability to send messages. Messages may be passed from player to player (including goalkeepers) or from soccer team to player. In this demo players do not pass messages to their team. (Although there is no reason why they couldn't. If you have a good reason for your players messaging their team, go ahead and do it.) All messages dispatched to field players or goalkeepers are handled via each class's respective global state, as you shall see later on in the chapter.

Since a player's team state dictates to some extent how the player should behave, your journey into the guts of the AI of Simple Soccer is probably best commenced with a description of the SoccerTeam class. After you understand what makes a team tick, I'll move on to describe how the players and goalkeepers work their soccer magic.

The SoccerTeam Class

The SoccerTeam class owns instances of the players that comprise the soccer team. It has pointers to the soccer pitch, the opposing team, the team's home goal, and its opponent's goal. Additionally, it has pointers to the "key" players on the pitch. Individual players can query their soccer team and use this information in their state machine logic.

First of all, I'll describe the roles of these key players and then move on to discuss the various states a Simple Soccer team utilizes. Here's how the key player pointers are declared in the class prototype:

```
class SoccerTeam
{
private:

  /* EXTRANEOUS DETAIL OMITTED */

  //pointers to "key" players
  PlayerBase*              m_pReceivingPlayer;
  PlayerBase*              m_pPlayerClosestToBall;
  PlayerBase*              m_pControllingPlayer;
```

```
  PlayerBase*              m_pSupportingPlayer;

  /* EXTRANEOUS DETAIL OMITTED */
};
```

The Receiving Player

When a player kicks the ball toward another player, the player waiting to receive the ball is, not surprisingly, known as the *receiver.* There will only ever be one receiver allocated at any one time. If there is no allocated receiver, this value is set to `NULL`.

The Closest Player to the Ball

This pointer points to the team member who is currently closest to the ball. As you can imagine, knowing this sort of information is useful when a player has to decide if he should chase after the ball or leave it for another team member to pursue. Each time step, the soccer team will calculate which player is the closest and keep this pointer continuously updated. Therefore, during play, `m_pPlayerClosestToBall` will never be `NULL`.

The Controlling Player

The *controlling player* is the player who is in command of the soccer ball. An obvious example of a controlling player is one who is about to make a pass to a teammate. A less obvious example is the player waiting to receive the ball *once the pass has been made*. In the latter example, even though the ball may be nowhere near the receiving player, the player is said to be in control since unless intercepted by an opponent, the receiver will be the next player able to kick the ball. The controlling player, when moving upfield toward the opponent's goal, is often referred to as the attacking player or, even more simply, as just *the attacker.* If the team does not control the ball, this pointer will be set to `NULL`.

The Supporting Player

When a player gains control of the ball, the team will designate a *supporting player.* The supporting player will attempt to move into a useful position farther upfield from the attacker. Supporting positions are rated based on certain qualities such as how easy it is for the attacker to pass the ball to the position and the likelihood of scoring a goal from the position. For example, position B in Figure 4.6 would be considered a good supporting position (good view of the opponent's goal, easy to pass to), position C a so-so supporting position (fair view of the opponent's goal, poor passing potential), and position D a very poor support position (little passing potential, no shot at the goal, not upfield of the attacker).

If there is no allocated supporting player, this pointer will point to `NULL`.

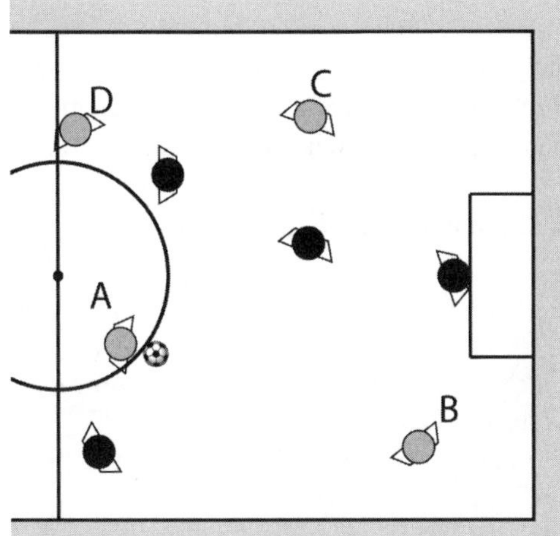

Figure 4.6. Support positions: the good, the bad, and the ugly

The supporting positions are calculated by sampling a series of locations on the playing field and running several tests on them, resulting in a cumulative score. The position with the highest score is deemed the *best supporting spot*, or BSS as I shall sometimes refer to it. This is achieved with the aid of a class named the `SupportSpotCalculator`. I guess right now might be a good time to go off on a small but important tangent to show you how this class operates.

Calculating the Best Support Spot

The `SupportSpotCalculator` class calculates the BSS by scoring a number of spot positions sampled from the opponent's half of the pitch. The default spot locations (for the red team) are shown in Figure 4.7.

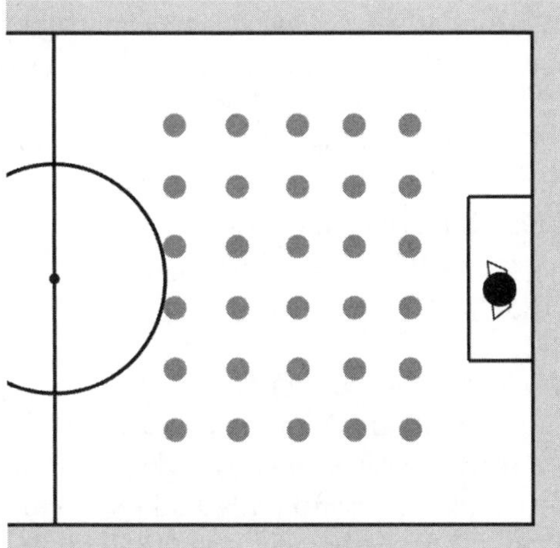

Figure 4.7. The red team considers these potential support spots.

As you can see, all the spots are located in the opponent's half of the pitch. There is no need to sample positions farther downfield, as the supporting player will always be trying to find the location that gives the best opportunity of a goal shot, and that will inevitably be situated close to the opponent's goal.

A support spot has a position and a score, like so:

```
struct SupportSpot
{
  Vector2D  m_vPos;

  double    m_dScore;

  SupportSpot(Vector2D pos, double val):m_vPos(pos),
                                        m_dScore(value)
  {}
};
```

The spots are scored by examining each one in turn and scoring them for a particular quality, such as whether or not a goal is possible from the spot's position or how far away from the controlling player the spot is situated. The scores for each quality are accumulated and the spot with the highest score is marked as the best supporting spot. The supporting player can then move toward the BSS's position in readiness for a pass from the attacker.

NOTE It's not essential that the BSS is calculated every update step; therefore the number of times the calculation is made is regulated to `SupportSpotUpdateFreq` times per second. The default value, set in params.ini, is once per second.

To determine exactly what these qualities should be, you have to think like a soccer player. If you were running up that soccer pitch trying to put yourself in an advantageous support position, what factors would you consider? Probably you would value positions where your fellow teammates could pass the ball to you. In your mental map of the soccer pitch, you would imagine yourself at each location and consider those positions where you think it would be safe for the attacker to pass the ball to you as good positions in which to place yourself. The `SupportSpotCalculator` does the same by giving each spot that satisfies this condition a score equivalent to the value: `Spot_CanPassScore` (set as 2.0 in params.ini). Figure 4.8 shows a typical position during a game, highlighting all the spots that have been rated for passing potential.

In addition, positions from which a goal can be scored are worthy of attention. Therefore the `SupportSpotCalculator` assigns a score of `Spot_CanScoreFromPositionScore` to each spot passing the goal-shot-is-possible test. I'm no expert soccer player (far from it!) but I reckon the ability to make a pass to a spot should be ranked higher than the ability to make a goal shot from a spot — after all, the attacker must be able to pass the ball

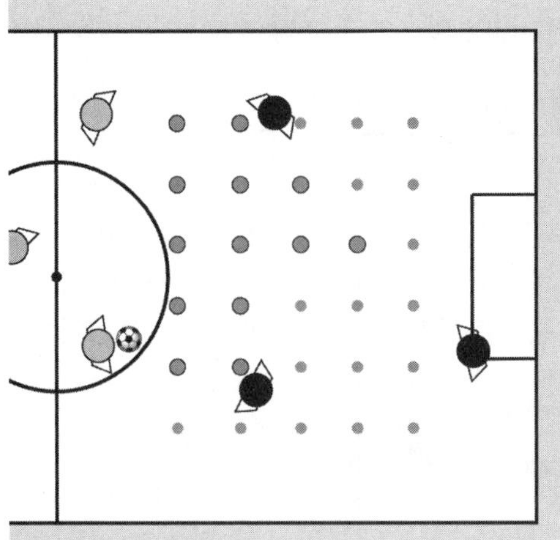

Figure 4.8. Spots rated for passing potential

to the supporting player before a goal attempt can be made. With this in mind, the default value for `Spot_CanScoreFromPositionScore` is 1.0. Figure 4.9 shows the same position as Figure 4.8 with the spots rated for goal shot potential.

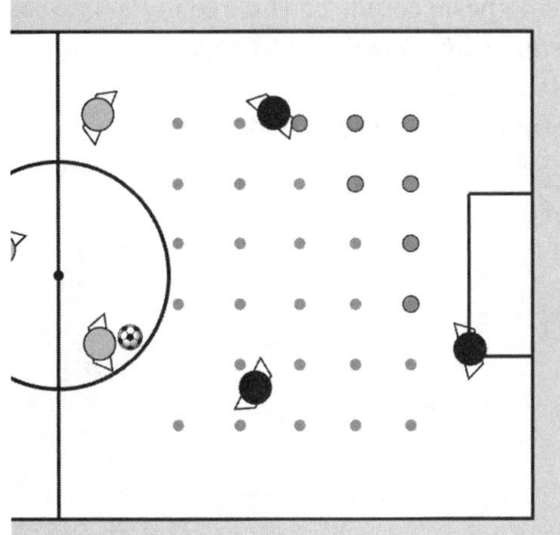

Figure 4.9. Spots rated by their goal scoring potential

Another consideration a supporting player may make is to aim for a position a specific distance away from its teammate. Not too far away to make the pass difficult and risky, and not too close to make the pass wasteful.

I've used a value of 200 pixels as the optimal distance a supporting player should be away from the controlling player. At this distance a spot will receive an optimal score of `Spot_DistFromControllingPlayerScore` (default 2.0), with scores trailing off for distances any closer or farther away. See Figure 4.10.

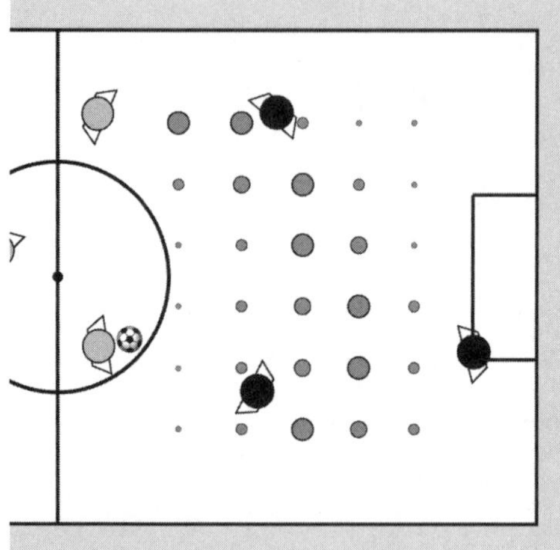

Figure 4.10. Spots rated according to their distance from the attacker. The larger the spot, the higher its score.

When each position has been examined and all the scores have been accumulated, the spot with the highest score is considered to be the best supporting spot, and the supporting attacker will move to occupy this position in readiness to receive a pass.

This procedure of determining the BSS is undertaken in the method `SupportSpotCalculator::DetermineBestSupportingPosition`. Here is the source code for you to examine:

```
Vector2D SupportSpotCalculator::DetermineBestSupportingPosition()
{
  //only update the spots every few frames
  if (!m_pRegulator->AllowCodeFlow()&& m_pBestSupportingSpot)
  {
    return m_pBestSupportingSpot->m_vPos;
  }

  //reset the best supporting spot
  m_pBestSupportingSpot = NULL;

  double BestScoreSoFar = 0.0;

  std::vector<SupportSpot>::iterator curSpot;

  for (curSpot = m_Spots.begin(); curSpot != m_Spots.end(); ++curSpot)
  {
    //first remove any previous score. (the score is set to one so that
    //the viewer can see the positions of all the spots if he has the
    //aids turned on)
    curSpot->m_dScore = 1.0;
```

```
    //Test 1. is it possible to make a safe pass from the ball's position
    //to this position?
    if(m_pTeam->isPassSafeFromAllOpponents(m_pTeam->ControllingPlayer()->Pos(),
                                           curSpot->m_vPos,
                                           NULL,
                                           Prm.MaxPassingForce))
    {
      curSpot->m_dScore += Prm.Spot_PassSafeStrength;
    }

    //Test 2. Determine if a goal can be scored from this position.
    if( m_pTeam->CanShoot(curSpot->m_vPos,
                          Prm.MaxShootingForce))
    {
      curSpot->m_dScore += Prm.Spot_CanScoreStrength;
    }

    //Test 3. calculate how far this spot is away from the controlling
    //player. The farther away, the higher the score. Any distances farther
    //away than OptimalDistance pixels do not receive a score.
    if (m_pTeam->SupportingPlayer())
    {
      const double OptimalDistance = 200.0;

      double dist = Vec2DDistance(m_pTeam->ControllingPlayer()->Pos(),
                                  curSpot->m_vPos);

      double temp = fabs(OptimalDistance - dist);

      if (temp < OptimalDistance)
      {

        //normalize the distance and add it to the score
        curSpot->m_dScore += Prm.Spot_DistFromControllingPlayerStrength *
                             (OptimalDistance-temp)/OptimalDistance;
      }
    }

    //check to see if this spot has the highest score so far
    if (curSpot->m_dScore > BestScoreSoFar)
    {
      BestScoreSoFar = curSpot->m_dScore;

      m_pBestSupportingSpot = &(*curSpot);
    }

  }

  return m_pBestSupportingSpot->m_vPos;
}
```

Well, I guess that "little tangent" to discuss the subject of support spots turned into quite a large one! Before I got distracted, I was telling you how the `SoccerTeam` class did its stuff, remember? As I've mentioned, a `SoccerTeam` owns a state machine. This gives it the ability to change its behavior according to what state it's in. Let's now take a close look at a team's available states and how they can affect the behavior of its players.

SoccerTeam States

At any moment in time, a soccer team can be in one of three states: **Defending**, **Attacking**, or **PrepareForKickOff**. I've kept the logic of these states very simple — my intention is to show you how to implement a tiered AI and not to demonstrate how to create complex soccer tactics — although they can be easily added to and modified to create just about any type of team behavior you can imagine.

As I mentioned earlier, players use the idea of "regions" to help position themselves correctly on the playing field. The team states use these regions to control where players should move if they are not in possession of the ball or supporting/attacking. When defending, for example, it's sensible for a soccer team to move its players closer to the home goal, and when attacking, the players should move farther upfield, closer to the opponent's goal.

Here are descriptions of each team state in detail.

PrepareForKickOff

A team enters this state immediately after a goal has been scored. The Enter method sets all the key player pointers to NULL, changes their home regions back to the kick-off positions, and sends each player a message requesting they move back to their home regions. Something like this, in fact:

```
void PrepareForKickOff::Enter(SoccerTeam* team)
{
  //reset key player pointers
  team->SetControllingPlayer(NULL);
  team->SetSupportingPlayer(NULL);
  team->SetReceiver(NULL);
  team->SetPlayerClosestToBall(NULL);

  //send Msg_GoHome to each player.
  team->ReturnAllFieldPlayersToHome();
}
```

Each Execute cycle, the team waits until all the players from both teams are situated within their home regions, at which point it changes state to **Defending** and the match recommences.

```
void PrepareForKickOff::Execute(SoccerTeam* team)
{
  //if both teams in position, start the game
  if (team->AllPlayersAtHome() && team->Opponents()->AllPlayersAtHome())
  {
    team->ChangeState(team, Defending::Instance());
  }
}
```

Defending

The Enter method of a soccer team's **Defending** state changes the home positions of all the team members to be located in the team's half of the pitch. Bringing all the players close to the home goal like this makes it harder for the opposing team to maneuver the ball through and score a goal. Figure 4.11 shows the home positions for the red team when they are in the **Defending** state.

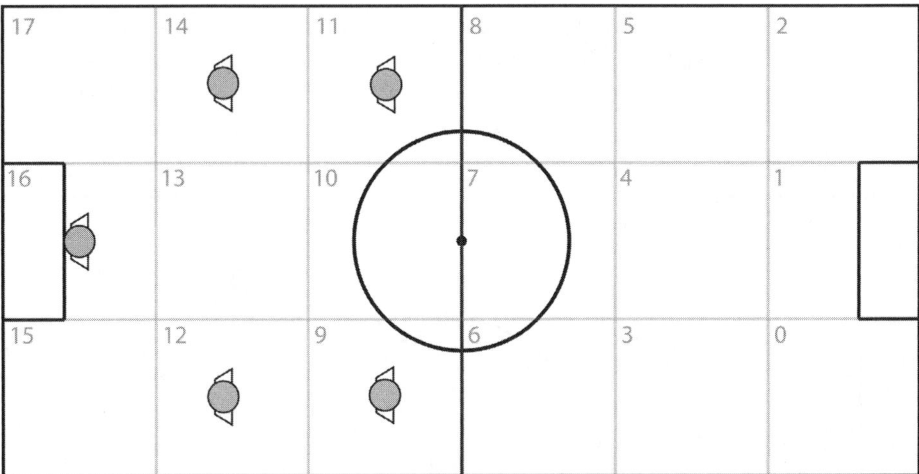

Figure 4.11. Players in their home regions for the Defending team state

```
void Defending::Enter(SoccerTeam* team)
{
  //these define the home regions for this state of each of the players
  const int BlueRegions[TeamSize] = {1,6,8,3,5};
  const int RedRegions[TeamSize] = {16,9,11,12,14};

  //set up the player's home regions
  if (team->Color() == SoccerTeam::blue)
  {
    ChangePlayerHomeRegions(team, BlueRegions);
  }
  else
  {
    ChangePlayerHomeRegions(team, RedRegions);
  }

  //if a player is in either the Wait or ReturnToHomeRegion states, its
  //steering target must be updated to that of its new home region
  team->UpdateTargetsOfWaitingPlayers();
}
```

The Execute method of the **Defending** state continuously queries the team to see if it has gained control of the ball. As soon as the team has control, the team changes state to **Attacking**.

```
void Defending::Execute(SoccerTeam* team)
{
  //if in control change states
  if (team->InControl())
  {
    team->ChangeState(team, Attacking::Instance()); return;
  }
}
```

Attacking

As the `Enter` method of the **Attacking** state looks identical to that for the **Defending** state, I'm not going to waste space and list it here. The only difference is that the players are assigned different home regions. The regions assigned to the red team's players when **Attacking** are shown in Figure 4.12.

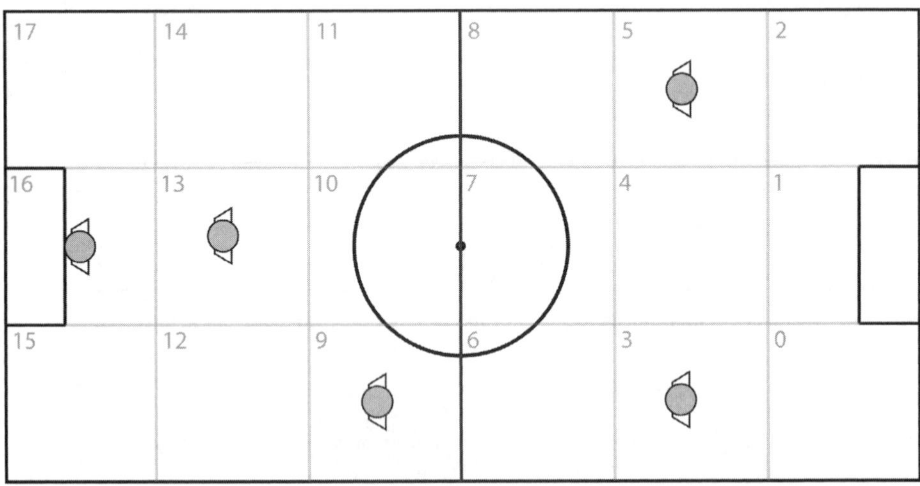

Figure 4.12. Players in their home regions for the Attacking team state

As you can see, the players position themselves much closer to the opponent's goal. This gives them an increased chance of keeping the ball in the opponent's half of the pitch and therefore more chance of scoring a goal. Notice how one player is kept back, positioned just ahead of the goalkeeper, in order to provide a modicum of defense should an opponent break free with the ball and make a run for the team's goal.

The `Execute` method of the **Attacking** state is also similar to that for the **Defending** state with one addition. When a team gains control of the ball, the team immediately iterates through all the players to determine which one will provide the best support for the attacker. Once a support player has been assigned, it will merrily move off toward the best supporting spot, as determined by the process we discussed earlier.

```
void Attacking::Execute(SoccerTeam* team)
{
  //if this team is no longer in control change states
  if (!team->InControl())
  {
    team->ChangeState(team, Defending::Instance()); return;
  }

  //calculate the best position for any supporting attacker to move to
  team->DetermineBestSupportingPosition();
}
```

That's enough about the SoccerTeam class for now. Let's take a look at how the players are implemented.

Field Players

The field players are the guys who run around the field, passing the ball and taking shots at their opponent's goal. There are two types of field players: *attackers* and *defenders*. Both are instantiated as objects of the same class, FieldPlayer, but an enumerated member variable is set to determine their role. Defenders mainly stay to the rear of the field protecting the home goal, and attackers are given more freedom to move up the field, toward the opponent's goal.

Field Player Motion

A field player has a velocity-aligned heading and utilizes steering behaviors to move into position and to chase the ball. When motionless, a field player rotates to face the ball. It doesn't do this to perceive the ball, as it always knows where the ball is (from querying the game world directly), but because it has a better chance of passing immediately after an intercept and because it looks better to our human eyes. Remember, this is about creating the illusion of intelligence, and not hard-core AI as studied by academics. Most human players will assume that if a computer player is tracking the ball with its head, then it *must* be "watching" the ball. By creating players that always track the ball we also ensure nothing odd happens — like a player receiving and controlling the ball when it's facing in the opposite direction. That sort of thing would break the illusion, leaving a human player feeling cheated and dissatisfied. I'm sure you have experienced this feeling yourself when playing games. It only takes a small dodgy-looking event to damage a player's confidence in the AI.

The field players move around the pitch utilizing the **arrive** and **seek** behaviors to steer toward the steering behavior target or using **pursuit** to chase the ball's predicted future position. Any required steering behavior is typically switched on in a state's Enter method and switched off in its Exit method, which brings me nicely around to discussing the states a field player can occupy.

Field Player States

In real life, soccer players must learn a set of skills in order to control the ball well enough to coordinate team play and to score goals. They do this by endless hours of practice and repetition of the same moves. Simple Soccer players don't have to practice, but they do rely on you, the programmer, to bestow them with the skills they need to play well.

A field player's finite state machine utilizes eight states:

- **GlobalPlayerState**
- **Wait**
- **ReceiveBall**
- **KickBall**
- **Dribble**
- **ChaseBall**
- **ReturnToHomeRegion**
- **SupportAttacker**

State changes are made either in the logic of a state itself or when a player is sent a message by another player (to receive a ball for example).

GlobalPlayerState

The main purpose of the field player's global state is to be a message router. Although much of a player's behavior is implemented by the logic contained within each of its states, it's also desirable to implement some form of player cooperation via a communication system. A good example of this is when a supporting player finds itself in an advantageous position and requests a pass from a teammate. To facilitate player communication, the trusty messaging system you learned about in Chapter 2 is implemented.

There are five messages used in Simple Soccer. They are:

- `Msg_SupportAttacker`
- `Msg_GoHome`
- `Msg_ReceiveBall`
- `Msg_PassToMe`
- `Msg_Wait`

The messages are enumerated in the file SoccerMessages.h. Let's take a look at how each of them is processed.

```
bool GlobalPlayerState::OnMessage(FieldPlayer* player, const Telegram& telegram)
{
  switch(telegram.Msg)
  {
  case Msg_ReceiveBall:
    {
      //set the target
      player->Steering()->SetTarget(*(Vector2D*)(telegram.ExtraInfo));

      //change state
      player->ChangeState(player, ReceiveBall::Instance());
```

```
      return true;
    }

    break;
```

Msg_ReceiveBall is sent to the receiving player when a pass is made. The position of the pass target is stored as the receiver's steering behavior target. The receiving player acknowledges the message by changing state to **ReceiveBall**.

```
  case Msg_SupportAttacker:
    {
      //if already supporting just return
      if (player->CurrentState() == SupportAttacker::Instance()) return true;

      //set the target to be the best supporting position
      player->Steering()->SetTarget(player->Team()->GetSupportSpot());

      //change the state
      player->ChangeState(player, SupportAttacker::Instance());

      return true;
    }

    break;
```

Msg_SupportAttacker is sent by the controlling player to request support as it attempts to move the ball farther up the field. When a player receives this message, it sets its steering target to the best supporting spot and then changes state to **SupportAttacker**.

```
  case Msg_GoHome:
    {
      player->SetDefaultHomeRegion();

      player->ChangeState(player, ReturnToHomeRegion::Instance());

      return true;
    }

    break;
```

When a player receives this message, it moves back to its home region. It's frequently broadcast by the goalkeepers prior to goal kicks and by the "pitch" to move the players back into their kick-off positions between goals.

```
case Msg_Wait:
    {
      //change the state
      player->ChangeState(player, Wait::Instance());

      return true;
    }

    break;
```

Msg_Wait instructs a player to wait at its current position.

```
case Msg_PassToMe:
  {
    //get the position of the player requesting the pass
    FieldPlayer* receiver = (FieldPlayer*)(telegram.ExtraInfo);

    //if the ball is not within kicking range or the player does not have
    //a window within which he can make the kick, this player cannot pass
    //the ball to the player making the request.
    if (!player->BallWithinKickingRange())
    {
      return true;
    }

    //make the pass
    player->Ball()->Kick(receiver->Pos() - player->Ball()->Pos(),
                         Prm.MaxPassingForce);

    //let the receiver know a pass is coming
    Dispatch->DispatchMsg(SEND_MSG_IMMEDIATELY,
                          player->ID(),
                          receiver->ID(),
                          Msg_ReceiveBall,
                          NO_SCOPE,
                          &receiver->Pos());


    //change state
    player->ChangeState(player, Wait::Instance());

    player->FindSupport();

    return true;
  }

  break;
```

Msg_PassToMe is used in a couple of situations, mainly when a supporting player has moved into position and thinks it has a good chance of scoring a goal. When a player receives this message, it passes the ball to the requesting player (if the pass can be made safely).

```
  }//end switch

  return false;
}
```

In addition to OnMessage, the global state also implements the Execute method. This lowers the maximum speed of a player if it's close to the ball to simulate the way that soccer players move slower when they have possession.

```
void GlobalPlayerState::Execute(FieldPlayer* player)
{
  //if a player is in possession and close to the ball reduce his max speed
```

```
  if((player->BallWithinReceivingRange()) &&
     (player->Team()->ControllingPlayer() == player))
  {
    player->SetMaxSpeed(Prm.PlayerMaxSpeedWithBall);
  }

  else
  {
     player->SetMaxSpeed(Prm.PlayerMaxSpeedWithoutBall);
  }
}
```

ChaseBall

When a player is in the **ChaseBall** state, it will **seek** to the ball's current position, attempting to get within kicking range.

When a player enters this state its **seek** behavior is activated like so:

```
void ChaseBall::Enter(FieldPlayer* player)
{
  player->Steering()->SeekOn();
}
```

During an update of the Execute method a player will change state to **KickBall** if the ball comes within kicking range. If the ball is not within range, a player will continue to chase the ball as long as that player remains the closest member of its team to the ball.

```
void ChaseBall::Execute(FieldPlayer* player)
{
  //if the ball is within kicking range the player changes state to KickBall.
  if (player->BallWithinKickingRange())
  {
    player->ChangeState(player, KickBall::Instance());

    return;
  }

  //if the player is the closest player to the ball then he should keep
  //chasing it
  if (player->isClosestTeamMemberToBall())
  {
    player->Steering()->SetTarget(player->Ball()->Pos());

    return;
  }

  //if the player is not closest to the ball anymore, he should return back
  //to his home region and wait for another opportunity
  player->ChangeState(player, ReturnToHomeRegion::Instance());
}
```

When a player exits this state, the **seek** behavior is deactivated.

```
void ChaseBall::Exit(FieldPlayer* player)
{
```

```
  player->Steering()->SeekOff();
}
```

Wait

When in the Wait state a player will stay positioned at the location given by its steering behavior target. If the player gets jostled out of position by another player, it will move back into position.

There are a couple of exit conditions for this state:

- If a waiting player finds itself upfield of a teammate that is controlling the ball, it will message the teammate with a request for it to pass the ball. This is because it's desirable to get the ball as far upfield as possible and as quickly as possible. If safe, the teammate will make the pass and the waiting player will change state to receive the ball.
- If the ball becomes closer to the waiting player than any other teammate and there is no allocated receiving player, it will change state to **ChaseBall**.

```
void Wait::Execute(FieldPlayer* player)
{
  //if the player has been jostled out of position, get back in position
  if (!player->AtTarget())
  {
    player->Steering()->ArriveOn();

    return;
  }

  else
  {
    player->Steering()->ArriveOff();

    player->SetVelocity(Vector2D(0,0));

    //the player should keep his eyes on the ball!
    player->TrackBall();
  }

  //if this player's team is controlling AND this player is not the attacker
  //AND is farther up the field than the attacker he should request a pass.
  if ( player->Team()->InControl()    &&
     (!player->isControllingPlayer()) &&
       player->isAheadOfAttacker() )
  {
    player->Team()->RequestPass(player);

    return;
  }

  if (player->Pitch()->GameOn())
  {
   //if the ball is nearer this player than any other team member AND
```

```
      //there is not an assigned receiver AND neither goalkeeper has
      //the ball, go chase it
     if (player->isClosestTeamMemberToBall() &&
         player->Team()->Receiver() == NULL  &&
         !player->Pitch()->GoalKeeperHasBall())
     {
       player->ChangeState(player, ChaseBall::Instance());

       return;
     }
   }
}
```

ReceiveBall

A player enters the **ReceiveBall** state when it processes a `Msg_ReceiveBall` message. This message is sent to the receiving player by the player that has just made the pass. The `ExtraInfo` field of the `Telegram` contains the target position of the ball so the receiving player's steering target can be set accordingly, allowing the receiver to move into position, ready to intercept the ball.

There can only ever be one player from each team in the **ReceiveBall** state — it wouldn't be good tactics to have two or more players attempting to intercept the same pass, so the first thing the `Enter` method of this state does is update the appropriate `SoccerTeam` pointers to enable the other team members to query them if necessary.

To create more interesting and natural-looking play, there are two methods of receiving a ball. One method uses the **arrive** behavior to steer toward the ball's target position; the other uses the **pursuit** behavior to pursue the ball. A player chooses between them depending on the value `ChanceOfUsingArriveTypeReceiveBehavior`, whether or not an opposing player is within a threatening radius, and whether or not the receiver is positioned in the third of the pitch closest to the opponent's goal (I call this area the "hot region").

```
void ReceiveBall::Enter(FieldPlayer* player)
{
  //let the team know this player is receiving the ball
  player->Team()->SetReceiver(player);

  //this player is also now the controlling player
  player->Team()->SetControllingPlayer(player);

  //there are two types of receive behavior. One uses arrive to direct
  //the receiver to the position sent by the passer in its telegram. The
  //other uses the pursuit behavior to pursue the ball.
  //This statement selects between them dependent on the probability
  //ChanceOfUsingArriveTypeReceiveBehavior, whether or not an opposing
  //player is close to the receiving player, and whether or not the receiving
  //player is in the opponent's "hot region" (the third of the pitch closest
  //to the opponent's goal)
  const double PassThreatRadius = 70.0;
```

```
  if ((player->InHotRegion() ||
       RandFloat() < Prm.ChanceOfUsingArriveTypeReceiveBehavior) &&
      !player->Team()->isOpponentWithinRadius(player->Pos(), PassThreatRadius))
  {
    player->Steering()->ArriveOn();
  }
  else
  {
    player->Steering()->PursuitOn();
  }
}
```

The Execute method is straightforward. A receiving player will move into position and will remain there unless the soccer ball comes within a specified distance or if its team loses control of the ball, at which time the player will change to the **ChaseBall** state.

```
void ReceiveBall::Execute(FieldPlayer* player)
{
  //if the ball comes close enough to the player or if his team loses control
  //he should change state to chase the ball
  if (player->BallWithinReceivingRange() || !player->Team()->InControl())
  {
    player->ChangeState(player, ChaseBall::Instance());

    return;
  }

  //the player's target must be continuously updated with the ball position
  //if the pursuit steering behavior is used to pursue the ball.
  if (player->Steering()->PursuitIsOn())
  {
    player->Steering()->SetTarget(player->Ball()->Pos());
  }

  //if the player has "arrived" at the steering target he should wait and
  //turn to face the ball
  if (player->AtTarget())
  {
    player->Steering()->ArriveOff();
    player->Steering()->PursuitOff();
    player->TrackBall();
    player->SetVelocity(Vector2D(0,0));
  }
}
```

KickBall

If there's one thing that soccer players like doing more than getting drunk and hugging each other, it's kicking soccer balls. Oh yes. They love it. Simple Soccer players are no different. Well, I guess they don't get drunk and hug each other, but they *do* enjoy a good kick around.

A Simple Soccer player must be able to control and kick the ball in a number of ways. It must be able to attempt shots at the opponent's goal, have the skills necessary to pass the ball to another player, and be able to dribble. When a player obtains control of the ball it should select the most appropriate option to use at any time.

The **KickBall** state implements the logic for goal shots and passing. If for some reason a player cannot take a shot or a pass is not necessary, the player's state will be changed to **Dribble**. A player cannot remain in the **KickBall** state for longer than one update cycle; whether the ball is kicked or not, the player will always change state somewhere in the journey through the state logic. A player enters this state if the ball comes within `PlayerKickingDistance` of its position.

Let me walk you through the source code:

```
void KickBall::Enter(FieldPlayer* player)
{
  //let the team know this player is controlling
   player->Team()->SetControllingPlayer(player);

   //the player can only make so many kick attempts per second.
   if (!player->isReadyForNextKick())
   {
     player->ChangeState(player, ChaseBall::Instance());
   }
}
```

The `Enter` method first lets the team know that this player is the controlling player and then checks to see if the player is permitted to kick the ball this update step. Players are only allowed to make kick attempts a few times a second, at a frequency stored in the variable `PlayerKickFrequency`. If the player cannot make a kick attempt, its state is changed to **ChaseBall** and it will continue running after the ball.

The number of times a player may kick a ball per second is restricted to prevent anomalies in behavior. For example, with no restriction, situations can occur where the ball is kicked, the player goes into the wait state, and then, because the ball is still in kicking range, a split second later the players kicks it again. Because of the way the ball physics is handled, this can result in jerky, unnatural ball motion.

```
void KickBall::Execute(FieldPlayer* player)
{
  //calculate the dot product of the vector pointing to the ball
  //and the player's heading
  Vector2D ToBall = player->Ball()->Pos() - player->Pos();
  double   dot    = player->Heading().Dot(Vec2DNormalize(ToBall));

  //cannot kick the ball if the goalkeeper is in possession or if it's
  //behind the player or if there is already an assigned receiver. So just
  //continue chasing the ball
  if (player->Team()->Receiver() != NULL   ||
      player->Pitch()->GoalKeeperHasBall() ||
      (dot < 0) )
  {
```

```
    player->ChangeState(player, ChaseBall::Instance());
    return;
  }
```

When the Execute method is entered, the dot product of the player's heading and the vector pointing toward the ball is calculated to determine if the ball is behind or in front of the player. If the ball is behind, or there is already a player waiting to receive the ball, or one of the goalkeepers has the ball, the player's state is changed so that it continues to chase the ball.

If the player is able to kick the ball, the state logic determines if there is a possible goal shot to be made. After all, goals are the aim of the game, so it naturally should be the first thing considered when a player obtains control of the ball.

```
  /* Attempt a shot at the goal */

  //the dot product is used to adjust the shooting force. The more
  //directly the ball is ahead of the player, the more forceful the kick
  double power = Prm.MaxShootingForce * dot;
```

Notice how the power of the shot is proportional to how directly ahead of the player the ball is. If the ball is situated to the side, the power with which the shot can be made is reduced.

```
  //if a shot is possible, this vector will hold the position along the
  //opponent's goal line the player should aim for.
  Vector2D    BallTarget;

  //if it's determined that the player could score a goal from this position
  //OR if he should just kick the ball anyway, the player will attempt
  //to make the shot
  if (player->Team()->CanShoot(player->Ball()->Pos(),
                               power,
                               BallTarget)                 ||
     (RandFloat() < Prm.ChancePlayerAttemptsPotShot))
  {
```

The CanShoot method determines if there is a potential shot at the goal. (You will find a detailed description of the CanShoot method toward the end of this chapter.) If there is a potential shot, CanShoot will return true and store the position the player should aim for in the vector BallTarget. If it returns false, we check to see whether or not a "cosmetic" potshot should be made (BallTarget will hold the location of the last position found invalid by CanShoot, so we know the shot is guaranteed to fail). The reason for making the occasional potshot is to liven up the gameplay, making it look far more exciting to the human observer; it can get tedious quickly if the computer players always score from a goal attempt. The occasional random potshot introduces a little uncertainty, and makes the game a much more enjoyable experience.

```
    //add some noise to the kick. We don't want players who are
    //too accurate! The amount of noise can be adjusted by altering
```

```
  //Prm.PlayerKickingAccuracy
  BallTarget = AddNoiseToKick(player->Ball()->Pos(), BallTarget);

  //this is the direction the ball will be kicked
  Vector2D KickDirection = BallTarget - player->Ball()->Pos();

  player->Ball()->Kick(KickDirection, power);
```

The ball is kicked by calling the `SoccerBall::Kick` method with the desired heading. Because perfect players making perfect kicks all the time does not make for very realistic-looking soccer, an amount of noise is added to the kick direction. This ensures the players will occasionally make poor kicks.

```
  //change state
  player->ChangeState(player, Wait::Instance());

  player->FindSupport();

  return;
}
```

Once the ball has been kicked, the player changes to the **Wait** state and requests assistance from another teammate by calling the `PlayerBase::FindSupport` method. `FindSupport` "asks" the team to determine the teammate best suited to provide support, and to send a request via the messaging system for the team member to enter the **SupportAttacker** state. The state then returns control to the player's `Update` method.

If no shot at the goal is possible, the player considers a pass. A player will only consider this option if it's threatened by an opposing player. A player is deemed to be threatened by another when the two are less than `PlayerComfortZone` pixels apart and the opponent is ahead of the facing plane of the player. The default is set in params.ini at 60 pixels. A larger value will result in players making more passes and a smaller value will result in more successful tackles.

```
/* Attempt a pass to a player */

//if a receiver is found, this will point to it
PlayerBase* receiver = NULL;

power = Prm.MaxPassingForce * dot;

//test if there are any potential candidates available to receive a pass
if (player->isThreatened()  &&
    player->Team()->CanPass(player,
                            receiver,
                            BallTarget,
                            power,
                            Prm.MinPassDist))
{
  //add some noise to the kick
  BallTarget = AddNoiseToKick(player->Ball()->Pos(), BallTarget);
```

```
    Vector2D KickDirection = BallTarget - player->Ball()->Pos();

    player->Ball()->Kick(KickDirection, power);

    //let the receiver know a pass is coming
    Dispatch->DispatchMsg(SEND_MSG_IMMEDIATELY,
                          player->ID(),
                          receiver->ID(),
                          Msg_ReceiveBall,
                          NO_SCOPE,
                          &BallTarget);
```

The method FindPass examines all the friendly players to find the teammate farthest up the playing field situated in a position where a pass can be made without getting intercepted. (A detailed description of FindPass can be found toward the end of this chapter.) If a valid pass is found, the kick is made (with added noise as before), and the receiver is notified by sending it a message to change state to **ReceiveBall**.

```
    //the player should wait at his current position unless instructed
    //otherwise
    player->ChangeState(player, Wait::Instance());

    player->FindSupport();

    return;
  }
```

If the game logic flows to this point, then neither an appropriate pass nor a goal attempt has been found. The player still has the ball though, so it enters the **Dribble** state. (It's worth noting that this is not the only time passes are made — teammates can request passes from players by sending them the appropriate message.)

```
  //cannot shoot or pass, so dribble the ball upfield
  else
  {
    player->FindSupport();

    player->ChangeState(player, Dribble::Instance());
  }
}
```

Dribble

Dribbling is something babies are excellent at, from both ends… but the word has also been adopted by the game of soccer to describe the art of moving a ball along the field in a series of small kicks and dashes. Using this skill, a player is able to rotate on the spot or move agilely around an opponent while retaining control of the ball.

Because one of the exercises at the end of this chapter will be for you to try to improve this skill, I've only implemented a simple method of dribbling, giving a player just enough ability to move the game along at a reasonable pace.

The Enter method simply lets the rest of the team know that the dribbling player is assumed to be in control of the ball.

```
void Dribble::Enter(FieldPlayer* player)
{
  //let the team know this player is controlling
  player->Team()->SetControllingPlayer(player);
}
```

The Execute method contains the majority of the AI logic. First, a check is made to see if the ball is between the player and its home goal (downfield of the player). This situation is undesirable, because the player wants to move the ball as far upfield as possible. Therefore the player must turn around *while still retaining control of the ball.* To achieve this, players make a series of very small kicks in a direction $\frac{\pi}{4}$ (45 degrees) away from their facing direction. After making each small kick, the player changes state to **ChaseBall**. When done several times in quick succession, this has the effect of rotating the player and ball until they are heading in the correct direction (toward the opponent's goal).

If the ball is positioned upfield of the player, the player will nudge it a short distance forward and then change state to **ChaseBall** in order to follow it.

```
void Dribble::Execute(FieldPlayer* player)
{
  double dot = player->Team()->HomeGoal()->Facing().Dot(player->Heading());

  //if the ball is between the player and the home goal, it needs to swivel
  //the ball around by doing multiple small kicks and turns until the player
  //is facing in the correct direction
  if (dot < 0)
  {
    //the player's heading is going to be rotated by a small amount (Pi/4)
    //and then the ball will be kicked in that direction
    Vector2D direction = player->Heading();

    //calculate the sign (+/–) of the angle between the player heading and the
    //facing direction of the goal so that the player rotates around in the
    //correct direction
    double angle = QuarterPi * -1 *
                 player->Team()->HomeGoal()->Facing().Sign(player->Heading());

    Vec2DRotateAroundOrigin(direction, angle);

    //this value works well when the player is attempting to control the
    //ball and turn at the same time
    const double KickingForce = 0.8;

    player->Ball()->Kick(direction, KickingForce);
  }
```

```
  //kick the ball down the field
  else
  {
    player->Ball()->Kick(player->Team()->HomeGoal()->Facing(),
                         Prm.MaxDribbleForce);
  }

  //the player has kicked the ball so he must now change state to follow it
  player->ChangeState(player, ChaseBall::Instance());

  return;
}
```

SupportAttacker

When a player obtains control of the ball he immediately requests support by calling the `PlayerBase::FindSupport` method. `FindSupport` examines each team member in turn to determine which player is closest to the best supporting spot (calculated every few time steps by `SupportSpot-Calculator`) and messages that player to change state to **SupportAttacker**.

On entering this state, the player's **arrive** behavior is switched on and its steering target is set to the location of the BSS.

```
void SupportAttacker::Enter(FieldPlayer* player)
{
  player->Steering()->ArriveOn();

  player->Steering()->SetTarget(player->Team()->GetSupportSpot());
}
```

There are a number of conditions that make up the logic of the `Execute` method. Let's step through them.

```
void SupportAttacker::Execute(FieldPlayer* player)
{
  //if his team loses control go back home
  if (!player->Team()->InControl())
  {
    player->ChangeState(player, ReturnToHomeRegion::Instance()); return;
  }
```

If a player's team loses control, the player should change state to move back toward its home position.

```
  //if the best supporting spot changes, change the steering target
  if (player->Team()->GetSupportSpot() != player->Steering()->Target())
  {
    player->Steering()->SetTarget(player->Team()->GetSupportSpot());

    player->Steering()->ArriveOn();
  }
```

As you have seen, the position of the best supporting spot changes according to many factors, so any supporting player must always make sure its steering target is kept updated with the latest position.

```
  //if this player has a shot at the goal AND the attacker can pass
  //the ball to him the attacker should pass the ball to this player
  if( player->Team()->CanShoot(player->Pos(),
                               Prm.MaxShootingForce) )
  {
    player->Team()->RequestPass(player);
  }
```

A supporting player spends the majority of its time in the opponent's half of the pitch. Therefore it should always be on the lookout for the possibility of a shot at the opponent's goal. These few lines use the `SoccerTeam::CanShoot` method to determine if there is a potential goal shot. If the result is affirmative, the player requests a pass from the player controlling the ball. In turn, if `RequestPass` determines that a pass from the controlling player to this player is possible without being intercepted, a `Msg_ReceiveBall` message will be sent and the player will change state accordingly in readiness to receive the ball.

```
  //if this player is located at the support spot and his team still has
  //possession, he should remain still and turn to face the ball
  if (player->AtTarget())
  {
    player->Steering()->ArriveOff();

    //the player should keep his eyes on the ball!
    player->TrackBall();

    player->SetVelocity(Vector2D(0,0));

    //if not threatened by another player request a pass
    if (!player->isThreatened())
    {
      player->Team()->RequestPass(player);
    }
  }
}
```

Finally, if the supporting player reaches the position of the BSS, it waits and makes sure it's always facing the ball. If there are no opponents within its immediate vicinity and it doesn't feel threatened, it requests a pass from the controlling player.

 **NOTE** Note that a request for a pass does not mean a pass will be made. A pass will only be made if the pass is considered safe from interception.

Goalkeepers

A goalkeeper's job is to keep the ball from traveling over the goal line. To do this, a goalkeeper utilizes a different set of skills than a field player and is therefore implemented as a separate class, `GoalKeeper`. A goalkeeper will move backward and forward along the goal mouth until the ball comes within a specific range, at which point it will move outward toward the ball in an attempt to intercept it. If a goalkeeper attains possession of the ball, it puts the ball back in play by kicking it to an appropriate team member.

A Simple Soccer goalkeeper is assigned to the region that overlaps its team's goal. Therefore the red goalkeeper is assigned to region 16 and the blue goalkeeper to region 1.

Goalkeeper Motion

Along with having a completely different set of states than a field player, the `GoalKeeper` class must employ a slightly different setup for its motion. If you observe a goalkeeper playing soccer you will notice that he is almost always looking directly at the ball and that many of his movements are from side to side, rather than along his facing direction like a field player. Because an entity using steering behaviors has a velocity aligned heading, a goalkeeper utilizes another vector, `m_vLookAt`, to indicate facing direction, and it's this vector that is passed to the `Render` function in order to transform the goalkeeper's vertices. The end result is an entity that appears to be always facing the ball and can move laterally from side to side as well as along its heading axis. See Figure 4.13.

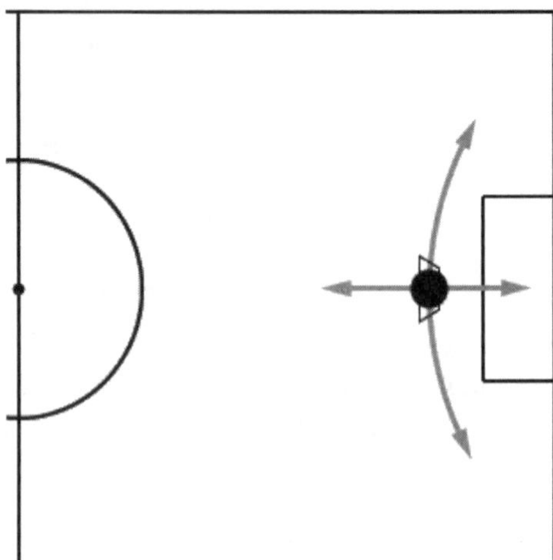

Figure 4.13. Goalkeeper movement

Goalkeeper States

A goalkeeper utilizes five states. These are:

- **GlobalKeeperState**
- **TendGoal**
- **ReturnHome**
- **PutBallBackInPlay**
- **InterceptBall**

Let's take a look at each one of these in detail to see what makes a goalkeeper tick.

GlobalKeeperState

Like the FieldPlayer global state, the GoalKeeper global state is used as the router for all the messages it can receive. A goalkeeper only listens for two messages: Msg_GoHome and Msg_ReceiveBall.

I think the code can speak for itself here:

```
bool GlobalKeeperState::OnMessage(GoalKeeper* keeper, const Telegram& telegram)
{
  switch(telegram.Msg)
  {
    case Msg_GoHome:
    {
      keeper->SetDefaultHomeRegion();

      keeper->ChangeState(keeper, ReturnHome::Instance());
    }

    break;

    case Msg_ReceiveBall:
      {
        keeper->ChangeState(keeper, InterceptBall::Instance());
      }

      break;

  }//end switch

  return false;
}
```

TendGoal

When in the **TendGoal** state, a goalkeeper will move laterally across the front of the goal mouth, attempting to keep its body between the ball and a moving position located to its rear somewhere along the goal line. Here is the state's Enter method:

```
void TendGoal::Enter(GoalKeeper* keeper)
{
  //turn interpose on
  keeper->Steering()->InterposeOn(Prm.GoalKeeperTendingDistance);
```

```
  //interpose will position the agent between the ball position and a target
  //position situated along the goal mouth. This call sets the target
  keeper->Steering()->SetTarget(keeper->GetRearInterposeTarget());
}
```

First, the **interpose** steering behavior is activated. **Interpose** will return a steering force that attempts to position the goalkeeper between the ball and a position situated along the goal mouth. This position is determined by the `GoalKeeper::GetRearInterposeTarget` method, which assigns a position to the target proportionally as far up the length of the goal mouth as the ball is positioned up the width of the pitch. (I hope that sentence made sense because I agonized over it for ten minutes and it's the best I could do!) Hopefully Figure 4.14 will help your understanding. From the goalkeeper's perspective, the farther the ball is to the left, the farther to the left along the goal line is the interpose rear target. As the ball moves to the goalkeeper's right, the interpose rear target moves to the right of the goal mouth with it.

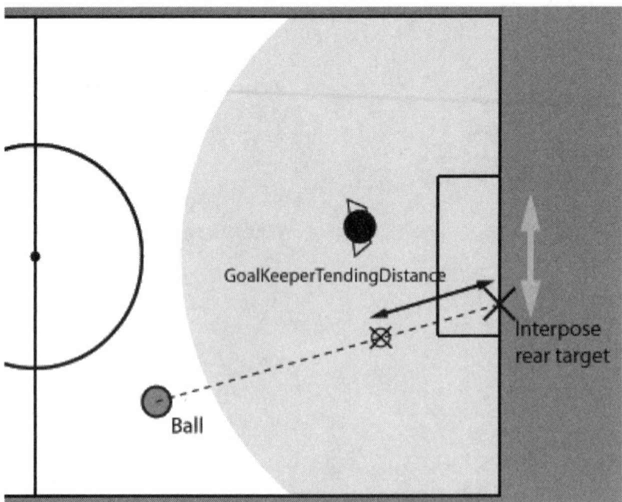

Figure 4.14. Tending the goal

The black double-headed arrow indicates the distance the goalkeeper attempts to keep between itself and the back of the net. This value is set in params.ini as `GoalKeeperTendingDistance`.

Let's move on to the `Execute` method.

```
void TendGoal::Execute(GoalKeeper* keeper)
{
  //the rear interpose target will change as the ball's position changes
  //so it must be updated each update step
  keeper->Steering()->SetTarget(keeper->GetRearInterposeTarget());
```

```
  //if the ball comes in range the keeper traps it and then changes state
  //to put the ball back in play
  if (keeper->BallWithinPlayerRange())
  {
    keeper->Ball()->Trap();

    keeper->Pitch()->SetGoalKeeperHasBall(true);

    keeper->ChangeState(keeper, PutBallBackInPlay::Instance());

    return;
  }

  //if ball is within a predefined distance, the keeper moves out from
  //position to try to intercept it.
  if (keeper->BallWithinRangeForIntercept())
  {
    keeper->ChangeState(keeper, InterceptBall::Instance());
  }
```

First, a check is made to see if the ball is close enough for the goalkeeper to grab hold of. If so, the ball is trapped and the keeper changes state to **PutBallBackInPlay**. Next, if the ball comes within intercept range, shown in Figure 4.14 as the area in light gray and set in params.ini as `GoalKeeperInterceptRange`, the keeper changes state to **InterceptBall**.

```
  //if the keeper has ventured too far away from the goal line and there
  //is no threat from the opponents he should move back toward it
  if (keeper->TooFarFromGoalMouth() && keeper->Team()->InControl())
  {
    keeper->ChangeState(keeper, ReturnHome::Instance());

    return;
  }
}
```

Occasionally, following a state change from **InterceptBall** to **TendGoal**, the goalkeeper can find itself too far away from the goal. The last few lines of code check for this eventuality and, if safe to do so, changes the keeper's state to **ReturnHome**.

The `TendGoal::Exit` method is very simple; it just deactivates the **interpose** steering behavior.

```
void TendGoal::Exit(GoalKeeper* keeper)
{
  keeper->Steering()->InterposeOff();
}
```

ReturnHome

The **ReturnHome** state moves the goalkeeper back toward its home region. When the home region is reached or if the opponents gain control over the ball, the keeper is put back into the **TendGoal** state.

```
void ReturnHome::Enter(GoalKeeper* keeper)
{
  keeper->Steering()->ArriveOn();
}

void ReturnHome::Execute(GoalKeeper* keeper)
{
  keeper->Steering()->SetTarget(keeper->HomeRegion()->Center());

  //if close enough to home or the opponents get control over the ball,
  //change state to tend goal
  if (keeper->InHomeRegion() || !keeper->Team()->InControl())
  {
    keeper->ChangeState(keeper, TendGoal::Instance());
  }
}

void ReturnHome::Exit(GoalKeeper* keeper)
{
  keeper->Steering()->ArriveOff();
}
```

PutBallBackInPlay

When a goalkeeper gains possession of the ball, it enters the **PutBallBack-InPlay** state. A couple of things happen in the `Enter` method of this state. First, the keeper lets its team know it has the ball, then all the field players are instructed to go back to their home regions via the call to the `SoccerTeam::ReturnAllFieldPlayersToHome` method. This ensures that there will be enough free space between the keeper and the players to make a goal kick.

```
void PutBallBackInPlay::Enter(GoalKeeper* keeper)
{
  //let the team know that the keeper is in control
  keeper->Team()->SetControllingPlayer(keeper);

  //send all the players home
  keeper->Team()->Opponents()->ReturnAllFieldPlayersToHome();
  keeper->Team()->ReturnAllFieldPlayersToHome();
}
```

The goalkeeper now waits until all the other players have moved far enough away and it can make a clean pass to one of its team members. As soon as an opportunity to pass becomes available, the keeper passes the ball, sends a message to the receiving player to let it know the ball is on its way, and then changes state to return to tending the goal.

```
void PutBallBackInPlay::Execute(GoalKeeper* keeper)
{
  PlayerBase*  receiver = NULL;
  Vector2D     BallTarget;

  //test if there are players farther forward on the field we might
  //be able to pass to. If so, make a pass.
```

```
  if (keeper->Team()->FindPass(keeper,
                               receiver,
                               BallTarget,
                               Prm.MaxPassingForce,
                               Prm.GoalkeeperMinPassDist))
  {
    //make the pass
    keeper->Ball()->Kick(Vec2DNormalize(BallTarget - keeper->Ball()->Pos()),
                         Prm.MaxPassingForce);

    //goalkeeper no longer has ball
    keeper->Pitch()->SetGoalKeeperHasBall(false);

    //let the receiving player know the ball's comin' at him
    Dispatcher->DispatchMsg(SEND_MSG_IMMEDIATELY,
                            keeper->ID(),
                            receiver->ID(),
                            Msg_ReceiveBall,
                            &BallTarget);

    //go back to tending the goal
    keeper->GetFSM()->ChangeState(TendGoal::Instance());

    return;
  }

  keeper->SetVelocity(Vector2D());
}
```

InterceptBall

A goalkeeper will attempt to intercept the ball if the opponents have control and if it comes into "threat range" — the gray area shown in Figure 4.15. It uses the **pursuit** steering behavior to steer it toward the ball.

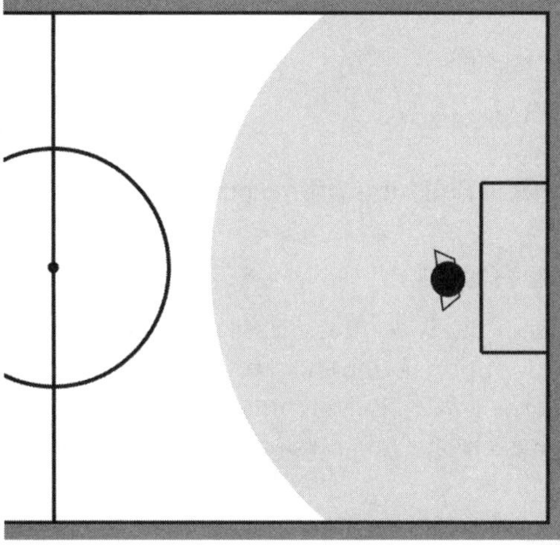

Figure 4.15. A goalkeeper's "threat range"

```
void InterceptBall::Enter(GoalKeeper* keeper)
{
  keeper->Steering()->PursuitOn();
}
```

As the goalkeeper moves outward, toward the ball, it keeps checking the distance to the goal to make sure it doesn't travel too far. If the goalkeeper does find itself out of goal range it changes state to **ReturnHome**. There is one exception to this: If the goalkeeper is out of goal range yet is the *closest player on the pitch to the ball*, he keeps running after it.

If the ball comes in range of the goalkeeper, he stops the ball using the `SoccerBall::Trap` method, lets everyone know he is in possession, and changes state in order to put the ball back in play.

```
void InterceptBall::Execute(GoalKeeper* keeper)
{
  //if the goalkeeper moves too far away from the goal he should return to his
  //home region UNLESS he is the closest player to the ball, in which case
  //he should keep trying to intercept it.
  if (keeper->TooFarFromGoalMouth() && !keeper->ClosestPlayerOnPitchToBall())
  {
    keeper->ChangeState(keeper, ReturnHome::Instance());

    return;
  }

  //if the ball becomes in range of the goalkeeper's hands he traps the
  //ball and puts it back in play
  if (keeper->BallWithinPlayerRange())
  {
    keeper->Ball()->Trap();

    keeper->Pitch()->SetGoalKeeperHasBall(true);

    keeper->ChangeState(keeper, PutBallBackInPlay::Instance());

    return;
  }
}
```

The exit method of **InterceptBall** turns off the pursuit behavior.

Key Methods Used by the AI

A number of the methods of the `SoccerTeam` class are used frequently by the AI, and thus a full description is important to your complete understanding of how the AI works. With this in mind, I'll spend the next few pages taking you through each one step by step. Put your math hat back on…

SoccerTeam::isPassSafeFromAllOpponents

A soccer player, whatever his role in the game, is continually assessing his position in relation to those around him and making judgments based upon those assessments. One calculation the AI undertakes frequently is to determine if a pass from position A to position B can be intercepted by any opposing player at any point in the ball's trajectory. It needs this information to judge whether or not it can make passes, whether it should request a pass from the current attacker, or if there is a chance of scoring a goal.

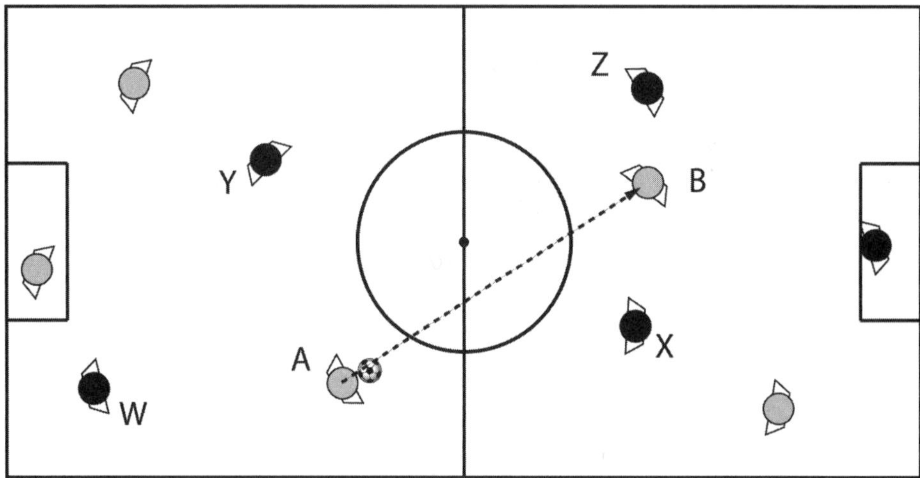

Figure 4.16. Player A passing directly to player B

Consider Figure 4.16. Player A would like to know if it can pass the ball to player B without it being intercepted by any of the opponents W, X, Y, or Z. To determine this it must consider each opponent in turn and calculate if an intercept is likely. `SoccerTeam::isPassSafeFromOpponent` is where all the work is done.

The method takes as parameters the start and end positions of the pass, a pointer to the opponent to be considered, a pointer to the receiver the ball is being passed to, and the force the ball is going to be kicked with. The method is called for each opponent in the opposing team by the method `SoccerTeam::isPassSafeFromAllOpponents`.

```
bool SoccerTeam::isPassSafeFromOpponent(Vector2D    from,
                                        Vector2D    target,
                                        const PlayerBase* const receiver,
                                        const PlayerBase* const opp,
                                        double      PassingForce)const
{
  //move the opponent into local space.
  Vector2D ToTarget = target - from;
```

```
Vector2D ToTargetNormalized = Vec2DNormalize(ToTarget);

Vector2D LocalPosOpp = PointToLocalSpace(opp->Pos(),
                                         ToTargetNormalized,
                                         ToTargetNormalized.Perp(),
                                         from);
```

The first step is to assume A is looking directly at the "target" position (in this example, the position of player B) and move the opponent into A's local coordinate system. Figure 4.17 shows how all the opposing players in Figure 4.16 are positioned when moved into player A's local space.

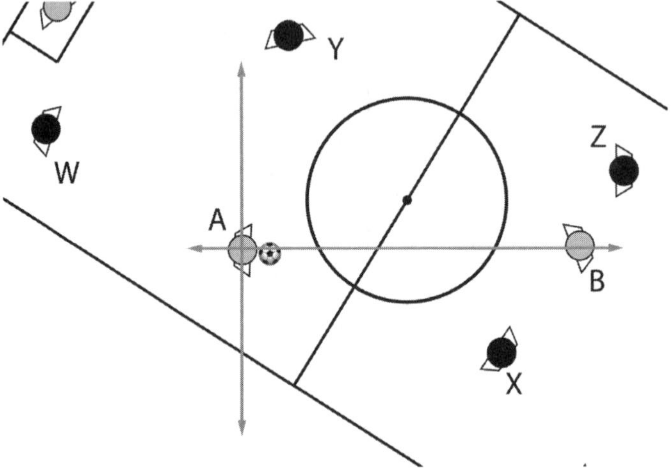

Figure 4.17. The players transformed into A's local space

```
//if opponent is behind the kicker then pass is considered okay (this is
//based on the assumption the ball is going to be kicked with a
//velocity greater than the opponent's max velocity)
if ( LocalPosOpp.x < 0 )
{
  return true;
}
```

An assumption is made that the ball will always be kicked with an initial velocity greater than a player's maximum speed. If this is true, any opponents situated behind the kicker's local *y*-axis may be removed from any further consideration. Therefore, given the example in Figure 4.17, W can be discarded.

Next, any opponents positioned farther away from the passing player than the target are considered. If the situation is as shown in Figure 4.16 and the target location of the pass is situated at the receiver's feet, then any opponent situated farther away than this may be immediately discarded. However, this method is also called to test the validity of potential passes that are situated to either side of the receiving player, such as the ones shown in Figure 4.18.

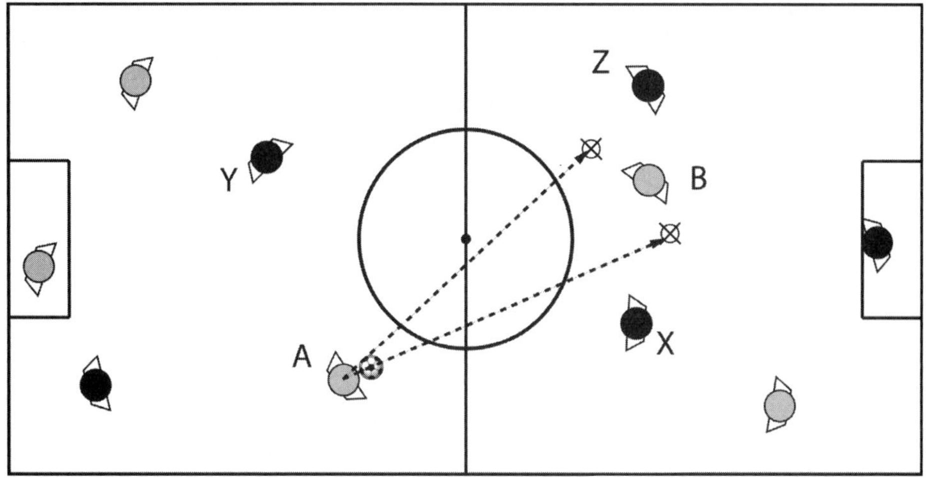

Figure 4.18. Passes to either side of the receiving player are also possible.

In this instance an additional test must be made to check that the opponent is farther away from the target position than the receiver. If so, then the opponent may be discarded.

```
//if the opponent is farther away than the target we need to consider if
//the opponent can reach the position before the receiver.
if (Vec2DDistanceSq(from, target) < Vec2DDistanceSq(opp->Pos(), from))
{
  //this condition is here because sometimes this function may be called
  //without reference to a receiver. (For example, you may want to find
  //out if a ball can reach a position on the field before an opponent
  //can get to it)
  if (receiver)
  {
    if (Vec2DDistanceSq(target, opp->Pos()) >
        Vec2DDistanceSq(target, receiver->Pos()))
    {
      return true;
    }
  }

  else
  {
    return true;
  }
}
```

The best chance an opponent situated between the two previous conditions has of intercepting the ball is to run to the point where the ball's trajectory is perpendicular to the opponent's position, shown as points Yp and Xp for players Y and X respectively in Figure 4.19.

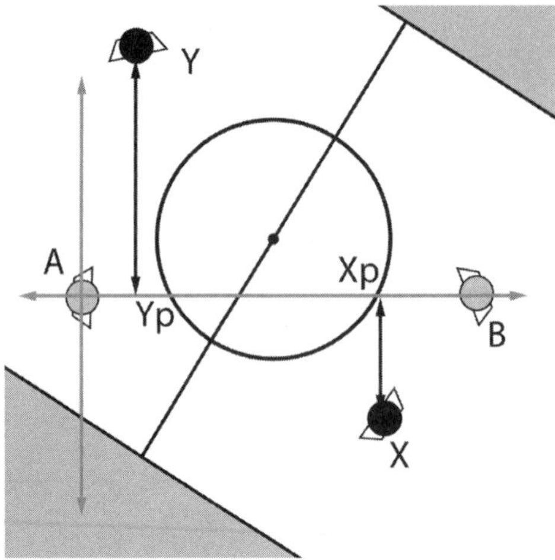

Figure 4.19. Testing the intercept points

To intercept the ball, an opponent must be able to reach this point before the ball gets there. To show you how to calculate if this is possible, let's examine the case of opponent Y.

First of all, the time taken for the ball to cover the distance from A to Yp is determined by calling `SoccerBall::TimeToCoverDistance`. This method was described in detail earlier, so you should understand how it works. Given this time, it's possible to calculate how far opponent Y can travel before the ball reaches point Yp (time * velocity). I call this distance Y's range, because it's the distance Y can travel in any direction in the specified amount of time. To this range must be added the radius of the soccer ball and the radius of the player's bounding circle. This range value now represents the player's "reach" given the time it takes for the ball to reach Yp.

The reach of Y and X are shown by the dotted circles in Figure 4.20.

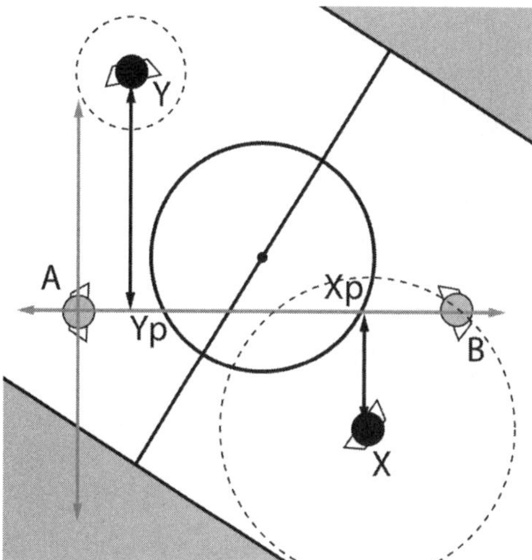

Figure 4.20. Opponent movement ranges

If the circle described by an opponent's reach intersects the *x*-axis, it indicates the opponent is able to intercept the ball within the allotted time. Therefore, in this example, it can be concluded that opponent Y is not a threat but opponent X is.

Here is the last snippet of code for you to examine.

```
  //calculate how long it takes the ball to cover the distance to the
  //position orthogonal to the opponent's position
  double TimeForBall =
  Pitch()->Ball()->TimeToCoverDistance(Vector2D(0,0),
                                       Vector2D(LocalPosOpp.x, 0),
                                       PassingForce);

  //now calculate how far the opponent can run in this time
  double reach = opp->MaxSpeed() * TimeForBall +
                 Pitch()->Ball()->BRadius()+
                 opp->BRadius();

  //if the distance to the opponent's y position is less than his running
  //range plus the radius of the ball and the opponent's radius, then the
  //ball can be intercepted
  if ( fabs(LocalPosOpp.y) < reach )
  {
    return false;
  }

  return true;
}
```

NOTE Technically speaking, the ranges shown in Figure 4.20 are incorrect. I've made the assumption that it takes zero time for the opponent to rotate to face its intercept point. To be accurate, the time needed to rotate should also be taken into consideration, in which case the range is described by an ellipse instead of a circle. Like so:

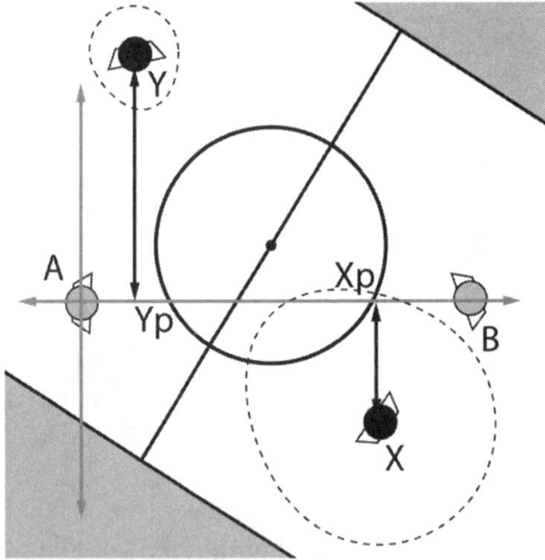

Figure 4.21

Obviously, it's a lot more expensive to calculate ellipse-line intersections, which is why circles are used instead.

SoccerTeam::CanShoot

One very important skill a soccer player has is, of course, the ability to score goals. A player who is in possession of the ball may query the `SoccerTeam::CanShoot` method to see if it's able to score a goal given the ball's current position and a value representing the force with which the player kicks the ball. If the method determines the player is able to shoot, it will return true and store the position the player should shoot at in a reference to a vector, `ShotTarget`.

The method works by randomly selecting a number of positions along the goal mouth and testing each of them in turn to check if the ball can be kicked to that point without being intercepted by any of the opposing players. See Figure 4.22.

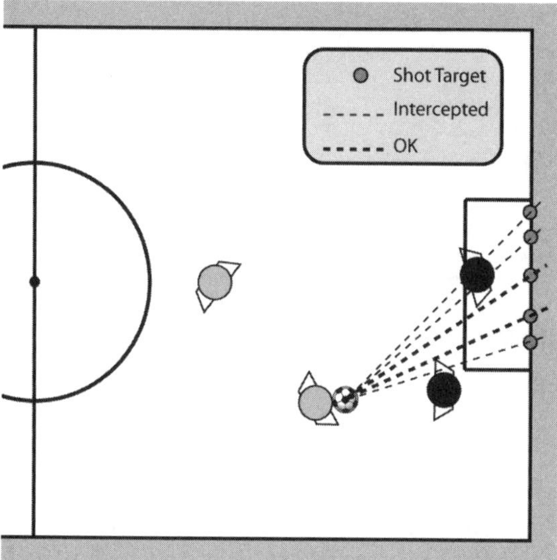

Figure 4.22. Randomly selected shot targets

Here is the code listing. (Notice how there is a check to make sure the kicking force is enough to move the ball over the goal line.)

```
bool SoccerTeam::CanShoot(Vector2D  BallPos,
                          double    power
                          Vector2D& ShotTarget)const
{
  //the number of randomly created shot targets this method will test
  int NumAttempts = Prm.NumAttemptsToFindValidStrike;

  while (NumAttempts--)
  {
    //choose a random position along the opponent's goal mouth. (making
    //sure the ball's radius is taken into account)
    ShotTarget = OpponentsGoal()->Center();

    //the y value of the shot position should lie somewhere between the two
    //goal posts (taking into consideration the ball diameter)
    int MinYVal = OpponentsGoal()->LeftPost().x + Pitch()->Ball()->BRadius();
    int MaxYVal = OpponentsGoal()->RightPost().x - Pitch()->Ball()->BRadius();

    ShotTarget.x = RandInt(MinYVal, MaxYVal);

    //make sure striking the ball with the given power is enough to drive
    //the ball over the goal line.
    double time = Pitch()->Ball()->TimeToCoverDistance(BallPos,
                                                       ShotTarget,
                                                       power);

    //if so, this shot is then tested to see if any of the opponents
    //can intercept it.
    if (time > 0)
```

```
    {
      if (isPassSafeFromAllOpponents(BallPos, ShotTarget, NULL, power))
      {
        return true;
      }
    }
  }

  return false;
}
```

SoccerTeam::FindPass

The FindPass method is called by a player to determine if a pass to a teammate is possible and, if so, which position and teammate is best to pass the ball to.

The method takes as parameters a pointer to the player requesting the pass; a reference to a pointer that will point to the receiving player (if a pass is found); a reference to a vector, PassTarget, to which will be assigned the position the pass will be made to; the power the ball will be kicked with; and a value representing the minimum distance a receiver should be from the passing player, MinPassingDistance.

The method then iterates through all the passer's teammates and calls GetBestPassToReceiver for each of those that are at least MinPassingDistance from the passer. GetBestPassToReceiver examines a number of potential passing locations for the teammate under consideration and, if a pass can be safely made, stores the best opportunity in the vector BallTarget.

After all the teammates have been considered, if a valid pass has been found, the one that is closest to the opponent's baseline is assigned to PassTarget and the pointer to the player that should receive the pass is assigned to receiver. The method then returns true.

Here is the listing for you to examine.

```
bool SoccerTeam::FindPass(const PlayerBase*const passer,
                         PlayerBase*&         receiver,
                         Vector2D&            PassTarget,
                         double               power,
                         double               MinPassingDistance)const
{

  std::vector<PlayerBase*>::const_iterator curPlyr = Members().begin();

  double    ClosestToGoalSoFar = MaxDouble;
  Vector2D BallTarget;

  //iterate through all this player's team members and calculate which
  //one is in a position to be passed the ball
```

```
  for (curPlyr; curPlyr != Members().end(); ++curPlyr)
  {
    //make sure the potential receiver being examined is not this player
    //and that it's farther away than the minimum pass distance
    if ( (*curPlyr != passer) &&
        (Vec2DDistanceSq(passer->Pos(), (*curPlyr)->Pos()) >
         MinPassingDistance*MinPassingDistance))
    {
      if (GetBestPassToReceiver(passer, *curPlyr, BallTarget, power))
      {
        //if the pass target is the closest to the opponent's goal line found
        //so far, keep a record of it
        double Dist2Goal = fabs(BallTarget.x - OpponentsGoal()->Center().x);

        if (Dist2Goal < ClosestToGoalSoFar)
        {
          ClosestToGoalSoFar = Dist2Goal;

          //keep a record of this player
          receiver = *curPlyr;

          //and the target
          PassTarget = BallTarget;
        }
      }
    }
  }//next team member

  if (receiver) return true;

  else return false;
}
```

SoccerTeam::GetBestPassToReceiver

Given a passer and a receiver, this method examines several different positions situated around the receiver to test if a pass may be made safely to any of them. If a pass can be made, the method stores the best pass — the one to the position closest to the opponent's baseline — in the parameter PassTarget, and returns true.

Let me talk you through the algorithm using the situation shown in Figure 4.23.

```
bool SoccerTeam::GetBestPassToReceiver(const PlayerBase* const passer,
                                       const PlayerBase* const receiver,
                                       Vector2D&               PassTarget,
                                       double                  power)const
{
```

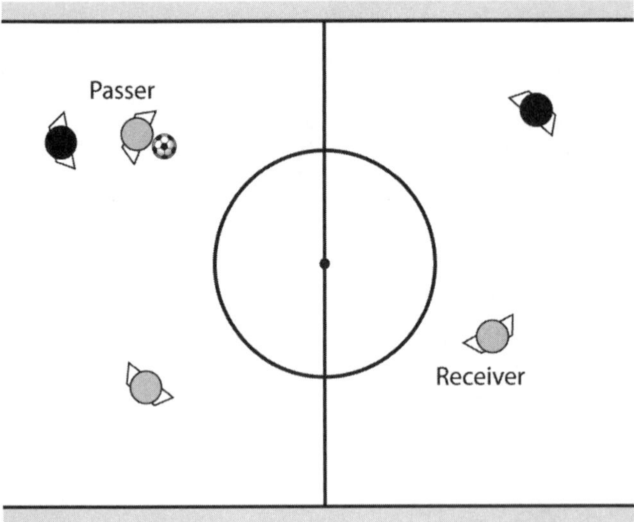

Figure 4.23. A typical passing situation

First of all, the method calculates how long it will take for the ball to reach the receiver's position and immediately returns false if it's impossible to reach this point given the kicking force, `power`.

```
//first, calculate how much time it will take for the ball to reach
//this receiver
double time = Pitch()->Ball()->TimeToCoverDistance(Pitch()->Ball()->Pos(),
                                                   receiver->Pos(),
                                                   power);

//return false if ball cannot reach the receiver after having been
//kicked with the given power
if (time <= 0) return false;
```

It's now possible to calculate how far the receiver is able to move within this time, using the equation $\Delta x = v\Delta t$. The intercept points of the tangents from the ball to this range circle represent the limits of the receiver's pass envelope. See Figure 4.24.

```
//the maximum distance the receiver can cover in this time
double InterceptRange = time * receiver->MaxSpeed();
```

In other words, assuming it does not waste time turning around or accelerating to maximum speed, the receiver can reach positions ip1 or ip2 *just* in time to intercept the ball. However in reality, this distance is often too large, especially if the distance between the receiver and passer is reaching the limits within which a pass can be made (often ip1 and ip2 will end up situated outside the playing area). It's much better to consider passes to positions that lay well within this region. This will reduce the chance of opponents intercepting the ball and also make the pass less prone to

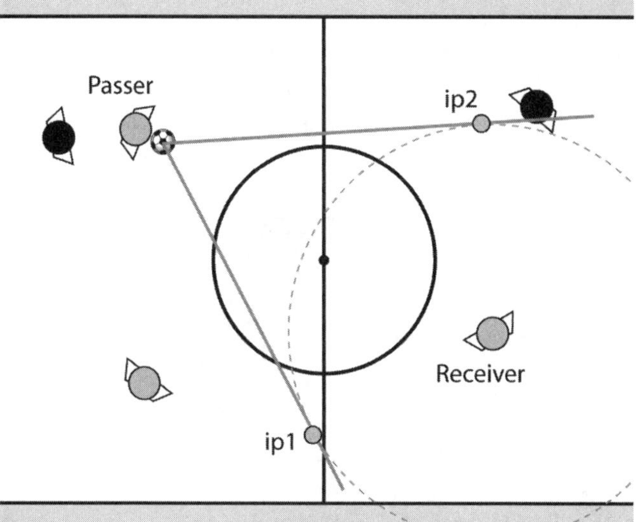

Figure 4.24. The limits of the receiver's range

unforeseen difficulties (such as the receiver having to maneuver around opponents to reach the pass target). It also gives the receiver some "space," some time in which it can reach the position and then orient itself properly in time to receive the pass. With this in mind, the intercept range is scaled down to about a third of its original size. See Figure 4.25.

```
//Scale down the intercept range
const double ScalingFactor = 0.3;
InterceptRange *= ScalingFactor;
```

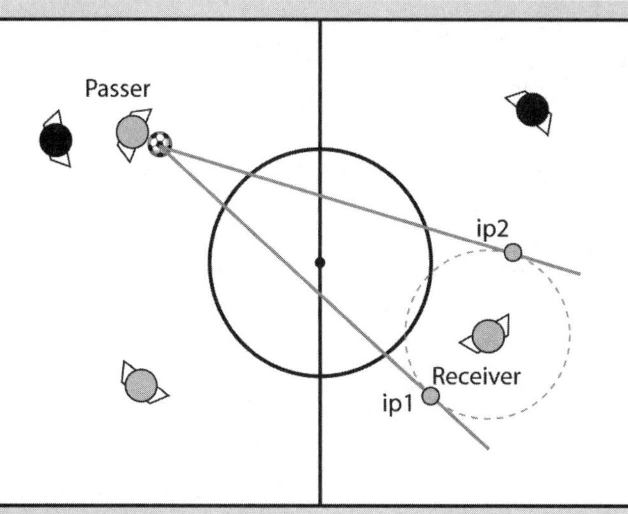

Figure 4.25. The receiver's range is reduced.

As you can see, this looks much more reasonable and more like the type of passing range a human soccer player would consider. The next step is to calculate the positions of ip1 and ip2. These will be considered as potential passing targets. In addition, the method will also consider a pass directly to the receiver's current location. These three positions are stored in the array `Passes`.

```
//calculate the pass targets that are positioned at the intercepts
//of the tangents from the ball to the receiver's range circle.
Vector2D ip1, ip2;

GetTangentPoints(receiver->Pos(),
                 InterceptRange,
                 Pitch()->Ball()->Pos(),
                 ip1,
                 ip2);

const int NumPassesToTry = 3;
Vector2D Passes[NumPassesToTry] = {ip1, receiver->Pos(), ip2};
```

Finally, the method iterates through each potential pass to make sure the position is located within the playing area and to ensure it's safe from an interception attempt by any opponents.

The loop makes a note of the best valid pass it examines and returns the result accordingly.

```
// this pass is the best found so far if it's:
//
// 1. Farther upfield than the closest valid pass for this receiver
//    found so far
// 2. Within the playing area
// 3. Cannot be intercepted by any opponents

double ClosestSoFar = MaxDouble;
bool   bResult      = false;

for (int pass=0; pass<NumPassesToTry; ++pass)
{
  double dist = fabs(Passes[pass].x - OpponentsGoal()->Center().x);

  if (( dist < ClosestSoFar) &&
      Pitch()->PlayingArea()->Inside(Passes[pass]) &&
      isPassSafeFromAllOpponents(Pitch()->Ball()->Pos(),
                                 Passes[pass],
                                 receiver,
                                 power))

  {
    ClosestSoFar = dist;
    PassTarget   = Passes[pass];
    bResult      = true;
  }
}
```

```
  return bResult;
}
```

Making Estimates and Assumptions Work for You

You have probably noticed I've used many estimates and assumptions throughout the calculations described in this chapter. At first, this may seem like a bad thing because, as programmers, we're used to making sure everything works "just so," like perfect clockwork automatons.

Sometimes, however, it's beneficial to design your game's AI in such a way that it *makes occasional mistakes.* This, as far as making computer game AI goes, can be a Good Thing. Why? Because it's more realistic. Humans make mistakes and misjudgments all the time, and therefore the occasional mistake made by the AI makes for a much more entertaining experience from a human player's perspective.

There are two ways of inducing mistakes. The first is to make the AI "perfect" and dumb it down. The second is to *allow* "errors" to creep in by making assumptions or estimates when designing the algorithms the AI uses. You have seen both of these methods used in Simple Soccer. An example of the former is when random noise is used to introduce a small amount of error in direction every time the ball is kicked. An example of the latter is where circles instead of ellipses are used to describe an opponent's intercept range.

When deciding how to create error and uncertainty in your AI, you must examine each appropriate algorithm carefully. My advice is this: If an algorithm is easy to code and doesn't require much processor time, do it the "correct" way, make it perfect, and dumb down to taste. Otherwise, check if it's possible to make any assumptions or estimates to help reduce the complexity of the algorithm. If your algorithm can be simplified in this way, code it, then make sure you test it thoroughly to ensure the AI performs satisfactorily.

Summing Up

Simple Soccer demonstrates how team-based AI for a sports game can be created using only a handful of basic AI techniques. Of course, as it stands, the behavior is neither particularly sophisticated nor complete. As your knowledge of AI techniques and experience increase you will see many areas where the design of Simple Soccer can be improved or added to. For starters, though, you might like to try your hand at some of the following practice exercises.

Practice Makes Perfect

The following exercises have been designed to reinforce each of the different skills you have learned so far in the book. I hope you have a lot of fun completing them.

1. As it stands, the dribbling behavior is poor: If the supporting player cannot move into a suitable position quickly enough, the attacker will happily dribble the ball in a straight line directly into the hands of the opposing team's goalkeeper (or into the rear wall, whichever comes first). Improve this behavior by adding logic to prevent the attacker from moving too far ahead of the supporting player. Found that easy? What other ways can you think of to improve an attacker's behavior? Can you create players that can dribble the ball *around* opponents?
2. Other than the change of home regions, there isn't any defensive play implemented in the example code. Create players that are able to interpose themselves between the opponent's attacking and supporting players.
3. Adjust the support spot calculator to try different scoring schemes. There are many options for you to experiment with here. For example, you could rate a position for the quality of being equidistant from all the opponents or for the quality of being ahead of the controlling player's position. You could even vary the rating scheme based on where the controlling and supporting players are located.
4. Create additional states at the team level to implement more varied tactics. In addition to just assigning different home regions to the players, create states that assign roles to some of the players too. One tactic might be to hem in the opposing team's attacking player by assigning players to surround it. Another could be to command some of the players to stay close — to "mark" in soccer terminology — any of the opponents the AI perceives as a threat (like one situated near the home goal for example).
5. Change the program so that a passing player kicks the ball with the correct force required for it to arrive at the receiver's feet with a velocity of your choice.
6. Introduce the idea of stamina. All players start off with the same amount of stamina and as they run around the field they use it up. The less stamina they have, the slower they can run and the less power they can put into their shots. They can only recover their stamina if they are motionless.
7. Implement a referee. This is not as easy as it first sounds. The referee must always try to position itself where it can see the ball and players without interfering with the action.

NOTE To assist you, I've left some of the debug code in the Simple Soccer project. When you compile and run the program, you will see an additional window to which you can output debug information. Any information sent to this window is also output to a file called DebugLog.txt that you can view after the program has been exited. (Be careful though — if you are outputting lots of debug info, this text file can grow quickly.)

To write to the debug console, use the format:

```
debug_con << "This is a number : " << 3 << "";
```

The "" at the end of the line gives a line return. You can send any type to the console that has overloaded the << operator.

When you have finished debugging you can remove the console by commenting out the line `#define DEBUG` in the DebugConsole.h file. This will route all your debugging comments to a dummy stream.

In addition to the debug console, the main program has options accessible through the menus to give you immediate visual feedback of some of the key concepts.

Chapter 5

The Secret Life of Graphs

This chapter focuses on a mind-bogglingly useful mathematical abstraction called a *graph*. You'll be using graphs a lot in game AI. In fact, you've already seen them: The state transition bubble diagrams from Chapter 1 are a type of graph. Graphs and their baby brothers, *trees*, are used by game AI programmers all the time. They can be used for a whole variety of things — from enabling game agents to travel between two points efficiently, to deciding what to build next in a strategy game and solving puzzles.

The first part of this chapter will be spent introducing you to the different kinds of graphs and the terminology associated with them. You'll learn what graphs actually are, how they can be used, and how to code them efficiently. The remainder of the chapter will describe, in lots of detail, many of the search algorithms available to exploit the full power of graphs.

Graphs

When developing the AI for games, one of the most common uses of graphs is to represent a network of paths an agent can use to navigate around its environment. When I first learned this I was confused, as all my life I'd known a graph to look like the graphs I was taught to draw at

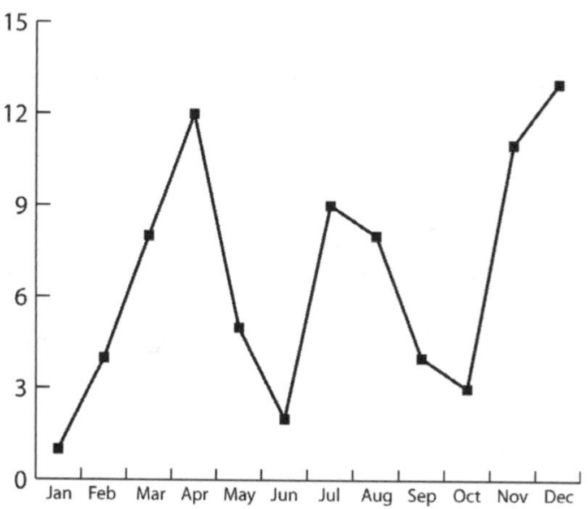

Figure 5.1. A typical graph

school — something like the familiar shape shown in Figure 5.1, for example.

I'd always thought of graphs as useful for visualizing the rise and fall of some property, like the temperature charts shown on TV weather reports or sales figures, stuff like that, and so I was left wondering how this sort of graph could possibly be used to represent the paths weaving around the walls and obstacles in a game environment. If you have never studied graph theory, then this is possibly the way you think about graphs too. I guess it's just the way we are conditioned. However, let me show you something interesting. Check out Figure 5.2.

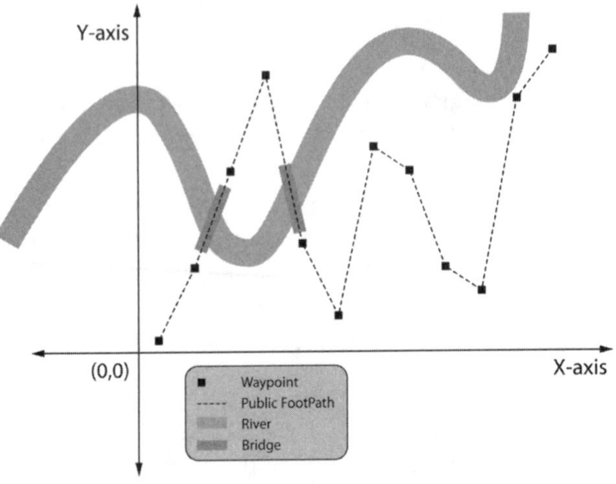

Figure 5.2

This is the same graph, but I've changed the axis labeling to represent the *x* and *y* coordinates of Cartesian space, adding a few cosmetic embellishments so that now it represents a path meandering close to a river. In fact it looks like something your average person on the street would refer to as a *map*. Indeed, the whole image *is* a map, but the series of waypoints and the footpath connecting them is represented by a very simple graph. Now I realize a few of you will be thinking this is no big deal, but I believe that for many this subtle shift in perspective can be a revelation. It certainly was for me. In graph terminology, the waypoints are called *nodes* (or sometimes vectors) and the footpaths connecting them are called *edges* (or sometimes *arcs*).

Figure 5.3 shows some more examples of graphs. As you can see, they can assume a wide variety of configurations.

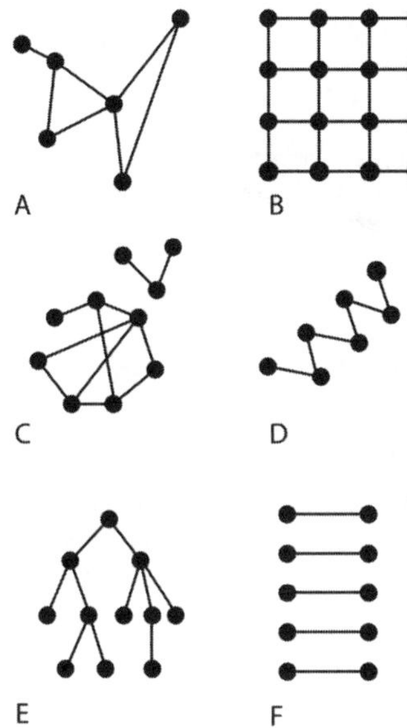

Figure 5.3. Examples of graphs

In a broader context, a graph is a symbolic representation of a network, and while the nodes and edges may represent a spatial relationship, such as the example previously discussed, this doesn't have to be the case. Graphs can be used to represent networks of any kind, from telephone networks and the World Wide Web to electronic circuits and artificial neural networks.

NOTE Graphs can be either *connected* or *unconnected*. A graph is considered to be connected when it's possible to trace a path from *every* single node to *every* other.

Graphs A, B, D, and E in Figure 5.3 are examples of connected graphs. Graphs C and F are examples of unconnected graphs.

A More Formal Description

A graph, G, can be formally defined as the set of nodes or vertices, N, linking with the set of edges, E. You will often find this written as:

$$G = \{N, E\} \tag{5.1}$$

If each node in a graph is labeled with an integer in the range 0 to (N-1), an edge can now be referred to by the nodes it connects, for example 3-5 or 19-7.

Many graphs have edges that are *weighted* — they contain information about the *cost* of moving from one node to another. For example, in the graph shown in Figure 5.2, the cost of traversing an edge is the distance between the two nodes it connects. In a graph representing the tech-tree for a Warcraft-like RTS game the edges might indicate the resources required to upgrade each unit.

NOTE Although a graph may have multiple connections to the same node or even looped connections connecting a node to itself, these features are rarely necessary for game AI and will not be considered in the following pages.

Trees

Most programmers are aware of the tree data structure. Trees are used profusely throughout all programming disciplines. However, you may not realize that trees are the subset of graphs comprising all graphs that are *acyclic* (containing no cyclic paths). Graph E in Figure 5.3 is a tree, and that's probably the shape you are familiar with, but graph D is also a tree. Graph F is a *forest* of trees.

Graph Density

The ratio of edges to nodes indicates whether a graph is *sparse* or *dense*. Sparse graphs have few connections per node and dense graphs many. Figure 5.4 shows an example of both types. In order to reduce complexity and keep CPU and memory usage to a minimum, you should prefer sparse graphs whenever possible, for example, when designing a graph for use in path planning (see Chapter 8).

Knowing whether a graph is dense or sparse is helpful when selecting an appropriate data structure to encode the graph's structure, since an implementation that is efficient for a dense graph is probably not going to be efficient for one that is sparse.

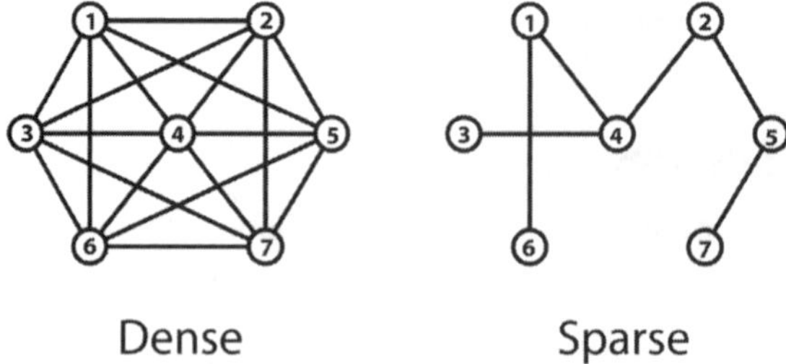

Figure 5.4. Examples of dense and sparse graphs

Digraphs

So far we have assumed that if it's possible to travel from node A to node B, then it's also possible to do the reverse. This may not always be the case. Sometimes you may need to implement a graph where the connections are directional. For example, your game may have a "death-slide" positioned across a river. An agent should only be able to traverse this one way — from the top to the bottom — so we have to find a way of representing this type of connection.

Alternatively, it may be possible to travel between two nodes in either direction but the *cost* of each traversal may be different. A good example of this is if you want your agents to take the terrain's gradients into consideration. After all, it's easy for a vehicle to travel efficiently and quickly downhill, but it takes a lot more fuel for a vehicle to move uphill, and its top speed will be much slower. We can reflect this information using a graph called a *digraph*, or DAG for short.

A digraph has edges that are *directed*, or one way. The nodes that define a directed edge are known as an *ordered pair* and specify the direction of the edge. For example, the ordered pair 16-6 indicates that it's possible to travel from node 16 to node 6 but not from node 6 to 16. In this example, node 16 is known as the *source* node and node 6 the *destination* node.

Figure 5.5 shows a small digraph. The edges are drawn using arrows to indicate their direction.

When designing a data structure for graphs it's often helpful to think of undirected graphs as digraphs with two edges connecting each connected pair of nodes. This is convenient because both types of graphs (directed and undirected) can then be represented by the same data structure. For example, the sparse undirected graph shown in Figure 5.4 can be represented by the digraph shown in Figure 5.6.

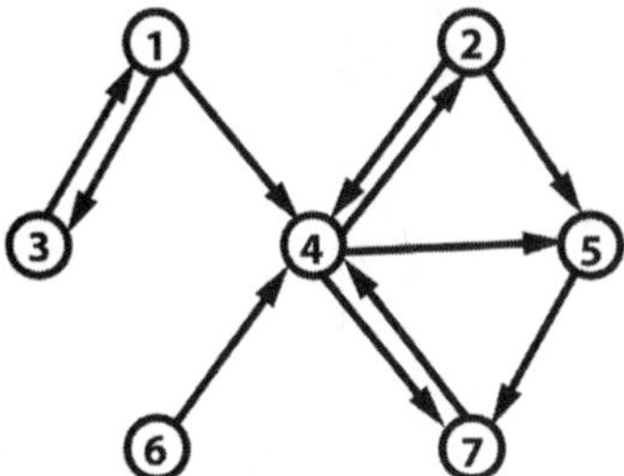

Figure 5.5. A simple digraph. Note that in the world of digraphs, unconnected graphs are more frequent as they may contain nodes that are only reachable from one direction.

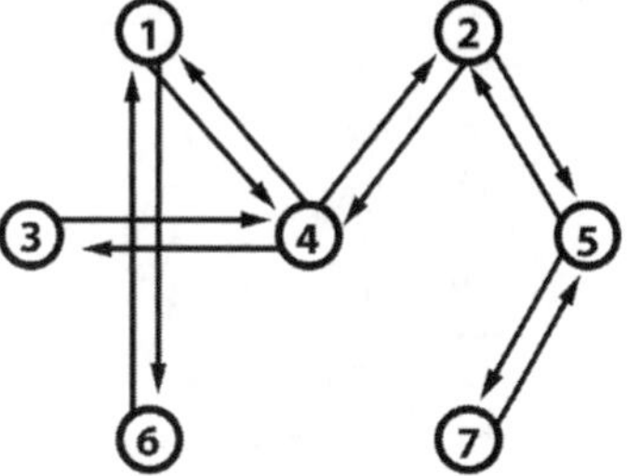

Figure 5.6. Representing an undirected graph as a digraph

Graphs in Game AI

Before we move on to the implementation of the code for a graph, let's take a quick look at some of the things you can use a graph for in the development of a game's AI, starting with the most popular use: navigation or pathfinding.

Navigation Graphs

A *navigation graph*, or *navgraph*, is an abstraction of all the locations in a game environment the game agents may visit and of all the connections between those points. Consequently, a well-designed navgraph is a data structure embodying *all* the possible paths through the game environment and is therefore extremely handy for helping your game agents decide how to get from A to B.

Each node in a navgraph usually represents the position of a key area or object within the environment and each edge represents the connections between those points. Furthermore, each edge will have an associated cost, which in the simplest case represents the distance between the nodes it connects. This type of graph is known to mathematicians as a *Euclidian graph*. Figure 5.7 shows a navigation graph created for a small walled environment and highlights a *path* through that graph.

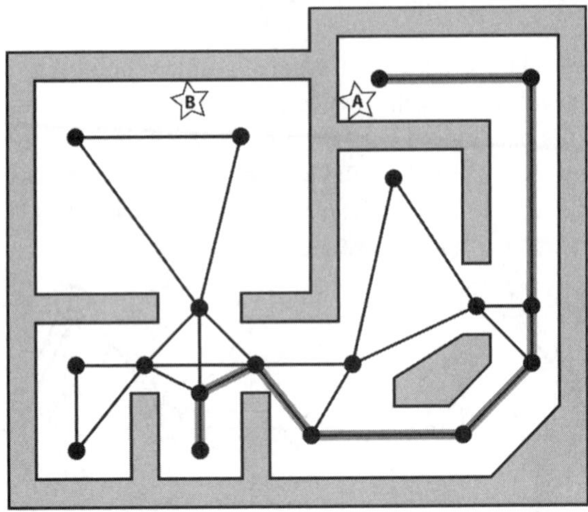

Figure 5.7. A simple navigation graph. The collection of all the edges and nodes constitute the graph. The highlighted edges represent a possible path through the graph.

I'd like to make it clear that a game agent is not restricted to moving along the graph edges as though it were a train traveling along rails. An agent can move to any unobstructed position within the game environment, but it uses the navigation graph to negotiate its environment — to plan paths between two or more points and to traverse them. For example, if an agent positioned at point A finds it necessary to move to position B, it can use the navgraph to calculate the best route between the nodes closest to those points.

Figure 5.7 is typical of a navigation graph created for a first-person shooter. Other types of games may find a different node layout more effective. RTS/RPG type games, for instance, are often based upon a grid of tiles or cells, where each tile represents a different type of terrain such as grass, road, mud, etc. Therefore, it's convenient to create a graph using the center points of each tile and assigning edge costs based upon the distance between cells weighted for the terrain type the edge moves over. This approach enables game agents to easily calculate paths that avoid water, prefer traveling on roads to mud, and meander around mountains. Figure 5.8 shows the sort of cell layout you can expect to see utilized in an RTS/RPG.

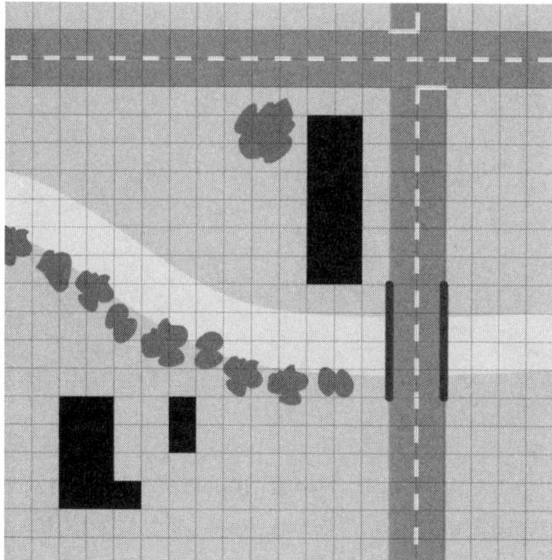

Figure 5.8. A typical cell-based environment. Although not shown for clarity, graph nodes are positioned in the centers of the cells with edges connecting adjacent nodes. The PathFinder demo for this chapter uses this type of navgraph.

Because some RTS/RPG games can use literally hundreds of thousands of cells, the disadvantage of this approach is that the graphs can be extremely large, costly to search, and take up large amounts of memory. Fortunately for AI developers, some of these problems can be avoided using techniques you will learn later in the book.

⌘ **TIP** If you are creating a "stealth 'em up" like the games Thief and Thief 2 by Looking Glass Studios/Eidos Interactive, you can use a navgraph that has its edges weighted by how much sound a character would make traversing the edge. Edges that are quiet to traverse such as those along carpet would have low edge weights, and loud edges high values. Designing your graphs this way enables your game characters to find the quietest path between two rooms.

Dependency Graphs

Dependency graphs are used in resource management type games to describe the dependencies between the various buildings, materials, units, and technologies available to a player. Figure 5.9 shows part of a dependency graph created for such a game. This kind of graph makes it easy to see what prerequisites are required for the creation of each type of resource.

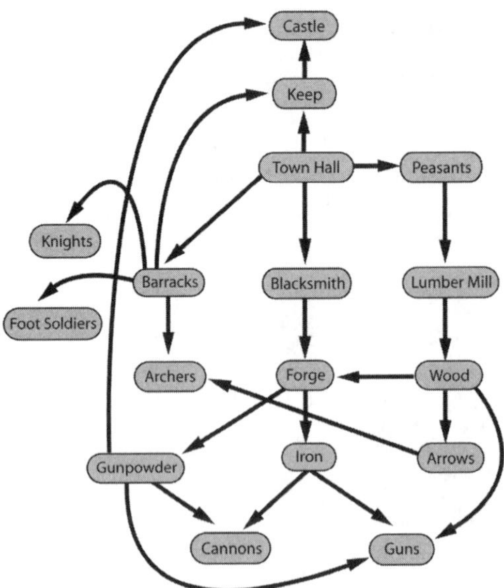

Figure 5.9. A simple dependency graph

Dependency graphs are invaluable when designing an AI for this type of genre because the AI can use them to decide on strategies, predict the future status of an opponent, and assign resources effectively. Here are some examples based upon the graph shown in the figure.

1. If the AI is preparing for battle and ascertains that archers are going to be advantageous, it can examine the dependency graph to conclude that before it can produce archers, it must first make sure it has a barracks and the technology of arrows. It also knows that in order to produce arrows it must have a lumber mill producing wood. Therefore, if the AI already has a lumber mill it can assign resources to building a barracks or vice versa. If the AI has neither a barracks nor a lumber mill it can inspect the technology graph further to determine that it's probably advantageous to build the barracks *before* the lumber mill. Why? Because the barracks is a prerequisite for three different kinds of fighting unit, whereas a lumber mill is only a prerequisite for producing wood. The AI has already determined a battle is imminent, so it should realize (if you've designed it correctly, of course) that it should be putting resources into making fighting units as soon as possible, because as we all know, knights and foot soldiers make better warriors than planks of wood!
2. If an enemy foot soldier carrying a *gun* comes into the AI's territory, the AI can work *backward* through the graph to conclude that:
   - The enemy *must* have already built a forge and a lumber mill.
   - The enemy *must* have developed the technology of gunpowder.
   - The enemy *must* be producing the resources of wood and iron.

Further examination of the graph would indicate that the enemy probably either has cannons or is currently building them. Nasty!

The AI can use this information to decide on the best plan of attack. For example, the AI would know that to prevent any more gun-toting enemies from reaching its territory, it should target the enemy's forge and lumber mill. It can also infer that sending an assassin to hit the enemy blacksmith would weaken its foe considerably, and perhaps devote resources toward creating an assassin for this purpose.

3. Often, a technology or specific unit is key to a team winning a game. If the costs of building each resource are assigned to the dependency graph's edges, then the AI can use this information to calculate the most efficient route to produce that resource.

State Graphs

A *state graph* is a representation of every possible state a system can be in and the transitions between those states. This collection of a system's potential states is known as its *state space*. A graph of this type can be searched to see if a particular state is possible or to find the most efficient route to a specific state.

Let's look at a simple example using the "Towers of Hanoi" puzzle.

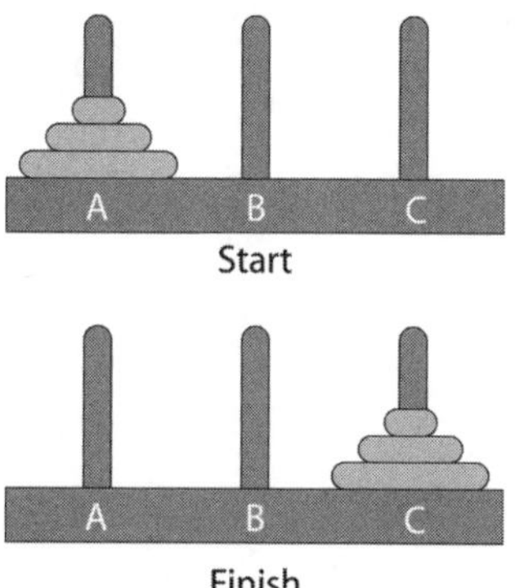

Figure 5.10. The Towers of Hanoi

In this simple version of the puzzle there are three pegs — A, B, and C — and three rings of varying sizes that fit over the pegs. The rings start off positioned in order of size over peg A. The aim of the puzzle is to move the rings until they are all positioned on peg C, also in order of size. Only one ring may be moved at a time. A ring may be placed either on an empty peg or on top of a ring that is bigger than itself.

We can represent the state space of this puzzle using a graph where each node represents one of the possible states the puzzle may occupy. The edges of the graph represent the transitions between the states: If it's possible to move directly from one state to another there will be an edge connecting the two states; otherwise there will be no connection. The graph is constructed by first creating a node that contains the start state of the puzzle. This is known as the *root node*. The root node is then expanded by adding all the states attainable from that node to the graph, and then each of those states is expanded, and so on, until all the possible states and transitions have been added to the graph. Each state's previous state is called its *parent* state, and the new state is called the *child* of the parent state.

Figure 5.11 shows this process. An arrow connecting two states means that one state can be reached from the other by moving one of the disks. The graph gets complicated quickly, so I've omitted many of the possible states to make it easier to see one of the paths leading to a solution.

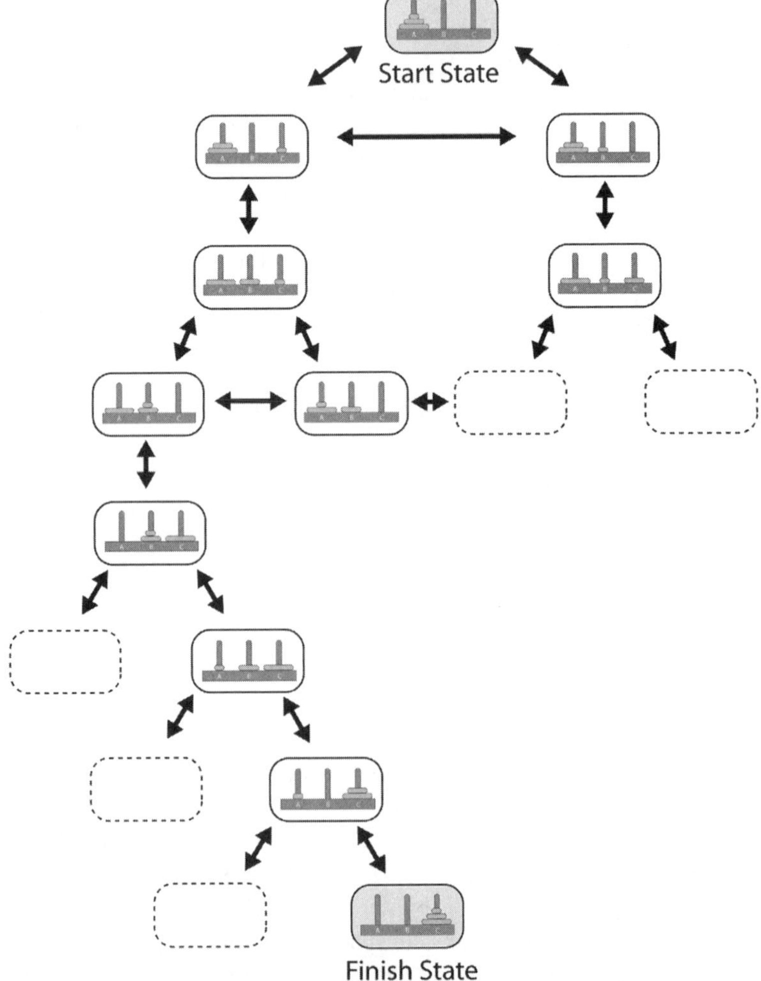

Figure 5.11. Expanding the states for the Towers of Hanoi puzzle. The dotted boxes indicate states that have not been expanded.

A state graph can easily be searched to find a goal state. In this example, the goal state is one where all the pieces are positioned on peg C in the correct order. By searching the state space it's possible to not only find a single solution, but to find every possible solution or the solution requiring the fewest moves (or the most moves if that's what you are looking for).

The average number of child nodes radiating from each parent node is known as a graph's *branching factor*. For some problems, such as the puzzle example we have discussed here, the branching factor is low — on the order of one to three branches per node — making it possible to represent with a graph the entire state space in a computer's memory. For many domains though, the branching factor is much higher and the number of potential states grows enormously as the distance from the root node (the depth of the graph) increases. With these types of systems it's impossible to represent the entire state space because it will quickly exceed the memory capabilities of even the most powerful computer. Even if such a graph could be stored, it would still take eons to complete a search. Consequently, these types of graphs are created and searched by expanding a few nodes at a time, typically (but not always) using algorithms that direct the search toward the goal state.

Implementing a Graph Class

Two popular data structures used to represent graphs are *adjacency matrices* and *adjacency lists*. Adjacency matrix graphs use a two-dimensional matrix of Booleans or floats to store a graph's connectivity information. Booleans are used if there is no cost associated with traversing an edge and floats are used when there is an associated cost, such as for a navigation graph where each edge represents the distance between two nodes. The exact implementation is, of course, up to the designer and the needs of his problem. Figure 5.12 shows what the adjacency matrix looks like for the digraph in Figure 5.6.

	①	②	③	④	⑤	⑥	⑦
①	0	0	0	1	0	1	0
②	0	0	0	1	1	0	0
③	0	0	0	1	0	0	0
④	1	1	1	0	0	0	0
⑤	0	1	0	0	0	0	1
⑥	1	0	0	0	0	0	0
⑦	0	0	0	0	1	0	0

Figure 5.12. An adjacency matrix

Each “1” represents a connection between two nodes, and each “0” represents the lack of a connection. By reading the values directly off the matrix from Figure 5.12, we know that there is no connection from node 2 to 6, but there is an edge connecting 4 to 2.

Adjacency matrices are intuitive, but for large sparse graphs this type of representation is inefficient as most of the matrix is used storing unnecessary zero values. A much better data structure for sparse graphs (the most commonly occurring graphs in game AI) is the adjacency list.

For each node present, an adjacency list graph stores a linked list of all its adjacent edges. Figure 5.13 shows how this works for the previous example.

①→4→6
②→4→5
③→4
④→1→2→3
⑤→2→7
⑥→1
⑦→5

Figure 5.13. An adjacency list representation of the digraph from Figure 5.6

Adjacency lists are efficient for storing sparse graphs because they don’t waste space storing null connections. The amount of space required to store a graph using this type of data structure is proportional to N + E (number of nodes + number of edges), whereas for an adjacency matrix it is proportional to N^2 (number of nodes squared).

As most of the graphs you will come across in AI game development are sparse, an adjacency list will frequently be your data structure of choice. With this in mind let’s take a look at the source code required to implement such a graph.

The GraphNode Class

GraphNode encapsulates the minimum information a node requires for an adjacency list graph representation: a unique identifying number, or index.

Here’s the listing of the graph node declaration:

```
class GraphNode
{
protected:

  //every node has an index. A valid index is >= 0
  int        m_iIndex;

public:
```

```
  GraphNode():m_iIndex(invalid_node_index){}
  GraphNode(int idx):m_iIndex(idx){}

  virtual ~GraphNode(){}

  int  Index()const;
  void SetIndex(int NewIndex);
};
```

Because often you will require that a node contains additional information, GraphNode is typically used as a base class from which to derive custom-built nodes. For example, a navigation graph's nodes must store spatial information, and a dependency graph's nodes must contain information about the assets they represent.

A node class designed for use within a navigation graph might look something like this:

```
template < class extra_info = void*>
class NavGraphNode : public GraphNode
{
protected:

  //the node's position
  Vector2D     m_vPosition;

  //often you will require a navgraph node to contain additional information.
  //For example a node might represent a pickup such as armor in which
  //case m_ExtraInfo could be an enumerated value denoting the pickup type,
  //thereby enabling a search algorithm to search a graph for specific items.
  //Going one step further, m_ExtraInfo could be a pointer to the instance of
  //the item type the node is twinned with. This would allow a search algorithm
  //to test the status of the pickup during the search. See Chapter 8 for further
  //info.
  extra_info  m_ExtraInfo;

public:

  /*INTERFACE OMITTED */
};
```

Please note that although the node class listed here uses a 2D vector to represent a node's position, a graph can exist in any number of dimensions you like. If you are creating a navigation graph for a 3D game, simply use 3D vectors. Everything will work just the same.

The GraphEdge Class

The GraphEdge class encapsulates the basic information required to denote a connection between two graph nodes. Here's the code:

```
class GraphEdge
{
protected:
```

```
  //An edge connects two nodes. Valid node indices are always positive.
  int     m_iFrom;
  int     m_iTo;

  //the cost of traversing the edge
  double   m_dCost;

public:

  //ctors
  GraphEdge(int from, int to, double cost):m_dCost(cost),
                                           m_iFrom(from),
                                           m_iTo(to)
  {}

  GraphEdge(int from, int to):m_dCost(1.0),
                              m_iFrom(from),
                              m_iTo(to)
  {}

  GraphEdge():m_dCost(1.0),
              m_iFrom(invalid_node_index),
              m_iTo(invalid_node_index)
  {}
```

Occasionally it's useful to be able to create a `GraphEdge` with either or both indices set to an "invalid" (negative) value. The enumerated value `invalid_node_index` found in the file NodeTypeEnumerations.h is used here to initialize `From` and `To` in the default constructor.

```
  virtual ~GraphEdge(){}

  int   From()const;
  void  SetFrom(int NewIndex);

  int   To()const;
  void  SetTo(int NewIndex);

  double Cost()const;
  void  SetCost(double NewCost);
};
```

If you are working on a platform where memory use is a much greater concern than the speed of searching a graph, you can get good savings on cell-based graphs (or graphs of equal or greater density) by not explicitly storing the cost of each edge. Instead, you can save memory by omitting the cost field from the `GraphEdge` class and calculate the cost "on-the-fly" using a function of attributes of its two adjacent nodes. For example, if the edge cost is equal to the distance between two nodes, the function would be the Euclidean distance. Something like:

```
//cost from A to B
cost = Distance(NodeA.Position, NodeB.Position)
```

Because there are usually eight times more edges than vertices in this type of graph, the memory savings can be considerable when large numbers of nodes are involved.

The SparseGraph Class

Graph nodes and edges are grouped together in the SparseGraph class. This is implemented as a class template, enabling this type of graph to use any appropriate node and edge types. Algorithms that operate on graphs should be able to access the node and edge data quickly. With this in mind, the SparseGraph class is designed so that each node's index number keys directly into a vector of graph nodes (m_Nodes) and a vector of adjacency edge lists (m_Edges), giving a lookup time of O(1). However, this creates a problem when a node is removed from the graph, since if it were to be removed from m_Nodes also, all the indexing for any higher indexed nodes would be invalidated. Therefore, instead of erasing the node from the vector, its index is set to the enumerated value invalid_node_index, and all the methods of SparseGraph treat this value as if there were no node present.

Here is the listing of SparseGraph's declaration.

```
template <class node_type, class edge_type>
class SparseGraph
{
public:

  //enable easy client access to the edge and node types used in the graph
  typedef edge_type                EdgeType;
  typedef node_type                NodeType;

  //a few more useful typedefs
  typedef std::vector<node_type>   NodeVector;
  typedef std::list<edge_type>     EdgeList;
  typedef std::vector<EdgeList>    EdgeListVector;


private:

  //the nodes that comprise this graph
  NodeVector      m_Nodes;

  //a vector of adjacency edge lists. (each node index keys into the
  //list of edges associated with that node)
  EdgeListVector  m_Edges;

  //is this a directed graph?
  bool            m_bDigraph;
```

```
  //the index of the next node to be added
  int            m_iNextNodeIndex;


  /* EXTRANEOUS DETAIL OMITTED */


public:

  //ctor
  SparseGraph(bool digraph): m_iNextNodeIndex(0), m_bDigraph(digraph){}

  //returns the node at the given index
  const NodeType&  GetNode(int idx)const;

  //non-const version
  NodeType&  GetNode(int idx);

  //const method for obtaining a reference to an edge
  const EdgeType& GetEdge(int from, int to)const;

  //non const version
  EdgeType& GetEdge(int from, int to);

  //retrieves the next free node index
  int   GetNextFreeNodeIndex()const;

  //adds a node to the graph and returns its index
  int   AddNode(NodeType node);

  //removes a node by setting its index to invalid_node_index
  void  RemoveNode(int node);

  //methods to add and remove edges
  void  AddEdge(EdgeType edge);
  void  RemoveEdge(int from, int to);
```

Note how the class has methods for removing nodes and edges. This is a necessary feature if your graph is *dynamic* and has the ability to change as the game progresses. For example, it's easy to represent the disruption wreaked by an earthquake by removing (and sometimes by adding) edges from a navigation graph. Alternatively, gameplay similar to that of Command & Conquer can add and remove edges as players build or blast away bridges and walls.

```
  //returns the number of active + inactive nodes present in the graph
  int   NumNodes()const;

  //returns the number of active nodes present in the graph
  int   NumActiveNodes()const;

  //returns the number of edges present in the graph
  int   NumEdges()const;
```

```
  //returns true if the graph is directed
  bool  isDigraph()const;

  //returns true if the graph contains no nodes
  bool  isEmpty()const;

  //returns true if a node with the given index is present in the graph
  bool isPresent(int nd)const;

  //methods for loading and saving graphs from an open file stream or from
  //a filename
  bool  Save(const char* FileName)const;
  bool  Save(std::ofstream& stream)const;
  bool  Load(const char* FileName);
  bool  Load(std::ifstream& stream);

  //clears the graph ready for new node insertions
  void Clear();

  //iterators clients may use to access nodes and edges
  class ConstEdgeIterator;
  class EdgeIterator;
  class NodeIterator;
  class ConstNodeIterator;
};
```

From the information in this section you have learned that graphs are a powerful tool to have at your disposal. However, the graph data structure alone has few uses. Much of the power of graphs is only realized when they are operated upon by algorithms designed to explore them, either to find a specific node or to find a path between nodes. The rest of this chapter is devoted to a study of several of those algorithms.

Graph Search Algorithms

Graph theory has been a popular area of study of mathematicians for many years and numerous algorithms have been devised to search and explore a graph's topology. Among other things, by utilizing search algorithms it is possible to:

- Visit every node in a graph, effectively mapping out the graph's topology.
- Find *any* path between two nodes. This is useful if you want to find a node but you don't really care how you get there. For example, this type of search can be used to find one (or more) of the solutions to the Towers of Hanoi puzzle.
- Find the *best* path between two nodes. What is "best" depends on the problem. If the graph to be searched is a navgraph, the best path may be the shortest path between two nodes, the path that takes an agent between two points in the fastest time, the path that avoids enemy line of sight, or the most quiet path (à la Thief). If the graph is a state

graph such as that for the Towers of Hanoi puzzle, then the best path will be the one reaching the solution in the fewest steps.

Before I get to the nitty-gritty I'd like to make it clear that many of you are initially going to find some of these algorithms difficult to understand. In fact I think graph search algorithms should come with a health warning. Something like the following would be appropriate:

WARNING!

Beware! Search algorithms have the ability to create in the average human brain terrible amounts of frustration and confusion, leading to headaches, nausea, and sleep deprivation. Spontaneous and excessive howling is not uncommon. Please be aware these symptoms are commonplace in the early stages of the learning curve and are not generally cause for concern. Normal service is usually resumed within a reasonable length of time. (If symptoms persist, however, stay clear of busy roads, razor blades, and loaded weapons. Seek medical advice at the earliest opportunity.)

Seriously though, for many people this stuff can be difficult to understand. For this reason I'm going to take my time explaining each algorithm. It's very important that you understand the theory and don't just use these techniques in a "cut and paste" fashion, because often you may want to modify an algorithm to suit your own requirements. Without an understanding of *how* these searches work, any modification will be almost impossible and you'll be left scratching your head in frustration.

Strap yourself into your seat then. Let's get on with it!

Uninformed Graph Searches

Uninformed graph searches, or *blind searches* as they are sometimes known, search a graph without regard to any associated edge costs. They can distinguish individual nodes and edges however, enabling them to identify a target node or to recognize previously visited nodes or edges. This is the only information required to either completely explore a graph (to visit every node) or find a path between two nodes.

Depth First Search

Meet little Billy. Billy is standing at the entrance to a typical theme park: a conglomeration of rides and other attractions and the paths meandering through the park that connect them. Billy doesn't have a map but he's eager to discover what rides and other entertainment the park has to offer.

Fortunately Billy knows about graph theory and he quickly spots the similarity between the layout of a theme park and a graph. He sees that each attraction can be represented by a node and the paths between them by edges. Knowing this, Billy can ensure he visits every attraction and walks down every path using a search algorithm called the *depth first search*, or DFS for short.

The depth first search is so named because it searches by moving as deep into the graph as possible. When it hits a dead end it backtracks to a shallower node where it can continue its exploration. Using the theme park as an example, this is how the algorithm works:

From the entrance to the park (the source node), Billy makes a note of its description and of the paths that extend outward from it (the edges) on a slip of paper. Next, he chooses one of the paths to walk down. It makes no difference which — he can choose one at random provided it's a path he hasn't already explored. Every time a path leads Billy to a new attraction he makes a note of its name and of the paths connected to it. The illustrations labeled A to D in Figure 5.14 demonstrate the first few steps of this process. The thin black lines represent unexplored paths and the highlighted lines show the paths Billy has chosen to walk down.

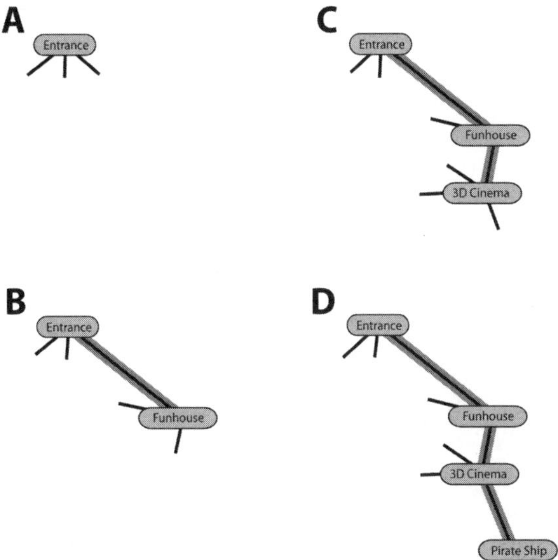

Figure 5.14

When he reaches the position shown at D, Billy notices that no new paths lead from the Pirate Ship (in graph parlance this node is known as a terminal node). Therefore, to continue the search he backtracks to the 3D Cinema where there are further unexplored paths to traverse. See Figure 5.15 E.

When he reaches the Ice Blaster there are four unexplored paths to try. The first two he navigates lead back to previously visited places — the Entrance and the Funhouse — so he marks each path as explored before backtracking to the Ice Blaster to try another route. Eventually he finds a path leading to the Slot Machines. See Figure 5.15 F, G, and H.

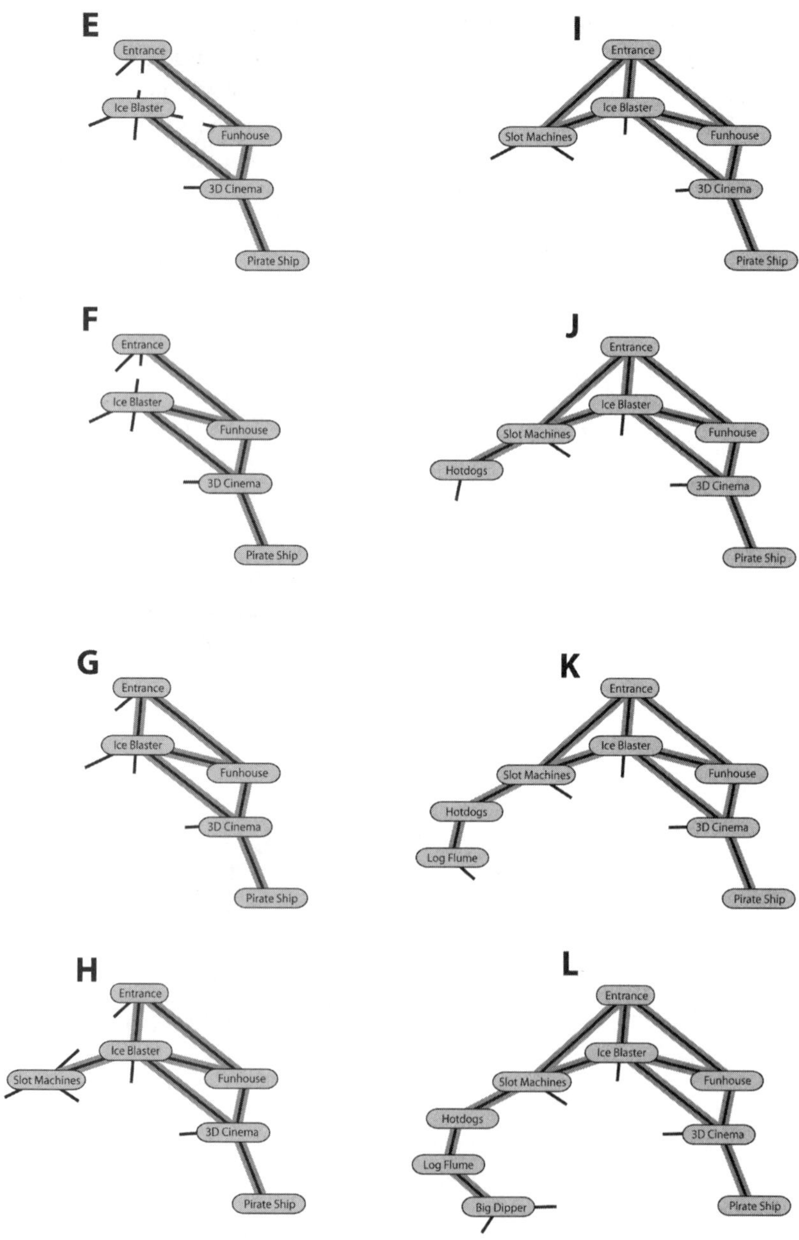

Figure 5.15

This process of moving forward through the graph as far as possible before backtracking to previously unexplored paths continues until the entire theme park has been mapped. Steps I to L in Figure 5.15 show the next few steps of the process. Figure 5.16 shows the finished graph after Billy has visited every attraction and walked down every path.

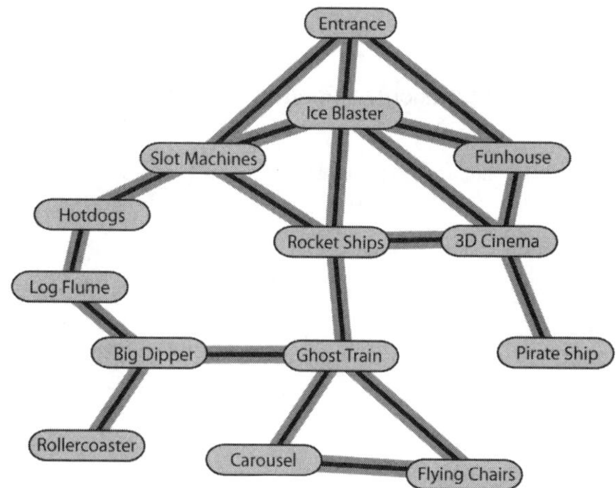

Figure 5.16. Billy's completed map

NOTE Given a source node, the depth first search can only guarantee that all the nodes and edges will be visited in a *connected* graph. Remember, a connected graph is one where any node can be reached from any other. If you are searching an unconnected graph, such as C in Figure 5.3, then the algorithm must be expanded to include a source node for each sub-graph.

Implementing the Algorithm

The DFS is implemented as a class template and can be used with any graph implementation (such as a dense graph) using the same interface as the SparseGraph class shown earlier. First let's walk through the class declaration, then I'll go on to describe the search algorithm itself.

```
template<class graph_type>
class Graph_SearchDFS
{
private:

  //to aid legibility
  enum {visited, unvisited, no_parent_assigned};

  //create typedefs for the edge and node types used by the graph
  typedef typename graph_type::EdgeType Edge;
  typedef typename graph_type::NodeType Node;

private:

  //a reference to the graph to be searched
  const graph_type &  m_Graph;

  //this records the indexes of all the nodes that are visited as the
  //search progresses
  std::vector<int>   m_Visited;
```

m_Visited contains the same number of elements as there are nodes in the graph. Each element is initially set to unvisited. As the search progresses, every time a node is visited its corresponding element in m_Visited will be set to visited.

```
//this holds the route taken to the target.
std::vector<int>  m_Route;
```

m_Route also contains the same number of elements as there are nodes in the graph. Each element is initially set to no_parent_assigned. As the graph search proceeds, this vector stores the route to the target node by recording the parents of each node at the relevant index. For example, if the path to the target follows the nodes 3 - 8 - 27, then m_Route[8] will hold 3 and m_Route[27] will hold 8.

```
//the source and target node indices
int               m_iSource,
                  m_iTarget;
```

When you explore a graph, more often than not you'll be searching for a specific target (or targets). To use the theme park analogy again, it's as though you are searching for a particular ride such as the rollercoaster. With this in mind, search algorithms usually make use of a termination condition, generally in the form of a target node index.

```
//true if a path to the target has been found
bool              m_bFound;

//this method performs the DFS search
bool Search();
```

This method is the code that implements the depth first search algorithm. We'll dive into its guts in just a moment.

```
public:

  Graph_SearchDFS(const graph_type& graph,
                  int               source,
                  int               target = -1 ):

                              m_Graph(graph),
                              m_iSource(source),
                              m_iTarget(target),
                              m_bFound(false),
                              m_Visited(m_Graph.NumNodes(), unvisited),
                              m_Route(m_Graph.NumNodes(), no_parent_assigned)

  {
    m_bFound = Search();
  }

  //returns true if the target node has been located
  bool              Found()const{return m_bFound;}

  //returns a vector of node indexes that comprise the shortest path
```

```
  //from the source to the target
  std::list<int> GetPathToTarget()const;
};
```

The DFS search algorithm is implemented using a `std::stack` of `const` pointers to the edges comprising the graph it is searching. A stack is a last in, first out data structure (usually abbreviated to LIFO). The stack is used in a similar way to the sheet of paper our friend Billy used to explore the theme park: Edges are pushed onto it as the search proceeds, just as Billy jotted down the paths as he explored.

Have a quick look at the code for the `Search` method and then I'll talk you through it with an example to make sure you understand how it does its magic.

```
template <class graph_type>
bool Graph_SearchDFS<graph_type>::Search()
{
  //create a std stack of pointers to edges
  std::stack<const Edge*> stack;

  //create a dummy edge and put on the stack
  Edge Dummy(m_iSource, m_iSource, 0);

  stack.push(&Dummy);

  //while there are edges on the stack keep searching
  while (!stack.empty())
  {
    //grab the next edge
    const Edge* Next = stack.top();

    //remove the edge from the stack
    stack.pop();

    //make a note of the parent of the node this edge points to
    m_Route[Next->To] = Next->From();

    //and mark it visited
    m_Visited[Next->To()] = visited;

    //if the target has been found the method can return success
    if (Next->To() == m_iTarget)
    {
      return true;
    }

    //push the edges leading from the node this edge points to onto
    //the stack (provided the edge does not point to a previously
    //visited node)
    graph_type::ConstEdgeIterator ConstEdgeItr(m_Graph, Next->To());

    for (const Edge* pE=ConstEdgeItr.begin();
        !ConstEdgeItr.end();
        pE=ConstEdgeItr.next())
```

```
    {
      if (m_Visited[pE->To()] == unvisited)
      {
        stack.push(pE);
      }
    }
  }//while

  //no path to target
  return false;
}
```

To help your understanding let's examine a simple example. Using the undirected graph shown in Figure 5.17, let's say we want to search for node 3 (the target node), commencing the search from node 5 (the source node).

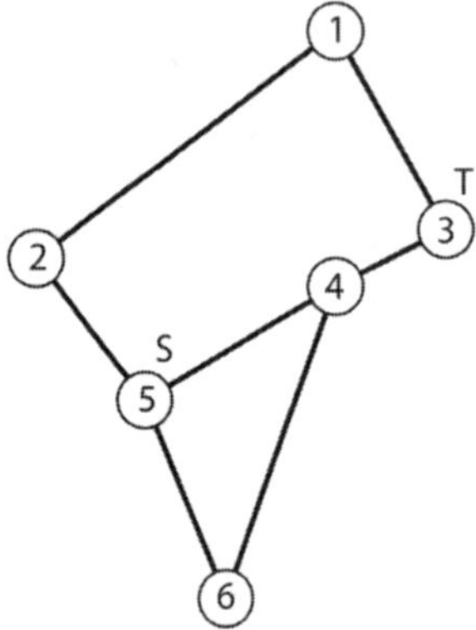

Figure 5.17. A simple graph search problem

`Search` begins by creating a dummy edge — one leading from the source node back to the source node — and putting it on the stack. See Figure 5.18. The highlight indicates that the edge is on the stack.

The search proceeds by entering a `while` loop. While there are still unexplored edges on the stack, the algorithm iterates through the following steps. The comments in brackets describe the situation for the first iteration through the loop.

1. Remove the topmost edge from the stack. (The dummy edge [5 - 5].)
2. Note the parent of the edge's destination node by inserting the parent's index in the vector `m_Routes`, at the element referred to by the destination node's index. (Because a dummy edge is used to start the algorithm, the parent of node 5 is also node 5. Therefore `m_Routes[5]` is set to 5.)

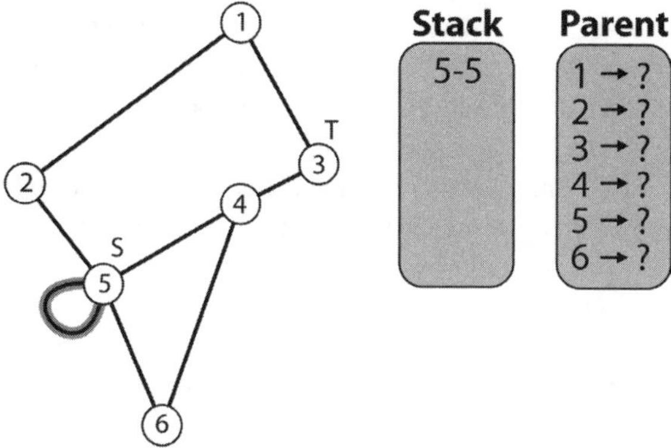

Figure 5.18. A dummy edge is placed on the stack.

3. Mark the edge's destination node as visited by assigning the enumeration `visited` to the relevant index in the `m_Visited` vector (`m_Visited[5] = visited`).
4. Test for termination. If the edge's destination node is the target node, then the search can return success. (5 is not the target node so the search continues.)
5. If the edge's destination node is not the target, then *provided the node the current edge points to has not already been visited*, all its adjacent edges are pushed onto the stack. (The edges [5 - 2], [5 - 4], and [5 - 6] are pushed into `stack`.)

Figure 5.19 shows the state of play of the algorithm after one iteration of the while loop. The gray color of the source node indicates that it's been marked as visited.

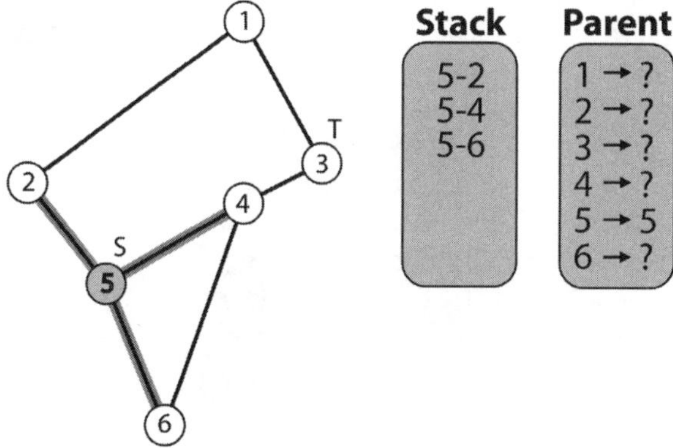

Figure 5.19. The edges leading from node 5 are placed on the stack.

At this point, the algorithm branches back to the beginning of the while loop, pops the next edge off the top of the stack (edge [5 - 2]), marks its destination node as visited (node 2), and makes a note of the parent of the destination node (node 5 is the parent of node 2).

Next, the algorithm considers what edges should be pushed onto the stack. Node 2 (which edge [5 - 2] points to) has two adjacent edges: [2 - 1] and [2 - 5]. Node 5 has been marked as visited so edge [2 - 5] does not get added to the stack. As node 1 hasn't been visited, the edge leading to it, [2 - 1], is pushed onto the stack. See Figure 5.20. The thick black line from [5 - 2] indicates that particular edge will not be considered further.

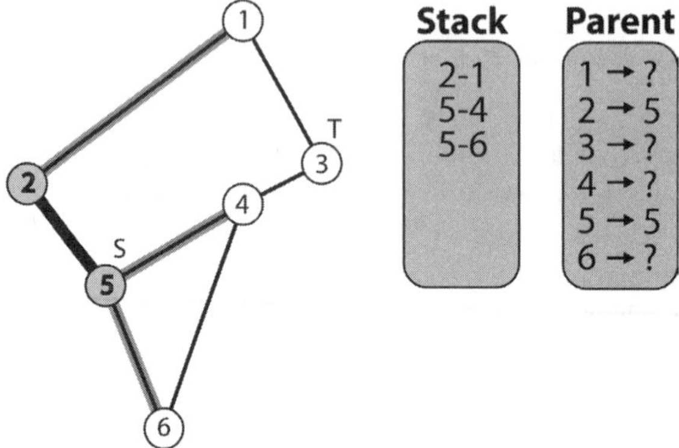

Figure 5.20

Once again the algorithm branches back to the beginning of the while loop and pops the next edge off the stack (edge [2 -1]), marks its destination node as visited (node 1), and makes a note of its parent (node 2 is the parent of node 1). Node 1 has edges leading to node 3 and node 2. Node 2 has already been visited so only the edge [1 - 3] is pushed onto the stack. See Figure 5.21.

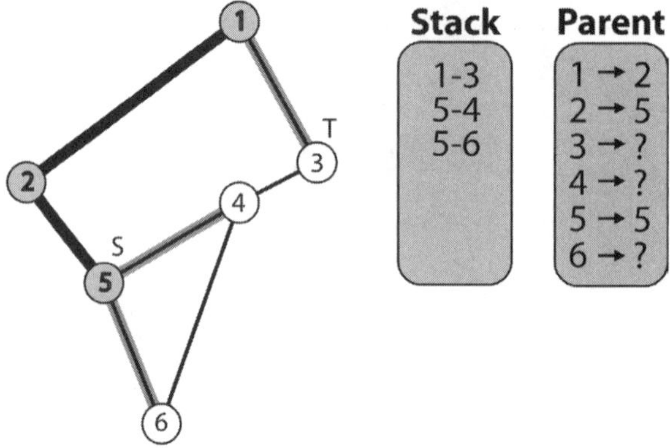

Figure 5.21

This time when the algorithm pops the next edge [1 - 3] from the stack, after the usual procedure of marking the destination node and noting the parent, the algorithm finds that it has located the target, at which point the algorithm exits. At this stage the status is as shown in Figure 5.22.

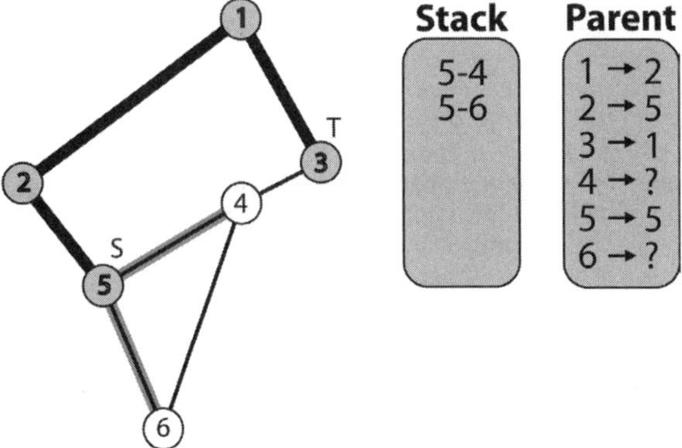

Figure 5.22

During the search, the path to the target node is stored in the vector `m_Route` (represented in the previous figures by the table used to store each node's parents). The method `GetPathToTarget` extracts this information and returns it as a vector of integers representing the indices of the nodes an agent must follow to move from source to target. Here's what the source code looks like:

```
template <class Graph>
std::list<int> Graph_SearchDFS<Graph>::GetPathToTarget()const
{
  std::list<int> path;

  //just return an empty path if no path to target found or if
  //no target has been specified
  if (!m_bFound || m_iTarget<0) return path;

  int nd = m_iTarget;

  path.push_back(nd);

  while (nd != m_iSource)
  {
    nd = m_Route[nd];

    path.push_back(nd);
  }

  return path;
}
```

This is a very simple method. It starts by testing to see what the parent of the target node is, and then the parent of that node, and so on until the source node is reached. In the example you have been following in the last few pages, the path this method returns is 5 - 2 - 1 - 3.

NOTE For speed and efficiency, the implementations of the search algorithms described in this chapter are designed to operate on graphs created prior to the search. However, for some problems it will be impossible to do this because the expected size of the graph is either too large to store in memory or because it's necessary to conserve memory by only creating those nodes and edges that are essential to the search. For example, if you wanted to search the state space of a game like chess, it's impossible to build a state graph prior to the search due to the massive number of possible states. Instead, nodes and edges must be created as the search proceeds.

The DFS in Action

To give you some useful visual feedback I've created a demo program to accompany this chapter, which demonstrates the various graph searches on a grid layout navigation graph. This type of node arrangement is commonly found in tile-based games where a node is positioned in the center of each tile and edges connect to the closest eight neighbors. See Screenshot 5.1. The vertical and horizontal lines represent the tile boundaries, the dots are the graph nodes, and the thin lines extending from the nodes are the connecting edges. Unfortunately, the screenshot is printed in grayscale, so it may not be easy to see everything clearly. If you are close to a computer I'd recommend you run the executable PathFinder.exe, and press the "G" key to see the graph displayed.

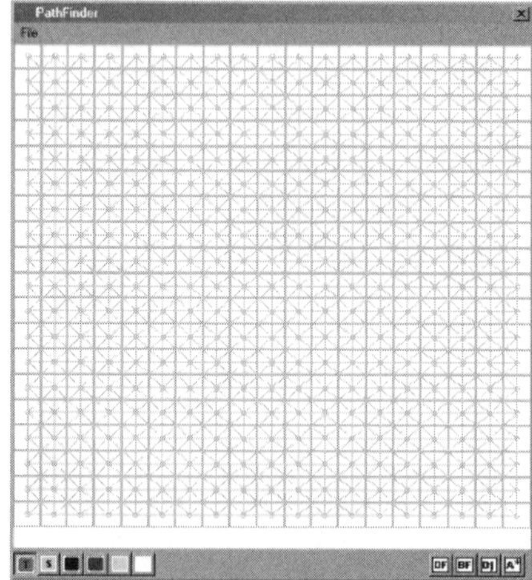

Screenshot 5.1

NOTE Although in the real world the diagonal connections in the PathFinder demo are longer than the vertical and horizontal connections, the depth first search has no knowledge of any associated edge cost and therefore treats all edges as equal.

I've used a grid-based node arrangement for the demo because it makes it easy to create experimental graphs by blocking in tiles to represent obstacles or varying terrain. However, *this does not mean that your game must use a grid-based graph.* I'm emphasizing this point because I frequently see newcomers struggle to understand how a graph can be in any shape other than a grid. They say things like, "*I know how the XYZ search algorithm works for tile-based RTS games, but is it possible to use it in my FPS?*" I see this sort of question a lot and I suppose it's because the majority of demos, tutorials, and articles about pathfinding show examples using a grid-based node layout (for the reasons already listed), and I guess people assume that's the way it's got to be. Please... I'm begging you, don't make the same mistake! *Graphs can be any shape you like (and in any number of dimensions).*

Anyway, let's get back to the DFS. Screenshot 5.2 shows a simple map I've created by blocking out some of the tiles as obstacles.

Screenshot 5.2. A simple test map (To aid clarity, the graph is not shown, just the tiles.)

As it's printed in grayscale, I've made the source and target nodes easier to see by marking them with a square and a cross, respectively. The numbers in the bottom right-hand corner show the number of nodes and edges in the underlying graph.

DFS Improvements

Some graphs can be very deep and the DFS can easily get delayed by going too far down the wrong path. In the worst-case scenario, the DFS may be unable to recover from a wrong choice early on in the search, becoming permanently stuck.

As an example, let's say you want to find the solution to a randomly mixed-up Rubik's Cube. The entire state space for this problem is enormous and prohibits the generation of the complete state graph prior to any search, therefore nodes are created on-the-fly as each state is expanded starting from the root node. At some point in the search, the DFS algorithm may choose an edge leading to a sub-graph of the state space that does not contain a solution state, but that is too large to expand fully given the computational power available. This results in a solution never being returned by the DFS, and the computer will effectively hang.

Fortunately, by limiting how many edges deep the DFS algorithm searches before it starts to backtrack, this can be prevented. This is called *depth limited search*. By utilizing depth limited search, provided the depth is one the algorithm can search given the computational power available, the DFS will always return a solution if there is one to be found *at that depth*.

However, depth limited search has a major drawback. How do you know what limit to set for the maximum search depth? For most problem domains it's impossible to judge what that limit should be. Using the Rubik's Cube as an example, a solution might be three moves away or fifteen. If the maximum search depth is set at ten, it may or may not find a solution. If it is set too high, the number of possible states may result in a search that hangs. Fortunately, there is a way around this problem: *iterative deepening DFS*.

Iterative deepening search works by using the DFS to search a graph with a depth limit of one, then depth two, then three, and so on until the search is complete. Although at first glance this may appear to be a waste of resources as the nodes at shallower depths are searched multiple times, in reality the majority of nodes are always on the fringe of the search. This is especially true of searches through graphs with a high branching factor. Given a branching factor of eight, like that of the graph in the PathFinder demo, the number of nodes on the fringe is shown in Table 5.1.

Table 5.1

Depth	Fringe Nodes	Total Nodes
0	1	1
1	8	9
2	64	73
3	512	585
4	4096	4681
n	$8n$	$1+ \ldots +8n-1+8n$

I imagine a few of you might be thinking something along the lines of "But if, during a normal DFS search, a depth of *n* hangs the computer, surely when the iterative deepening DFS reaches the same depth it will also hang the computer!" The answer is yes, if the IDDFS is permitted to go that deep you will get problems, but the secret to using the iterative deepening approach is to impose a cutoff, usually defined as a time limit. When the time allocated to the search expires, the algorithm terminates, regardless of what level it has reached.

A spin-off from this methodical approach is that given enough time and a valid target, the iterative deepening DFS will not only find the target, but it will find the target in the fewest steps possible.

The line in Screenshot 5.3 illustrates the path the DFS has made in its quest for the target. As you can see, it meanders around over almost the entire map area before stumbling upon the target node, clearly demonstrating that, although the DFS finds the target, it doesn't guarantee to find the best route to the target.

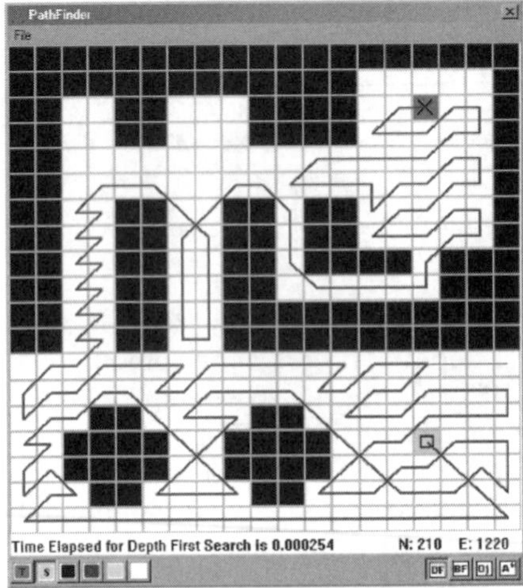

Screenshot 5.3. The DFS in action

Also note in this example that the DFS has not explored any edges not on the path to the target node. When the target node can be reached via multiple paths this is a common trait of the DFS, making it a speedy algorithm to employ when the path length is unimportant (i.e., if searching a state space to see whether a particular state exists as opposed to determining the fastest route to that state).

Breadth First Search

Although the plain-vanilla DFS guarantees to find a target node in a connected graph, it does not guarantee to find the *best* path to that node — the path containing the fewest edges. In the previous example, the DFS resulted in a path spanning three edges even though the best path spans two: 5 - 4 - 3. See Figure 5.22 on page 219.

The BFS algorithm fans out from the source node and examines each of the nodes its edges lead to before fanning out from those nodes and examining all the edges they connect to and so on. You can think of the search as exploring all the nodes that are one edge away from the source node, then all the nodes two edges away, then three edges, and so on until the target node is found. Therefore, as soon as the target is located, the path leading to it is guaranteed to contain the fewest edges possible. (There may be other paths of equal length, but there will be no shorter path.)

Implementing the Algorithm

The algorithm for BFS is almost exactly the same as for DFS except it uses a first in, first out (FIFO) *queue* instead of a stack. Consequently, this time edges are retrieved from the queue in the same order they are put onto the queue. Take a look at the source code for the BFS `Search` method.

```
template <class graph_type>
bool Graph_SearchBFS< graph_type>::Search()
{
  //create a std queue of pointer's edges
  std::queue<const Edge*> Q;

  //create a dummy edge and put on the queue
  const Edge Dummy(m_iSource, m_iSource, 0);
  Q.push(&Dummy);

  //mark the source node as visited
  m_Visited[m_iSource] = visited;

  //while there are edges in the queue keep searching
  while (!Q.empty())
  {
    //grab the next edge
    const Edge* Next = Q.front();

    Q.pop();

    //mark the parent of this node
    m_Route[Next->To()] = Next->From();

    //exit if the target has been found
    if (Next->To() == m_iTarget)
    {
      return true;
    }

    //push the edges leading from the node at the end of this edge
    //onto the queue
    graph_type::ConstEdgeIterator ConstEdgeItr(m_Graph, Next->To());

    for (const Edge* pE=ConstEdgeItr.begin();
        !ConstEdgeItr.end();
         pE=ConstEdgeItr.next())
    {
      //if the node hasn't already been visited we can push the
      //edge onto the queue
      if (m_Visited[pE->To()] == unvisited)
      {
        Q.push(pE);

        //the node is marked as visited here, BEFORE it is examined, because
        //it ensures a maximum of N edges are ever placed in the queue,
        // rather than E edges.
        m_Visited[pE->To()] = visited;
```

```
      }
    }
  }

  //no path to target
  return false;
}
```

To clarify the algorithm for you, let's go through the same example used previously. Figure 5.23 will refresh your memory.

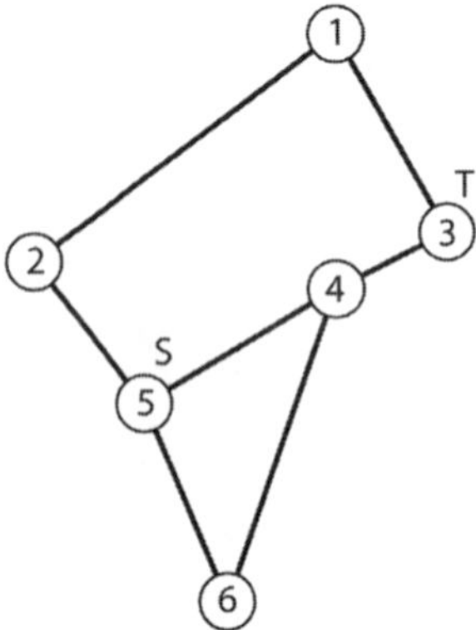

Figure 5.23. Find the shortest path from node 5 to node 3.

The BFS commences like the DFS. First a dummy edge [5 - 5] is created and pushed onto the queue. Then the source node is marked as visited. See Figure 5.24.

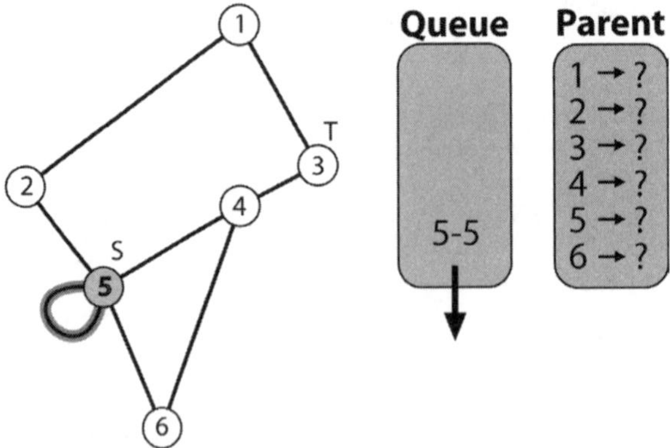

Figure 5.24

Next the algorithm makes a note of 5's parent. As before, because the first edge to be considered is a dummy edge, node 5 is set to be the parent of itself. This edge is then removed from the front of the queue and all of node 5's adjacent edges (the ones pointing to unvisited nodes) are added. See Figure 5.25.

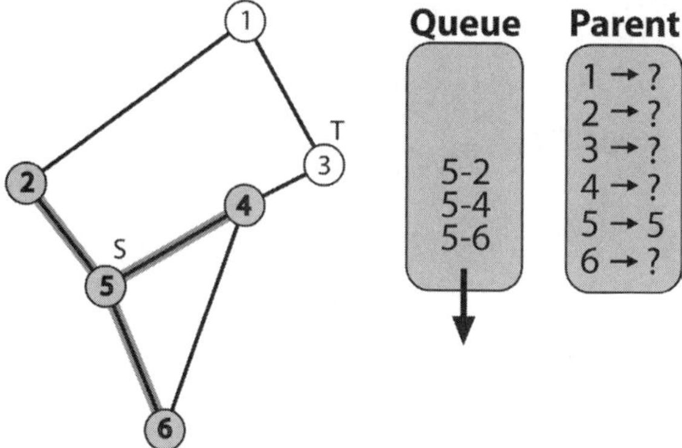

Figure 5.25

So far everything has looked very similar to the DFS, but this is where the algorithm starts to differ. Next, the edge [5 - 6] is removed from the queue. Node 5 is noted to be the parent of node 6. As both of node 6's adjacent edges point to previously visited nodes, they are not added to the queue. See Figure 5.26.

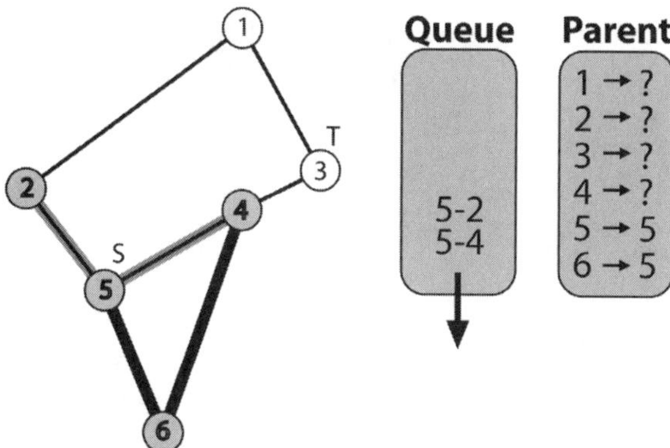

Figure 5.26

Next off the queue is edge [5 - 4]. Node 5 is noted to be node 4's parent. Node 4 has three adjacent edges but only the edge [4 - 3] points to an unmarked node, so this is the only one that is put on the queue. See Figure 5.27.

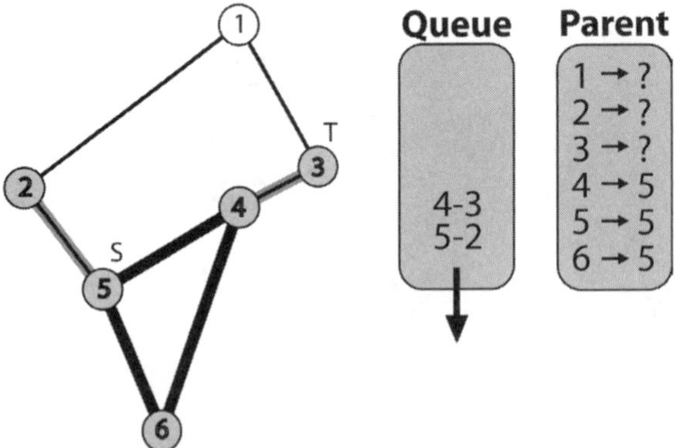

Figure 5.27

Next is the edge [5 - 2]. Node 5 is noted to be node 2's parent and the edge [2 - 1] placed on the queue. See Figure 5.28.

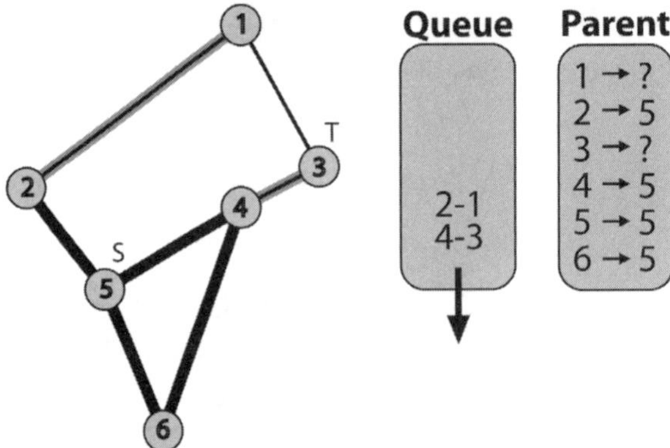

Figure 5.28

The edge [4 - 3] is next. Node 4 is noted to be node 3's parent. As node 3 is also the target node, it is at this point the algorithm exits. See Figure 5.29.

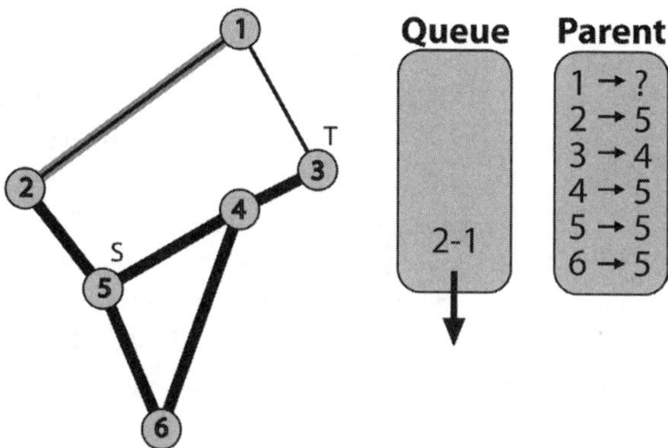

Figure 5.29

Using the `m_Routes` vector to work back through the parents from the target node to the source, we get the path 3 - 4 - 5. This is the path between the two containing the fewest edges… the best path.

⌘ **TIP** You can speed up the BFS (and many other graph search algorithms) by running two searches simultaneously, one started at the source node and the other at the target node, and stopping the search when they meet. This is called a *bidirectional* search.

The BFS in Action

Let's fire up the PathFinder program again to see the BFS operating in the real world. First of all I think it will be useful for you to examine the simple example shown in Screenshot 5.4. (If you are running the PathFinder program, load up the file no_obstacles_source_target_close.map, and click the BF button on the toolbar.)

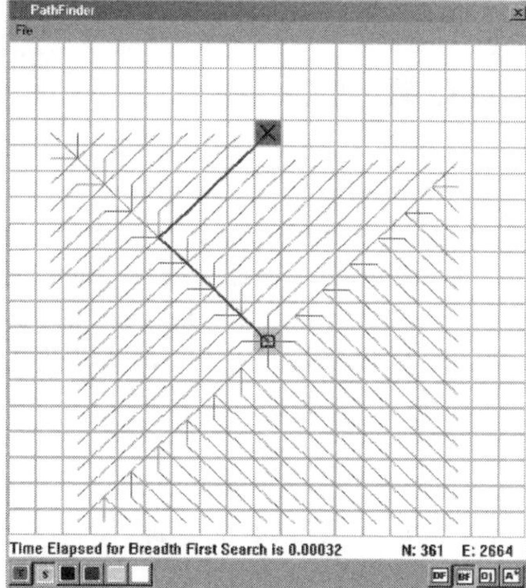

Screenshot 5.4

In this case there are no obstacles present. The source node is positioned close to the target node with only a few other nodes (tiles) separating them. Once again the thick line shows the path the BFS algorithm has found. The thin lines represent all the edges the algorithm has visited on its way to the target. This clearly demonstrates how the BFS fans out from the source node until the target node has been found. The visited edges form a square shape because the BFS, like the DFS, treats all edges as though they are of equal length. The path veers to the left and then to the right instead of directly toward the target node for the same reason. They both take the same number of steps but the path shape is entirely dependent on the order in which each node's edges are explored.

Screenshot 5.5 shows the BFS operation on the same map we saw earlier. The improvement in path length is clear, although this is to be expected as the plain DFS is not suited for shortest path searches. Once more, note how each and every edge up to the same depth away from the source node as the target has been visited.

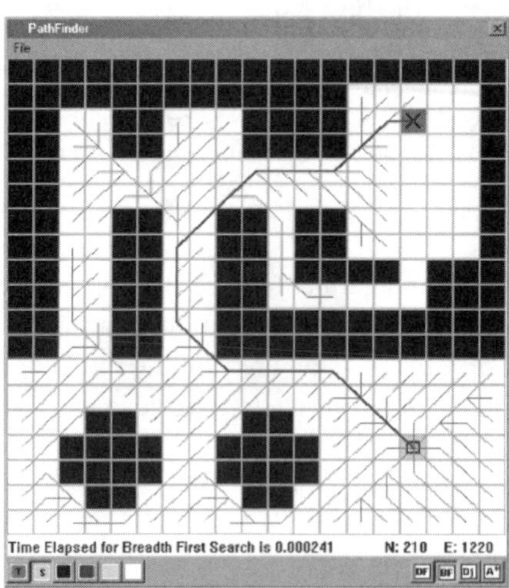

Screenshot 5.5

Unfortunately, because the BFS is so systematic in its exploration, it can prove unwieldy to use on anything other than small search spaces. If we denote the branching factor as *b* and the number of edges the target node is away from the source as *d* (the depth), then the number of nodes examined is given by equation 5.2.

$$1 + b + b^2 + b^3 + \ldots + b^d \qquad (5.2)$$

If the graph to be explored is very large and has a high branching factor, then the BFS will hog a lot of memory and perform poorly. Even worse, if the state space has a branching factor so high it prohibits the creation of a complete graph prior to the search, requiring the BFS to expand the nodes as it explores, a search could take literally *years* to terminate. In their book *Artificial Intelligence: A Modern Approach*, Russell and Norvig give an example of a puzzle with a branching factor of 10; assuming that it takes one millisecond to expand each node, the BFS will take 3,500 years to reach a depth of 14! Computers have become much faster beasts since the first edition of that book was published, but even so you would still be an old man in the amount of time the BFS takes to get to this depth.

Cost-Based Graph Searches

For many problem domains, the related graph will have a *cost* (sometimes referred to as a weight) associated with traversing an edge. For instance, navigation graphs usually have edges with a cost proportional to the distance between the nodes they connect. To find the shortest paths through the graph these costs must be taken into account. It's simply not enough — as we did previously with the BFS — to find the path containing the fewest number of edges because, with an associated cost, it can be much cheaper to travel down many short edges than two long ones. See Figure 5.30.

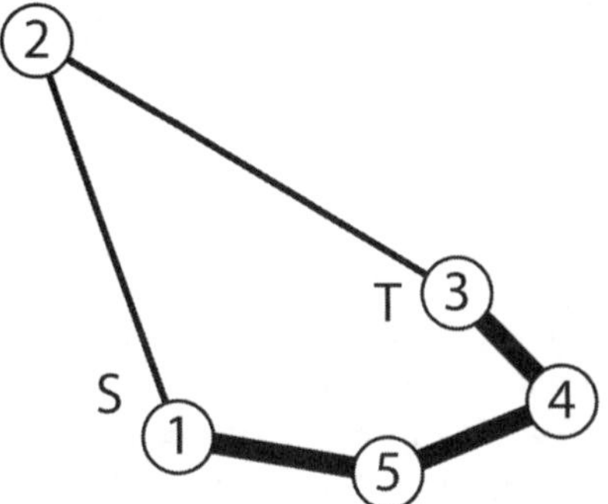

Figure 5.30. The path 1 - 5 - 4 - 3 is shorter than the path 1 - 2 - 3 even though it contains more edges.

Although it's possible to use the BFS or DFS to exhaustively search through all the routes to a target node, adding up the costs of each path as it goes and then selecting the lowest cost path, it's obviously a very inefficient solution. Fortunately there are much better methods at our disposal.

Edge Relaxation

The search algorithms discussed in the remainder of this chapter are based on a technique called *edge relaxation*. As an algorithm proceeds it gathers information about the best path found so far (BPSF) from the source node to any of the other nodes en route to the target. This information is updated as new edges are examined. If a newly examined edge infers that the path to a node may be made shorter by using it in place of the existing best path, then that edge is added and the path is updated accordingly.

This relaxation process, as with all graph operations, is much easier to understand by observing a diagram. Take a look at Figure 5.31. With the graph shown in A, the best path from 1 to 4 via 3 is not improved by examining the edge [5 - 4]. Therefore no relaxation is necessary. With graph B, however, the edge [5 - 4] can be utilized to create a shorter path to 4; as a result the BPSF must be updated accordingly by changing node 4's parent from 3 to 5 (giving the path 1 - 2 - 5 - 4).

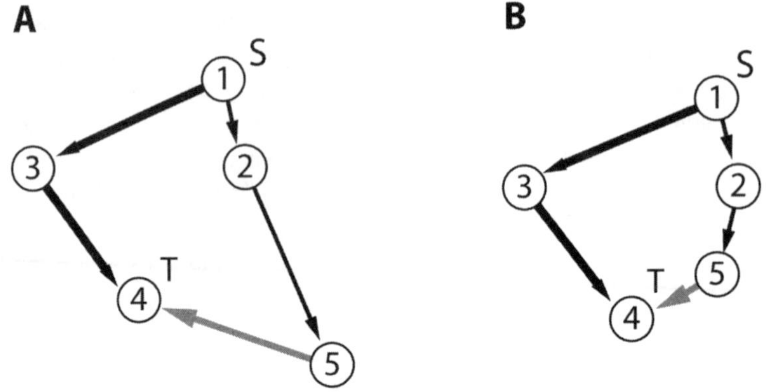

Figure 5.31

This process is called edge relaxation because it mimics the way a piece of elastic stretched along the edges of the BPSF would relax (become less taut) when an edge is found that facilitates a shorter path.

Each algorithm keeps a `std::vector` of floats (indexed by node) representing the best total cost to each node found by the algorithm so far. Given the general case shown in Figure 5.32, pseudocode to relax a path would look something like this:

```
if (TotalCostToThisNode[t] > TotalCostToThisNode[n] + EdgeCost(n-to-t))
{
  TotalCostToThisNode[t] = TotalCostToThisNode[n] + EdgeCost(n-to-t));

  Parent(t) = n;
}
```

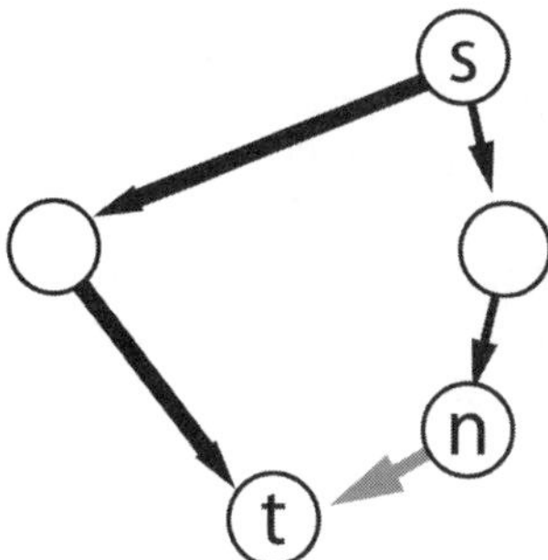

Figure 5.32

Shortest Path Trees

Given a graph, G, and a source node, the *shortest path tree* (SPT) is the sub-tree of G that represents the shortest path from any node on the SPT to the source node. Again, a picture is worth a thousand words, so take a look at Figure 5.33. It shows an SPT with its root positioned at node 1.

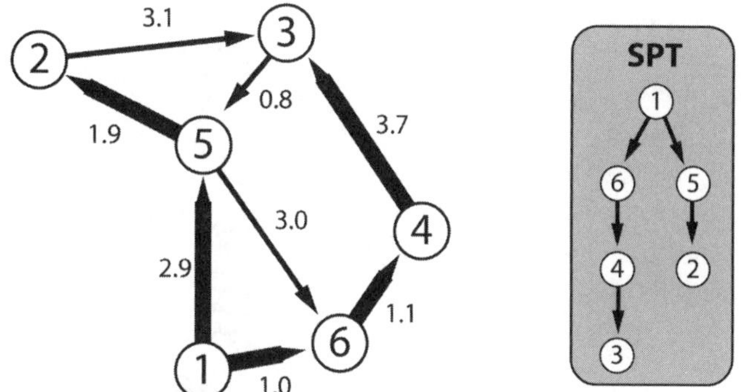

Figure 5.33. The shortest path tree for node 1 is shown on the left by the thick edges and represented again on the right by a directed tree. To find the shortest path from any node in the graph to node 1, all you have to do is trace the route backward through the SPT from the node in question. For example, tracing the path from node 3 to node 1 gives the path 1 - 6 - 4 - 3.

The following algorithms find the shortest paths in weighted graphs by "growing" a shortest path tree outward from the source node.

Dijkstra's Algorithm

Professor Edsger Wybe Dijkstra has provided computer science with many valuable contributions, but one of the most famous is his algorithm for finding shortest paths in weighted graphs.

Dijkstra's algorithm builds a shortest path tree one edge at a time by first adding the source node to the SPT and then by adding the edge that gives the shortest path from the source to a node not already on the SPT. This process results in an SPT containing the shortest path from every node in the graph to the source node. If the algorithm is supplied with a target node, the process will terminate as soon as it is found. At the point the algorithm terminates, the SPT it has generated will contain the shortest path to the source node from the target node, and from every node visited during the search.

HISTORICAL NOTE Dijkstra is also famous for having designed and coded the Algol 60 compiler and for fervently denouncing the use of the goto statement in programming. I am also rather fond of his saying that "the question of whether computers can think is like the question of whether submarines can swim." Regrettably, Dijkstra died in 2002 of cancer.

Let's step through an example using the same graph you saw in Figure 5.33 but in this instance the source node will be node 5.

First, node 5 is added to the SPT and the edges leaving it are placed on the search frontier. See Figure 5.34.

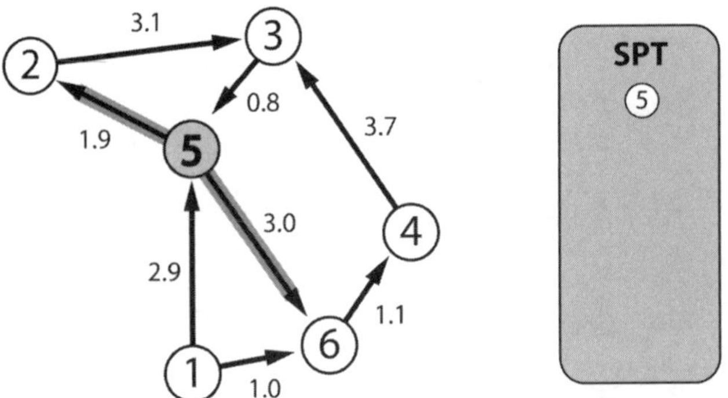

Figure 5.34. Node 5 is added to the SPT. Edges on the search frontier are highlighted.

The algorithm then examines the destination nodes of the edges on the frontier — 6 and 2 — and adds the one closest to the source (node 2 at distance 1.9) to the SPT. Next, any edges leaving node 2 are added to the frontier. See Figure 5.35.

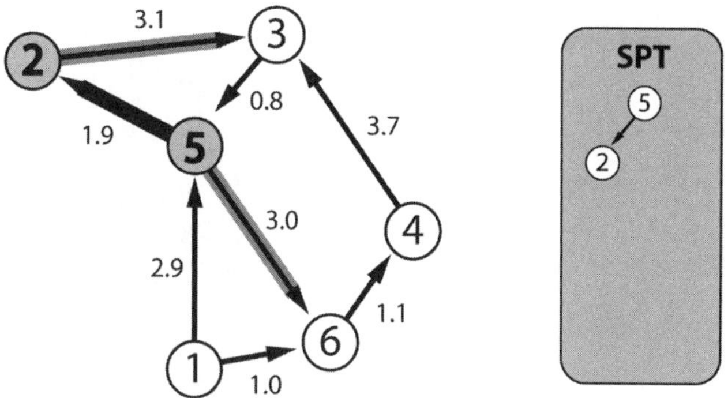

Figure 5.35. Thick black edges represent those on the SPT.

Again the algorithm examines the destination nodes of the edges on the frontier. The cost to get to node 3 from the source is 5.0 and the cost to get to node 6 is 3.0. Node 6 is therefore the next node to be added to the SPT, and all the edges leaving it are added to the frontier. See Figure 5.36.

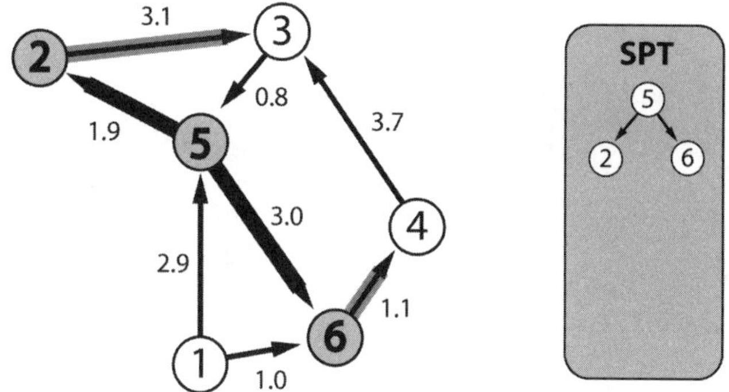

Figure 5.36

The process is repeated once more. As the cost to node 4 is less than the cost to node 3, this is added to the SPT. This time, however, the only edge from node 4 leads to node 3 — a node that is already the destination node of an edge on the frontier. This is where edge relaxation comes into play. Examining both the possible paths to 3, the algorithm sees that path 5 - 2 - 3 has a cost of 5.0 and path 5 - 6 - 4 - 3 a higher cost of 7.8. Therefore, the edge [2 - 3] remains on the SPT and the edge [4 - 3] is removed from further consideration. See Figure 5.37.

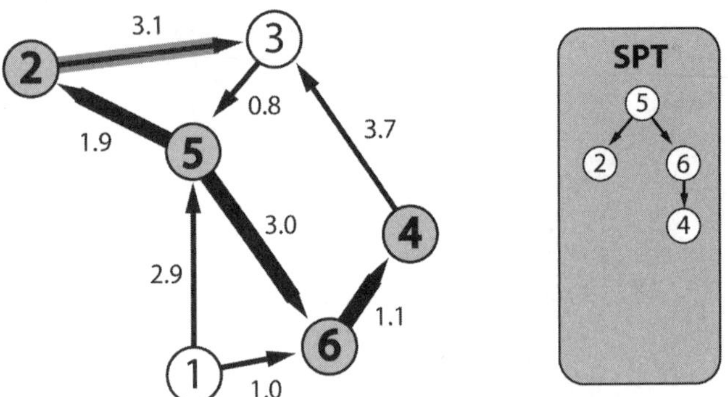

Figure 5.37

Finally node 3 is added to the SPT. See Figure 5.38. Notice how the edge [3 - 5] has not been added to the frontier. This is because node 5 is already on the SPT and does not require further consideration. Additionally, notice how node 1 has not been added to the SPT. Since there are only edges leading away from node 1 it is effectively isolated from the other nodes in the graph.

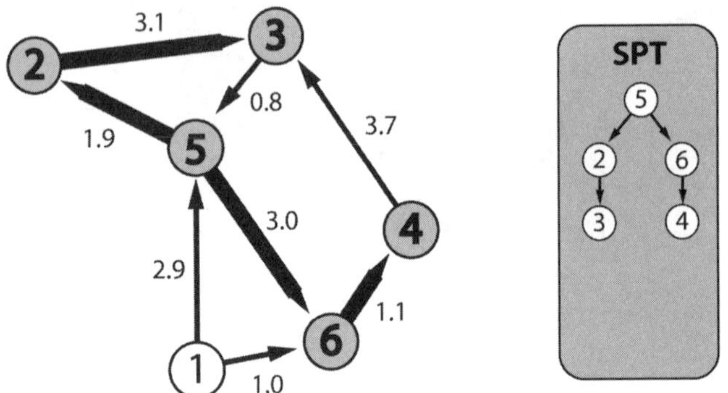

Figure 5.38

Implementing Dijkstra's Algorithm

The implementation of Dijkstra's shortest path algorithm can be gnarly to understand at first and I confess I've not been looking forward to writing this part of the chapter because I reckon it's not going to be any easier to explain! I think we both need to take a deep breath before we move on: breathe in… hold it… three, two, one… and out.

That's much better. Okay, let me begin by showing you the class declaration. The comments within the code provide explanations of each of the member variables, most of which should by now sound familiar.

```
template <class graph_type >
class Graph_SearchDijkstra
{
private:

  //create typedefs for the node and edge types used by the graph
  typedef typename graph_type::EdgeType Edge;
  typedef typename graph_type::NodeType Node;

private:

  const graph_type &             m_Graph;

  //this vector contains the edges that comprise the shortest path tree -
  //a directed sub-tree of the graph that encapsulates the best paths from
  //every node on the SPT to the source node.
  std::vector<const Edge*>      m_ShortestPathTree;

  //this is indexed into by node index and holds the total cost of the best
  //path found so far to the given node. For example, m_CostToThisNode[5]
  //will hold the total cost of all the edges that comprise the best path
  //to node 5 found so far in the search (if node 5 is present and has
  //been visited of course).
  std::vector<double>           m_CostToThisNode;

  //this is an indexed (by node) vector of "parent" edges leading to nodes
  //connected to the SPT but that have not been added to the SPT yet.
  std::vector<const Edge*> m_SearchFrontier;

  int                           m_iSource;
  int                           m_iTarget;

  void Search();

public:

  Graph_SearchDijkstra(const graph_type& graph,
                       int               source,
                       int               target = -1):m_Graph(graph),
                                     m_ShortestPathTree(graph.NumNodes()),
                                     m_SearchFrontier(graph.NumNodes()),
                                     m_CostToThisNode(graph.NumNodes()),
                                     m_iSource(source),
                                     m_iTarget(target)
  {
    Search();
  }

  //returns the vector of edges defining the SPT. If a target is given
  //in the constructor, then this will be the SPT comprising all the nodes
  //examined before the target is found, else it will contain all the nodes
```

```
  //in the graph.
  std::vector<const Edge*> GetAllPaths()const;

  //returns a vector of node indexes comprising the shortest path
  //from the source to the target. It calculates the path by working
  //backward through the SPT from the target node.
  std::list<int>        GetPathToTarget()const;

  //returns the total cost to the target
  double                GetCostToTarget()const;

};
```

This search algorithm is implemented using an indexed priority queue. A *priority queue*, or PQ for short, is a queue that keeps its elements sorted in order of priority (no surprises there then). This type of data structure can be utilized to store the destination nodes of the edges on the search frontier, in order of increasing distance (cost) from the source node. This method guarantees that the node at the front of the PQ will be the node *not* already on the SPT that is *closest* to the source node. Am I making sense so far? If not, please berate me under your breath before reading this paragraph again.

A PQ must be able to maintain the elements stored within it in sorted order. This implies each graph node must have an additional member variable to store the costs accumulated to that node, in order that the ≤ or ≥ operators may be overloaded to give the correct behavior. Although using an additional member variable is certainly a valid solution, I'd rather not have to change the existing graph node, and besides, this can be problematic when multiple searches are run simultaneously, since each individual search will be utilizing the same data record. This can be overcome by creating copies of the nodes, but then precious memory and speed is forfeited.

The alternative is to use an *indexed priority queue* (iPQ for short). This type of PQ indexes into a vector of *keys*. In this example, the keys are the accumulated costs for each node stored in the vector `m_CostToThisNode`. A node is added to the queue by inserting its *index*. Similarly, when a node is retrieved from the iPQ, it is its *index* that is returned and not the node itself (or a pointer to the node). This index can then be used to access the node and its data via `m_Graph::GetNode`.

It's time to show you some source code. Make sure you take your time and understand every line of this algorithm; it will pay dividends for you in the long run. I have made copious comments within the source to aid your understanding but, if you are a mere mortal, I doubt the comments alone will be enough for it to "click" on first reading. (If after a few readings you still find yourself having difficulty with the algorithm, I *strongly* recommend you step through the code on a sheet of paper using a simple example.)

```
template <class graph_type>
void Graph_SearchDijkstra<graph_type>::Search()
```

```
{
  //create an indexed priority queue that sorts smallest to largest
  //(front to back). Note that the maximum number of elements the iPQ
  //may contain is NumNodes(). This is because no node can be represented
  // on the queue more than once.
  IndexedPriorityQLow<double> pq(m_CostToThisNode, m_Graph.NumNodes());

  //put the source node on the queue
  pq.insert(m_iSource);

  //while the queue is not empty
  while(!pq.empty())
  {
    //get the lowest cost node from the queue. Don't forget, the return value
    //is a *node index*, not the node itself. This node is the node not already
    //on the SPT that is the closest to the source node
    int NextClosestNode = pq.Pop();

    //move this edge from the search frontier to the shortest path tree
    m_ShortestPathTree[NextClosestNode] = m_SearchFrontier[NextClosestNode];

    //if the target has been found exit
    if (NextClosestNode == m_iTarget) return;

    //now to relax the edges. For each edge connected to the next closest node
    graph_type::ConstEdgeIterator ConstEdgeItr(m_Graph, NextClosestNode);
    for (const Edge* pE=ConstEdgeItr.begin();
        !ConstEdgeItr.end();
        pE=ConstEdgeItr.next())
    {
      //the total cost to the node this edge points to is the cost to the
      //current node plus the cost of the edge connecting them.
      double NewCost = m_CostToThisNode[NextClosestNode] + pE->Cost();

      //if this edge has never been on the frontier make a note of the cost
      //to reach the node it points to, then add the edge to the frontier
      //and the destination node to the PQ.
      if (m_SearchFrontier[pE->To()] == 0)
      {
        m_CostToThisNode[pE->To()] = NewCost;

        pq.insert(pE->To());

        m_SearchFrontier[pE->To()] = pE;
      }

      //else test to see if the cost to reach the destination node via the
      //current node is cheaper than the cheapest cost found so far. If
      //this path is cheaper we assign the new cost to the destination
      //node, update its entry in the PQ to reflect the change, and add the
      //edge to the frontier
      else if ( (NewCost < m_CostToThisNode[pE->To()]) &&
                (m_ShortestPathTree[pE->To()] == 0) )
      {
        m_CostToThisNode[pE->To()] = NewCost;
```

```
            //because the cost is less than it was previously, the PQ must be
            //resorted to account for this.
            pq.ChangePriority(pE->To());

            m_SearchFrontier[pE->To()] = pE;
          }
        }
      }
    }
```

⌘ **TIP** The indexed priority queue implementation utilizes a two-way heap to store the elements. For sparse graphs, if every edge examined produces an improvement in cost (requiring that `IndexedPriorityQLow::ChangePriority` is called), the algorithm gives a worst-case running time of $E\log_2 N$, although in practice the running time will be significantly lower.

It's possible to gain further speed improvements by using a *d*-way heap where *d* is a function of the graph density. This time the worst-case running time will be $E\log_d N$.

When all's said and done, Dijkstra's shortest path algorithm is a pretty good performer and is guaranteed to find the shortest path between two nodes if one exists.

Dijkstra's Algorithm in Action

Let's start up the PathFinder program once more and check out how Dijkstra's algorithm performs on the examples we saw earlier. Screenshot 5.6 illustrates the algorithm operating on the simple problem.

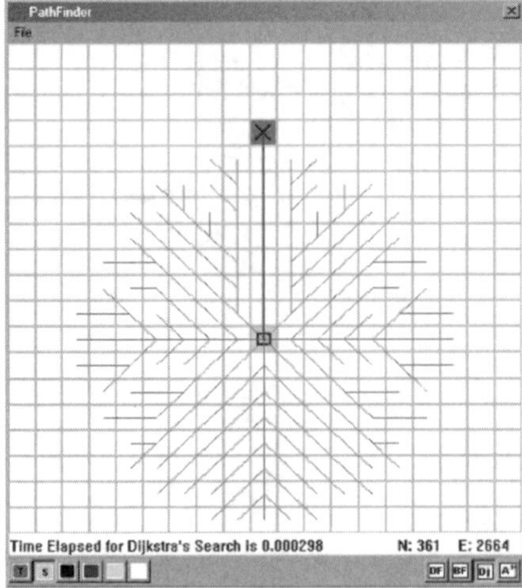

Screenshot 5.6

The result is similar to breadth first search, although now the tree comprising the examined edges is circular in appearance. This is due to Dijkstra's algorithm working with the actual costs of the edges, and so this time diagonal edges cost more to traverse than horizontal or vertical ones. With this in mind you can see how the algorithm has searched a similar distance in every direction before reaching the target.

Screenshot 5.7 shows Dijkstra's algorithm operating on the more complex map.

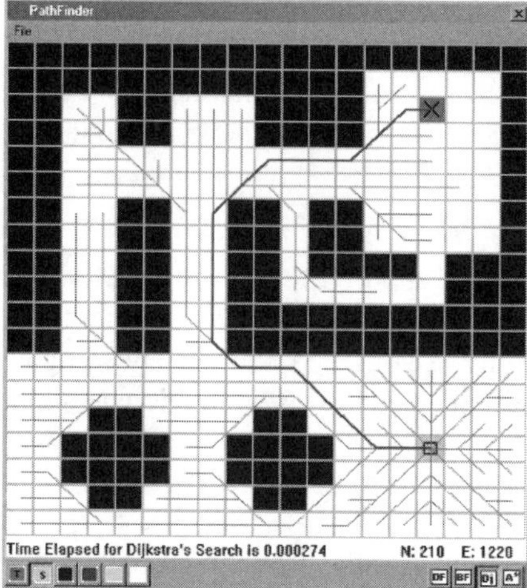

Screenshot 5.7

Like the BFS, Dijkstra's algorithm examines an awful lot of edges. Wouldn't it be great if the algorithm could be given hints as it progresses to nudge the search along in the correct direction? Well, luckily for us, this is possible. Ladies and gentlemen, please put your hands together in a round of applause and welcome A*!

Dijkstra with a Twist: A*

Dijkstra's algorithm searches by minimizing the cost of the path so far. It can be improved significantly by taking into account, when putting nodes on the frontier, an *estimate* of the cost to the target from each node under consideration. This estimate is usually referred to as a *heuristic*, and the name given to the algorithm that uses this method of heuristically directed search is A* (pronounced ay-star). And jolly good it is too!

If the heuristic used by the algorithm gives the *lower bound* on the actual cost (underestimates the cost) from any node to the target, then A* is guaranteed to give optimal paths. For graphs that contain spatial information, such as navigation graphs, there are several heuristic functions you can use, the most straightforward being the straight-line distance between the nodes in question. This is sometimes referred to as the *Euclidean distance*.

A* proceeds in an almost identical fashion to Dijkstra's search algorithm. The only difference is in the calculation of the costs of the nodes on the search frontier. The adjusted cost, *F*, to the node when positioned on the priority queue (the search frontier), is calculated as:

$$F = G + H \tag{5.3}$$

where *G* is the cumulative cost to reach a node and *H* is the heuristic estimate of the distance to the target. For an edge E that has just come off the frontier and been added to the SPT, the pseudocode to calculate the cost to its destination node looks like this:

```
Cost = AccumulativeCostTo(E.From) + E.Cost + CostTo(Target)
```

Utilizing a heuristic in this way, the modified costs *direct* the search toward the target node instead of radiating outward equally in all directions. This results in fewer edges needing to be examined, thereby speeding up the search and is the primary difference between A* and Dijkstra's algorithm.

NOTE If you set the heuristic cost to zero in A*, the resulting search behaves exactly the same as Dijkstra's algorithm.

Let's take a peek at how A* operates on the problem graphs used in the PathFinder program.

A in Action*

Screenshot 5.8 shows the result of A* operating on the simple source-target example problem. As you can see, no extraneous edges have been considered, and the path leads directly to the target. The heuristic function used is the straight-line distance between two nodes.

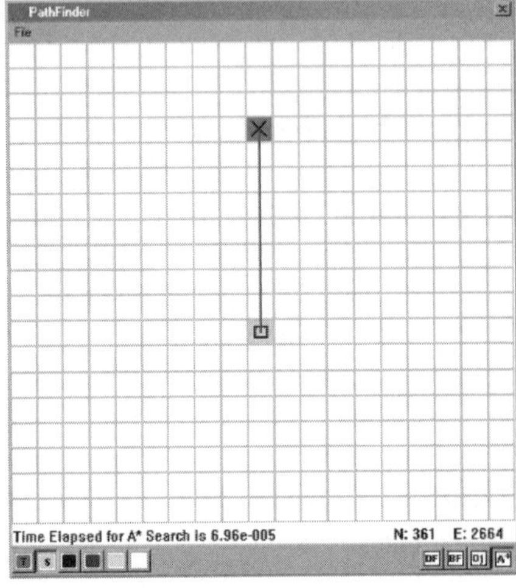

Screenshot 5.8. Do not pass Go, do not collect £200.

Screen shot 5.9 is just as impressive. Observe how few edges the A* algorithm had to consider before finding the target. As a consequence of this, the time taken to perform the search is considerably less than for any of the other searches (even though an evil square root is required to calculate the heuristic cost).

Screen shot 5.9

NOTE A* is proven to be optimally efficient. In other words, no other search algorithm will expand fewer nodes in the quest for the least cost path between source and target.

*Implementing A**

The A* class is very similar to `Graph_SearchDijkstra`. The implementation of the search requires that two `std::vectors` of costs are maintained: one for the *F* cost to each node, which is indexed into by the priority queue, and one for the *G* cost to each node. In addition, when creating an instance of this class you must specify, as a template parameter, the heuristic to be used. This design makes it easy for custom-built heuristics to be used with the class, like the Manhattan distance heuristic mentioned toward the end of this chapter.

Here's the class declaration for you to peruse:

```
template <class graph_type, class heuristic>
class Graph_SearchAStar
{
private:

  //create a typedef for the edge type used by the graph
  typedef typename graph_type::EdgeType Edge;

private:
```

```
  const graph_type&              m_Graph;

  //indexed into by node. Contains the "real" cumulative cost to that node
  std::vector<double>            m_GCosts;

  //indexed into by node. Contains the cost from adding m_GCosts[n] to
  //the heuristic cost from n to the target node. This is the vector the
  //iPQ indexes into.
  std::vector<double>            m_FCosts;

  std::vector<const Edge*>       m_ShortestPathTree;
  std::vector<const Edge*>       m_SearchFrontier;

  int                            m_iSource;
  int                            m_iTarget;

  //the A* search algorithm
  void Search();

public:

  Graph_SearchAStar(graph_type& graph,
                    int         source,
                    int         target):m_Graph(graph),
                                  m_ShortestPathTree(graph.NumNodes()),
                                  m_SearchFrontier(graph.NumNodes()),
                                  m_GCosts(graph.NumNodes(), 0.0),
                                  m_FCosts(graph.NumNodes(), 0.0),
                                  m_iSource(source),
                                  m_iTarget(target)
  {
    Search();
  }

  //returns the vector of edges that the algorithm has examined
  std::vector<const Edge*> GetSPT()const;

  //returns a vector of node indexes that comprise the shortest path
  //from the source to the target
  std::list<int>           GetPathToTarget()const;

  //returns the total cost to the target
  double                   GetCostToTarget()const;
};
```

Heuristic policies for use with this class must provide a static `Calculate` method with the following signature:

```
  //calculate the heuristic cost from node nd1 to node nd2
  static double Calculate(const graph_type& G, int nd1, int nd2);
```

Since the graph used by the PathFinder demo represents spatial information, the heuristic cost is calculated to be the straight-line distance (also known as the Euclidean distance) to the target node from each node under consideration. The following code shows how such a heuristic is implemented as a class that can be used as a template parameter for `Graph_SearchAStar`.

```
class Heuristic_Euclid
{
public:

  Heuristic_Euclid(){}

  //calculate the straight-line distance from node nd1 to node nd2
  template <class graph_type>
  static double Calculate(const graph_type& G, int nd1, int nd2)
  {
    return Vec2DDistance(G.GetNode(nd1).Position, G.GetNode(nd2).Position);
  }
};
```

The heuristic type is passed as a template parameter when an instance of the A* search class is created. Here is how the PathFinder demo program creates an instance of the A* search using the Euclidean heuristic:

```
  //create a couple of typedefs so the code will sit comfortably on the page
  typedef SparseGraph<NavGraphNode<>, GraphEdge>         NavGraph;
  typedef Graph_SearchAStar<NavGraph, Heuristic_Euclid> AStarSearch;

  //create an instance of the A* search using the Euclidean heuristic
  AStarSearch AStar(*m_pGraph, m_iSourceCell, m_iTargetCell);
```

The implementation of the A* `Search` method is almost identical to that used for Dijkstra's shortest path algorithm. The only exception is that the cost to reach a specific node before it is put on the frontier is now calculated as $G + H$ (instead of just G). The value of H is determined by calling the static method of the heuristic policy class.

```
template <class graph_type, class heuristic>
void Graph_SearchAStar<graph_type, heuristic>::Search()
{
  //create an indexed priority queue of nodes. The queue will give priority
  //to nodes with low F costs. (F=G+H)
  IndexedPriorityQLow<double> pq(m_FCosts, m_Graph.NumNodes());

  //put the source node on the queue
  pq.insert(m_iSource);

  //while the queue is not empty
  while(!pq.empty())
  {
    //get lowest cost node from the queue
    int NextClosestNode = pq.Pop();

    //move this node from the frontier to the spanning tree
    m_ShortestPathTree[NextClosestNode] = m_SearchFrontier[NextClosestNode];

    //if the target has been found exit
    if (NextClosestNode == m_iTarget) return;
```

```
    //now to test all the edges attached to this node
    graph_type::ConstEdgeIterator ConstEdgeItr(m_Graph, NextClosestNode);

    for (const Edge* pE=ConstEdgeItr.begin();
        !ConstEdgeItr.end();
         pE=ConstEdgeItr.next())
    {
      //calculate the heuristic cost from this node to the target (H)
      double HCost = heuristic::Calculate(m_Graph, m_iTarget, pE->To());

      //calculate the "real" cost to this node from the source (G)
      double GCost = m_GCosts[NextClosestNode] + pE->Cost();

      //if the node has not been added to the frontier, add it and update
      //the G and F costs
      if (m_SearchFrontier[pE->To()] == NULL)
      {
        m_FCosts[pE->T()] = GCost + HCost;
        m_GCosts[pE->To()] = GCost;

        pq.insert(pE->To());

        m_SearchFrontier[pE->To()] = pE;
      }

      //if this node is already on the frontier but the cost to get here this
      //way is cheaper than has been found previously, update the node costs
      //and frontier accordingly.
      else if ((GCost < m_GCosts[pE->To()]) &&
               (m_ShortestPathTree[pE->To()]==NULL))
      {
        m_FCosts[pE->To()] = GCost + HCost;
        m_GCosts[pE->To()] = GCost;

        pq.ChangePriority(pE->To());

        m_SearchFrontier[pE->To()] = pE;
      }
    }
  }
}
```

⌘ TIP If you are working with strict memory requirements you can curb the amount of memory the A* or Dijkstra's search uses by limiting the number of nodes put on the priority queue. In other words, only the *n* best nodes are kept on the queue. This has become known as a *beam search*.

The Manhattan Distance Heuristic

You have seen how the A* search algorithm class can be used with the Euclidean (straight-line distance) heuristic. Another heuristic function popular with programmers of games that have navgraphs with grid-like topology, such as tile-based war games, is the *Manhattan distance* between two nodes: the sum of the displacement in tiles vertically and horizontally.

For example, the Manhattan distance between the nodes *v* and *w* in Figure 5.39 is 10 (6 + 4).

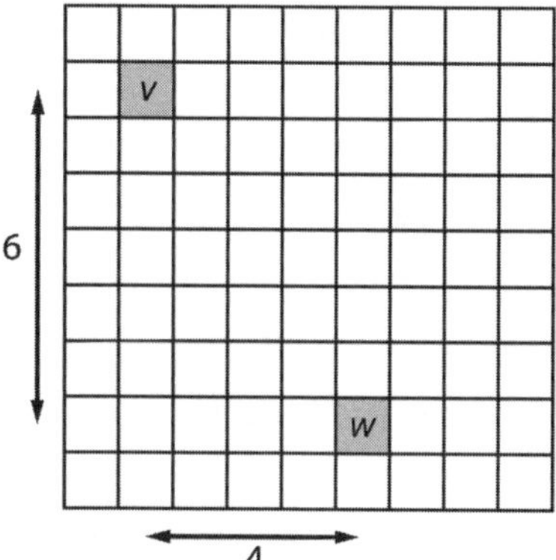

Figure 5.39. Calculating the Manhattan distance between two nodes

The Manhattan distance gives a speed increase over the Euclidean heuristic because no square root is required for the calculation.

Summing Up

You should now have a decent understanding of graphs and of the algorithms you can use to search them. As with most AI techniques, your understanding will grow enormously through practical experience, so I urge you to attempt at least some of the following problems.

Practice Makes Perfect

1. Using a pencil and paper, trace out the DFS, BFS, and Dijkstra's algorithm for the following graph. Use a different start and finish node for each search. Extra points will be awarded for use of style and color.

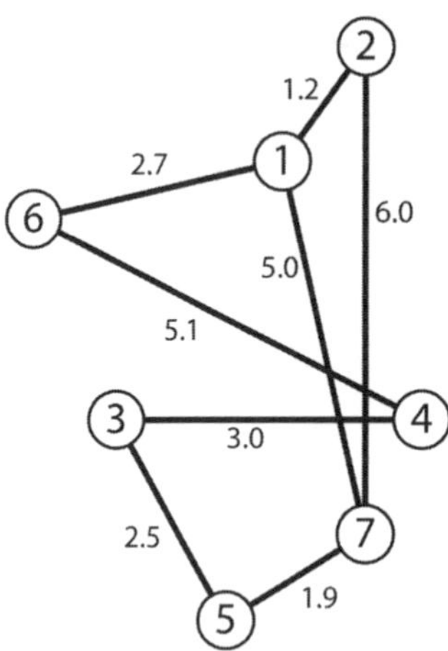

Figure 5.40

2. Create a Manhattan distance heuristic policy class to estimate the distance between a node and the target in a navigation graph. Try the heuristic out with different graphs. Is it better or worse than the Euclidean heuristic for grid-based graphs?
3. The Euclidean heuristic calculates the straight-line distance between nodes. This calculation requires the use of a square root. Create a heuristic that works in distance-squared space and note the shape of the paths it creates.
4. Create a program to find the best solution to the *n*-disk Towers of Hanoi puzzle where *n* can be any positive integer. To do this you must rewrite the BFS algorithm so that nodes and edges are added to the state graph as the search proceeds. This is an excellent way to test your understanding of the material presented in this chapter.
5. Now modify the algorithm you created in 4 to search for the best solution using iterative deepening DFS. How does it compare?
6. Use the A* algorithm to solve a shuffled Rubik's Cube. Give much consideration to the design of the heuristic function. This is a difficult problem, searching a potentially enormous search space, so first try your algorithm on a cube that is only one rotation away from a solution, then two, and so on. (Tip: If you are having difficulty designing a heuristic, do a search on the Internet… there are several interesting papers and articles on the subject.)

Chapter 6

To Script, or Not to Script, That Is the Question

Scripting languages are rapidly gaining popularity with game developers. You only have to listen to the buzz at developer conferences or see the amount of discussion regarding scripting on the Internet developer forums to know what a hot topic they have become. Several big-name developers have started to use scripting extensively in their titles. Epic Games' Unreal Tournament series, BioWare's Neverwinter Nights, and Crytek's Far Cry all utilize scripting languages.

Screenshot 6.1. Unreal Tournament 2003

© Epic Games, Inc.

To appreciate what all the fuss is about you need to know what a scripting language is before you understand how a game can benefit from using one.

Just What Is a Scripting Language?

As projects grow in size, the time required to compile the source code increases. As we all know, this can be a real pain in the backside. Changing just a couple of constants can result in a lengthy rebuild. For this reason, it's common practice to place many of the constants in a separate initialization file and create code to read and parse that file. This way, if you want to change some values, you don't need to recompile the project; you only have to change the values in the initialization/configuration file — usually a simple text file. You may be surprised to know the use of an initialization file like this is a rudimentary form of scripting and the text the initialization file contains is a very basic scripting language.

A more advanced scripting language increases the interaction between the script and the executable, enabling you to not only initialize variables but to create game logic or even game objects, all from one or more script files. These script files are run from within your program by something called a *virtual machine*, or VM for short. I'm not going to go into the details of virtual machines in this book — it's too low level and I don't think it's appropriate — but it helps to think of a VM as an *emulated* CPU sitting snugly inside your game's executable (your web browser, for example, uses a virtual machine to run Java code). You write functions in the syntax of the scripting language, which are read and then run inside the virtual machine. The beauty of scripting is that the virtual machine can communicate with the language inside which it resides (in our case C++), enabling data to easily be passed back and forth.

Scripts can either be *interpreted* or *compiled*. An interpreted script exists in the same format in which it is written — the human readable scripting language itself — and is read, parsed, and executed line by line by something called an *interpreter*. As this can be a slow process to do on-the-fly, some interpreted scripting languages automatically compile the script before it's executed. Another problem with interpreted scripts is that they can easily be understood and edited by game players who like nothing better than to give themselves an unfair advantage.

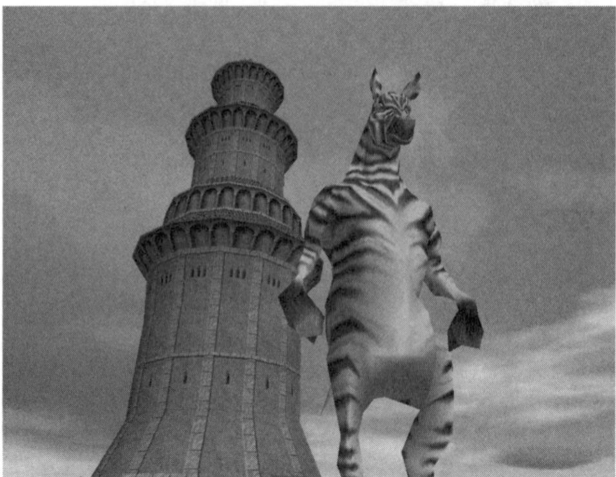

© Lionhead Studios Limited
Screenshot 6.2. Black & White

Compiled scripts are scripts that have been converted by the scripting language's compiler into a form of machine code the VM can execute directly. This machine code, or *byte code*, is completely platform independent because it's not been compiled to run on a type of machine, it's been compiled to run inside the virtual machine. Compiled scripts run faster, are smaller in size, and are therefore quicker to load. An additional benefit is that byte code is illegible to humans and therefore less prone to misuse by the end user.

What a Scripting Language Can Do for You

Scripting languages can assist the development process in many ways:

They can be used as a quick and easy way of reading variables and game data from initialization files. There's no need to write a parser of your own — just plug in the scripting language and off you go. And although this is a little like using a snowplow instead of a shovel to shift the snow from your driveway, it makes the job quick and easy and you don't get blisters on your hands.

They can save time and increase productivity. As game projects grow in size, so too does the time required to build them. Full engine compiles frequently take several minutes to complete and in some instances, well over an hour. This can be a nightmare for the AI programmer who has just implemented his latest brainwave and needs to test its performance before moving on to the next stage of his master plan. The last thing you want to do is sit around drinking yet *another* coffee, drumming the rhythm to the "Ace of Spades" on your thighs while your machine chugs away. However, if some of the AI logic is transferred from C++ to a script, changes can be made easily and quickly without need for recompilation. In projects where

Screenshot 6.3. Impossible Creatures

© Relic Entertainment, Inc.

you know in advance that compile times are going to be a daily thorn in your side, it's worth considering scripting the majority of the AI decision logic while the game is in development, and then transferring the speed-critical stuff back to C++ prior to shipping. This keeps your productivity and cranial juices flowing while simultaneously reducing caffeine jitters to a minimum, which means it's good for the heart as well as the cash flow.

They can increase creativity. Scripting languages usually operate at a higher level than languages such as C++ and utilize syntax that is more intuitive to non-programmers. This is advantageous because it allows other members of the development team like level designers, artists, and producers to make adjustments to the gameplay (or any other aspect of the design) without having to pester you every few minutes. They are able to do this from the comfort of their own workstations, making as many adjustments as they like to the exposed functionality of the AI without any need for major rebuilds. This is beneficial to both productivity and creativity. The former promotes experimentation and the latter enables you, the programmer, to work uninterrupted. Since this ability to play with the engine allows any interested members of the development team to get their hands dirty and fool around with the gameplay, giving them a greater sense of involvement in the final product, it's also good for morale.

They provide extensibility. In recent years there has been an upsurge in players customizing games to create "mods." Some of these mods are unrecognizable from the original game because just about everything has changed. The maps are different, the textures are unique, the weapons more kick-ass, and the bad guys badder. Using a scripting language, it's possible to expose as much or as little of your game engine as you like, putting its power directly into the hands of the mod makers. Increasingly, game developers are electing to give game players the opportunity to tinker with their

© Atari/BioWare

Screenshot 6.4. Neverwinter Nights

products, and this trend is likely to continue well into the future. This has become a big selling point for many games. Probably the two best known examples in recent times are Epic Games' Unreal Tournament 2004 (and UT2003) and BioWare's Neverwinter Nights. Both provide the gamer with a powerful scripting engine, enabling individuals and teams to create rich, custom-built scenarios.

Now that you've seen some of the advantages of using scripting in your games, let's take a look at some specific examples of how scripting languages have been used by game developers.

Dialogue Flow

One of the simplest and earliest uses of scripting languages in games is to manage the vast amounts of dialogue found in RPG type games. In these, scripts are used to control the flow of dialogue between a character and the player. A typical script might look something like this:

```
** Dialogue script 1 for Eric the Gross Nosed **

FUNCTION DialogueWithGrossNosedEric(Player plyr)

  Speak("Welcome stranger. What brings thee amongst us gentle folk?")

  int reply = plyr.SpeakOption(1, "Yo dude, wazzup?",
                               2, "I want your money, your woman, and that chicken")

  IF reply == 1 THEN

    Speak("Wazzuuuuuup!")

  ELSE IF reply == 2 THEN

    Speak( "Well, well. A fight ye wants, is it? Ye can't just go around these parts demandin' chickens
           from folk. Yer likely to get that ugly face smashed in. Be off with thee!")

  END IF

END FUNCTION
```

This sort of script would be called by the main game code on the occurrence of a specific event. In this example, it would be the player entering the vicinity of Eric the Gross Nosed. Utilizing scripts in this way makes it easy for game designers to write humongous amounts of dialogue quickly and easily.

There's no need to stop at just dialogue. Scripts can be written to control a character's actions and the camera positioning, and handle sounds and animation, providing a kind of…

Stage Direction

Stage direction is probably the most common utilization of scripting in games at the time of this book's publication. These types of scripts turn the common or garden-variety game designer into a virtual film director, a veritable cyber-Spielberg capable of manipulating the actions of the game characters and environments at will, enabling the designer to create immersive and entertaining game scenarios without so much as a whisper in the AI or engine programmer's ear. These type of scripts open up the guts of the game engine to the wannabe Scorseses on your development team, allowing game objects and events to be easily handled and created. Here's how such a script might look:

```
FUNCTION script_castle_guard (player)

  ** create a guard situated at the castle's drawbridge
  guard = Guard(GetPos(Drawbridge))

  **focus and lock the camera on the guard
  LockCamera(guard)

  **move the guard toward the player
  guard.Move(GetPos(player))

  IF Player.Has(GetFlag(AUTHORIZATION_FROM_KING)) THEN

    **welcome the player and escort him to the king
    guard.Speak("Good Evening" + player.Name()+" His Majesty is expecting you. Come this way")

    guard.Move(GetPos(Throne_Room))

    player.Follow(guard)

  ELSE

    **give the player some verbal abuse, then dump him in the dungeon
    guard.Speak("OI! Wot are you doin' on my bridge! You are coming with me, my son!")

    guard.Move(GetPos(Dungeon))

    player.Follow(guard)

  END IF

  **move guard back to drawbridge
  guard.Move(GetPos(Drawbridge))

END FUNCTION
```

Used correctly, scripted sequences enhance the game playing experience and are an ideal vehicle to move a story line forward. Lionhead's Black & White made great use of this type of stage direction to control the game's quests.

Screenshot 6.5. Black & White
© Lionhead Studios Limited

AI Logic

Tweaking the AI of game characters is a big part of an AI programmer's job. If the project is particularly large, this can prove to be a very frustrating experience as each change to the code may involve a lengthy recompile. Fortunately, this can be avoided by utilizing a scripting language. I don't mean by this that scripting languages should be used to write speed-critical portions of AI code — such as the code required to do a graph search, for example — but that scripts may be used to write the decision logic of your game agents. For example, if your agent uses a finite state machine, rather than hard-coding the states, you can expose the interface of your agent class (and any other relevant classes) to the scripting language and write scripts for each state, enabling the agent's flow of logic to be easily adjusted. This means you can tweak until your heart bursts without any of the usual inconvenience of sitting around waiting for recompiles. Far Cry and Unreal Tournament are a couple of examples of games that use scripts in this way.

Scripting in Lua

Over the last five years a scripting language called *Lua* has increased in popularity with game developers and has been used to provide scripting for many notable games including:

- Escape from Monkey Island
- MDK 2
- Grim Fandango
- Baldur's Gate
- Impossible Creatures

- Homeworld 2
- Far Cry

Lua has gained this popularity because it's extremely powerful and fast (for a scripting language), yet lightweight and simple to use. The icing on the cake is that it's also very portable, free, and open-source.

Screenshot 6.6. Impossible Creatures

© Relic Entertainment, Inc.

It's impossible within the space of one chapter to describe all the features of Lua, but I can provide you with a decent introduction, certainly enough to whet your appetite and to show you how Lua can be used effectively in your own games.

Let's get started then…

Setting Up Your Compiler to Work with Lua

The Lua headers and libraries can be found in the common/lua-5.0 folder in the downloadable files. You must direct your compiler to search for the Lua header files in the common/lua-5.0/include folder, and for the lua libraries in the common/lua-5.0/lib folder. When you create a project, make sure you add the Lua libraries: lua.lib, lualib.lib, and lauxlib.lib.

Getting Started

Before you learn how to interface your C/C++ programs with Lua, you need to know how to program using the Lua programming language. With this in mind, the next few pages will be spent giving you a tour of Lua to familiarize you with the data types and syntax. Fortunately, Lua is very easy to learn and it will only take you a short while before you feel competent enough to start writing your own scripts. Once you are familiar with the language, I'll demonstrate how Lua variables and functions can be accessed from within C++ and vice versa. We'll then spend some time examining how C++ classes can be exposed to Lua before moving on to a little project that ties everything together.

NOTE Although this chapter will show you enough to get you started, it's impossible to do the language justice in just one chapter. Therefore, I highly recommend you read the Lua documentation and visit the Lua user's wiki online at http://lua-users.org/wiki/.

Lua comes with an interactive interpreter (common/lua-5.0/bin/lua.exe) you can use to try out little snippets of code by typing them directly into the console at the command prompt, but for anything more than a couple of lines you may find this tedious. I think the best way to start your journey into Lua is by showing you how to run a script using the C/C++ Lua API. This way you can use the familiar environment of your compiler's IDE to write and run scripts.

Let me talk you through the code required to run a Lua script from a C/C++ program.

```
extern "C"
{
  #include <lua.h>
  #include <lualib.h>
  #include <lauxlib.h>
}
```

First you have to include the relevant header files. Since Lua is a pure C library, you must let the compiler know this explicitly or you'll experience problems. This is done by encasing the `#includes` with `extern "C"`.

```
//include the lua libraries. If your compiler doesn't support this pragma
//then don't forget to add the libraries in your project settings!
#pragma comment(lib, "lua.lib")
#pragma comment(lib, "lualib.lib")

#include <iostream>

int main()
{
  //create a lua state
  lua_State* pL = lua_open();
```

Each script file you run will be executed in a dynamically allocated structure called a `lua_State`. Every function in the Lua library requires that a pointer to a `lua_State` be passed to it as a parameter. Therefore, before running a script file you must create a Lua state by calling `lua_open`.

```
  //enable access to the standard libraries
  luaopen_base(pL);
  luaopen_string(pL);
  luaopen_table(pL);
```

```
luaopen_math(pL);
luaopen_io(pL);
```

Lua comes with several standard libraries. They provide input/output, mathematical, and string manipulation functions, among other things. These lines of code make sure the library commands can be called from within your Lua script. Of course, if your Lua scripts don't use these library functions, they may be omitted. For now though, let's include all of them.

```
if (int error = lua_dofile(pL, "your_first_lua_script.lua") != 0)
{
  std::cout << "\n[C++]: ERROR(" << error << "): Problem with lua"
            << "script file!\n\n" << std::endl;

  return 0;
}
```

The command `lua_dofile` loads, compiles, and executes a Lua script. If there is a problem with running the script the function returns an error code.

It is also possible to precompile a Lua script using luac.exe, which you can find in the common/lua-5.0/bin folder. As mentioned earlier, compiled scripts load quicker and are effectively sealed from the eyes of the end user. Precompiled scripts are loaded into your program in the same way as regular scripts.

```
//tidy up
lua_close(pL);
```

To tidy up, `lua_close` must be called. This function destroys all the objects in the Lua state and frees up any dynamically allocated memory.

```
  return 0;
}
```

If you boot up the project StartHere, you can try out your own Lua programs as you work your way through the first section of this chapter by typing them out in the your_first_lua_script.lua file and then hitting the run button.

Lua Variables

Lua is a *dynamically typed* language. This means that unlike C/C++, variables can be assigned any type. In other words, you can do stuff like this:

```
--start lua script

--assign the string "Bilbo Baggins" to the variable 'name'
name = "Bilbo Baggins"

print ("name = "..name)
```

```
--now assign the floating-point number 3.14159 to the variable pi
pi = 3.14159

--assigning pi to name is also valid
name = pi

--as is this
pi = false
```

Notice that comments in Lua are proceeded by -- instead of the double slash or /* … */ used for C++/C comments. You can also write comments over multiple lines using the following syntax:

```
--[[this is an extremely long
   comment separated
   over several lines]]
```

Although statements spread over multiple lines must be terminated with a semicolon, this is not mandatory for single line statements. Consequently, all the following statements are correct syntax:

```
A = 10

B = 10; A = 10;

B = 10; A = 10

B = 10  A = 10

print (
"It is possible to span over multiple lines"
);
```

If the semicolon at the end of the print statement had not been present, it would have given an error.

It's also possible to assign values to several variables simultaneously. For example, you can do stuff like this:

```
a, b, c, d = 1, 2, 3, 4

x, y, z = a, b, c
```

If the number of variables on the left-hand side is greater than the number on the right, then the *nil* value is applied to the extraneous variables. `nil` is a special Lua type and indicates the absence of meaning. For example:

```
x, y, z = 1, 2

print (x, y, z)
```

gives the output:

```
1  2  nil
```

If the number of terms on the right-hand side is greater, then the additional values are simply discarded. For example:

```
x, y, z = 1, 2, 3, 4, 5

print (x, y, z)
```

gives the output:

```
1 2 3
```

There are three different kinds of variables in Lua: global, local, and table fields. *Variables are considered to be global unless they are explicitly defined as local using the local keyword*, like so:

```
local name = "sally"
```

Before a value is assigned to a variable its value is nil.

I'm starting to get a little ahead of myself here, so let me break off and discuss the Lua variable types in detail.

Lua Types

Lua uses eight basic types. They are as follows:

Nil

nil has been defined to be distinct from any other value and is used to represent the absence of meaning. Once you have created a variable, it's possible to "delete" it by assigning the nil type to it. The nil type is Lua's magic wand: If a variable is assigned this value, it vanishes as though it never existed. Poof!

Number

The **number** type is used to represent floating-point numbers. Internally, this value is treated as a double. Therefore, when you pass numbers to your C/C++ program, you must remember to cast them to the correct type.

String

The **string** type is an array of 8-bit characters. You can join strings together using the concatenation operator .. (two dots). If either side of the .. operator is not a string, then it is converted prior to concatenation. Therefore:

```
age = 25
print ("I am "..age.." years of age")
```

gives the output:

```
I am 25 years of age
```

Boolean

This represents a true or false value. A zero or nil signifies a false value, and anything else, true.

Functions

Functions in Lua are also a type and can be assigned to variables. The function can then be called using that variable's name. Because Lua is typeless, no types have to be specified either in the parameter list or as a return value. Here's an example of a simple function to add two numbers together. Note how the function block ends with the end keyword.

```
add = function(a, b)

 return a+b

end
```

This syntax is a little unfamiliar to us, so Lua provides another way of declaring a function, which looks a little more like C++:

```
function add(a, b)

 return a+b

end
```

Unlike C++, Lua functions can return several variables at once, so the following is perfectly acceptable:

```
function IncrementTwoValues(a, b)

 return a+1, b+1

end


a = 2; b = 10;

print (a, b)


a, b = IncrementTwoValues(a, b);

print (a, b)
```

The output from this script is:

```
2  10
3  11
```

Tables

A **table** is a very powerful data type. You can think of a table as a kind of associative array or hash table, which means not only can you index a table with integers, but you can also index into a table using any type of key. In addition, Lua tables are *heterogeneous* — they can mix data types.

A C/C++ style syntax is used to access tables. Here are some examples using integers as indexes:

```
--create a table
test_table = {}

--assign some values to it
test_table[1] = 4
test_table[2] = 5.6
test_table[3] = "Hello World"
```

It's also possible to construct the same table using this syntax:

```
test_table = {4, 5.6, "Hello World"}
```

Now let's add a couple of associative indices:

```
test_table["eight"] = 8
test_table[3.141] = "Pi"
```

n-dimensional tables are easy also. Let's say you want to create a lookup table to decide who wins the game of rock-paper-scissors as shown in Figure 6.1.

Human \ Computer	Rock	Paper	Scissors
Rock	draw	lose	win
Paper	win	draw	lose
Scissors	lose	win	draw

Figure 6.1

The table tells us a rock played against scissors is a win, paper played against paper is a draw, and so on. This is how the table can be reproduced as a Lua table:

```
lookup = {}

lookup["rock"] = {}
lookup["rock"]["rock"]     = "draw"
lookup["rock"]["paper"]    = "lose"
lookup["rock"]["scissors"] = "win"

lookup["paper"] = {}
lookup["paper"]["rock"]     = "win"
lookup["paper"]["paper"]    = "draw"
lookup["paper"]["scissors"] = "lose"

lookup["scissors"] = {}
lookup["scissors"]["rock"]     = "lose"
```

```
lookup["scissors"]["paper"]   = "win"
lookup["scissors"]["scissors"] = "draw"
```

Fortunately, this can be reduced in size to something more pleasing to the eye:

```
lookup = {}
lookup["rock"]  = {rock = "draw", paper =  "lose", scissors = "win"}
lookup["paper"] = {rock = "win", paper = "draw", scissors =  "lose"}
lookup["scissors"] = {rock =  "lose", paper = "win", scissors = "draw"}
```

In addition to using the square brackets ([]) to retrieve a value, the access operator (.) may also be used, like so:

```
test_table.eight = 8
```

Functions can also be assigned to tables, so you can do stuff like this:

```
function add(a, b)
  return a+b
end

op = {}
op["add"] = add

print(op.add(4, 7));
```

UserData

The **userdata** type is provided to allow Lua variables to store custom C/C++ data. A variable of the type userdata cannot be created or modified inside Lua, only through the C/C++ interface. Because userdata corresponds to a raw block of memory, there are no predefined operations (other than assignment and an identity test), but it is possible to define operations using metatables.

 **NOTE** A metatable may be assigned to Lua userdata or table types and can be used to define the behavior of the type it is attached to. Each metatable is a table in its own right and defines the behavior for the type it is attached to for specific operations such as +, ==, or concatenate. You use them in a similar way to operator overloading in C++. Please see the Lua documentation for some good examples of how you may use metatables.

Threads

The **thread** type enables individual threads of execution to be spawned.

Logical Operators

Lua has three logical operators: and, or, and not. They operate very much like their C++ counterparts &&, ||, and !. Like C++, they only evaluate the second term if necessary. The values False and `nil` are false; everything else is considered to be true.

Conditional Structures

Lua provides the conditional structures if, while, repeat, and for. Lua's versions of the `if` and `while` control structures are very similar to those used in C/C++, except the conditions are not required to be supplied inside parentheses. Here is an example of the former:

```
if a == 4 then
  print ("yup")
 else
  print ("nope")
end
```

And here is an example of a while loop:

```
while a > 1 do
 a = a - 1
end
```

Notice how both the if and while structures end their blocks with the end keyword.

repeat's dancing partner is until. They work together like this:

```
repeat
 a = a - 1
 print (a)
until a == 0
```

There are two versions of the familiar `for` structure. One is numeric and the other is used with tables. The numeric for has the syntax:

```
for var = lower_value, upper_value, step do
 something()
end
```

This means the loop will be executed for each value of var between lower_value and upper_value in increments of `step`. Therefore, the code:

```
for a = 10, 14, 2 do
 print (a)
end
```

gives the output of:

```
10
12
14
```

The variable a is automatically declared as a local variable and is only visible within the loop. For loops may be exited using the break keyword.

The other type of for loop is used to traverse tables. This has a different syntax.

```
for k, v in t do

  something()

end
```

The k and v refer to the table t's key-value pair. Here's an example to clarify how it works:

```
data = {a=1, b=2, c=3}

for k, v in data do

  print (k, v)

end
```

Running this snippet of code produces the output:

```
a  1
c  3
b  2
```

As you can see, the values are not listed in the expected order. This is because the order is undefined in Lua; it depends on how the table has been stored internally.

Rock-Paper-Scissors in Lua

As a simple example to demonstrate some of the syntax of the Lua programming language, here's some simple code that plays the game rock-paper-scissors. (The AI is extremely dumb; it just picks randomly.)

```
-------------------------------------------------------------------------------

--Name:   rock_paper_scissors2.lua

--Author: Mat Buckland

--Desc:   lua script to implement a rock-paper-scissors game

-------------------------------------------------------------------------------

--[[seed the random number generator]]
```

```
math.randomseed(os.time())


--[[these global variables will hold the scores of the player
  and the computer]]

user_score = 0
comp_score = 0


--[[ this table is used to determine who wins which round ]]

lookup = {};
lookup["rock"]  = {rock = "draw", paper = "lose", scissors = "win" }
lookup["paper"] = {rock = "win", paper = "draw", scissors =  "lose"}
lookup["scissors"] = {rock =  "lose", paper = "win", scissors = "draw"}


--[[this function returns the computer's best guess]]

function GetAIMove()

   --create a table so we can convert an integer to a play string
   local int_to_name = {"scissors", "rock", "paper"}

   --get a random integer in the range 1-3 and use it as an index
   --into the table we've just made so that the function can return
   --a random play
   return int_to_name[math.random(3)]

end


--[[this function uses the lookup table to decide the winner and
   allocates scores accordingly]]

function EvaluateTheGuesses(user_guess, comp_guess)

   print ("user guess... "..user_guess.."  comp guess... "..comp_guess)

   if (lookup[user_guess][comp_guess] == "win") then

       print ("You Win the Round!")

       user_score = user_score + 1

   elseif (lookup[user_guess][comp_guess] ==  "lose") then

      print ("Computer Wins the Round")

       comp_score = comp_score + 1
```

```
    else

      print ("Draw!")

      print (lookup[user_guess][comp_guess])

    end

end


--[[   main game loop    ]]

print ("Enter q to quit game");
print()

loop = true
while loop == true do

   --let the user know the current score
   print("User: "..user_score.." Computer: "..comp_score)

   --grab input from the user via the keyboard
   user_guess = io.stdin:read '*l'

   --[[declare a table to convert the user's input into a string]]

   local letter_to_string = {s = "scissors", r = "rock", p = "paper"}


   if user_guess == "q" then

      loop = false   --quit the game if user enters 'q'

   elseif (user_guess == "r") or (user_guess == "p") or (user_guess == "s") then

      comp_guess = GetAIMove()

      EvaluateTheGuesses(letter_to_string[user_guess], comp_guess)

   else

      print ("Invalid input, try again")

   end
end
```

Now that you've got a feel for the Lua language, let's get on with what you really want to know: how to interface Lua with your C/C++ programs.

TIP When compiling you may get a whole load of linker errors with this signature:

```
libcmt.lib(blahblah.obj) : error LNK2005: __blahblah already defined in LIBCD.lib
```

or the warning:

```
defaultlib "LIBCMT" conflicts with use of other libs; use /NODEFAULTLIB:library
```

This is because the Lua libraries will have been compiled with a different set of runtime libraries than your application. In 99% of cases you can remove these by telling your compiler to ignore the libcmt library. (In VC6 go to Project Settings -> Link -> Input, then enter libcmt in the Ignore Libraries field.) If this doesn't work then you will need to create the Lua libraries yourself with the correct settings (see the docs).

Interfacing with C/C++

C++ and Lua use different syntax and data types, so it's impossible for them to "talk" directly to one another. You can view this conceptually as two pirates shipwrecked on separate islands situated too far apart for them to be able to converse with each other, no matter how loudly they shout. Fortunately, one of the pirates owns a very vocal parrot named Bernie. Bernie remembers and repeats the last thing said to him and regularly flies between the islands in search of food. The pirates quickly realize Bernie can be used as a means of communicating with each other. If Pirate One wants to know Pirate Two's name, he can say to Bernie "Ahoy there matey! Who be I speakin' to?" and wait for the parrot to fly across the waters. When he returns, Bernie will speak the last thing Pirate Two uttered: "I be Black Beard. Arrr, harrr. Yes I be."

In the same way the pirates use Bernie to route their conversation, Lua and C++ are able to communicate using a *virtual stack*, which grows and shrinks according to the demands of the script. As a quick example, let's say the string "Captain Hook" has been assigned to the variable `Pirates_Name` in a Lua script file.

```
Pirates_Name = "Captain Hook"
```

A C++ function can access this variable by following these steps:

1. The C++ function puts the string Pirates_Name on the Lua stack.
2. Lua reads the stack and finds the string Pirates_Name.
3. Lua looks up the value of Pirates_Name in its global table and places whatever is assigned to it — "Captain Hook" — on the stack.
4. The C++ function grabs the string Captain Hook from the top of the stack.

Presto! Lua and C++ have just passed data between each other. Of course, when passing data back and forth for arrays and function calls and so forth, this process becomes much more complicated but is still essentially the same.

In customary stack implementations elements can only be "popped" and "pushed" on or off the stack, but with Lua the stack is also accessible by index. If *n* is the number of elements in the stack, then the elements are numbered from 1 to *n*, from the bottom (first in) of the stack upward. It's also possible to index into the stack using the negative integers: –1 to –*n*. In this case, the elements are counted from the top (last in) downward to –*n*. See Figure 6.2.

7	"g"	-1
6	"f"	-2
5	"e"	-3
4	"d"	-4
3	"c"	-5
2	"b"	-6
1	"a"	-7

Figure 6.2. A Lua virtual stack containing the characters "a" to "g"

In the figure, "e" can be said to be at position 5 *or* at position –3. In Lua, either value is correct. Many programmers prefer to work with negative indices because that way you don't need to know the exact size of the stack and only need to keep track of any recent values pushed onto it.

Don't be concerned if you feel a little confused right now. You'll see many examples of exactly how the Lua stack is used in the following pages and soon it will become second nature.

NOTE The default stack size `LUA_MINSTACK` is defined in lua.h as 20. You don't need to worry about adjusting this unless you create functions that push lots of values onto the stack (like recursive functions).

Accessing Lua Global Variables from within Your C++ Program

Let's say you have a Lua script file that has the global variables `name` and `age` defined and you'd like to access those values in your C++ program.

```
--global string and number types

name = "Spiderman"

age = 29
```

To be able to access those variables you must first put them on the Lua stack. You can do this by passing a pointer to the Lua state they have been defined in, and their name to the API function `lua_getglobal`. First of all though, it's wise to make sure the stack's top is set to index 0 (0 is empty) by using the function `lua_settop`. Here's the C++ code to do just that:

```
//reset the stack index
lua_settop(pL, 0);
```

And here's the code to put the variables we want to access on the stack:

```
//put the lua global variables "age" and "name" on the stack.
lua_getglobal(pL, "age");
lua_getglobal(pL, "name");
```

Now they are at our mercy! Before the C++ code grabs them, however, it's wise to make sure the values you *think* are on the top of the stack are *actually* at the top. This is done using one of the following:

```
int lua_type (lua_State *L, int index);
int lua_isnil (lua_State *L, int index);
int lua_isboolean (lua_State *L, int index);
int lua_isnumber (lua_State *L, int index);
int lua_isstring (lua_State *L, int index);
int lua_istable (lua_State *L, int index);
int lua_isfunction (lua_State *L, int index);
int lua_iscfunction (lua_State *L, int index);
int lua_isuserdata (lua_State *L, int index);
```

where `index` is the stack index you'd like to check. In our small example, we want to make sure the two values at positions 1 and 2 in the stack are a number and string respectively. Here's the code to do just that:

```
//check that the variables are the correct type. (notice how the
//stack index starts at 1, not 0)
if (!lua_isnumber(pL, 1) || !lua_isstring(pL, 2))
{
  cout << "\n[C++]: ERROR: Invalid type!";
}
```

At this point we know that values of the correct type are where they should be in the stack so it's time for C++ to grab them. However, because the values on the stack are Lua types, they need to be converted to C++ types. This is done using one of the following Lua API functions:

```
int             lua_toboolean (lua_State *L, int index);
lua_Number      lua_tonumber (lua_State *L, int index);
const char*     lua_tostring (lua_State *L, int index);
size_t          lua_strlen (lua_State *L, int index);
lua_CFunction   lua_tocfunction (lua_State *L, int index);
void*           lua_touserdata (lua_State *L, int index);
lua_State*      lua_tothread (lua_State *L, int index);
void*           lua_topointer (lua_State *L, int index);
```

This is how the appropriate conversion function is used to retrieve the values of `age` and `name` from the stack.

```
//now assign the values to C++ variables
string name = lua_tostring(pL, 2);

//notice the cast to int with this.
int    age = (int)lua_tonumber(pL, 1);
```

Notice how the number had to be cast to the correct type. This is because all numbers in Lua are treated as doubles.

Obviously, going through all these calls to grab just one variable can get extremely tedious very quickly, so it's best if you create your own functions to speed this process up. Here's an example of a function template to grab a number from the stack:

```
template <class T>
inline T PopLuaNumber(lua_State* pL, const char* name)
{
  lua_settop(pL, 0);

  lua_getglobal(pL, name);

  //check that the variable is the correct type.
  if (!lua_isnumber(pL, 1))
  {
    cout << "\n[C++]: ERROR: Invalid type!";
  }

  //grab the value, cast to the correct type, and return
  T val = (T)lua_tonumber(pL, 1);

  //remove the value from the stack
  lua_pop(pL, 1);

  return val;
}
```

Okay, that was easy. Let's move on to something a little more complicated.

⌘ TIP Because it's so easy to retrieve values from a script file, and because the Lua code itself is so lightweight, Lua provides a quick and simple way to create your game's initialization/configuration files.

Accessing a Lua Table from within Your C++ Program

Accessing a Lua table is a little more involved because there is a key associated with each element. Let's take a look at the simple table defined in the following Lua script.

```
--global table creation

simple_table = {name="Dan Dare", age=20}
```

To retrieve one or more of the elements, first of all `simple_table` must be added to the stack. This is done in a similar way to what you've already seen, by using `lua_getglobal`.

```
//reset the stack index
lua_settop(pL, 0);

//put the table on the stack
lua_getglobal(pL, "simple_table");
```

Next a check is made to ensure the correct type is in the expected position.

```
if (!lua_istable(pL, 1))
{
  cout << "\n[C++]: ERROR: simple_table is not a valid table";
}
```

```
else
{
```

Now to retrieve the element indexed into by the key "name." To do that, the key must be pushed onto the stack so Lua knows what it's looking for. You can push values from C/C++ onto the stack using one of these API calls:

```
void lua_pushboolean (lua_State *L, int b);
void lua_pushnumber (lua_State *L, lua_Number n);
void lua_pushlstring (lua_State *L, const char *s, size_t len);
void lua_pushstring (lua_State *L, const char *s);
void lua_pushnil (lua_State *L);
void lua_pushcfunction (lua_State *L, lua_CFunction f);
void lua_pushlightuserdata (lua_State *L, void *p);
```

The keys in this example are strings, so `lua_pushstring` is used to push "name" onto the stack.

```
  //push the key onto the stack
  lua_pushstring(pL, "name");
```

`lua_gettable` is a function that pops the key off the stack, grabs the corresponding element, and puts it back on the stack. Notice how I've used negative indices to index backward from the top of the stack (–1 is the top, remember).

```
  //table is now at -2 (key is at -1). lua_gettable now pops the key off
  //the stack and then puts the data found at the key location on the stack
  lua_gettable(pL, -2);
```

Once the desired element is on the top of the stack, as before, it's a good idea to ensure it is of the correct type.

```
  //check that element is the correct type
  if (!lua_isstring(pL, -1))
  {
    cout << "\n[C++]: ERROR: invalid type";
  }
```

Finally, grab the data.

```
  //grab the data
  name = lua_tostring(pL, -1);

  cout << "\n\n[C++]: name = " << name;
```

And remove it from the stack.

```
  lua_pop(pL, 1);
}
```

By now you should be getting a feel for how the stack is used, so let's move on to accessing functions defined in Lua from within a C++ program.

Accessing a Lua Function from within C++

Using a similar process to that used in the last two sections, you can allow your C/C++ program to access Lua functions. Let's use the simple function add as an example:

```
--function to add two numbers together and return the result

function add(a, b)

  return (a + b)

end;
```

A Lua function is a type just like a number, string, or table, so the process for accessing one is familiar. First, place the function on the stack and make sure what's there is what you are expecting.

```
//get the function from the global table and push it on the stack
lua_getglobal(pL, "add");

//check that it is there
if (!lua_isfunction(pL, -1))
{
  cout << "\n\n[C++]: Oops! The lua function 'add' has not been defined";
}
```

Next the parameters are pushed onto the stack. The first parameter is pushed first, followed by any others. The add function takes two parameters, so the following code pushes the numbers 5 and 8 onto the stack.

```
//push some variables onto the lua stack
lua_pushnumber(pL, 5);
lua_pushnumber(pL, 8);
```

At this point the Lua stack contains all the information required to call the function: the function name and the parameters we want to pass to it. The function is called using the API function lua_call. Its prototype looks like this:

```
void lua_call (lua_State *L, int nargs, int nresults);
```

nargs is the number of parameters that have been pushed onto the stack, and nresults is the number of parameters the function will return. The parameters are returned in direct order, so the last parameter returned will be on the top of the stack.

Here's how lua_call is used to call the add function.

```
//calling the function with parameters to set the number of parameters in
//the lua func and how many return values it returns. Puts the result at
//the top of the stack.
lua_call(pL, 2, 1);
```

Finally the result is retrieved and removed from the top of the stack.

```
//grab the result from the top of the stack
int result = lua_tonumber(pL, -1);

lua_pop(pL, 1);
```

All these examples can be found in the project cpp_using_lua.

NOTE Most of the Lua API "functions" mentioned in this chapter are actually `#defines`. I recommend you check them out at some point by examining the lua.h, lualib.h, and lauxlib.h files.

Exposing a C/C++ Function to Lua

To call a C/C++ function from a Lua script it must be of the type `lua_CFunction`, which is defined as:

```
int (lua_CFunction*) (lua_State*)
```

In other words, you must make sure your C/C++ function takes the form:

```
int function_name(lua_State*)
```

Let's take a look at an example. I'm going to alter the rock-paper-scissors example shown earlier so that some of the functions are written in C++ and are called from within the Lua script. You can find the project file under the name lua_using_cpp.

In the RockPaperScissors.h file you'll see a C++ function called `EvaluateTheGuesses`, which has the prototype:

```
void EvaluateTheGuesses(std::string  user_guess,
                        std::string  comp_guess,
                        int&         user_score,
                        int&         comp_score);
```

To be able to call this function from Lua, the prototype has to be changed to conform to the correct signature. This is easy to do by wrapping it *inside* another function that has the required footprint. Inside the wrapper, any parameters are retrieved from the stack as before and used to call the function proper. Any return values are then pushed onto the stack.

Let me demonstrate by showing you how the `EvaluateTheGuesses` function is wrapped. First we create a similarly named function with the correct footprint.

```
int cpp_EvaluateTheGuesses(lua_State* pL)
{
```

`lua_gettop` is then used to return the index of the top element of the stack. When a function call is made from Lua, the top of the stack is reset and then any parameters are pushed onto the stack. Therefore, the value `lua_gettop` returns is equal to the number of parameters Lua is attempting to pass.

```
//get the number of parameters passed to this function from the lua
//stack and make sure it is equal to the correct number of parameters
```

```
//for EvaluateTheGuesses.
int n = lua_gettop(pL);
```

It's always a good idea at this point to confirm that the number of parameters Lua is passing is correct.

```
if (n!=4)
{
  std::cout << "\n[C++]: Wrong number of arguments for"
            << " cpp_EvaluateTheGuesses";

  return 0;
}
```

And that the parameters are of the correct type.

```
 //check that the parameters are of the correct type.
if (!lua_isstring(pL, 1) || !lua_isstring(pL, 2) ||
    !lua_isnumber(pL, 3) || !lua_isnumber(pL, 4))
{
  std::cout << "\n[C++]: ERROR: Invalid types passed to"
            << " cpp_EvaluateTheGuesses";
}
```

At this point we know we have the correct amount of parameters and that they are of the correct type, so we can proceed by grabbing them from the stack and calling the function proper.

```
//grab the parameters off the stack
std::string user_guess = lua_tostring(pL, 1);
std::string comp_guess = lua_tostring(pL, 2);
int         user_score = (int)lua_tonumber(pL, 3);
int         comp_score = (int)lua_tonumber(pL, 4);

//call the C++ function proper
EvaluateTheGuesses(user_guess, comp_guess, user_score, comp_score);
```

`user_score` and `comp_score` have been updated, so it's time to pass them back to Lua.

```
  //now push the updated scores onto the stack
  lua_pushnumber(pL, user_score);
  lua_pushnumber(pL, comp_score);

  //return the number of values pushed onto the stack
  return 2;
}
```

Once your C/C++ function has been wrapped, you must register it with Lua using the API function `lua_register` before your Lua script attempts to use it. `lua_register` takes as parameters a pointer to a Lua state, a string defining the name of the function, and a pointer to the function, like so:

```
lua_register(pL, "cpp_EvaluateTheGuesses", cpp_EvaluateTheGuesses);
```

Once a function has been registered with Lua it can be called from a Lua script as normal.

NOTE Unlike C++, Lua handles memory management automatically. It uses something called a garbage collector to periodically delete all the dead objects. The performance of the garbage collector can be customized to your taste, ranging from immediate deletion of dead objects to no deletion. See the Lua documentation for further details.

Exposing a C/C++ Class to Lua

This is where things start to get tricky! Exposing a C++ class to a Lua script can be pretty gnarly. You basically have to create a Lua table that has as its elements the class data and methods you require to expose. You may also have to create a metatable that defines how your class behaves with any appropriate operators such as == or *. As you have seen, simply exposing a C-like function to Lua can get longwinded, so you can imagine the amount of work required to expose a C++ class. Fortunately, someone has already done the hard work for us and created an API allowing for pain-free class (and function) registration. It's called *Luabind*, and just like Lua it's free, open-source, and easy to use and understand.

Luabind to the Rescue!

Luabind is a library for creating bindings between Lua and C++. It is implemented using the magic of template meta-programming so the source code is not for the faint hearted, but it makes exposing your C/C++ classes and functions a cinch. It handles inheritance and templated classes and you can even use it to create classes in Lua. It's still in the early days of development, so it is not without its problems, but these are few and the developers, Daniel Wallin and Arvid Norberg, have put in a lot of time to iron out the bugs and to provide fast and helpful support should you need it.

Setting Up Luabind

Before you can use Luabind you must set up your compiler correctly. Luabind (6.0) requires you to have the Boost library 1.30.0 or later headers installed. You can download Boost from www.boost.org. Unzip and add the boost header folder to your compiler's include paths.

The required files for Luabind are in the folder common/luabind. You must set this path in your compiler for the Luabind headers, and the path common/luabind/src for the source files. Although you can build the Luabind libraries, it's much easier (unless you are using UNIX) to just include all the files found in common/luabind/src in your project.

TIP For those of you who use .NET, there is a Lua and Luabind .NET wrapper called LuaDotNet available from codeproject. You can grab it from: http://www.codeproject.com/managedcpp/luanetwrapper.asp.

To use Luabind you must include the Luabind header along with the Lua files, and then call the function `luabind::open(lua_State*)`. This registers all the functions Luabind uses to expose your classes and functions.

You eventually end up with code that flows like this:

```
extern "C"
{
  #include <lua.h>
  #include <lualib.h>
  #include <lauxlib.h>
}

#include <luabind/luabind.hpp>


int main()
{
  //create a lua state
  lua_State* pLua = lua_open();

  //open luabind
  luabind::open(pLua);

  /* Register functions and classes with luabind here */

  /* load and run the script here */

  //tidy up
  lua_close(pLua);

  return 0;
}
```

Now let me show you how easy Luabind is to use.

Scopes

Any function or class you register using Luabind must be registered in a scope. This can be either a namespace of your choice or in the global scope, which Luabind calls `module`. To create a scope you use `luabind::module`. It is used like this:

```
luabind::module(pL)
[
  //register stuff here
];
```

This will register functions and classes in the global scope. To place your functions or classes in a namespace, you call `luabind::module` using the desired name like so:

```
luabind::module(pL, "MyNamespace")
[
  //register stuff here
];
```

Luabind represents namespaces using a table, so in this example, all the functions and classes registered will be put into the table MyNameSpace.

Exposing C/C++ Functions Using Luabind

To expose a C/C++ function to Lua use the luabind::def function. As an example, let's take two simple functions, add and HelloWorld, and bind them to Lua. Here are the functions:

```
void HelloWorld()
{
  cout << "\n[C++]: Hello World!" << endl;
}

int add(int a, int b)
{
  return a + b;
}
```

And here's how you bind them:

```
module(pL)
[
  def("HelloWorld", &HelloWorld),
  def("add", &add)
];
```

How easy is that! Following is a Lua script file that calls the exposed functions.

```
--lua script to demonstrate exposing C++ functions to Lua using luabind

print("[lua]: About to call the C++ HelloWorld() function")

HelloWorld()


print("\n[lua]: About to call the C++ add() function")

a = 10
b = 5

print ("\n[lua]: "..a.." + "..b.." = "..add(a, b))
```

Running this script gives the output:

```
[lua]: About to call the C++ HelloWorld() function
[C++]: HelloWorld!
[lua]: About to call the C++ add() function
[lua]: 10 + 5 = 15
```

The project file containing this script is called ExposingCPPFunctions-ToLua.

If you have overloaded functions then you must explicitly give their signature when you register them. So if you have the functions:

```
int  MyFunc(int);
void MyFunc(double);
```

they should be registered as:

```
module(pLua)
[
  def("MyFunc", (int (*)(int)) &MyFunc),
  def("MyFunc", (void (*)(double)) &MyFunc),
];
```

NOTE When using Luabind, your compiler may complain that its internal heap limit has been exceeded. In MSVC 6.0 you can increase the limit by going to Project Settings, clicking on the C++ tab, and adding /ZmXXX to the end of the options string where XXX is a value between 100 and 2000. The default value is 100, so just increase it a little. Make sure you add /Zm in both the debug and release versions.

Exposing C/C++ Classes Using Luabind

Binding classes to Lua is not much more complicated. It's done using the class template `class_` and one of its methods, `def`, to register any constructors, methods, member variables, and destructors. `class_::def` returns a `this` pointer to enable chaining. The following show how you use it.

The class `Animal`:

```
class Animal
{
private:

  int         m_iNumLegs;

  std::string  m_NoiseEmitted;

public:

  Animal(std::string NoiseEmitted,
         int         NumLegs):m_iNumLegs(NumLegs),
                              m_NoiseEmitted(NoiseEmitted)
  {}

  virtual ~Animal(){}

  virtual void Speak()const
  {std::cout << "\n[C++]: " << m_NoiseEmitted << std::endl;}

  int         NumLegs()const{return m_iNumLegs;}
};
```

is registered like so:

```
module(pLua)
[
  class_<Animal>("Animal")
    .def(constructor<string, int>())
    .def("Speak", &Animal::Speak)
    .def("NumLegs", &Animal::NumLegs)
];
```

Once registered, it's possible to create an instance of the class inside a Lua script. Here's an example:

```
--create an animal object and call its methods

cat = Animal("Meow", 4);

print ("\n[Lua]: A cat has "..cat:NumLegs().. " legs.");

cat:Speak();
```

Notice how the : operator is used to call the methods. This is a shorthand way of writing cat.Speak(cat). Methods must be called this way because classes in Lua are represented by tables. Each element of the table represents a class member variable or method.

It's almost as easy to bind a derived class. Here's an example of a class derived from the `Animal` class.

```
class Pet : public Animal
{
private:

  std::string  m_Name;

public:

  Pet(std::string name,
      std::string noise,
      int         NumLegs):Animal(noise, NumLegs),
                           m_Name(name)
  {}

  std::string GetName()const{return m_Name;}
};
```

Using Luabind, the `Pet` class is exposed to Lua, making use of the template parameter `bases<`*`base class`*`>` to specify its base class. Here's how:

```
module(pLua)
[
  class_<Pet, bases<Animal> >("Pet")
     .def(constructor<string, string, int>())
     .def("GetName", &Pet::GetName)

];
```

If your class is derived from multiple classes, each base class must be named with bases<> and separated by commas, like this:

```
class_<Derived, bases<Base1, Base2, Base3> >("Derived")
```

Creating Classes in Lua Using Luabind

It's also possible to define classes within your Lua scripts using Luabind. Here's how you would go about creating a class similar to `Animal`.

```
--Lua script to define the class: Animal

class 'Animal'

function Animal:__init(num_legs, noise_made)

   self.NoiseMade = noise_made
   self.NumLegs = num_legs

end

function Animal:Speak()

   print(self.NoiseMade)

end

function Animal:GetNumLegs()

   return self.NumLegs

end
```

The self keyword is like the `this` keyword in C++. Here's an example of the Animal class being used:

```
--example of use

cat = Animal(4, "meow")

cat:Speak()

print ("a cat has "..cat:GetNumLegs().." legs")
```

When this Lua script is executed the output is:

```
meow
a cat has 4 legs
```

It's also possible to use inheritance with Luabind classes. Here's how a Pet class — derived from an Animal — is defined:

```
class 'Pet' (Animal)

function Pet:__init(name, num_legs, noise_made) super(num_legs, noise_made)
```

```
   self.Name = name
end
function Pet:GetName()
   return self.Name
end
```

Notice how the super keyword is used to call the constructor of the base class before initializing any of the derived class's data members. Here's a short script that demonstrates the use of a Pet:

```
dog = Pet("Albert", 4, "woof")
dog:Speak()
print ("my dog's name is "..dog:GetName())
```

Running this script gives the output:

```
woof
my dog's name is Albert
```

The project CreatingClassesUsingLuabind demonstrates the use of Luabind to create classes.

luabind::object

To facilitate passing Lua types to your C++ functions and objects, Luabind provides a class named `object`. This class has the ability to represent any Lua type and comes in very handy indeed. Here's the prototype cut and pasted straight from the Luabind docs. Have a good look at it and then I'll talk you through some of the member functions.

```
class object
{
public:
  class iterator;
  class raw_iterator;
  class array_iterator;

  template<class T>
  object(lua_State*, const T& value);
  object(const object&);
  object(lua_State*);
  object();

  ~object();

  iterator begin() const;
  iterator end() const;
  raw_iterator raw_begin() const;
```

```
  raw_iterator raw_end() const;
  array_iterator abegin() const;
  array_iterator aend() const;

  void set();
  lua_State* lua_state() const;
  void pushvalue() const;
  bool is_valid() const;
  operator bool() const;

  template<class Key>
  <implementation-defined> operator[](const Key&);

  template<class Key>
  object at(const Key&) const;

  template<class Key>
  object raw_at(const Key&) const;

  template<class T>
  object& operator=(const T&);
  object& operator=(const object&);

  template<class T>
  bool operator==(const T&) const;
  bool operator==(const object&) const;
  bool operator<(const object&) const;
  bool operator<=(const object&) const;
  bool operator>(const object&) const;
  bool operator>=(const object&) const;
  bool operator!=(const object&) const;

  void swap(object&);
  int type() const;

  <implementation-defined> operator()();

  template<class A0>
  <implementation-defined> operator()(const A0& a0);

  template<class A0, class A1>
  <implementation-defined> operator()(const A0& a0, const A1& a1);

  /* ... */
};
```

at() and []

Once a Lua type is assigned to a `luabind::object` you can use the [] operator or the `at()` method to access the data. `at()` provides read-only access and [] read and write access. The parameter passed to [] or `at()` must be a Lua type name in the global scope. (Remember, all Lua variables are defined in the global scope unless explicitly declared local.) To convert a `luabind::object` to a C++ type you must use `luabind::object_cast`.

For example, let's say a Lua script defines some values like this:

```
Mat = 37
Sharon = 15
Scooter = 1.5
```

The Lua global table, in which those values reside, can be assigned to a `luabind::object` using `get_globals`, like this:

```
luabind::object global_table = get_globals(pLua);
```

The data can now be retrieved from the `luabind::object` like this:

```
float scooter = luabind::object_cast<float>(global_table.at("Scooter"));
```

Or changed like this:

```
global_table["Mat"] = 10;
```

One of the more useful things possible with a `luabind::object` is to use it to call functions defined in Lua. You can even include `luabind::objects` as member variables of a C++ class, enabling the functionality of that class to be changed whenever you want by reassigning different Lua functions to the `objects`. You'll see an example of this later in the chapter when I show you how to design a scripted finite state machine class.

is_valid and bool

`is_valid` and `operator bool` provide a way of checking that a `luabind::object` contains a valid type. For example:

```
//assign the Lua global environment to a luabind::object
luabind::object MyObject = get_globals(pLua);

//check if the object is valid and if so do something with the value indexed
//into by "key"
if (MyObject.is_valid())
{
   DoSomething(MyObject[key]);
}
```

This can also be written as:

```
if (MyObject)
{
   DoSomething(MyObject[key]);
}
```

A `luabind::object` is invalid when it has been created using the default constructor and has not yet been assigned a value.

Object Iterators

The methods `end()` and `begin()` return `luabind::iterator` objects. These iterators work in the forward direction only and can be used to step through the elements of any table the `luabind::object` is holding.

⌘ **TIP** In addition to `luabind::object`, Luabind also provides `luabind::functor`, which is a more lightweight object you can use if you only need to store functions. See the Luabind documentation for more details.

Creating a Scripted Finite State Machine

To end the chapter I'm going to demonstrate how Lua, together with Luabind, can be used to create a scripted finite state machine class. This class is used in a similar way to the state machine class you've already seen described in this book, except now the game agent's state logic can be written in the Lua scripting language. Not only will this be a demonstration of the power of scripting languages, but it will help consolidate everything you have learned in this chapter.

As we have discussed, a scripted FSM has many advantages over a hard-coded state machine. Because any new logic can immediately be tested without recompiling the source, the frustration of the testing and tweaking phases of an agent's AI is reduced, resulting in faster development cycles. Additionally, once the AI framework has been exposed to a scripting language, you can hand your designer, artists, or whoever a copy of the compiled game, together with a little documentation, and they can fool around with the AI to their heart's content *without having to pester you any further.* Well, okay, you may have to work on the interface a little until everyone is happy, but that's about all. When the game is released you can choose to either compile the script files, effectively encrypting them from the prying eyes of the game player, or leave the scripts as they are, provide a little documentation, and put the power of your engine into the game player's hands.

 **NOTE** Luabind can be a great tool but, because it relies heavily on template programming, the addition of it to a project will result in increased compile times. This, alas, is the price we have to pay for its functionality.

How It Works

To be able to write state logic within a script file, the scripting language must be able to access the interfaces of the relevant C++ objects. For this example, I'm going to show you how the WestWorld demo from Chapter 1 can be converted to use a scripted state machine. As a result, the relevant classes to expose to Lua will be `Miner` and `Entity`. In addition, the methods of the scripted state machine class itself must also be exposed to enable state changes to be made from within a script.

The `StateMachine` class used up to now has made use of the state design pattern to implement its functionality. The `StateMachine` class has a data member of base class type `State`, representing the current state of the agent. This member variable can be exchanged at any time with any other derived type of `State` in order to change the functionality of the class. To provide similar behavior, the scripted state machine class has a member variable of type `luabind::object`, which represents the current state of the agent. The states are created in Lua as Lua tables. Each table contains three functions, providing the logic for the Enter, Execute, and Exit phases of the state. This is easier to show than to describe. A Lua table providing similar functionality to a C++ `State` class is created like this:

```
--create a table to represent the state
State_DoSomething = {}

--now create the Enter, Execute, and Exit methods
State_DoSomething["Enter"] = function(pAgent)
  --logic goes here
end

State_DoSomething["Execute"] = function(pAgent)
  --logic goes here
end

State_DoSomething["Exit"] = function(pAgent)
  --logic goes here
end
```

You'll see some concrete examples of `Miner` states in a moment, but for now it is enough to know that a Lua table like this can be assigned to a `luabind::object`. Once assigned, it is a straightforward matter to call the appropriate function using the `luabind::object::at()` method.

Let's take a look at the `ScriptedStateMachine` class to see how these ideas are put together. Check out the following code carefully. Notice how the `m_CurrentState` member variable acts as the holder for the current state and how it is changed by passing a `luabind::object` type to the `ChangeState` method. Other than a few small alterations, the class looks very similar to its C++ `StateMachine` cousin — and so it should because it provides the same functionality.

```
template <class entity_type>
class ScriptedStateMachine
{
private:

  //pointer to the agent that owns this instance
  entity_type*      m_pOwner;

  //the current state is a Lua table of Lua functions. A table may be
  //represented in C++ using a luabind::object
  luabind::object   m_CurrentState;

public:

  ScriptedStateMachine(entity_type* owner):m_pOwner(owner){}

  //this method assigns a state to the FSM
```

```
  void SetCurrentState(const luabind::object& s){m_CurrentState = s;}


  //this method makes sure the current state object is valid before calling
  // the Execute function of the Lua table it represents
  void  UpdateScriptedStateMachine()
  {
    //make sure the state is valid before calling its Execute "method"
    if (m_CurrentState.is_valid())
    {
      m_CurrentState.at("Execute")(m_pOwner);
    }
  }

  //change to a new state
  void  ChangeState(const luabind::object& new_state)
  {
    //call the Exit method of the existing state
    m_CurrentState.at("Exit")(m_pOwner);

    //change state to the new state
    m_CurrentState = new_state;

    //call the Entry method of the new state
    m_CurrentState.at("Enter")(m_pOwner);
  }

  //retrieve the current state
  const luabind::object&  CurrentState()const{return m_CurrentState;}
};
```

The state logic contained within the Lua scripts must be able to call some of the methods of `ScriptedStateMachine` to permit state transitions. Consequently, Luabind is used to expose the relevant member functions like this:

```
void RegisterScriptedStateMachineWithLua(lua_State* pLua)
{
  luabind::module(pLua)
    [
      class_<ScriptedStateMachine<Miner> >("ScriptedStateMachine")

        .def("ChangeState", &ScriptedStateMachine<Miner>::ChangeState)
        .def("CurrentState", &ScriptedStateMachine<Miner>::CurrentState)
        .def("SetCurrentState", &ScriptedStateMachine<Miner>::SetCurrentState)
    ];
}
```

Notice how only the methods required by the state logic are exposed. There's no point exposing `UpdateScriptedStateMachine` because, in this example, it should never be called from within a script.

Following are listings of the `Entity` class, the `Miner` class, and the functions that are called to bind them. You needn't dwell on these listings as the classes will be familiar in structure, but be sure to observe how the pertinent methods are registered with Lua.

Here's the `Entity` class declaration:

```
class Entity
{

private:

  int          m_ID;

  std::string  m_Name;

  //used by the constructor to give each entity a unique ID
  int NextValidID(){static int NextID = 0; return NextID++;}

public:

  Entity(std::string name = "NoName"):m_ID(NextValidID()), m_Name(name){}

  virtual ~Entity(){}

  //all entities must implement an update function
  virtual void  Update()=0;

  //accessors
  int         ID()const{return m_ID;}
  std::string Name()const{return m_Name;}
};
```

And here's the function that registers the class with Lua:

```
void RegisterEntityWithLua(lua_State* pLua)
{
  module(pLua)
    [
      class_<Entity>("Entity")

        .def("Name", &Entity::Name)
        .def("ID", &Entity::ID)
    ];
}
```

The `Miner` class is a cut-down version of the one from Chapter 2. It looks like this:

```
class Miner : public Entity
{
private:

  ScriptedStateMachine<Miner>* m_pStateMachine;

  //how many nuggets the miner has in his pockets
  int                          m_iGoldCarried;

  //the higher the value, the more tired the miner
  int                         m_iFatigue;
```

```
public:

  Miner(std::string name);

  ~Miner(){delete m_pStateMachine;}

  //this must be implemented
  void Update();

  int          GoldCarried()const{return m_iGoldCarried;}
  void         SetGoldCarried(int val){m_iGoldCarried = val;}
  void         AddToGoldCarried(int val);

  bool         Fatigued()const;
  void         DecreaseFatigue(){m_iFatigue -= 1;}
  void         IncreaseFatigue(){m_iFatigue += 1;}

  ScriptedStateMachine<Miner>* GetFSM()const{return m_pStateMachine;}
};
```

Here's how the Miner class is registered. Note how the bases<> parameter is used to specify the Miner's base class.

```
void RegisterMinerWithLua(lua_State* pLua)
{
  module(pLua)
    [
      class_<Miner, bases<Entity> >("Miner")

        .def("GoldCarried", &Miner::GoldCarried)
        .def("SetGoldCarried", &Miner::SetGoldCarried)
        .def("AddToGoldCarried", &Miner::AddToGoldCarried)
        .def("Fatigued", &Miner::Fatigued)
        .def("DecreaseFatigue", &Miner::DecreaseFatigue)
        .def("IncreaseFatigue", &Miner::IncreaseFatigue)
        .def("GetFSM", &Miner::GetFSM)
    ];
}
```

Now that it's possible to access the Miner, Entity, and ScriptedStateMachine interfaces from within a Lua script, we can write the AI logic for each state.

The States

As discussed previously, the Miner states will be written in the Lua scripting language. Instead of a C++ class, each state is represented by a Lua table that has elements containing Enter, Execute, and Exit functions.

To keep it simple and concise there are only three states implemented for a Miner — GoHome, Sleep, and GoToMine — but this will be sufficient to demonstrate the idea.

Here's how the three states are implemented:

GoHome

```
State_GoHome = {}

State_GoHome["Enter"] = function(miner)
  print ("[Lua]: Walkin' home in the hot n' thusty heat of the desert")
end

State_GoHome["Execute"] = function(miner)
  print ("[Lua]: Back at the shack. Yes siree!")
  if miner:Fatigued() then
    miner:GetFSM():ChangeState(State_Sleep)
  else
    miner:GetFSM():ChangeState(State_GoToMine)
  end
end

State_GoHome["Exit"] = function(miner)
  print ("[Lua]: Puttin' mah boots on n' gettin' ready for a day at the mine")
end
```

Sleep

```
State_Sleep = {}

State_Sleep["Enter"] = function(miner)
  print ("[Lua]: Miner "..miner:Name().." is dozin' off")
end

State_Sleep["Execute"] = function(miner)
  if miner:Fatigued() then
    print ("[Lua]: ZZZZZZ... ")
    miner:DecreaseFatigue()
```

```
    else

      miner:GetFSM():ChangeState(State_GoToMine)

    end

  end

  State_Sleep["Exit"] = function(miner)

    print ("[Lua]: Miner "..miner:Name().." is feelin' mighty refreshed!")

  end
```

GoToMine

```
State_GoToMine = {}


State_GoToMine["Enter"] = function(miner)

  print ("[Lua]: Miner "..miner:Name().." enters gold mine")

end


State_GoToMine["Execute"] = function(miner)

  miner:IncreaseFatigue()

  miner:AddToGoldCarried(2)

  print ("[Lua]: Miner "..miner:Name().." has got "..miner:GoldCarried().." nuggets")


  if miner:GoldCarried() > 4 then

    print ("[Lua]: Miner "..miner:Name().." decides to go home, with his pockets full of nuggets")

    miner:GetFSM():ChangeState(State_GoHome)

  end

end


State_GoToMine["Exit"] = function(miner)

  print ("[Lua]: Miner "..miner:Name().." exits gold mine")

end
```

And that's it. The scripted state machine class calls the relevant functions of each table to give the Enter, Execute, and Exit behavior of each state.

State changes are made by switching the table the `luabind::object m_CurrentState` points to.

You can check out firsthand how everything works by compiling the ScriptedStateMachine project. Fool around with it a little, add some additional states, and play around for a while to get a feel for how everything integrates.

Useful URLs

If you start to use Lua and Luabind seriously, you will probably run into many problems requiring assistance. Fortunately, you can find a lot of support on the Internet. The following is a list of some of the more useful resources available to help you out of difficulty:

- http://www.lua.org/

  The home page of Lua and the place where you can subscribe to the Lua mailing list
- http://lua-users.org/wiki/LuaDirectory

  This is the Lua wiki. It has many useful articles and links to help you out.
- http://lua-users.org/lists/lua-l/

  This is a searchable database of the Lua mailing list.
- http://luabind.sourceforge.net/

  The home of Luabind. Luabind also has a mailing list you can subscribe to.

It Doesn't All Smell of Roses

By now, I bet you're thinking that scripting languages are the code equivalent of a trip to Willy Wonka's chocolate factory. Everything you want and more, all wrapped up in pretty ribbons. Well, I have to give it to you straight… it's not. There are a few downsides. For starters, all those lovely helper apps you've come to know and love aren't going to help you when you type your scripts (not without modification, anyway). Say farewell to auto-complete and a teary adieu to those lovely little info boxes that appear when your mouse hovers over a variable. Oh boy! Like electricity or doughnuts, you don't realize how much you rely on these things until you have to make do without.

⌘ **TIP** There are a number of editors available that are useful for writing scripts (providing colored syntax and auto indent, for example). Two of the best free editors are SciTE (www.scintilla.org/SciTE.html) and Crimson Editor (www.crimsoneditor.com).

In addition, debugging a script can be hell. Languages such as C/C++ have matured over many years and your typical development environment comes with a powerful suite of debugging utilities. You can step through code a line at a time, break into the code at will, and create watches to track the peskier of your variables. Programmers have never had it so easy. However, when you start to use scripting languages, the simplest of bugs can take an age to track down. Even a plain old syntactical error can seem like a bug from hell.

Of course, the level of evil inherent in scripting languages varies tremendously. Some languages provide no assistance whatsoever, while others (Lua for example) provide a few error codes, may throw exceptions, and can halt the script before too much damage is done. Very few, however, provide the sort of facilities you are used to, so most of the time you will end up writing your own.

Summing Up

Scripting is such an enormous topic that it is impossible to teach everything about it in just one chapter. However, by now you should know enough to be able to create reasonably complex scripts using the Lua scripting language and integrate them seamlessly in your own games and applications. If this chapter has got you excited about the possibilities provided by Lua and Luabind, then I strongly recommend you put a day or two aside and read the documentation from cover to cover. It's also a good idea to visit some of the URLs I've mentioned and browse through the mailing list archives. You'll find all sorts of unusual and interesting ways of using the Lua language.

Happy scripting!

Chapter 7

Raven: An Overview

This chapter will present an overview of a game named Raven. Raven will be used as the framework within which all the remaining techniques described in this book will be implemented (in addition to most of the ones you've already learned). First, some time will be spent familiarizing you with the game architecture before concluding with an outline of the components that make up the AI. Full descriptions of some of these components will be provided within this chapter. Others will have entire chapters dedicated to them.

The Game

Raven is a top-down 2D game environment that is simple, yet complex enough to adequately demonstrate the techniques described in this book. A typical Raven map consists of a number of rooms and corridors, several spawn points from which the agents ("bots") are generated, and items such as health packs or weapons the bots can pick up and use. See Screenshot 7.1.

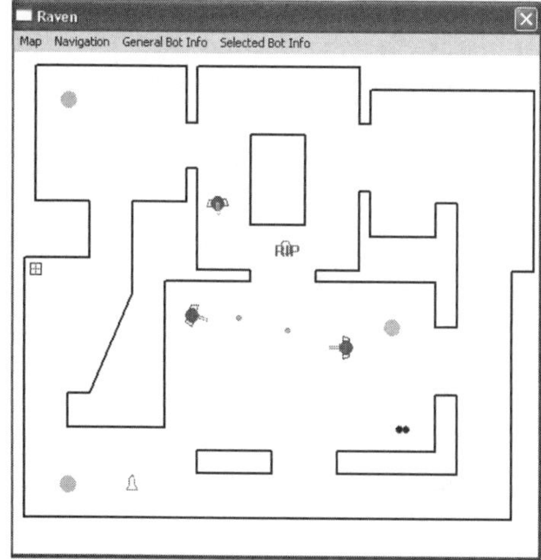

Screenshot 7.1. This looks better in motion. Honest!

The gameplay is similar to a Quake-style deathmatch. When commencing a game, several AI controlled bots are spawned that run around the map attempting to make as many kills as possible and picking up weapons and health as needed. If a bot is killed, it immediately respawns with full health from a random spawn point and the position where it was killed is marked by a "grave" for several seconds.

A bot can be selected by right-clicking on it *once*. When selected, a red circle will be drawn around the bot and additional AI-related information will be drawn to the screen depending on what options are set in the menu.

Right-click on a *selected* bot, and you will "possess" it — it will be under your control. A possessed bot is encircled in blue and can be moved by right-clicking on the part of the map you'd like it to travel to. The navigation AI of the bot will automatically provide assistance by planning the shortest path to the chosen location. The aim of the bot is controlled by the mouse. Because a bot is able to aim independently of the direction of its movement, a possessed bot will always face in the direction of the mouse cursor. A left click will fire the bot's current weapon in the direction of the mouse cursor. (For ranged weapons, such as the rocket launcher, the target *is* the cursor position.) You can change weapons (provided the bot is carrying more than one) by pressing the keys "1" to "4". A bot is released from your control by right-clicking on a different bot or by pressing the "X" key.

NOTE Although when you play the game you can see all the other bots clearly, each bot's AI is only able to see other bots that are within its field of view and not obscured by walls. This makes the design of the AI much more interesting. The FOV is set in the Raven/params.lua file.

Overview of the Game Architecture

In this section we'll examine the key classes that comprise the game framework. Figure 7.1 shows an overview of how the high-level objects interrelate.

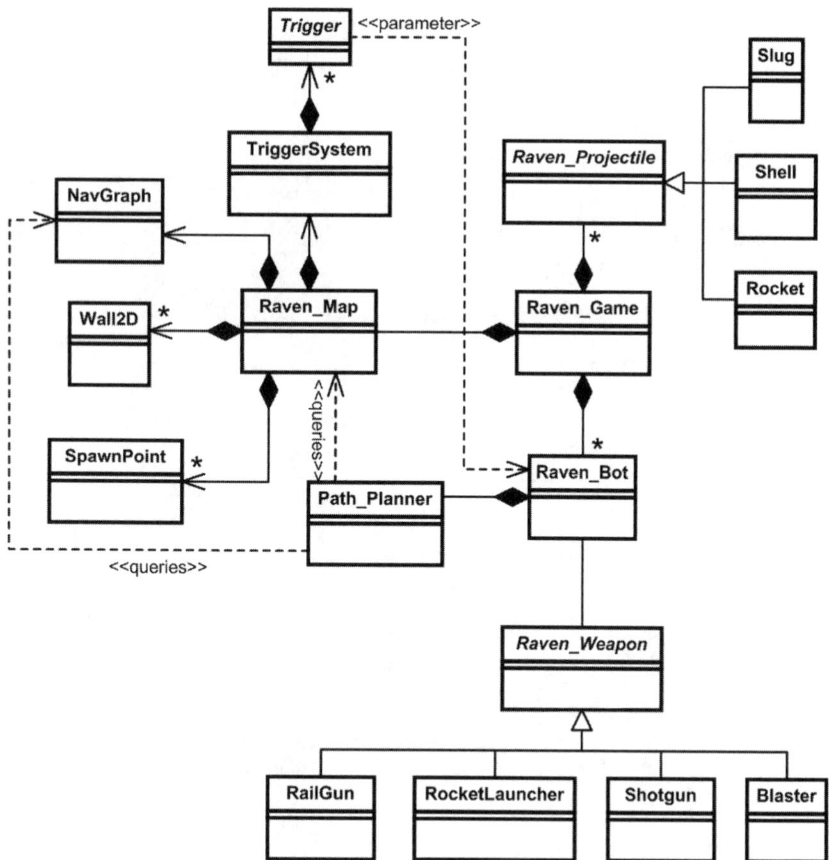

Figure 7.1. The Raven architecture

Let's take a look at some of these classes in more detail.

The Raven_Game Class

The `Raven_Game` class is the project's hub. This class owns an instance of a `Raven_Map`, a container of bots, and a container of any active projectiles (rockets, slugs, etc.). Among others, the `Raven_Game` class has methods for loading maps and their associated navigation graphs, updating and rendering the game entities and geometry, querying the world with line-of-sight requests, and handling user input.

Following is a partial listing of the Raven_Game class declaration. Have a quick glance to familiarize yourself with it.

```
class Raven_Game
{
private:

  Raven_Map*                       m_pMap;

  std::list<Raven_Bot*>            m_Bots;

  //the user may select a bot to control manually. This member
  //holds a pointer to that bot
  Raven_Bot*                       m_pSelectedBot;

  //this list contains any active projectiles (slugs, rockets,
  //shotgun pellets, etc.)
  std::list<Raven_Projectile*>     m_Projectiles;

  /* EXTRANEOUS DETAIL OMITTED FOR CLARITY */

public:

  //the usual suspects
  void Render();
  void Update();

  //loads an environment from a file
  bool LoadMap(const std::string& FileName);

  //returns true if a bot of size BoundingRadius cannot move from A to B
  //without bumping into world geometry
  bool isPathObstructed(Vector2D A, Vector2D B, double BoundingRadius = 0)const;

  //returns a vector of pointers to bots in the FOV of the given bot
  std::vector<Raven_Bot*> GetAllBotsInFOV(const Raven_Bot* pBot)const;

  //returns true if the second bot is unobstructed by walls and in the field
  //of view of the first.
  bool        isSecondVisibleToFirst(const Raven_Bot* pFirst,
                                     const Raven_Bot* pSecond)const;

  /* EXTRANEOUS DETAIL OMITTED FOR CLARITY */
};
```

⌘ **TIP** Note that GetAllBotsInFOV does not limit the number of bots returned by the method. This is not necessary for the demo, but for games where there might frequently be dozens or even hundreds of other agents in view, it's a good idea to cap the number to the *n* closest the agent can see.

The Raven Map

The Raven_Map class owns containers of all the objects that make up the game world geometry — walls, triggers, spawn points, etc. — and also owns an instance of the map's navigation graph. These items are created when a file of the Raven map format is opened.

When Raven is run, the default map (Raven_DM1) and its corresponding navigation graph are read from file. A number of Raven bots are then created at randomly selected, unoccupied spawn points.

NOTE The parameters for Raven are stored in the Lua script file params.lua. Access to the scripts is made convenient through the use of a singleton class Raven_Scriptor, which in turn is derived from the Scriptor class. This class is simply an encapsulation of all the commonly used methods for accessing Lua variables like LuaPopNumber and LuaPopString. If you need further clarification, check out the file common/script/Scriptor.h.

Here is a partial listing of Raven_Map's declaration.

```
class Raven_Map
{
public:

  typedef NavGraphNode<GraphEdge, Trigger<Raven_Bot>*>   GraphNode;
  typedef SparseGraph<GraphNode>                          NavGraph;
  typedef TriggerSystem<Trigger<Raven_Bot> >              Trigger_System;

private:

  //the walls that comprise the current map's architecture.
  std::vector<Wall2D*>                 m_Walls;

  //triggers are objects that define a region of space. When a raven bot
  //enters that area, it "triggers" an event. That event may be anything
  //from increasing a bot's health to opening a door or requesting a lift.
  Trigger_System                       m_TriggerSystem;

  //this holds a number of spawn positions. When a bot is instantiated
  //it will appear at a randomly selected point chosen from this vector.
  std::vector<Vector2D>                m_SpawnPoints;

  //this map's accompanying navigation graph
  NavGraph*                            m_pNavGraph;

  /* EXTRANEOUS DETAIL OMITTED */

public:

  Raven_Map();
  ~Raven_Map();

  void Render();

  //loads an environment from a file
```

```
  bool    LoadMap(const std::string& FileName);

  void    AddSoundTrigger(Raven_Bot* pSoundSource, double range);

  double  CalculateCostToTravelBetweenNodes(unsigned int nd1,
                                            unsigned int nd2)const;


  void    UpdateTriggerSystem(std::list<Raven_Bot*>& bots);

  /* EXTRANEOUS DETAIL OMITTED */
};
```

Raven map files are created in the editor that accompanies the project. Although simple, it is more than adequate for creating Raven maps and their accompanying navigation graphs. See the following sidebar.

The Raven Map Editor

I've coded a simple map editor to help create and edit Raven maps. See Screenshot 7.2.

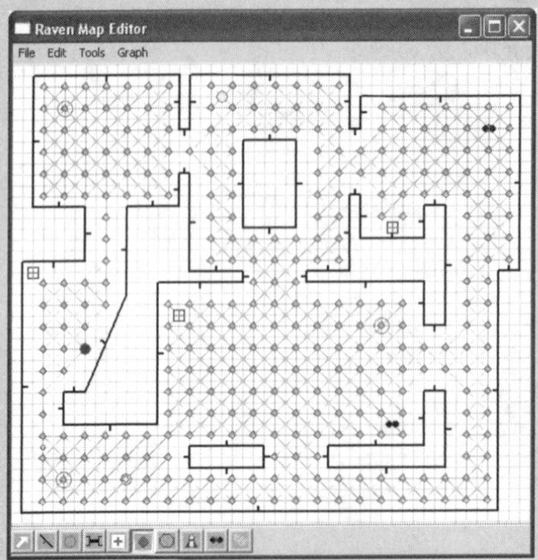

Screenshot 7.2. The Raven Map Editor

The editor is easy to use. Just click on the buttons at the bottom of the window to select the object you want to add, then click in the display window to add it. Save the map when it's finished into the Raven/Maps folder. Further instructions are provided by the ReadMe.doc in the Map Editor folder.

Raven Weapons

There are four weapons available. They are:

- **The Blaster**: This is a bot's default weapon. It fires green bolts of electricity at the rate of three per second. This weapon automatically recharges so it can never run out of ammo. It inflicts only one unit of damage per hit.
- **The Shotgun**: A shotgun can only be fired once per second. Each cartridge contains ten balls of shot, which spread out as they leave the gun. This means the shotgun is far more accurate and deadly at close to medium distances than it is at long range. Each ball of shot inflicts one unit of damage.
- **The Rocket Launcher**: The rocket launcher has a firing rate of 1.5 rockets per second. The rockets travel fairly slowly and explode on impact. Any entity caught in a rocket's blast radius will incur ten units of damage. Because rockets travel fairly slowly and can be easily dodged, the rocket launcher is best used as a medium range weapon.
- **The Railgun**: A railgun fires slugs at the rate of one per second. The slugs travel almost instantaneously to the target, making this weapon ideal for sniping and long-distance shots. (Railgun shots are only stopped by walls, so if several bots standing in a line are hit, the slug will penetrate all of them.)

A Raven bot starts each game holding a blaster and gains possession of the other types of weapons by locating them on the map and running over them. If a bot already has a weapon of the type it has run over, only the weapon's ammo is added to the inventory.

Each of the weapon types inherit from the Raven_Weapon class. The public interface of the class looks like this:

```
class Raven_Weapon
{
public:

  Raven_Weapon(unsigned int TypeOfGun
               unsigned int DefaultNumRounds,
               unsigned int MaxRoundsCarried,
               double       RateOfFire,
               double       IdealRange,
               double       ProjectileSpeed,
               Raven_Bot*   OwnerOfGun);

  virtual ~Raven_Weapon(){}

  //this method aims the weapon at the given target by rotating the weapon's
  //owner's facing direction (constrained by the bot's turning rate). It
  //returns true if the weapon is directly facing the target.
```

```
  bool           AimAt(Vector2D target)const;

  //this discharges a projectile from the weapon at the given target position
  //(provided the weapon is ready to be discharged... every weapon has its
  //own rate of fire)
  virtual void  ShootAt(Vector2D target) = 0;

  //each weapon has its own shape and color
  virtual void  Render() = 0;

  //this method returns a value representing the desirability of using the
  //weapon. This is used by the AI to select the most suitable weapon for
  //a bot's current situation. This value is calculated using fuzzy logic.
  //(Fuzzy logic is covered in Chapter 10)
  virtual double GetDesirability(double DistToTarget)=0;

  //returns the maximum speed of the projectile this weapon fires
  double         GetProjectileSpeed()const;

  int            NumRoundsRemaining()const;
  void           DecrementNumRounds();
  void           IncrementRounds(int num);

  //returns an enumerated value representing the gun type
  unsigned int   GetTypeOfGun()const;
};
```

Both AI and human players use this interface to aim and shoot weapons. If you are interested in seeing how each weapon type is implemented, please check out the relevant files in the Raven/Armory folder.

Projectiles

The projectiles (slugs, pellets, rockets, and bolts) fired by the weapons are derived from the `Raven_Projectile` class, which in turn inherits from the familiar `MovingEntity` class. The class hierarchy is shown in Figure 7.2. Each projectile is modeled as a point mass and obeys real-world physics. (This is overkill for this type of game, but given that a `MovingEntity` class had already been defined it was a piece of cake to implement.)

When a weapon is fired, an instance of the correct type of projectile is created and added to `Raven_Game::m_Projectiles`. Once the projectile has impacted (and any animation sequence has terminated) it is removed from the list. Whenever a projectile intersects a bot, it sends it a message informing it of who fired the shot and the amount of damage done.

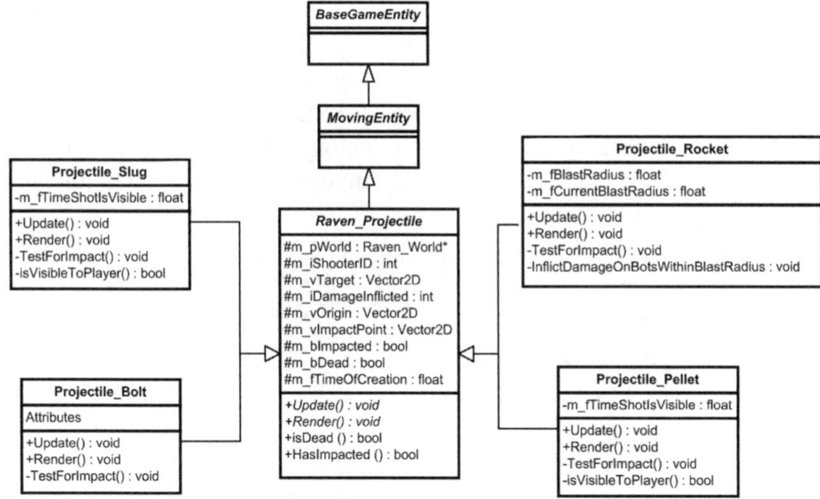

Figure 7.2. UML class diagram showing the Raven projectile hierarchy

Triggers

A *trigger* is an object that defines a condition, which, when satisfied by an agent, generates an action (it is triggered). Many of the triggers utilized in commercial games have the property that they are triggered when a game entity enters a *trigger region:* a predefined region of space that is attached to the trigger. These regions can be any arbitrary shape but are usually circular or rectangular for 2D environments and spherical, cubic, or cylindrical for 3D environments.

Triggers are a wonderfully useful tool for both game designers and AI programmers. You can use them to create all sorts of events and behaviors. For instance, triggers make doing stuff like this easy:

- A game character wanders down a gloomy corridor. It steps onto a pressure-sensitive plate and triggers a mechanism that rams forty pointy sticks through its respiratory cavity. (This is one of the most obvious uses for a trigger.)
- You shoot a guard. When it dies a trigger is added to the game that alerts other guards to the body if they wander within a specified distance of it.
- A game character shoots its gun. A trigger is added to the game that alerts any other character within a specified radius to the noise.
- A lever on a wall is implemented as a trigger. If an agent pulls it, it opens a door.
- You've implemented a puzzle in one corner of a room but you think a few players will have difficulty solving it. As an aid, you can

attach a trigger to the puzzle that activates if the player stands near it more than three times. When activated, the trigger flashes up some kind of hint system to help the player solve the puzzle.

- A troll whacks an ogre on its head with a spiky stick. The ogre runs off but is bleeding. As each drop of blood falls to the ground it leaves a trigger. The troll can then chase the ogre by following the trail of blood.

Raven makes use of several types of triggers. The class hierarchy is given in Figure 7.3.

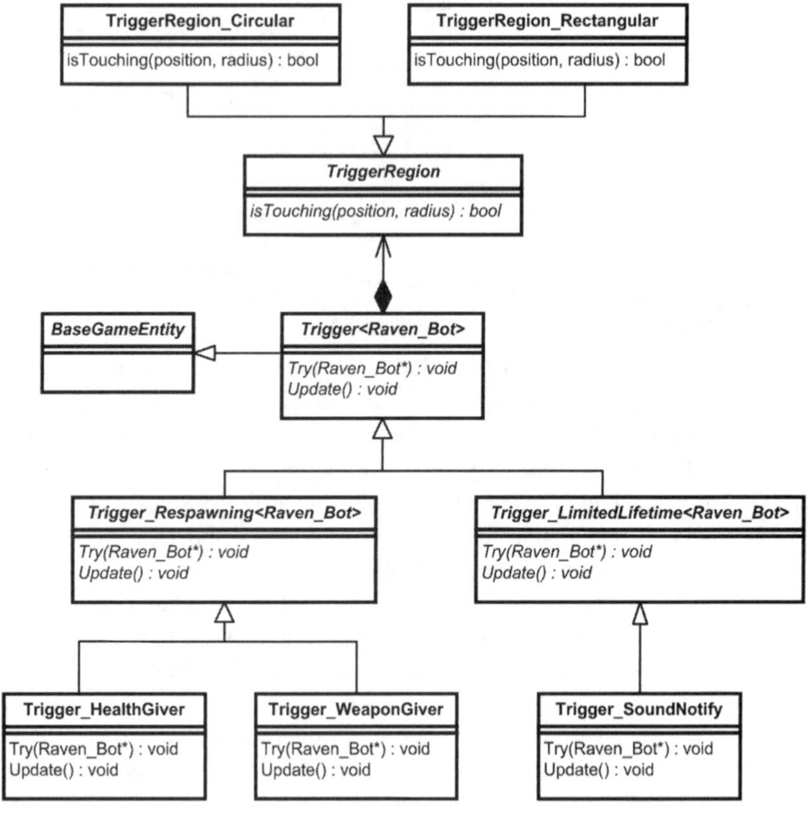

Figure 7.3. The `Trigger` class hierarchy

It's worthwhile spending some time examining each of these objects in detail. First let's take a quick look at the `TriggerRegion` class.

TriggerRegion

The `TriggerRegion` class defines a method `isTouching` that all trigger regions must implement. `isTouching` returns true if an entity of the given size and position is overlapping the trigger region. Each trigger type owns an instance of a TriggerRegion and utilizes the isTouching method to determine when it should be triggered.

Here is its declaration:

```
class TriggerRegion
{
public:

  virtual ~TriggerRegion(){}

  virtual bool isTouching(Vector2D EntityPos, double EntityRadius)const = 0;
};
```

And here is an example of a concrete trigger region that defines a circular region of space:

```
class TriggerRegion_Circle : public TriggerRegion
{
private:

  //the center of the region
  Vector2D m_vPos;

  //the radius of the region
  double   m_dRadius;

public:

  TriggerRegion_Circle(Vector2D pos,
                       double   radius):m_dRadius(radius),
                                        m_vPos(pos)
  {}

  bool isTouching(Vector2D pos, double EntityRadius)const
  {
    //distances calculated in squared-distance space
    return Vec2DDistanceSq(m_vPos, pos) <
           (EntityRadius + m_dRadius)*(EntityRadius + m_dRadius);
  }
};
```

As you can see, the method isTouching will return true as soon as the entity overlaps with the circle defined by the region.

Trigger

The Trigger class is a base class from which all other trigger types are derived. It has two methods that must be implemented by all child classes: Try and Update. These methods are called each iteration of the game's update loop. Update updates a trigger's internal state (if any). Try tests if the entity passed to it as a parameter is overlapping the trigger region and takes action appropriately.

Trigger's declaration is straightforward. Here's the listing:

```
template <class entity_type>
class Trigger : public BaseGameEntity
{
private:

  //Every trigger owns a trigger region. If an entity comes within this
  //region the trigger is activated
  TriggerRegion* m_pRegionOfInfluence;

  //if this is true the trigger will be removed from the game on the
  //next update
  bool           m_bRemoveFromGame;

  //it's convenient to be able to deactivate certain types of triggers
  //on an event. Therefore a trigger can only be triggered when this
  //value is true (respawning triggers make good use of this)
  bool           m_bActive;

  //some types of triggers are twinned with a graph node. This enables
  //the pathfinding component of an AI to search a navgraph for a specific
  //type of trigger.
  int            m_iGraphNodeIndex;

protected:

  void SetGraphNodeIndex(int idx){m_iGraphNodeIndex = idx;}

  void SetToBeRemovedFromGame(){m_bRemoveFromGame = true;}
  void SetInactive(){m_bActive = false;}
  void SetActive(){m_bActive = true;}

  //returns true if the entity given by a position and bounding radius is
  //overlapping the trigger region
  bool isTouchingTrigger(Vector2D EntityPos, double EntityRadius)const;

  //child classes use one of these methods to add a trigger region
  void AddCircularTriggerRegion(Vector2D center, double radius);
  void AddRectangularTriggerRegion(Vector2D TopLeft, Vector2D BottomRight);

public:

  Trigger(unsigned int id);
  virtual ~Trigger();

  //when this is called the trigger determines if the entity is within the
  //trigger's region of influence. If it is then the trigger will be
  //triggered and the appropriate action will be taken.
  virtual void  Try(entity_type*) = 0;

  //called each update step of the game. This method updates any internal
  //state the trigger may have
  virtual void  Update() = 0;
```

```
  int  GraphNodeIndex()const{return m_iGraphNodeIndex;}
  bool isToBeRemoved()const{return m_bRemoveFromGame;}
  bool isActive(){return m_bActive;}
};
```

Triggers have the m_iGraphNodeIndex member variable because it's occasionally useful to link certain types of triggers with a node of a navigation graph. For example, in Raven, item types such as health and weapons are implemented as a special type of trigger called giver-triggers. Because giver-triggers are linked with a graph node, the path planner is able to easily search the navgraph for a particular item type, such as the closest instance of a health item when a bot is running low on health (Chapter 8 will explain this in more detail).

Respawning Triggers

The Trigger_Respawning class is derived from Trigger and defines a trigger that becomes inactive for a certain period of time after it has been triggered by an entity. This type of trigger is utilized within Raven to implement item types a bot can "pick up," such as health or weapons. In this way an item can be made to respawn (reappear) at its original location a period of time after it is picked up.

```
template <class entity_type>
class Trigger_Respawning : public Trigger<entity_type>
{
protected:

  //When a bot comes within this trigger's area of influence it is triggered
  //but then becomes inactive for a specified amount of time. These values
  //control the amount of time required to pass before the trigger becomes
  //active once more.
  int   m_iNumUpdatesBetweenRespawns;
  int   m_iNumUpdatesRemainingUntilRespawn;

  //sets the trigger to be inactive for m_iNumUpdatesBetweenRespawns
  //update steps
  void Deactivate()
  {
    SetInactive();
    m_iNumUpdatesRemainingUntilRespawn = m_iNumUpdatesBetweenRespawns;
  }

public:

  Trigger_Respawning(int id);
  virtual ~Trigger_Respawning();

  //to be implemented by child classes
  virtual void  Try(entity_type*) = 0;
```

```
  //this is called each game-tick to update the trigger's internal state
  virtual void Update()
  {
    if ( (--m_iNumUpdatesRemainingUntilRespawn <= 0) && !isActive())
    {
      SetActive();
    }
  }

  void SetRespawnDelay(unsigned int numTicks);
};
```

NOTE Since Raven utilizes a fixed update rate, the triggers use update steps as their representation of time (each update step is one unit of time). If, however, you choose to implement a variable update frequency for your trigger system, remember to program your trigger's update method to use the time difference between updates.

Giver-Triggers

The health and weapon items in Raven are implemented using a type of trigger called a *giver-trigger*. Whenever an entity enters a giver-trigger's trigger region, it is "given" the corresponding item. Health givers obviously increase a bot's health and weapon givers provide a bot with an instance of the weapon type they represent. Another way of looking at it is that the bot "picks up" the item the trigger represents.

To enable health and weapon items to respawn after they have been picked up by a bot, giver-triggers inherit from the Trigger_Respawning class.

Weapon Givers

Here is the declaration of the Trigger_WeaponGiver class.

```
class Trigger_WeaponGiver : public Trigger_Respawning<Raven_Bot>
{
private:

 /* EXTRANEOUS DETAIL OMITTED */

public:

  //this type of trigger is created when reading a map file
  Trigger_WeaponGiver(std::ifstream& datafile);

  //if triggered, this trigger will call the PickupWeapon method of the
  //bot. PickupWeapon will instantiate a weapon of the appropriate type.
  void Try(Raven_Bot*);

  //draws a symbol representing the weapon type at the trigger's location
  void Render();

  /* EXTRANEOUS DETAIL OMITTED */
};
```

The Try method is implemented like so:

```
void Trigger_WeaponGiver::Try(Raven_Bot* pBot)
{
  if (isActive() && isTouchingTrigger(pBot->Pos(), pBot->BRadius()))
  {
    pBot->PickupWeapon( EntityType() );

    Deactivate();
  }
}
```

If the trigger is active and the bot is overlapping the trigger region, the Raven_Bot::PickupWeapon method is called. This method instantiates a weapon of the given type and adds it (or ammo only if already held) to the bot's inventory. Finally, the logic deactivates the trigger. The trigger will remain deactivated for a specific amount of time before it reactivates. When deactivated, the trigger will not be rendered.

Health Givers

Health giver-triggers are implemented very similarly.

```
void Trigger_HealthGiver::Try(Raven_Bot* pBot)
{
  if (isActive() && isTouchingTrigger(pBot->Pos(), pBot->BRadius()))
  {
    pBot->IncreaseHealth(m_iHealthGiven);

    Deactivate();
  }
}
```

As you can see, this is almost the same code as used previously except this time the triggering bot's health is increased.

Limited Lifetime Triggers

Occasionally a trigger with a fixed lifespan is needed — one that remains in the environment for a certain number of update steps before getting automatically removed. Trigger_LimitedLifetime provides such an object.

```
template <class entity_type>
class Trigger_LimitedLifetime : public Trigger<entity_type>
{
protected:

  //the lifetime of this trigger in update steps
  int m_iLifetime;

public:

  Trigger_LimitedLifetime(int lifetime);
  virtual ~Trigger_LimitedLifetime(){}
```

```
  //children of this class should always make sure this is called from within
  //their own update method
  virtual void Update()
  {
    //if the lifetime counter expires set this trigger to be removed from
    //the game
    if (--m_iLifetime <= 0)
    {
      SetToBeRemovedFromGame();
    }
  }

  //to be implemented by child classes
  virtual void  Try(entity_type*) = 0;
};
```

The sound notification trigger is a good example of how limited lifespan triggers are used.

Sound Notification Triggers

This type of trigger is used in Raven to notify other entities of gunshot sounds. Every time a weapon is fired a `Trigger_SoundNotify` is created and left at the position of the shot. This type of trigger has a circular trigger region with a radius proportional to the loudness of the weapon. It is derived from `Trigger_LimitedLifetime` and is designed to only be active for one bot trigger update. When a bot triggers this type of trigger, it sends a message to the bot notifying it which bot made the sound.

```
class Trigger_SoundNotify : public Trigger_LimitedLifetime<Raven_Bot>
{
private:

  //a pointer to the bot that has made this sound
  Raven_Bot*  m_pSoundSource;

public:

  Trigger_SoundNotify(Raven_Bot* source, double range);

  void Trigger_SoundNotify::Try(Raven_Bot* pBot)
  {
    //is this bot within range of this sound
    if (isTouchingTrigger(pBot->Pos(), pBot->BRadius()))
    {
      Dispatcher->DispatchMsg(SEND_MSG_IMMEDIATELY,
                              SENDER_ID_IRRELEVANT,
                              pBot->ID(),
                              Msg_GunshotSound,
                              m_pSoundSource);
    }
  }
};
```

Managing Triggers: The TriggerSystem Class

The `TriggerSystem` class is responsible for managing a collection of triggers. The `Raven_Map` class owns an instance of a `TriggerSystem` and registers each trigger with the system as it is created. The trigger system takes care of updating and rendering all registered triggers and removes triggers as their lifetime expires.

Here's the source for `TriggerSystem`. I've listed the method bodies of `UpdateTriggers` and `TryTriggers` so you can see exactly how they work.

```
template <class trigger_type>
class TriggerSystem
{
public:

  typedef std::list<trigger_type*> TriggerList;

private:

  //a container of all the triggers
  TriggerList   m_Triggers;

  //this method iterates through all the triggers present in the system and
  //calls their Update method in order that their internal state can be
  //updated if necessary. It also removes any triggers from the system that
  //have their m_bRemoveFromGame field set to true.
  void UpdateTriggers()
  {
    TriggerList::iterator curTrg = m_Triggers.begin();
    while (curTrg != m_Triggers.end())
    {
      //remove trigger if dead
      if ((*curTrg)->isToBeRemoved())
      {
        delete *curTrg;

        curTrg = m_Triggers.erase(curTrg);
      }
      else
      {
        //update this trigger
        (*curTrg)->Update();

        ++curTrg;
      }
    }
  }

  //this method iterates through the container of entities passed as a
  //parameter and passes each one to the Try method of each trigger provided
  //the entity is alive and is ready for a trigger update.
  template <class ContainerOfEntities>
```

```
  void TryTriggers(ContainerOfEntities& entities)
  {
    //test each entity against the triggers
    ContainerOfEntities::iterator curEnt = entities.begin();
    for (curEnt; curEnt != entities.end(); ++curEnt)
    {
      //an entity must be ready for its next trigger update and it must be
      //alive before it is tested against each trigger.
      if ((*curEnt)->isReadyForTriggerUpdate() && (*curEnt)->isAlive())
      {
        TriggerList::const_iterator curTrg;
        for (curTrg = m_Triggers.begin(); curTrg != m_Triggers.end(); ++curTrg)
        {
          (*curTrg)->Try(*curEnt);
        }
      }
    }
  }


public:

  ~TriggerSystem()
  {
    Clear();
  }

  //this deletes any current triggers and empties the trigger list
  void Clear();

  //This method should be called each update step of the game. It will first
  //update the internal state of the triggers and then try each entity against
  //each active trigger to test if any should be triggered.
  template <class ContainerOfEntities>
  void Update(ContainerOfEntities& entities)
  {
    UpdateTriggers();
    TryTriggers(entities);
  }

  //this is used to register triggers with the TriggerSystem (the TriggerSystem
  //will take care of tidying up memory used by a trigger)
  void Register(trigger_type* trigger);

  //some triggers are required to be rendered (like giver-triggers for example)
  void Render();

  const TriggerList& GetTriggers()const{return m_Triggers;}
};
```

Okay, that should be enough insight into the Raven game framework. Let's now take a look at the design of the bot AI.

AI Design Considerations

The design of the Raven bot AI is approached in the usual manner: We consider what behavior is required of the bots to be successful within their environment and decompose that behavior into a list of components we are able to implement and coordinate.

I'm sure you have either played or watched someone play a Quake-like deathmatch game, so let's mull over that experience and see what observations can be made about how a human player plays this sort of game. Two obvious skills required are the ability to move around and the ability to aim and shoot a weapon at other players. What isn't so immediately obvious is that if you watch experienced players you will notice that they are almost always aiming and shooting at an enemy (provided one is in their vicinity) whether they are attacking or defending, and regardless of the direction they are moving. For instance, they might be strafing from side to side or running away backward while laying down defensive fire. We'll take a tip from this observation and implement the weapon handling and movement components of the AI so that they operate independently of each other.

What sort of movement related skills will the AI need? It's clear a bot should be able to move in any direction while avoiding walls and other bots. We can also see it's necessary to implement some type of search algorithm to enable the AI to plan paths to specific locations or items.

What about weapon handling? What kind of weapon related decisions does a player have to make? Well, first of all, a player has to decide which weapon is best suited for the current situation. In Raven there are four kinds of weapons: the blaster, the shotgun, the rocket launcher, and the railgun. Each of these weapons has pros and cons. For example, a shotgun is devastating when an enemy is close, but because of the way the shot spreads outward as it travels away from the gun muzzle it becomes much less effective with distance (see Figure 7.4). A rocket launcher is great at medium distance but is dangerous to use up close because of the splashback from the explosion. Any AI we implement must be able to weigh the pros and cons of each weapon and select one accordingly.

A player also has to be able to aim his chosen weapon effectively. For weapons that fire high-velocity projectiles, such as the railgun and shotgun, a player must aim directly at an enemy's position, but in the case of weapons that fire slower-moving projectiles, such as the blaster or rocket launcher, a player must be able to predict the enemy's movement and aim accordingly. The bot AI must be able to do the same.

Often in games of this sort a player will be pitted against multiple opponents. If two or more enemies are visible, the player must decide which one to target. As a result, any AI we design must also be able to select a single target from a group. This brings us to another issue: that of perception. Human players select targets from the opponents perceived by their senses.

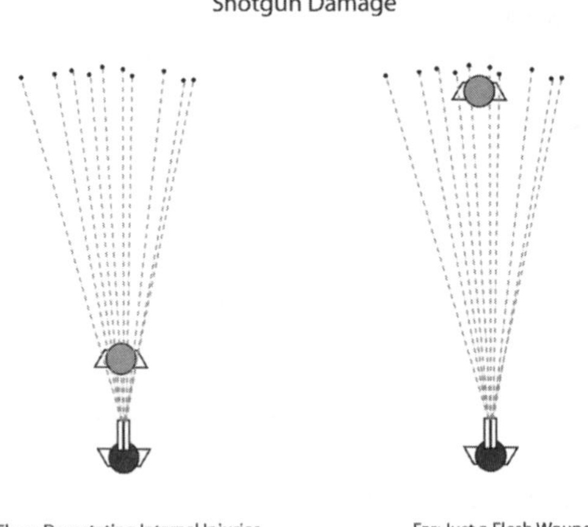

Figure 7.4. Shotgun damage

In Raven this includes visible opponents and opponents that are noisy enough to be heard. In addition, humans also use their short-term memory to keep track of any bots they have encountered recently; human players do not instantly forget about opponents that have recently moved out of their sensory range. For example, if a player is chasing a target that then disappears around a corner, he will keep chasing the target even though it cannot be seen. To be convincing, any bot AI must also exhibit similar sensory abilities.

Of course, all the skills mentioned thus far operate at a fairly low level. For many games of this type, it's simply not enough to run around a map at random, firing at enemies only when they're stumbled upon. A decent AI must be able to reflect upon its own state and that of the world around it and choose actions it thinks will help improve its state. For example, a bot should be able to recognize when it is running low on health and formulate a plan to locate and navigate to a health item. If a bot is fighting an enemy but is short on ammo, it should be able to consider the possibility of breaking off the fight in order to locate a few extra rockets. Therefore some type of high-level decision-making logic must be implemented.

AI Implementation

To imbue a bot with the illusion of intelligence we need to employ quite a list of skills and abilities. Let's walk through them and discuss how each is implemented by the Raven bot AI.

Decision Making

For their decision-making processes Raven bots use an architecture based around the arbitration of goals. The behavior necessary for a bot to win a game is decomposed into several high-level goals such as "attack," "find health," or "chase target." Goals can be nested and it's common for high-level goals to be composed of two or more subgoals. For instance, the "find health" goal is composed of the subgoals "find path to closest active health item" and "follow path to item." In turn, the goal "follow path" can be decomposed into several "move to position" type goals.

Every time the decision-making component of a bot's AI is updated, each of the high-level goals is evaluated for its suitability given the bot's current status and the one with the highest score is selected as the current goal. The bot will then decompose this goal into its constituent subgoals and attempt to satisfy each one in turn.

This type of decision-making architecture is covered in detail in Chapter 9.

Movement

For low-level movement the Raven bots make use of the steering behaviors **seek**, **arrive**, **wander**, **wall avoidance**, and **separation**. There is no collision detection or response between the bots and world geometry; the bots rely entirely on **wall avoidance** and **separation** steering behaviors to negotiate their environment. (I'm not advocating that you should use this approach in your own projects — your game will probably require much stricter collision detection — but it's adequate for the demos that accompany this book. It's also a rather good demonstration of just how effective steering behaviors can be if used correctly.)

Steering behaviors are implemented in the usual way described in previous chapters. The `Raven_Bot` class inherits from a `MovingEntity` and instantiates its own instance of the familiar steering behavior object. AI components that influence a bot's movement use the interface to this instance to control the movement of the bot.

Path Planning

The bots in Raven must be able to plan paths through their environment in order to move to a target location or toward an instance of a game item such as a weapon or health. To facilitate this process, each bot owns a dedicated path planning class that its decision-making component can use to request paths.

The evolution of the Raven path planner component is discussed in detail in Chapter 8.

Perception

For many game genres (but not all), modeling perception accurately is one of the keys to maintaining the illusion of intelligence since an agent's awareness of its environment should be consistent with its embodiment. If a game character has two eyes and two ears situated on its head in a similar fashion to a human, then it should perceive its environment accordingly. This is not to say we have to model stereo vision and hearing, but it is paramount that in a game of this type an agent's decision logic is consistent with what it should and should not be able to perceive within its sensory horizon. If there is any inconsistency the player will grow disillusioned and his enjoyment of the game will be greatly diminished. For instance, I'm sure most of us have witnessed behavior similar to the following.

- You approach a bot *silently* from the rear, but it immediately turns around (maybe it hears you blink) and fragments your intestines with a chaingun.
- You run and hide. It's impossible for your enemy to know you have shut yourself in a tiny storage room, but nevertheless it proceeds directly to your location, opens the door, and lobs a grenade inside.
- You notice two guards in a guard tower. They sweep the ground with a powerful searchlight but you notice a path to the base of the tower that is always in darkness. You quietly and confidently crawl along your chosen route. The searchlight never goes near you, yet one of the guards shouts "Achtung" and pops a cap in your ass.

These types of events occur because the programmer has given the AI total access to the game's data, thereby bestowing the agents with the gift of *sensory omnipotence*. He's done it because it was easier, or because he didn't have time to separate out truth vs. perception, or perhaps just because he didn't give it any thought. In any event, this is a big "no-no" with gamers. They will lose interest in the game because they will believe the AI is cheating (which, of course, it is).

NOTE This type of sensory modeling is not as important for RTS-type games where the CPU/memory overhead of implementing such a system for hundreds of agents will likely be prohibitive. It's also doubtful that significant improvements in gameplay will be made from implementing such a system.

To prevent these perceptual inconsistencies an agent's sense of vision and hearing must be filtered to ensure consistency with its visual and aural capabilities. For example, in a game where each bot must exhibit similar sensory capabilities to the human player, if a human player's view is restricted to 90 degrees, the bots should share the same restriction. If a player's sight is occluded by walls and obstacles, this should also apply to the bots. If a player cannot hear a character blink or hear sounds farther away than a certain range, then neither should the bots; and if light levels play an important part in the gameplay, a bot should not be able to see in the dark (unless it's wearing night-vision goggles of course).

Another type of perception related problem often seen in computer games is what I like to call *selective sensory nescience*: the inability of agents to sense specific types of events or entities. Here are some typical examples.

- You enter a room. There are two trolls in the distance with their backs to you. They are close enough for you to make out their muttering. They are discussing lunch. An ogre leaps out from the darkness to your left, startling you. You slay the ogre by unleashing your largest and loudest spell: Death By Thunder Cannon. The ogre explodes magnificently in a rip-roaring explosion of apocalyptic magnitude yet the two trolls don't hear it — they simply keep on discussing the merits of mint sauce with roast lamb.
- You stab a Nazi guard in the back. As he slumps to the floor you hear more guards approach, so you slink off into a dark corner. The guards enter the room and your mouse hand tenses, ready for the moment when they start looking around for the intruder. However, the guards do not see the body on the floor, even when they walk right over it.
- You find yourself in a hack and slash fight with a ghostly warrior. Unfortunately, you have misjudged the situation and are on the receiving end of a serious kicking. In desperation you turn and run out the nearest doorway only to find that as soon as you are out of sight the warrior forgets all about you.

Once again the illusion of intelligence is broken because the game characters are not behaving consistently with what is expected from their perceptual capability. In these examples though, it's not because the agents perceive too much information, but rather too little. The latter example is particularly interesting as it demonstrates how, in order to be convincing, an agent must also be bestowed with a mechanism for simulating short-term memory. Without short-term memory an agent is incapable of considering potential opponents that lie outside its sensory horizon. This can result in spectacularly stupid-looking behavior.

In Figure 7.5, two opponents — Gnasher and Basher — are in Billy's field of view and he selects one, Basher, to be his target. Billy then turns to face Basher and shoots him. See Figure 7.6.

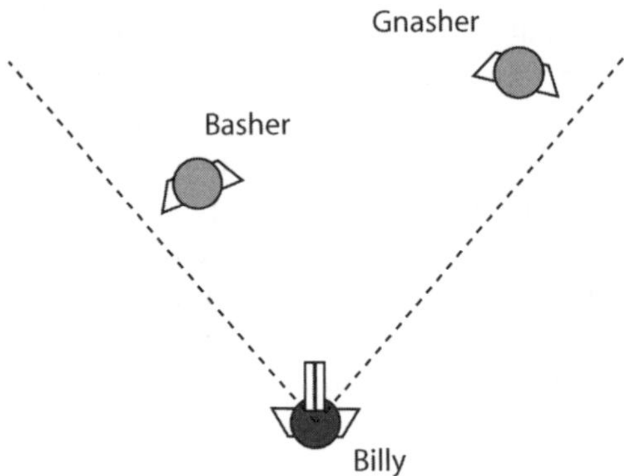

Figure 7.5. Billy and two opponents. The dotted lines describe Billy's field of view.

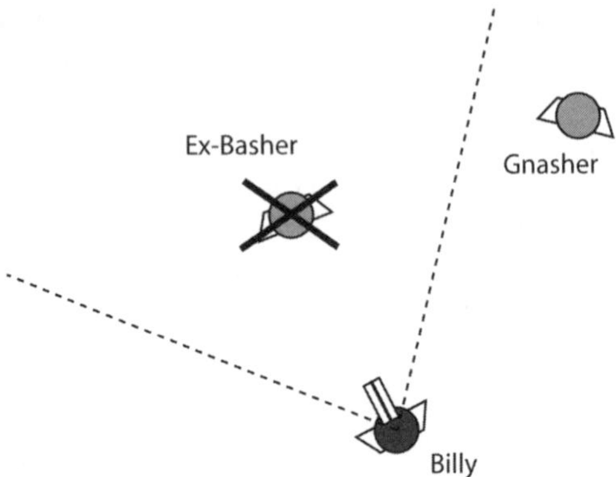

Figure 7.6. Billy slays Basher.

Unfortunately for Billy, as his programmer has not bestowed him with any short-term memory, as soon as Gnasher leaves his field of view he is forgotten. This gives Gnasher the opportunity to sneak up on Billy and bite his head off. See Figure 7.7.

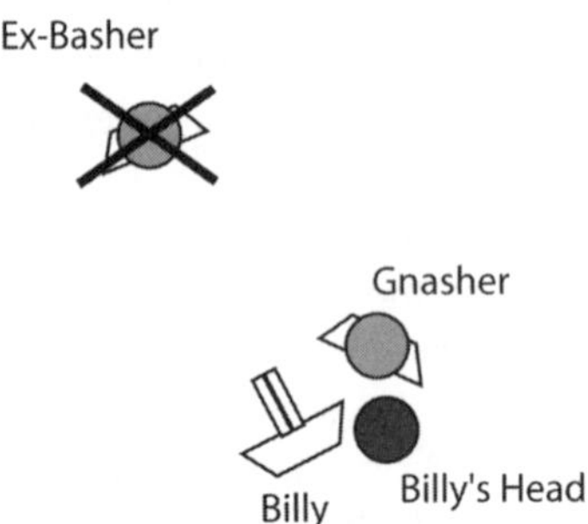

Figure 7.7. Billy loses his head.

This type of sequence is easily avoided if agents are able to remember what they have recently sensed for a period of time.

In Raven, the task of managing, filtering, and remembering sensory input is encapsulated by the class Raven_SensoryMemory, which each bot owns an instance of. This object manages a std::map of MemoryRecords, which is a simple data structure that looks like this:

```
struct MemoryRecord
{
  //records the time the opponent was last sensed (seen or heard). This
  //is used to determine if a bot can "remember" this record or not.
  //(if CurrentTime() - dTimeLastSensed is greater than the bot's
  //memory span, the data in this record is made unavailable to clients)
  double       dTimeLastSensed;

  //it can be useful to know how long an opponent has been visible. This
  //variable is tagged with the current time whenever an opponent first becomes
  //visible. It's then a simple matter to calculate how long the opponent has
  //been in view (CurrentTime - dTimeBecameVisible)
  double       dTimeBecameVisible;

  //it can also be useful to know the last time an opponent was seen
  double       dTimeLastVisible;

  //a vector marking the position where the opponent was last sensed. This can
  // be used to help hunt down an opponent if it goes out of view
  Vector2D    vLastSensedPosition;

  //set to true if opponent is within the field of view of the owner
  bool        bWithinFOV;

  //set to true if there is no obstruction between the opponent and the owner,
  //permitting a shot.
  bool        bShootable;
};
```

Each time a bot encounters a *new* opponent, an instance of a MemoryRecord is created and added to the memory map. Once a record has been made, whenever the corresponding opponent is heard or seen its record is updated with the relevant information. A bot is able to use this memory map to determine what opponents it has sensed recently and to react accordingly. In addition, because each memory record caches visibility information, many line-of-sight calculations can be avoided. Instead of requesting time-consuming line-of-sight requests from the game world object, a bot can simply and quickly retrieve the Boolean value stored in its memory map.

The declaration of Raven_SensoryMemory is as follows:

```
class Raven_SensoryMemory
{
private:
```

```
  typedef std::map<Raven_Bot*, MemoryRecord> MemoryMap;

private:

  //the owner of this instance
  Raven_Bot* m_pOwner;

  //this container is used to simulate memory of sensory events. A MemoryRecord
  //is created for each opponent in the environment. Each record is updated
  //whenever the opponent is encountered. (when it is seen or heard)
  MemoryMap  m_MemoryMap;

  //a bot has a memory span equivalent to this value. When a bot requests a
  //list of all recently sensed opponents, this value is used to determine if
  //the bot is able to remember an opponent or not.
  double     m_dMemorySpan;

  //this methods checks to see if there is an existing record for pBot. If
  //not, a new MemoryRecord record is made and added to the memory map.(Called
  //by UpdateWithSoundSource & UpdateVision)
  void       MakeNewRecordIfNotAlreadyPresent(Raven_Bot* pBot);

public:

  Raven_SensoryMemory(Raven_Bot* owner, double MemorySpan);

  //this method is used to update the memory map whenever an opponent makes
  //a noise
  void     UpdateWithSoundSource(Raven_Bot* pNoiseMaker);

  //this method iterates through all the opponents in the game world and
  //updates the records of those that are in the owner's FOV
  void     UpdateVision();

  bool     isOpponentShootable(Raven_Bot* pOpponent)const;
  bool     isOpponentWithinFOV(Raven_Bot* pOpponent)const;
  Vector2D GetLastRecordedPositionOfOpponent(Raven_Bot* pOpponent)const;
  double   GetTimeOpponentHasBeenVisible(Raven_Bot* pOpponent)const;
  double   GetTimeSinceLastSensed(Raven_Bot* pOpponent)const;
  double   GetTimeOpponentHasBeenOutOfView(Raven_Bot* pOpponent)const;

  //this method returns a list of all the opponents that have had their
  //records updated within the last m_dMemorySpan seconds.
  std::list<Raven_Bot*> GetListOfRecentlySensedOpponents()const;
};
```

Whenever a sound event occurs, the `UpdateWithSoundSource` method is called with a pointer to the source of the sound. `UpdateVision` is called from `Raven_Bot::Update` at a specified frequency. Together, these methods ensure that a bot's sense of hearing and vision are always up to date. A bot may then request information from its sensory memory using one of the listed methods, the most interesting being `GetListOfRecentlySensedOpponents`. This iterates through the memory map and builds a list of all those opponents sensed within recent memory. Here's what the method looks like:

```
std::list<Raven_Bot*>
Raven_SensoryMemory::GetListOfRecentlySensedOpponents()const
{
  //this will store all the opponents the bot can remember
  std::list<Raven_Bot*> opponents;

  double CurrentTime = Clock->GetCurrentTime();

  MemoryMap::const_iterator curRecord = m_MemoryMap.begin();
  for (curRecord; curRecord!=m_MemoryMap.end(); ++curRecord)
  {
    //if this bot has been updated in the memory recently, add to list
    if ( (CurrentTime - curRecord->second.dTimeLastSensed) <= m_dMemorySpan)
    {
      opponents.push_back(curRecord->first);
    }
  }

  return opponents;
}
```

As you can see, if a particular record has not been updated within the last `m_dMemorySpan` seconds it is not added to the list, and the bot effectively forgets all about that opponent. This ensures that a bot will remember an opponent for a short while after it has been sensed even if it goes out of view.

Target Selection

The class that handles target selection is called `Raven_TargetingSystem`. Each `Raven_Bot` owns an instance of this class and delegates target selection to it. Its declaration looks like this:

```
class Raven_TargetingSystem
{
private:

  //the owner of this system
  Raven_Bot*  m_pOwner;

  //the current target (this will be null if there is no target assigned)
  Raven_Bot*  m_pCurrentTarget;


public:

  Raven_TargetingSystem(Raven_Bot* owner);

  //each time this method is called the opponents in the owner's sensory
  //memory are examined and the closest is assigned to m_pCurrentTarget.
  //if there are no opponents that have had their memory records updated
```

```
  //within the memory span of the owner then the current target is set
  //to zero
  void       Update();

  //returns true if there is a currently assigned target
  bool       isTargetPresent()const;

  //returns true if the target is within the field of view of the owner
  bool       isTargetWithinFOV()const;

  //returns true if there is unobstructed line of sight between the target
  //and the owner
  bool       isTargetShootable()const;

  //returns the position where the target was last seen. Throws an exception if
  //there is no target currently assigned
  Vector2D   GetLastRecordedPosition()const;

  //returns the amount of time the target has been in the field of view
  double     GetTimeTargetHasBeenVisible()const;

  //returns the amount of time the target has been out of view
  double     GetTimeTargetHasBeenOutOfView()const;

  //returns a pointer to the target. null if no target current.
  Raven_Bot* GetTarget()const;

  //sets the target pointer to null
  void       ClearTarget();
};
```

At a specified interval, the targeting system `Update` method is called from `Raven_Bot::Update`. `Update` obtains a list of recently perceived opponents from the sensory memory and selects one of them to be the current target.

The selection criterion used by the Raven bots is very simple: The closest opponent is assigned to be the current target. This works adequately for Raven but your game may demand alternative or more rigorous selection criteria. For instance, you might prefer to design a selection method that incorporates one or more of the following:

- An opponent's angle of deviation from the bot's heading (in other words, he's right in front of you)
- An opponent's facing direction (he can't see you — sneak attack!)
- The range of the weapon the opponent is carrying (he can't get me)
- The range of the weapon the bot is carrying (I can't get him)
- Any power-ups the opponents or bot may be using (how tough is he?)
- How long an opponent has been visible (he probably knows about me if I know about him)

- How much damage an opponent has inflicted on the bot in the last few seconds (that makes me mad!)
- How many times an opponent has been killed by the bot (ha, ha!)
- How many times the bot has been killed by an opponent (meanie!)

Weapon Handling

The Raven bots use the `Raven_WeaponSystem` class to manage all operations specific to weapons and their deployment. This class owns a `std::map` of instances of weapons, keyed into by their type, a pointer to the currently held weapon, and variables denoting the aiming accuracy of the bot and the bot's reaction time. These last two variables are used by the weapon aiming logic to prevent a bot from hitting its target 100 percent of the time or shooting at an opponent the instant it comes into view. This is important because if an AI performs too well most players will quickly become frustrated and stop playing the game. These values allow the game testers to adjust the bots' skill level until they put up a tough battle, but lose more often than win. This, for most players, will provide the most enjoyable gaming experience.

In addition to the member variables, the class has methods for adding weapons, changing the current weapon, aiming and shooting the current weapon, and selecting the best weapon for the current game state.

Here's the declaration for you to look over.

```
class Raven_WeaponSystem
{
private:

  //a map of weapon instances keyed into by type
  typedef std::map<int, Raven_Weapon*>  WeaponMap;

private:

  Raven_Bot*       m_pOwner;

  //pointers to the weapons the bot is carrying (a bot may only carry one
  //instance of each weapon)
  WeaponMap        m_WeaponMap;

  //a pointer to the weapon the bot is currently holding
  Raven_Weapon*    m_pCurrentWeapon;

  //this is the minimum amount of time a bot needs to see an opponent before
  //it can react to it. This variable is used to prevent a bot from shooting at
  //an opponent the instant it becomes visible.
  double           m_dReactionTime;
```

```
  //each time the current weapon is fired a certain amount of random noise is
  //added to the angle of the shot. This prevents the bots from hitting
  //their opponent 100% of the time. The lower this value the more accurate
  //a bot's aim will be. Recommended values are between 0 and 0.2 (the value
  //represents the max deviation in radians that can be added to each shot).
  double          m_dAimAccuracy;

  //the amount of time a bot will continue aiming at the position of the target
  //even if the target disappears from view.
  double          m_dAimPersistance;

  //predicts where the target will be by the time it takes the current weapon's
  //projectile type to reach it. Used by TakeAimAndShoot
  Vector2D    PredictFuturePositionOfTarget()const;

  //adds a random deviation to the firing angle not greater than m_dAimAccuracy
  //rads
  void        AddNoiseToAim(Vector2D& AimingPos)const;

public:

  Raven_WeaponSystem(Raven_Bot* owner,
                     double     ReactionTime,
                     double     AimAccuracy,
                     double     AimPersistance);

  ~Raven_WeaponSystem();

  //sets up the weapon map with just one weapon: the blaster
  void          Initialize();

  //this method aims the bot's current weapon at the target (if there is a
  //target) and, if aimed correctly, fires a round. (Called each update step
  //from Raven_Bot::Update)
  void          TakeAimAndShoot()const;

  //this method determines the most appropriate weapon to use given the current
  //game state. (Called every n update steps from Raven_Bot::Update)
  void          SelectWeapon();

  //this will add a weapon of the specified type to the bot's inventory.
  //If the bot already has a weapon of this type only the ammo is added.
  //(called by the weapon giver-triggers to give a bot a weapon)
  void          AddWeapon(unsigned int weapon_type);

  //changes the current weapon to one of the specified type (provided that type
  //is in the bot's possession)
  void          ChangeWeapon(unsigned int type);

  //returns a pointer to the current weapon
  Raven_Weapon* GetCurrentWeapon()const{return m_pCurrentWeapon;}
```

```
    //returns a pointer to the specified weapon type (if in inventory, null if
    //not)
    Raven_Weapon* GetWeaponFromInventory(int weapon_type);

    //returns the amount of ammo remaining for the specified weapon
    int           GetAmmoRemainingForWeapon(unsigned int weapon_type);

    double        ReactionTime()const{return m_dReactionTime;}
};
```

The method `SelectWeapon` uses fuzzy logic to decide the best weapon to use for the current game state. Fuzzy logic is logic that has been extended to encompass partial truths. In other words, an object doesn't have to be either a member of a set or not; with fuzzy logic an object can be a member of a set to a *matter of degree*. Fuzzy logic and its application to weapon selection is covered in detail in Chapter 10.

Each update step the `TakeAimAndShoot` method is called from `Raven_Bot::Update`. This method first queries the targeting system to ensure the current target is either shootable (the targeting system in turn retrieves this information from the bot's sensory memory) or has only very recently moved out of view. The latter condition ensures that a bot will continue aiming its weapon at the target even if it briefly dodges behind a wall or other obstacle. If neither condition is true, the weapon's facing direction will be aligned with the bot's heading.

If one of the conditions is true, the best place to aim the current weapon is determined. For "instant hit" weapons, such as the shotgun or railgun, this will be directly at the target. For weapons that fire slower-moving projectiles, such as the rocket launcher or blaster, the method must predict where the target will be by the time the projectile reaches it. This calculation is similar to that used for the pursuit steering behavior and is undertaken by the method `PredictFuturePositionOfTarget`.

⌘ TIP As the Raven code stands, the prediction of a target's future position for weapon aiming is based upon its instantaneous velocity — the velocity at which it is moving at the time of the calculation. However, this can give poor results, especially if the target is dodging around a lot. A more accurate method is to take the average of the target's velocity sampled over the last *t* time steps.

Once an aiming position has been determined the logic rotates the facing position of the bot toward it and shoots the weapon, provided it is aimed correctly and that the target has been in view longer than the time required for the bot to react.

All this logic is much clearer in code, so here is the method's listing:

```
void Raven_WeaponSystem::TakeAimAndShoot()const
{
  //aim the weapon only if the current target is shootable or if it has only
  //very recently gone out of view (this latter condition is to ensure the
  //weapon is aimed at the target even if it temporarily dodges behind a wall
  //or other cover)
  if (m_pOwner->GetTargetSys()->isTargetShootable() ||
     (m_pOwner->GetTargetSys()->GetTimeTargetHasBeenOutOfView() <
      m_dAimPersistance) )
  {
    //the position the weapon will be aimed at
    Vector2D AimingPos = m_pOwner->GetTargetBot()->Pos();

    //if the current weapon is not an instant hit type gun the target position
    //must be adjusted to take into account the predicted movement of the
    //target
    if (GetCurrentWeapon()->GetType() == type_rocket_launcher ||
        GetCurrentWeapon()->GetType() == type_blaster)
    {
      AimingPos = PredictFuturePositionOfTarget();

      //if the weapon is aimed correctly, there is line of sight between the
      //bot and the aiming position, and it has been in view for a period longer
      //than the bot's reaction time, shoot the weapon
      if ( m_pOwner->RotateFacingTowardPosition(AimingPos) &&
          (m_pOwner->GetTargetSys()->GetTimeTargetHasBeenVisible() >
           m_dReactionTime) &&
           m_pOwner->GetWorld()->isLOSOkay(AimingPos, m_pOwner->Pos()))
      {
        AddNoiseToAim(AimingPos);

        GetCurrentWeapon()->ShootAt(AimingPos);
      }
    }

    //no need to predict movement, aim directly at target
    else
    {
      //if the weapon is aimed correctly and it has been in view for a period
      //longer than the bot's reaction time, shoot the weapon
      if ( m_pOwner->RotateFacingTowardPosition(AimingPos) &&
          (m_pOwner->GetTargetSys()->GetTimeTargetHasBeenVisible() >
           m_dReactionTime) )
      {
        AddNoiseToAim(AimingPos);

        GetCurrentWeapon()->ShootAt(AimingPos);
      }
    }
```

```
    }

    //no target to shoot at so rotate facing to be parallel with the bot's
    //heading direction
    else
    {
      m_pOwner->RotateFacingTowardPosition(m_pOwner->Pos()+ m_pOwner->Heading());
    }
}
```

Notice how when the aiming position is predicted, a line-of-sight test must be made to ensure the predicted position is unobstructed by walls. This is not necessary if the weapon is aimed directly at the target because the LOS to the target position is cached when the target's memory record is updated. Notice also how immediately before the weapon is fired, some noise is added to the aiming position in order to prevent the shot from hitting the target 100 percent of the time.

⌘ **TIP** For some games it's a good idea to ensure an AI controlled agent *always* misses the first time it takes a shot at the player. This is because the shot will warn the player to the presence of the agent, enabling him to take appropriate action without getting hurt immediately. This is particularly useful for scenarios where a player often enters unexplored rooms full of baddies because it gives him a chance to retreat a little and take stock of the situation instead of getting unexpectedly slaughtered.

Also, when deliberately shooting to miss, if the projectile or its trajectory can easily be seen (like a rocket or arrow), you can add to the excitement by ensuring the shot passes close by and within the player's field of view.

Another good aiming tip is this: If the player's health is very low, reduce the aiming accuracy of any bots shooting at him. This way he gets a chance to pull off an amazing recovery, which will enhance his game playing experience significantly. (He gets to feel like Aragorn in the Battle for Helm's Deep instead of like Paul Newman and Robert Redford in the last few minutes of *Butch Cassidy and the Sundance Kid*!)

Putting It All Together

Figure 7.8 shows how the AI components discussed in the last few pages interrelate. Note how the `Goal_Think` object has no direct control of low-level components such as movement and weapon handling. Its purpose is to arbitrate between and manage the processing of high-level goals. Individual goals utilize the lower-level components as and when required.

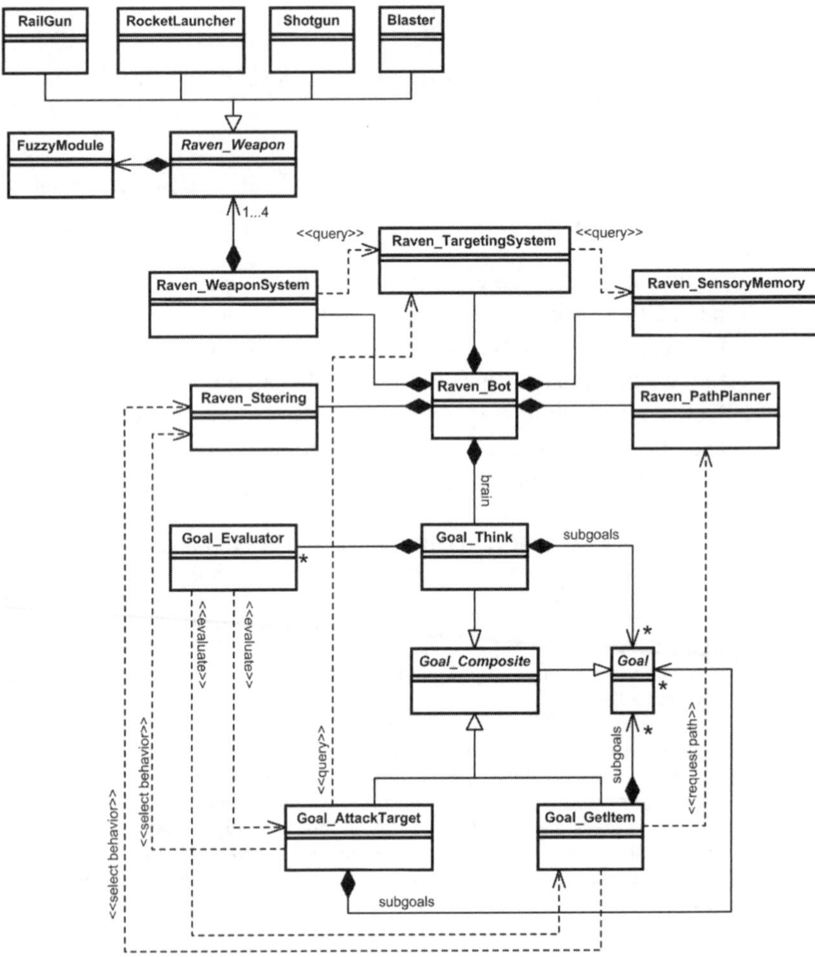

Figure 7.8. The Raven bot AI. Only a couple of high-level goals are shown to aid clarity.

All these components are updated with a specific frequency from the `Raven_Bot::Update` method so I guess that's where we should cast our eyes next.

Updating the AI Components

It's not essential for all the components of a bot's AI to be updated each time step. Many of the components are very CPU intensive and updating them all at the same rate would be folly. Instead, each component is examined to see how time critical or processor intensive it is and an update frequency is assigned accordingly. For instance, it's generally essential for the movement component of the AI to be updated every time step in order for obstacles and walls to be avoided correctly. A component such as weapon selection is not so time critical and therefore its update frequency can occur at a much slower rate; say, twice a second. Similarly, the component of a bot's sensory memory that polls the game world for visible opponents is very processor intensive because of the number of line-of-sight tests undertaken. For this reason, the polling is restricted to a low frequency — by default four times a second — and the results are cached.

This is not rocket science of course. Often you will have no way of knowing what the ideal update frequency is, so you must make an informed guess and tweak until you're happy with the results.

The Raven bots use instances of `Regulator` objects to control the updates of each of their AI components. This is a straightforward class that is instantiated using the required update frequency and has a single method, `isReady`, that returns true if it's time to allow the next update. The declaration of the class looks like this:

```
class Regulator
{
private:

  //the time period between updates
  double m_dUpdatePeriod;

  //the next time the regulator allows code flow
  DWORD  m_dwNextUpdateTime;

public:

  Regulator(double NumUpdatesPerSecondRqd);

  //returns true if the current time exceeds m_dwNextUpdateTime
  bool isReady();
};
```

The `Regulator` class automatically ensures updates are staggered over multiple time steps by adding a small random offset (between 0 and 1 second) to `m_dwNextUpdateTime` upon instantiation. (Without this offset, the same component of all active agents will be updated on the same time step.)

⌘ **TIP** By using regulators it's also possible to implement a kind of "level of detail" AI by lowering the update rate of some of the AI components of agents that are far away from the player and insignificant to his immediate experience. Raven doesn't do this since the game world is small, but you might like to experiment with this idea for your own games.

The `Raven_Bot` class instantiates several regulators and uses the majority of them in its `Update` method like so:

```
void Raven_Bot::Update()
{
  //process the currently active goal. Note this is required even if the bot
  //is under user control. This is because goals are created whenever a user
```

```
  //clicks on an area of the map that necessitates a path planning request.
  m_pBrain->Process();

  //Calculate the steering force and update the bot's velocity and position
  UpdateMovement();

  //if the bot is under AI control
  if (!isPossessed())
  {
    //update the sensory memory with any visual stimulus
    if (m_pVisionUpdateRegulator->isReady())
    {
      m_pSensoryMem->UpdateVision();
    }

    //examine all the opponents in the bot's sensory memory and select one
    //to be the current target
    if (m_pTargetSelectionRegulator->isReady())
    {
      m_pTargSys->Update();
    }

    //appraise and arbitrate between all possible high-level goals
    if (m_pGoalArbitrationRegulator->isReady())
    {
       m_pBrain->Arbitrate();
    }

    //select the appropriate weapon to use from the weapons currently in
    //the inventory
    if (m_pWeaponSelectionRegulator->isReady())
    {
      m_pWeaponSys->SelectWeapon();
    }

    //this method aims the bot's current weapon at the current target
    //and takes a shot if a shot is possible
    m_pWeaponSys->TakeAimAndShoot();
  }
}
```

The update frequencies for each component can be found in params.lua. The default settings are shown in Table 7.1.

Table 7.1. AI update frequencies

Component	Frequency (updates per second)
Vision	4
Target selection	2
Goal arbitration	2
Weapon selection	2

NOTE For this book, I chose to aggregate the `Regulator` instances in the `Raven_Bot` class because it makes their use more explicit. You may prefer for the objects requiring regulation to instantiate their own instances and use them to control the flow of logic in the appropriate method (usually their `Update` method).

Summing Up

This chapter has provided an overview of the design of AI for agents capable of playing a deathmatch type game. Although your understanding is still incomplete, you have seen how an agent's AI can be decomposed into several small, easily managed components, which are capable of communicating and working together to form a unified behavior. The remaining chapters will provide the plaster to plug the gaps in your knowledge.

Practice Makes Perfect

1. So far, Raven bots can only sense opponents they see or hear. However, they are still unable to feel the terrible burning and ripping sensation of a steel bullet casing tearing through their flesh. Write code to update their sensory system so that a bot is able to sense when it is being shot at. Create another field in the `MemoryRecord` structure to record the amount of damage each opponent has inflicted in the last few seconds. This value could be used as part of the target selection criterion.
2. Try out different target selection criteria. Observe how they affect the gameplay. Change the code so that each bot uses a unique criterion and play them off against each other to see which one performs best.

Chapter 8

Practical Path Planning

You saw in Chapter 5 how navigation graphs can be utilized by agents to plan paths between locations in the environment. However, when it comes down to implementing that theory in practice, you'll find there are all sorts of problems to overcome before your agents start moving around like you want them to. This chapter addresses many of the practical issues encountered when designing the path planning module(s) of game agents. Although the demos in this chapter are based around the Raven framework, most of the techniques are applicable across a wide range of game genres.

Navigation Graph Construction

To determine a path from A to B using a search algorithm such as those discussed in Chapter 5, a game environment must be partitioned into a data structure the algorithms can explore: a navigation graph. Because there are many ways of representing the geometry that makes up a game world — tile-, vector-, or polygon-based for example — it's hardly surprising there are numerous methods of converting the pertinent spatial information into a graph-like data structure. Let's examine several of the popular methods utilized in modern games.

Tile Based

Tile- or cell-based games like those found abundantly in the RTS and war game genres have large and sometimes complex environments based on squares or hexes. It therefore makes sense to design the game's navigation graph around these cells: Each graph node represents the center of a cell, with the graph edges denoting the connections between adjacent cells. In games of this type there will occasionally be a cost for maneuvering a game unit — like a tank or soldier — across the varying types of terrain. Water and mud are, after all, much more difficult for a Sherman tank to cross than tarmac or compacted earth. Since each cell is normally assigned a specific terrain type by the map designer, it's a trivial matter to use this information to weight the edges of the navigation graph accordingly. The algorithms employed to search the graph can make use of this additional information to determine appropriate paths through the terrain, ones that avoid water and mud or go around hills rather than over the top of them.

The downside to using cells as the skeleton for a navgraph is that the search spaces can quickly become extremely large. Even a modest 100 x 100 cell map will need a graph made up of up to 10,000 nodes and 78,000 (or so) edges. Given that RTS games usually have dozens or even hundreds of AI units active at any one time, with many of them requesting graph searches each update step, that's a hell of a lot of number crunching to be done, not to mention the related memory cost. Fortunately there are a number of methods available to ease the burden, which we'll be taking a look at later in the chapter.

Points of Visibility

A *points of visibility* (POV) navigation graph is created by placing graph nodes, usually by hand, at important points in the environment such that each graph node has line of sight to at least one other. Positioned carefully, the graph nodes will make a graph connecting all the important areas in the world geometry. Figure 8.1 shows a simple POV graph created for a Raven map (Raven_DM1).

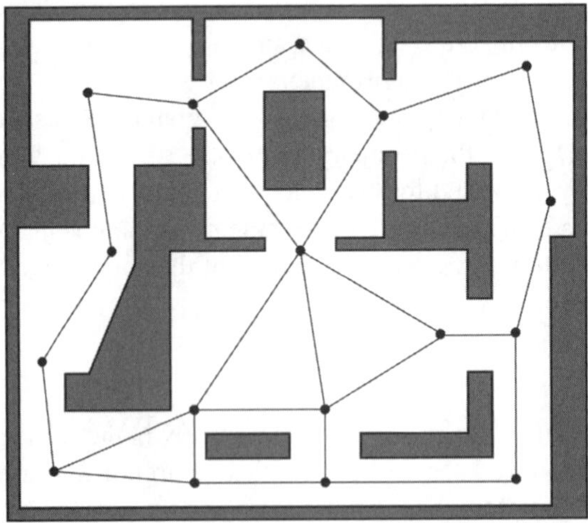

Figure 8.1. Points of visibility navigation graph

One feature of POV graphs is that they may be easily expanded to include nodes that proffer information over and above the connectivity data. For example, nodes can easily be added to a POV graph to represent good sniping, cover, or ambush positions. The downside is that if a game map is large and complex the map designer can spend an awful lot of precious development time positioning and tweaking the graph. A POV graph can also be problematic if you plan to include any type of map generation feature, since you must then develop some automated method to generate the POV graph structure as well for the new maps to be of any use. (This is why some games don't have random map generation features.) One solution for this problem, however, is to use *expanded geometry* techniques.

Expanded Geometry

If a game environment is constructed from polygons it's possible to use the information present in those shapes to *automatically* create a POV graph, which, for large maps can be a real time-saver. This is achieved by first expanding the polygons by an amount proportional to the bounding radius of the game agents. See Figures 8.2 A and B. The vertices defining this expanded geometry are then added as nodes to a navigation graph. Finally, an algorithm is run to test for line of sight between the vertices, and edges are added to the graph appropriately. Figure 8.2 C shows the finished navigation graph.

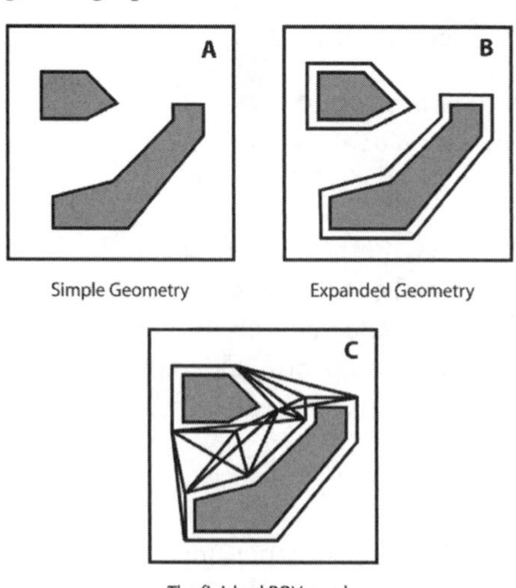

Figure 8.2. Creating a POV using expanded geometry

As the polygons are expanded by an amount not less than an agent's bounding radius, an agent can search the resulting navigation graph to create paths that safely negotiate the environment without bumping into walls.

NavMesh

One approach growing in popularity with game developers is to use a network of convex polygons, called a *navmesh*, to describe the walkable areas of a game environment. A convex polygon has the valuable property that it allows unobstructed travel from any point in the polygon to any other. This is useful because it enables an environment to be represented using a graph where each node represents a convex space (instead of a point). Figure 8.3 shows the map from Figure 8.1 partitioned in such a way.

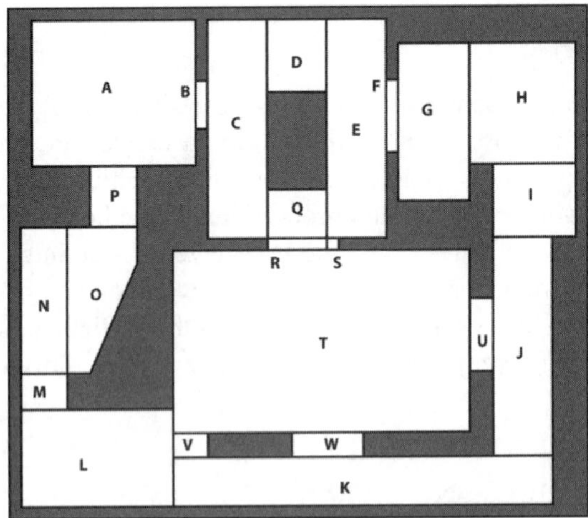

Figure 8.3. Raven_DM1 partitioned into a navmesh

Why is this a good thing? Well, navmeshes are efficient. The data structure required to store one is compact and can be searched very quickly. In addition, where environments are constructed entirely from polygons — like the majority of 3D FPS type games — it's possible to use algorithms to partition the walkable areas of the maps automatically.

The Raven Navigation Graph

Because they provide me with the greatest opportunity for demonstrating a varied range of techniques, the navigation graphs for Raven maps are created using the POV method. You saw earlier how the navgraph shown in Figure 8.1 was created by positioning nodes by hand inside a map editor. In this example a small number of nodes have been positioned at important intersections. Since each node is effectively representing a large spatial region, this type of graph can be said to be *coarsely granulated* (or *grained*). Coarsely granulated graphs are very compact data structures. They use very little memory and are quick to search and relatively easy to create, although they do have several limitations. Let's take a look at some of their faults.

Coarsely Granulated Graphs

If a game restricts its agents to movement along the edges of a navigation graph only, such as the movement of the characters in the Pac-Man range of games (see Screenshot 8.1), then a coarsely granulated navgraph is the perfect choice. However, if you are designing a navgraph for a game where the characters are given more freedom, coarse graphs can be harbingers of all sorts of problems.

Screenshot 8.1: Pacmen at play

For example, most RTS/RPG games use a control system where the user is free to command characters to move to any navigable area of the map. Normally this is done with a couple of mouse clicks, one to select the NPC and another to select the position it should move to. To move the NPC into position the AI must follow these steps:

1. Find the closest visible graph node to the NPC's current location, say, node A.
2. Find the closest visible graph node to the target location, say, node B.
3. Use a search algorithm to find the least cost path from A to B.
4. Move the NPC to node A.
5. Move the NPC along the path calculated in step 3.
6. Move the NPC from B to the target location.

If these steps are followed with a coarsely grained graph, such as the one shown earlier, unsightly paths will regularly occur. See Figure 8.4 for an example.

Some of these kinks can be ironed out using a path smoothing algorithm, such as the one discussed later in this chapter, but due to the coarseness of the navigation graph there will still be many occasions where an agent will zigzag unnaturally at the start and end points of a path. Even worse, when using coarse graphs there are almost always a few positions on the map to which there is no line of sight from any of the graph nodes, effectively rendering those areas invisible to any path planner. Figure 8.5 illustrates two positions on the Raven_DM1 map that are inaccessible to

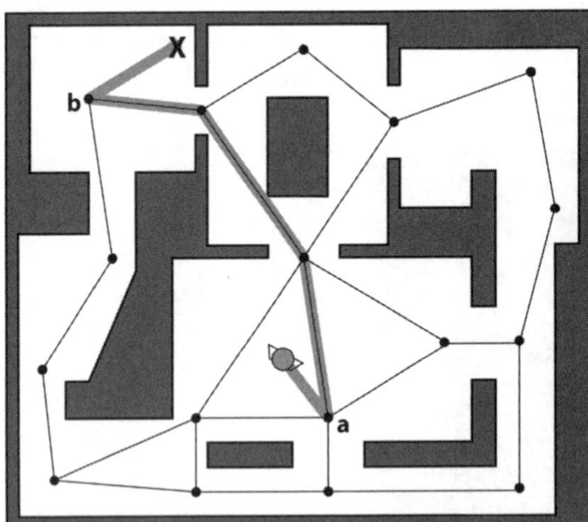

Figure 8.4. The path of an agent moving from its current position to the one marked by the X. (The closest node to the agent and the closest node to the target are shown by a and b respectively.) Notice how the agent must double back on itself twice to get to the target location. Nasty.

the path planner. These "invisible" areas are fairly easy to spot when testing a small map, but are much harder to find as the complexity of a map increases. This is reflected in a number of games that have been released with such problems.

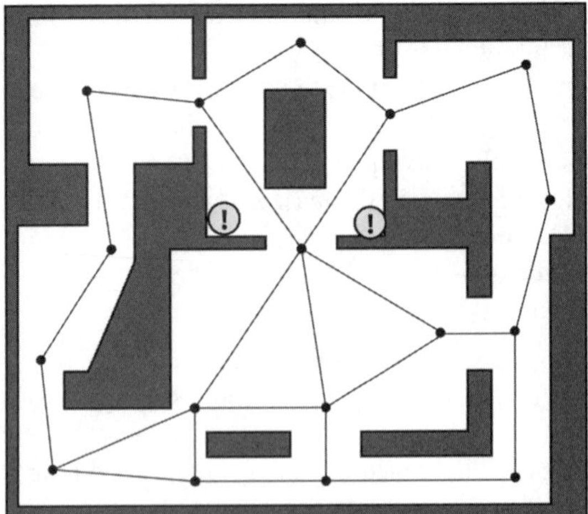

Figure 8.5. Map positions that are "invisible" to the navigation graph

You can observe these problems first hand by running the Raven_CoarseGraph executable. When the demo is run the bot will explore the environment by creating paths to randomly selected graph nodes. Right-click on the bot to select it and you will be able to see the path it's following shown as a series of red dots. Notice how the bot's movement looks okay as long as it sticks to positions along the navigation graph. Now right-click on the bot again to "possess" it. Once possessed, you can right-click anywhere else in the environment and the bot will attempt to calculate a path to that point (as long as the point is located within a navigable area of the map). Observe how the bot has to backtrack to follow certain paths.

Finely Grained Graphs

Poor paths and inaccessible positions can be improved by increasing the granularity of the navigation graph. Figure 8.6 is an example of a very finely granulated graph created for the Raven_DM1 map. Creating a graph like this by hand is extremely tedious, so a flood fill algorithm is utilized by the map editor to do the majority of the work. See the following sidebar for further details.

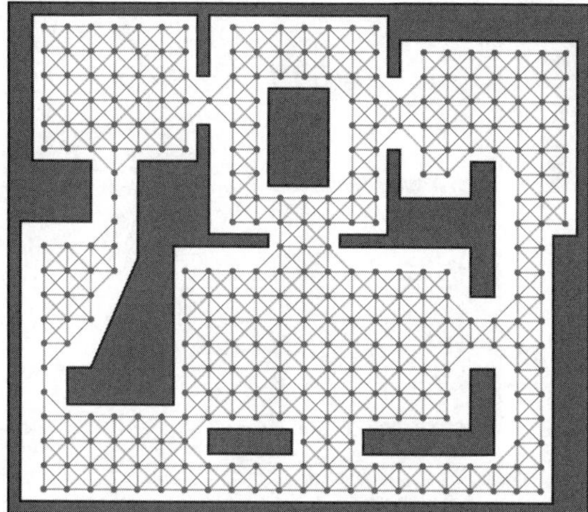

Figure 8.6. A finely granulated navigation graph

Since finely grained graphs are similar in topology to tile-based navigation graphs — and therefore present similar challenges to the AI programmer — I'll be using them as a basis to demonstrate the techniques described in the remainder of this chapter. This way I hope to kill several birds with one stone, and by the end of the chapter you'll understand how to create an agent capable of planning paths through any game environment, be it an FPS, RTS, or RPG.

Using the Flood Fill Algorithm to Create a Navigation Graph

To use the flood fill algorithm to create a navigation graph a single "seed" node is first placed somewhere in the map. See Figure 8.7, top left. The algorithm then "grows" a graph by expanding nodes and edges outward from the seed in each available direction, and then from the nodes on the fringe of the graph, until all the navigable area is filled. The figure shows the first six iterations of such a process.

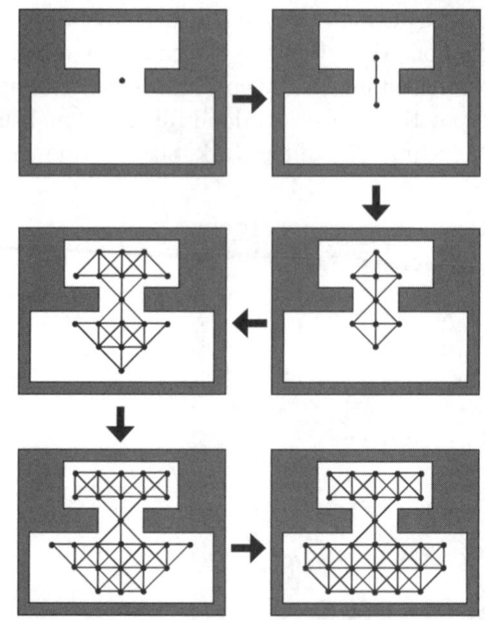

Figure 8.7. The first six iterations of the flood fill algorithm

This is a similar sort of technique paint programs use to fill an irregular shape, except instead of flooding a shape with a color the editor uses the algorithm to flood a map with graph nodes and edges. Individual nodes can then be moved, deleted, or added by the designer to give the desired result. To ensure that an agent's movement is unrestricted, during the process the algorithm ensures that all nodes and edges are positioned a minimum distance equal to the agent's bounding radius from any walls.

Adding Items to the Raven Navigation Graph

Most games include items an agent can pick up and use in some way. These items can be added as nodes to the navigation graph, enabling the path planning AI to easily search for the items and plan paths to them. Where there are multiple instances of the same item, the AI can use the navgraph to quickly determine which is the least costly to reach.

Remember back in Chapter 5 I showed you an example of a graph node class designed specifically for use with navigation graphs? Just in case your memory is as poor as mine, here's the listing again:

```
template <class extra_info = void*>
class NavGraphNode : public GraphNode
{
protected:

  //the node's position
  Vector2D     m_vPosition;

  //often you will want a navgraph node to contain additional information.
  //(for example a node might represent the position of an item type
  //such as health, thereby enabling a search algorithm to search a graph
  //for that item type)
  extra_info  m_ExtraInfo;

public:

  //ctors
  NavGraphNode():m_ExtraInfo(extra_info()){}


  NavGraphNode(int      idx,
               Vector2D pos):GraphNode(idx),
                             m_vPosition(pos),
                             m_ExtraInfo(extra_info())
  {}

  virtual    ~NavGraphNode(){}

  Vector2D   Pos()const;
  void       SetPos(Vector2D NewPosition);

  extra_info ExtraInfo()const;
  void       SetExtraInfo(extra_info info);

  /* EXTRANEOUS DETAIL OMMITTED */
};
```

This is the node class used by the Raven navigation graph. As mentioned in the previous chapter, item types in Raven are derived from the `Trigger` class. When a giver-trigger is added to a map using the map editor, a graph node is also added. That node's `m_ExtraInfo` member is assigned a pointer to the item it's twinned with, thereby enabling a modified search algorithm to query the navigation graph for particular item types as well as for specific node indexes. You'll be seeing exactly how this is done later in the chapter.

 **TIP** When designing the maps for some games it's a good idea to place frequently used items such as ammunition and armor directly in the most commonly used paths of the game agents. This helps the agents because they will tend to stay focused on the more important game objectives instead of having to run around searching for weapons and ammo.

Using Spatial Partitioning to Speed Up Proximity Queries

One of the most frequently used methods of a path planning class is a function that determines the closest visible node to a given position. If this search is undertaken by iterating through all the nodes in order to find the closest, the performance will be in $O(n^2)$ time: Each time the number of nodes doubles, the time taken to search them increases fourfold. As you saw in Chapter 3, the efficiency of such searches can be improved by using a spatial partitioning technique such as cell-space partitioning, BSP trees, quad-trees, or any other of the numerous methods available. For navigation graphs of over a couple hundred nodes, spatial partitioning gives dramatic speed increases as the search time becomes a function of the node density, $O(d)$, rather than the number of nodes; and since the density of nodes throughout navgraphs tends to be fairly consistent, the time taken to do a node proximity query will be constant. Consequently, the `Raven_Game` class partitions a navgraph's nodes using the cell-space method when a map is loaded.

NOTE There is no code written for this chapter per se. All the demos have been created by compiling the Raven project files with certain options switched on or off to demonstrate each technique I discuss. Because of this, the demos use *compiled* Lua script files to prevent you from twiddling with options that may crash the demos. For full twiddling rights, please compile the Raven project proper!

Creating a Path Planner Class

The majority of the remainder of this chapter will be spent following the development of a path planning class capable of executing and managing the numerous graph search requests required by a Raven bot. This class is called `Raven_PathPlanner` and each bot will own an instance of it. The class will start off simple, but as the chapter progresses its capabilities will be expanded incrementally, providing the opportunity to demonstrate how to solve many of the typical problems encountered when developing a path planning AI.

First let's consider the minimum functionality a path planning object must provide. A Raven bot at the very least should be able to plan a path from its current position to any other *location*, given that both positions are valid and navigable, and a path is possible. A Raven bot should also be capable of planning the least cost path between its current position and a specific *item type*, such as a health pack. As a result, the path planning class must have methods for searching the navgraph for such paths and for accessing the resultant path data. With these features in mind let's have a first try at a path planning class.

```
class Raven_PathPlanner
{
private:

  //for legibility
  enum {no_closest_node_found = -1};

private:

  //A pointer to the owner of this class
  Raven_Bot*                    m_pOwner;

  //a local reference to the navgraph
  const Raven_Map::NavGraph&    m_NavGraph;

  //this is the position the bot wishes to plan a path to reach
  Vector2D                      m_vDestinationPos;

  //returns the index of the closest visible and unobstructed graph node to
  //the given position. If none is found it returns the enumerated value
  //"no_closest_node_found"
  int   GetClosestNodeToPosition(Vector2D pos)const;

public:

  Raven_PathPlanner(Raven_Bot* owner);

  //finds the least cost path between the agent's position and the target
  //position. Fills path with a list of waypoints if the search is successful
  //and returns true. Returns false if unsuccessful
  bool   CreatePathToPosition(Vector2D TargetPos, std::list<Vector2D>& path);

  //finds the least cost path to an instance of ItemType. Fills path with a
  //list of waypoints if the search is successful and returns true. Returns
  //false if unsuccessful
  bool   CreatePathToItem(unsigned int ItemType, std::list<Vector2D>& path);
};
```

This class provides the minimum functionality a game agent requires. Let's take a closer look at the methods that create the paths.

Planning a Path to a Position

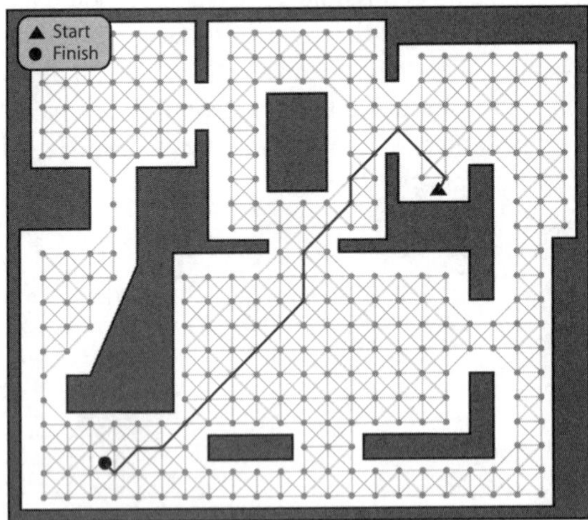

Figure 8.8. Planning a path to a position

Planning a path from a bot's current location to a target location is straightforward. The path planner must:

1. Find the closest visible unobstructed graph node to the bot's current location.
2. Find the closest visible unobstructed graph node to the target location.
3. Use a search algorithm to find the least cost path between the two.

The following code uses these steps. The comments should be adequate explanation.

```
bool Raven_PathPlanner::CreatePathToPosition(Vector2D TargetPos,
                                             std::list<Vector2D>& path)
{
  //make a note of the target position
  m_vDestinationPos = TargetPos;

  //if the target is unobstructed from the bot's position, a path does not need
  //to be calculated, and the bot can ARRIVE directly at the destination.
  //isPathObstructed is a method that takes a start
  //position, a target position, and an entity radius and determines if an
  //agent of that size is able to move unobstructed between the two positions.
  //It is used here to determine if the bot can move directly to the target
  //location without the need for planning a path.
  if (!m_pOwner()->GetWorld()->isPathObstructed(m_pOwner->Pos(),
                                                TargetPos,
                                                m_pOwner->BRadius()))
  {
    path.push_back(TargetPos);

    return true;
  }
  //find the closest unobstructed node to the bot's position.
```

```
  //GetClosestNodeToPosition is a method that queries the navigation graph
  //nodes (via the cell-space partition) to determine the closest unobstructed
  //node to the given position vector. It is used here to find the closest
  //unobstructed node to the bot's current location.
  int ClosestNodeToBot = GetClosestNodeToPosition(m_pOwner->Pos());

  //if no visible node found return failure. This will occur if the
  //navgraph is badly designed or if the bot has managed to get itself
  //*inside* the geometry (surrounded by walls) or an obstacle.
  if (ClosestNodeToBot == no_closest_node_found)
  {
    return false;
  }

  //find the closest visible unobstructed node to the target position
  int ClosestNodeToTarget = GetClosestNodeToPosition(TargetPos);

  //return failure if there is a problem locating a visible node from
  //the target.
  //This sort of thing occurs much more frequently than the above. For
  //example, if the user clicks inside an area bounded by walls or inside an
  //object.
  if (ClosestNodeToTarget == no_closest_node_found)
  {
    return false;
  }

  //create an instance of the A* search class to search for a path between the
  //closest node to the bot and the closest node to the target position. This
  //A* search will utilize the Euclidean straight line heuristic
  typedef Graph_SearchAStar< Raven_Map::NavGraph, Heuristic_Euclid> AStar;

  AStar search(m_NavGraph,
               ClosestNodeToBot,
               ClosestNodeToTarget);

  //grab the path
  std::list<int> PathOfNodeIndices = search.GetPathToTarget();

  //if the search is successful convert the node indices into position vectors
  if (!PathOfNodeIndices.empty())
  {
    ConvertIndicesToVectors(PathOfNodeIndices, path);

    //remember to add the target position to the end of the path
    path.push_back(TargetPos);

    return true;
  }
  else
  {
     //no path found by the search
     return false;
  }
}
```

Planning a Path to an Item Type

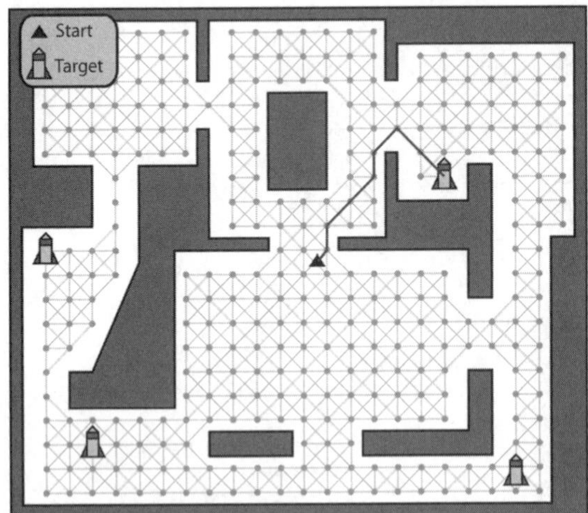

Figure 8.9. Planning a path to an item type

A* is the better algorithm to search for the least cost path from the bot's current position to a *specific* target position, but what about when the least cost path is required to a item type — such as a rocket launcher — where there may be *many* instances in the environment of the particular type? To calculate the heuristic cost during an A* search, the algorithm must have both a source position *and* a target position. Consequently, when using A* to search for the closest instance of an item type, a search must be completed for *each* instance present in the game world before the one with the least cost path can be chosen as the best item to move toward. This is okay if your map contains only a handful of instances of an item, but what if it contains many? After all, it's not uncommon for RTS game environments to include dozens or even hundreds of instances of resources like trees or gold. That means numerous A* searches will be necessary to locate just one item. This is not good.

When *many* similar item types are present, Dijkstra's algorithm is the better choice. As you've learned, Dijkstra's algorithm "grows" a shortest path tree outward from the root node until either the target has been reached or the entire graph has been explored. As soon as the item searched for is located, the algorithm will terminate and the SPT will contain the path from the root to the closest item of the desired type. In other words, no matter how many instances of an item type are present in the game world, Dijkstra's algorithm only needs to be run *once* to find the least cost path to one of them

As it stands, the Dijkstra's algorithm class used thus far in this book will only terminate when a particular node *index* is found. As a result, the code needs to be altered so the search will terminate upon the location of an active *item type* (a giver-trigger). This can easily be achieved by specifying as a template parameter a policy that acts as a termination condition. For example:

```
template <class graph_type, class termination_condition>
class Graph_SearchDijkstra
{
  /* OMITTED */
};
```

A termination condition policy is a class containing a single static method, `isSatisfied`, which returns true if the conditions required for termination are fulfilled. The signature of `isSatisfied` looks like this:

```
static bool isSatisfied(const graph_type& G, int target, int CurrentNodeIdx);
```

A modified Dijkstra's algorithm can use such a policy to determine when the search should conclude. To facilitate this, the line:

```
    //if the target has been found exit
    if (NextClosestNode == m_iTarget) return;
```

found in `Graph_SearchDijkstra::Search` is replaced with:

```
    //if the target has been found exit
    if (termination_condition::isSatisfied(m_Graph,
                                           m_iTarget,
                                           NextClosestNode))
    {
      //make a note of the node index that has satisfied the condition. This
      //is so we can work backward from the index to extract the path from
      //the shortest path tree.
      m_iTarget = NextClosestNode;

      return;
    }
```

Before this adapted algorithm can be used though, an appropriate termination condition policy must be created. In Raven, item types are represented by giver-triggers. Therefore, when searching for an item type, a search should terminate when a graph node that has its `m_ExtraInfo` field pointing to an active trigger of the correct type is located.

Here is the termination condition policy class that ends a search based upon those criteria:

```
template <class trigger_type>
class FindActiveTrigger
{
public:

  template <class graph_type>
  static bool isSatisfied(const graph_type& G, int target, int CurrentNodeIdx)
  {
    bool bSatisfied = false;
```

```
    //get a reference to the node at the given node index
    const graph_type::NodeType& node = G.GetNode(CurrentNodeIdx);

    //if the extra info field is pointing to a giver-trigger, test to make sure
    //it is active and that it is of the correct type.
    if ((node.ExtraInfo() != NULL) &&
         node.ExtraInfo()->isActive() &&
        (node.ExtraInfo()->EntityType() == target) )
    {
      bSatisfied = true;
    }

    return bSatisfied;
  }
};
```

Armed with this termination condition and the customized Dijkstra search algorithm, it's a simple matter to find the path with the least cost to an active item of a specific type. Let's say you want to find the closest health pack to the graph node with index 6. Here's how:

```
typedef FindActiveTrigger<Trigger<Raven_Bot> > term_con;
typedef Graph_SearchDijkstra_TS<RavenMap::NavGraph, term_con> SearchDij;

//instantiate the search
SearchDij dij(G,               //the graph
              6,               //the source node
              type_health);    //the item type we are searching for

//grab the path
std::list<int> path = dij.GetPathToTarget();
```

where `type_health` is an enumerated value.

3D NOTE By now I hope you understand there is *no difference* between pathfinding in 3D and pathfinding in 2D. Sure, for an agent to get around in most 3D environments it might have to do stuff like jump ravines and use lifts, but these considerations should be transparent to a path planner. They simply manifest themselves as edge cost adjustments so that the search algorithm can account for the cost of doing the jump, traversing the ledge, using a lift, or doing whatever when it is searching for the least cost path to a target position. If this is still not evident, I strongly recommend you backtrack and reread Chapter 5 while keeping in mind that a graph may exist in any number of dimensions.

Paths as Nodes or Paths as Edges?

So far we've been thinking about paths as a series of position vectors, or waypoints. Often though, paths comprised of graph edges give the AI programmer additional flexibility. As an example, let's consider a game with NPCs that must have their movement between certain points in the environment constrained to a specific type such as "tiptoe across here," "crawl under here," or "run quickly here." You may think that the game's relevant navgraph nodes could be annotated with flags indicating the desired behavior (for example, a node could be tagged with the "tiptoe" behavior to make an agent start tiptoeing as soon as it reaches that node), but in practice there are problems with this approach.

For example, Figure 8.10 shows part of a navgraph where one of the edges, A - B, traverses a river. The game design requires that agents must change to the "swim" behavior when traveling from A to B (or vice versa), so the nodes A and B are annotated to reflect this. Let's say an agent is following the path e - A - B - h. When the agent reaches node A its behavior will change to swimming and it can cross the edge to B safely. So far so good, but unfortunately at this point it runs into problems. When it reaches node B, which is also annotated with the swim behavior, it will continue *swimming* along the edge B - h. Not good. If this isn't bad enough, let's say an agent wants to follow the path e - A - c. As soon as it reaches A it will still start swimming even though it has no intention of crossing the river!

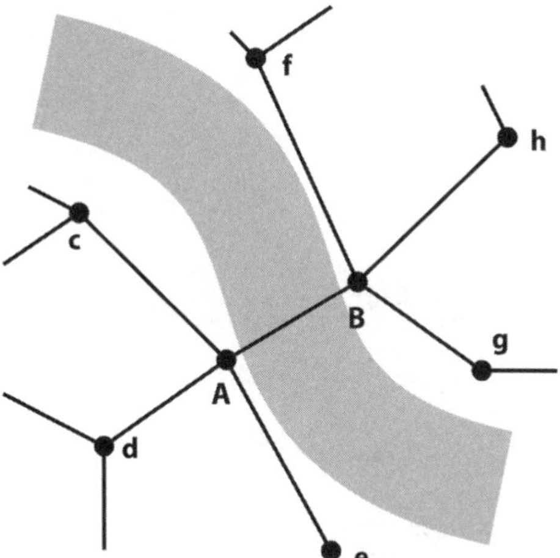

Figure 8.10. A navgraph spanning a river

This problem can easily be resolved, however, if the graph edges are annotated instead of the nodes. This way an agent can easily query the edge information as it follows the path and change behavior accordingly. Given the previous example this means that the edge A - B is annotated with the instruction to swim and all the other edges with the instruction to walk (or whatever else might be appropriate). Now, when an agent follows the path e - A - B - h its movement will be correct.

⌘ **TIP** Using annotation you can easily specify edge behavior that is modified during gameplay. For instance, you could design a map that has a makeshift bridge — like a fallen log — crossing a stream, which agents traverse normally until the bridge is destroyed or moved. When the bridge is removed, the annotation of the edge is changed to "swim" and its cost increased to reflect the additional amount of time required to move along it. In this way, agents still consider the edge when planning paths and will modify their animation appropriately when they traverse it. (You could even remove/disable the edge to represent conditions making the stream impassable, like a flood.)

An Annotated Edge Class Example

An annotated edge is easily created by deriving from GraphEdge and adding an additional data member to represent the flag (or flags, depending on what sort of information you'd like the edge to represent). Here's an example:

```
class NavGraphEdge : public GraphEdge
{
public:

  //enumerate some behavior flags
  enum BehaviorType
  {
    normal    = 1 << 0,
    tippy_toe = 1 << 1,
    swim      = 1 << 2,
    crawl     = 1 << 3,
    creep     = 1 << 4
  };

protected:

  //the behavior associated with traversing this edge
  BehaviorType   m_iBehavior;

  /* EXTRANEOUS DETAIL OMITTED */
};
```

⌘ **TIP** If your game design requires edge and/or node annotation you will often find that the extra fields in the node/edge classes are unused (or set to "normal") for the majority of instances in the navgraph. This can be a significant waste of memory if your graph is large. In such cases I recommend you use a hash-map type lookup table or, in the case where there is a large amount of annotation per instance, create a special data structure that each edge or node can store a pointer to.

Modifying the Path Planner Class to Accommodate Annotated Edges

To accommodate edge annotation, the path planner and search algorithm classes must be modified to return paths that contain the additional information. To facilitate this, Raven makes use of the PathEdge class — a simple data structure that stores node position and edge annotation information. Here is its listing:

```
class PathEdge
{
private:
```

```
  //positions of the source and destination nodes this edge connects
  Vector2D m_vSource;
  Vector2D m_vDestination;

   //the behavior associated with traversing this edge
  int      m_iBehavior;

public:

  PathEdge(Vector2D Source,
           Vector2D Destination,
           int      Behavior):m_vSource(Source),
                              m_vDestination(Destination),
                              m_iBehavior(Behavior)
  {}

  Vector2D Destination()const;
  void     SetDestination(Vector2D NewDest);

  Vector2D Source()const;
  void     SetSource(Vector2D NewSource);

  int      Behavior()const;
};
```

The `Raven_PathPlanner::CreatePath` methods and the corresponding search algorithms are altered slightly to create `std::lists` of `PathEdges`. Here's the listing of the modified `CreatePathToPosition` method with the changes in bold.

```
bool Raven_PathPlanner::CreatePathToPosition(Vector2D TargetPos,
                                             std::list<PathEdge>& path)
{
  //if the target is unobstructed from the bot's position, a path does not need
  //to be calculated, and the bot can ARRIVE directly at the destination.
  if (!m_pOwner()->GetWorld()->isPathObstructed(m_pOwner->Pos(),
                                                TargetPos,
                                                m_pOwner->BRadius()))
  {
    //create an edge connecting the bot's current position and the
    //target position and push it on the path list (flagged to use the
    //"normal" behavior)
    path.push_back(PathEdge(m_pOwner->Pos(), TargetPos, NavGraphEdge::normal));

    return true;
  }
  //find the closest unobstructed node to the bot's position.
  int ClosestNodeToBot = GetClosestNodeToPosition(m_pOwner->Pos());
  if (ClosestNodeToBot == no_closest_node_found)
  {
    //no path possible
    return false;
  }
```

```
  //find the closest visible unobstructed node to the target position
  int ClosestNodeToTarget = GetClosestNodeToPosition(TargetPos);
  if (ClosestNodeToTarget == no_closest_node_found)
  {
    //no path possible
    return false;
  }

  //create an instance of the A* search class.
  typedef Graph_SearchAStar<Raven_Map::NavGraph, Heuristic_Euclid> AStar;

  AStar search(m_NavGraph, ClosestNodeToBot, ClosestNodeToTarget);

  //grab the path as a list of PathEdges
  path = search.GetPathAsPathEdges();

  //if the search has been successful add the first and last edges manually to
  //the path
  if (!path.empty())
  {
    path.push_front(PathEdge(m_pOwner->Pos(),
                             path.front().GetSource(),
                             NavGraphEdge::normal));

    path.push_back(PathEdge(path.back().GetDestination(),
                            TargetPos,
                            NavGraphEdge::normal));

    return true;
  }

  else
  {
     //no path found by the search
     return false;
  }
}
```

A bot can now easily query the annotation of path edges and make appropriate behavior adjustments. In pseudocode, each time a bot pops a new edge of the list it does something like this:

```
if (Bot.PathPlanner.CreatePathToPosition(destination, path))
{
  PathEdge next = GetNextEdgeFromPath(path)
  switch(next.Behavior)
  {
     case behavior_stealth:
        set stealth mode
        break

     case behavior_swim
        set swim mode
        break

     etc
```

```
    }
    Bot.MoveTo(NavGraph.GetNodePosition(next.To))
}
```

You can assume from here onward that any demos using the Raven framework will use edge paths instead of waypoint paths.

⌘ **TIP** Some game worlds include teleporters or "portals" that agents can use to move magically and instantaneously between locations. If your game makes use of such devices, you will not be able to use the A* search algorithm to accurately plan paths because it's impossible to accommodate them within the heuristic. Instead you must utilize an alternative search algorithm such as Dijkstra's.

Path Smoothing

Quite often, and especially if a game's navigation graph is in the shape of a grid, the paths created by the path planner tend to contain unnecessary edges, producing kinks like those shown in Figure 8.11. These look unnatural to the human eye — after all, a human wouldn't zigzag needlessly like this, so it looks bad when a game agent does it. (Of course this is perfectly acceptable if you are modeling domestic cats, which appear to have their own secret agenda when moving from A to B ☺.)

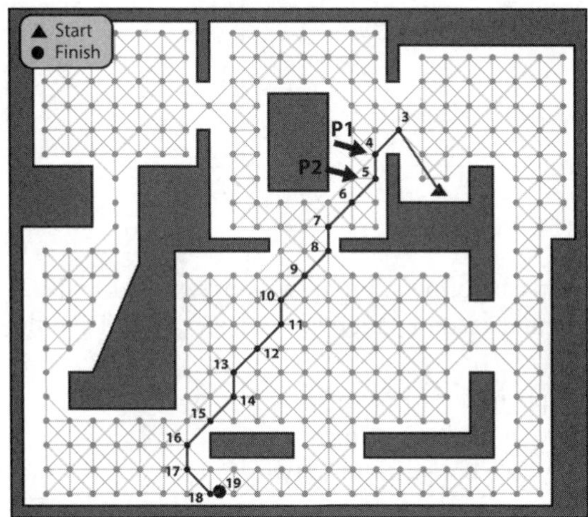

Figure 8.11. A kinky path

Using A* and a grid-based navgraph, better-looking paths can be created using the Manhattan distance heuristic in combination with a function that penalizes each change in direction. (The Manhattan distance, remember, is the sum of the number of tiles displaced horizontally and vertically between the nodes under consideration.) However, the paths produced are still far from ideal due to the graph's topology restricting turns to increments of 45 degrees. This method also fails with another common problem.

As we have seen, before a path planner can search for a path it must find the graph nodes closest to the start and destination positions, and these will not always be the ones that give a natural-looking path. The solution to both these problems is to post-process paths to "smooth" out the unwanted kinks. There are a couple of methods for doing this — one rough and one precise.

Path Smoothing Rough but Quick

A reasonably quick method for smoothing a path works by checking the "passability" between adjacent edges. If one of the edges is superfluous, the two edges are replaced with one. See Figure 8.12.

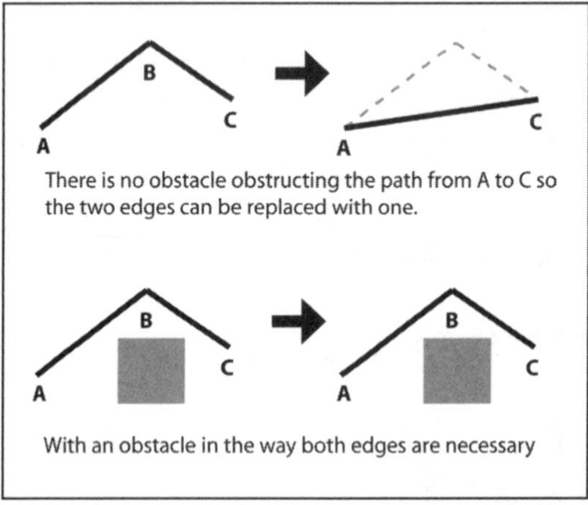

Figure 8.12

The algorithm proceeds as follows: First, two iterators, E1 and E2, are positioned at the first and second path edges respectively. Then these steps are followed:

1. Grab the source position of E1.
2. Grab the destination position of E2.
3. If the agent *can* move between these two positions unobstructed by the world geometry, assign the destination of E1 to that of E2 and remove E2 from the path. Reassign E2 to the new edge following E1. (Note that this is not a simple line-of-sight test as an entity's size must be taken into consideration — it must be able to move between the two positions without bumping into any walls.)
4. If the agent *cannot* move unobstructed between the two positions, assign E2 to E1 and advance E2.
5. Repeat steps until the destination of E2 is equal to the destination of the path.

Let's see this algorithm in action and smooth the path shown in Figure 8.13. First, E1 is pointed at the first edge in the path and E2 to the second.

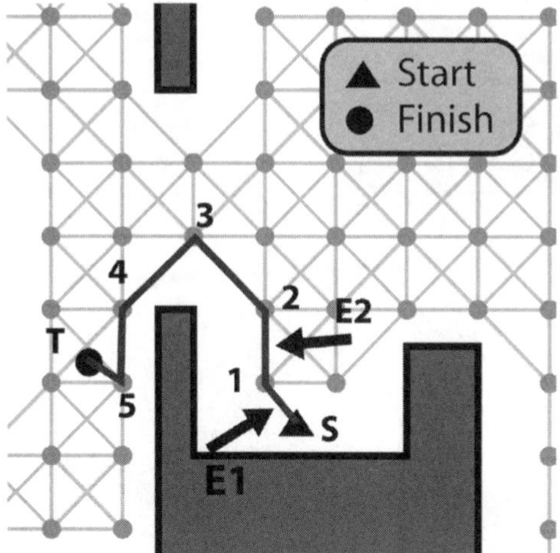

Figure 8.13

E1 is the edge S - 1 and E2 the edge 1 - 2. We can see that an agent is able to move unobstructed between E1->Source (S) and E2->Destination (2) so the position of node index 2 is assigned to E1->Destination, the edge 1 - 2 is removed from the path, and E2 is advanced to point to the edge 2 - 3. See Figure 8.14. (Notice the edge pointed to by E1 is now linking S - 2.)

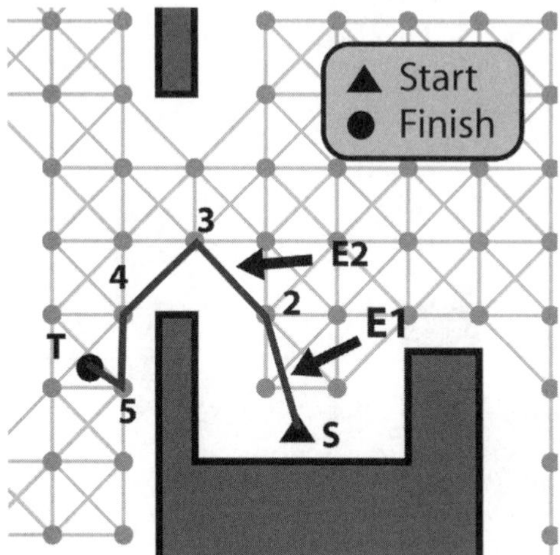

Figure 8.14

Once again we can see that an agent is able to move unobstructed between E1->Source (S) and E2->Destination (3), so again the path and iterators are updated, giving the situation shown in Figure 8.15.

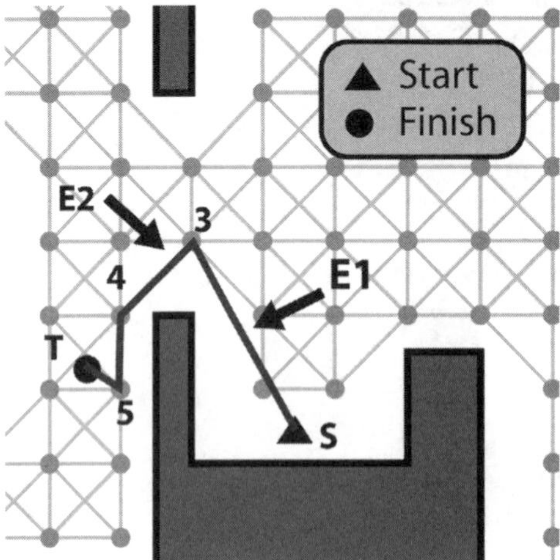

Figure 8.15

This time, however, the positions E1->Source (S) and E2->Destination (4) are obstructed. Therefore, E1 and E2 are both advanced one edge. See Figure 8.16.

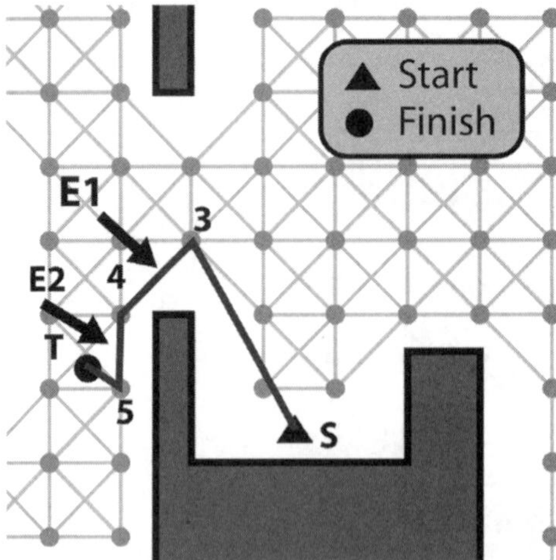

Figure 8.16

Again, the path between nodes 3 and 5 is obstructed so E1 and E2 are advanced. This time, as the path between 4 and T is passable, the edges are updated to reflect this, giving the final smoothed path shown in Figure 8.17.

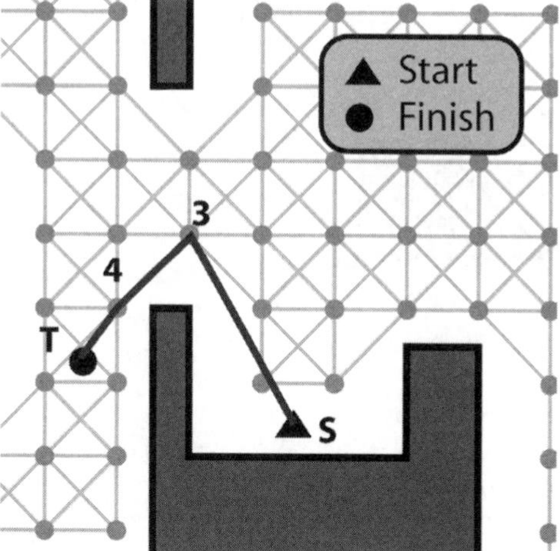

Figure 8.17. The finished path

The source code to smooth a path using this algorithm looks like this:

```
void Raven_PathPlanner::SmoothPathEdgesQuick(std::list<PathEdge>& path)
{
  //create a couple of iterators and point them at the front of the path
  std::list<PathEdge>::iterator e1(path.begin()), e2(path.begin());

  //increment e2 so it points to the edge following e1.
  ++e2;

  //while e2 is not the last edge in the path, step through the edges, checking
  //to see if the agent can move without obstruction from the source node of
  //e1 to the destination node of e2. If the agent can move between those
  //positions then the two edges are replaced with a single edge.
  while (e2 != path.end())
  {
    //check for obstruction, adjust and remove the edges accordingly
    if ( m_pOwner->canWalkBetween(e1->Source(), e2->Destination()) )
    {
      e1->SetDestination(e2->Destination());
      e2 = path.erase(e2);
    }

    else
    {
      e1 = e2;
      ++e2;
    }
  }
}
```

Path Smoothing Precise but Slow

Alas, the previous algorithm is not perfect. If you examine Figure 8.17 again you can see that the last two edges could have easily been replaced with just one as shown in Figure 8.18.

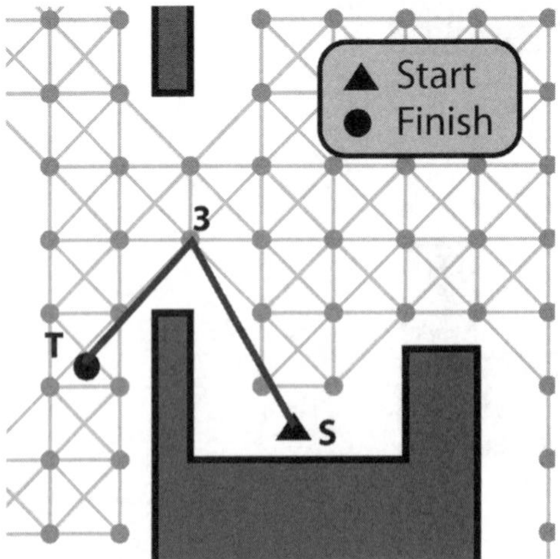

Figure 8.18. A better path

The algorithm missed this because it only checked the passability between adjacent edges. A more precise smoothing algorithm must iterate through all the edges from E1 to the final edge each time E1 is advanced. However, although precise, this method is much slower because many additional intersection tests have to be made. Of course, which smoothing algorithm you use, or whether you decide to use smoothing at all, depends on how much processor time you have available and the requirements of your game.

The code to smooth a path more precisely looks like this:

```
void Raven_PathPlanner::SmoothPathEdgesPrecise(std::list<PathEdge>& path)
{
  //create a couple of iterators
  std::list<PathEdge>::iterator e1, e2;

  //point e1 to the beginning of the path
  e1 = path.begin();

  while (e1 != path.end())
  {
    //point e2 at the edge immediately following e1
    e2 = e1;
    ++e2;

    //while e2 is not the last edge in the path, step through the edges,
    //checking to see if the agent can move without obstruction from the
```

```
    //source node of e1 to the destination node of e2. If the agent can move
    //between those positions then any edges between e1 and e2 are
    //replaced with a single edge.
    while (e2 != path.end())
    {
      //check for obstruction, adjust and remove the edges accordingly
      if ( m_pOwner->canWalkBetween(e1->Source(), e2->Destination()) )
      {
        e1->SetDestination(e2->Destination());
        e2 = path.erase(++e1, ++e2);
        e1 = e2;
        --e1;
      }

      else
      {
        ++e2;
      }
    }

    ++e1;
  }
}
```

You can see both of these algorithms in action by running the Raven_PathSmoothing demo.

NOTE If your map makes use of graph edges annotated with special behaviors or if your agents have other constraints like a restricted turning circle, the smoothing algorithms must be modified to prevent deletion of important edges. See the Raven project source for an example.

Methods for Reducing CPU Overhead

Load spikes take place when the amount of processor cycles required by a game engine is in excess of the number of cycles available. If a game has oodles of AI controlled agents running around, all able to request paths at any time, then load spikes can occur when too many of them simultaneously request searches. When this happens, the fluid flow of the game will be interrupted as the CPU attempts to keep up with the demands put on it, thus creating a jerky, stuttering motion. Obviously this is a bad thing and should be avoided wherever possible. The next few pages will be devoted to methods that lessen the likelihood of load spikes by reducing the per-update overhead of path planning requests.

Precalculated Paths

If your game environment is static and you have memory to spare, a good option for lessening the CPU load is to use precalculated lookup tables, enabling paths to be determined extremely quickly. These may be calculated at any convenient time, such as when a map is read from file or created by the map editor and stored along with the map data. A lookup table must include routes from every node in the navgraph to every other node in the navgraph. This can be calculated using Dijkstra's algorithm to create the shortest paths tree (SPT) for every node in the graph. (Remember, the SPT is a sub-tree of the navgraph rooted at the target node that contains the shortest path to every other node.) The information is then extracted and stored in a two-dimensional array of integers.

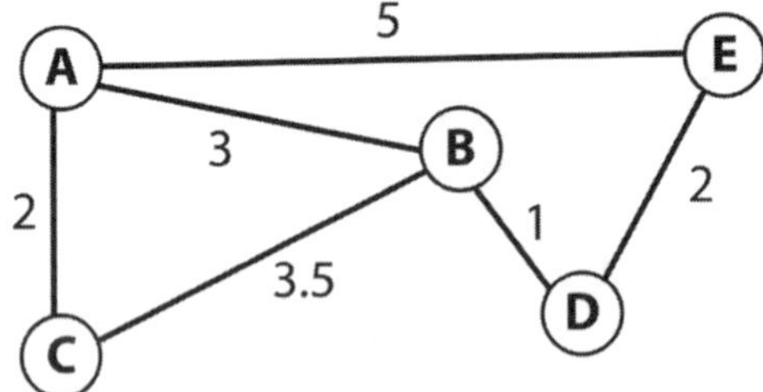

Figure 8.19. A simple graph

For example, given the graph shown in Figure 8.19, the corresponding lookup table is as shown in Figure 8.20. The entries in the table show the next node the agent should travel to on the path from start to destination. For instance, to determine the least cost path from C to E, we cross-reference C with E, giving node B. Node B is then cross-referenced with the destination to give D, and so on, until the table entry is equivalent to the target node. In this instance, we get the path C - B - D - E, which is the shortest path from C to E.

	A	B	C	D	E
A	A	B	C	B	E
B	A	B	C	D	D
C	A	B	C	B	B
D	B	B	B	D	E
E	A	D	D	D	E

Figure 8.20. The shortest paths lookup table for the graph shown in Figure 8.19

The source code to create such a table can be found in the file common/graph/HandyGraphFunctions.h. It will create an all-pairs lookup table for any graph type with an interface similar to SparseGraph. It looks like this:

```
template <class graph_type>
std::vector<std::vector<int> > CreateAllPairsTable(const graph_type& G)
{
  enum {no_path = -1};

  //create a 2D table of elements all set to the enumerated value no_path
  std::vector<int> row(G.NumNodes(), no_path);

  std::vector<std::vector<int> > shortest_paths(G.NumNodes(), row);

  for (int source=0; source<G.NumNodes(); ++source)
  {
    //calculate the SPT for this node
    Graph_SearchDijkstra<graph_type> search(G, source);

    std::vector<const GraphEdge*> spt = search.GetSPT();

    //now that we have the SPT it's easy to work backward through it to find
    //the shortest paths from each node to this source node
    for (int target = 0; target<G.NumNodes(); ++target)
    {
      if (source == target)
      {
        shortest_paths[source][target] = target;
      }

      else
      {
        int nd = target;

        while ((nd != source) && (spt[nd] != 0))
        {
          shortest_paths[spt[nd]->From][target]= nd;

          nd = spt[nd]->From;
        }
      }
    }//next target node
  }//next source node

  return shortest_paths;
}
```

Precalculated Costs

Sometimes it's necessary for a game agent to calculate the *cost* of traveling from one place to another. For example, together with other features, an agent may factor in the cost of a game object when deciding if it wants to pick up that item. A search to determine these costs for each item type each AI update step will be very expensive if the navigation graph is large and/or there are many items of the same type. In situations like this a pre-calculated costs table may prove invaluable. This is constructed in a similar way to the all-pairs route table discussed in the last section, except this time the elements of the table represent the total cost to follow the shortest path from one node to any other. See Figure 8.21.

	A	B	C	D	E
A	0	3	2	4	5
B	3	0	3.5	1	3
C	2	3.5	0	4.5	6.5
D	4	1	4.5	0	2
E	5	3	6.5	2	0

Figure 8.21. The path cost lookup table for the graph shown in Figure 8.19

The code to create such a table is as follows:

```
template <class graph_type>
std::vector<std::vector<double> > CreateAllPairsCostsTable(const graph_type& G)
{
  std::vector<double> row(G.NumNodes(), 0.0);

  std::vector<std::vector<double> > PathCosts(G.NumNodes(), row);

  for (int source=0; source<G.NumNodes(); ++source)
  {
    //do the search
    Graph_SearchDijkstra<graph_type> search(G, source);

    //iterate through every node in the graph and grab the cost to travel to
    //that node
    for (int target = 0; target<G.NumNodes(); ++target)
    {
      if (source != target)
      {
        PathCosts[source][target]= search.GetCostToNode(target);
      }
    }//next target node
```

```
  }//next source node

  return PathCosts;
}
```

The Raven bots will make use of cost lookup tables to evaluate goals later in the book.

⌘ **TIP** If you look closely at the path cost lookup table shown in Figure 8.21 you will notice that it is symmetrical about the top-left to bottom-right diagonal. Provided your graphs are not directed (the cost of traveling from A to B is always the same as from B to A), you can make the table much more efficient by storing the table as a one-dimensional array of size $\sum_{i=1}^{i=(n-1)} i$, where *n* is the number of nodes in the graph. (The Σ symbol, by the way, is the Greek capital letter *Sigma* and indicates summation. In this example the Sigma symbol indicates that you should sum all the integers between $i=1$ and $i=(n-1)$. In other words, if *n* is 5, the result of $\sum_{i=1}^{i=(n-1)} i$ would be 1+2+3+4=10).

Time-Sliced Path Planning

An alternative to precalculating lookup tables to lighten the CPU load is to allocate a fixed amount of CPU resources per update step for *all* the search requests and to distribute these resources evenly between the searches. This is achieved by dividing up the searches over multiple time steps, a technique known as *time slicing*. A considerable amount of extra work is required to get this idea working but it's worth the effort for some games because the load on the CPU from the graph searches is guaranteed to be constant, no matter how many agents are making requests.

NOTE I'd like to make it clear that time-sliced pathfinding is overkill for a game with only a handful of agents such as Raven, but it's a great technique to consider if your game has dozens or hundreds of agents, and especially if you're developing for a console platform, because it helps you to live within the constraints of the hardware.

First of all, the Dijkstra and A* searches must be modified in such a way that they can search a graph over multiple update steps. Then, as agents request searches, their path planners create instances of the relevant searches (A* or Dijkstra) and register themselves with a *path manager* class. The path manager keeps a list of pointers to all active path planners, which it iterates through each time step, evenly sharing the available CPU resources between them. When a search is either completed successfully or a path is not located, the path planner notifies its owner by sending it a message. Figure 8.22 shows a UML type sequence diagram of the process.

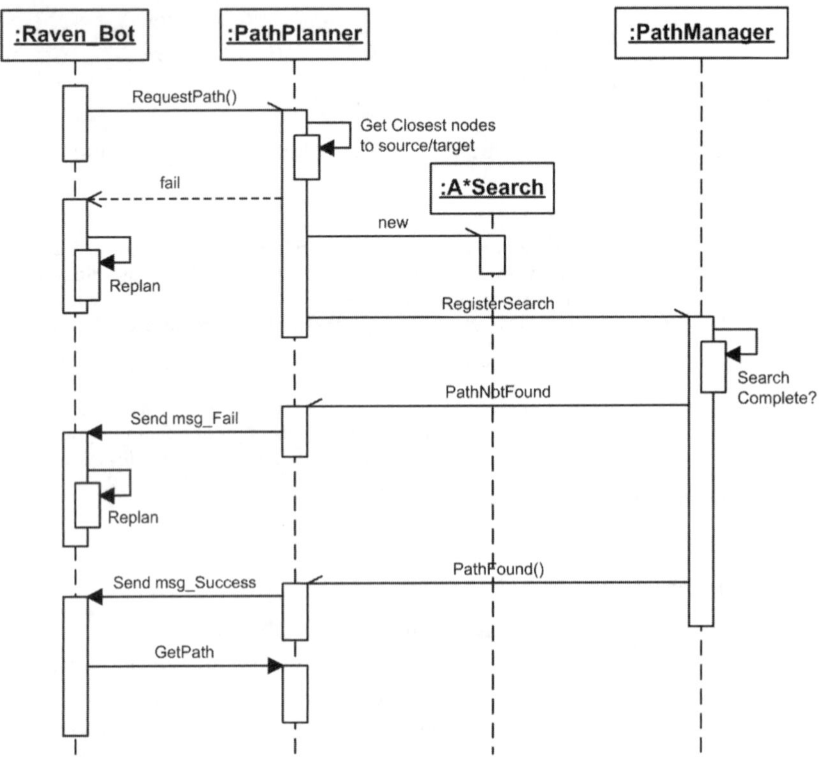

Figure 8.22. The process sequence for a time-sliced A* search

It's time to take a detailed look at the modifications required to effect this process. Let's start by examining how the A* and Dijkstra's search algorithm classes are adapted.

Modifying the Search Algorithms to Accommodate Time-Slicing

The A* and Dijkstra's search algorithms contain a loop that repeats the following steps:

1. Grab the next node from the priority queue.
2. Add the node to the shortest paths tree.
3. Test to see if the node is the target.
4. If the node is not the target, examine the nodes it is connected to, placing them on the priority queue when appropriate. If the node is the target, return success.

We'll refer to a single iteration of these steps as a *search cycle*. Because repeated iterations will eventually complete a search, search cycles can be used to divide a search over multiple time steps. Consequently, the A* and Dijkstra's search algorithm classes are modified to contain a method called `CycleOnce`, which contains the code required to undertake a single search cycle. This is relatively easy to do by instantiating the priority queue as a class member and initializing it with the source node index in the constructor. In addition the algorithm must be modified slightly so that CycleOnce returns an enumerated value indicating the status of the search. The status can be one of the following: target_found, target_not_found, or search_incomplete. A client is then able to call CycleOnce repeatedly until the return value indicates completion of the search.

Here is the listing of the time-sliced A* algorithm's CycleOnce method.

```
template <class graph_type, class heuristic>
int Graph_SearchAStar_TS<graph_type, heuristic>::CycleOnce()
{
  //if the PQ is empty the target has not been found
  if (m_pPQ->empty())
  {
    return target_not_found;
  }

  //get lowest cost node from the queue
  int NextClosestNode = m_pPQ->Pop();

  //put the node on the SPT
  m_ShortestPathTree[NextClosestNode] = m_SearchFrontier[NextClosestNode];

  //if the target has been found exit
  if (NextClosestNode == m_iTarget)
  {
    return target_found;
  }

  //now to test all the edges attached to this node
  Graph::ConstEdgeIterator EdgeItr(m_Graph, NextClosestNode);

  for (const GraphEdge* pE=EdgeItr.beg(); !EdgeItr.end(); pE=EdgeItr.nxt())
  {
    /* SAME AS IN PREVIOUS A* ALGORITHM */
  }

  //there are still nodes to explore
  return search_incomplete;
}
```

⌘ **TIP** If your game utilizes agents deployed in squads or platoons, you don't need to plan a path for each member of the platoon every time the platoon needs to move from A to B; just plan a single path for the platoon leader and make all the other members of the platoon follow that leader (using an appropriate steering behavior).

Creating a Common Interface for the Search Algorithms

Given that it's possible for both A* and Dijkstra's searches to be used by the path planner (to search for positions or items respectively), it's convenient for them to share a common interface. As a result, both the time-sliced A* class and the time-sliced Dijkstra's class derive from a virtual class named Graph_SearchTimeSliced.

Here is the declaration of the interface:

```
template <class edge_type>
class Graph_SearchTimeSliced
{
public:

  enum SearchType{AStar, Dijkstra};

private:

  SearchType m_SearchType;


public:

  Graph_SearchTimeSliced(SearchType type):m_SearchType(type){}

  virtual ~Graph_SearchTimeSliced(){}

  //When called, this method runs the algorithm through one search cycle. The
  //method returns an enumerated value (target_found, target_not_found,
  //search_incomplete) indicating the status of the search
  virtual int                           CycleOnce()=0;

  //returns the vector of edges that the algorithm has examined
  virtual std::vector<const edge_type*> GetSPT()const=0;

  //returns the total cost to the target
  virtual double                         GetCostToTarget()const=0;

  //returns the path as a list of PathEdges
  virtual std::list<PathEdge>           GetPathAsPathEdges()const=0;

  SearchType                            GetType()const{return m_SearchType;}
};
```

The path planner class is now able to instantiate either kind of search and assign it to a single pointer. The following listing is the updated version of the Raven_PathPlanner class and illustrates the extra data and methods required to facilitate the creation of time-sliced path requests.

```
class Raven_PathPlanner
{
private:

  //a pointer to an instance of the current graph search algorithm.
  Graph_SearchTimeSliced*         m_pCurrentSearch;

  /* EXTRANEOUS DETAIL OMITTED */

public:
```

```
  //creates an instance of the Dijkstra's time-sliced search and registers
  //it with the path manager
  bool      RequestPathToItem(unsigned int ItemType);

  //creates an instance of the A* time-sliced search and registers it with
  //the path manager
  bool      RequestPathToTarget(Vector2D TargetPos);

  //the path manager calls this to iterate once though the search cycle
  //of the currently assigned search algorithm. When a search is terminated
  //the method messages the owner with either the msg_NoPathAvailable or
  //msg_PathReady messages.
  int       CycleOnce()const;

  //called by an agent after it has been notified that a search has terminated
  //successfully. The method extracts the path from m_pCurrentSearch, adds
  //additional edges appropriate to the search type and returns it as a list of
  //PathEdges.
  Path      GetPath();
};
```

The `Raven_PathPlanner::CycleOnce` method calls the `CycleOnce` method of the currently instantiated search and checks the result. If the result indicates success or failure, a message is dispatched to the owner of the class to enable any appropriate action to be taken. To clarify, here is the listing of that method:

```
int Raven_PathPlanner::CycleOnce()const
{
  assert (m_pCurrentSearch &&
         "<Raven_PathPlanner::CycleOnce>: No search object instantiated");

  int result = m_pCurrentSearch->CycleOnce();

  //let the bot know of the failure to find a path
  if (result == target_not_found)
  {
     Dispatcher->DispatchMsg(SEND_MSG_IMMEDIATELY,
                             SENDER_ID_IRRELEVANT,
                             m_pOwner->ID(),
                             Msg_NoPathAvailable,
                             NO_ADDITIONAL_INFO);

  }

  //let the bot know a path has been found
  else if (result == target_found)
  {
    //if the search was for an item type then the final node in the path will
    //represent a giver trigger. Consequently, it's worth passing the pointer
    //to the trigger in the extra info field of the message. (The pointer
    //will just be NULL if no trigger)
    void* pTrigger =
    m_NavGraph.GetNode(m_pCurrentSearch->GetPathToTarget().back()).ExtraInfo();
```

```
    Dispatcher->DispatchMsg(SEND_MSG_IMMEDIATELY,
                            SENDER_ID_IRRELEVANT,
                            m_pOwner->ID(),
                            Msg_PathReady,
                            pTrigger);
  }

  return result;
}
```

Let's now examine the class that manages all the search requests.

The Path Manager

The path manager is a class template called, not surprisingly, `PathManager`. When a bot makes a path request via its path planner, the planner creates an instance of the correct type of search (A* for positions, Dijkstra's for types) and registers itself with the path manager. The path manager keeps a list of all active search requests, which it updates each time step.

Here is its declaration:

```
template <class path_planner>
class PathManager
{
private:

  //a container of all the active search requests
  std::list<path_planner*>  m_SearchRequests;

  //this is the total number of search cycles allocated to the manager.
  //Each update step these are divided equally among all registered path
  //requests
  unsigned int              m_iNumSearchCyclesPerUpdate;

public:

  PathManager(unsigned int NumCyclesPerUpdate);

  //every time this is called, the total amount of search cycles available will
  //be shared out equally between all the active path requests. If a search
  //completes successfully or fails, the method will notify the relevant bot
  void UpdateSearches();

  //a path planner should call this method to register a search with the
  //manager. (The method checks to ensure the path planner is only registered
  //once)
  void Register(path_planner* pPathPlanner);

  //an agent can use this method to remove a search request.
  void UnRegister(path_planner* pPathPlanner);
};
```

The path manager is allocated a number of search cycles it can use to update all active searches each update step. When `UpdateSearches` is called, the allocated cycles are shared equally between the registered path planners and each active search's CycleOnce method is called the appropriate number of times. When a search ends in success or failure the path manager removes the search request from its list.

Here is the listing of the method for your perusal.

```
template <class path_planner>
inline void PathManager<path_planner>::UpdateSearches()
{
  int NumCyclesRemaining = m_iNumSearchCyclesPerUpdate;

  //iterate through the search requests until either all requests have been
  //fulfilled or there are no search cycles remaining for this update step.
  std::list<path_planner*>::iterator curPath = m_SearchRequests.begin();
  while (NumCyclesRemaining-- && !m_SearchRequests.empty())
  {
    //make one search cycle of this path request
    int result = (*curPath)->CycleOnce();

    //if the search has terminated remove from the list
    if ( (result == target_found) || (result == target_not_found) )
    {
      //remove this path from the path list
      curPath = m_SearchRequests.erase(curPath);

    }
    //move on to the next
    else
    {
      ++curPath;
    }

    //the iterator may now be pointing to the end of the list. If this is so,
    // it must be reset to the beginning.
    if (curPath == m_SearchRequests.end())
    {
      curPath = m_SearchRequests.begin();
    }

  }//end while
}
```

NOTE Instead of restricting the path manager to a number of search cycles, you may prefer to allocate a specific amount of *time* to use each update for the path searches. This is easily accomplished by adding code to exit the PathPlanner::UpdateSearches method when the allotted time has been exceeded.

Creating and Registering a Search

As we have seen, each Raven bot owns an instance of the Raven_PathPlanner class. To permit the creation of time-sliced path requests, this class has been modified to own a pointer to an instance of a time-sliced search algorithm (an instance of the Graph_SearchDijkstra_TS class when a bot requests a path to an item type and an instance of the Graph_SearchAStar_

TS class if a bot requests a path to a target position). These instances are created and registered with the search manager in the methods RequestPathToTarget or RequestPathToItem.

Here is how the request for an item search is made:

```
bool Raven_PathPlanner:: RequestPathToItem(unsigned int ItemType)
{
  //clear the waypoint list and delete any active search
  GetReadyForNewSearch();

  //find the closest visible node to the bot's position
  int ClosestNodeToBot = GetClosestNodeToPosition(m_pOwner->Pos());

  //remove the destination node from the list and return false if no visible
  //node found. This will occur if the navgraph is badly designed or if the bot
  //has managed to get itself *inside* the geometry (surrounded by walls)
  //or an obstacle
  if (ClosestNodeToBot == no_closest_node_found)
  {
    return false;
  }

  //create an instance of the Dijkstra search class
  typedef FindActiveTrigger<Trigger<Raven_Bot> > term_con;
  typedef Graph_SearchDijkstra_TS<Raven_Map::NavGraph, term_con> DijSearch;

  m_pCurrentSearch = new DijSearch(m_pWorld->GetNavigationGraph(),
                                   ClosestNodeToBot,
                                   ItemType);

  //and register the search with the path manager
  m_pWorld->GetPathManager()->Register(this);

  return true;
}
```

Once registered, the path manager will call the CycleOnce method of the relevant algorithm each update step until the search terminates in success or failure. When an agent is notified that a path has been found, it grabs the path from the path planner by calling the Raven_PathPlanner::GetPath method.

Preventing the Twiddling of Thumbs

One consequence of time-sliced path planning is that there will be a delay from the time an agent requests a path to the time it receives notification that the search has been successful or unsuccessful. This delay is proportional to the size of the navigation graph, the number of search cycles per update allocated to the search manager, and the number of active search requests. The delay may be very small, just a few update steps, or it may be large, even as much as a couple of seconds. For some games it may be okay for an agent to sit around twiddling its thumbs during this period, but for many it will be important that the agent responds immediately in some way. After all, when a game player clicks on an NPC and then clicks on a location for that NPC to move to, he expects it to react without delay and will not be impressed with the game if this does not happen. So what is our poor little game agent to do in this situation? It must start moving before a path has been formulated, but where to?

A simple option, and the one I have used for Raven, is for the agent to **seek** toward its goal until it receives notification from the search manager that a path is ready, at which time it follows the path. However, if the bot requests a search to an item type, then the goal location is unknown until a search is completed (because there may be many instances of that item). In this situation the bot simply **wanders** until it receives notification. This works fine in most cases but it does present another problem: By the time a path is formulated, an agent may have moved quite a distance from the position where the search was initially requested. Consequently, the first few nodes of the path returned from the planner will be located in such a way that the agent will need to backtrack to follow them. For an example of this, examine Figure 8.23. In A the bot has requested a path from the path planner and during the delay is **seeking** toward the target. Figure 8.23 B shows the position at the time when the bot receives notification that a path has been formulated. As you can see, left to its own devices the bot will turn around and backtrack to follow the waypoints. Bad bot! Naughty bot!

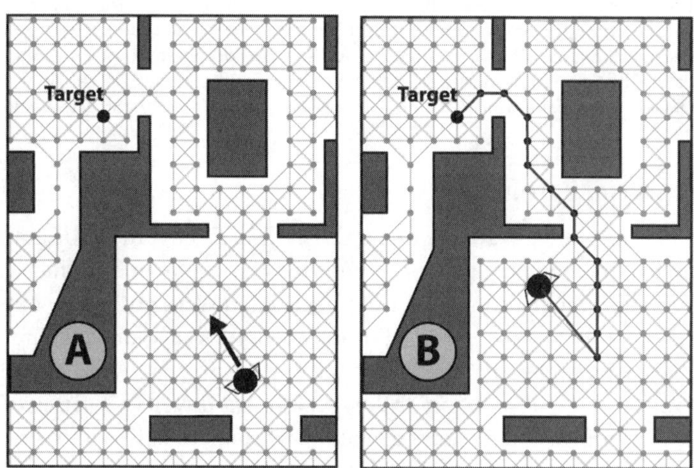

Figure 8.23. A bot seeks, then backtracks (bot shown at increased scale for clarity).

Fortunately, we already have a solution to this problem. When the smoothing algorithm described earlier is used on the path, all the excess waypoints are automatically deleted, resulting in the more natural-looking path shown in Figure 8.24. Time-sliced path planning therefore should always be used in conjunction with some sort of path smoothing.

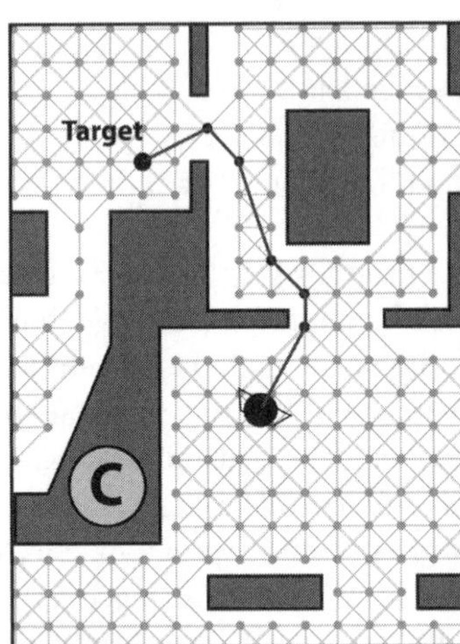

Figure 8.24. Result after smoothing

You can observe these effects firsthand by running the Raven_TimeSlicing demo and watching the bots navigate the environment with smoothing turned on or off. (The number of search cycles available to the search manager per update has been made extremely small to highlight the effect.)

⌘ **TIP** If you see that your agents are often following each other in single file to reach a location or item, and you are utilizing A* to generate the paths, you can vary the path produced by the search algorithm by adding some noise to the heuristic. This will result in slightly different paths for the same search. An example of such a heuristic can be found in the file common/graph/AStarHeuristicPolicies.h.

Hierarchical Pathfinding

Another technique available to cut down the CPU overhead of graph searches is named *hierarchical pathfinding*. It works in a similar way to how humans move around their environment. (Well, not really, but it makes for a good example ☺.) For instance, let's say you wake up in the middle of the night and decide to fetch a glass of milk. At one level of awareness you will probably follow a path that traverses a series of rooms (e.g., bedroom to top of stairs to bottom of stairs to hallway to dining room to kitchen) but at another you will be planning the paths between the rooms as you reach them. For instance, when you arrive at the dining room your brain will automatically calculate a path into the kitchen that may involve walking around the dining table, avoiding a dresser full of plates, opening a door, and trying not to kick the dog's water bowl. As such your mind is planning paths on several different levels — at different granularities. Another way of looking at it is that at one level the path is planned using a series of areas (dining room, kitchen, etc.), and at the lower level it is planned using a series of points through those areas.

This concept can be replicated in a computer by designing a path planner that utilizes two superimposed navgraphs of different granularities — one coarse, one fine. For example, imagine a strategy game based upon the American Civil War. A hierarchical path planner for this game could utilize a coarsely granulated graph to represent connectivity information at the state level and a finely granulated one at the level of towns and roads. When a military unit requests a path from Atlanta to Richmond, the path planner determines what states these towns lie in — Georgia and Virginia — and calculates a path between them using the state navgraph: Georgia to South Carolina to North Carolina to Virginia. This path can be calculated extremely quickly as the graph only contains a few dozen nodes, one for each state represented in the game. The planner then uses the finely grained navgraph to calculate paths between the states as and when the unit requires them. In this way searches of the finely grained graph are kept shallow, and therefore quick.

NOTE Although the use of two graph layers is the most typical implementation of hierarchical pathfinding, there's nothing to prevent you from using more layers if your game environment is complex enough to warrant it.

Applying the same idea to the Raven_DM1 map, the path planner could use the graphs shown in Figure 8.25. The graph on the left can be used to quickly determine paths at the "room" level and the one on the right to determine the paths between the rooms, at the "point" level.

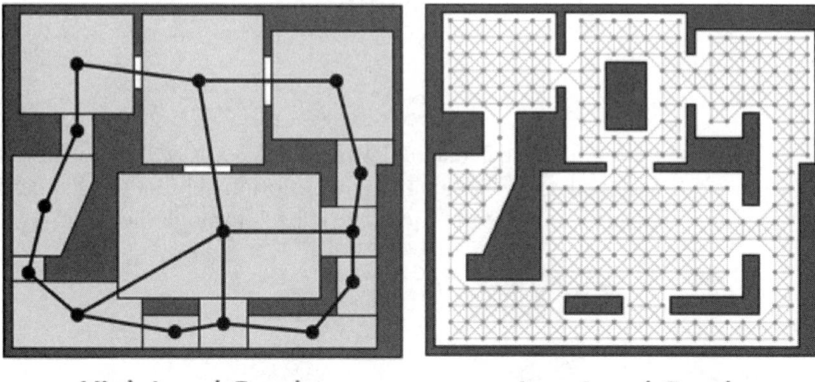

Figure 8.25. Hierarchical path planning

Of course, this is a trivial example; you should only consider hierarchical pathfinding when a game requires path planning over large and/or complex environments.

NOTE It's worth mentioning that a kind of two-tiered hierarchical pathfinding is implicit when a world is partitioned using a navmesh. (Note how the high-level graph in Figure 8.25 closely resembles the navmesh shown in Figure 8.3).

Getting Out of Sticky Situations

A problem players of computer games witness far too regularly is that of NPCs getting stuck. This can happen for all sorts of reasons. In particular, it occurs frequently when an environment contains lots of agents and the geometry has bottlenecks. A bottleneck could be a small space between two obstacles, a narrow doorway, or a tight corridor. If too many agents simultaneously attempt to navigate a bottleneck, then some of them may be pushed backward and end up wedged against a wall or obstacle. Let's have a look at this happening with a simple example.

Figure 8.26 shows a bot — we'll call him Eric — following the path A to B to C. It also shows a number of other bots traveling in the opposite direction. Eric is in for a nasty surprise.

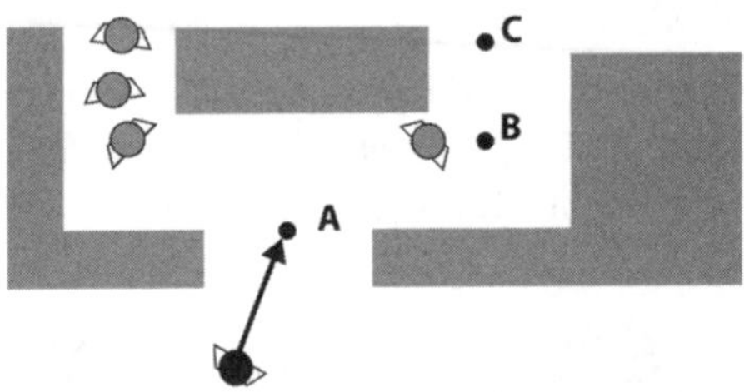

Figure 8.26

In Figure 8.27, Eric has reached waypoint A so it's removed from the list and B assigned as the next waypoint. Unfortunately, as this happens, the other bots arrive and start to jostle Eric back through the doorway.

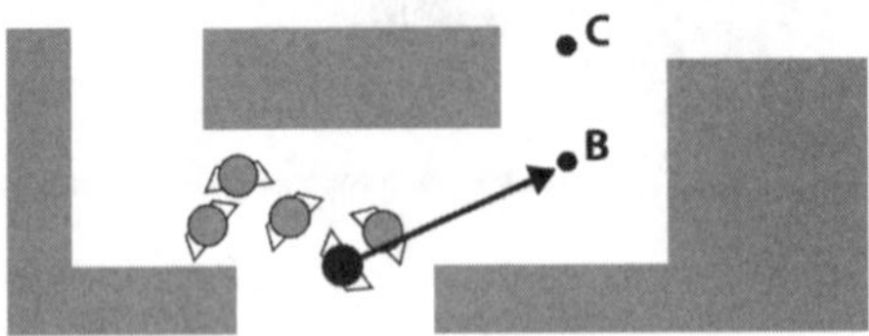

Figure 8.27

In Figure 8.28, Eric has been pushed all the way back out of the doorway, but he still keeps seeking to waypoint B. Silly old Eric.

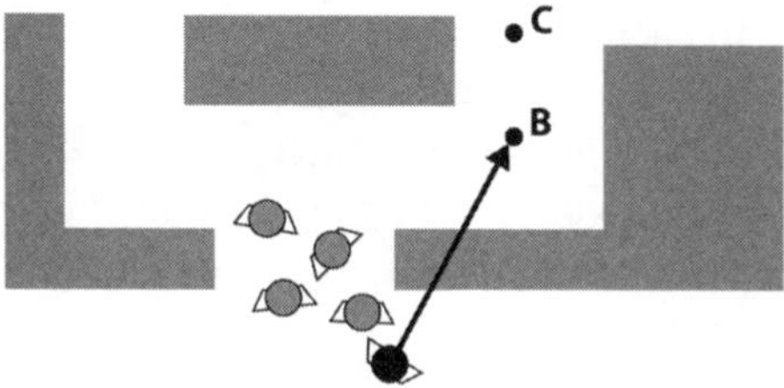

Figure 8.28

Finally Eric ends up wedged against the wall, struggling furiously, still hopelessly trying to seek to his next waypoint as shown in Figure 8.29. Tsk, tsk.

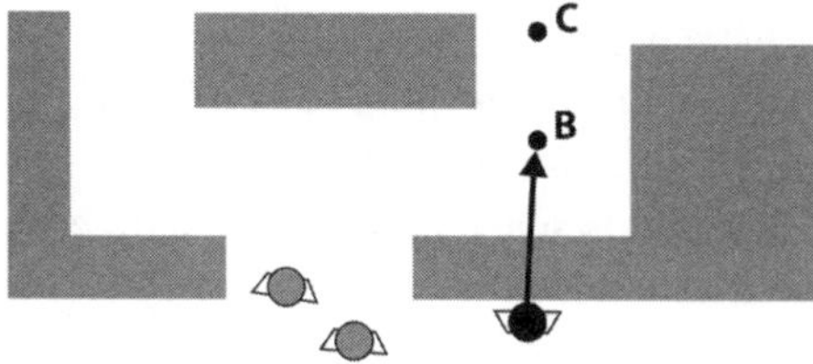

Figure 8.29

Obviously we don't want this sort of thing to happen, so any AI worth its salt should make regular tests for such situations and plan accordingly. But how to do this? Well, one way is for the agent to calculate the distance to its current waypoint each update step. If this value remains about the same or consistently increases, then it's a fair bet the agent is either stuck or being pushed backward by the separation force from neighboring agents. Another way is to calculate an expected arrival time for each waypoint and replan if the current time exceeds the expected. This is the approach adopted in Raven. It is very simple to implement. Whenever a new edge is pulled off the path, the expected time to traverse it is calculated as follows (in pseudocode):

```
Edge next = GetNextEdgeFromPath(path)

//in a simple navgraph the edge cost is the length of the edge
ExpectedTimeToReachPos = next.cost / Bot.MaxSpeed

//factor in a margin of error
MarginOfError = 2.0;

ExpectedTimeToReachPos += MarginOfError;
```

The margin of error is used to take into account any reactive behavior the bot undertakes during its journey, such as veering to the side to avoid another bot or jostling in doorways and narrow passages. This margin should be small enough to prevent your agents from looking dumb, yet large enough to prevent the agents from frequently requesting new paths from the path planner.

NOTE You can observe bots getting stuck if you run the Raven_BotsGetting-Stuck demo. In the demo several bots are exploring the map. An arrow is drawn from their current position to their current destination. As they jostle around the doorways some of them will get stuck, a few of them permanently.

Summing Up

This chapter has presented many methods and techniques related to path planning. Most of the ideas have been incorporated into the Raven game framework so you can see them working in situ and examine the code to see how it all works together. Please note that this is only by way of example. You wouldn't normally use all these techniques at one time. Just use whatever your game demands and no more.

Practice Makes Perfect

When moving to a target position, the Raven bots fill the gap created by the time required to undertake a graph search by **seeking** to that position. This is cheap and easy to implement, but in games with hundreds of agents or huge navgraphs the delay may be too long for this approach to be effective. Given too long a delay, the agents will start walking stupidly into walls and other obstacles. Also there are times when the best path to a position involves walking away from, or perpendicular to, the target before bending back around to face it. See Figure 8.30.

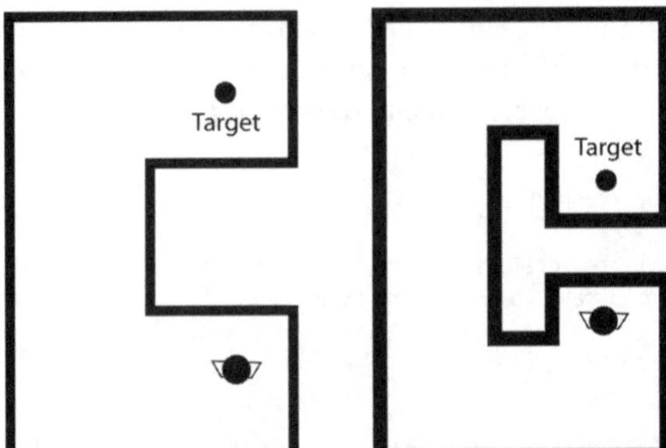

Figure 8.30. Problem situations

Seeking in situations like this for any length of time is a definite no-no. What agents must do instead is determine a partial path to the target position. That is to say, the A* algorithm must be modified to return the path to the node closest to the target after a user-defined number of search cycles or search depth has been reached. The agent can then follow this path until the complete path is created. This will produce much better-looking behavior and reduce the chances of making the agent look stupid.

Your mission, should you choose to accept it, is to modify the PathPlanner project to produce partial paths between the source and target nodes.

Chapter 9

Goal-Driven Agent Behavior

So far, we've examined agents utilizing a finite state machine-based architecture where behavior is decomposed into several states, each of which contains the logic to enable transitions to other states. This chapter introduces a subtly different approach. Instead of states, an agent's behavior is defined as a collection of hierarchical *goals*.

Goals are either atomic or composite in nature. Atomic goals define a single task, behavior, or action, such as **seek to position** or **reload weapon**, whereas composite goals are comprised of several subgoals, which in turn may be either atomic or composite, thereby defining a nested hierarchy. Composites usually describe more complex tasks than their atomic brethren such as **build weapons factory** or **retreat and find cover**. Both types of goals are able to monitor their status and have the capability to replan if they fail.

This hierarchical architecture provides the AI programmer with an intuitive mechanism for defining agent behavior because it shares many similarities with the human thought process. Humans select high-level abstract goals based upon their needs and desires and then recursively decompose them into a plan of action that can be followed. For instance, on a rainy day you might decide to **visit the cinema**. This is an abstract goal that cannot be acted upon until it's decomposed into smaller subgoals such as **leave house**, **travel to cinema**, and **enter cinema**. In turn, each of these is abstract and must be broken down further. This process is usually transparent of course, but we occasionally become conscious of it when the decomposition involves choice. For example, the subgoal **travel to cinema** can be satisfied in any number of ways — you may travel there by car, public transport, cycle, or on foot — and you may find yourself spending a few moments deliberating your choice. (This is especially true if you are collaborating with several other humans to satisfy a goal — think back to the last time you visited a video/DVD rental store with your friends. Argh!) This process continues until the goals have been decomposed into basic motor actions your body is able to execute. The **leave house** goal, for example, can be broken down into these component goals: **walk to closet**, **open closet door**, **remove coat from coat hook**, **put coat on**, **walk to kitchen**, **put shoes on**, **open door**, **walk outside**, and so on. Furthermore, humans don't like to squander energy so we generally don't waste precious calories thinking about a goal until it is absolutely necessary. For instance, you wouldn't decide how to open a can of beans until you have it in your hand or how to tie your shoelaces until your shoes are on your feet.

A goal-directed agent mimics this behavior. Each think update the agent examines the game state and selects from a set of predefined high-level goals, or *strategies* — the one it believes will most likely enable it to satisfy its strongest desire (usually, to win the game). The agent will then attempt to follow this goal by decomposing it into any constituent subgoals, satisfying each one in turn. It will continue doing this until the goal is either satisfied or has failed, or until the game state necessitates a change of strategy.

The Return of Eric the Brave

Let's walk through an example using our favorite game agent Eric, who has recently found employment in the RPG "Dragon Slayer 2." Eric's AI programmer has created several strategies for him to select from including **Defend from Dragon**, **Attack Dragon**, **Buy Sword**, **Get Food**, and **Get Drunk**. These strategies represent high-level abstract goals that are comprised of smaller subgoals such as **Create Path**, **Follow Path**, **Traverse Path Edge**, **Stab Dragon, Slice Dragon**, **Run Away**, and **Hide**. Therefore, to complete a strategy Eric must decompose it into its relevant subgoals and satisfy each in turn (decomposing them further if necessary).

Eric has just entered the game world and since he's not carrying a weapon and is therefore feeling vulnerable, his strongest desire is to find some sort of pointy stick before a dragon spots him. His "brain" (a special type of goal capable of making decisions) considers all the strategies available and finds that **Buy Sword** fits the bill admirably, so this is assigned as the goal to pursue until he elects otherwise. See Figure 9.1.

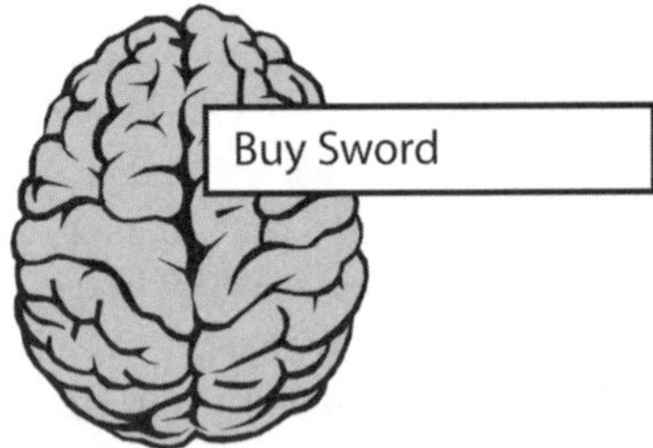

Figure 9.1. The Buy Sword goal slotted into Eric's brain

Eric cannot act upon this goal though because at this level it's too abstract and needs to be decomposed — or expanded, if you prefer to think of it that way — into its constituent subgoals. For the purposes of this example we'll assume **Buy Sword** consists of the subgoals shown in Figure 9.2. To obtain a sword Eric must first find some gold, then walk to the smithy where the blacksmith will gladly accept it as payment.

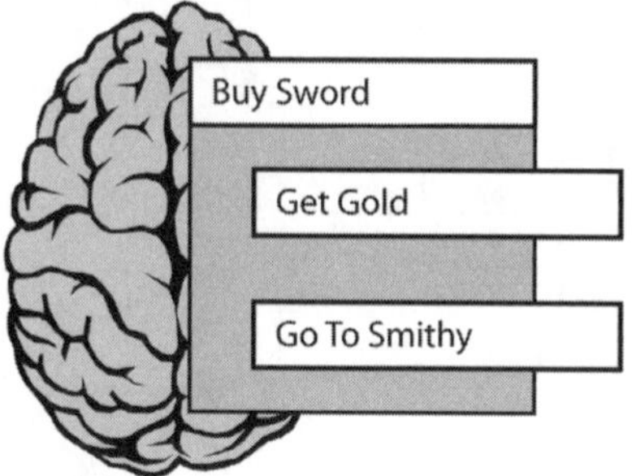

Figure 9.2. The Buy Sword goal is expanded into its constituent parts.

Agents satisfy goals consecutively so **Go To Smithy** will not be evaluated until **Get Gold** has been completed. This is another composite goal, however, so to complete it Eric must expand the hierarchy further. **Get Gold** consists of the subgoals **Plan Path (Goldmine)**, **Follow Path**, and **Pick Up Nugget**. See Figure 9.3.

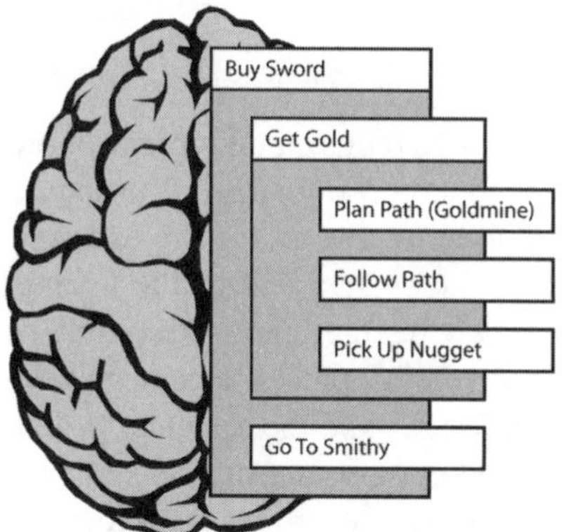

Figure 9.3. Expansion of the Get Gold goal

The **Plan Path (Goldmine)** goal is satisfied by sending a request to the path planner to plan a path to the gold mine. It is then removed from the goal list. The next one Eric considers is **Follow Path**, which can be further decomposed into several atomic **Traverse Edge** goals, each of which contain the logic required to follow an edge of the path leading to the gold mine. See Figure 9.4.

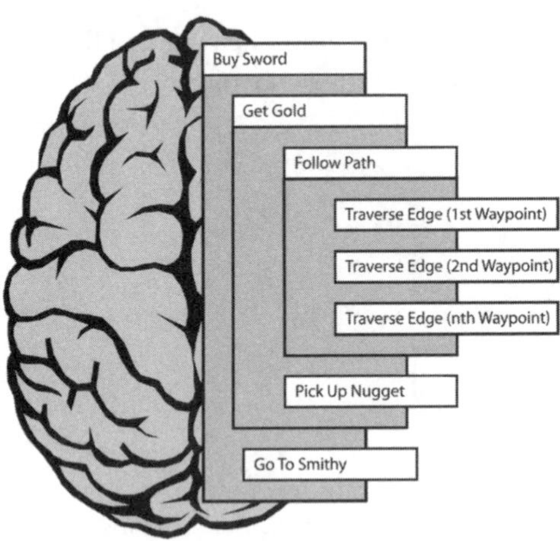

Figure 9.4. Expanding the Follow Path goal

This process of decomposing and satisfying goals continues until the entire hierarchy has been traversed and Eric is left with a gleaming new sword in his hands.

Well, that's the *what*; let's now look at the *how*.

Implementation

Nested object hierarchies, such as those required to implement hierarchical goal-based agents, are commonly found in software. For instance, word processors like the one I'm using to write this book store documents as collections of atomic and composite components. The smallest components, alphanumeric characters, are grouped together into increasingly complex collections. For example, the word "philosophy" is a composite component comprised of several atomic components, and the sentence "I think therefore I am" is a composite component comprised of three composite and two atomic objects. In turn, sentences can be grouped together into paragraph objects, which can be grouped into pages and so on. I'm sure you get the idea. The important point to note is that the application is able to handle composite and atomic objects uniformly, regardless of their size or complexity — it's just as easy to cut and paste a word as it is several pages of text. This is exactly the property required by hierarchical goals. But how do we code it?

The composite design pattern provides a solution. It works by defining an abstract base class that represents *both* composite and atomic objects. This enables clients to manipulate all goals identically, no matter how simple or complex they may be. See Figure 9.5.

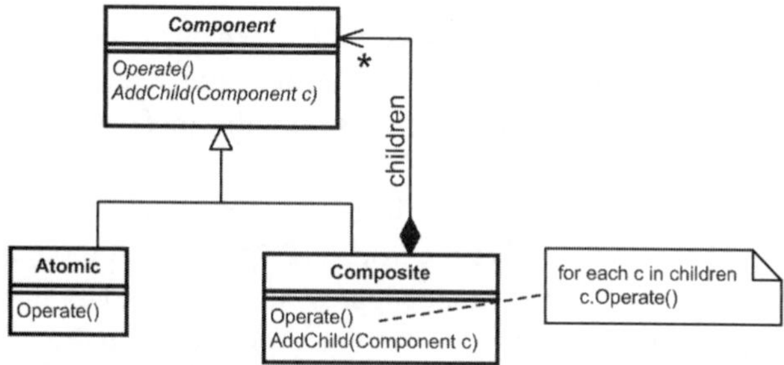

Figure 9.5 The archetypal composite design pattern

The figure clearly shows how `Composite` objects aggregate instances of `Components`, which in turn may be either `Composite` or `Atomic`. Notice how `Composite` objects forward client requests to their children. In this archetypal example requests are forwarded to all children. However, other designs may require a slightly different implementation, as is the case with goals.

Figure 9.6 shows the composite pattern applied to the design of hierarchical goals. Subgoals are added by pushing them onto the front of the subgoal container and are processed in LIFO (last in, first out) order in the same way as a stack-like data structure. Notice how client requests are only forwarded to the frontmost subgoal, ensuring that subgoals are evaluated in sequence.

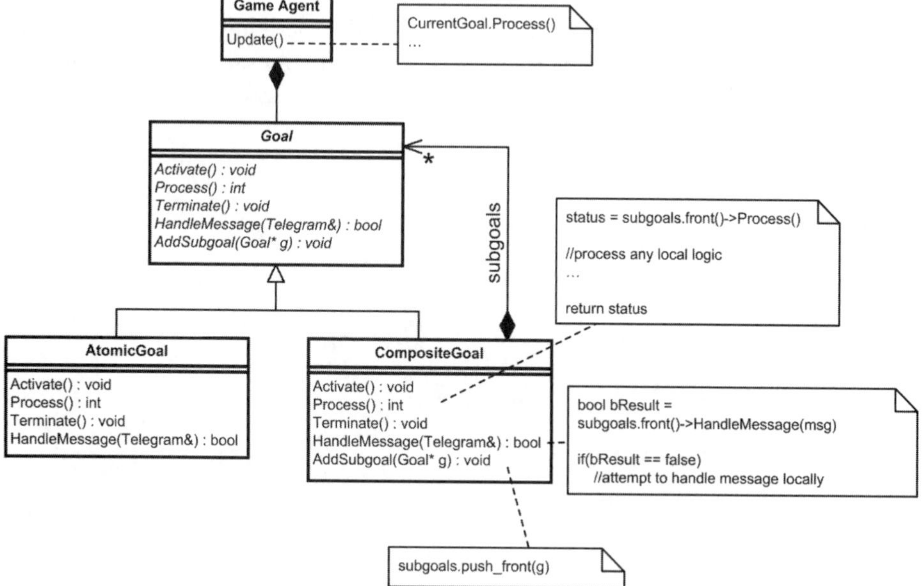

Figure 9.6. The composite pattern applied to goals

`Goal` objects share a lot of similarities with the `State` class. They have a method for handling messages just like `State`, and `Activate`, `Process`, and `Terminate` methods, which share similarities with the `Enter`, `Execute`, and `Exit` methods of `State`.

The `Activate` method contains initialization logic and represents the planning phase of the goal. Unlike the `State::Enter` method though, which is only called once when a state first becomes current, a `Goal` is able to call its `Activate` method any number of times to replan if the situation demands.

`Process`, which is executed each update step, returns an enumerated value indicating the status of the goal. This can be one of four values:

- `inactive`: The goal is waiting to be activated.
- `active`: The goal has been activated and will be processed each update step.
- `completed`: The goal has completed and will be removed on the next update.
- `failed`: The goal has failed and will either replan or be removed on the next update.

The `Terminate` method undertakes any necessary tidying up before a goal is exited and is called just before a goal is destroyed.

In practice, a chunk of the logic implemented by composite goals is common to all composites and can be abstracted out into a `Goal_Composite` class, which all concrete composite goals can inherit from, resulting in the final design fleshed out in Figure 9.7.

The UML diagrams do an adequate job of describing the `Goal` class hierarchy so I won't waste paper listing their declarations, but I think it will be helpful if I list the source for a couple of the `Goal_Composite` methods.

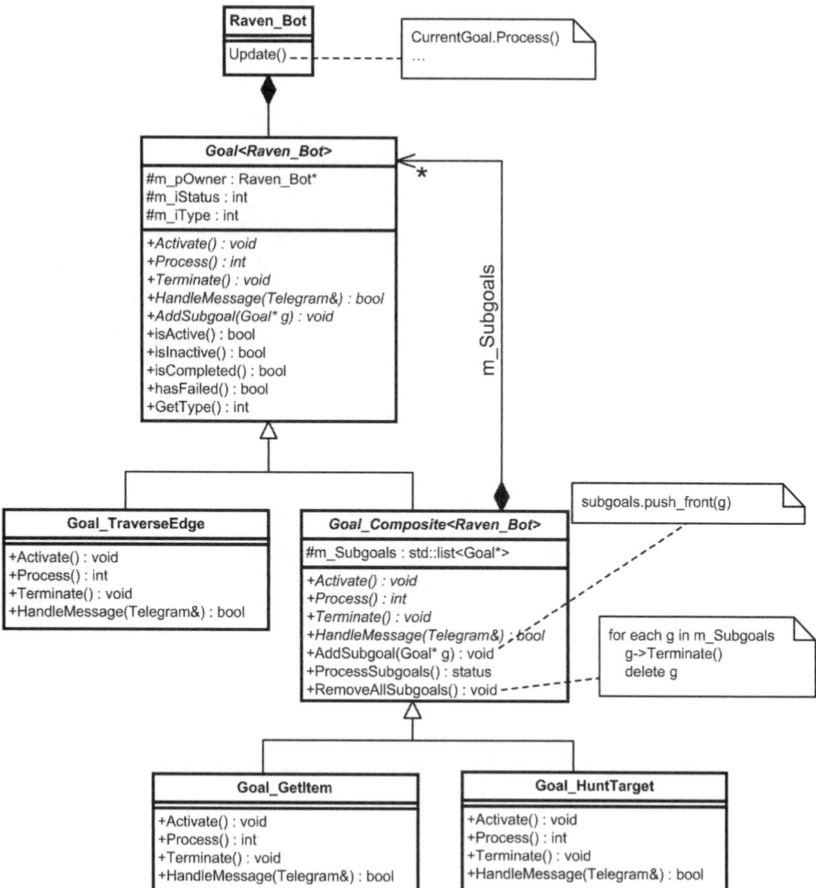

Figure 9.7. The final design. The figure shows three examples of concrete classes used by the Raven bots.

Goal_Composite::ProcessSubgoals

All composite goals call this method each update step to process their subgoals. The method ensures that all completed and failed goals are removed from the list before processing the next subgoal in line and returning its status. If the subgoal list is empty, `completed` is returned.

```
template <class entity_type>
int Goal_Composite<entity_type>::ProcessSubgoals()
{
  //remove all completed and failed goals from the front of the subgoal list
  while (!m_SubGoals.empty() &&
         (m_SubGoals.front()->isComplete() || m_SubGoals.front()->hasFailed()))
  {
    m_SubGoals.front()->Terminate();
    delete m_SubGoals.front();
    m_SubGoals.pop_front();
```

```
  }

  //if any subgoals remain, process the one at the front of the list
  if (!m_SubGoals.empty())
  {
    //grab the status of the frontmost subgoal
    int StatusOfSubGoals = m_SubGoals.front()->Process();

    //we have to test for the special case where the frontmost subgoal
    //reports "completed" and the subgoal list contains additional goals.
    //When this is the case, to ensure the parent keeps processing its
    //subgoal list,the "active" status is returned
    if (StatusOfSubGoals == completed && m_SubGoals.size() > 1)
    {
      return active;
    }

    return StatusOfSubGoals;
  }

  //no more subgoals to process - return "completed"
  else
  {
    return completed;
  }
}
```

Goal_Composite::RemoveAllSubgoals

This method clears the subgoal list. It ensures that all subgoals are destroyed cleanly by calling each one's `Terminate` method before deletion.

```
template <class entity_type>
void Goal_Composite<entity_type>::RemoveAllSubgoals()
{
  for (SubgoalList::iterator it = m_SubGoals.begin();
       it != m_SubGoals.end();
       ++it)
  {
    (*it)->Terminate();

    delete *it;
  }

  m_SubGoals.clear();
}
```

NOTE Some of you might be wondering how atomic goals implement the `AddSubgoal` method. After all, this method is meaningless in this context (because an atomic goal cannot by definition aggregate child goals), but it still has to be implemented in order to provide the common interface we require.

Since clients should know if a goal is composite or not and therefore shouldn't ever call `AddSubgoal` on an atomic goal, I've chosen for the method to throw an exception.

Examples of Goals Used by Raven Bots

The Raven bots utilize the goals listed in Table 9.1 to define their behavior.

Table 9.1 Goals used by Raven bots

Composite Goals	Atomic Goals
Goal_Think	Goal_Wander
Goal_GetItem	Goal_SeekToPosition
Goal_MoveToPosition	Goal_TraverseEdge
Goal_FollowPath	Goal_DodgeSideToSide
Goal_AttackTarget	
Goal_Explore	
Goal_HuntTarget	

Goal_Think is the highest-level goal of all. Each bot instantiates a copy of this goal, which persists until the bot is destroyed. Its task is to select between other high-level (strategy) goals according to their suitability to the current game state. We'll be taking a closer look at Goal_Think shortly, but first I think it will be a good idea to examine the code of a few of the other goals so you get a feel for how they work.

Goal_Wander

This is the easiest goal to understand and the simplest in a Raven bot's palette. It is an atomic goal that activates the **wander** steering behavior. Here is its declaration.

```
class Goal_Wander : public Goal<Raven_Bot>
{
public:

  Goal_Wander(Raven_Bot* pBot):Goal<Raven_Bot>(pBot, goal_wander){}

  //must be implemented
  void Activate();
  int  Process();
  void Terminate();
};
```

As you can see, the declaration is very straightforward. The class inherits from Goal and has methods that implement Goal's interface. Let's take a look at each method in turn.

```
void Goal_Wander::Activate()
{
  m_Status = active;
```

```
  m_pOwner->GetSteering()->WanderOn();
}
```

The Activate method simply turns on the **wander** steering behavior (see Chapter 3 if you need a refresher) and sets the goal's status to active.

```
int Goal_Wander::Process()
{
  //if status is inactive, call Activate() and set status to active
  ActivateIfInactive();

  return m_Status;
}
```

Goal_Wander::Process is just as straightforward. ActivateIfInactive is called at the beginning of every goal's Process logic. If a goal's status is inactive (as it always will be the first time Process is called because m_Status is set to inactive in the constructor), the Activate method is called, thereby initializing the goal.

Finally, the Terminate method switches the wander behavior off.

```
void Goal_Wander::Terminate()
{
  m_pOwner->GetSteering()->WanderOff();
}
```

Now let's examine a more complex atomic goal.

Goal_TraverseEdge

This directs a bot along a path edge and continuously monitors its progress to ensure it doesn't get stuck. To facilitate this, along with a local copy of the path edge, it owns data members for recording the time the goal is activated and the time the bot is expected to take to traverse the edge. It also owns a Boolean data member to record whether the edge is the last in the path. This value is needed to determine what steering behavior should be used to traverse the edge (**seek** for normal path edges, **arrive** for the last).

Here's its declaration:

```
class Goal_TraverseEdge : public Goal<Raven_Bot>
{
private:

  //the edge the bot will follow
  PathEdge  m_Edge;

  //true if m_Edge is the last in the path.
  bool      m_bLastEdgeInPath;

  //the estimated time the bot should take to traverse the edge
  double    m_dTimeExpected;

  //this records the time this goal was activated
  double    m_dStartTime;
```

```
  //returns true if the bot gets stuck
  bool      isStuck()const;

public:

  Goal_TraverseEdge(Raven_Bot* pBot,
                    PathEdge   edge,
                    bool       LastEdge);

  //the usual suspects
  void Activate();
  int  Process();
  void Terminate();
};
```

Prior to determining the estimated time required to traverse it, the `Activate` method queries the flag field of the graph edge to ascertain if any special terrain type is associated with it — mud, snow, water, etc. — and the bot's behavior is changed accordingly. (This feature is not used by Raven but I wanted to show you how to handle it should your game use specific terrain types.)

The method ends with code for activating the appropriate steering behavior. Here's the source:

```
void Goal_TraverseEdge::Activate()
{
  m_Status = active;

  //the edge behavior flag may specify a type of movement that necessitates a
  //change in the bot's behavior as it follows this edge
  switch(m_Edge.GetBehaviorFlag())
  {
    case NavGraphEdge::swim:
    {
      m_pOwner->SetMaxSpeed(script->GetDouble("Bot_MaxSwimmingSpeed"));

      //set appropriate animation
    }

    break;

    case NavGraphEdge::crawl:
    {
       m_pOwner->SetMaxSpeed(script->GetDouble("Bot_MaxCrawlingSpeed"));

      //set appropriate animation
    }

    break;
  }

  //record the time the bot starts this goal
  m_dStartTime = Clock->GetCurrentTime();
```

```
  //calculate the expected time required to reach this waypoint. This value
  //is used to determine if the bot becomes stuck
  m_dTimeExpected =
  m_pOwner->CalculateTimeToReachPosition(m_Edge.GetDestination());

  //factor in a margin of error for any reactive behavior. 2 seconds
  //should be plenty
  static const double MarginOfError = 2.0;

  m_dTimeExpected += MarginOfError;

  //set the steering target
  m_pOwner->GetSteering()->SetTarget(m_Edge.GetDestination());

  //Set the appropriate steering behavior. If this is the last edge in the path
  //the bot should arrive at the position it points to, else it should seek
  if (m_bLastEdgeInPath)
  {
     m_pOwner->GetSteering()->ArriveOn();
  }

  else
  {
    m_pOwner->GetSteering()->SeekOn();
  }
}
```

Once the goal has been activated it's a straightforward matter to process it. Each time the `Process` method is called, the code tests to see if the bot has become stuck or reached the end of the edge and sets `m_Status` accordingly.

```
int Goal_TraverseEdge::Process()
{
  //if status is inactive, call Activate()
  ActivateIfInactive();

  //if the bot has become stuck return failure
  if (isStuck())
  {
    m_Status = failed;
  }

  //if the bot has reached the end of the edge return completed
  else
  {
    if (m_pOwner->isAtPosition(m_Edge.GetDestination()))
    {
      m_Status = completed;
    }
  }

  return m_Status;
}
```

The `Terminate` method turns off the steering behaviors and resets the bot's maximum speed back to normal.

```
void Goal_TraverseEdge::Terminate()
{
  //turn off steering behaviors
  m_pOwner->GetSteering()->SeekOff();
  m_pOwner->GetSteering()->ArriveOff();

  //return max speed back to normal
  m_pOwner->SetMaxSpeed(script->GetDouble("Bot_MaxSpeed"));
}
```

Let's now move on to examine some composite goals.

Goal_FollowPath

This directs a bot along a path by repeatedly popping edges from the front of the path and pushing traverse edge type goals onto the front of its subgoal list.

Here's its declaration:

```
class Goal_FollowPath : public Goal_Composite<Raven_Bot>
{
private:

  //a local copy of the path returned by the path planner
  std::list<PathEdge>  m_Path;

public:

  Goal_FollowPath(Raven_Bot* pBot, std::list<PathEdge> path);

  //the usual suspects
  void Activate();
  int  Process();
  void Terminate(){}
};
```

In addition to having specific terrain types associated with them, graph edges may also require a bot to use a specific action to move along them. For example, an edge may require that an agent fly, jump, or even use a grappling hook to move along it. This type of movement constraint cannot be handled by simply adjusting the maximum speed and animation cycle of the agent. Instead, a unique traverse edge type goal must be created for each action. The follow path goal can then query the edge flags within its `Activate` method and add the correct type of traverse edge goal to its subgoal list as it pops edges from the path. To clarify, here's the listing for the `Activate` method:

```
void Goal_FollowPath::Activate()
{
  m_iStatus = active;
```

```
  //get a reference to the next edge
  PathEdge edge = m_Path.front();

  //remove the edge from the path
  m_Path.pop_front();

  //some edges specify that the bot should use a specific behavior when
  //following them. This switch statement queries the edge behavior flag and
  //adds the appropriate goals(s) to the subgoal list.
  switch(edge.GetBehaviorFlags())
  {
  case NavGraphEdge::normal:
    {
      AddSubgoal(new Goal_TraverseEdge(m_pOwner, edge, m_Path.empty()));
    }

    break;

  case NavGraphEdge::goes_through_door:
    {

      //also add a goal that is able to handle opening the door
      AddSubgoal(new Goal_NegotiateDoor(m_pOwner, edge, m_Path.empty()));
    }

    break;

  case NavGraphEdge::jump:
    {
      //add subgoal to jump along the edge
    }

    break;

  case NavGraphEdge::grapple:
    {
      //add subgoal to grapple along the edge
    }

    break;

  default:

    throw
    std::runtime_error("<Goal_FollowPath::Activate>: Unrecognized edge type");
  }
}
```

For efficiency, notice how only one edge at a time is removed from the path. To facilitate this, the `Process` method calls `Activate` each time it detects its subgoals are complete and the path is not empty. Here's how:

```
int Goal_FollowPath::Process()
{
  //if status is inactive, call Activate()
```

```
  ActivateIfInactive();

  //if there are no subgoals and there is still an edge left to traverse, add
  //the edge as a subgoal
  m_Status = ProcessSubgoals();

  //if there are no subgoals present check to see if the path still has edges.
  //if it does call Activate to grab the next edge.
  if (m_Status == completed && !m_Path.empty())
  {
    Activate();
  }

  return m_Status;
}
```

The `Goal_FollowPath::Terminate` method contains no logic since there is nothing to tidy up.

⌘ TIP When the Raven executable is run, there's an option to view the goal list of a selected agent in the menu. See Screenshot 9.1.

Screenshot 9.1

The figure is in grayscale but when you run the demo active goals will be drawn in blue, completed in green, inactive in black, and failed in red. The indenting shows how the goals are nested.

Goal_MoveToPosition

This composite goal is used to move a bot to any position on a map. Here is its declaration:

```
class Goal_MoveToPosition : public Goal_Composite<Raven_Bot>
{
private:

  //the position the bot wants to reach
  Vector2D m_vDestination;

public:
```

```
  Goal_MoveToPosition(Raven_Bot* pBot, Vector2D  pos);

 //the usual suspects
  void Activate();
  int  Process();
  void Terminate(){}

  //this goal is able to accept messages
  bool HandleMessage(const Telegram& msg);
};
```

Goal_MoveToPosition is instantiated with the location of the desired destination. When the goal is activated it requests a path to that position from the bot's path planner. Since time-sliced pathfinding is used, the bot may have a short wait until the path is formulated so in the interim Goal_SeekToPosition is added. (See the section in Chapter 8 called "Preventing the Twiddling of Thumbs" for further explanation.)

```
void Goal_MoveToPosition::Activate()
{
  m_Status = active;

  //make sure the subgoal list is clear
  RemoveAllSubgoals();

  //requests a path to the target position from the path planner. Because, for
  //demonstration purposes, the Raven path planner uses time slicing when
  //processing the path requests, the bot may have to wait a few update cycles
  //before a path is calculated. Consequently, for appearance sake, it just
  //seeks directly to the target position while it's awaiting notification
  //that the path planning request has succeeded/failed
  if (m_pOwner->GetPathPlanner()->RequestPathToTarget(m_vDestination))
  {
    AddSubgoal(new Goal_SeekToPosition(m_pOwner, m_vDestination));
  }
}
```

Once the path is created, the path planner will notify the bot via a telegram, which will be forwarded to any active goals. Therefore Goal_MoveToPosition must have the capability to handle messages, enabling it to respond appropriately — either by adding the **follow path** goal to its subgoal list or by signaling failure if the planner reports no path is possible. The listing is shown below. (Note how the message is forwarded to goals farther down the hierarchy before this goal attempts to handle it.)

```
bool Goal_MoveToPosition::HandleMessage(const Telegram& msg)
{
  //first, pass the message down the goal hierarchy
  bool bHandled = ForwardMessageToFrontMostSubgoal(msg);

  //if the msg was not handled, test to see if this goal can handle it
  if (bHandled == false)
  {
```

```
    switch(msg.Msg)
    {
    case Msg_PathReady:

      //clear any existing goals
      RemoveAllSubgoals();

      AddSubgoal(new Goal_FollowPath(m_pOwner,
                                     m_pOwner->GetPathPlanner()->GetPath()));

      return true; //msg handled


    case Msg_NoPathAvailable:

      m_Status = failed;

      return true; //msg handled

    default: return false;
    }
  }

  //handled by subgoals
  return true;
}
```

Goal_MoveToPosition's subgoals are processed and continuously monitored for failure. If one of the subgoals fails, then this goal reactivates itself in order to replan.

```
int Goal_MoveToPosition::Process()
{
  //if status is inactive, call Activate() and set status to active
  ActivateIfInactive();

  //process the subgoals
  m_Status = ProcessSubgoals();

  //if any of the subgoals have failed then this goal replans
  ReactivateIfFailed();

  return m_Status;
}
```

Let's now move on to see how one of the other strategy-level goals works: Goal_AttackTarget.

Goal_AttackTarget

A bot selects this strategy when it's feeling healthy and well armed enough to attack its current target. Goal_AttackTarget is a composite goal and its declaration is straightforward.

```
class Goal_AttackTarget : public Goal_Composite<Raven_Bot>
{
public:

  Goal_AttackTarget(Raven_Bot* pOwner);

  void Activate();

  int  Process();

  void Terminate(){m_iStatus = completed;}
};
```

All the action happens in the `Activate` method. First of all any existing subgoals are removed and then a check is made to ensure the bot's target is still current. This is essential because the target may die or move out of the bot's sensory horizon while this goal is still active. In the event of this happening the goal must exit.

```
void Goal_AttackTarget::Activate()
{
  m_iStatus = active;

  //if this goal is reactivated then there may be some existing subgoals that
  //must be removed
  RemoveAllSubgoals();

  //it is possible for a bot's target to die while this goal is active so we
  //must test to make sure the bot always has an active target
  if (!m_pOwner->GetTargetSys()->isTargetPresent())
  {
     m_iStatus = completed;

     return;
  }
```

Next the bot queries its targeting system to find out if it has a direct shot at the target. If a shot is possible it selects a movement tactic to follow. Remember, the weapon system is a completely separate component of the AI and will *always automatically* select the best weapon and aim and shoot at the current target, no matter what goal the bot is pursuing (see Chapter 7 if you need to refresh your memory). This means that this goal must only dictate how the bot should *move* while attacking. I have provided Raven bots with just two choices: If there is space to the left or right of the bot, it will strafe from side to side by adding `Goal_DodgeSideToSide` to its subgoal list. If there is no room to dodge, the bot simply **seeks** to the target's current position.

```
  //if the bot is able to shoot the target (there is LOS between bot and
  //target), then select a tactic to follow while shooting
  if (m_pOwner->GetTargetSys()->isTargetShootable())
  {
    //if the bot has space to strafe then do so
```

```
    Vector2D dummy;
    if (m_pOwner->canStepLeft(dummy) || m_pOwner->canStepRight(dummy))
    {
      AddSubgoal(new Goal_DodgeSideToSide(m_pOwner));
    }

    //if not able to strafe, head directly at the target's position
    else
    {
      AddSubgoal(new Goal_SeekToPosition(m_pOwner,
                                         m_pOwner->GetTargetBot()->Pos()));
    }
  }
```

Depending on the requirements of your game you will probably want to give your bot a much wider choice of aggressive movement tactics from which to select. For instance, you might like to add a tactic that moves the bot to the perfect range for shooting its current (or favorite) weapon or one that selects a good sniping or cover position (don't forget, navgraph nodes can be annotated with this sort of information).

If there is no direct shot at the target — because it may have just run around a corner — the bot adds `Goal_HuntTarget` to its subgoal list.

```
  //if the target is not visible, go hunt it.
  else
  {
    AddSubgoal(new Goal_HuntTarget(m_pOwner));
  }
}
```

The `Process` method for `Goal_AttackTarget` is trivial. It just makes sure the subgoals are processed and that the goal replans if a problem is detected.

```
int Goal_AttackTarget::Process()
{
  //if status is inactive, call Activate()
  ActivateIfInactive();

  //process the subgoals
  m_iStatus = ProcessSubgoals();

  ReactivateIfFailed();

  return m_iStatus;
}
```

I'm not going to go into the details of `Goal_HuntTarget` and `Goal_DodgeSideToSide`. It's pretty obvious what they do and you can always examine the source code if you want to look at the nitty-gritty.

Goal Arbitration

You now understand how goals work and have seen some concrete examples, but you're probably still wondering how the bots select between strategy-level goals. This is accomplished by the composite goal `Goal_Think`, which each bot owns a persistent instance of, forming the root of its goal hierarchy. `Goal_Think`'s function is to arbitrate between available strategies, choosing the most appropriate to be pursued. There are six strategy-level goals. They are:

- **Explore**: An agent picks an arbitrary point in its environment and plans and follows a path to that point.
- **Get Health**: An agent finds the least cost path to an instance of a health item and follows the path to that item.
- **Get Weapon (Rocket Launcher)**: An agent finds the least cost path to an instance of a rocket launcher and follows the path to it.
- **Get Weapon (Shotgun)**: An agent finds the least cost path to an instance of a shotgun and follows the path to it.

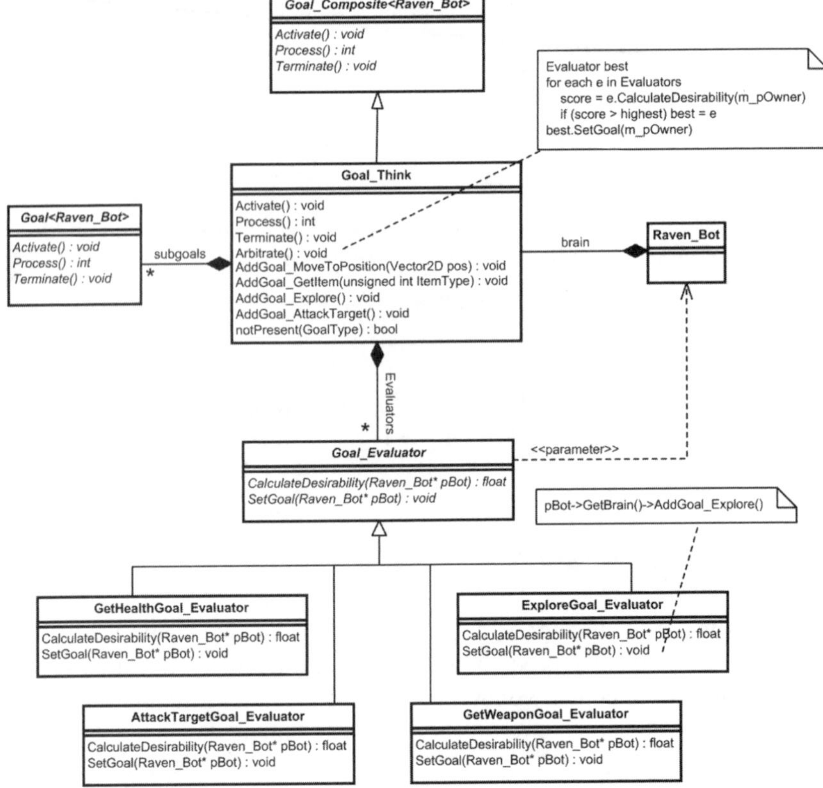

Figure 9.8. Although not explicitly shown, each `Goal_Think` instance instantiates three `GetWeaponGoal_Evaluator` objects, one for each weapon type the bot can pick up.

- **Get Weapon (Railgun)**: An agent finds the least cost path to an instance of a railgun and follows the path to it.
- **Attack Target**: An agent determines a strategy for attacking its current target.

Every think update each of these strategies is evaluated and given a score representing the desirability of pursuing it. The strategy with the highest score is assigned to be the one the agent will attempt to satisfy. To facilitate this process each `Goal_Think` aggregates several `Goal_Evaluator` instances, one for each strategy. These objects have methods for calculating the desirability of the strategy they represent, and for adding that goal to `Goal_Think`'s subgoal list. Figure 9.8 illustrates the design.

Each `CalculateDesirability` method is a hand-crafted algorithm that returns a value indicating the desirability of a bot pursuing the respective strategy. These algorithms can be tricky to create so it's often useful to first construct some helper functions that map feature specific information from the game to a numerical value in the range 0 to 1. These are then utilized in the formulation of the desirability algorithms. It's not especially important what range of values your feature extraction methods return — 0 to 1, 0 to 100, or –10000 to 1000 are all okay — but it helps if they are standardized across all methods. This will make it easier on your brain when you begin to create the algorithms for desirability.

To decide what information needs extracting from the game world, consider each strategy goal in turn and what game features have bearing upon the desirability of pursuing it. For instance, the **GetHealth** evaluation is going to require information regarding the status of a bot's health and the location of a health item. Similarly, the **AttackTarget** evaluator is going to require information in respect to the weapons and ammo a bot is carrying, in addition to its health levels (a bot low on health is much less likely to attack an opponent than a bot that is feeling fit as a fiddle). The **ExploreGoal** evaluator is a special case as you'll see shortly, but the **GetWeapon** evaluator will require additional knowledge about how far away a specific weapon is and the current ammo a bot is carrying for that weapon.

Raven uses four such feature extraction functions, implemented as static methods of the `Raven_Feature` class. Here is the listing of the class declaration, which contains a description of each method in the comments:

```
class Raven_Feature
{
public:

  //returns a value between 0 and 1 based on the bot's health. The better
  //the health, the higher the rating
  static double Health(Raven_Bot* pBot);

  //returns a value between 0 and 1 based on the bot's distance to the
```

```
  //given item. The farther the item, the higher the rating. If there is no
  //item of the given type present in the game world at the time this method
  //is called the value returned is 1
  static double DistanceToItem(Raven_Bot* pBot, int ItemType);

  //returns a value between 0 and 1 based on how much ammo the bot has for
  //the given weapon, and the maximum amount of ammo the bot can carry. The
  //closer the amount carried is to the max amount, the higher the score
  static double IndividualWeaponStrength(Raven_Bot* pBot, int WeaponType);

  //returns a value between 0 and 1 based on the total amount of ammo the
  //bot is carrying for each of the weapons. Each of the three weapons a bot
  //can pick up can contribute a third to the score. In other words, if a bot
  //is carrying an RL and an RG and has max ammo for the RG but only half max
  //for the RL, the rating will be 1/3 + 1/6 + 0 = 0.5
  static double TotalWeaponStrength(Raven_Bot* pBot);
};
```

I'll not list the method bodies here, but you may find it interesting to check them out at some point. You can find them in the file Raven/goals/Raven_Feature.cpp.

Now that we have some helper functions let's take a look at how they can be used to calculate the desirability scores for each strategy, which are also standardized to be in the range 0 to 1.

Calculating the Desirability of Locating a Health Item

Generally speaking, the desirability of locating a health item is proportional to the current health level of a bot and is inversely proportional to the distance away from the closest instance. Because each of these features is extracted by the methods discussed earlier and represented as a number in the range 0 to 1, this can be written as:

$$Desirability_{health} = k \times \left(\frac{1 - Health}{DistToHealth} \right)$$

where k is a constant used to tweak the result. This relationship makes sense because the farther you have to travel to retrieve an item the less you desire it, whereas the lower your health level, the greater your desire. (Note that we don't have to worry about a divide by zero error because it's impossible for an agent to get closer than its bounding radius away from an item before the item is triggered.)

Here is the source code from Raven that implements this algorithm.

```
double GetHealthGoal_Evaluator::CalculateDesirability(Raven_Bot* pBot)
{
  //first grab the distance to the closest instance of a health item
  double Distance = Raven_Feature::DistanceToItem(pBot, type_health);

  //if the distance feature is rated with a value of 1 it means that the
```

```
  //item is either not present on the map or too far away to be worth
  //considering, therefore the desirability is zero
  if (Distance == 1)
  {
    return 0;
  }
  else
  {
    //value used to tweak the desirability
    const double Tweaker = 0.2;

    //the desirability of finding a health item is proportional to the amount
    //of health remaining and inversely proportional to the distance from the
    //nearest instance of a health item.
    double Desirability = Tweaker * (1-Raven_Feature::Health(pBot)) /
                          (Raven_Feature::DistanceToItem(pBot, type_health));

    //ensure the value is in the range 0 to 1
    Clamp(Desirability, 0, 1);

    return Desirability;
  }
}
```

Calculating the Desirability of Locating a Specific Weapon

This is very similar to the previous algorithm. The desirability of locating a specific weapon can be given as:

$$Desirability_{weapon} = k \times \left(\frac{Health \times (1 - WeaponStrength)}{DistToWeapon} \right)$$

Notice how both the weapon strength and health features contribute to the desirability of retrieving a weapon. This is sensible because as a bot becomes more badly damaged or the amount of ammo it's carrying for that particular weapon increases, its desire for retrieving it should diminish.

This is how the algorithm looks in code:

```
double GetWeaponGoal_Evaluator::CalculateDesirability(Raven_Bot* pBot)
{
  //grab the distance to the closest instance of the weapon type
  double Distance = Raven_Feature::DistanceToItem(pBot, m_iWeaponType);

  //if the distance feature is rated with a value of 1 it means that the
  //item is either not present on the map or too far away to be worth
  //considering, therefore the desirability is zero
  if (Distance == 1)
  {
    return 0;
  }
  else
  {
    //value used to tweak the desirability
```

```
    const double Tweaker = 0.15f;

    double Health, WeaponStrength;

    Health = Raven_Feature::Health(pBot);

    WeaponStrength = Raven_Feature::IndividualWeaponStrength(pBot, m_iWeaponType);

    double Desirability = (Tweaker * Health * (1-WeaponStrength)) / Distance;

    //ensure the value is in the range 0 to 1
    Clamp(Desirability, 0, 1);

    return Desirability;
  }
}
```

The bonus of using distance as a factor in the desirability calculation for picking up weapon and health items is that, given the correct circumstances, bots will temporarily change strategy and divert their course to pick up nearby items.

⌘ **TIP** The influence of distance in the desirability algorithms we've examined so far is linear. In other words, the desirability is directly proportional to the distance from the item. However, you may prefer the "pull" of the item on the bot to become stronger more quickly as the bot approaches (like the force you feel when you move two magnets toward each other), instead of at a constant rate (like the force you feel when you stretch a spring). This is best explained with a graph. See Figure 9.9.

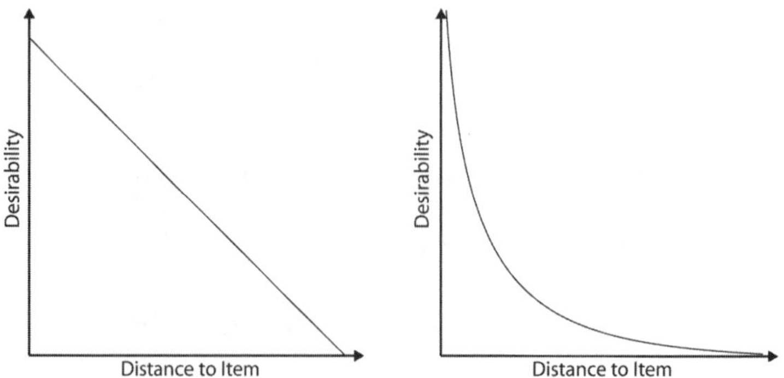

Figure 9.9. The graph on the left shows a linear relationship with distance; the one on the right is non-linear.

To create an algorithm that produces a desirability-distance curve similar to the graph on the right you must divide by the square (or even cube) of the distance. In other words, the equation is changed to:

$$Desirability_{weapon} = k \times \left(\frac{Health \times (1 - WeaponStrength)}{DistToWeapon^2} \right)$$

Don't forget that you will also have to tweak *k* to give you the results you desire.

Calculating the Desirability of Attacking the Target

The desirability of attacking an opponent is proportional to how healthy and powerful a bot is feeling. The "powerful" feature, in the context of Raven, is an indication of the number of guns and ammo a bot is carrying and is evaluated by the method `Raven_Feature::TotalWeaponStrength`. (I recommend you take a peek inside this method next time you're sitting at your computer.) Using these two features we can calculate the desirability of pursuing the **AttackTarget** goal:

$$Desirability_{attack} = k \times TotalWeaponStrength \times Health$$

Here's how it looks written in code:

```
double AttackTargetGoal_Evaluator::CalculateDesirability(Raven_Bot* pBot)
{
  double Desirability = 0.0;

  //only do the calculation if there is a target present
  if (pBot->GetTargetSys()->isTargetPresent())
  {
     const double Tweaker = 1.0;

     Desirability = Tweaker *
                    Raven_Feature::Health(pBot) *
                    Raven_Feature::TotalWeaponStrength(pBot);
  }

  return Desirability;
}
```

⌘ **TIP** Depending on how sophisticated you need your agent to be you can add and remove strategies from the arbiter. (Remember, `Goal_Think` is the arbiter of a Raven bot's strategy goals.) Indeed, you can even switch in and out entire sets of strategy goals to provide an agent with a whole new suite of behaviors to select from. Far Cry, for instance, uses this sort of technique to good effect.

Calculating the Desirability of Exploring the Map

This one is easy. Imagine yourself playing the game. You're only likely to go exploring the map if there are no other things requiring your immediate attention like attacking an opponent or looking for ammo or health. Consequently, the desirability of exploring the map is fixed as a low constant value, thus ensuring the option to explore is only selected if all alternatives have lower desirability scores. Here's the code:

```
double ExploreGoal_Evaluator::CalculateDesirability(Raven_Bot* pBot)
{
  const double Desirability = 0.05;

  return Desirability;
}
```

Putting It All Together

Once a desirability function has been defined for each evaluator object, all that remains is for Goal_Think to iterate through them each think update and select the highest to be the strategy a bot will pursue. Here's the code to clarify:

```
void Goal_Think::Arbitrate()
{
  double best = 0;
  Goal_Evaluator* MostDesirable = NULL;

  //iterate through all the evaluators to see which produces the highest score
  GoalEvaluators::iterator curDes = m_Evaluators.begin();
  for (curDes; curDes != m_Evaluators.end(); ++curDes)
  {
    double desirabilty = (*curDes)->CalculateDesirability(m_pOwner);

    if (desirabilty >= best)
    {
      best = desirabilty;
      MostDesirable = *curDes;
    }
  }

  MostDesirable->SetGoal(m_pOwner);
}
```

⌘ **TIP** Human players have the ability to anticipate what another player is about to do and act accordingly. We can do this because we are able to briefly shift our point of view to that of any other player and think about what their desires might be given our understanding of their state and the state of the game world. Here's an example:

> *You observe from a distance two players, Sid and Eric, battling it out with rocket launchers when all of a sudden, after getting hit twice in succession, Eric breaks off and starts running down a corridor. You shift your point of perspective to Eric and, because you know he's low on health, you anticipate it's very likely he's heading toward the health pack you know he knows is located in a room at the end of the corridor. You also realize that you are positioned closer to the health than Eric so you decide to "steal" it away from him and wait out of view until he arrives, whereupon you smear his intestines along a wall with your plasma rifle.*

The ability to anticipate another's actions like this is an innate characteristic of human behavior — we do it all the time — but it is possible to give an agent a similar, if somewhat much lessened, capability. Because the desires of goal arbitration agents are determined algorithmically, you can have a bot run the relevant attributes (health, ammo, etc.) of the *human player* through its own (or custom) arbiter to make a *guess* at what the player's desires might be at that time. Of course the accuracy of this guess very much depends on how closely the bot's desires match the player's — and that's up to your behavioral modeling skills — but it's usually not too difficult to make the occasional accurate prediction that enables a bot to give the player a nasty surprise, even with a very basic model.

Spin-offs

One great thing about a hierarchical goal-based arbitration design is that extra features are provided with little additional effort from the programmer. We'll spend the remainder of the chapter taking a look at them.

Personalities

Because the desirability scores are constrained to the same range, it's a simple matter to create agents with different personality traits by multiplying each score with a constant that biases it in the required direction. For instance, to create a Raven bot that plays aggressively with little regard for its own safety, you can bias its desire to get health by 0.6 and its desire to attack targets by 1.5. To create one that plays cautiously you can bias a bot's desires so it's more likely to pick up weapons and health than attack. If you were to design goal-directed agents for an RTS game you could create one opponent that favors exploration and researching technology, another that prefers to create huge armies as quickly as possible, and one other that is obsessive about establishing city defenses.

To facilitate such personality traits, the `Goal_Evaluator` base class contains a member variable `m_dCharacterBias`, which is assigned a value by the client in the constructor like so:

```
class Goal_Evaluator
{
protected:

  //when the desirability score for a goal has been evaluated it is multiplied
  //by this value. It can be used to create bots with preferences based upon
  //their personality
  double       m_dCharacterBias;

public:

  Goal_Evaluator(double CharacterBias):m_dCharacterBias(CharacterBias){}

  /* EXTRANEOUS DETAIL OMITTED */
};
```

`m_dCharacterBias` is utilized in the `CalculateDesirability` method of each subclass to adjust the desirability score calculation. Here's how it is added to the desirability calculation for **AttackTarget**:

```
double AttackTargetGoal_Evaluator::CalculateDesirability(Raven_Bot* pBot)
{
  double Desirability = 0.0;

  //only do the calculation if there is a target present
  if (pBot->GetTargetSys()->isTargetPresent())
  {
     const double Tweaker = 1.0;
```

```
    Desirability = Tweaker *
                   Raven_Feature::Health(pBot) *
                   Raven_Feature::TotalWeaponStrength(pBot);

    //bias the value according to the personality of the bot
    Desirability *= m_dCharacterBias;
  }

  return Desirability;
}
```

If your game design requires that the bots' personalities persist between games, you should create a separate script file for each bot containing the biases (plus any other bot character-specific data, such as weapon aiming accuracy, weapon selection preferences, etc.). There are no bots of this type in Raven, however; each time you run the program the bots' desirability biases are assigned random values in the constructor of `Goal_Think`, like so:

```
  //these biases could be loaded in from a script on a per bot basis
  //but for now we'll just give them some random values
  const double LowRangeOfBias = 0.5;
  const double HighRangeOfBias = 1.5;

  double HealthBias = RandInRange(LowRangeOfBias, HighRangeOfBias);
  double ShotgunBias = RandInRange(LowRangeOfBias, HighRangeOfBias);
  double RocketLauncherBias = RandInRange(LowRangeOfBias, HighRangeOfBias);
  double RailgunBias = RandInRange(LowRangeOfBias, HighRangeOfBias);
  double ExploreBias = RandInRange(LowRangeOfBias, HighRangeOfBias);
  double AttackBias = RandInRange(LowRangeOfBias, HighRangeOfBias);

  //create the evaluator objects
  m_Evaluators.push_back(new GetHealthGoal_Evaluator(HealthBias));
  m_Evaluators.push_back(new ExploreGoal_Evaluator(ExploreBias));
  m_Evaluators.push_back(new AttackTargetGoal_Evaluator(AttackBias));
  m_Evaluators.push_back(new GetWeaponGoal_Evaluator(ShotgunBias,
                                                     type_shotgun));
  m_Evaluators.push_back(new GetWeaponGoal_Evaluator(RailgunBias,
                                                     type_rail_gun));
  m_Evaluators.push_back(new GetWeaponGoal_Evaluator(RocketLauncherBias,
                                                     type_rocket_launcher));
```

⌘ **TIP** Goal arbitration is essentially an algorithmic process defined by a handful of numbers. As a result, it is not driven by logic (like an FSM) but by *data*. This is hugely advantageous because all you have to do to change the behavior is tweak the numbers, which you may prefer to keep in a script file so that other members of your team can easily experiment with them.

State Memory

The stack-like (LIFO) nature of composite goals automatically endows agents with a memory, enabling them to temporarily change behavior by pushing a new goal (or goals) onto the front of the current goal's subgoal list. As soon as the new goal is satisfied it will popped from the list and the agent will resume whatever it was doing previously. This is a very powerful feature that can be exploited in many different ways.

Here are a couple of examples.

Example One — Automatic Resuming of Interrupted Activities

Imagine that Eric, who is on his way to the smithy, gold in pocket, is set upon by a thief with a Rambo knife. This occurs just before he reaches the third waypoint of the path he is following. His brain's subgoal list at this point resembles Figure 9.10.

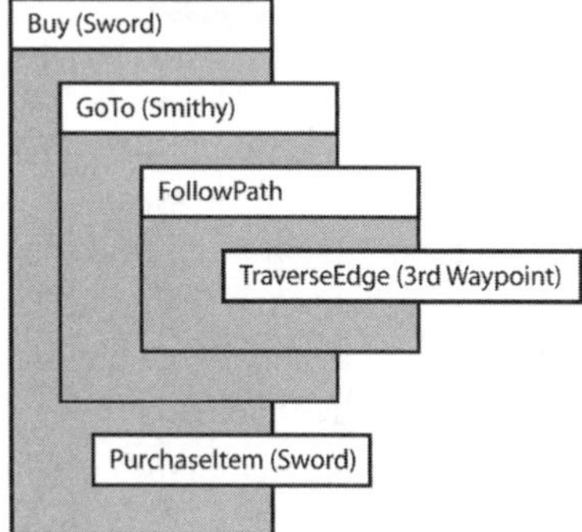

Figure 9.10

Eric didn't expect this to happen, but fortunately the AI programmer has created a goal for dealing with just this sort of thing called **DefendAgainstAttacker**. This goal is pushed onto the front of his subgoal list and remains active until the thief either runs away or is killed by Eric. See Figure 9.11.

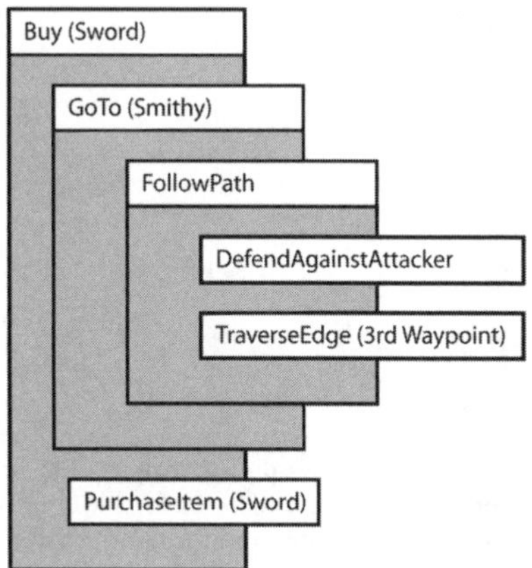

Figure 9.11

The great thing about this design is that when **DefendAgainstAttacker** is satisfied and removed from the list, Eric automatically resumes following the edge to waypoint three.

Some of you will probably be thinking "*Ah, but what if while chasing after the thief Eric loses sight of waypoint three?*" Well, that's the fantastic thing about this design. Because the goals have built-in logic for detecting failure and for replanning, if a goal fails the design moves backward up through the hierarchy until a parent is found that is capable of replanning the goal.

Example Two — Negotiating Special Path Obstacles

Many game designs necessitate that agents are capable of negotiating one or more types of path obstacles, such as doors, elevators, drawbridges, and moving platforms. Often this requires the agent to follow a short sequence of actions. For example, to use an elevator an agent must find the button that calls it, walk toward the button, press it, and then walk back and stand in front of the doors until the elevator arrives. Using a moving platform is a similar process: The agent must walk toward the mechanism that operates the platform, press/pull it, walk to the embarking point, wait for the platform to arrive, and finally, step onto the platform and wait until it gets to wherever it's going. See Figure 9.12.

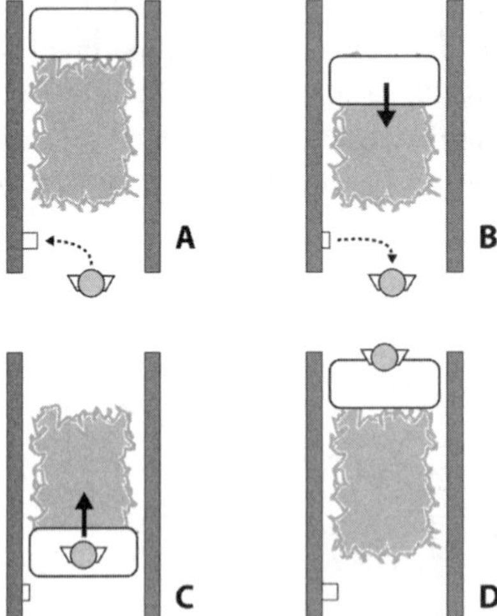

Figure 9.12. An agent uses a moving platform to cross a pit of fire. A) The agent walks to the button and presses it. B) The agent walks back and waits for the platform to arrive. C) The agent steps on the platform and remains stationary as it travels across the fiery pit. D) The agent continues on its way.

These "obstacles" should be transparent to the path planner since they are not barriers to an agent's movement. It takes time to negotiate them of course, but this can be reflected in the navgraph edge costs.

In order for agents to deal with such obstacles, the graph edge that passes through them must be annotated with information reflecting their type. The **FollowPath** goal can then check this information and ensure that the correct type of goal is pushed onto the front of an agent's goal list when such an edge is encountered. As in the previous example, the agent will pursue this new subgoal until it is completed and then resume whatever it was doing before.

To demonstrate this principle I've added support for negotiating sliding doors to the Raven bots' repertoires. Sliding doors are opened by touching a "button" located somewhere close to the door (one at each side). When a door is added in the map editor any graph edges that cross the door boundary are marked with the `goes_through_door` flag. If a bot encounters an edge flagged like this (as they are pulled off the path in `Goal_FollowPath::Activate`), a **NegotiateDoor** goal is added to its subgoal list like so:

```
void Goal_FollowPath::Activate()
{
  //get a reference to the next edge
  const PathEdge& edge = m_Path.front();

  switch(edge.GetBehaviorFlags())
  {
  case NavGraphEdge::goes_through_door:
    {
      //add a goal that is able to handle opening the door
      AddSubgoal(new Goal_NegotiateDoor(m_pOwner, edge));
    }

    break;
  //etc
```

The **NegotiateDoor** goal directs a bot through the sequence of actions required to open and pass through the door. As an example, let's consider the case of the bot shown in Figure 9.13 whose path takes it along the edge AB, which is obstructed by a sliding door.

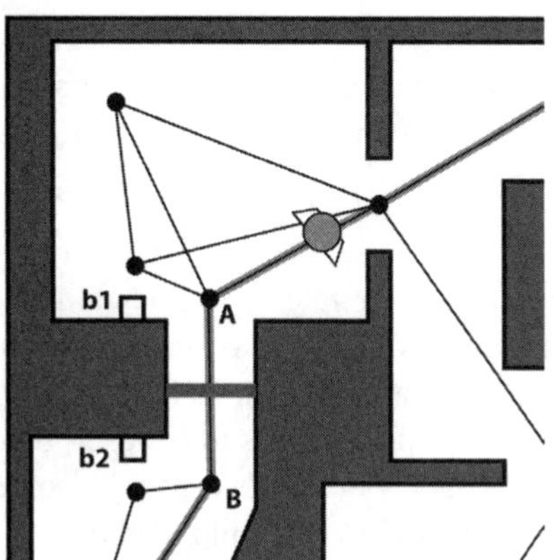

Figure 9.13

To get through the sliding door, the bot must follow these steps

1. Get the list of buttons that open the door (b1 and b2).
2. From the list, select the closest navigable button (b1).
3. Plan and follow a path to button b1 (the button will trigger, opening the door).
4. Plan and follow a path to node A.
5. Traverse the edge AB.

Goal_NegotiateDoor addresses each of these steps in its Activate method, adding the subgoals necessary to complete the task. The listing will help clarify.

```
void Goal_NegotiateDoor::Activate()
{
  m_iStatus = active;

  //if this goal is reactivated then there may be some existing subgoals that
  //must be removed
  RemoveAllSubgoals();

  //get the position of the closest navigable switch
  Vector2D posSw = m_pOwner->GetWorld()->GetPosOfClosestSwitch(m_pOwner->Pos(),
                                                               m_PathEdge.GetDoorID());

  //because goals are *pushed* onto the front of the subgoal list they must
  //be added in reverse order.

  //first, the goal to traverse the edge that passes through the door
  AddSubgoal(new Goal_TraverseEdge(m_pOwner, m_PathEdge));

  //next, the goal that will move the bot to the beginning of the edge that
  //passes through the door
  AddSubgoal(new Goal_MoveToPosition(m_pOwner, m_PathEdge.GetSource()));

  //finally, the goal that will direct the bot to the location of the switch
  AddSubgoal(new Goal_MoveToPosition(m_pOwner, posSw));
}
```

You can see Raven's bots navigating doors by running Raven and loading the map Raven_DM1_With_Doors.map. It uses a sparse navgraph so you can clearly see how the **NegotiateDoor** goal works.

Command Queuing

Real-time strategy games have grown in complexity tremendously over the last few years. Not only has the number of NPCs a player is able to control increased, but also the number of commands he can instruct the NPCs to follow. This has necessitated several improvements to the user interface, one being the ability for a player to queue an NPC's orders — something that has become known as *command queuing* (or build queuing).

One of the first uses of queuing was to position waypoints for an NPC to follow as a path. To do this a player holds down a key while clicking on the map to create a series of waypoints. The NPC stores the waypoints in a FIFO (first in, first out) data structure and follows them in order, stopping when its queue is empty. See Figure 9.14.

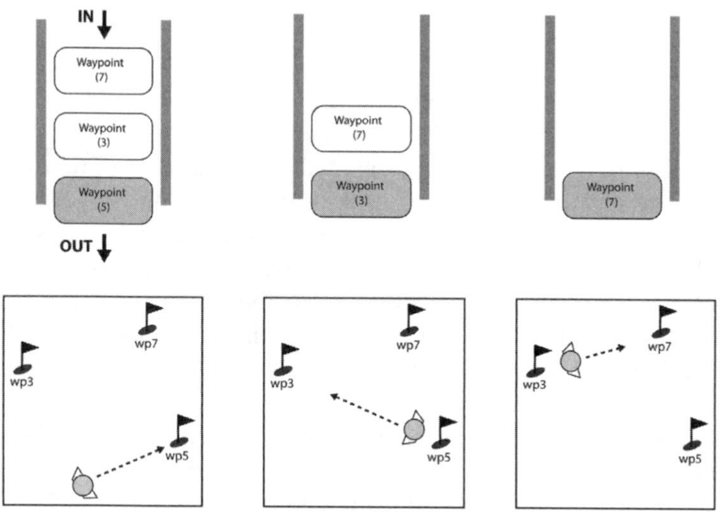

Figure 9.14. Queuing path waypoints

Designers quickly realized that with slight modification, the user could also assign patrol points to an NPC. If the waypoints are assigned by the player as patrol points (by holding down a different key while clicking), they are returned to the back of the queue as the NPC reaches them. In this way an

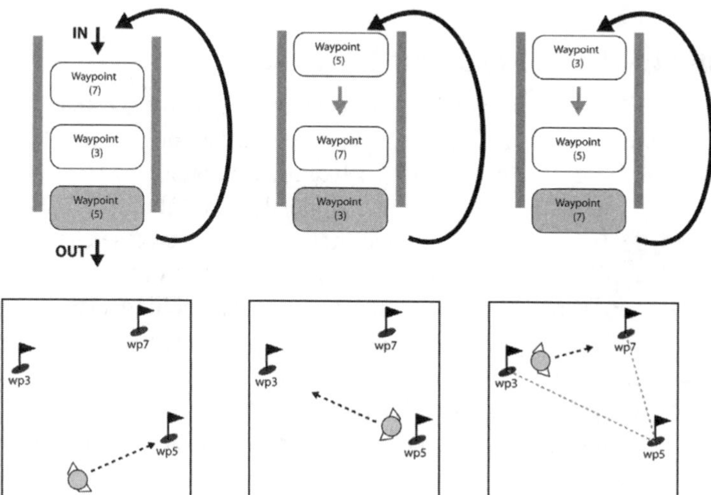

Figure 9.15. Queuing patrol waypoints

NPC will endlessly loop through its patrol points until instructed otherwise. See Figure 9.15.

Very shortly after this innovation, it was realized that not only could position vectors be queued, but so could any type of command. Subsequently, rather than issuing only one order at a time, by simply holding down a key while selecting orders, the player could queue multiple commands. For example, an NPC can be instructed to collect some gold, then build a barracks, then attack an enemy unit. Once the orders are issued the player can focus his attention elsewhere, confident the NPC will follow orders.

Command queuing significantly reduces the amount of time a player has to spend on micromanagement and increases the time available for more enjoyable aspects of the game. It therefore has become an indispensable feature within the RTS genre. Fortunately, using the composite goal architecture, this sort of functionality is incredibly easy to implement. All you have to do is allow clients to add goals to the *rear* of the subgoal list in addition to the front. That's it! Five minutes of work and you get command queuing.

You can observe command queuing in action in Raven. Unfortunately, unlike an RTS, Raven does not have lots of interesting commands, but you can queue multiple **MoveToPosition** goals by holding down the "Q" key while clicking on the map. I implemented this by adding the `QueueGoal_MoveToPosition` method to `Goal_Think` and some additional code for calling that method if the player clicks on the map while holding down the appropriate key. If you release the "Q" key and right-click on the map again, the queue is cleared and replaced with the single new goal. This would be just as easy to implement with any goal of your choosing though, because the queuing takes care of itself.

Using the Queue to Script Behavior

Another benefit of turning the subgoal list into a queue is that it enables you to script linear action sequences without too much difficulty. For example, you can create behavior like the following:

- A player enters a room and a ghostly game character appears that floats to a chest positioned in the corner, opens the chest, takes out a scroll, floats back to the player, and hands him the scroll.
- A player enters a hotel lobby with a glass ceiling. After a brief time spent in the room, a helicopter is heard. Seconds later the ceiling shatters into a million shards and several armed men in black are seen rappelling from the helicopter. When they hit the floor they scatter, each finding cover in a separate location, and start firing at the player.

- A player finds an old brass lamp. He rubs it and a genie appears. The genie says “Follow me” and leads the player to the opening to a secret tunnel, where it promptly vanishes in a puff of smoke.

To do this you have to ensure you define a goal for each step of the sequence and the triggers required to activate the script. In addition, you have to expose the relevant C++ code to your scripting language.

For example, to script the third example from the previous list in Lua you’d need to complete these tasks.

1. Create three goals:
   - A **SayPhrase** goal, which would output some text to the screen for a specified amount of time.
   - A **LeadPlayerToPosition** goal. This is similar to the **MoveTo-Position** goal seen in Raven except it has additional logic for making sure the genie does not lose sight of the player while leading him to the secret tunnel.
   - A **VanishInPuffOfSmoke** goal, which would remove the instance of the genie from the game world and leave behind a puff of smoke.
2. Create a trigger that is activated when a player performs the “rub” action on a specific “lamp” object. When activated, the trigger should call the appropriate Lua function.
3. Expose the relevant parts of the game architecture to Lua. Ideally you’d like to write a script that looks a little like this:

```
function AddGenieTourGuide(LampPos, TunnelPos, Player)

  --create an instance of a genie at the position of the lamp
  genie = CreateGenie(LampPos)

  --first welcome the player, text stays on screen for 2 seconds
  genie:SayPhrase("Welcome oh great "..Player:GetName().. "!", 2)

  --order the player to follow the genie. text stays on screen for
  --3 seconds
  genie:SayPhrase("Follow me for your three wishes", 3)

  --lead the player to the tunnel entrance
  genie:LeadPlayerToPosition(Player, TunnelPos)

  --vanish
  genie:VanishInPuffOfSmoke

end
```

Therefore you need to expose a C++ method that creates a genie, adds it to the game world, and returns a pointer to it, along with methods for adding the appropriate goals to a genie’s goal queue.

Summing Up

This chapter has presented a flexible and powerful goal-based agent architecture. You have learned how an agent's behavior can be modeled as a set of high-level strategies, each of which is comprised of a nested hierarchy of composite and atomic goals. You've also learned how agents can arbitrate between those strategies to select the most appropriate one to pursue given the current game state.

Although it shares many similarities, this type of architecture is far more sophisticated than a state-based design and will require some practice before you are able to use it confidently. As usual, I'm going to end the chapter with a few ideas you can play around with to help improve your understanding.

Practice Makes Perfect

1. Decent human FPS players get a "feel" for when a particular item is about to respawn. Indeed it's not unknown for some deathmatch players to play with an alarm clock by the side of their monitor! The Raven bots, however, currently haven't a clue when an item is going to respawn. Create a termination condition for the Dijkstra's search algorithm that calculates if an inactive (invisible) item type will respawn in the time it takes to reach it, thereby enabling a bot to preempt it.
2. The Raven bots have no defensive strategy. At the moment they just attempt to hunt down an item type if they do not feel strong enough to attack and hope this will lead them out of harm's way. You will notice when you watch the demo that this behavior often gets them into trouble since they make no attempt to dodge shots when pursuing an item. Write the logic and any extra goals required to enable bots to detect such situations and to dodge from side to side while still pursuing an item type.
3. Add character scripting to Raven and create one or two scripted sequences. This is a great exercise and will reinforce many of the things you've learned so far. You don't need to script anything complex. For instance, you could do something similar to the genie example described earlier. Create a script from the player's point of view that goes like this: When the player stands in a certain position, a bot enters the location from somewhere "out of view" (of course, this isn't really possible given the top-down nature of Raven, but you know what I mean), stops in front of the player, says "Follow Me," and then leads the player to a random location.

Chapter 10

Fuzzy Logic

Humans have the incredible ability to communicate skills simply and accurately by using vague linguistic rules. For example, a TV chef might instruct you how to make perfect cheese on toast like this:

1. Cut two slices of bread **medium thick**.
2. Turn the heat on the griddle on **high**.
3. Grill the slices on one side until **golden brown**.
4. Turn the slices over and add a **generous helping** of cheese.
5. Replace and grill until the top of the cheese is **slightly brown**.
6. Remove, sprinkle on a **small amount** of black pepper, and eat.

The words shown in bold are all vague linguistic terms, yet we would all be confident of following these instructions to create a delicious snack. Humans do this sort of thing all the time. It's a transparent and natural process for us to interpret instructions like this in a meaningful and accurate way.

When designing the AI for computer games, wouldn't it be great to be able to communicate with a computer in a similar fashion — to quickly and simply map expert knowledge from the human domain to the digital one? If computers were able to understand vague linguistic terms then we could sit down with an expert in the domain of interest (more often than not that will be you), ask questions pertinent to the skill necessary to be successful within that domain, and from the answers quickly create some linguistic rules for the computer to interpret — just like the ones shown for making toast.

Conventional logic is inadequate for processing such rules. As an example, imagine you are programming a golfing game and you've been given the job of spending the day with Tiger Woods to determine some ground rules for playing golf. At the end of the day your notepad is full of words of wisdom such as these:

> When putting: *If the **ball is far from the hole** and the **green is sloping gently downward from left to right**, then **hit the ball firmly** and at an **angle slightly to the left of the flag**.*
>
> When putting: *If the **ball is very close to the hole**, and the **green between the ball and hole is level**, then **hit the ball gently** and **directly at the hole**.*

When driving from the tee: *If the **wind is of strong force** and **blowing right to left**, and the **hole is far away**, then **hit the ball hard** and at an **angle far to the right of the flag**.*

These rules are very descriptive and make perfect sense to a human but are difficult to translate into a language a computer can understand. Words like "far," "very close," and "gently" do not have sharp, well-defined boundaries, and when we attempt to describe them in code the result often looks clumsy and artificial. For instance, we might encode the descriptive term "Distance" as the set of intervals:

Close = the ball is between 0 meters and 2 meters from the hole.
Medium = the ball is between 2 meters and 5 meters from the hole.
Far = the ball is greater than 5 meters from the hole.

But what if the ball is 4.99 meters away from the hole? Using these intervals to represent distances, a computer will put the ball firmly in the "Medium" slot, even though the addition of a couple more centimeters will transform it to being far away! It's not hard to see that when manipulating data presented in such a way any AI's reasoning about a domain is going to be fundamentally flawed. Of course, it's possible to reduce the effect of this problem by creating smaller and smaller intervals, but the underlying problem remains because the distance terms are still represented by discrete intervals.

Compare this to how a human reasons. When considering linguistic terms such as "far" and "close" or "gently" and "firmly," a human being is able to place vague boundaries on those terms and allow a value to be associated with a term to a *matter of degree*. When the ball is 4.99 meters away from the hole, a human will regard it to be *partly* associated with the term "medium distance" but *mostly* with the term "far distance." In this way humans perceive the distance quality of the ball *gradually* shifting between linguistic terms instead of changing abruptly, allowing us to reason accurately about linguistic rules such as the ones given for playing golf or making toast.

Fuzzy logic, invented by a man named Lotfi Zadeh in the mid-sixties, enables a computer to reason about linguistic terms and rules in a way similar to humans. Concepts like "far" or "slightly" are not represented by discrete intervals, but by fuzzy *sets*, enabling values to be assigned to sets to a matter of a degree — a process called *fuzzification*. Using fuzzified values computers are able to interpret linguistic rules and produce an output that may remain fuzzy or — more commonly, especially in video games — can be *defuzzified* to provide a crisp value. This is known as *fuzzy rule-based inference*, and is one of the most popular uses of fuzzy logic. See Figure 10.1.

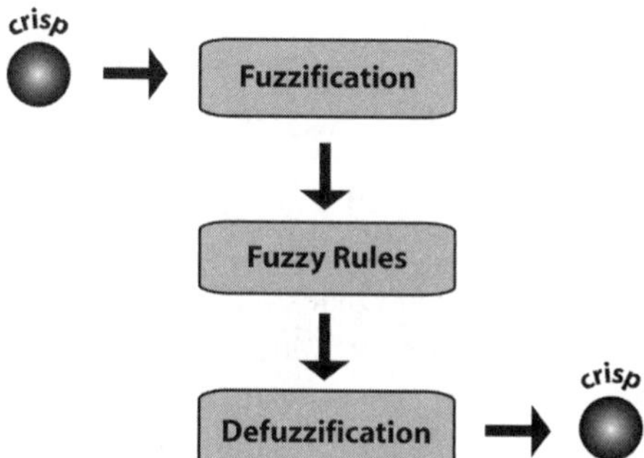

Figure 10.1. Fuzzy rule-based inference

We'll look into the fuzzy process in more detail shortly but, before you can begin to understand fuzzy sets, it helps to understand the mathematics of crisp sets, so our journey into fuzzydom will commence there.

NOTE Interpreting linguistic rules is only one of the many uses of fuzzy logic. I've focused on this application here because it's one of the most useful features for game AI programmers. Fuzzy logic has been successfully applied to many other areas including control engineering, pattern recognition, relational databases, and data analysis. You more than likely have several solid state fuzzy logic controllers in your home. They might be regulating your central heating system or stabilizing the image in your video camera.

Crisp Sets

Crisp sets are the mathematical concepts taught in school. They have clearly defined boundaries: An object (sometimes called an *element*) either completely belongs to a set or it doesn't. This is fine for many problems since many objects can be precisely classified. After all, a spade is a spade; it's not partly a spade and partly a pair of garden shears.

The domain of all elements a set belongs to is called the *universe of discourse*. The white rectangle of Figure 10.2 represents the universe of discourse of integers in the range 1 to 15. The circles inside the UOD denote the set of even integers and the set of odd integers.

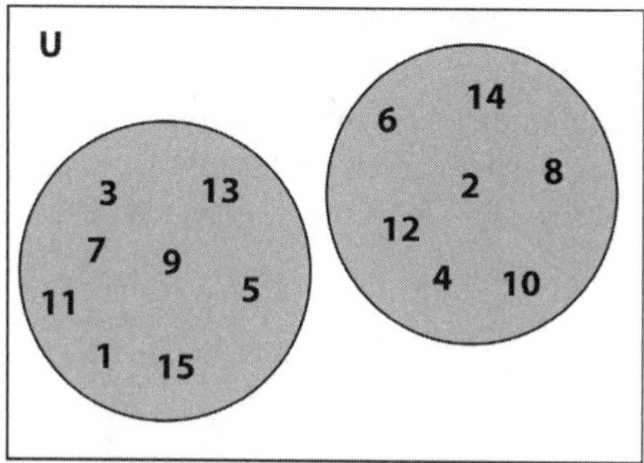

Figure 10.2

Using mathematical notation these sets can be written as:

Odd = {1, 3, 5, 7, 9, 11, 13, 15}
Even = {2, 4, 6, 8, 10, 12, 14}

As is evident, the *degree of membership* of a number to a crisp set is either true or false, 1 or 0. The number 5 is 100 percent odd and 0 percent even. In classical set theory all the integers are black and white in this way — they are members of one set to a degree of 1 and to the other to a degree of 0. It's also worth highlighting that an element can be contained in more than one crisp set. For example, the integer 3 is a member of the set of odd numbers, the set of prime numbers, and the set of all numbers less then 5. But in all these sets its degree of membership is 1.

Set Operators

There are a number of operations that can be performed on sets. The most common are *union*, *intersection*, and *complement*.

The union of two sets is the set that contains all the elements from both sets. The union operator is usually written using the symbol ∪. Given the two sets A = {1, 2, 3, 4} and B = {3, 5, 7}, the union of A and B can be written as:

$$A \cup B = \{1,2,3,4,3,5,7\} \qquad (10.1)$$

The union of two sets is equivalent to ORing the sets together — a given element is in one OR the other.

The intersection of two sets, written using the symbol ∩, is the set containing all the elements present in both sets. Using the sets A and B from above, their intersection is written as:

$$A \cap B = \{3\} \qquad (10.2)$$

The intersection of two sets is equivalent to ANDing the sets together. Using our two sets above there is only one element that is in set A AND in set B, making the intersection of sets A and B {3}.

The complement of a set is the set containing all the elements in the universe of discourse not present in the set. In other words, it is the *inverse* of the set. Let's say the universe of discourse of A and B is A ∪ B as given in equation (10.1), then A's complement is B, and B's complement is A. The complement operator is usually written using the ' symbol, although sometimes it is denoted by a bar across the top of the set's name. Both options are shown in equation 10.3.

$$\begin{aligned} A' &= B \\ \overline{B} &= A \end{aligned} \qquad (10.3)$$

The complement operator is equivalent to NOT.

Fuzzy Sets

Crisp sets are useful but problematic in many situations. For instance, let's examine the universe of discourse of all IQs, and let's define sets for *Dumb*, *Average*, and *Clever* like so:

Dumb = {70, 71, 72, … 89}
Average = {90, 91, 92, … 109}
Clever = {110, 111, 112, … 129}

A graphical way of showing these crisp sets is shown in Figure 10.3. Note how the degree of membership of an element in any of the sets can be either 1 or 0.

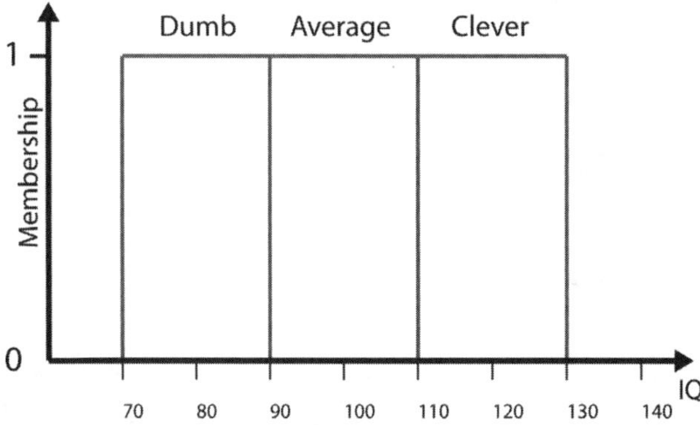

Figure 10.3

People's intelligence can now be categorized by assigning them to one of these sets based upon their IQ score. Clearly though, a person with an IQ of 109 is well above average intelligence and probably the majority of his peers would categorize him as clever. He's certainly much more intelligent than a person who has a score of 92 even though both fall into the same category. It's also ridiculous to compare a person with an IQ of 79 and a person of IQ 80 and come to the conclusion that one is dumb and the other isn't! This is where crisp sets fall down. Fuzzy sets allow elements to be assigned to them to a matter of degree.

Defining Fuzzy Boundaries with Membership Functions

A fuzzy set is defined by a *membership function*. These functions can be any arbitrary shape but are typically triangular or trapezoidal. Figure 10.4 shows a few examples of membership functions. Notice how they define a gradual transition from regions completely outside the set to regions completely within the set, thereby enabling a value to have *partial membership* to a set. This is the essence of fuzzy logic.

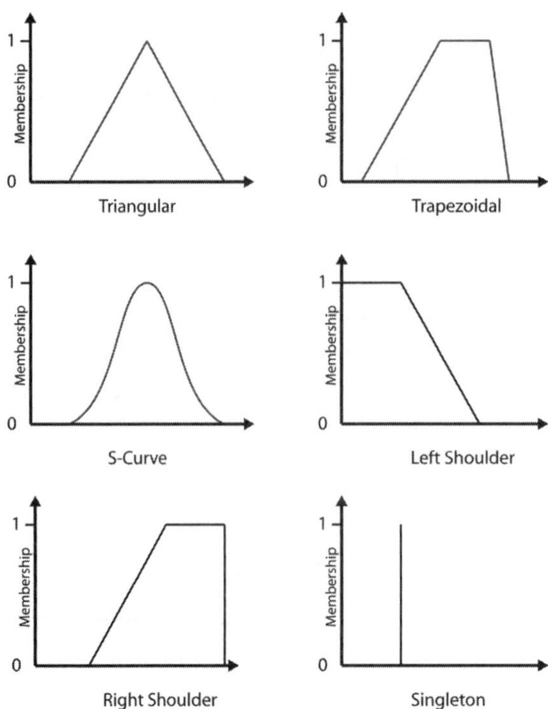

Figure 10.4. Some example membership functions. The singleton membership function is not really fuzzy — it's a special type of set that behaves like a discrete value. I've included it here though because singletons are occasionally used in the creation of fuzzy rules.

Figure 10.5 shows how the linguistic terms *Dumb*, *Average*, and *Clever* can be represented as fuzzy sets comprised of triangular membership functions. The dotted line shows how Brian, who has an IQ of 115, is a member of two sets. His degree of membership in *Clever* is 0.75 and in *Average* is 0.25. This is consistent with how a human would reason about Brian's

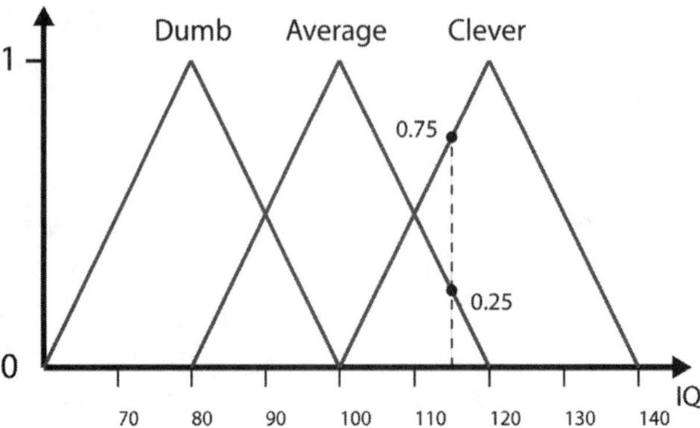

Figure 10.5. Dumb, Average, and Clever as fuzzy sets. The dotted line represents an IQ of 115, and its points of intersection with the sets Clever and Average represent its degree of membership in those sets.

intelligence. A human will consider him to be mostly clever, above average, which is exactly what can be inferred from his fuzzy set membership values.

NOTE It's worth noting that the linguistic terms associated with fuzzy sets can change their meaning when used in differing frames of reference. For example, the meaning of the fuzzy sets *Tall*, *Medium*, and *Short* will be different for Europeans than it would be for the pygmies of South America. All fuzzy sets, therefore, are defined and used within a context.

A membership function can be written in mathematical notation like this:

$$F_{Name\_of\_set}(x) \tag{10.4}$$

Using this notation we can write Brian's degree of membership, or DOM for short, in the fuzzy set *Clever* as:

$$Clever_{(Brian)} = F_{Clever}(115) = 0.75 \tag{10.5}$$

Fuzzy Set Operators

Intersections, unions, and complements of fuzzy sets are possible, just as they are with crisp sets. The fuzzy intersection operation is mathematically equivalent to the AND operator. The result of ANDing two or more fuzzy sets together is another fuzzy set. The fuzzy set of people who are *Average* AND *Clever* is shown graphically in Figure 10.6.

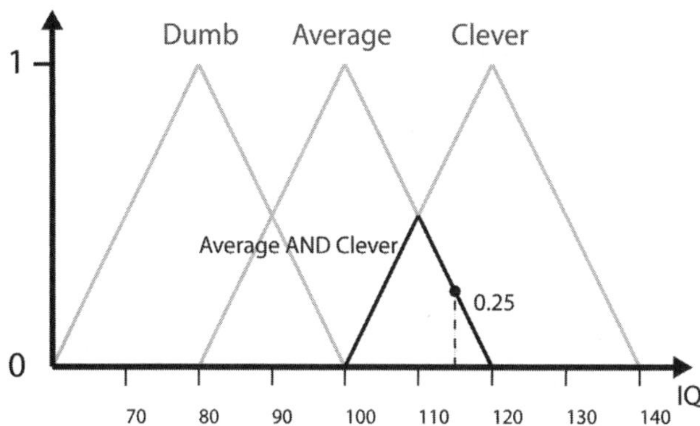

Figure 10.6. The set of people who are Average AND Clever

The graphical example illustrates well how the AND operator is equivalent to taking the minimum DOM (degree of membership) for each set a value is a member of. This is written mathematically as:

$$F_{Average \cap Clever}(x) = \min\left\{F_{Average}(x), F_{Clever}(x)\right\} \tag{10.6}$$

Brian's degree of membership in the set of people who are *Average* AND *Clever* is 0.25.

The union of fuzzy sets is equivalent to the OR operator. The compound set that is the result of ORing two or more sets together uses the *maximum* of the DOMs of the component sets. For the sets *Average* and *Clever* this is written as:

$$F_{Average \cup Clever}(x) = \max\left\{F_{Average}(x), F_{Clever}(x)\right\} \qquad (10.7)$$

Figure 10.7 shows the set of people who are *Average* OR *Clever*. Brian's membership in this set is 0.75.

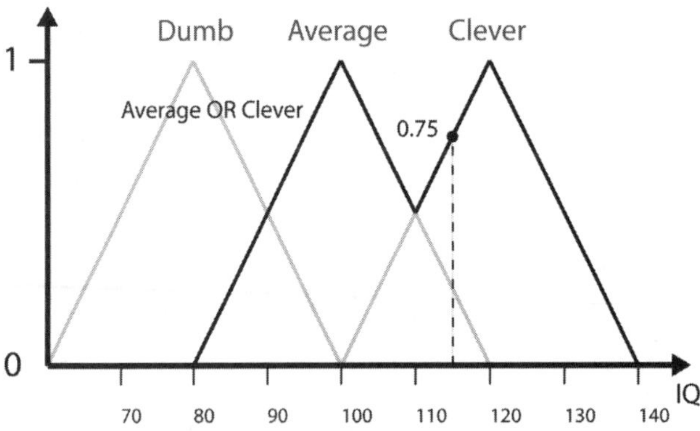

Figure 10.7. The set of people who are Average OR Clever

The complement of a value with a DOM of *m* is 1–*m*. Figure 10.8 describes the set of people who are NOT *Clever*. We saw earlier how Brian's degree of membership to *Clever* is 0.75, so his DOM to NOT *Clever* should be 1 – 0.75 = 0.25, which is exactly what we can see in the figure.

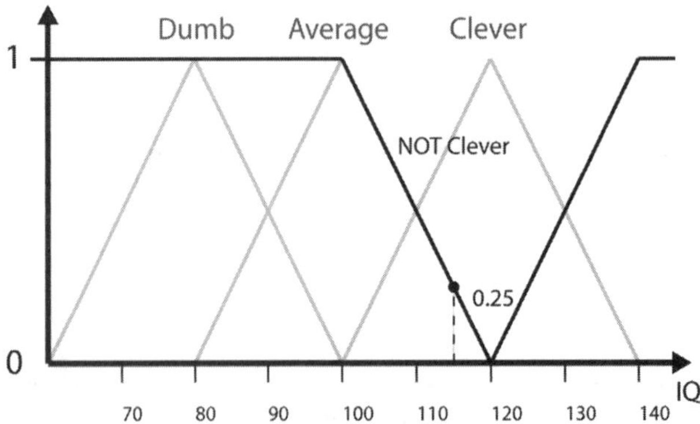

Figure 10.8. The complement of Clever

NOT *Clever* can be written mathematically as:

$$F_{Clever}(x)' = 1 - F_{Clever}(x) \tag{10.8}$$

Hedges

Hedges are unary operators that can be employed to modify the meaning of a fuzzy set. Two commonly used hedges are VERY and FAIRLY. For a fuzzy set A, VERY modifies it like so:

$$F_{VERY(A)} = (F_A(x))^2 \tag{10.9}$$

In other words, it results in the square of the membership degree. FAIRLY modifies a fuzzy set by taking the square root of the membership degree, like so:

$$F_{FAIRLY(A)} = \sqrt{F_A(x)} \tag{10.10}$$

The effect of these hedges is best seen graphically. Figure 10.9 shows how VERY narrows the membership function and how FAIRLY widens it. This is intuitive because the criteria for membership in a set modified by FAIRLY should be more relaxed than for the set itself. And the opposite holds for VERY — the criterion is tightened.

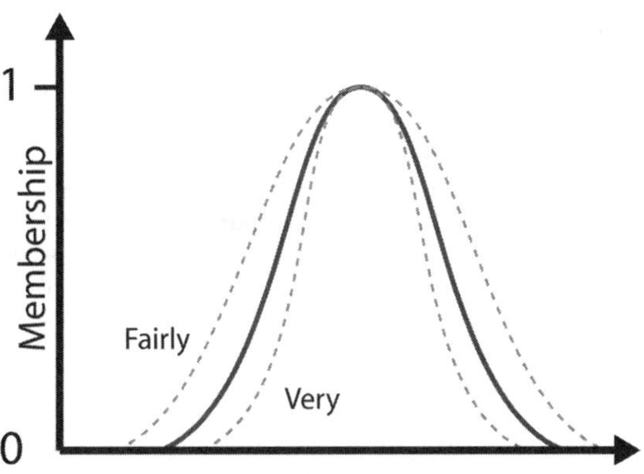

Figure 10.9. Modifying the shape of a membership function using fuzzy hedges

Fuzzy Linguistic Variables

A *fuzzy linguistic variable* (or FLV) is the composition of one or more fuzzy sets to represent a concept or domain qualitatively. Given our earlier example, the sets *Dumb*, *Average*, and *Clever* are members of the fuzzy linguistic variable **IQ**. This can be written in set notation as:

IQ = {*Dumb, Average, Clever*}

Here are some other examples of fuzzy linguistic variables and their component fuzzy sets:

Speed = {*Slow, Medium, Fast*}
Height = {*Midget, Short, Medium, Tall, Giant*}
Allegiance = {*Friend, Neutral, Foe*}
Target Heading = {*Far Left, Left, Center, Right, Far Right*}

Figure 10.10 shows the FLV **Target Heading** in graphical form. Notice how the membership functions of the member sets can be varied in shape and asymmetrical if the problem demands it. The collection of shapes (membership functions) that comprise the FLV is known as a *fuzzy manifold*, or *fuzzy surface*.

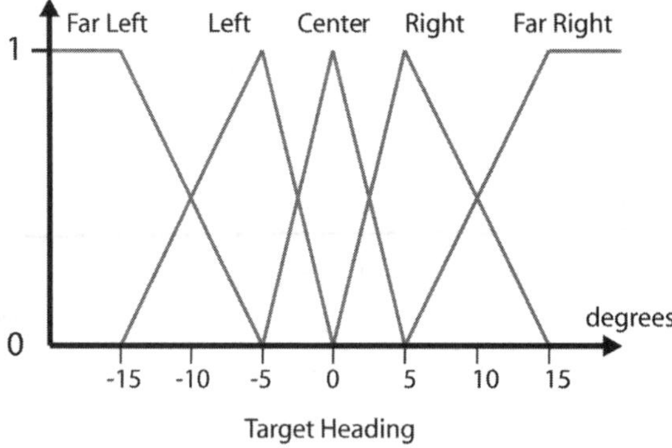

Figure 10.10. The FLV Target Heading

NOTE Practitioners of fuzzy logic seem unable to agree upon consistent terminology for describing the linguistic elements that comprise a fuzzy system (oh, the irony). Often you will find the expression "fuzzy linguistic variable" (or just "linguistic variable") applied to a collection of fuzzy sets *and* to the individual sets themselves. This can be confusing when reading the available literature.

Fuzzy Rules

This is where everything starts to come together. I realize you may be confused at the moment but hang in there; enlightenment will shortly be yours!

Fuzzy rules are comprised of an *antecedent* and a *consequent* in the form:

IF *antecedent* THEN *consequent*

The antecedent represents a condition and the consequent describes the consequence if that condition is satisfied. This type of rule is familiar to all programmers. We've all written code like:

IF Wizard.Health() <= 0 THEN Wizard.isDead()

The difference with fuzzy rules is that unlike conventional rules where the consequent either fires or not, in fuzzy systems the consequent can fire to a matter of degree. Here are some examples of fuzzy rules:

IF *Target_isFarRight* THEN *Turn_QuicklyToRight*

IF VERY(*Enemy_BadlyInjured*) THEN *Behavior_Aggressive*

IF *Target_isFarAway* AND *Allegiance_isEnemy* THEN *Shields_OnLowPower*

IF *Ball_isCloseToHole* AND *Green_isLevel* THEN *HitBall_Gently* AND *HitBall_DirectlyAtHole*

IF (*Bend_HairpinLeft* OR *Bend_HairpinRight*) AND *Track_SlightlyWet* THEN *Speed_VerySlow*

The antecedent, then, can be a single fuzzy term or the set that is the result of a combination of several fuzzy terms. The degree of membership of the antecedent defines the degree to which the consequent fires. A fuzzy inference system is typically comprised of many such rules, the number of which is proportional to the number of FLVs required for the problem domain and the number of membership sets those FLVs contain. Each time a fuzzy system iterates through its rule set it combines the consequents that have fired and defuzzifies the result to give a crisp value. More on the details of this in a moment but first, before we delve deeper, let's design some FLVs we can use to solve a real-world problem. Given a practical example you can sink your teeth into, I'm sure you'll find it much easier to see how all this stuff works together.

Designing FLVs for Weapon Selection

Because the rules a human player uses to decide when to change weapons can easily be described using linguistic terms, weapon selection is a good candidate for the application of fuzzy logic. Let's see how this idea can be applied to Raven.

To keep the example simple, we'll say the desirability of selecting a particular weapon from the inventory is dependent on two factors: the distance to the target and the amount of ammo. Each weapon class owns an instance of a fuzzy module, and each module is initialized with FLVs representing the linguistic terms **Distance to Target**, **Ammo Status** (antecedents), and **Desirability** (consequent), and also with rules pertinent to that weapon. The rules infer how desirable that weapon is for any given scenario, enabling a bot to select the weapon with the highest desirability score to be the current weapon.

The FLVs **Distance to Target** and **Desirability** are defined identically for each weapon type. **Ammo Status** and the rule set are custom built. The examples given in this chapter will focus on designing the FLVs and rule set for the rocket launcher.

Designing the Desirability FLV

We'll start by designing the fuzzy linguistic variable required to denote the consequent set: **Desirability**. There are a couple of important guidelines to adhere to when designing FLVs. They are:

- For any vertical line (representing an input value) drawn through the FLV, the sum of the DOMs in each of the fuzzy sets it intersects with should be approximately 1. This ensures a smooth transition between values over the FLV's fuzzy manifold (the combined shape of all membership sets).
- For any vertical line drawn through the FLV, it should only intersect with two or fewer fuzzy sets.

An FLV that breaks the first guideline is shown in Figure 10.11 A, and an FLV that breaks the second is shown in Figure 10.11 B.

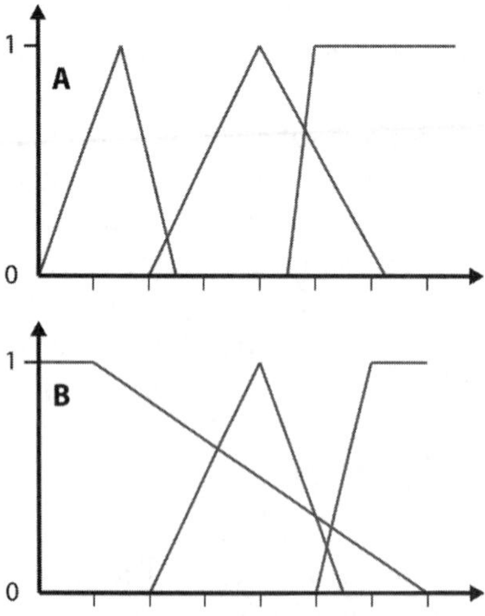

Figure 10.11. Badly designed FLVs

The FLV **Desirability** is required to represent the domain of all scores from 0 to 100. Therefore its member sets must adequately cover that range (while adhering to the guidelines). I have chosen to use three member sets: a left-shouldered set, a triangular set, and a right-shouldered set, representing the linguistic terms *Undesirable*, *Desirable*, and *VeryDesirable* as shown in Figure 10.12.

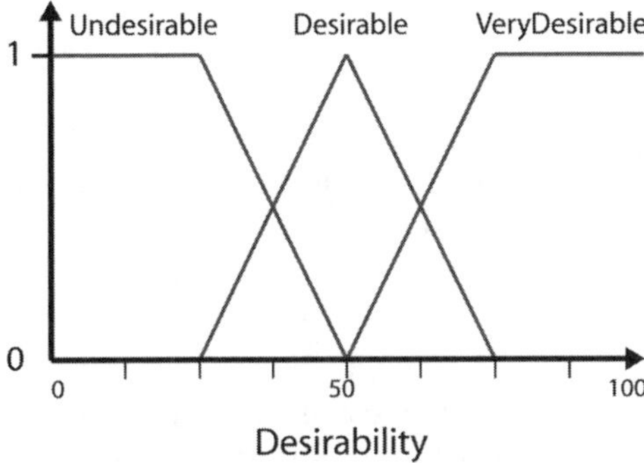

Figure 10.12. Desirability

Designing the Distance to Target FLV

Next, we'll consider the antecedent: **Distance to Target**. Once again the FLV is comprised of three sets, named *Target_Close*, *Target_Medium*, and *Target_Far*. These three terms are perfectly adequate to enable an expert (that's us folks) to determine rules for weapon selection. When I'm playing a game I think of the term "close" to mean almost next to me — at the sort of range where you might consider hand-to-hand combat. Therefore I've set the peak of the fuzzy set *Target_Close* at the distance 25 pixels, which I feel is about right given the scale of a typical Raven map (a bot has a bounding radius of about 10 pixels). I've chosen to use 150 pixels as the peak for *Target_Medium* because that feels about right, and I've chosen to make *Target_Far* a shoulder shape that peaks at 300 and then plateaus to 400. Notice how I'm not too concerned about the specific values; I'm just using values that "feel" correct. **Distance to Target** is shown in Figure 10.13.

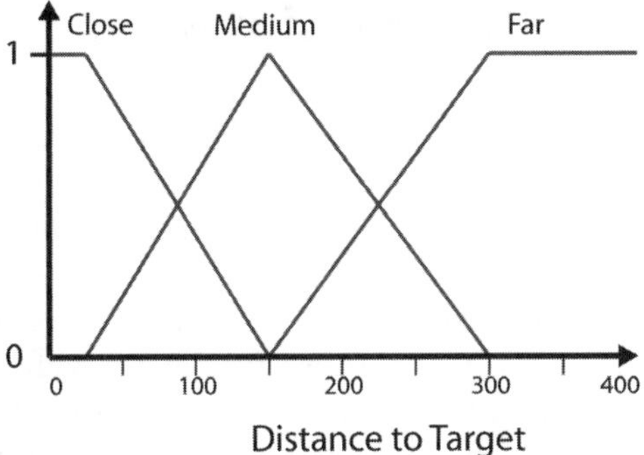

Figure 10.13. Distance to Target

Designing the Ammo Status FLV

Finally, we'll tackle **Ammo Status**, which will utilize the fuzzy sets *Ammo_Low*, *Ammo_Okay*, and *Ammo_Loads*. Because linguistic terms are *defined within a context* (since what you might consider an okay amount of ammo for, say, a grenade launcher, is unlikely to be an okay amount for a machine gun), this FLV varies from weapon to weapon.

A rocket launcher is able to shoot two rockets per second, so I'd say that an okay amount of ammo is about 10 rockets. If carrying 30 or so rockets, I'd consider myself to have loads of ammo and anything less than 10 is low. With this in mind I've designed **Ammo Status** as shown in Figure 10.14.

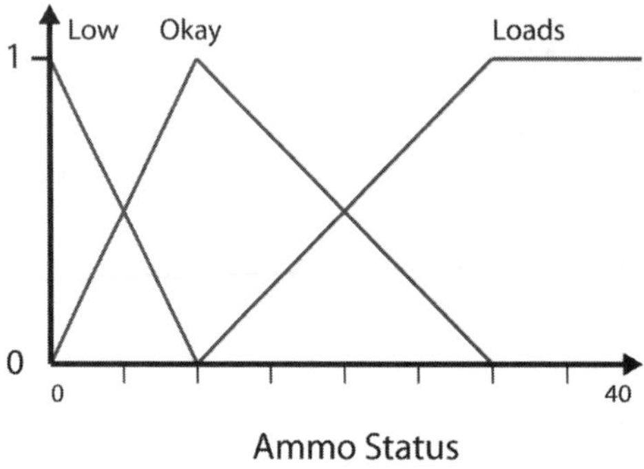

Figure 10.14. Ammo Status for the rocket launcher

As you can see, designing FLVs is mainly common sense: You simply examine and translate your own or, even better, an expert's knowledge about the domain.

Designing the Rule Set for Weapon Selection

Now that we have some fuzzy terms to play with, let's work on the rules. To cover all the possibilities, a rule must be created for each possible combination of antecedent sets. The FLVs **Ammo Status** and **Distance to Target** each contain three member sets, so to cover every combination nine rules must be defined.

Once again I'm going to play the role of expert. In my "expert" opinion, a rocket launcher is a great medium distance weapon but it's dangerous to use close up because you're likely to get damaged by the blast of the explosion. Also, because rockets move slowly, it's a poor choice of weapon when the target is far away since the rockets can be easily dodged. With these facts in mind, here are the nine rules I've created for determining the desirability of using a rocket launcher:

Rule 1. IF *Target_Far* AND *Ammo_Loads* THEN *Desirable*
Rule 2. IF *Target_Far* AND *Ammo_Okay* THEN *Undesirable*
Rule 3. IF *Target_Far* AND *Ammo_Low* THEN *Undesirable*
Rule 4. IF *Target_Medium* AND *Ammo_Loads* THEN *VeryDesirable*
Rule 5. IF *Target_Medium* AND *Ammo_Okay* THEN *VeryDesirable*
Rule 6. IF *Target_Medium* AND *Ammo_Low* THEN *Desirable*
Rule 7. IF *Target_Close* AND *Ammo_Loads* THEN *Undesirable*
Rule 8. IF *Target_Close* AND *Ammo_Okay* THEN *Undesirable*
Rule 9. IF *Target_Close* AND *Ammo_Low* THEN *Undesirable*

Note that these rules are only my opinion and will reflect my level of expertise in the game. When you design the rules for your own game, consult the best player you have on your development team because the more expert the player you derive the rules from, the better your AI will perform. This makes sense in the same way that Michael Schumacher will be able to describe a much better set of rules for driving a Formula One racing car than you or me.

Fuzzy Inference

It's now time to study the fuzzy inference procedure. This is where we present the system with some values to see which rules fire and to what degree. Fuzzy inference follows these steps:

1. For each rule,
   - 1a. For each antecedent, calculate the degree of membership of the input data.
   - 1b. Calculate the rule's inferred conclusion based upon the values determined in 1a.
2. Combine all the inferred conclusions into a single conclusion (a fuzzy set).
3. For crisp values, the conclusion from 2 must be defuzzified.

Let's now work through these steps using some of the rules we've created for weapon selection and some crisp input values. Let's say the target is at a distance of 200 pixels and the amount of ammo remaining is 8 rockets.

One rule at a time then…

Rule One

IF *Target_Far* AND *Ammo_Loads* THEN *Desirable*

The degree of membership of the value 200 to the set *Target_Far* is 0.33. The degree of membership of the value 8 in the set *Ammo_Loads* is 0. The AND operator results in the minimum of these values so the inferred conclusion for Rule 1 is *Desirable* = 0. In other words, the rule doesn't fire. Figure 10.15 shows this rule graphically.

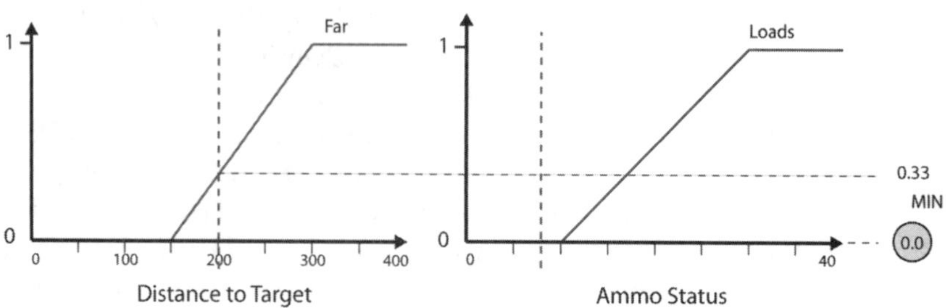

Figure 10.15. The value enclosed by the circle indicates the inferred conclusion.

Rule Two

IF *Target_Far* AND *Ammo_Okay* THEN *Undesirable*

For the second rule the degree of membership of the value 200 to the set *Target_Far* is 0.33. The degree of membership of the value 8 in the set *Ammo_Okay* is 0.78. The inferred conclusion for Rule 2 therefore is *Undesirable* = 0.33. See Figure 10.16.

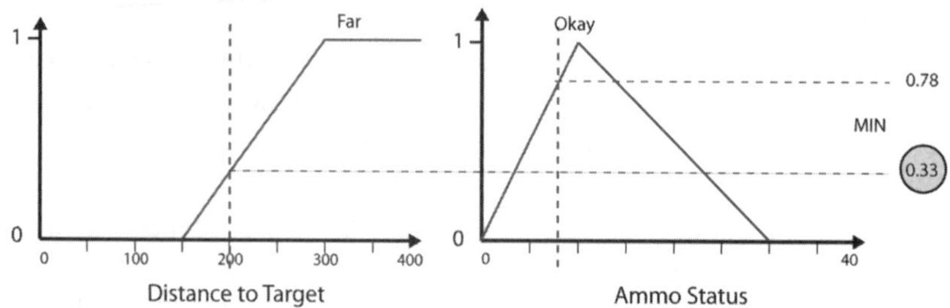

Figure 10.16. Rule 2

Rule Three

IF *Target_Far* AND *Ammo_Low* THEN *Undesirable*

Appling the same values to the third rule, the degree of membership of the value 200 to the set *Target_Far* is 0.33. The degree of membership of the value 8 in the set *Ammo_Low* is 0.2. The inferred conclusion for Rule 3 therefore is *Undesirable* = 0.2. See Figure 10.17.

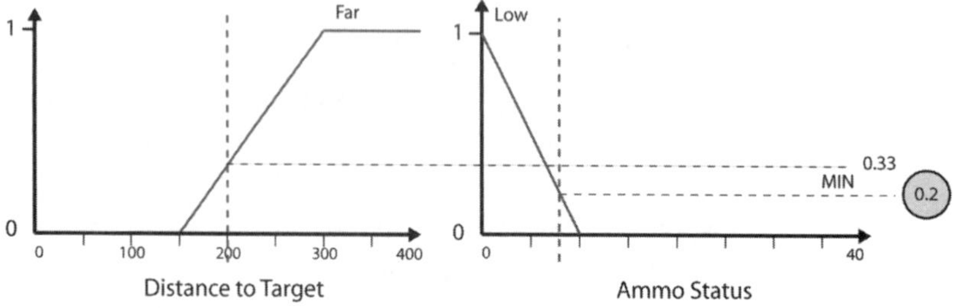

Figure 10.17. Rule 3

I'm sure you've got the gist of this by now so to spare a lot of repetition the inferred results for all the rules are summarized by the matrix shown in Figure 10.18. (This type of matrix is known as a *fuzzy associative matrix*, or FAM for short.)

	Target_Close	Target_Medium	Target_Far
Ammo_Low	Undesirable 0	Desirable 0.2	Undesirable 0.2
Ammo_Okay	Undesirable 0	VeryDesirable 0.67	Undesirable 0.33
Ammo_Loads	Undesirable 0	VeryDesirable 0	Desirable 0

Figure 10.18. The FAM for the weapon selection rule base given the input values target distance = 200 and ammo status = 8. The shaded cells highlight rules that have fired.

Note that *VeryDesirable* has fired once to a degree of 0.67. *Desirable* has fired once to a degree of 0.2, and *Undesirable* has fired twice with the degrees 0.2 and 0.33. One way to think of these values is as confidence levels. Given the input data, the fuzzy rules have inferred the result *VeryDesirable* with a confidence of 0.67 and the result *Desirable* with a confidence of 0.2. But what conclusion is inferred for *Undesirable*, which has fired twice? Well, there are a few ways of handling multiple confidences. The two most popular are bounded sum (sum and bound to 1) and maximum value (equivalent to ORing the confidences together). It doesn't make a vast amount of difference which method you choose. I prefer to OR the values together, which in this example results in a confidence for *Undesirable* of 0.33.

To summarize, Table 10.1 lists the inferred conclusions of applying the values of distance to target = 200 and ammo status = 8 to all the rules.

Table 10.1

Consequent	Confidence
Undesirable	0.33
Desirable	0.2
Very Desirable	0.67

These results are shown graphically in Figure 10.19. Notice how the membership function of each consequent is clipped to the level of confidence.

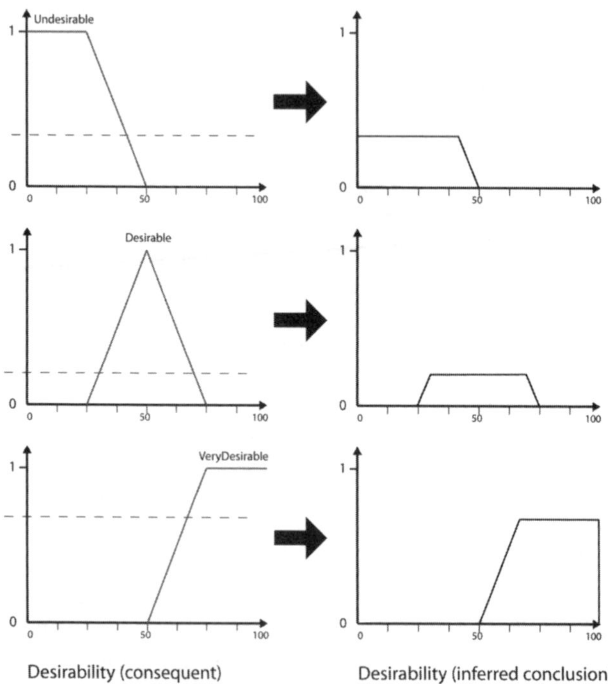

Figure 10.19. The inferred results of processing the rule set for weapon selection

The next step is to combine the inferred results into a single fuzzy manifold. See Figure 10.20.

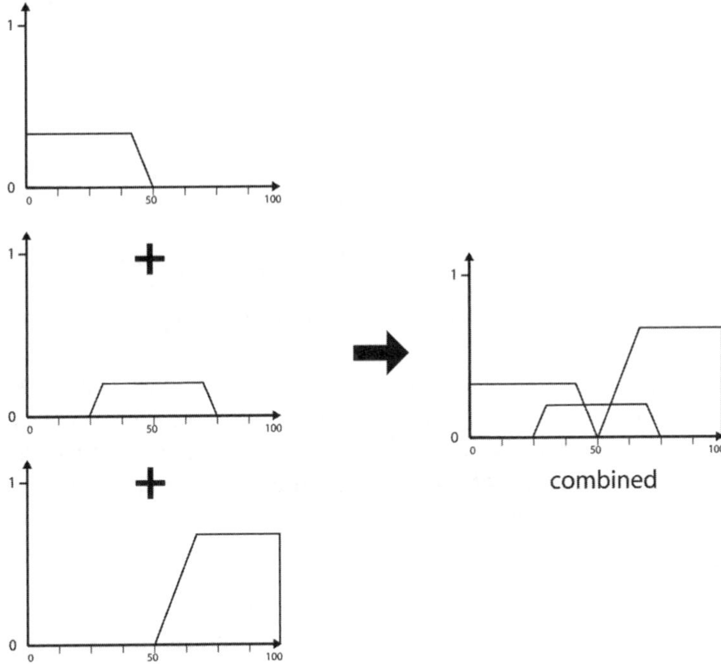

Figure 10.20. Combining the conclusions

Now that we have a composite fuzzy set representing the inferred conclusion of all the rules in the rule base, it's time to turn the process around and convert this output set into a single crisp value. This is achieved by a process called defuzzification.

Defuzzification

Defuzzification is the reverse of fuzzification: the process of turning a fuzzy set into a crisp value. There are many techniques for doing this and the next few pages will be spent examining the most common.

Mean of Maximum (MOM)

The mean of maximum — MOM for short — method of defuzzification calculates the average of those output values that have the highest confidence degrees. Figure 10.21 shows how this technique can be used to determine a crisp value from the output distribution for **Desirability** calculated earlier.

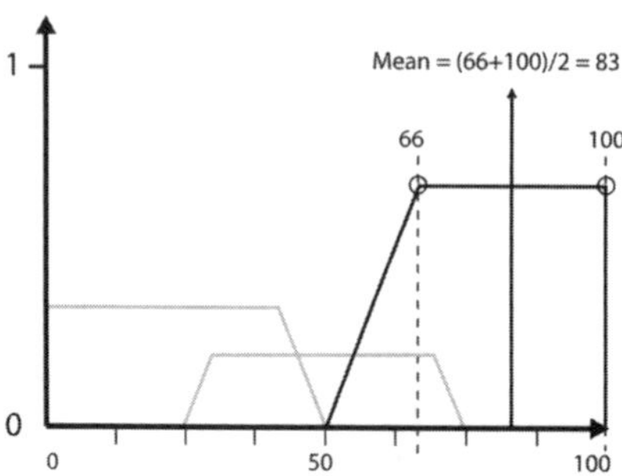

Figure 10.21. The mean of maximum method results in a desirability score of 83.

One problem with this method is it doesn't take into account those sets in the output that do not have confidences equal to the highest (like those shown in the figure in gray), which can bias the resultant crisp value to one end of the domain. More accurate fuzzification methods such as the ones listed below resolve this problem.

Centroid

The centroid method is the most accurate but is also the most complex to calculate. It works by determining the center of mass of the output sets. If you imagine each member set of the output set cut out of card stock and then glued together to form the shape of the fuzzy manifold, the center of mass is the position where the resultant shape would balance if placed on a ruler. See Figure 10.22.

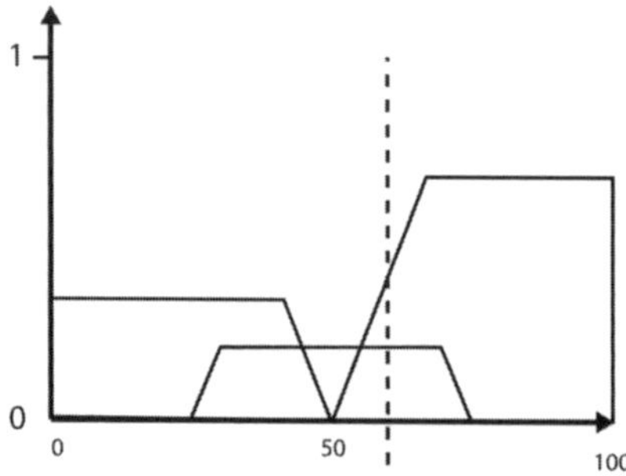

Figure 10.22. Finding the centroid

The centroid of a fuzzy manifold is calculated by slicing up the manifold into *s* sample points and calculating the sum of the contribution of the DOM at each sample point to the total, divided by the sum of the DOMs of the samples. The formula is given in (10.11).

$$CrispValue = \frac{\sum_{s=DomainMin}^{s=DomainMax} s \times DOM(s)}{\sum_{s=DomainMin}^{s=DomainMax} DOM(s)} \qquad (10.11)$$

where s is the value at each sample point and DOM(s) is the degree of membership in the FLV of that value. The more sample points chosen to do the calculation, the more accurate the result, although in practice 10 to 20 samples usually suffice.

Now I realize some of you may be having palpitations at this point so it's probably best if I clarify using an example. We'll defuzzify the fuzzy manifold resulting from running the weapon selection rules using the 10 sample points shown in Figure 10.23.

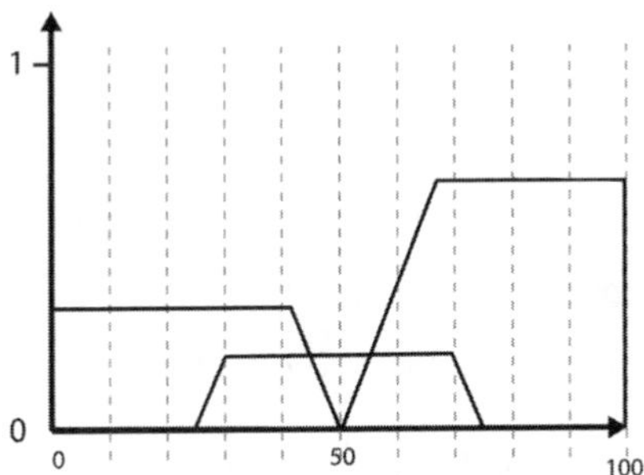

Figure 10.23. Calculating the centroid

For each sample point, the DOM in each member set is calculated. Table 10.2 summarizes the results. (Note: The values given for the samples at 30 and 70 are imprecise as they are simply estimated from Figure 10.23, but they are sufficiently accurate for this demonstration.)

Table 10.2

Value	Undesirable	Desirable	VeryDesirable	Sum
10	0.33	0	0	0.33
20	0.33	0	0	0.33
30	0.33	0.2	0	0.53
40	0.33	0.2	0	0.53
50	0	0.2	0	0.2
60	0	0.2	0.4	0.6
70	0	0.2	0.67	0.87
80	0	0	0.67	0.67
90	0	0	0.67	0.67
100	0	0	0.67	0.67

Now to plug the numbers into equation (10.11). First let's calculate the numerator (the part of the equation above the line).

$$
\begin{aligned}
&10 \times 0.33 + \\
&20 \times 0.33 + \\
&30 \times 0.53 + \\
&40 \times 0.53 + \\
&50 \times 0.2 + \\
&60 \times 0.6 + \\
&70 \times 0.87 + \\
&80 \times 0.67 + \\
&90 \times 0.67 + \\
&100 \times 0.67 = 334.8
\end{aligned} \tag{10.12}
$$

And now the denominator (the part below the line):

$$0.33 + 0.33 + 0.53 + 0.53 + 0.2 + 0.6 + 0.87 + 0.67 + 0.67 + 0.67 = 5.4 \tag{10.13}$$

Dividing the numerator by the denominator gives the crisp value:

$$
\begin{aligned}
Desirability &= \frac{334.8}{5.4} \\
&= 62
\end{aligned} \tag{10.14}
$$

Average of Maxima (MaxAv)

The maximum or *representative value* of a fuzzy set is the value where membership in that set is 1. For triangular sets this is the simply the value at the midpoint; for sets containing plateaus — such as right shoulder, left shoulder, and trapezoidal sets — this value is the average of the values at the beginning and end of the plateau. The *average of maxima* (MaxAv for short) defuzzification method scales the representative value of each consequent by its confidence and takes the average, like so:

$$\text{Crisp Value} = \frac{\sum \text{representative value} \times \text{confidence}}{\sum \text{confidence}} \tag{10.15}$$

The representative values of the sets comprising the output manifold are summarized in Table 10.3.

Table 10.3

Set	Representative Value	Confidence
Undesirable	12.5	0.33
Desirable	50	0.2
VeryDesirable	87.5	0.67

Plugging these values into the equation gives the desirability as a crisp value:

$$Desirability = \frac{12.5 \times 0.33 + 50 \times 0.2 + 87.5 \times 0.67}{0.33 + 0.2 + 0.67}$$
$$= \frac{72.75}{1.2} \quad (10.16)$$
$$Desirability = 60.625$$

As you can see, this method has produced a value very close to that calculated by the more accurate but costlier to calculate centroid technique (and it would have been closer had I not estimated some of the values in the centroid calculation) and therefore, this is the one I'd advise you use in your games and applications.

Well, that's it! We've gone from crisp values (distance to target = 200, ammo status = 8) to fuzzy sets, to inference, and back to a crisp value representing the desirability of using the rocket launcher (83, 62, or 60.625 depending on the defuzzification method). If this process is repeated for each weapon type a bot is carrying, it's a simple matter to select the one with the highest desirability score to be the weapon the bot should use given its current situation.

From Theory to Application: Coding a Fuzzy Logic Module

It's now time to see exactly how the classes required to implement fuzzy logic have been designed and how they are integrated with Raven.

The FuzzyModule Class

The `FuzzyModule` class is the heart of the fuzzy system. It contains a `std::map` of fuzzy linguistic variables and a `std::vector` containing the rule base. In addition, it has methods for adding FLVs and rules to the module and for running the module through the process of fuzzification, inference, and defuzzification.

```
class FuzzyModule
{
private:

  typedef std::map<std::string, FuzzyVariable*> VarMap;

public:

  //a client must pass one of these values to the defuzzify method.
  //This module only supports the MaxAv and centroid methods.
  enum DefuzzifyType{max_av, centroid};

  //when calculating the centroid of the fuzzy manifold this value is used
  //to determine how many cross sections should be sampled
  enum {NumSamplesToUseForCentroid = 15};

private:

  //a map of all the fuzzy variables this module uses
  VarMap                  m_Variables;

  //a vector containing all the fuzzy rules
  std::vector<FuzzyRule*>   m_Rules;

  //zeros the DOMs of the consequents of each rule. Used by Defuzzify()
  inline void SetConfidencesOfConsequentsToZero();


public:

  ~FuzzyModule();

  //creates a new "empty" fuzzy variable and returns a reference to it.
  FuzzyVariable&  CreateFLV(const std::string& VarName);

  //adds a rule to the module
  void            AddRule(FuzzyTerm& antecedent, FuzzyTerm& consequence);

  //this method calls the Fuzzify method of the named FLV
  inline void     Fuzzify(const std::string& NameOfFLV, double val);

  //given a fuzzy variable and a defuzzification method this returns a
  //crisp value
  inline double   DeFuzzify(const std::string& key, DefuzzifyType method);
};
```

A client will typically create an instance of this class for each AI that requires a unique fuzzy rule set. FLVs can then be added to the module using the `CreateFLV` method. This method returns a reference to the newly created FLV. Here's an example of how a module is used to create the fuzzy linguistic variables required for the weapon selection example:

```
FuzzyModule fm;
FuzzyVariable& DistToTarget = fm.CreateFLV("DistToTarget");
```

```
FuzzyVariable& Desirability = fm.CreateFLV("Desirability");
FuzzyVariable& AmmoStatus   = fm.CreateFLV("AmmoStatus");
```

At this point in time though, each of these FLVs is "empty." To be useful, an FLV must be initialized with some member sets. Let's take a look at how the different types of fuzzy sets are encapsulated.

The FuzzySet Base Class

Since it's necessary to manipulate fuzzy sets using a common interface, all fuzzy set types are derived from the abstract class FuzzySet. Each class contains a data member to store the degree of membership of the value to be fuzzified. Concrete FuzzySets own additional data for describing the shape of their membership function.

```
class FuzzySet
{
protected:

  //this will hold the degree of membership in this set of a given value
  double         m_dDOM;

  //this is the maximum of the set's membership function. For instance, if
  //the set is triangular then this will be the peak point of the triangle.
  //If the set has a plateau then this value will be the midpoint of the
  //plateau. This value is set in the constructor to avoid run-time
  //calculation of midpoint values.
  double         m_dRepresentativeValue;

public:

  FuzzySet(double RepVal):m_dDOM(0.0), m_dRepresentativeValue(RepVal){}

  //return the degree of membership in this set of the given value. NOTE:
  //this does not set m_dDOM to the DOM of the value passed as the parameter.
  //This is because the centroid defuzzification method also uses this method
  //to determine the DOMs of the values it uses as its sample points.
  virtual double     CalculateDOM(double val)const = 0;

  //if this fuzzy set is part of a consequent FLV and it is fired by a rule,
  //then this method sets the DOM (in this context, the DOM represents a
  //confidence level) to the maximum of the parameter value or the set's
  //existing m_dDOM value
  void                ORwithDOM(double val);

  //accessor methods
  double              GetRepresentativeVal()const;
  void                ClearDOM(){m_dDOM = 0.0;}
  double              GetDOM()const{return m_dDOM;}
  void                SetDOM(double val);
};
```

Let's now take a close look at a couple of concrete fuzzy set classes.

The Triangular Fuzzy Set Class

A triangular fuzzy set is defined by three values: a peak point, a left offset, and a right offset. See Figure 10.24.

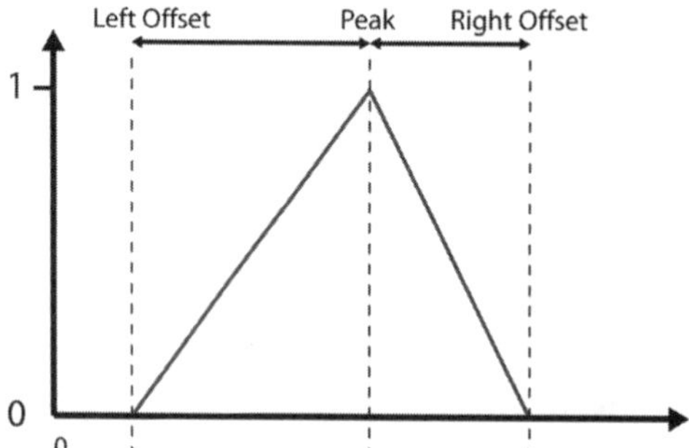

Figure 10.24. A triangular membership function

The declaration of the class encapsulating this data is as follows:

```
class FuzzySet_Triangle : public FuzzySet
{
private:

  //the values that define the shape of this FLV
  double   m_dPeakPoint;
  double   m_dLeftOffset;
  double   m_dRightOffset;

public:

  FuzzySet_Triangle(double mid,
                    double lft,
                    double rgt):FuzzySet(mid),
                                m_dPeakPoint(mid),
                                m_dLeftOffset(lft),
                                m_dRightOffset(rgt)
  {}

  //this method calculates the degree of membership for a particular value
  double CalculateDOM(double val)const;
};
```

As you can see, it's very straightforward. Notice how the midpoint of the triangle is passed to the constructor of the base class as the representative value for this shape. The interface from `FuzzySet` only defines one method that must be implemented: `CalculateDOM`, the method that determines the degree of membership of a value to the set. The following is the code for that implementation:

```
double FuzzySet_Triangle::CalculateDOM(double val)const
{
  //test for the case where the triangle's left or right offsets are zero
```

```
  //(to prevent divide by zero errors below)
  if ( (isEqual(m_dRightOffset, 0.0) && (isEqual(m_dPeakPoint, val))) ||
       (isEqual(m_dLeftOffset, 0.0) && (isEqual(m_dPeakPoint, val))) )
  {
    return 1.0;
  }

  //find DOM if left of center
  if ( (val <= m_dPeakPoint) && (val >= (m_dPeakPoint - m_dLeftOffset)) )
  {
    double grad = 1.0 / m_dLeftOffset;

    return grad * (val - (m_dPeakPoint - m_dLeftOffset));
  }

  //find DOM if right of center
  else if ( (val > m_dPeakPoint) && (val < (m_dPeakPoint + m_dRightOffset)) )
  {
    double grad = 1.0 / -m_dRightOffset;

    return grad * (val - m_dPeakPoint) + 1.0;
  }

  //out of range of this FLV, return zero
  else
  {
    return 0.0;
  }
}
```

The Right Shoulder Fuzzy Set Class

A right-shouldered fuzzy set is also parameterized by three values: a peak point, a left offset, and a right offset. See Figure 10.25.

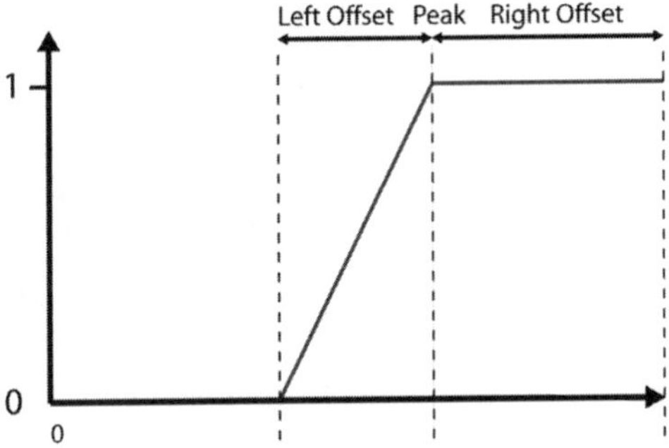

Figure 10.25. A right shoulder membership function

Once again the class definition is straightforward:

```
class FuzzySet_RightShoulder : public FuzzySet
{
private:
```

```
  //the values that define the shape of this FLV
  double   m_dPeakPoint;
  double   m_dLeftOffset;
  double   m_dRightOffset;

public:

  FuzzySet_RightShoulder(double peak,
                         double LeftOffset,
                         double RightOffset):

                  FuzzySet( ((peak + RightOffset) + peak) / 2),
                  m_dPeakPoint(peak),
                  m_dLeftOffset(LeftOffset),
                  m_dRightOffset(RightOffset)

  {}

  //this method calculates the degree of membership for a particular value
  double CalculateDOM(double val)const;
};
```

This time the representative value is the midpoint of the plateau of the shoulder.

The `CalculateDOM` method is also slightly different.

```
double FuzzySet_RightShoulder::CalculateDOM(double val)const
{
  //check for case where the offset may be zero
  if (isEqual(0, m_dLeftOffset) && isEqual(val,m_dMidPoint))
  {
    return 1.0;
  }

  //find DOM if left of center
  if ( (val <= m_dMidPoint) && (val > (m_dMidPoint - m_dLeftOffset)) )
  {
    double grad = 1.0 / m_dLeftOffset;

    return grad * (val - (m_dMidPoint - m_dLeftOffset));
  }

  //find DOM if right of center
  else if (val > m_dMidPoint)
  {
    return 1.0;
  }

  //out of range of this FLV, return zero
  else
  {
    return 0.0;
  }
}
```

Again, it's all very straightforward. I don't want to waste paper listing the code for the other fuzzy sets; they're just as clear-cut and easy to understand. Let's move on to the fuzzy linguistic variable class.

Creating a Fuzzy Linguistic Variable Class

The fuzzy linguistic variable class `FuzzyVariable` contains a `std::map` of pointers to instances of `FuzzySets` — the sets that make up its manifold. In addition, it has methods for adding fuzzy sets and for fuzzifying and defuzzifying values.

Whenever a member set is created and added to an FLV, the min/max ranges of the FLV are recalculated and assigned to the values `m_dMinRange` and `m_dMaxRange`. Keeping a record of the range of the domain of the FLV in this way allows the logic to determine if a value presented for fuzzification is out of bounds and to exit with an assertion if necessary.

Here's the class declaration:

```
class FuzzyVariable
{
private:

  typedef std::map<std::string, FuzzySet*>  MemberSets;

private:

  //disallow copies
  FuzzyVariable(const FuzzyVariable&);
  FuzzyVariable& operator=(const FuzzyVariable&);

private:

  //a map of the fuzzy sets that comprise this variable
  MemberSets   m_MemberSets;

  //the minimum and maximum value of the range of this variable
  double       m_dMinRange;
  double       m_dMaxRange;


  //this method is called with the upper and lower bound of a set each time a
  //new set is added to adjust the upper and lower range values accordingly
  void AdjustRangeToFit(double min, double max);

  //a client retrieves a reference to a fuzzy variable when an instance is
  //created via FuzzyModule::CreateFLV(). To prevent the client from deleting
  //the instance the FuzzyVariable destructor is made private and the
  //FuzzyModule class made a friend.
  ~FuzzyVariable();

  friend class FuzzyModule;
```

```
public:

  FuzzyVariable():m_dMinRange(0.0),m_dMaxRange(0.0){}

  //the following methods create instances of the sets named in the method
  //name and adds them to the member set map. Each time a set of any type is
  //added the m_dMinRange and m_dMaxRange are adjusted accordingly. All of the
  //methods return a proxy class representing the newly created instance. This
  //proxy set can be used as an operand when creating the rule base.
  FzSet  AddLeftShoulderSet(std::string name,
                            double      minBound,
                            double      peak,
                            double      maxBound);

  FzSet  AddRightShoulderSet(std::string name,
                             double      minBound,
                             double      peak,
                             double      maxBound);

  FzSet  AddTriangularSet(std::string name,
                          double      minBound,
                          double      peak,
                          double      maxBound);

  FzSet  AddSingletonSet(std::string name,
                         double      minBound,
                         double      peak,
                         double      maxBound);


  //fuzzify a value by calculating its DOM in each of this variable's subsets
  void        Fuzzify(double val);

  //defuzzify the variable using the MaxAv method
  double       DeFuzzifyMaxAv()const;

  //defuzzify the variable using the centroid method
  double       DeFuzzifyCentroid(int NumSamples)const;
};
```

Notice how the methods for creating and adding sets do not use the same parameters used by the fuzzy set classes themselves. For example, in addition to a string representing the name, the `AddLeftShoulderSet` method takes as parameters the minimum bound, a peak point, and a maximum bound, whereas the `FuzzySet_Triangle` class uses values specifying a midpoint, a left offset, and a right offset. This is simply to make the methods more instinctive for clients to use. Typically, when creating FLVs you will sketch out their member sets on paper (or imagine them in your head), making it a lot easier to read off the values left to right instead of calculating all the offsets.

Let's build on our example and add some member sets to DistToTarget.

```
FuzzyModule fm;
FuzzyVariable& DistToTarget = fm.CreateFLV("DistToTarget");

FzSet Target_Close = DistToTarget.AddLeftShoulderSet("Target_Close",
                                                      0,
                                                      25,
                                                      150);

FzSet Target_Medium = DistToTarget.AddTriangularSet("Target_Medium",
                                                     25,
                                                     50,
                                                     300);

FzSet Target_Far = DistToTarget.AddRightShoulderSet("Target_Far",
                                                     150,
                                                     300,
                                                     500);
```

These few lines of code create the FLV shown in Figure 10.26.

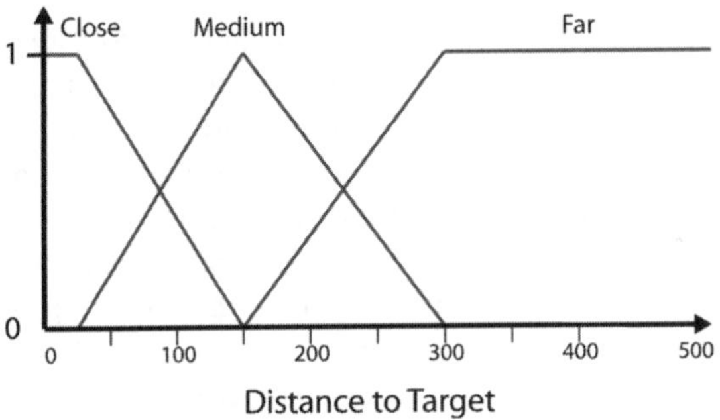

Figure 10.26

Notice how an instance of a FzSet is returned by each of the set addition methods. This is a proxy class that mimics the functionality of a concrete FuzzySet. The concrete instances themselves are contained within FuzzyVariable::m_MemberSets. These proxies are used as operands when constructing a fuzzy rule base.

Designing Classes for Building Fuzzy Rules

This is undoubtedly the gnarliest part of coding a fuzzy system. As you've learned, each fuzzy rule takes the form:

IF *antecedent* THEN *consequent*

where the antecedent and consequent can be single fuzzy sets or composite sets that are the results of operations. To be flexible the fuzzy module must be able to handle rules using not only the AND operator but also the OR and NOT operators and fuzzy hedges such as VERY and FAIRLY. In other words, the module should be able to cope with rules like the following:

IF a1 and a2 THEN c1

IF VERY(a1) AND (a2 OR a3) THEN c1

IF [(a1 AND a2) OR (NOT(a3) AND VERY(a4))] THEN [c1 AND c2]

Within the final rule observe how the OR operator is operating on the result of (a1 AND a2) and the result of (NOT(a3) AND VERY(a4)). In turn, the AND in the second term is operating on the results of NOT(a3) and VERY(a4). If that isn't complex enough, the rule has two consequents ANDed together. Obviously this example is well over the top and it's *extremely* unlikely a game AI programmer will ever require a rule such as this (although it wouldn't be too uncommon a sight in many fuzzy expert systems), but it illustrates my point well — any operator class worth its salt must be able to handle individual operands and compositions of operands and operators identically. This is clearly another area where the composite design pattern comes to the rescue.

To reiterate: The idea behind the composite pattern is to design a common interface for both composite and atomic objects to implement; when a request is made of the composite it will forward it to one or more of its children (see Chapter 9 if you require a more detailed explanation of the composite pattern). In fuzzy rules, operands (fuzzy sets) are atomic objects, and operators (AND, OR, VERY, etc.) are composites. Therefore, a class is required that defines a common interface for both these types of objects to implement. That class is called `FuzzyTerm` and it looks like this:

```
class FuzzyTerm
{
public:

  virtual ~FuzzyTerm(){}

  //all terms must implement a virtual constructor
  virtual FuzzyTerm* Clone()const = 0;

  //retrieves the degree of membership of the term
  virtual double      GetDOM()const=0;

  //clears the degree of membership of the term
  virtual void       ClearDOM()=0;

  // method for updating the DOM of a consequent when a rule fires
  virtual void       ORwithDOM(double val)=0;
};
```

Because any type of fuzzy operation on one or more sets results in a composite fuzzy set, this small interface is adequate to define objects for use in the construction of fuzzy rules. Figure 10.27 shows the relationship between the FuzzyTerm class, the fuzzy AND operator class FzAND (composite), and the FzSet fuzzy set proxy object (atomic).

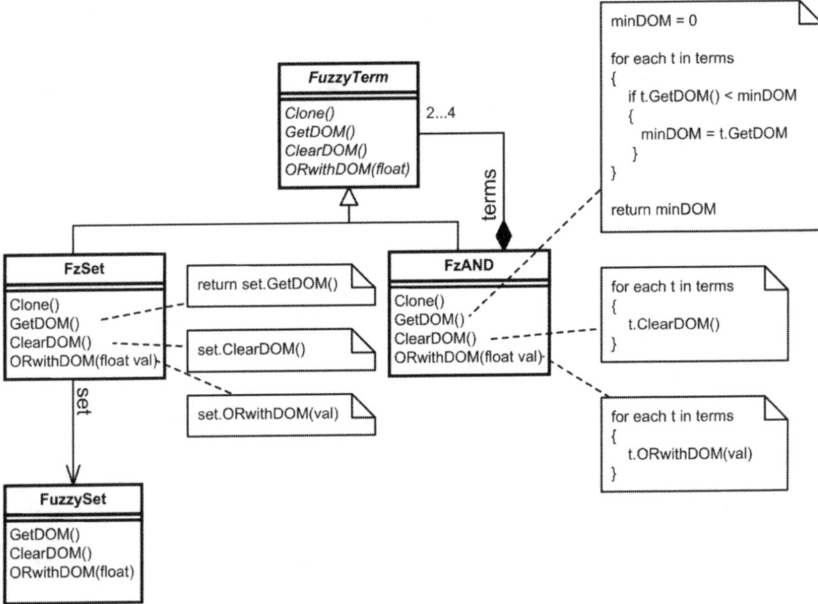

Figure 10.27. The composite pattern applied to fuzzy operators and operands

Observe how the FzAND object may contain from two to four FuzzyTerms and that when one of its methods is called it iterates through each of them and delegates the call to each child's corresponding method or uses their interface to calculate a result. Also notice how a FzSet acts as a proxy for a FuzzySet object. A proxy class is used to hide a real class from a client; it acts as a surrogate to the real class in order to control access to it. Proxy classes maintain a reference to the class they are a surrogate for and when a client calls a method of the proxy class, it forwards the call to the equivalent method of the reference.

Whenever a FuzzySet is added to a FuzzyVariable the client is handed a proxy to it in the form of a FzSet. This proxy can be copied and used multiple times in the creation of the rule base. No matter how many times it is copied it will always surrogate for the same object, which tidies up the design considerably since we don't have to worry about keeping track of copies of FuzzySets as rules are created.

Using this design for all operators and operands it's possible to produce a very user-friendly interface for creating fuzzy rules. Clients use syntax like the following to add rules:

```
fm.AddRule(FzAND(Target_Far, Ammo_Low), Undesirable);
```

Even the complex term shown earlier is easy to construct:

```
fm.AddRule(FzOR(FzAND(a1,a2), FzAND(FzNOT(a3), FzVery(a4))), FzAND(c1, c2));
```

To understand this better let's delve into the guts of the AddRule method. Here's the implementation:

```
void FuzzyModule::AddRule(FuzzyTerm& antecedent, FuzzyTerm& consequence)
{
  m_Rules.push_back(new FuzzyRule(antecedent, consequence)));
}
```

As you can see, all this method does is create a local copy of a FuzzyRule class. A FuzzyRule contains an instance of a FuzzyTerm denoting the antecedent and another denoting the consequent. These instances are copies of the FuzzyTerms used to construct the FuzzyRule. This is one reason why each FuzzyTerm subclass must implement the virtual constructor method Clone.

Here's the listing so you can see exactly what's going on.

```
class FuzzyRule
{
private:

  //antecedent (usually a composite of several fuzzy sets and operators)
  const FuzzyTerm*  m_pAntecedent;

  //consequence (usually a single fuzzy set, but can be several ANDed together)
  FuzzyTerm*        m_pConsequence;

  //it doesn't make sense to allow clients to copy rules
  FuzzyRule(const FuzzyRule&);
  FuzzyRule& operator=(const FuzzyRule&);

public:

  FuzzyRule(FuzzyTerm& ant,
            FuzzyTerm& con):m_pAntecedent(ant.Clone()),
                            m_pConsequence(con.Clone())
  {}

  ~FuzzyRule(){delete m_pAntecedent; delete m_pConsequence;}

  void SetConfidenceOfConsequentToZero(){m_pConsequence->ClearDOM();}

  //this method updates the DOM (the confidence) of the consequent term with
  //the DOM of the antecedent term.
  void Calculate()
  {
    m_pConsequence->ORwithDOM(m_pAntecedent->GetDOM());
  }
};
```

Okay, I think that's enough comment on the design of classes used to create and execute fuzzy rules. If you want to dig into the guts a little further, I advise you to check out the implementation of the FzAND, FzOR, FzVery, and

`FzFairly` classes, which you can find in the common/fuzzy folder. The UML diagram in Figure10.28 will also help you to understand how all the objects used by the fuzzy module interrelate.

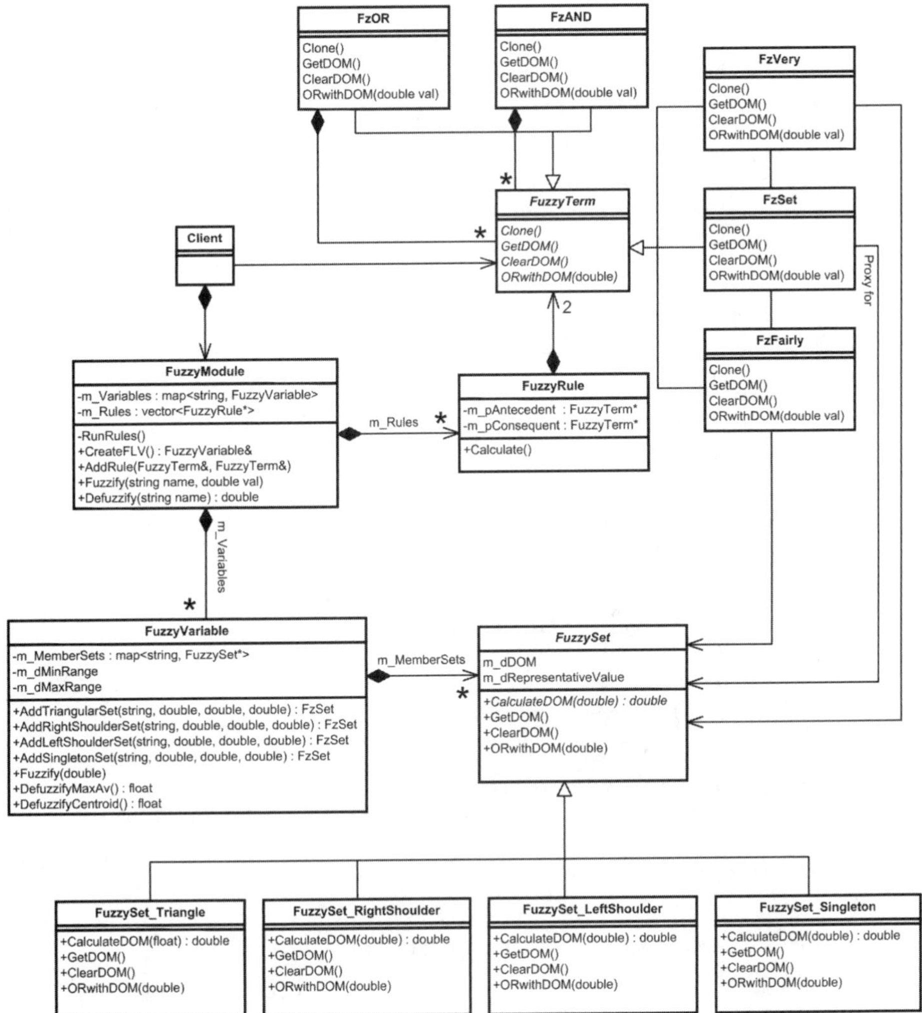

Figure 10.28

Continuing with the code shown earlier in this section, here is how the rule base for the rocket launcher can be added to the fuzzy module:

```
/* first initialize the fuzzy module with FLVs */

/* now add the rule set */
fm.AddRule(FzAND(Target_Close, Ammo_Loads), Undesirable);
fm.AddRule(FzAND(Target_Close, Ammo_Okay), Undesirable);
fm.AddRule(FzAND(Target_Close, Ammo_Low), Undesirable);
fm.AddRule(FzAND(Target_Medium, Ammo_Loads), VeryDesirable);
```

```
fm.AddRule(FzAND(Target_Medium, Ammo_Okay), VeryDesirable);
fm.AddRule(FzAND(Target_Medium, Ammo_Low), Desirable);
fm.AddRule(FzAND(Target_Far, Ammo_Loads), Desirable);
fm.AddRule(FzAND(Target_Far, Ammo_Okay), Desirable);
fm.AddRule(FzAND(Target_Far, Ammo_Low), Undesirable);
```

Once a FuzzyModule has been initialized, it's a painless matter to input values and calculate a crisp conclusion. Here's a method that does just that:

```
double CalculateDesirability(FuzzyModule& fm, double dist, double ammo)
{
   //fuzzify the inputs
   fm.Fuzzify("DistToTarget", dist);
   fm.Fuzzify("AmmoStatus", ammo);

  //this method automatically processes the rules and defuzzifies
  //the inferred conclusion
  return fm.DeFuzzify("Desirability", FuzzyModule::max_av);
}
```

When the DeFuzzify method is called, the rules are processed and the inferred conclusion defuzzified into a crisp value. Here's the method for your perusal:

```
inline double
FuzzyModule::DeFuzzify(const std::string& NameOfFLV, DefuzzifyMethod method)
{
  //first make sure the named FLV exists in this module
  assert ( (m_Variables.find(NameOfFLV) != m_Variables.end()) &&
          "<FuzzyModule::DeFuzzifyMaxAv>:key not found");

  //clear the DOMs of all the consequents
  SetConfidencesOfConsequentsToZero();

  //process the rules
  std::vector<FuzzyRule*>::iterator curRule = m_Rules.begin();
  for (curRule; curRule != m_Rules.end(); ++curRule)
  {
    (*curRule)->Calculate();
  }

  //now defuzzify the resultant conclusion using the specified method
  switch (method)
  {
  case centroid:

    return m_Variables[NameOfFLV]->DeFuzzifyCentroid(NumSamples);

  case max_av:

    return m_Variables[NameOfFLV]->DeFuzzifyMaxAv();
  }

  return 0;
}
```

How Raven Uses the Fuzzy Logic Classes

Each Raven weapon owns an instance of a fuzzy module, which is initialized with FLVs and rules specific to the weapon. All weapons are derived from the Raven_Weapon abstract base class and implement the method GetDesirability, which updates the fuzzy module and returns a crisp desirability score.

Here are the relevant parts of Raven_Weapon:

```
class Raven_Weapon
{
protected:

  FuzzyModule   m_FuzzyModule;

  /* EXTRANEOUS DETAIL OMITTED */

public:

  virtual double GetDesirability(double DistToTarget)=0;

  /* EXTRANEOUS DETAIL OMITTED */
};
```

Every few update cycles (twice a second by default) the bots query each of the weapons in their inventory to determine which of them is the most desirable given the distance to the bot's target and the ammo remaining, and selects the one with the highest desirability score. The code that implements this logic is listed below.

```
void Raven_Bot::SelectWeapon()
{
  //only need to run this code if a target is present
  if (m_pTargSys->isTargetPresent())
  {
    //calculate the distance to the target
    double DistToTarget = Vec2DDistance(Pos(), m_pTargSys->GetTarget()->Pos());

    //for each weapon in the inventory calculate its desirability given the
    //current situation. The most desirable weapon is selected
    double BestSoFar = MinDouble;

    std::vector<Raven_Weapon*>::const_iterator curWeap;
    for (curWeap = m_Weapons.begin(); curWeap != m_Weapons.end(); ++curWeap)
    {
      //grab the desirability of this weapon (desirability is based upon
      //distance to target and ammo remaining)
      double score = (*curWeap)->GetDesirability(DistToTarget);

      //if it is the most desirable so far select it
      if (score > BestSoFar)
      {
        BestSoFar = score;
```

```
            //place the weapon in the bot's hand.
            m_pCurrentWeapon = *curWeap;
          }
        }
      }
    }
```

The Combs Method

One major problem with fuzzy inference systems is that as the complexity of the problem increases, the number of rules required escalates at an alarming rate. For example, the simple module created to solve the weapon selection problem only required nine rules — one for each possible combination of the antecedent sets — but if we add just one more FLV, again consisting of three member sets, then 27 rules are necessary. It gets much worse if the number of member sets in each FLV has to be increased to obtain more precision. For instance, 125 rules are required for a system with three FLVs each containing five member sets. Add another FLV consisting of five member sets and the number skyrockets to 625 rules! This effect is known as *combinatorial explosion* and is a huge problem when designing fuzzy systems for time-critical applications, which of course is what computer games are.

Luckily for us, we have a knight in shining armor in the form of William Combs, an engineer with Boeing. In 1997 Combs proposed a system that enables the number of rules to grow linearly with the number of member sets instead of exponentially. Table 10.4 shows the number of rules required using the traditional method versus the Combs method (assume each FLV contains five member sets).

Table 10.4

Number of FLVs	Rules Rqd. (traditional)	Rules Rqd. (Combs)
2	25	10
3	125	15
4	625	20
5	3,125	25
6	15,625	30
7	78,125	35
8	390, 625	40

A big difference, I'm sure you'll agree!

The theory behind the Combs method works on the principle that a rule such as:

IF *Target_Far* AND *Ammo_Loads* THEN *Desirable*

is logically equivalent to:

IF *Target_Far* THEN *Desirable*

OR

IF *Ammo_Loads* THEN *Desirable*

Using this principle, a rule base can be defined that contains only one rule per consequent member set. For example, the nine rules for the desirability of the rocket launcher given previously:

Rule 1. IF *Target_Far* AND *Ammo_Loads* THEN *Desirable*
Rule 2. IF *Target_Far* AND *Ammo_Okay* THEN *Undesirable*
Rule 3. IF *Target_Far* AND *Ammo_Low* THEN *Undesirable*
Rule 4. IF *Target_Medium* AND *Ammo_Loads* THEN *VeryDesirable*
Rule 5. IF *Target_Medium* AND *Ammo_Okay* THEN *VeryDesirable*
Rule 6. IF *Target_Medium* AND *Ammo_Low* THEN *Desirable*
Rule 7. IF *Target_Close* AND *Ammo_Loads* THEN *Undesirable*
Rule 8. IF *Target_Close* AND *Ammo_Okay* THEN *Undesirable*
Rule 9. IF *Target_Close* AND *Ammo_Low* THEN *Undesirable*

can be reduced to six rules:

Rule 1. IF *Target_Close* THEN *Undesirable*
Rule 2. IF *Target_Medium* THEN *VeryDesirable*
Rule 3. IF *Target_Far* THEN *Undesirable*

Rule 4. IF *Ammo_Low* THEN *Undesirable*
Rule 5. IF *Ammo_Okay* THEN *Desirable*
Rule 6. IF *Ammo_Loads* THEN *VeryDesirable*

This is not a great reduction of course, but as you saw in Table 10.4, the Combs method becomes an increasingly attractive alternative as the number of member sets used by the linguistic variables rises.

One of the drawbacks with this method is that the changes to the rule base required to accommodate the logic are not intuitive. Combs gives a good example in his paper "The Combs Method for Rapid Inference":

When I got my first driver's license, my insurance agent reminded me that since I was sixteen AND male AND single, my insurance premium would be high. Later, after college, he said that since I was in my mid-twenties AND male AND married, my insurance premium would be moderately low.

This latter statement seems to make more intuitive sense than our alternative format: since I was in my mid-twenties, my insurance premium would be moderately low, OR since I was a male, my insurance premium would be moderately high, OR since I was married, my insurance premium would be low.

No agent wanting to close a sale would utter such a seemingly conflicting statement. One of the problems with [this method] is that the transformation from [(p and q) then r] to [(p then r) or (q then r)] shifts our focus from one rule to what appears to be the union of two (or more) rules. In addition, since each of these alternative rules can contain different consequent subsets, they seem to be contradicting each other: either my premium is high OR my premium is low. How can it be both?

For many of you, the counterintuitiveness of this method may be a stumbling block but if so, persevere — it's definitely worth the effort if you find yourself working with large rule bases.

Fuzzy Inference and the Combs Method

When using the Combs method, rules are processed as normal. To clarify, let's work through an example with the same figures used in the example shown earlier in the chapter: 200 pixels for distance and 8 for ammo status. Calculating the result of each rule we get:

Target_Close → *Undesirable* (0.0)
Target_Medium → *VeryDesirable* (0.67)
Target_Far → *Undesirable* (0.33)
Ammo_Low → *Undesirable* (0.22)
Ammo_Okay → *Desirable* (0.78)
Ammo_Loads → *VeryDesirable* (0.0)

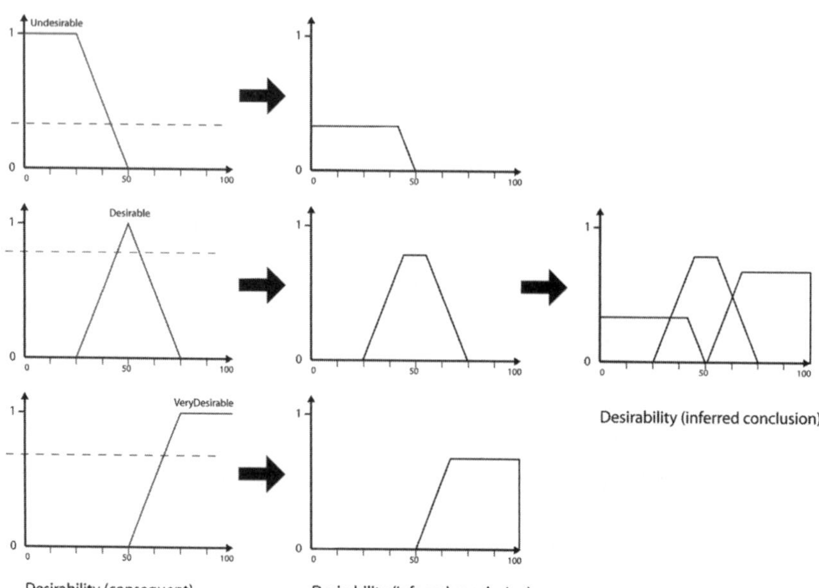

Figure 10.29

Now all we have to do is clip the relevant member sets of the consequent to the maximum of those values (ORing them together). This procedure and the resulting set is shown in Figure 10.29.

Using the `MaxAv` defuzzification method on this set results in a crisp value of 57.16, a very similar result to that received from the traditional fuzzy logic inference procedure.

Implementation

One fantastic aspect of this method is that no changes have to be made to the fuzzy logic classes to implement it. You only have to rewrite the rules to conform to the Combs logic. Bonus!

NOTE If you are curious about the logic behind the Combs method, I recommend you examine his paper. He gives a very detailed proof of the logic behind the method, which is well worth reading when you have a few minutes to spare.

Summing Up

You should now have a firm understanding of the theory behind fuzzy logic, but you'll need to get some practical experience under your belt before you recognize just how powerful and flexible it is. With this in mind I strongly suggest you try your hand at some of the following tasks (they start easy and become increasingly complex).

Practice Makes Perfect

1. Delve into the Raven code and increase the number of sets used in the fuzzy linguistic variables to five. This means you will have to completely redefine the FLVs and the accompanying rules for each weapon (or for just one of the weapons if you are feeling lazy ☺).
2. If you completed task 1 successfully you will have ended up with 25 rules. Your second challenge is to reduce the number of rules to 10 by converting them to the Combs method.
3. As it stands, the bot aiming logic is weak. Adding random noise to the aiming is okay but it's not very realistic. With random noise a bot will still occasionally make very stupid and obvious aiming errors. For instance, on occasions when a lot of noise is added, a bot might miss a shot that a human player — no matter how poor — would never miss. Alternatively, when very little is added a bot will from time to time make shots that no mortal player could ever make. (Don't you just *hate* it when that happens!)

The bot aiming can be made a lot more realistic by using fuzzy logic to calculate the deviation of each shot from perfect based upon variables like distance to target, relative lateral velocity, and how long the opponent has been visible. (Other considerations might be size, visibility, and profile — standing up, crouching, face on, side on, etc. — but these aren't relevant to Raven.) Use the skills you've learned in this chapter to implement fuzzy rules for accomplishing this.

Last Words

Wow! The end of the book is here. No more late nights (for a short while at least). I can go out and party. See my friends. I wonder how old they'll look. Maybe my girlfriend will even start talking to me again!

Seriously though, I hope you've enjoyed reading this book, have learned from it, and are ready to start implementing the techniques in your own games (if you haven't started already). If you'd like to discuss any of the topics in this book or anything else related to AI, please visit the forum at my web site, www.ai-junkie.com.

I'd like to end the book with a few guidelines I recommend you revisit from time to time… to *keep it real*, as rappers are fond of saying.

- There is very rarely just *one* correct way of creating a good game AI solution. Experiment with various methods as much as time permits before committing yourself to a design.
- Playtest often, and *listen* to your playtesters. If possible, *watch* them play. Make sure you take a notepad and pen, as you'll be using them a lot.
- During your learning curve you will find yourself drawn — inevitably, like a moth to a flame — to one or two AI techniques that really make your whiskers curl. Do not fall into the trap of obsessing over such techniques and contriving problems to apply them to. This is akin to finding a hammer and then walking around looking for stuff to hit with it.
- Do at least one brainstorming session devoted to AI with *everyone* else on your team, not just the game designer/producer (yes, even the artists). This will result in several new and possibly exciting ideas for you to mull over.
- The design of game AI is an iterative process. There's no way you're going to get it right the first time. It's just not possible to consider all the intricacies of anything more complex than the simplest of problems, so do not become disheartened when your first attempt performs poorly. Persevere, learn from your mistakes, and keep repeating the design cycle until you get it right.

- Don't limit your reading to game AI related topics. Many of your best ideas will come when reading around the subject. Cognitive science, robotics, philosophy, psychology, social science, biology, and even military tactics are all topics worthy of your time.
- A hugely clever and almost unbeatable opponent is rarely the goal of a game AI programmer. Good AI has *one* purpose: to make the gameplay fun. You will be wise to remind yourself of this from time to time because, believe me, it is *very easy* to miss the point and get bogged down with trying to make the most intelligent game agent known to man instead of one that makes a player laugh and shout with glee.
- Above all, when designing AI, always bear in mind that *the sophistication of your game agent should be proportional to its life span*. There is little point designing an agent that utilizes all the latest technological bells and whistles if it's only expected to live for three seconds before a player blows its head off.

Appendix A

C++ Templates

This appendix has been written as a quick and *very brief* introduction to C++ templates. It only skims the surface of what you can achieve with templates, but I cover enough ground for you to understand the code that accompanies this book.

Function Templates

If you have never used templates before then you will have almost certainly at some time created several versions of the same function to cater to each type you require the function to operate on. For example, you may create a function called `Clamp` that takes an integer and makes sure its value is between two limits. Something like this:

```
void Clamp(int& Val, int MinVal, int MaxVal)
{
  if (Val < MinVal) {Val = MinVal; return;}
  if (Val > MaxVal) {Val = MaxVal; return;}
}
```

Later on in your project, you realize that you want the same functionality but for floats. So you create another version of `Clamp`:

```
void Clamp(float& Val, float MinVal, float MaxVal)
{
  if (Val < MinVal) {Val = MinVal; return;}
  if (Val > MaxVal) {Val = MaxVal; return;}
}
```

And you may find that you want to add more versions for other types too. Repeating all this code every time you want to support a new type can become a pain in the butt. Fortunately for us, C++ templates provide a mechanism to allow classes and functions to be *parameterized* so that they provide the *same behavior* for *different types*. The declaration of a function template is very similar to a normal function declaration except the type is left unspecified. Here's how the `Clamp` function shown previously looks as a function template:

```
template <typename T>
void Clamp(T& Val, T MinVal, T MaxVal)
{
  if (Val < MinVal) {Val = MinVal; return;}
```

```
  if (Val > MaxVal) {Val = MaxVal; return;}
}
```

The template keyword is basically stating that this definition specifies a family of functions that are parameterized by the template parameter T. When this function template is called, an instance of Clamp will be generated by the compiler for each type for which the template is used. So, given the following program:

```
int main()
{
  int intVal = 10;
  int iMin   = 20;
  int iMax   = 30;

  cout < "\nintVal before Clamp = " < intVal;

  Clamp(intVal, iMin, iMax);

  cout < "\nintVal after Clamp = " < intVal;

  float floatVal = 10.5;
  float fMin     = 25.5;
  float fMax     = 35.5;

  cout < "\n\nfloatVal before Clamp = " < floatVal;

  Clamp(floatVal, fMin, fMax);

  cout < "\nfloatVal after Clamp = " < floatVal;

  return 0;
}
```

the compiler will create two instances of Clamp, one taking integers as parameters and the other taking floats, giving the output:

```
intVal before Clamp = 10
intVal after Clamp = 20

floatVal before Clamp = 10.5
floatVal after Clamp = 25.5
```

Adding More Types

So far so good, but what if you wanted to do something like:

```
Clamp(floatVal, iMin, iMax);
```

Now that the parameters include one float and two integers, the function template for Clamp given previously will not compile. You will get the error: “template parameter 'T' is ambiguous” or something similar. To provide support for more types you must add them to the parameterized list like so:

```
template <typename T, typename M>
void Clamp(T& Val, M MinVal, M MaxVal)
{
  if (Val < MinVal) {Val = MinVal; return;}
  if (Val > MaxVal) {Val = MaxVal; return;}
}
```

Using this definition the `Clamp` family of functions will accept different types for the value and for the range (a little contrived I know, but it gets the point across). Now you can do stuff like this:

```
int main()
{
  int   intVal    = 10;
  int   iMin      = 20;
  int   iMax      = 30;
  float floatVal  = 10.5;
  float fMin      = 25.5;
  float fMax      = 35.5;

  cout < "\nintVal before Clamp = " < intVal;
  Clamp(intVal, fMin, fMax);
  cout < "\nintVal after Clamp = " < intVal;

  cout < "\n\nfloatVal before Clamp = " < floatVal;
  Clamp(floatVal, iMin, iMax);
  cout < "\nfloatVal after Clamp = " < floatVal;

  return 0;
}
```

giving the output:

```
intVal before Clamp = 10
intVal after Clamp = 25

floatVal before Clamp = 10.5
floatVal after Clamp = 20
```

Class Templates

Just like functions, classes can be parameterized with one or more types. For example, the STL container classes you are probably familiar with are class templates you can use to manipulate collections of objects, whatever their type.

A common way of demonstrating how a class template works is to implement a stack-like data structure. Here's the declaration of `Stack`, a class that acts as a stack and can hold five elements of the parameterized type `T`:

```
template <class T>
class Stack
{
private:
```

```
  enum {MaxEntries = 5};

  T   m_Slots[MaxEntries];

  int m_NextFreeSlot;

public:

  Stack():m_NextFreeSlot(0){}

  //add an object to the stack
  void Push(const T& t);

  //remove an object from the stack
  T    Pop();

  bool Full()const{return m_NextFreeSlot == MaxEntries;}
  bool Empty()const{return m_NextFreeSlot == 0;}
};
```

As you can see, there is little difference between a class template and a function template. You may have noticed that this time I declared the parameterized type as `<class T>` and not `<typename T>` as I did for the function template. You can use either of these keywords interchangeably as they are for all intents and purposes identical.

Inside the class template the type identifier `T` can be used just like any other type. In this example it's used to declare an array, `m_Slots`, of size 5, as the parameter type to be passed to the member function `Push`, and as the return type of the member function `Pop`.

The definition of a class member function is made by first specifying that it is a function template and then by using the full type of the class template itself: `Stack<T>`. That was a horrible sentence so perhaps I'd better show you explicitly. Here's the implementation of the `Stack::Push` member function:

```
template <class T>
void Stack<T>::Push(const T& t)
{
  if (m_NextFreeSlot < MaxEntries)
  {
    m_Slots[m_NextFreeSlot++] = t;
  }
  else
  {
    throw std::out_of_range("stack empty");
  }
}
```

And here's the implementation of `Stack::Pop`:

```
template <class T>
T Stack<T>::Pop()
{
  if (m_NextFreeSlot >= 0)
```

```
  {
    return m_Slots[--m_NextFreeSlot];
  }
  else
  {
    throw std::range_error("stack empty");
  }
}
```

An instance of a Stack is created by specifying the template arguments explicitly. Here's a small program showing how Stack can be used with the types int and float:

```
int main()
{
  Stack<int>   iStack;
  Stack<float> fStack;

  //add some values to the stacks
  for (int i=0; i<10; ++i)
  {
    if (!iStack.Full())   iStack.Push(i);

    if (!fStack.Full()) fStack.Push(i*0.5);

  }

  //pop the values from the int stack
  cout < "Popping the ints... ";
  for (i=0; i<10; ++i)
  {
    if (!iStack.Empty())
    {
      cout < iStack.Pop() < ", ";
    }
  }

  //pop the values from the float stack
  cout < "\n\nPopping the floats... ";
  for (i=0; i<10; ++i)
  {
    if (!fStack.Empty())
    {
      cout < fStack.Pop() < ", ";
    }
  }

  return 0;
}
```

The output from this program is:

```
Popping the ints... 4, 3, 2, 1, 0,

Popping the floats... 2, 1.5, 1, 0.5, 0,
```

When the compiler tackles the line:

```
Stack<float> fStack
```

the compiler creates code resembling the class `Stack` where all instances of `T` are replaced by the type `float`. One important point to note here is that *only the member functions that are called within your program are instantiated.* This has the bonus that you can instantiate a class template for types that cannot be operated on by certain member functions as long as those member functions are not used. To clarify this point, imagine the `Stack` class implements a method `Write` that sends the contents of the stack to an `ostream` (by calling each element's < operator), and imagine you have another class, `MyDodgyClass`, which does not overload the < operator. Because only those member functions that are called are instantiated in code, you could still use a `Stack<MyDodgyClass>` as long as you never call its `Write` method.

Linker Confusion

Finally, let me show you a problem with C++ templates. Normally, we are used to splitting up our classes and functions into declarations, which go into a header file (*.h/*.hpp), and their definitions, which go into a *.c/*.cpp file. Unfortunately, if you try to organize templates in the same way you will get linker errors. This is because when your code is compiling, the compiler needs to know what templates to instantiate and for what types. The only way it can do this is by examining code in (usually) another file, which has been compiled separately. When the compiler sees that a function template or class is being used it assumes that the definition is provided elsewhere and leaves a note for the linker to resolve the issue. But of course the linker cannot because no template code has been created, hence the error.

Unfortunately, the best way of resolving this problem at the moment is to put both class and function template declarations and definitions in one big header file. This is, of course, undesirable, as our compile times will soar, but alas it is the most reliable option as I write this. There are alternatives, such as explicit instantiation or by using the poorly supported `export` keyword, but these are usually more trouble than they are worth at the moment. Hopefully something will be done about this problem in the next few years.

Appendix B

UML Class Diagrams

The Unified Modeling Language (UML) is a useful tool for object-oriented analysis and design. One part of the UML, the *class diagram*, is utilized frequently throughout this book because this type of diagram is especially good at clearly and succinctly describing the static relationships between objects.

Figure 1 shows the class diagram utilized in Chapter 7 to describe the relationships between some of the objects used in one of the book's projects.

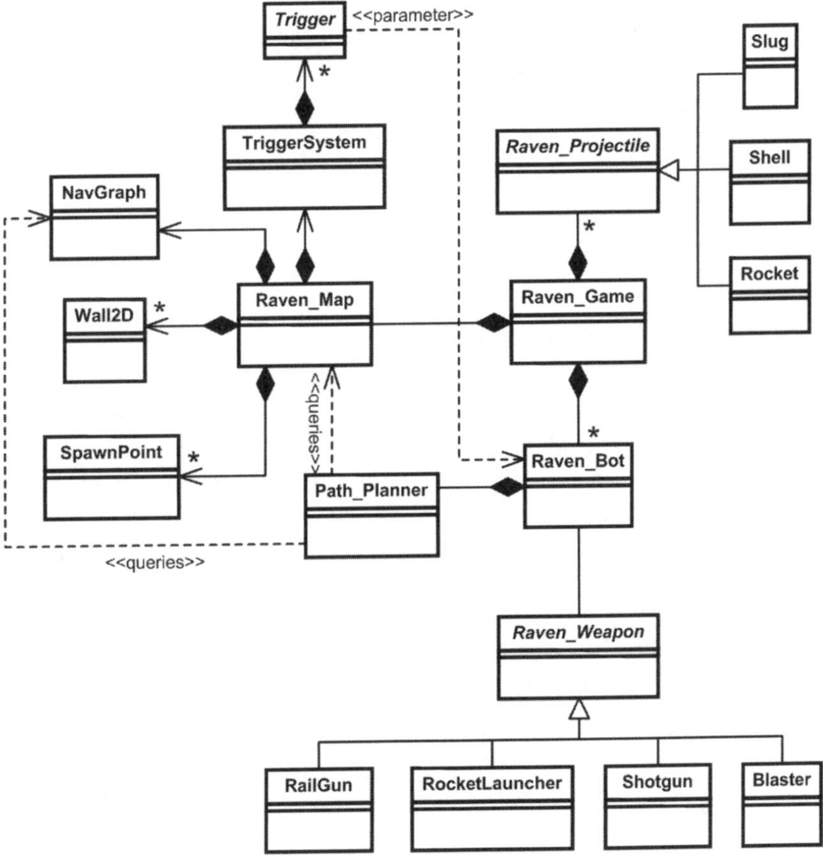

Figure 1. Example UML class diagram

If this is the first time you've seen a UML class diagram you'll probably find the figure perplexing, but by the time you've finished reading this appendix it will make perfect sense (knock on wood ☺).

Class Names, Attributes, and Operations

First of all let's start off with the name, attributes, and operations of a class. Classes are represented by a rectangle divided into three compartments. The name of the class is in bold at the top of the rectangle, attributes are written beneath, and operations are listed in the bottom compartment. See Figure 2.

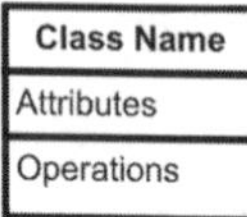

Figure 2. The class/object rectangle

For example, if one of the objects in a game is a racing car, it can be specified as shown in Figure 3.

RacingCar

velocity
position

Steer(amount)
Accelerate(amount)
GetPosition()

Figure 3. Example of attributes and operations

Of course, a racing car object is likely to be much more complex than this, but we only need to list the attributes and operations of immediate interest. The class can easily be fleshed out more fully at a later stage if necessary. (Quite often, I don't show any attributes or operations at all and use class diagrams simply to show the relationships between objects, as demonstrated by Figure 1.) Note that the operations of a class define its interface.

The type of an attribute can be shown listed after its name and separated by a colon. The return value of an operation may also be shown in the same way, as can the type of a parameter. See Figure 4.

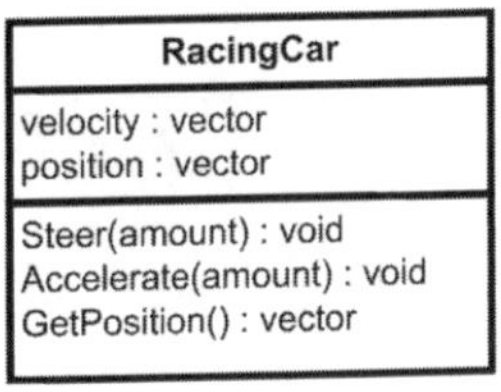

```
RacingCar
---------------------------------
velocity : vector
position : vector
---------------------------------
Steer(amount) : void
Accelerate(amount) : void
GetPosition() : vector
```

Figure 4. Specifying the type

Throughout the book I rarely use the "name : type" format for parameters as it often makes the diagrams too large to fit on the page comfortably. Instead, I just list the type, or sometimes a descriptive name if the type can be inferred from it.

Visibility of Attributes and Operations

Each class attribute and operation has a visibility associated with it. For instance, an attribute may either be public, private, or protected. This property is shown using the symbols + for public, - for private, and # for protected. Figure 5 shows the RacingCar object with the visibility of its attributes and operations listed.

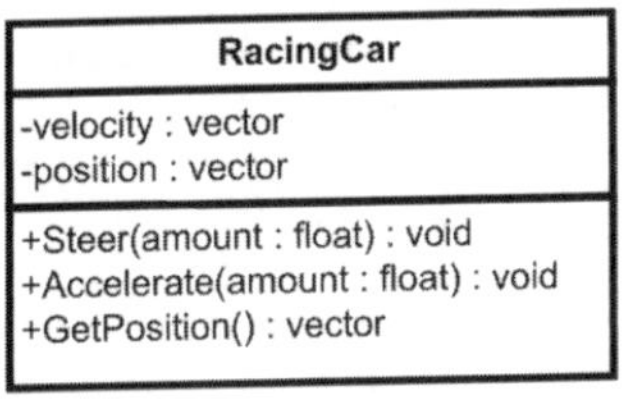

```
RacingCar
---------------------------------
-velocity : vector
-position : vector
---------------------------------
+Steer(amount : float) : void
+Accelerate(amount : float) : void
+GetPosition() : vector
```

Figure 5

As with the types, it's not imperative that you list the visibilities when drawing class diagrams; they only need to be shown if they are immediately important to the part of the design you are modeling (or, as in my case, describing).

When all the attributes, operations, types, visibilities, etc., are specified it's very easy to convert the class into code. For example, C++ code for the RacingCar object looks like this:

```
class RacingCar
{
private:

  vector m_vPosition;

  vector m_vVelocity;

public:

  void Steer(float amount){...}
```

```
  void Accelerate(float amount){...}

  vector GetPosition()const{return m_vPosition;}
};
```

Relationships

Classes are not much use on their own. In object-oriented design each object usually has a relationship with one or more other objects, such as the child-parent type relationship of inheritance or the relationship between a class method and its parameters. The following describe the notation the UML specifies to denote each particular type of relationship.

Association

An *association* between two classes represents a *connection or link between instances of those classes*, and is denoted using a solid line. Unfortunately, at the time of writing, UML practitioners seem unable to agree upon what the italicized text in the previous sentence actually means, so for the purposes of this book an association is said to exist between two classes if *one of them contains a persistent reference to the other.*

Figure 6 shows the association between a RacingCar object and a Driver object.

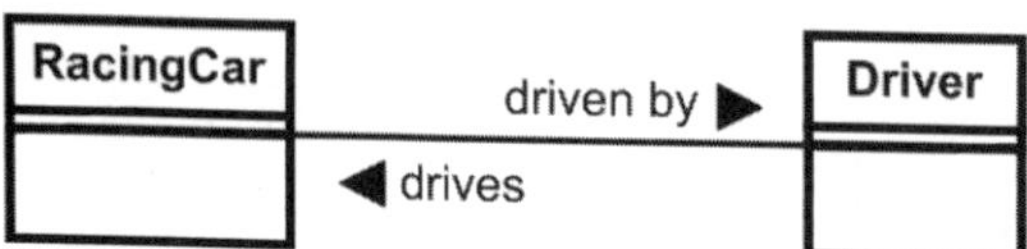

Figure 6. An association

This class diagram tells us that a racing car is driven by a driver and that a driver drives a racing car. It also tells us that a RacingCar instance maintains a persistent reference to a Driver instance (via a pointer, instance, or reference) and vice versa. In this example both ends have been explicitly named with a descriptive label called a role name, although much of the time this is not necessary as the role is usually implicit given the names of the classes and the type of association linking them. I prefer to only name the roles when I believe it is absolutely necessary as I feel it makes a complex class diagram simpler to comprehend.

Multiplicity

The end of an association may also have *multiplicity*, which is an indication of the number of instances participating in the relationship. For instance, a racing car can only have one or zero drivers, and a driver is either driving a car or not. This can be shown as in Figure 7 using 0..1 to specify the range.

Relationships

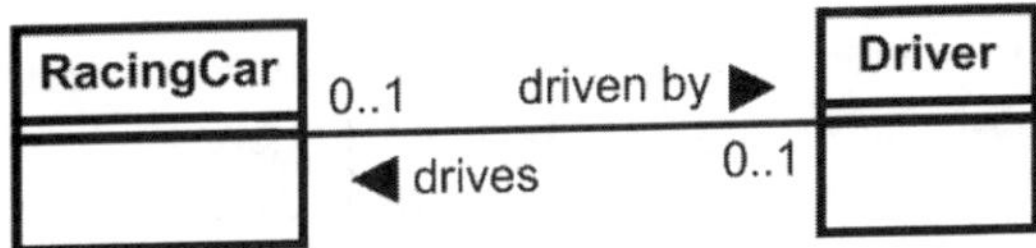

Figure 7. An association showing multiplicity

Figure 8 demonstrates how a RacingCar object can be shown to be associated with any number of Sponsor objects (using an asterisk to indicate infinity as the upper bound of the range), and how a Sponsor can only be associated with one RacingCar at any time.

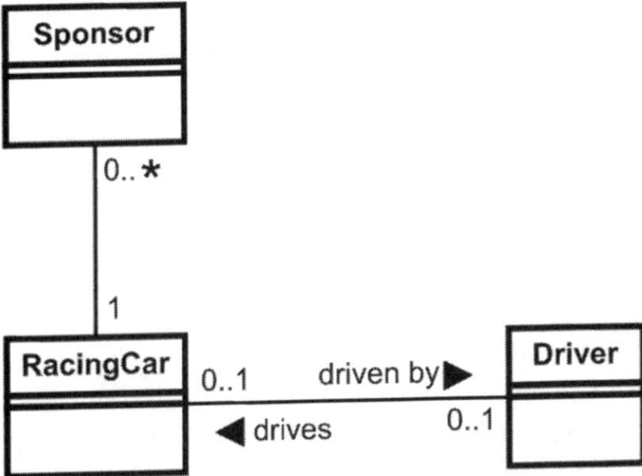

Figure 8

Figure 8 shows the longhand way of specifying an unlimited range and a range of 1, but often (and certainly within this book) you will see these relationships expressed in shorthand, as shown in Figure 9. The single asterisk denotes an unbounded range between 0 and infinity, and the absence of any numbers or an asterisk at the end of an association implies a singular relationship.

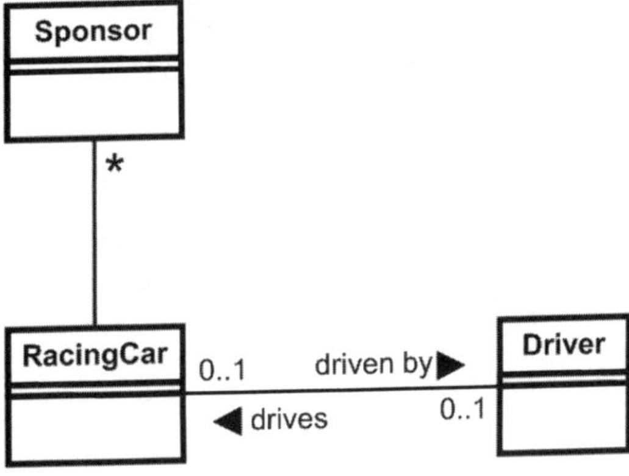

Figure 9

It is also possible for a multiplicity to represent a combination of discrete values. For instance, a car may have two or four doors — 2, 4.

Given only the associations shown in Figure 9, we can infer how an interface for a RacingCar class might look:

```
class RacingCar
{
public:

  Driver* GetDriver()const;
  void    SetDriver(Driver* pNewDriver);
  bool    isBeingDriven()const;

  void    AddSponsor(Sponsor* pSponsor);
  void    RemoveSponsor(Sponsor* pSponsor);
  int     GetNumSponsors()const;

  ...
};
```

Navigability

So far the associations you've seen have been bidirectional: A RacingCar knows about a Driver instance, and that Driver instance knows about the RacingCar instance. A RacingCar knows about each Sponsor instance and each Sponsor knows about the RacingCar. Often however, you will need to express a *unidirectional* association. For example, it's unlikely that a RacingCar need be aware of the Spectators watching it, but it is important that a Spectator is aware of the car it is watching. This is a one-way relationship and is expressed by adding an arrow to the appropriate end of the association. See Figure 10.

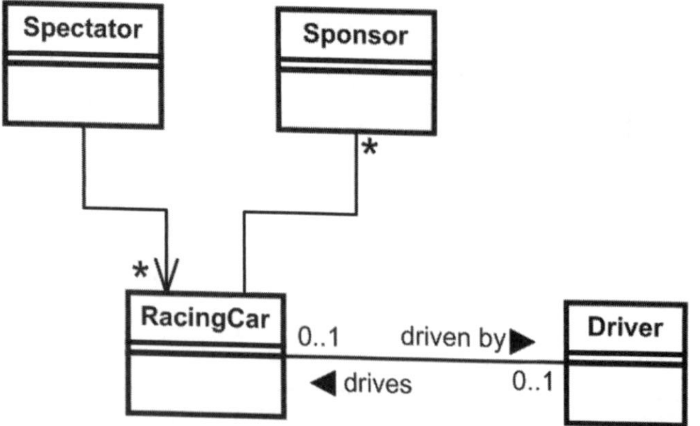

Figure 10. A Spectator has a unidirectional association with a RacingCar.

Notice also how the figure clearly shows how a Spectator may be watching any number of racing cars.

Shared and Composite Aggregation

Aggregation is a special case of association and denotes the *part of* relationship. For instance, an arm is a part of a body. There are two types of aggregation: *shared* and *composite*. Shared aggregation is when the parts can be shared between wholes and composite aggregation is when the parts are owned by the whole.

For example, the mesh (3D polygon model) that describes the shape of a racing car and is textured and rendered to a display can be shared by many racing cars. As a result, this can be represented as shared aggregation, which is denoted by a hollow diamond. See Figure 11.

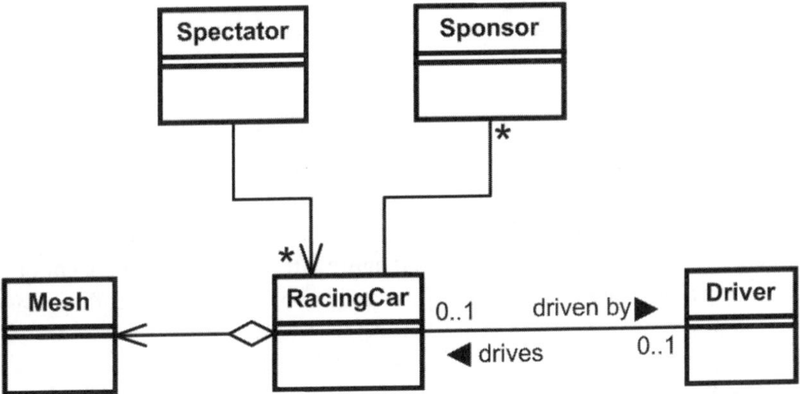

Figure 11. The relationship between a Mesh and a RacingCar is shown as a shared aggregation.

Note that shared aggregation implies that when a RacingCar is destroyed its Mesh is not destroyed. (Also note how the diagram shows that a Mesh object knows nothing about a RacingCar object.)

Composite aggregation is a much stronger relationship and implies the parts live and die with the whole. Sticking with our RacingCar example, we could say that a Chassis has this type of relationship with a car. A Chassis is wholly owned by a RacingCar and is destroyed when the car is destroyed. This kind of relationship is denoted using a filled diamond as shown in Figure 12.

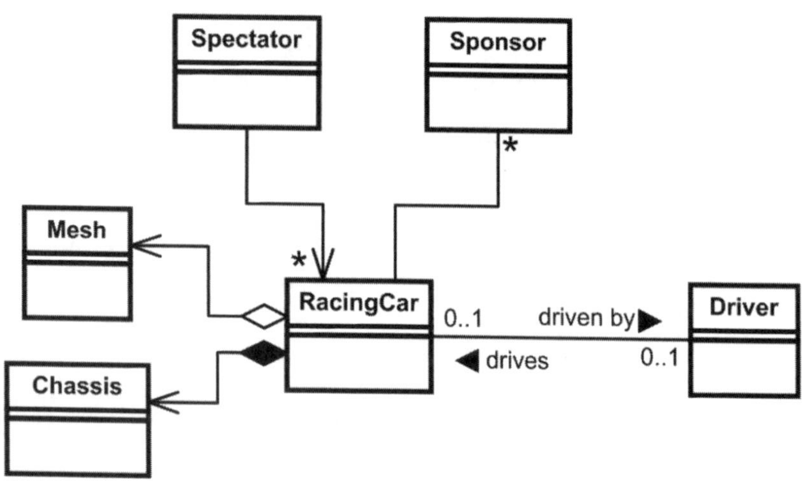

Figure 12. The relationship between a Chassis and a RacingCar is a composite aggregation.

There is a very subtle difference between shared aggregation and association. For example, in the design discussed thus far the relationship between a Spectator and a RacingCar has been shown as an association, but as many different Spectators can watch the same car you might think it's okay to show the relationship as shared aggregation. However, a spectator is not part of the whole of a racing car and the relationship therefore is association, not aggregation.

Generalization

Generalization is a way of describing the relationship between classes that have common properties. With regard to C++, generalization describes the *is a* relationship of inheritance. For example, a design might require that different types of RacingCar are subclassed from RacingCar to provide vehicles for specific kinds of races, such as rally, Formula One, or touring. This type of relationship is shown using a hollow triangle on the base class end of the association as shown in Figure 13.

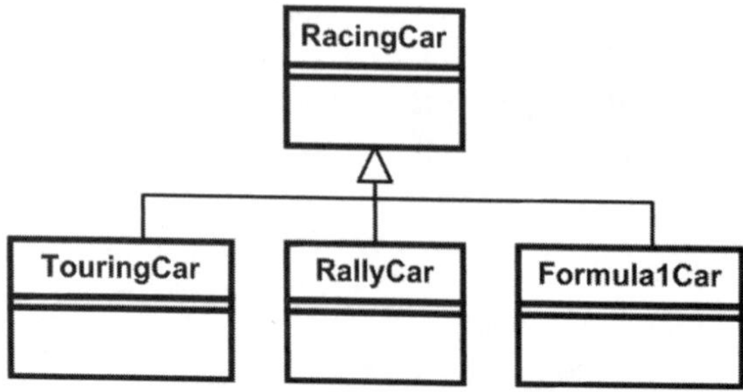

Figure 13. Expressing the base-derived class relationship

Often in object-oriented design we use the concept of an abstract class to define an interface to be implemented by any subclasses. This is described explicitly by the UML using italicized text for the class name and for any of its abstract operations. Therefore, if RacingCar is to be implemented as an abstract class with one pure virtual method `Update`, the relationship between it and other racing cars is shown as in Figure 14.

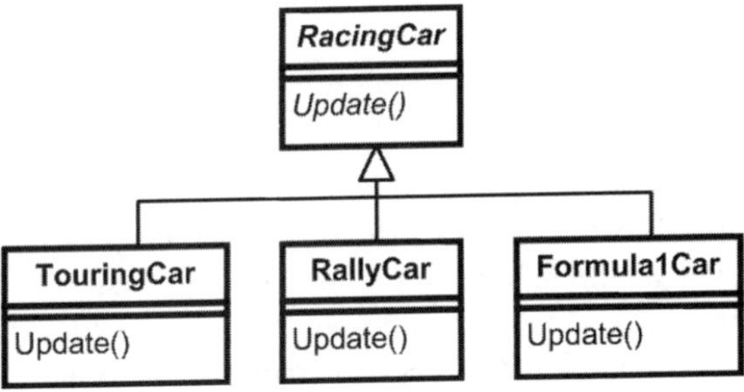

Figure 14. Describing an abstract base class

Note that some people prefer to make the relationship more explicit by adding "{abstract}" beneath the class name or after any abstract operation's name. This is shown in Figure 15.

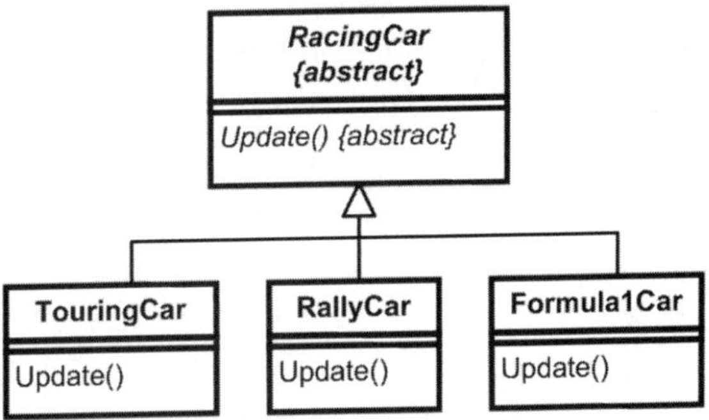

Figure 15. Describing an abstract base class more explicitly

Dependencies

Often you will find that a class *depends* on another for some reason, yet the relationship between them is not an association (as defined by the UML). This occurs for all sorts of reasons. For instance, if a method of class A takes a reference to class B as a parameter, then A has a dependency on B. Another good example of a dependency is when A sends a message to B via a third party, which would be typical of a design incorporating event handling.

A dependency is shown using a dashed line with an arrow at one end, and can be optionally qualified by a label. Figure 16 shows how a RacingCar has a dependency to a RaceTrack.

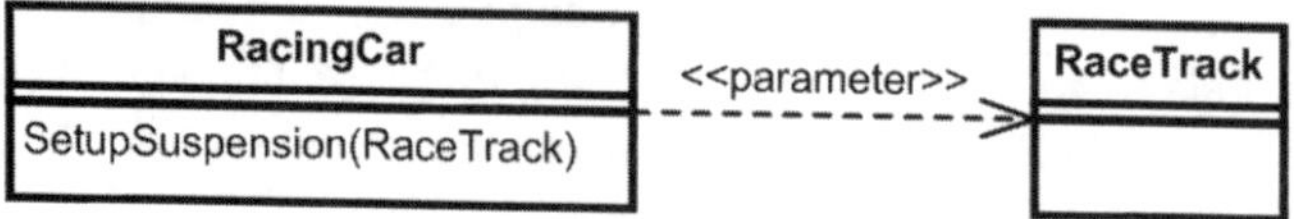

Figure 16. The dependency relationship

Notes

Notes are an additional feature you can use to zoom in on specific features that need further explanation in some way. For instance, I use notes in the class diagrams printed in this book to add pseudocode where necessary. A note is depicted as a rectangle with a "folded" corner and has a dashed line connecting it to the area of interest. Figure 17 shows how a note is used to explain how the UpdatePhysics method of a RacingCar iterates through its four wheels, calling each one's Update method.

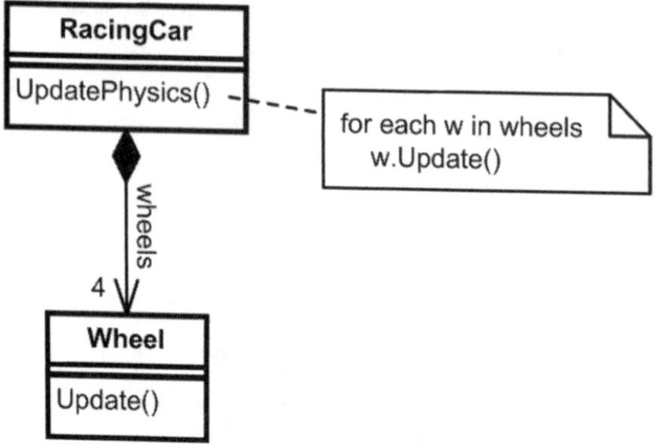

Figure 17. A note can be used to provide further detail.

Summing Up

Did you follow all that okay? To test yourself, flip back to Figure 1 and see how much sense it makes. If you still find it confusing, read through this appendix again. If you understood it, well done! Now you can get back to the AI!

Appendix C

Setting Up Your Development Environment

Downloading the Demo Executables

You can download the demo executables discussed in the book from the following URL: www.wordware.com/files/ai. Then click on Buckland_AIExecutables.zip.

Downloading and Installing the Source Code

To set up your development environment in order to compile and run the projects discussed in the book, follow these steps:

1. Download the zip file containing the source code from www.wordware.com/files/ai. Then click on Buckland_AISource.zip. Unzip and extract to a folder of your choice (for example, C:\AI Source).
2. Download and install the Boost library headers from www.boost.org. (By default this will be something like C:\ boost_1_31_0.)
3. Assuming you have unzipped Boost and the source code into the folders specified in steps 1 and 2, add the following paths to the general settings of your compiler in your development environment.

Include file paths

- C:\ boost_1_31_0
- C:\AI Source\Common
- C:\AI Source\Common\lua-5.0\include
- C:\AI Source\Common\luabind

Source file paths

- C:\AI Source\Common
- C:\AI Source\Common\lua-5.0
- C:\AI Source\Common\luabind

Library file paths

- C:\AI Source\Common\lua-5.0\lib

References

"A Generic Fuzzy State Machine in C++," *Game Programming Gems 2*, Eric Dysband

Algorithms in C++: Parts 1-4, Robert Sedgewick

Algorithms in C++: Part 5, Robert Sedgewick

Applying UML and Patterns, Craig Larman

Artificial Intelligence: A Modern Approach, Stuart Russell and Peter Norvig

Artificial Intelligence: A New Synthesis, Nils J. Nilsson

C++ Templates: The Complete Guide, David Vandevoorde and Nicolai M. Josuttis

Design Patterns, Erich Gamma, Richard Helm, Ralph Johnson, and John Vlissides

Effective C++, Scott Meyers

"Enhancing a State Machine Language through Messaging," *AI Game Programming Wisdom*, Steve Rabin

Fuzzy Logic: Intelligence, Control, and Information, John Yen and Reza Langari

"How Autonomous is an Autonomous Agent?" Bertil Ekdahl

"Interactions with Groups of Autonomous Characters," Craig Reynolds

"It Knows What You're Going To Do: Adding Anticipation to a Quakebot," John E. Laird

Layered Learning in Multiagent Systems: A Winning Approach to Robotic Soccer, Peter Stone

Lua 5.0 Reference Manual

More Effective C++, Scott Meyers

"Navigating Doors, Elevators, Ledges and Other Obstacles," *AI Game Programming Wisdom*, John Hancock

Newtonian Physics, Benjamin Crowell

"Pathfinding Design Architecture," *AI Game Programming Wisdom*, Dan Higgins

Pattern Hatching, John Vlissides

Physics for Game Developers, David M. Bourg

"Polygon Soup for the Programmer's Soul," Patrick Smith

"Smart Moves: Intelligent Pathfinding," Bryan Stout

"Steering Behaviors," Christian Schnellhammer and Thomas Feilkas

"Steering Behaviors for Autonomous Characters," Craig Reynolds

"Steering Behaviours," Robin Green

"Stigmergy, Self-Organisation, and Sorting in Collective Robotics," Owen Holland and Chris Melhuish

The C++ Programming Language, Bjarne Stroustrup

The C++ Standard Library, Nicolai Josuttis

"The Combs Method for Rapid Inference," William E. Combs

"The Integration of AI and Level Design in *Halo*," Jaime Griesemer and Chris Butcher

"The Quake 3 Arena Bot," J.M.P. van Waveren

"Toward More Realistic Pathfinding," Marco Pinter

UML Distilled, Martin Fowler and Kendall Scott

UML Tutorial: Finite State Machines, Robert C. Martin

Bugs and Errata

As you've seen, I've written a lot of code to accompany this book. Since I don't have the support of a group of playtesters to test it, it will be a miracle if there are no bugs lurking within.

You will be able to download bug fixes from the following URL:

www.ai-junkie.com/ai_book2/bugs

If you find a bug that hasn't been reported, please let me know by sending an email to bugs@ai-junkie.com so I can address it.

Similarly, although my editors and I have made every effort to ensure the text is error free, a few typos always seem to slip through the net. Any corrections to the text will be made available at the following URL:

www.ai-junkie.com/ai_book2/errata

I'd be very appreciative if you could email errata@ai-junkie.com with the details of any such errors you discover.

Index

Gamedev.net

The most comprehensive game development resource

- The latest news in game development
- The most active forums and chatrooms anywhere, with insights and tips from experienced game developers
- Links to thousands of additional game development resources
- Thorough book and product reviews
- Over 1000 game development articles!

Game design
Graphics
DirectX
OpenGL
AI
Art
Music
Physics
Source Code
Sound
Assembly
And More!

OpenGL is a registered trademark of Silicon Graphics, Inc.
Microsoft, DirectX are registered trademarks of Microsoft Corp. in the United States and/or other countries.

Looking for more?

Check these and other titles from Wordware's complete list.

Introduction to 3D Game Programming with DirectX 9.0
1-55622-913-5 • $49.95
6 x 9 • 424 pp.

Advanced 3D Game Programming with DirectX 9.0
1-55622-968-2 • $59.95
6 x 9 • 552 pp.

Learn Vertex and Pixel Shader Programming with DirectX 9
1-55622-287-4 • $34.95
6 x 9 • 304 pp.

Programming Multiplayer Games
1-55622-076-6 • $59.95
6 x 9 • 576 pp.

ShaderX²: Introductions & Tutorials with DirectX 9
1-55622-902-X • $44.95
6 x 9 • 384 pp.

ShaderX²: Shader Programming Tips & Tricks with DirectX 9
1-55622-988-7 • $59.95
6 x 9 • 728 pp.

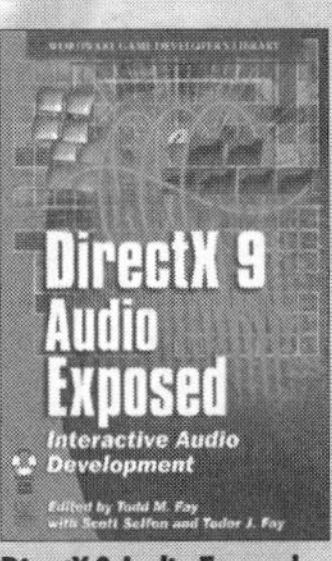

DirectX 9 Audio Exposed
1-55622-288-2 • $59.95
6 x 9 • 568 pp.

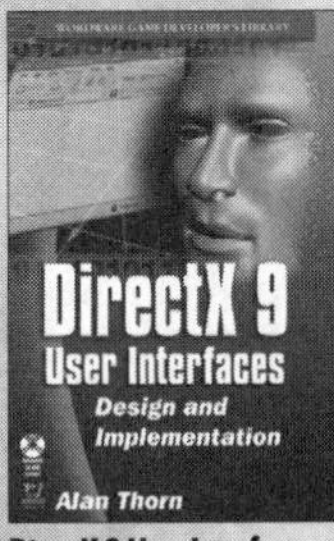

DirectX 9 User Interfaces
1-55622-249-1 • $44.95
6 x 9 • 376 pp.

Just Released

SQL Anywhere Studio 9 Developer's Guide
1-55622-506-7 • $49.95
6 x 9 • 488 pp.

Wireless Game Development in Java with MIDP 2.0
1-55622-998-4 • $39.95
6 x 9 • 360 pp.

Game Design Theory and Practice 2nd Ed.
1-55622-912-7 • $54.95
6 x 9 • 728 pp.

Official Butterfly.net Game Developer's Guide
1-55622-044-8 • $49.95
6 x 9 • 424 pp.

Visit us online at www.wordware.com for more information.

Use the following coupon code for online specials: ai0782

LightWave 3D 8 Texturing
1-55622-285-8 • $49.95
6 x 9 • 504 pp.

LightWave 3D 8 Lighting
1-55622-094-4 • $54.95
6 x 9 • 536 pp.

LightWave 3D 8: 1001 Tips & Tricks
1-55622-090-1 • $39.95
6 x 9 • 648 pp.

LightWave 3D 7.5 Lighting
1-55622-354-4 • $69.95
6 x 9 • 496 pp.

Essential LightWave 3D 7.5
1-55622-226-2 • $44.95
6 x 9 • 424 pp.

CGI Filmmaking: The Creation of Ghost Warrior
1-55622-227-0 • $49.95
9 x 7 • 344 pp.

Coming Soon

LightWave 3D 8 Cartoon Character Creation Vol. I
1-55622-253-X • $49.95
6 x 9 • 500 pp.

LightWave 3D 8 Cartoon Character Creation Vol. II
1-55622-254-8 • $49.95
6 x 9 • 550 pp.

3DS Max Lighting
1-55622-401-X • $49.95
6 x 9 • 536 pp.

Advanced Lighting and Materials with Shaders
1-55622-292-0 • $59.95
9 x 7 • 500 pp.

Visit us online at **www.wordware.com** for more information.
Use the following coupon code for online specials: **ai0782**